tenth edition

SuperVision
and Instructional Leadership
A DEVELOPMENTAL APPROACH

Carl D. Glickman
Professor Emeritus of Education, The University of Georgia

Stephen P. Gordon
Professor of Education and Community Leadership, Texas State University

Jovita M. Ross-Gordon
Professor of Adult, Professional, and Community Education, Texas State University

330 Hudson Street, NY NY 10013

VP and Editorial Director: *Kevin Davis*
Executive Portfolio Manager: *Julie Peters*
Content Producer: *Miryam Chandler*
Portfolio Management Assistant: *Maria Feliberty*
Executive Product Marketing Manager:
Christopher Barry
Executive Field Marketing Manager: *Krista Clark*
Procurement Specialist: *Deidra Smith*
Cover Design: *Taylor Reed, Cenveo*

Cover Art: *selensergen/Fotolia*
Media Producer: *Allison Longley*
Editorial Production and Composition Services:
SPi Global
Full-Service Project Manager: *Michelle Gardner*
Printer/Binder: *RRD Owensville*
Cover Printer: *RRD Owensville*
Text Font: *Sabon LT Pro*

Credits and acknowledgments for materials borrowed from other sources and reproduced, with permission, in this textbook appear on the appropriate page within the text.

Every effort has been made to provide accurate and current Internet information in this book. However, the Internet and information posted on it are constantly changing, so it is inevitable that some of the Internet addresses listed in this textbook will change.

Library of Congress Cataloging-in-Publication Data

Names: Glickman, Carl D., author. | Gordon, Stephen P., 1948- author. |
   Ross-Gordon, Jovita M., author.

Title: Supervision and instructional leadership : a developmental approach /
   Carl D. Glickman, Professor Emeritus of Education, The University of Georgia, Athens, Georgia,
   Stephen P. Gordon, Professor of Education and Community Leadership, Texas State University,
   Jovita M. Ross-Gordon, Professor of Adult, Professional, and Community Education, Texas State
   University.

Description: Tenth edition. | New York : Pearson, [2017]

Identifiers: LCCN 2016028429 | ISBN 9780134449890

Subjects: LCSH: School supervision.

Classification: LCC LB2806.4 .G56 2017 | DDC 371.2/03—dc23

LC record available at https://lccn.loc.gov/2016028429

1 16

ISBN 10:   0-13-444989-4
ISBN 13: 978-0-13-444989-0

About the Authors

Carl D. Glickman is Professor Emeritus of Education at the University of Georgia. He began his career as a Teacher Corps intern in the rural South and later was a principal of award-winning schools in New Hampshire. At the University of Georgia he and colleagues founded the Georgia League of Professional Schools, a nationally validated network of high-functioning public schools dedicated to the principles of democratic education. He is the author or editor of 14 books on school leadership, educational renewal, and the moral imperative of education.

Stephen P. Gordon is a professor of Education and Community Leadership at Texas State University. He is author of the book *Professional Development for School Improvement,* coauthor of the books *The Basic Guide to Supervision and Instructional Leadership* and *How to Help Beginning Teachers Succeed,* and editor of the books *Collaborative Action Research* and *Standards for Instructional Supervision: Enhancing Teaching and Learning.* Dr. Gordon, the former director of the National Center for School Improvement, also was lead consultant for the ASCD video series *Improving Instruction through Observation and Feedback.*

Jovita M. Ross-Gordon is a professor of Adult, Professional and Community Education at Texas State University. Dr. Ross-Gordon is the author, editor, or coeditor of several books including the 2010 *Handbook of Adult and Continuing Education.* She has also published numerous chapters and articles on the teaching and learning of adults, particularly in the setting of higher education. She is currently coeditor-in-chief of *New Directions for Adult and Continuing Education,* and has served in numerous leadership positions with professional organizations focusing on adult education.

Preface

New to This Edition

Highlights of new features of this 10th edition include the following:

- The Pearson eText, access to which is sold with each new copy of this text, contains video links aligned with content and an end of chapter digital self-assessment "Check Your Understanding" set of open-ended questions with feedback, designed to deepen understanding of the concepts and practices presented in the text.
- Differentiated instructional leadership roles for supervisors, formal teacher leaders, and informal teacher leaders (Chapter 1)
- The Newtonian paradigm and traditional schools (Chapter 2)
- The quantum paradigm and dynamic schools (Chapter 3)
- Update on self-directed learning and introduction to heutagogy (Chapter 4)
- Role-plays on beliefs about teaching and supervision (Chapter 5)
- Introductory activity on Johari Window (Chapter 6)
- Characteristics of teachers best matched with directive control, directive informational, collaborative, and nondirective behaviors (Chapters 7, 8, 9, 10)
- Schoolwide classroom observations (Chapter 12)
- Process decision program charts (Chapter 13)
- Implementation skills (Chapter 14)
- Mentoring (chapter 15)
- A new chapter on teacher evaluation (Chapter 16)
- The new wave of teacher evaluation systems (Chapter 17)
- Stages of group development (Chapter 17)
- Characteristics of effective groups (Chapter 17)
- Curriculum mapping—and remapping (Chapter 19)
- Appreciative inquiry (Chapter 20)
- Comparing chaos theory, postmodern theory, and educational change theory (Chapter 21)
- Equity for students with disabilities (Chapter 22)
- Comparing classic organizations with authentic communities (Chapter 23)

Details of the New Edition

This 10th edition continues to call for a collegial approach to instructional supervision, and Part 1 of the book expands on that call by emphasizing the need for teacher leadership as a critical component of collegial supervision. Responsibilities of supervisors as well as formal and informal teacher leaders are suggested as part of a collective approach to supervision described in Chapter 1.

Part 2 considers the knowledge necessary for successful supervision. In Chapter 2, we describe the characteristics of conventional schools that hinder teaching and learning, and ask the reader to examine the Newtonian paradigm as the worldview that undergirds conventional schools. Chapter 3 turns the reader's attention to the positive side as we explore the characteristics of dynamic schools and how such schools reflect the quantum paradigm. Teachers, of course, are adults, and we are proud that this was the first book on instructional supervision with extensive discussions of adult learning and development. This edition adds to the knowledge on adult and teacher development presented in Chapter 4 with an update on self-directed learning and an introduction to the concept of *heutagogy*, an alternative to andragogy that focuses on an even more autonomous, self-determined adult learner. Successful supervisors need to not only know about the different belief systems that influence teaching and supervision, but also to clarify their own beliefs about education and supervision. Chapter 5 provides both a review of various belief systems and activities designed to assist understanding and clarification of beliefs.

Part 3 shifts to a discussion of interpersonal skills. Chapter 6 introduces the supervisory behavior continuum and shows how interpersonal behaviors along the continuum represent different approaches to supervision. This chapter also includes methods supervisors can use to assess their own supervisory behaviors. The next four chapters describe each of four interpersonal approaches: directive control (Chapter 7), directive informational (Chapter 8), collaborative (Chapter 9), and nondirective (Chapter 10), and discuss characteristics of teachers best matched with each approach, the sequence of behaviors for each approach, and issues related to each approach. Finally, developmental supervision is reviewed in Chapter 11. The three phases of the model—choosing the best approach, applying the chosen approach, and fostering teacher development—are presented, along with case studies of the four supervisory approaches incorporated into the developmental model.

Part 4 is concerned with the technical skills of supervision. Observation skills, addressed in Chapter 12, can be used to carry out both quantitative and qualitative classroom observations, either for the purpose of assisting individual teachers to improve their instruction or for schoolwide observations as part of a needs assessment or evaluation of the school's instructional program. Chapter 13 begins with assessing and planning for personal improvement, and then shifts to a discussion of schoolwide assessment and planning as the first two components of instructional improvement across the organization. The discussion of skills for schoolwide instructional improvement continues in Chapter 14, which addresses skills for implementation and evaluation, the third and fourth components of the improvement process.

Part 5, on the technical tasks of supervision, begins with Chapter 15's treatment of direct assistance, including clinical supervision, peer coaching, and a new section on mentoring. Chapter 16 in this edition is a new chapter focused on the evaluation of teaching. In this chapter we examine the new wave of teacher evaluation systems, many of which include a "value added" component requiring the consideration of student test scores as part of teacher evaluation. We also discuss the difference between summative and formative evaluation of teachers, urge that these two types of evaluation of teaching be kept separate, and argue for more emphasis on formative evaluation. Chapter 17, on group development, includes new sections on the stages of group development and the characteristics of effective groups as well as long-standing discussions of group roles, resolving conflict, and preparing for group meetings. Chapter 18 includes information on the characteristics of successful professional development; suggestions for integrating schoolwide, group, and individual professional development; descriptions of alternative professional development formats; discussion of three stages of professional development; and ideas for evaluating professional development programs. Chapter 19, on curriculum development, describes the effects of legislated learning on the school curriculum and urges that teachers become more involved in curriculum development as a vehicle for enhancing their thinking about instruction. Five key issues that must be addressed during curriculum development are presented, the need for a culturally diverse curriculum is discussed, and a new section on "curriculum mapping and remapping" is introduced. Chapter 20 proposes action research as a vehicle for integrating all of the other technical tasks of supervision. The characteristics of successful action research are reviewed, and three alternative approaches to action research are offered for consideration. Shared governance for action research is described, and suggestions for assisting action research are offered.

Part 6 deals with the cultural tasks of supervision. Chapter 21 looks at three very different sources of change theory—chaos theory, postmodern theory, and education change theory—and presents a variety of comparisons across the three theories. The chapter concludes with a call to change the conditions of teaching if we wish schools to improve. Chapter 22 is concerned with the need to address diversity in our schools, and examines the need to work toward equity for diverse economic, racial, and ethnic groups; males and females; sexual and gender minorities; and students with disabilities. Finally, Chapter 23, on building community, proposes that schools are more likely to foster student growth and development if they are viewed as communities rather than organizations, and suggests five attributes of a fully functioning school community.

To the Instructor

We recommend that students be asked to consider the "Questions to Reflect On . . . " at the beginning of each chapter as they read the chapter. One way of doing this is to ask students to keep a reflective journal throughout the course, with journal entries for each chapter focused on that chapter's reflective questions. Students then can share their responses to the questions as part of a class discussion on the chapter.

The reflective exercise at the end of each chapter can be completed independently outside of class or be adopted for use as a small-group, in-class activity. Individual students or small groups can share reflective exercise products with the class.

Acknowledgments

It is impossible to acknowledge all those who have contributed to the development of this book. We would like to acknowledge the contribution of our colleague Edward Pajak, who developed with Glickman the directive informational supervisory approach in the early 1980s; throughout his career, Ed provided a guiding influence on the field of supervision. A host of colleagues—school practitioners, graduate students, and university faculty members—have provided us with settings, collaborations, and discussion for field-testing developmental and democratic propositions about supervision. Thanks to Dr. Jeff King, Dr. Rachel Solis, and doctoral research assistant Zane Wubbena for their assistance in various phases of the writing process. A special thanks to doctoral research assistant Susan Croteau, who conducted literature reviews, contributed to the writing of learning outcomes and our discussion of equity for students with disabilities, and assisted with editing.

Brief Contents

Contents

4 Adult and Teacher Development Within the Context of the School   62

5 Reflections on Educational Beliefs, Teaching, and Supervision   93

13 Assessing and Planning Skills   220

14 Implementation and Evaluation Skills   248

part five
Technical Tasks of Supervision   265

15 Direct Assistance to Teachers   267

16 Evaluation of Teaching   284

17 Group Development   302

18 Professional Development   325

part **six**
Cultural Tasks of Supervision   **387**

part **1**

Introduction

chapter 1

SuperVision for Successful Schools

Learning Outcomes for This Chapter

After reading this chapter, you should be able to:

1. Compare congenial, conventional, and collegial schools.
2. List the five purposes of teacher leadership.
3. Explain the moral purpose of supervision.

Questions to Reflect On as You Read This Chapter

1. The authors describe three very different schools in this chapter: Finnie Tyler High School, Germando Elementary, and Progress Middle School. Have you taught in or observed schools with instructional environments similar to any of these schools? If so, what were the effects of the school's environment on teachers? On students?

2. What surprises you about the authors' concept of instructional supervision? Do you agree with the authors' ideas about what instructional supervision should be?

3. Can teachers carry out instructional supervision as the authors define it? *Should* teachers carry out what the authors call instructional supervision?

4. Have you served in any of the instructional leadership activities listed in Table 1.1? Which activities do you believe would be the best new activities to initiate in a school you work at or are familiar with?

5. In this first chapter the authors provide a chart (see Figure 1.1) that demonstrates the scope and organization of the entire book. What topics on the chart are you especially interested in reading and discussing?

Take a walk with us. First, let's step into Finnie Tyler High School, with a student body of 1,200, in a lower- to middle-class urban neighborhood. A sign by the entrance tells all visitors to report to the office. In the halls, we see students milling around, boys and girls talking in groups, couples holding hands, one couple intertwined romantically in a corner. The bell rings and students scurry to the next class. We find the school office and introduce ourselves to the secretary and school principal, who are expecting our visit. They welcome us and assure us that we may move around the school and talk to students, teachers, and other staff. The school population has been notified of our visit and understands that we have come to see how Tyler High School operates. The principal tells us we will find Tyler a pleasant place. Equipped with a floor plan of classrooms and other facilities, we continue on our way.

The principal's description is accurate: Students seem happy and uninhibited, socializing easily with each other even during instruction time. Teachers joke with students. In the faculty lounge, we hear laughter that rises, falls, and then rises again. Several teachers have told us about the traditional Friday after-school gatherings at the local pizza parlor, where teachers and administrators socialize over a drink.

Classrooms vary considerably from each other; teachers tell us they can teach however they wish. Most teachers stand at the front of the room, lecturing, asking questions, and assigning seatwork. Some, however, take a less structured approach, allowing students to work alone or in small groups. There is an unhurried atmosphere. Students move at a leisurely pace, and classes seldom start on time. Teachers of the same subjects use the same textbooks but otherwise seem to have discretion to function as they please. As one seven-year veteran teacher at this school sums it up: "We have an ideal situation. We like each other, and the administration leaves us alone. I am observed once a year. I have one faculty meeting a month to attend. I love the other teachers and we have a great time together. The kids are fine, not as academic as they should be, but this school is a nice place for them. I wouldn't want to teach anyplace else."

Now let's drive across town to Germando Elementary School, with 600 students, located in a wealthy, suburban part of the city. Again, we follow the sign to the office. A few students are standing with their noses against the wall by their classroom doors. Otherwise, the halls are vacant and still; all classroom doors are shut. In the principal's office sit two students with tears in their eyes, obviously fearful of their impending conference with the principal. The principal welcomes us and hands us a preplanned schedule of times to visit particular teachers. She tells us not to visit any classroom during instructional time. "I think you will find that I run a tight ship," she says. "Teachers and students know exactly what is expected of them and what the consequences are for ignoring those expectations. Teachers are here to teach, and I see to it that it happens."

Moving down the halls, we are struck by the similarity of the classrooms. The desks are in rows; the teacher is in front; the school rules are posted on the right of the chalkboard. At the first recess time, the students seem to erupt onto the playground. Expecting to find a group of teachers in the faculty lounge, we are surprised to find only two people. One is knitting and the other is preparing a cup of coffee. All the other teachers have remained in the classrooms, either alone or with one other teacher.

Continuing our observation after recess, we find that teachers at each grade level not only work with the same textbooks but are on the same pages as well. When we ask about this, one teacher tells us that the principal has standardized the entire curriculum and knows what is being taught in every classroom at each moment of the day. At the first faculty meeting in August, the principal lays out materials, schedules, and time lines developed by the central office. We ask how the principal can enforce such procedures, and the teacher replies, "She asks for weekly lesson plans, visits my room at least once every two weeks, and has other central office personnel visit and report back to her."

In the classrooms we visit, students are generally quiet but restless. They appear attentive; those who are not are disciplined. Teachers are mostly businesslike; some show warmth toward their students, others do not. We conclude our visit with three separate interviews of teachers. It seems that teaching in Germando is perceived as a job to do. Whether one likes them or not, the principal's rules and regulations are to be followed. Teachers mention that when they have attempted to make modest changes in their instruction, they have been told to drop the changes and return to the school plan. All three mention the teacher who last year refused to follow the reading textbook and was subsequently forced to resign.

Finnie Tyler High School and Germando Elementary School are examples of real schools. Which is the successful school? Which has better attendance, attitudes, and achievement? *Neither does!* Both are ineffective, mediocre schools. The successful schools in the same system are quite different from either. Our first conclusion might be that these schools are very different. Tyler High School appears to have little supervision of instruction, whereas Germando has too much. According to the definition of instructional supervision presented in this book, however, *neither* school has effective instructional supervision. It also might appear that Tyler meets teachers' individual needs, whereas Germando meets organizational goals set by the principal. In successful schools, however, individual needs are fulfilled through organizational goals. In these two schools, *neither* need is being met. Finally, the working environments in these two schools only appear to be dissimilar; soon we will see how similar they really are.

The last school on our tour is Progress Middle School. Our first stop at Progress is the school office, where we are informed by the school secretary that the principal will meet with us at the end of the period. The principal is teaching Mr. Simmons's class while Simmons observes another teacher as part of a peer-coaching program involving a number of teachers. The secretary invites us to wait for the principal in the teachers' lounge, where several teachers are spending their preparation period. As we relax with a soda, we listen to an animated discussion among the teachers concerning an interdisciplinary unit of instruction they are planning. The teachers are brainstorming alternative teaching and assessment strategies for the unit and discussing how these strategies could be connected to the unit's theme.

Soon the principal joins us and invites us on a tour of the school. During the tour, we note that classroom environments are work oriented, as well as warm and supportive. In some classrooms, students are involved in hands-on inquiry. In other classrooms, cooperative learning is taking place. In still others, teachers are challenging students to reflect on lesson content by using higher-level questioning and inviting student opinions on the lesson topic. A commonality across all classrooms is students engaged in active learning. Teachers give students feedback on their performance and provide alternative learning opportunities and special attention to those experiencing difficulties.

After school, we attend a meeting of the school leadership council, made up primarily of teachers. The council is considering action research proposals submitted by faculty liaison groups. Each proposal is focused on improvement of curriculum and instruction. Much of the debate among council members is concerned with whether or not the proposed research will assist in meeting the school's vision, mission, and goals agreed on two years earlier by the entire faculty. At times the debate becomes heated. Clearly the council is taking its decision making seriously. The principal is a voting member of the council but does not have veto power over council decisions, which are made by majority rule.

Germando Elementary is an example of a *conventional school*—characterized by dependency, hierarchy, and professional isolation. Finnie Tyler is an example of a *congenial school*—characterized by friendly social interactions and professional isolation. A successful school like Progress Middle School is a *collegial school*—characterized by purposeful adult interactions about improving schoolwide teaching and learning. Professional respect is a byproduct of discussing issues with candor, accepting disagreements as integral to change, and respecting the wisdom and care of all for arriving at educational decisions for students.

Collegial schools establish learning goals for all students consistent with the responsibility of education in a democratic society. These schools are always studying teaching and learning, setting common priorities, making decisions about internal changes and resource allocations, and assessing effects on student learning (Sergiovanni, 2006). These schools are driven by (1) a covenant of learning—mission, vision, and goals; (2) a charter for schoolwide, democratic decision making; and (3) a critical study process for informing decisions and conducting action research (Glickman, 1993, 2003). In effect, successful schools create a "SuperVision" of instruction, democratically derived and studied, that gives purpose and direction to the common world of adults.

SuperVision: A New Name for a New Paradigm

Like schools, supervision can be conventional, congenial, or collegial. Throughout most of its history supervision has operated from within a conventional paradigm (worldview), attempting to control teachers' instructional behaviors (Nolan & Hoover, 2010; Sullivan & Glanz, 2009). Based on what we know about successful schools, the time has come to move from conventional schools (still dominant in the United States) and congenial schools (less prevalent but still present throughout the nation) toward collegial schools (growing in number and success). A *paradigm shift toward the collegial model, if it is to succeed, must include a shift away from conventional or congenial supervision toward collegial supervision.* This view of supervision includes all of the following:

1. A collegial rather than a hierarchical relationship between teachers and formally designated supervisors
2. Supervision as the province of teachers as well as formally designated supervisors
3. A focus on teacher growth rather than teacher compliance
4. Facilitation of teachers collaborating with each other in instructional improvement efforts
5. Teacher involvement in ongoing reflective inquiry (Gordon, 1997, p. 116 see also Fallon & Barnett, 2009; Kohm & Nance, 2009; Snow-Gerono, 2008).

Jo Blase captures the spirit of this new, collegial approach to supervision in the following description:

> Leadership is shared with teachers, and it is cast in coaching, reflection, collegial investigation, study teams, explorations into the uncertain, and problem solving. It is position-free supervision wherein the underlying spirit is one of expansion, not traditional supervision. Alternatives, not directives or criticism, are the focus, and the community of learners perform professional—indeed, moral—service to students (cited in Gordon, 1995; see also Printy, Marks, & Bowers, 2009).

Collegial supervision, then, stands in sharp contrast to traditional approaches to supervision (Zepeda, 2005).

▶ Video Illustration

In this video, a supervisor is being interviewed about his work with teachers during his first year as principal. On a scale of 1 to 10, with 1 representing no commitment and 10 representing the highest possible commitment, how would you rate the principal's commitment to collegial supervision? What information from the video supports your rating?

Given the fact that the historic role of supervision has been inspection and control, it is not surprising that most teachers do not equate supervision with collegiality. When teachers have been asked to make word associations with the term *instructional supervision,* most of the associations have been negative, as indicated by the following list (Gordon, 1997, p. 118):

Control	Directive
Step-by-step	Irrelevant
Lack of creativity	Waste of time
Lack of free choice	Restricting
Evaluation	Rules
Negative	Dog and pony show
Nonexistent	Big brother
Jumping through hoops	Intimidating
Boring	Constantly under watch
Paperwork	Anxiety
Bureaucrat	Boss
Monitoring instruction	Stress
Guidelines for testing	Need for detailed lesson plans
Authority	Micromanagement
Unrealistic	Yuck!

The dictionary definition of *supervision* is to "watch over," "direct," "oversee," "superintend." The history of instructional supervision is viewed most often as an instrument for controlling teachers. The flight from education of both new and experienced educators is due, in part, to the external control of teachers' work lives (Lavié, 2006). It seems that a new term for describing the collegial model of instructional leadership espoused in this book is in order. Therefore, the first word in the title of this new edition is *SuperVision,* a term that denotes a common vision of what teaching and learning can and should be, developed collaboratively by formally designated supervisors, teachers, and other members of the school community. The word also implies that these same persons will work together to make their vision a reality—to build a democratic community of learning based on moral principles calling for all students to be educated in a manner enabling them to lead fulfilling lives and be contributing members of a democratic society (Lavié, 2006).*

---

*To avoid awkwardness of writing, from here on we will use the spelling SuperVision only in particular headings. But the point is that SuperVision and instructional leadership are integrated and interchangeable concepts.

Supervisory Glue as a Metaphor for Success

We can think of supervision as the *glue* of a successful school. Supervision is the function in schools that draws together the discrete elements of instructional effectiveness into whole-school action. In other words, when teachers accept common goals for students and therefore complement each other's teaching, and when supervisors work with teachers in a manner consistent with the way teachers are expected to work with students, then—and only then—does the school reach its goals. Regardless of a school's grade span, socioeconomic setting, or physical characteristics, successful schools have a common glue that keeps a faculty together and creates consistency among a school's various elements. The glue is the process by which some person or group of persons is responsible for providing a link between individual teacher needs and organizational goals so that individuals within the school can work in harmony toward their vision of what the school *should* be.

Effective supervision requires knowledge, interpersonal skills, and technical skills. These are applied through the technical supervisory tasks of direct assistance to teachers, curriculum development, professional development, group development, and action research; and the cultural tasks of facilitating change, addressing diversity, and building community. This adhesive pulls together organizational goals and teacher needs and provides for improved learning.

New Roles for Supervisors and Teachers

In this chapter we have argued that teachers and supervisors should have a collegial relationship, that supervision should be the province of teachers as well as supervisors, and that teachers should collaborate with each other for instructional improvement. In many schools, however, both supervisors and teachers will need to change how they think about leadership and instructional supervision before teachers can collaborate fully with supervisors as instructional leaders.

Many supervisors have been prepared in educational leadership preparation programs to be *heroic individuals,* described by Bogotch (2002) as possessing "a single-mindedness to pursue their own vision tenaciously and apart from others who may not share their particular vision" (p. 148). To fully engage teachers as instructional leaders, supervisors need to move away from heroic individualism, toward *communal leadership,* which, according to Furman (2004), "shifts the locus of moral agency to the community as a whole" (p. 222). Applied to instructional supervision, communal leadership means that the supervisor becomes the facilitator of a community of practice that uses collaborative inquiry, reflection, and dialogue to develop a collective vision of what it wants teaching and learning to look like, explores ways of moving toward that vision, and assesses its progress for the purpose of continuous improvement. Communal supervision involves all professionals in the school community accepting moral responsibility for improving instruction in order to improve learning for *all* students.

Why should teachers participate in instructional leadership? Why not just let supervisors supervise and teachers teach? Hart's (1995) five purposes of teacher leadership address the why questions. Teacher leadership:

1. Promotes democratic schools and democratic education
2. Allows the school to take advantage of teacher experience and expertise
3. Helps the school to recruit and retain highly qualified teachers
4. Increases the likelihood that teachers will accept curriculum and instructional innovations, since teachers are involved in designing the innovations
5. Promotes a more professional work environment

Hart's rationale for teacher leadership is powerful, but given the history of authoritarian supervision in many schools, neither a supervisor's willingness to involve teachers in instructional leadership nor the benefits of teacher leadership described in the literature ensures that teachers will accept instructional leadership responsibilities. We are warned by Kohm and Nance (2009) that in a school where they have not previously participated in schoolwide instructional decisions, "teachers see problems as somebody else's fault and solutions as somebody else's responsibility" (p. 72). A supervisor wishing to move teachers who are used to traditional supervision toward communitarian, collegial supervision can begin by opening two-way communication with teachers about strengths and weaknesses of instruction in the school, their vision of the optimal environment for teaching and learning, and their ideas for moving toward that vision. It is important that the purpose of such discussions not be to merely create a traditional vision statement, but to engage in open, reflective, ongoing discussion about how the school community can improve student learning by improving instruction at both the school and the classroom levels. The collective vision that emerges from instructional dialogue should be flexible and subject to change if it does not lead to the improvement of teaching and learning.

We believe that all teachers have a moral obligation to be concerned about all students in the school community, and that this obligation includes being an instructional leader at some level. The accountability movement, coupled with the increasing realization by educators that designated supervisors can no longer do it all, has led to the assignment of teacher leaders in schools across the nation. If the teacher-leader movement is to succeed, districts and schools must provide some basic types of support for teachers who assume formal leadership roles. Teacher leaders need the following types of support:

- Clearly defined roles and responsibilities of both supervisors and teacher leaders, disseminated to all stakeholders.
- Professional development to prepare teacher leaders for their roles, including development of general leadership skills such as communication, collaboration,

planning, organizing, time management, group process, technology, and data analysis skills; as well as skills for promoting adult learning, reflective inquiry, and cultural responsiveness. Teacher leaders also should be provided differentiated professional development to learn skills for specific leadership activities they are assigned, such as mentoring, peer coaching, group presentations, curriculum development, action research, and so on.

- Moral support from supervisors and teachers. Even the best teacher leaders cannot do it alone; they need the trust, encouragement, and cooperation of coworkers.

- Released time to prepare for leadership activities, meet with teachers, work on projects, and so forth. Even teachers provided with released time can be overloaded with leadership responsibilities, thus the assignment of an appropriate workload is another necessary support.

- Ongoing consultation, which can take a variety of forms, such as mentoring of new teacher leaders by supervisors or experienced teacher leaders, seminars that address issues in teacher leadership, and critical friends from outside the school consulting with teacher leaders.

- Provision of necessary resources and materials, such as books, software, curriculum materials, workshop supplies, and so forth.

- Rewards such as increased salary or stipends, funding for continuing education, memberships in educational associations and networks related to teacher leadership, and public recognition. The primary rewards of teacher leadership are intrinsic, but extrinsic rewards are a way for the district and school to support the concept of teacher leadership and acknowledge the work of teacher leaders (Gordon, 2011; Gordon, Jacobs, & Solis, 2013; Jacobs, Gordon, & Solis, 2013).

Not all teachers are able or willing to be designated as teacher leaders. Novice teachers, and some experienced teachers, need to focus on developing teaching expertise before assuming formal leadership roles. Although teacher leaders should be expert teachers, some expert teachers do not possess the qualities necessary to assume formal leadership roles and are of greater value to students if they continue teaching fulltime. And some teachers simply prefer to focus primarily on teaching and have no desire to assume formal leadership roles, at least in the present. The wishes of teachers who do not wish to be designated as teacher leaders should be honored; however, all teachers should practice informal teacher leadership to varying degrees, depending on their individual situations, interests, and talents.

Informal teacher leadership can take place at the school, team, or classroom level. Teachers can serve on school-level committees, participate in schoolwide needs assessment and goal setting, assist in schoolwide change efforts, be part of school outreach to the community, and so on. Informal teacher leadership at the team level can include reciprocal peer coaching, collaborative learning walks, membership in professional learning communities, service on curriculum development teams, participation in team action research, and so forth. Examples of classroom leadership can take the form of self-evaluation of teaching, self-directed improvement, democratic pedagogy, teaching for equity and social justice, classroom-based curriculum development, collaboration with parents and community members, classroom action research, and establishing the classroom as a moral community and a community of inquiry.

As is evident from our discussion thus far, communal supervision does not mean that everyone has the same leadership role and responsibilities. Communal supervision can be distributed so that designated supervisors, designated teacher leaders, and informal teacher leaders have different roles and responsibilities, but this does not in any way imply a three-tiered hierarchy. Rather, the model we propose involves coequal community members with differentiated leadership and teaching responsibilities, mutually committed to each other, their students, and a collective vision of what they want teaching and learning to be in their school.

In communal supervision, the supervisor moves from sole provider to coordinator of instructional leadership. It's important to recognize that teacher leadership in the model we present is fluid. Designated teacher leaders typically are not responsible for all of the activities we list; different teacher leaders assume different leadership responsibilities, and teacher leaders' roles and responsibilities tend to evolve over time. For example, a teacher leader serving as an expert coach for a few years may eventually shift to leading a curriculum development team. After serving as a designated teacher leader for a few years, a teacher may return to full-time teaching and informal teacher leadership. Conversely, a teacher who has been successful in informal teacher leadership may be asked to become a designated teacher leader. Instructional leadership can take many different forms and be distributed in a variety of different ways in communal supervision. Regardless of the specific instructional leadership activities of designated supervisors, designated teacher leaders, and informal teacher leaders, and how those activities are distributed, all of those activities should (1) focus on the schools' collective vision for teaching and learning, and (2) complement each other in order to form a coherent system of instructional leadership. Table 1.1 provides examples of distributed instructional leadership activities for designated supervisors, designated teacher leaders, and informal teacher leaders across nine tasks of supervision.

▶ Video Illustration

The principal in this video is attempting to move away from traditional supervision. What aspects of communal supervision do you see taking place in the high school? How could the principal increase the communal nature of supervision in the school? How could the principal further distribute instructional leadership among teachers?

t a b l e **1.1** **Distributed Instructional Leadership in Communal Supervision**

Task	Designated Supervisors	Designated Teacher Leaders	Informal Teacher Leaders
Direct Assistance	• Provide clinical supervision • Coordinate, support, and monitor peer coaching throughout the school • Mentor novice supervisors, aspiring supervisors, teacher leaders, and aspiring teacher leaders • Lead collaborative learning walks • Share new teaching methods, resources, and materials with teachers • Be present for teachers and students	• Provide expert peer coaching • Coordinate peer coaching teams • Mentor experienced teachers, new teacher leaders, aspiring teacher leaders, beginning teachers, and teachers new to the school • Co-teach • Lead collaborative learning walks • Share new teaching methods, resources, and materials with other teachers	• Participate in reciprocal peer coaching • Mentor beginning teachers and teachers new to the school • Co-teach • Participate in collaborative learning walks • Share new teaching methods, resources, and materials with other teachers
Evaluation of Teaching	• Conduct formative teacher evaluation* • Conduct summative teacher evaluation* • Coordinate formative evaluation of instructional teams • Coordinate formative evaluation of teaching at the school level	• Conduct formative self-evaluation of own teaching • Conduct formative evaluation of other teachers • Assist with formative self-evaluation of instructional teams • Assist with formative evaluation of teaching at the school level	• Conduct formative self-evaluation of teaching • Participate in formative coevaluation with other teachers • Participate in formative self-evaluation of instructional teams • Participate in formative evaluation of teaching at the school level
Group Development	• With stakeholder input, form new collegial groups as needed • Model successful facilitation of collegial groups • Support and monitor collegial groups throughout the school • Coordinate communication, collaboration, and coherence across collegial groups	• Facilitate formal groups • Serve as liaison across formal groups and between formal groups and school leadership	• Facilitate informal groups • Serve as liaison across informal groups and between informal groups and school leadership

(Continued)

Task	Designated Supervisors	Designated Teacher Leaders	Informal Teacher Leaders
Professional Development	• Engage in own professional development • Coordinate professional development needs assessment • With stakeholder input, introduce and plan professional development • Coordinate, support, and monitor professional development • Deliver professional development • Promote a school culture that fosters transformative learning • Coordinate assessment of professional development	• Provide input on professional development needs, and assist in professional development needs assessment • Assist in planning professional development • Participate in teacher-leader and teacher professional development • Deliver professional development • Participate in assessment of professional development	• Provide input on professional development needs • Assist in planning professional development • Participate in professional development • Deliver professional development • Participate in assessment of professional development
Curriculum Development	• Assign curriculum development teams and team leaders • Introduce innovative ideas and research on curriculum • Facilitate schoolwide decisions about the curriculum's purpose, content, organization, and format • Facilitate schoolwide efforts to make the curriculum more culturally responsive • Coordinate curriculum development to ensure appropriate sequence, continuity, scope, and balance • Coordinate monitoring and assessment of curriculum implementation and results	• Facilitate team discussions on decisions about the curriculum's purpose, content, organization, and format • Introduce innovative ideas and research on curriculum • Participate in curriculum writing at the school level • Coordinate and participate in curriculum writing at the team level • Facilitate team efforts to make the curriculum more culturally responsive • Gather and analyze data on assigned areas of the curriculum • Pilot, assess, and modify curriculum in the classroom	• Participate in decisions about the curriculum's purpose, content, organization, and format • Participate in making the curriculum more culturally responsive • Participate in curriculum writing at the school and team level • Pilot, assess, and modify curriculum in the classroom

Task	Designated Supervisors	Designated Teacher Leaders	Informal Teacher Leaders
Action Research	• Conduct individual action research • Facilitate school action research council • Coordinate, support, and monitor action research liaison groups and task forces • Support and monitor action research projects and assess results • Promote an inquiry stance among teachers and staff	• Conduct individual action research • Serve as member of school's action research council • Serve on action research liaison group and task forces • Participate in schoolwide action research • Coordinate instructional teams' action research • Promote an inquiry stance among teachers and staff	• Conduct individual action research • Serve as member of school's action research council • Serve on action research liaison group and task forces • Participate in instructional teams' action research • Participate in schoolwide action research • Use student action research as pedagogy
Facilitating Change	• Focus on building capacity for change • Seek input from all stakeholders regarding needed change • Develop partnerships to assist change • Promote norms present in school cultures of continuous improvement • Foster coherence among change efforts • Coordinate and support change efforts • Engage in open and respectful dialogue with those resistant to change • Coordinate gathering and analyzing data to monitor and assess change efforts	• Focus on building capacity for change • Assist in gathering feedback from stakeholders regarding needed change • Participate in decisions about needed change • Coordinate with other teacher leaders and supervisors on schoolwide change • Facilitate change at the instructional team and classroom level • Engage in open and respectful dialogue with those resistant to change • Assist with gathering and analyzing data to monitor and assess change efforts	• Participate in decisions about needed change • Collaborate with other teachers in implementing change at the school and team level • Seek parent and student input and support for change at the classroom level • Adapt schoolwide and instructional team change to classroom teaching • Engage in self-directed change at the classroom level • Provide classroom data to assist monitoring and assessment of change efforts
Addressing Diversity	• Learn about and from other cultures • Develop culturally responsive teaching and leadership skills • In collaboration with stakeholders, establish policies for equitable treatment of all groups	• Learn about and from other cultures • Develop culturally responsive teaching and leadership skills • Build personal, caring relationships • Model cultural responsiveness	• Learn about and from other cultures • Develop culturally responsive teaching skills • Build personal, caring relationships • Model cultural responsiveness

(Continued)

Task	Designated Supervisors	Designated Teacher Leaders	Informal Teacher Leaders
	• Build personal, caring relationships • Model cultural responsiveness • Coordinate and share schoolwide equity audits • Coordinate schoolwide efforts to develop teacher and staff cultural responsiveness • In collaboration with stakeholders, develop schoolwide structures and processes that promote equity and social justice • Coordinate schoolwide development of culturally responsive curriculum, instruction, and student assessment • Collaborate with families and community in promoting equity and social justice	• Assist in coordination of schoolwide equity audits • Assist in coordination of schoolwide efforts to promote equity and social justice • Coordinate and share subgroup equity audits • Coordinate instructional teams' work with parents and community to promote equity and social justice • Coordinate instructional teams' work to develop culturally responsive curriculum, instruction, and assessment • Work with individual teachers to promote their cultural responsiveness	• Participate in schoolwide equity audits • Participate in schoolwide efforts to promote equity and social justice • Participate in subgroup equity audits • Participate in instructional teams' efforts to promote equity and social justice • Conduct and share classroom and individual student equity audits • Recognize and utilize diverse cultural assets of community, families, and students in classroom teaching • Use culturally responsive teaching and student assessment strategies
Building Community	• Lead the school as a democratic community that embraces democratic values, relationships, and governance • Support democratic pedagogy • Practice the principles of moral community • Lead the school as a moral community • Lead the school as a professional learning community, and foster subgroups as professional learning communities • Lead the school as a community of inquiry • Form partnerships and provide leadership to the larger community	• Support the school as a democratic community and lead instructional teams as democratic communities • Practice and support democratic pedagogy • Practice the principles of moral community • Support the school as a moral community and lead instructional teams as moral communities • Lead and participate in professional learning communities • Lead instructional teams in the cycle of inquiry • Assist in coordination of school-based or school-linked community service	• Participate in democratic community at the school and team level • Practice democratic pedagogy • Practice the principles of moral community • Teach students moral principles • Participate in professional learning communities • Work with other teachers through the cycle of inquiry • Make the classroom a community of inquiry • Assist in coordination of school-based or school-linked community service • Participate in community development • Use the community as a learning environment.

Task	Designated Supervisors	Designated Teacher Leaders	Informal Teacher Leaders
	• Coordinate school-based or school-linked community service • Lead community development • Promote community-based learning	• Participate in community development • Coordinate community-based learning	

Formative and summative evaluation should be carried out separately (see Chapter 16)

Supervision and Moral Purpose

Supervision based on moral purpose begins with the school community asking two broad questions:

1. What type of society do we desire?
2. What type of educational environment should supervision promote in order to move toward the society we desire?

If even part of the answer to the first question involves a democratic society in which all members are considered equal, then the answer to the second question must involve creating an educational environment that prepares students to be members of that democratic society. We can take this one step further and say that the answer involves creating a school that mirrors the democratic society that we desire.

We ground this book in a SuperVision of schools that deliver on the promise of education that promotes a better democracy for all (Glickman, 2003; Lavié, 2006). To do so, we cannot think of ourselves as first-grade teachers, high school mathematics teachers, middle school counselors, central office specialists, high school principals, or superintendents. These positions are reflections of where we locate our bodies to go to work, but the names don't reflect where we need to locate our minds and our hearts. Educators are the primary stewards of the democratic spirit. The total of our efforts is far greater than the particulars of our job (Glickman, 1998; Lavié, 2006).

The democratic impulse for renewing education continues to resonate in the thoughts of many local teachers, parents, administrators, and citizens in schools throughout this country—perhaps among more people than ever before. However, schools blessed with such far-sighted people are still in the margin. The challenge to bring an inclusive definition of democracy as the guiding principle into public education is enormous (Glickman, 1998). We have been here before and we might fall short once again. But whether we succeed or simply keep the spirit alive, we will have let other generations of educators and citizens know that this is the most important fight in which to engage—the democratic education of our students for a just and democratic society.

Organization of This Book

Figure 1.1 demonstrates the scope and organization of this text. For those in supervisory roles, the challenge to improving student learning is to apply certain knowledge, interpersonal skills, and technical skills to the technical tasks of direct assistance, evaluation of teaching, group development, curriculum development, professional development, and action research, as well as the cultural tasks of facilitating change, addressing diversity, and building community to enable teachers to teach in a collective, purposeful manner, uniting organizational goals and teacher needs. As the supervisor allows teachers to take greater control over their own professional lives, a school becomes a dynamic setting for learning.

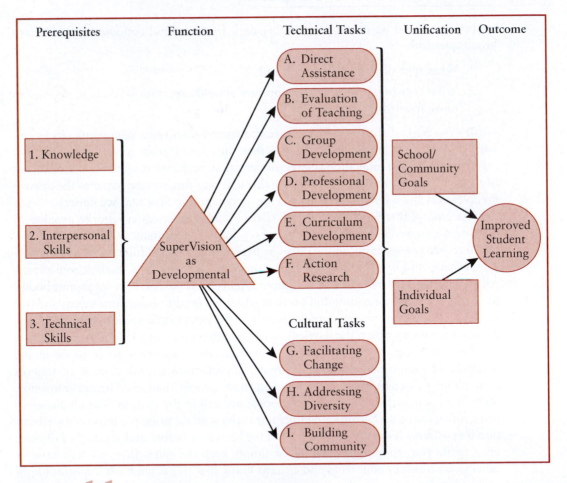

figure **1.1**   **SuperVision and Successful Schools**

To facilitate such collective instructional improvement, those responsible for supervision must have certain prerequisites. The first is a *knowledge* base. Supervisors need to understand the exception—what teachers and schools can be—in contrast to the norm—what teachers and schools typically are. They need to understand how knowledge of adult and teacher development and alternative supervisory practices can help break the norm of mediocrity found in typical schools. Second, there is an *interpersonal skills* base. Supervisors must know how their own interpersonal behaviors affect individuals as well as groups of teachers and then study ranges of interpersonal behaviors that might be used to promote more positive and change-oriented relationships. Third, the supervisor must have *technical skills* in observing, planning, assessing, implementing, and evaluating instructional improvement. Knowledge, interpersonal skills, and technical competence are three complementary aspects of supervision as a developmental function.

Supervisors have certain educational tasks at their disposal that enable teachers to evaluate and modify their instruction. In planning each task, the supervisor needs to plan specific ways of giving teachers a greater sense of professional power to teach students successfully. Technical supervisory tasks that have such potential to affect teacher development are direct assistance, evaluation of teaching, group development, professional development, curriculum development, and action research. Direct assistance *(A)* is the provision of personal, ongoing contact with the individual teacher to observe and assist in classroom instruction. Evaluation of teaching *(B)* includes the assessment of teaching at the individual, team, and school levels. Group development *(C)* is the gathering together of teachers to make decisions on mutual instructional concerns. Professional development *(D)* includes the learning opportunities for faculty provided or supported by the school and school system. Curriculum development *(E)* is the revision and modification of the content, plans, and materials of classroom instruction. Action research *(F)* is the systematic study by a faculty of what is happening in the classroom and school with the aim of improving learning. Cultural tasks that can assist both school and teacher development include facilitating change, addressing diversity, and building community. Facilitating change *(G)* includes both assisting innovation and developing the capacity of the school and teachers to change with a changing environment. Addressing diversity *(H)* means developing both culturally responsive teachers and culturally responsive schools to ensure equity for all. Building community *(I)* involves fostering democracy, moral action, professional learning, and inquiry in the school as well as engaging the larger community in collaborative efforts to improve the school and community.

By understanding how teachers grow optimally in a supportive and challenging environment, the supervisor can plan the tasks of supervision to bring together the school community's goals and teacher needs into a single fluid entity. The unification of individual teacher needs with organizational goals in "a cause beyond oneself" has been demonstrated to promote powerful instruction and improved student learning.

Figure 1.1, therefore, presents the organization of this text in a nutshell. Part 2 will be devoted to essential knowledge. Part 3 will deal with interpersonal skills. Part 4 will explain technical skills the supervisor needs, and Part 5 will discuss the application of such knowledge and skills to the technical tasks of supervision. Finally, Part 6 will introduce the cultural tasks of supervision and show how supervision can integrate individual needs with school community goals to improve schools, teaching, and learning.

> ✔ **Check Your Understanding 1.0**   Click here to gauge your understanding of the key concepts presented in this chapter.

REFLECTIVE EXERCISE

For the purpose of this reflective exercise, assume that you recently accepted a position as school principal in a district where the principal is assigned the primary responsibility for instructional supervision at each school. When you interviewed for the position with the superintendent, you made it clear to her that you would take a collegial approach to supervision, including the fostering of teachers as instructional leaders.

It is now just a few weeks prior to when you are to become principal, and earlier today you received a call from the superintendent during which she informed you that the results of the state's annual high-stakes achievement test have just been received and your new school has failed the state test. The superintendent states that, while she agrees in principle with your ideas on collegial supervision, your first year as principal will not be a good time for collegiality. The superintendent tells you that in light of the failing test score, the coming school year will be a time for demanding that teachers focus on improving students' test performance and closely monitoring teachers' instruction to make sure it is focused on the state's test objectives. You remain committed to collegial supervision, but you also prefer not to be relieved of your new position as principal because of a conflict with the superintendent over the best approach to instructional supervision. As principal and instructional supervisor, how will you address the superintendent's concerns? How will you work with the school's teachers over the next year to improve teaching and learning?

part 2

Knowledge

Part 2 examines the prerequisite knowledge for supervision. Chapter 2 will consider the pessimistic news—why schools are typically ineffective. The causes of ineffectiveness will be traced to the teaching career and the school environment. Chapter 3 will explain the optimistic news about the characteristics of dynamic schools. Chapter 4 will explain the relevance of adult learning and development to supervision. Chapter 5 will look at how beliefs about education and supervision provide the foundation for supervisory practice. While moving from pessimism to optimism to realism, we will be riding through highly explosive grounds. Reactions of delight, anger, chagrin, hope, and disagreement are to be expected as current research challenges us to rethink current supervisory practices.

chapter 2

The Norm: Why Traditional Schools Are as They Are

Learning Outcomes for This Chapter

After reading this chapter, you should be able to:

1. Explain the long-term effects of teachers' psychological isolation.
2. Explain the appropriate response to the presence of different cultures within the same school.
3. Describe how the Newtonian characteristic of atomism is reflected in traditional schools.

Questions to Reflect On as You Read This Chapter

1. What are some ways that the problems of teacher isolation can be addressed?
2. If you are or have been a teacher, think back on your first year of teaching. Did you experience the problems of beginning teachers described in this chapter? Did you receive support from one or more educators that helped you cope with the challenges of your first year of teaching?
3. What can be done to attract and retain the most qualified teachers to schools serving low-income communities?
4. What are some different cultures within a school you are familiar with that are either isolated from each other or in conflict with each other? What do you believe is responsible for the isolation or conflict?
5. The last section of this chapter describes several ways that traditional schools reflect the Newtonian paradigm. What are some additional ways that traditional schools mirror the Newtonian worldview?

Our eyes must be wide open as we examine historical aspects of schools, teachers, and leadership. We must acknowledge that the traditional school culture must be changed if we are serious about lasting instructional improvement.

The Work Environment or Culture of Schools: The Legacy of the One-Room Schoolhouse

The study of values, beliefs, myths, rituals, symbols, heroes, shamans, and storytellers in organizations is well documented in the literature (Bolman & Deal, 2002). It may seem technically incorrect to apply the term *culture* to professional settings; the term is appropriated from the anthropological studies of largely intact and isolated communities of people. However, the concept of culture helps us reexamine schools as places of human community with peculiar histories and stories. When we grasp the underlying values of our particular school as a work environment, we can consciously act to reshape the organization into a purposeful collection of individuals who believe that schools are for students, for learning, and for improvement rather than for insularity, self-protection, and complacency.

Discussing the present work environment of schools without discussing the one-room schoolhouse would be comparable to talking about issues in Western democracies without acknowledging the Magna Carta. Much of what exists in beliefs and expectations about schools can be traced to the idyllic-looking, clapboard, one-room schoolhouses of pioneer times. The teacher was responsible for the total instruction of all students, the maintenance of the building, keeping the stove filled with wood, and cleaning the floors. Our first schoolteachers were seen as working in an honorable but menial profession, poorly paid but second only to the preacher in prestige.

The work environment of teachers in the Frontier West is described by McMillan and Price (2005):

> Classrooms in the West often were in sod dugouts with little, if any furniture. The one room schoolhouse often housed upward of 20 students varying in age from 5 to 22. The teacher relied on parents sending books and resources that were of questionable use and adapted the curriculum to what was available in terms of pedagogical tools. The women teachers of the West withstood the lack of funding, lack of proper schoolhouse, limited supplies, and very little encouragement, yet maintained the attitude that theirs' was a noble profession. . . . The parallel with modern teaching conditions is remarkable, with overcrowded classrooms, underpaid professionals, scarce resources, funding difficulties and yet an unwavering attitude on the part of the teacher as to the nobility of the job. (p. 146)

In the one-room schoolhouse, the teacher was responsible for all that transpired within its four walls; therefore, collective action in a school was automatic. What the teacher wanted to do about curriculum and instruction was what the school did! This legacy of independence, isolation, and privatization of teaching remains alive and well in many schools today. Instead of having physically separated one-room school-houses, we often see the one-room schoolhouses repeated every few yards down a school corridor. Teachers each see their students, within the four walls, as their own school. Although the old one-room school is physically gone, it still holds a pervasive grip on the minds and actions of many teachers and schools.

The sense of classrooms as being private places is in direct contrast to the research on norms of improving schools: "There is abundant research linking higher levels of student achievement to educators that work in the collaborative culture of a professional learning community" (DuFour, 2011, p. 59).

The one-room schoolhouse of pioneer times has spawned a deep-seated institutional belief among educators that is characterized by isolation, psychological dilemmas, routine, inadequate induction of beginning teachers, inequity, lack of career stages, lack of professional dialogue, lack of involvement in school decisions, and conservatism. Many educators accept that these characteristics are simply part of a school culture, and there is little doubt that they pervade the minds and beliefs of many teachers and administrators. However, instructional leaders question whether beliefs and practices acceptable in the past are appropriate for the present, when we need to initiate a new culture based on purposeful and collective beliefs about school, students, and teaching. Let's look at the characteristics of today's education that are derived from the one-room schoolhouse of bygone days.

Isolation

The isolation and individualism of teachers has been observed in all major studies of their work environment. DuFour (2011) notes:

> Teachers work in isolation from one another. They view their classrooms as their personal domains, have little access to the ideas or strategies of their colleagues, and prefer to be left alone rather than engage with their colleagues or principals. Their professional practice is shrouded in a veil of privacy and personal autonomy and is not a subject for collective discussion or analysis. Their schools offer no infrastructure to support collaboration or continuous improvement, and, in fact the very structure of their schools serves as a powerful force for preserving the status quo. (p. 57)

Classrooms are set up structurally in such a way that teachers are difficult to supervise, do not receive feedback from others, and cannot work collaboratively. During a typical workday, a teacher will talk to only a few other adults—on the way to the classroom in the morning, for 20 minutes or so at lunch and recess, and at the end of the day on the way out of the building. While teaching, teachers in most schools are invisible to each other and lack any concrete knowledge of what other teachers are doing in their classrooms.

Physical teacher isolation can lead to *psychological* isolation: "Due to the isolated culture, teachers may become frustrated, bored, and depleted as they privately struggle with their anxieties" (Chang, 2009, p. 193). Teachers who have experienced long-term psychological isolation tend to view their work environment as limited to *their* classroom, *their* students, and *their* teaching. Although their isolation was initially involuntary, over time they have adapted to and accepted the tradition of isolation (Brooks, Hughes, & Brooks, 2008; Price & Collett, 2012); they now resist opportunities for professional dialogue and collaboration with other teachers that might arise.

Psychological Dilemma and Frustration

The teacher's work environment is marked by incessant psychological encounters. In just a few minutes of observation, one might see a teacher ask a question, reply with a smile to a student's answer, frown at an inattentive student, ask a student to be quiet, put a hand on a student's shoulder, and begin to lecture. Teachers have thousands of such psychological encounters in a normal school day (Grayson & Alvarez, 2008). A look, a shrug, and a word all have intended meanings between teacher and students.

Each day an elementary teacher meets with 25 to 35 students for 6.5 hours. A secondary teacher meets with 100 to 150 students for five to seven 50-minute periods. All this human interaction takes place in a 900-square-foot room, where a teacher must instruct, manage, discipline, reinforce, socialize, and attend to multiple occurrences. This crowded professional life makes teachers wish for fewer problems and smaller classes to reduce the psychological demand of constant decision making (Chang, 2009; Pietarinen, Pyhalto, Soini, & Salmela-Aro, 2013; Van Droogenbroeck, Spruyt, & Vanroelen, 2014).

> Students always have brought their ills to school: headaches, respiratory ailments, broken bones. Today, students arrive at school with much more serious medical conditions. Teachers are asked to accommodate students with such conditions as autism, attention deficit disorder, and effects of fetal alcohol syndrome. Classroom environments are changing as well. Forty-five students are squeezed into spaces designed for 30, and students and teachers often work in conditions that most business, legal, or medical professionals would not tolerate. As budgets dwindle and buildings decay, environmental conditions take a toll over time and affect student learning on a daily basis. (Garrett, 2006, p. 12)

To maintain their own sanity in the face of an overload of psychological encounters and an inability to attend to the psychological needs of each student in a confined and regulated workplace, teachers often cope by routinizing classroom activity. The classroom routine for students becomes similar to the outside routine for teachers. For example, a science teacher might have students listen to a 20-minute presentation, followed by a 10-minute question-and-answer period and then by 20 minutes of seatwork. An elementary teacher might teach three reading groups who rotate for 15 minutes each; the groups each read aloud, respond to teacher questions, and then complete worksheets. By routinizing what happens within the classroom, a teacher avoids making hundreds of decisions. The routinization of teaching allows the teacher to avoid the inherent conflict between being overwhelmed psychologically by the responsibility for teaching a large number of students and being aware of neglecting the personal needs of individual students. In interpersonal terms, teaching closely resembles clinical psychology, but it takes place in an environment more like that of factory production.

Routine of the Teaching Career

The routine of the teaching day is imposed by administrative fiat, school board policy, and state guidelines. Every classroom teacher is required to be at school before students enter and to remain until they have departed. In primary or elementary schools, a teacher has specific times for recess and lunch, as well as approximate time allocations for teaching a given subject (e.g., 45 minutes for reading, 30 minutes for mathematics, 30 minutes twice a week for social studies). The teacher is assigned a certain number of students and has responsibility for them for the entire day and school year. The teacher is expected to remain physically in the assigned classroom for the entire school day, with the exception of recess, lunch, or special classes. Outside the classroom, teachers also have scheduled responsibilities for lunch, recess, and dismissal. In middle school, junior high school, and senior high school, the school day is different from that of elementary school but still has a set routine. A secondary teacher will have four to seven different classes of students meeting at specific times each day for an extended period (11, 18, or 36 weeks). Again, the teacher begins and dismisses each class at a prescribed time and has regular duties outside the classroom (e.g., monitoring the lunchroom, halls, or bathrooms).

Regardless of grade level, teachers do not schedule their own time or determine the number or type of students. Unlike more autonomous professionals, teachers do not put up a shingle on the door, ask clients to arrange for appointments, or take Wednesday mornings off. Teachers do not have the right to make changes in their schedule. Imagine a teacher asking the school secretary to clear his or her schedule for several hours, to attend to other business. School goes on, students keep coming, the bells keep ringing, and teachers cannot make individual readjustments of their professional time.

Of course, elementary and secondary teachers often make readjustments within the assigned time, within their four walls, with their assigned students, and with instruction. School time, however, is imposed. Starting and ending times, numbers of students, physical locations for teaching, and extra duties are set for the duration, and a teacher has little control. The routines the school as a workplace imposes are more like those of a factory than a high-status profession. The punch-in, punch-out clock may not be visible in the entryway of the school, but nonetheless it exists. Chang (2009) notes "teaching is often marked by a myopic focus on day-to-day, separation from other adults, and limited opportunities for reflection"(p. 193).

Inadequate Induction of Beginning Teachers*

Teaching has been a career in which those with the least experience face the greatest challenges and most difficult responsibilities—a strange state of affairs, indeed! Beginning teachers in many schools face a number of environmental difficulties: inadequate resources, difficult work assignments, unclear expectations, a sink-or-swim mentality, and reality shock (Anhorn, 2008; Colley, 2002; Gordon & Maxey, 2000; Johnson & Kardos, 2002; McCann & Johannesen, 2004). As we describe these difficulties, we invite you to reflect on your own first year of teaching and to recall if they were part of your entrance to the profession.

Inadequate Resources.   If a teacher makes known that he or she will not be returning in the fall, then after the last day of school other teachers will often descend on the vacant classroom and remove materials that will be useful to them. They remove not only instructional materials but also desks, tables, and chairs! In return, they discard their unwanted items and furniture in the vacant room. Additionally, teachers may jockey around for the more spacious, better-lighted classrooms. Thus, for the incoming year, the neophyte teacher with the least amount of experience often steps into the physically least desirable classroom in the school, with discards for furniture and equipment and few instructional materials.

Difficult Work Assignments.   Experienced staff and administration will often arrange for the so-called problem children and/or lowest-achieving groups of students to be assigned to the newest teacher. In addition, the least interesting and most difficult courses usually are assigned to beginners (Angelle, 2006; Hoigaard, Giske, & Sundsli, 2012; Johnson, 2001; Stansbury, 2001). New teachers are often given larger classes and more duties than experienced teachers (Birkeland & Johnson, 2002; Gallant & Riley, 2014; Imig & Imig, 2006).

Unclear Expectations.   A common complaint among first-year teachers is that they are never sure what is expected of them as professionals (Gallant & Riley, 2014; Johnson & Kardos, 2002; Maistre & Paré, 2010). Administrators, other teachers, parents, and students express conflicting expectations of the beginner, leaving the neophyte in a quandary about whose expectations he or she should try to meet.

Sink-or-Swim Mentality.   For a variety of reasons, beginning teachers are left on their own to "sink or swim." Administrators and experienced teachers tend to view the first year of teaching as a necessary "trial by fire" through which all neophytes must pass. Many experienced colleagues are reluctant to provide assistance to beginning teachers. Some veterans think it is only fair that new teachers should pass through the same trials and tribulations that they navigated when they were beginners. Some see

*Parts of this section are adapted from Stephen P. Gordon and Susan Maxey, *How to Help Beginning Teachers Succeed* (2nd ed.), pp. 1–8. Reprinted by permission of the Association for Supervision and Curriculum Development, Alexandria, VA. Copyright © 2000 by the Association for Supervision and Curriculum Development. All rights reserved.

it as a process that "weeds out" weak teachers, allowing only the strong to survive. Other experienced teachers are reluctant to assist beginners because of the norms of individualism and privacy that pervade the school culture.

Beginners often are reluctant to ask the principal or colleagues for help when they are experiencing management or instructional problems because of the fact that teaching is the only profession in which a novice is expected to assume the same (or more) responsibilities at the same level of competence as experienced colleagues. Novice teachers often do not ask for help because they fear that a request for assistance will call into question their professional competence. In fact, neophytes often go to great lengths to conceal their classroom problems (Buchanan, Prescott, Schuck, Aubusson, & Burke, 2013; Cherubini, 2009; Gallant & Riley, 2014; Schaefer, 2013).

Reality Shock. Veenman defined *reality shock* as "the collapse of the missionary ideals formed during teacher training by the harsh and rude reality of classroom life" (1984, p. 143). Individuals tend to enter teaching with idealized visions of what it will be like. Classroom management problems, student learning difficulties, and the environmental difficulties already discussed tend to destroy those ideals rather quickly. Moreover, neophytes are faced with the numbing realization that they are unprepared to deal with the harsh realities of teaching. This realization can lead to disillusionment and professional paralysis (Chubbuck, Clift, & Alland, 2001; Gallant & Riley, 2014).

Effects of Environmental Difficulties. The environmental problems just discussed can cause tremendous stress and eventually lead to physical and emotional problems. Novice teachers tend to have more negative attitudes about themselves, their teaching, their profession, and students at the end than at the beginning of their first year of teaching (Craig, 2013; Gordon & Maxey, 2000; Mitchell, Reilly, & Logue, 2009; Scherff, Ollis, & Rosencrans, 2006). Between 33% and 50% of teachers drop out of the profession within their first 7 years of teaching (DeAngelis & Presley, 2011; Henry, Fortner, & Bastian, 2012; Imig & Imig, 2006; Ingersoll & Smith, 2003), with up to 15% leaving each of the first 2 years (Darling-Hammond, 2006; Kaiser, 2011). Many of the most promising teachers are the ones who leave the profession early in their careers (Fantilli & McDougall, 2009; Feiman-Nemser, 2003). Finally, as a result of their initial negative experiences, many teachers who stay in the profession develop a survival mentality, a narrow set of teaching methods, and resistance to experimentation and change that may last throughout their teaching careers (Collie, Shapka, & Perry, 2012; Gordon & Maxey, 2000; Hoy & Spero, 2005).

Inequity

The inequity between experienced and beginning teachers is not the only type of disparity often found in conventional districts and schools. Schools located in lower-income communities often are not provided the same resources as other schools in the same district. The physical facilities in low-income schools may be in ill repair and even present health and safety hazards. Class sizes often are larger than those in middle- or upper-class schools. Textbooks and instructional materials may be woe-fully out of date or nonexistent. Low-income schools may be shortchanged on human resources as well. Many teachers in low-income schools are teaching outside of their field (Achinstein, Ogawa, & Speiglman, 2004; Desimone & Long, 2010; Haycock & Hanushek, 2010; Ingersoll, 2002). New teachers often stay at low-income schools only until they are eligible to transfer to other schools, creating problems with faculty and school stability. The personnel problems in low-income schools often are blamed on the difficulty and frustration of teaching low-achieving students, but the major cause of the problem is that districts often provide neither sufficient resources and incentives to attract the most qualified teachers nor sufficient support to retain them.

Inequity for low-income and racial/ethnic minority students and students in at-risk situations also can be a problem within conventional schools that include a diverse student body. Large percentages of low-income groups often are placed in remedial tracks where they miss out on the richer, higher-level curriculum taught to other students (Bass & Gerstl-Pepin, 2011; Gomez & Futrell, 2008; Lleras, 2008; Welton, 2013). In many conventional schools, there is little or no attempt to consider the culture or learning styles of racial/ethnic minority students when designing curric-ulum, selecting instructional materials, or preparing lessons (Rios et al., 2009). Worse still, both unconscious and overt racism go unchallenged by supervisors and teachers in some schools. It may not be easy or comfortable for educators in conventional schools to critically examine inequity, but admitting the presence of inequity is the first step toward removing it from our schools.

Unstaged Career

More prestigious professions avoid such an abrupt transition from student to full professional. Physicians, lawyers, engineers, and scientists all experience several tran-sition years of apprenticeship, internship, and junior membership on the job before they qualify for full rights and responsibilities in the profession.

This set of circumstances leads to the negative characteristic of the teaching profession that perhaps most significantly differentiates it from others—namely, an unstaged career. More prestigious occupations have rigorous screening and require-ments. Furthermore, they have a transitional or proving-ground stage; only when an aspirant has been judged competent by senior members does the junior member step into the next stage of the career, which provides high visibility, greater challenge, a substantial increase in salary, and responsibility for monitoring and judging the next wave of junior members. For example, a law school graduate must pass the bar exam and then serve as a clerk, legal aide, or junior member of a law firm. This person works behind the scenes on writing and research that are credited to his or her supe-rior. After proving competence over time, however, the lawyer then becomes a partner in a firm, a public prosecutor or defender, or an independent attorney. This movement brings visibility and stature in the profession and the right to have one's own appren-tices to do the less challenging, less exciting work.

Teaching, on the other hand, has been unstaged from entry to exit. Education majors take courses, spend time in schools, perform as student teachers, and then graduate from college into their own classrooms as teachers. After that, no matter how many years they continue to teach, they do not move into another stage. The 20-year veteran teacher has the same classroom space, number of students, and requirements as the first-year teacher. Furthermore, for each year of experience, a teacher realizes a salary increase identical to that received by all others of comparable experience.

Lack of Dialogue about Instruction

Generally, people in schools do not talk about their work—teaching—with each other (Kohm & Nance, 2009; Morrison, 2013; Shuck et al., 2011). In successful schools, by contrast, they constantly talk with each other, in a problem-solving, action-oriented way, about teaching (David, 2009; Morrison, 2013; Shuck et al., 2011). This talk is generated through faculty and committee meetings, in-service workshops, observations and conferences, faculty lounge contacts, and other informal occasions. This talk is of a specific nature: teaching and learning of students. Of course, teachers talk with each other in all schools, but the talk is of a more social nature—telling stories about students, parents, administrators, community, and school events.

For teachers to talk often and seriously with each other about the core of their job—instruction and curriculum—is a rarity in many schools. Time is not planned for it to occur. Faculty meetings are information giving, and when school concerns are raised, they are often deflected to noninstructional matters such as schedules, district policies, extracurricular responsibilities, and building maintenance.

The public school as a work institution is unique in that a collection of adults can be employed as professionals within the same physical setting, with a common responsibility for providing their particular services to the same group of clients (students) and not be frequently and intensively engaged with each other in discussions on how to improve their services. Again, the lack of such dialogue is related to the one-room schoolhouse legacy, which accepts isolation, privacy, and lack of career stages as the norms of teaching.

▶ **Video Illustration**

This video shows a portion of a faculty meeting called to discuss progress on students' writing scores. In what ways does the meeting address the need for dialogue about instruction that the authors say is missing in many schools? In what ways could the supervisor leading the meeting have increased the quality of the dialogue?

Lack of Involvement in Schoolwide Curricular and Instructional Decisions

If teachers don't see each other at work, don't talk with each other about their work, and see teaching as what goes on within their own four walls, it is not surprising that they are not given the opportunity, time, or expectations to be involved in decisions about curriculum and instruction beyond their four walls. The norm in most schools is that teachers are not expected to contribute experience, knowledge, and wisdom to decisions about the common good of educating students.

> In contrast to schools in high-achieving European and Asian countries, American factory-model schools offer fewer opportunities for teachers to come to know students well over long periods of time and much less time for teachers to spend working with one another to develop curriculum, plan lessons, observe and discuss teaching strategies, and assess student work in authentic ways. (Darling-Hammond, 2006, p. 302)

Conservatism

All of the previously discussed characteristics of traditional schools contribute to teacher conservatism. One aspect of this conservatism is a set of restricted, teacher-centered instructional methods. Beyond reliance on traditional teaching methods, less obvious aspects of conservatism can be observed in most schools, including the following:

- An emphasis on short-range rather than long-range instructional goals
- Satisfaction with successes with individual lessons, students, and projects rather than with the continuous growth of all students
- Reliance on personal experience rather than educational research
- Narrow limits on the types and degree of collegiality and collaboration in which teachers are willing to engage
- A reflexive resistance to curricular or instructional innovations

Such conservatism is not surprising considering the isolation and psychological dilemma found in the traditional school environment. The irony is that conservatism, which results largely from the other environmental problems we have described, tends to hinder efforts to solve those very same problems!

Cultures Within Cultures

Some cautions are in order concerning our discussion of school culture. Although there clearly is such a thing as a traditional school culture, each school also has cultural characteristics of its own, based on the community it serves and its unique combination of educators and students. Moreover, there are multiple cultures *within* each school. The presence of diverse cultures should be a positive aspect of any school, but the norms, structures, and customs of a traditional school can cause different cultures to become isolated from and in conflict with each other.

- There is, of course, an adult culture and a student culture in every school. The teacher-centered instruction in traditional schools tends to ignore students' lives outside of school, student interests, and the need for students to be actively involved in the learning process. Failing to understand and consider student culture can hinder the development of teacher–student relationships and lower the quality of teaching and learning.

- There are a variety of different cultures within the student population of any school. The different cultures may be based on race or socioeconomic status, but even in a school that is homogeneous in terms of race and class there are differences in gender, sexual orientation, and religion, among others. Chapter 22 will focus on diverse cultures, but for now let us say that traditional schools tend to neither emphasize understanding or meeting the needs of different student cultures, nor help students from different cultures to learn together. Ignoring the differences between student cultures can lead to some students feeling they are not welcome at school, student frustration, and conflicts among students and between students and teachers, all of which can lead to a negative educational environment for students and teachers.

- Teachers also belong to different cultural groups within a school. Different academic departments, instructional teams, and grade-level teams may become professional islands within a school, with members of the group collaborating with each other but isolated from other groups of teachers. In times of scarce resources, different academic units may view other groups as competitors for available resources, which can lead to intergroup conflict. Teachers from different age groups or career stages might also join together in groups that separate themselves from the larger school community. Small groups of teachers working together can do much to improve teaching and learning. However, when groups of teachers become isolated from each other and view the group they affiliate with as more important than the school as a whole, there is little likelihood for schoolwide collegiality or whole-school improvement.

All schools include multiple cultures and subcultures. The problem is that traditional supervision tends to ignore these different cultures, treating all teachers the same and expecting teachers to treat all students the same. This leads to cultural clashes and morale problems that hinder collective action for instructional improvement. The correct response to the reality of multiple cultures is to work to understand those cultures and to build bridges connecting those cultures so they can find common purpose and work together for the improvement of teaching and learning. In Chapter 3 we will describe how dynamic, successful schools promote common purpose and collective action.

Looking Deeper: The Newtonian Paradigm and Traditional Schools

The characteristics of traditional schools described earlier in this chapter have had negative effects on teachers and students, so why do they persist? True, all organizations tend to resist change, but this statement simply brings us back to the original question, "Why?" One way to address the question is through the concept "paradigm," originally used to discuss scientific paradigms in Thomas Kuhn's (1970) seminal work, *The Structure of Scientific Revolutions*. Kilmann (2001) defines paradigm as "a coherent, internally consistent approach for making sense of the universe and coping with life: essentially how one sees, thinks, and behaves"(p. 13). The Newtonian paradigm dominated Western science and culture from the 17th century, its influence spreading beyond physics to economics, politics, psychology, management, organization development, and not least of all, education (Wheatley, 1994; Zohar, 1997). Now we will explore the characteristics of the Newtonian paradigm that drives traditional schools.

Atomism

One characteristic of the Newtonian paradigm present in traditional schools is atomism. The Newtonian supposition is that space is primarily an empty void, with some isolated objects traveling through it as objects or parts of a system, similar to parts of a machine. Indeed, the Newtonian metaphor for a system, and for the universe in general, is the machine. Like individual objects, particular systems are separate from other systems.

The Newtonian paradigm treats human organizations, including schools, as machines. A problem with the school indicates that some working part of the school is broken; fix the broken part and the school runs smoothly. With the Newtonian emphasis on individual parts, there is a tendency to separate the school organization into components. Persons in the school community are separated according to distinct roles: the role of the supervisor is to lead, the role of teachers is to teach, and the role of students is to learn. Components can be broken into subcomponents: students are "gifted," "learning disabled," "ESL," "minorities," and so forth. Teachers teach "core" or "special" classes. Individual members of the school community are even split into component parts. Teachers are expected to separate their personal and professional lives, students are expected to separate their personal interests from school academics, and parents are expected to be parents at home, but passive supporters of school policies and docile recipients of assessments of their children at school.

The Newtonian paradigm leads to divisions beyond role separation. In traditional schools, the curriculum is broken into separate subjects, the school year into terms, and the school day into periods; and there is considerable separation between the school itself and its immediate external environment—the community it serves. The school is considered the sum of its visible parts, with little consideration of the less tangible relationships among those parts. One problem with atomism in schools is that it leads to fragmentation among persons and processes that are part of the school, and isolation of the school from the parents and community that it is supposed to be serving. Also, if educators focus only on the parts and the immediate interactions of those parts with each other, they lose the opportunity to see the big picture of what is going on in the school and community.

Prediction and Control

Newtonian physics assumes that if we know the position and velocity of an object we can calculate future positions of that object. According to the Newtonian paradigm, equally accurate predictions can be made of the activity of systems of objects in motion:

> A more complicated dynamic system is composed of many constituent parts, and its motion is not necessarily limited to one-dimensional space. Nevertheless, no matter how complicated the system and the actions on the system are, the dynamics of the system can, in principle, be understood or predicted on the basis of those same principles. (Tang, 2009, p. 2)

Newtonian physics holds that objects that make up natural systems travel and interact according to laws of physics that can be discovered, and that once we discover these laws, we can both predict and control the objects and the system. Again, natural systems and their parts act like machines that can be inspected and adjusted.

The Newtonian paradigm applied to schools treats the school organization as a machine, with persons, structures, policies, curriculum, instruction, and assessment all parts of that machine. For the machine to work efficiently, its parts must be controlled, and understanding how the machine works through the gathering of (usually quantitative) data is the first step in being able to control it. Data are used to determine if the machine is working effectively, and if it is not, to pinpoint problem parts so they can be fixed. Hierarchical relationships and bureaucracy are used to control the parts of the Newtonian school and keep it running smoothly. Designated figures (superintendent, principal, teachers) control persons below them in the hierarchy and are controlled by those above them. The bureaucracy consists of special parts of the organization—structures, rules, and procedures—integrated across the system to assist with control. The Newtonian approach tends to create schools that see parents and community members as a threat to control, thus it sets up clear boundaries between the school and the external environment. Although parents and community members can of course visit the school, activities and interactions during those visits are prescribed and tightly controlled by supervisors and teachers. The school is more concerned with traditional public relations strategies than with school–community collaboration.

A school following the Newtonian paradigm may well have a vision, but that vision is a predetermined destination the school is traveling toward (Wheatley, 1994) rather than an unfolding vision based on deep-seated values and a cause beyond oneself. The school ruled by the Newtonian paradigm first decides on its destination and then seeks the most efficient way to reach that destination. For example, the destination might be a particular school mean on the state's high-stakes achievement test, and the most efficient way of achieving that destination could be perceived as more classroom exercises, homework, and quizzes using the test format; special remediation provided to "bubble students"; and motivational talks on test preparation and test-taking strategies delivered by outside experts.

There are a number of problems with a prediction and control approach to school improvement. First, the hierarchy and bureaucracy used to assure control tend to either cause educators to leave the school in pursuit of a less restrictive environment or to become passive workers. Some students may rebel against such environments and become chronic discipline problems, and others will become passive learners, with their natural desire for relevant learning slowly giving way to boredom. A school that decides on a single, concrete vision gives up the opportunity to consider alternative visions or an unfolding vision, and if it commits all of its resources to a predetermined route to its vision it eliminates other, possibly better paths (Zohar, 1997). Finally, the school that attempts to control parent and community input and participation runs the risk of isolating itself from the very groups that it was created to serve.

Objective Measurement

Newtonian physics focuses on objects and their interactions. The classic Newtonian metaphor is billiard balls striking each other. Objective measurement is used to determine the current state of objects and to predict future states. Corresponding constructs in schools are objective measurements of teacher, student, and school performance. As with atomism, prediction, and control, there are problems with objective measurement in schools. First, most supervisors and teachers who have been involved with an "objective" teacher evaluation system or reviewed the results of an "objective" achievement test tend to question whether true objectivity is really possible. Second, any measurement tool only measures certain aspects of a teacher's instruction, a student's learning, or a school's performance. What about those aspects of teaching, learning, or schools—some of which may be critically important—that are not being measured? Critics argue that purely objective measurement is an illusion, and that the use of traditional measurement tools is a reflection of atomism and a tool for prediction and control.

Connecting the Dots: The Newtonian Paradigm and the Traditional School Environment

The characteristics of traditional schools that we discussed earlier in this chapter are eerily reflective of the Newtonian paradigm. Although the *isolation* of teachers was originally due to the one-room schoolhouse, the continuation of that norm is clearly in sync with Newtonian atomism. The atomistic nature of traditional schools means that teachers are on their own to deal with large numbers of students and the resulting *psychological dilemma and frustration,* which leads to Newtonian control through routinizing of classroom activity. The *routine of the teaching career* imposed by state legislatures and school districts, with its prescribed schedule and responsibilities, is clearly intended to maintain Newtonian control of teachers and schools. An atomistic school environment that results in their being forced to sink or swim in isolation especially hurts beginning teachers in schools with *inadequate induction support*.

A school based on the Newtonian paradigm contributes to *inequity*. Students from marginalized groups typically are exposed to the most atomistic curriculum and instruction, with simplistic material broken down into isolated bits of learning with little relevance to the students' culture or the outside world, taught through repetitious, boring learning activities. Traditional schools tend to focus on Newtonian control of racial, ethnic, and economic minorities, who are disciplined more often and more severely than students from the dominant group. And students from marginalized groups suffer from theoretically objective measurement tools that are in reality culturally biased, resulting in over placement in remedial programs and under placement in gifted and advanced placement programs.

The *unstaged career* in traditional schools means that as teachers develop increasing expertise (as opposed to merely more experience) there is no corresponding increase in responsibility, prestige, or salary, and no opportunity for formal leadership roles. This means that the school organization maintains the same level of control over an experienced, expert teacher as a newly tenured teacher. Also, the experienced teacher is subject to the same "objective measurement" of teaching performance as beginning teachers. *The lack of dialogue about instruction* in traditional schools is partly due to the atomistic isolation of teachers from each other, and partly due to the tightly controlled schedule of the teaching day that does not allow time for teachers to meet. Additionally, the high-stakes achievement tests ("objective measures") that dominate K-12 education tend to lead teachers toward "test prep" and away from dialogue about higher levels of teaching and learning. In traditional schools, the curriculum is based on mandated state standards, high-stakes achievement tests, or curriculum guides developed in the district's central office, and such external control of the curriculum results in a *lack of involvement in schoolwide curricular and instructional decisions*. Finally, if teachers in traditional schools are isolated from their colleagues by an atomistic organization, are part of a system that seeks to predict and control their behavior and the behavior of their students, and are subject to "objective measurement" of their teaching and their students' learning, we can understand why *conservatism* prevails in such school environments.

The Need to Move Beyond the Newtonian Paradigm

The Newtonian paradigm was responsible for significant gains in our understanding of the universe for over three centuries, and still can be applied today to many aspects of physics. However, since the early 20th century, quantum physics has answered questions about the subatomic world for which Newtonian physics was not suited. We can argue about whether the Newtonian paradigm was *ever* appropriate for education, but given the increasingly complex, diverse, and global world in which we live, it is clearly time for a change of educational paradigms. In the next chapter we will discuss a new paradigm more appropriate for 21st-century schools.

> ✔ **Check Your Understanding 2.0**   Click here to gauge your understanding of the key concepts presented in this chapter.

REFLECTIVE EXERCISE

Assume you are the leader of an outside team that has been asked to assess the work environment of a school that you have not visited in the past. During the weeklong visit to the school you will have access to school administrators, teachers, students, parents, classrooms, common areas, a whole-school faculty meeting, meetings of various teacher groups, and school records.

- What questions about the school work environment will the assessment team ask school administrators? teachers? students? parents?

- What will your team focus on during classroom observations? Observation of common areas? Observation of the whole-school faculty meeting? Observations of meetings of various teacher groups?

- What school records will you review, and what specific data will you gather from those records?

chapter 3

The Dynamic School

Learning Outcomes for This Chapter

After reading this chapter, you should be able to:

1. Define *collegiality* and explain how it can be used to improve schools.
2. Define a *cause beyond oneself*.
3. Identify the characteristics of effective professional development.
4. List the four broad characteristics of a positive learning climate.
5. Explain how students and teachers benefit from the use of authentic curriculum, instruction, and assessment.
6. Explicate each of the three characteristics of strong democracy in schools: inclusion, integration, and internalization.
7. Describe ways in which the supervisor can assist teachers with collaborative action research.
8. Describe a culturally responsive school.
9. Give examples of school partnerships and networks, and explain how they can contribute to school improvement.
10. Explain, in general terms, the assumptions of the quantum paradigm concerning observation and measurement.

Questions to Reflect On as You Read This Chapter

1. How does the environment of the dynamic school described in this chapter contrast with the traditional school environment described in Chapter 2?
2. Are you familiar with a school in which teachers, school leaders, and parents all share "a cause beyond oneself" that underlies the school's improvement efforts? If so, define the school's cause beyond oneself.

3. If you were to conduct a weeklong visit to a school with which you are unfamiliar, what indicators would you look for to determine if the school was implementing authentic curriculum, instruction, and assessment?

4. What is the relationship between data, reflection, and action? Reflect on a potential school renewal effort for which all three of these elements would be essential.

5. To what extent do you believe the aspects of the quantum paradigm discussed in this chapter are relevant to schools?

The characteristics of traditional schools described in Chapter 2 represent *static systems*. Organizations that are static are unable to grow, develop, or adapt to a changing environment. Given the rapid changes we are experiencing in demographics, technology, and geopolitics, schools that remain static systems will encounter increasing difficulty in educating students for today's—and tomorrow's—world. Dynamic schools, in contrast to traditional, static schools, possess the capacity for continuous change to meet the evolving needs of students, communities, and society. Different authors have defined dynamic schools in various ways. Rallis and Goldring (2000) focus on the roles assumed by principals of dynamic schools: facilitator, balancer, flag bearer and bridger, inquirer, learner, and leader. Carr, Herman, and Harris (2005) present collaborative processes for creating dynamic schools, including mentoring, coaching, and study groups. Rallis and associates center on ethical policies of the dynamic school, addressing such topics as inclusion, immigrants, English language learners, consideration of the whole child, and bullying (Rallis, Rossman, Cobb, Reagan, & Kuntz, 2008). And Edwards and Chapman (2009) propose six "pillars of dynamic schools": communication and relationships, leadership and empowerment, planning and evaluation, collaboration, accountability and responsibility, and consistency and redundancy.

Our own model of the dynamic school begins with a general description of a dynamic system that we then use as a framework to present research and theory on successful schools. A dynamic system is driven by an energizing force that enables and compels the system to act in a certain way. The action of a dynamic system is not random (although it may appear to be), but purposeful. The energizing force in a dynamic social system motivates and guides its members toward action for a common purpose. Dynamic systems are interactive, and when they are fully functioning, different forces, structures, or processes within the system interact in a coherent manner, allowing the system to maintain equilibrium. More complex dynamic systems have the capacity for continuous growth and development. The most complex systems interact with their external environment, use feedback loops to adapt to a changing environment, and even engage in mutual adaptation with their environment. Dynamic schools are dynamic systems, but what educational factors characterize dynamic schools? The remainder of this chapter attempts to answer that question. Many of the characteristics of dynamic schools we introduce in this chapter are addressed in more detail later in the book.

Shared Leadership, Collegiality, and Collaboration

The supervisor who shares leadership understands that knowledge and skills to improve instruction are distributed throughout the school community (Larsen & Rieckhoff, 2014; Watson & Scribner, 2007; Youngs, 2014). Shared decision making leads to better decisions and increases the likelihood those decisions will be implemented. Shared instructional leadership includes the supervisor providing time and resources for teachers to engage in leadership activities and buffering teachers from bureaucratic work not focused on instructional leadership (Heck & Hallinger, 2014; Printy, Marks, & Bowers, 2009; Wahlstrom & Louis, 2008).

Shared instructional leadership frequently consists of the supervisor facilitating groups of teachers working together to improve instruction. Peer coaching teams, professional learning communities, action research teams, study groups, and curriculum development teams are a few examples of teacher leadership teams. One advantage of leadership teams is the reciprocal influence described by Watson and Scribner (2007): "Individuals experience a sense of synergy in these situations because each person gains something from the others in their development of innovative ideas"(p. 257). The supervisor wishing to promote teachers' collaborative work needs to keep in mind that not all collaborative work is carried out within formal structures; much of it is informal (Fairman & Mackenzie, 2015; Goddard, & Tschannen-Moran, 2007). Thus, both formal and informal collaborative work should be encouraged and supported.

Shared leadership and collaborative work are connecting pathways to the collegial school culture we described in Chapter 1. In collegial cultures, teachers take collective responsibility for helping all of their colleagues to become better teachers and for the growth and development of all students. In addition to mutual support, professional community "includes shared values, a common focus on student learning, collaboration in the development of curriculum and instruction, the sharing of practices, and reflective dialogue" (Wahlstrom & Louis, 2008, p. 463). Collegiality replaces the isolation and privatism of traditional school cultures. In collegial cultures, teachers' "energy, creative thinking, efficiency, and goodwill increase, and the cynicism and defensiveness that hamper change decrease" (Kohm & Nance, 2009, p. 68). Fullan (2000) argues, "The development of professional community must become the key driver of improvement. When this happens, deeper changes in both culture and structure can be accomplished"(p. 582).

A Cause Beyond Oneself

One characteristic of successful schools is "a cause beyond oneself." In dynamic schools, teachers do not view their work as simply what they carry out within their own four walls but see themselves as part of the larger enterprise of complementing and working with each other to educate students. A cause beyond oneself thus is a *common cause* based on shared beliefs and core values. We can refer to this common cause as the school's vision, but to do so accurately we must understand what goes into its development. The type of vision we refer to is not one that a supervisor convinces other members of the school community to "buy into," nor is it a statement written by teachers during a one-day retreat. Rather, an authentic shared vision develops over a period of time through the shared leadership, collaborative work, and collegiality discussed in the previous section.

Each school is a unique blend of students, adults, and educational needs in interaction with the unique community the school serves, and thus each school must develop its own vision. Ultimately, however, a school's common cause must connect to the universal purpose of all schools: student learning. Gajda and Koliba (2008) state it well: "The most important organizational practices around which school-based communities of practice should form is the systematic examination and improvement of instruction so as to achieve universal and equitable increases in student achievement, engagement, and performance"(p. 139). Because student populations, faculties, and educational needs change over time, dynamic schools—through shared leadership, collaborative work, and collegial relationships—develop the capacity to adapt to internal and external change.

Because school development is inextricably intertwined with development of the larger community the school services, dynamic schools make *school–community development* part of their vision. A cause beyond oneself becomes a cause beyond one's school. Mutual adaptation and development are based on a common cause as well as continuous, two-way communication and feedback enabling the common cause to evolve over time.

> ▶ **Video Illustration**
>
> In this video, the supervisor is leading a school through a "revitalization" process. Do the members of the school community depicted in the video have what the authors describe as "a cause beyond oneself"? If so, how would you describe the school's cause?

Professional Development

Professional development in PK–12 schools historically has been ineffective; however, effective professional development is critical to the dynamic school. Professional development in the dynamic school is focused on the school's vision and integrated with the previously discussed shared leadership, collaborative work, and collegiality. Effective professional development is job embedded and ongoing; it involves teachers in the planning, delivering, and assessing of learning activities; and it provides follow-up for adapting new learning to the classroom (Balan, Manko, & Phillips, 2011; Gordon, 2004; Hansen-Thomas, Casey, & Grosso, 2013; Larsen & Rieckhoff, 2014).

An assistance program for beginning teachers is an important component of a school's professional development program. Effective support programs include but go beyond an orientation to the school and community, providing ongoing support for 1 to 3 years. Beginners' support comes in a variety of formats, including the assignment of an experienced teacher as mentor, skill training, support seminars, and so forth. Beginning teachers report that having an assigned mentor, especially one who observes and discusses their teaching, is a powerful form of support (Gilles, Carrillo, Wang, Stegall, & Bumgarner, 2013; LoCasale-Crouch, Davis, Wiens, & Pianta, 2012; Wang, Odell, & Schwille, 2008). After reviewing 15 studies on beginning teacher support programs, Ingersoll and Strong (2011) concluded that support programs result in increased retention of beginners, improved teaching, and higher student achievement. Beginning teacher assistance programs also can socialize new teachers into the shared leadership, collaborative work, collegiality, and common cause associated with dynamic schools.

Schools need not limit career assistance to beginning teachers. All teachers are influenced by their sociocultural backgrounds and adult learning styles as they progress through adult stages, lifecycle phases, transition events, and role development, which all affect one's teaching career. Differentiated professional development can provide different types of assistance to teachers at different career stages and with different learning needs.

Chapter 4 presents a comprehensive discussion of adult and teacher development and Chapter 18 provides a full discussion of professional development.

Positive Learning Climate

The dynamic school provides a positive learning climate for all students. Positive learning climates possess a number of characteristics (Allodi, 2010; Cohen, 2007; Cohen, McCabe, Michelli, & Pickeral, 2009; Doll, 2010; Gillen, Wright, & Spink, 2011; Marshall, 2004). We place those characteristics into four categories: safe environment, moral tone, relationships, and sense of empowerment.

Safe Environment: Students in a positive learning climate feel physically and emotionally safe. School facilities are clean and well maintained. Positive, proactive discipline techniques are used. An antibullying policy is in place and strictly adhered to. Adults are present throughout the school, monitoring student behavior and available to provide assistance. Procedures for managing conflict are in place.

Moral Tone: In a positive learning climate, adults care for students and are deeply committed to student success. Students are respected and treated fairly; adults listen to them and take their concerns seriously. Students are accepted as individuals—with their unique personal histories, needs, and interests considered by teachers—but also are treated as members of a community of learners with a mutual obligation to care for and assist one another.

Relationships: Students in positive learning climates develop relationships with peers, teachers, and school leaders. Students feel connected to the school; they have a sense that they are welcome, that they belong. Relationships that contribute to a positive learning climate go beyond the school walls; they include school–family and school–community relationships. Students in dynamic schools associate the school with their family and community.

Sense of Empowerment: We include a number of related elements in this category, including self-efficacy. Doll (2010) writes, "Efficacy expectations saturate the social and psychological climate of high-performing schools. Self-efficacy is a person's belief that he or she will succeed on the tasks he or she attempts; self-efficacy often becomes a self-fulfilling prophecy"(p. 13). Self-efficacy and achievement can be cyclical; early achievement can increase self-efficacy, which in turn can lead to higher levels of achievement. Allowing students to participate in decisions about their learning environment, what they learn, and how they learn it can foster student empowerment. Allowing students to participate in decisions about their own learning will not only make learning more relevant, but also help develop student responsibility and autonomy. Another way to facilitate students' sense of empowerment is to allow them to express their creativity during the learning process and in demonstrations of learning.

▶ Video Illustration

This video includes a discussion about positive learning environments and a portion of a classroom lesson. Which of the four general characteristics of a positive learning environment—safe environment, moral tone, relationships, and sense of empowerment—are represented in the video? For each of the four characteristics that appear to be present, what are the indicators of that presence?

Authentic Curriculum, Instruction, and Assessment

Curriculum is the "missing link" in effective schools and school improvement research. Most research has used standardized test scores as the criteria for effective or improved schools, without attention to either the school curriculum or whether the learning measured by the test was valuable. Similarly, the emphasis in schools in recent years has been on teaching mandated content and preparing students for the test, not on assessing the value of the content students are being taught or on improving the curriculum. In one way, current practice makes sense; externally mandated standards and high-stakes achievement tests provide schools with a ready-made curriculum of sorts. Yet, when PK–12 educators allow external mandates to completely displace local curriculum, they have abdicated their responsibility to participate in an incredibly important moral decision: *What should students learn?* If each school exists within a unique context and serves a unique population of students and families, then it makes sense that at least some of the school curriculum should be tailored to the local context and community. Moreover, Starratt (2007) argues that the school's curriculum needs to be integrated with the students' journey toward self-understanding:

> . . . the moral agenda that young people feel, namely their obligation to become whole, to be real, to own themselves, to make their way, to say their truth, to make a contribution, to be involved in matters of public importance, to be engaged in real work, is by and large ignored, disregarded, actively rejected in many schools. Instead learners are expected to study for the right answers in a curriculum that remains detached from the journey of self-definition and self-commitment. (p. 172)

The key to developing an authentic curriculum that meets the needs of the local community and individual students, addressing higher-level learning not typically reflected in external mandates, is to develop a comprehensive curriculum that subsumes and goes beyond external mandates.

The concept of authentic instruction, developed by Newmann and Associates (1996) and studied more recently by others (Dennis & O'Hair, 2010; Preus, 2012), includes four principles that can be applied to curriculum and assessment as well as instruction. The first principle is higher-order thinking, in which students differentiate, synthesize, hypothesize, and generate new meaning. Another principle is deep knowledge, for which students examine a complex topic in depth, discovering relationships and interactions among different aspects of the topic. The third principle is substantive conversation between the teacher and students or among the students that leads to shared knowledge and meaning. The final principle of authentic instruction is the connection of new knowledge to the student's life beyond the school.

Authentic assessment entails the student applying new learning to the world outside of school or to a simulation of the outside world. Problem-based learning, project-based learning, service learning, portfolios, presentations, and performances all can be used for authentic assessment.

Authentic curriculum, authentic instruction, and authentic assessment are very much interrelated; the lines between what students learn, how they learn it, and how their learning is assessed become blurred in a more coherent design for learning.

Video Illustration

Compare the description of authentic assessment in the video to the four principles of authentic instruction identified by Newmann and Associates.

> ▶ **Video Illustration**
>
> This video is about the student portfolio as a tool for authentic assessment. As you watch the video, reflect on how the four principles of authentic instruction identified by Newmann and Associates could be incorporated into a student portfolio.

Democracy

Those who espouse democratic schools argue that a democratic school community prepares students for democratic citizenship, promotes ongoing school improvement, fosters teacher growth, and results in improved student learning. Here we will provide a brief overview of how democratic community enables school, teacher, and student development, with more in-depth discussions of democratic schools in later chapters.

Let's begin our discussion of democratic community by distinguishing between what Gordon and Boone (2012) call weak and strong democracy. A weak democracy functions at a surface level and is concerned primarily with individual privacy and majority rule. Strong democracy, by contrast, is based on social morality, open inquiry, and interdependence. Furman and Starratt's (2002) definition of democratic community reflects strong democracy:

> Democratic community is processual and moral. It is the enactment of participatory processes of open inquiry in working for the common good in regard to both local and global concerns; it is guided by a social morality that recognizes the worth of individuals and the social value of community (however temporal and provisional), celebrates differences, and understands the ultimate and pragmatic interdependence of all. (p. 116)

Three characteristics of strong democracy discussed by Gordon and Boone (2012) are inclusion, integration, and internalization. *Inclusion* is defined as involving all groups in discussion, inquiry, decision making, and service. In schools this means involving teachers, educational specialists, students, parents, and community groups as well as different cultural groups and groups with different points of view. *Integration* means embedding democracy in all aspects of school and classroom life.

> A teacher calling a classroom meeting when a class conflict breaks out or a serious discipline problem arises *is not* integrated democracy; democracy that is part of the daily interactions between teachers and students and among students, that is evident in the overall classroom climate, and that is incorporated throughout the curriculum, teaching, learning, and student assessment *is* integrated democracy. (pp. 51–52)

Finally, democracy becomes *internalized* when it becomes interwoven with the school culture: "democracy becomes an assumption, a habitual way of dealing with people and situations, a way of life"(p. 52).

Democratic community increases school, teacher, and student capacity for growth and development, and is "essential to continuous school improvement" (Mallory & Reavis, 2007, p. 10). Democratic community also increases the likelihood that teachers will trust school leaders and colleagues and, in turn, engage in ongoing collaboration and professional learning (Kensler, Caskie, Barber, & White, 2009). Students in schools committed to democratic community have consistently performed better than comparison groups on standardized tests and other achievement measures (Glickman, 1993, 1998).

Democracy is an essential component of the dynamic school; without it, the school community and its individual members cannot experience optimal moral, social, and intellectual development.

Chapter 20 presents a model for school governance based on democratic principles, and Chapter 23 includes a more extensive discussion of democratic community.

Inquiry

At the broadest level, inquiry can be viewed as a cycle that includes identifying a focus area, gathering and analyzing data on the focus area, reflecting on the data and planning for action, and implementing and evaluating the planned action. Inquiry can take place at the individual, group, or school level, but collaborative inquiry is an especially powerful attribute of the dynamic school. Gajda and Koliba (2008) emphasize that the action component of inquiry is essential: "If teacher teams and their members do not take action as a result of their decisions, the cycle of inquiry ceases to move forward and school improvement falters"(p. 145).

Inquiry can take many forms. Currently, action research is the most popular structure for inquiry in schools. Traditional educational research tends to be carried out separately from action to improve schools. Not so with action research:

Collaborative action research integrates research and action in a number of ways that traditional research does not. First, action research integrates the investigation of problems with the solving of those problems. Second, in action research the researchers and the action-takers are the same. This means that those who best know the learners and the educational environment can embed their knowledge and concerns in the research, and play the central role in deciding the implications of the research for action. Third, the research and action take place in the same context, meaning that the research can directly inform and validate action. (Gordon, 2008, pp. 3–4)

Supervisors can assist teachers with collaborative action research by providing professional development on the purpose and phases of action research and the skills needed to carry out the process, including data gathering, data analysis, planning, and problem-solving skills. The supervisor can be present to facilitate meetings of teachers new to action research, or provide an outside "critical friend" to assist teachers in their early action research ventures. As is the case with other types of teacher collaboration, the most important support the supervisor can provide to teachers engaged in collaborative action research is the time needed to work together on the research.

Typically, it is teachers who carry out action research in schools, but students also can participate. Students can carry out individual action research, or collaborative action research at the classroom or school level. Preble and Taylor (2009), for example, report on student participation in collaborative action research to improve school climate in which students helped to survey adults and students, reviewed data, identified problem areas, presented assessment results to the faculty, and worked with teachers and administrators to develop and implement improvement plans. School climate improved in two-thirds of the participating schools, and the academic achievement in schools with improved climates increased significantly more than in the schools where school climate had not improved.

The ultimate goal of the inquiry process is to develop schools as *cultures of inquiry* in which inquiry becomes a way of life, with the cycle of data gathering, reflective dialogue, and action improving teachers' instruction and students' learning. At the school level, inquiry "is ongoing, nonlinear, and iterative, involving reflection, action, and communication. . . The School Improvement Plan becomes a living process, with the team collecting, evaluating, and disseminating information all of the time to monitor their progress and revisit priorities" (Earl & Katz, 2006, p. 108).

Chapter 20 provides a full discussion of action research, and Chapter 23 addresses inquiry within the context of building community.

Cultural Responsiveness

Dynamic schools are culturally responsive. They not only respect but also celebrate diverse cultures and tap into the assets of those cultures for the benefit of all students. Adults who work in culturally responsive schools genuinely care for all students, develop personal relationships with students, and promote positive relationships among students from different cultures. Dynamic schools believe that all students can succeed; these schools do not have ability tracks, and are determined that all students will not only master basic skills but also achieve higher-order learning.

Cultural responsiveness is integrated across the curriculum in dynamic schools. The curriculum incorporates the values, customs, and languages of diverse students and their families. Supervisors, teachers, and students from different cultures learn about each other's cultures, families, and lives outside of school. Students learn about the perspectives of different cultural groups on social issues, and become involved in service learning and social action projects.

Teachers in culturally responsive schools have an understanding of their own cultural backgrounds, the cultures of the students they teach, and cultural issues that need to be addressed in the classroom. Teachers have conversations with their students about their lives outside of the classroom, *listen* to their students, and treat students' concerns seriously. Teachers in dynamic schools both nourish and hold high expectations for their students. Culturally responsive teachers are continuously using classroom conversations, discussions with parents, and community visits to better understand their students' cultures and to use that understanding in their teaching. Responsive teachers also keep parents informed of their children's progress in school, and work collaboratively with parents to address problems that arise.

Dynamic schools use culturally sensitive assessments to measure students' progress and diagnose learning problems. Students are given multiple opportunities for and alternative ways of demonstrating learning. The focus is on assessment to assist student learning rather than to label students or to place them in "remediation" that could actually harm their academic and social development.

The supervisory task of addressing diversity is the topic of Chapter 22, which includes discussions on achievement gaps, cultural clashes, cultural responsiveness, and equity for different cultural groups.

Partnerships and Networks

Several years ago, one of the authors visited 14 schools across the United States that had been recognized either by the U.S. Department of Education or nationally recognized experts for their exemplary professional development programs focused on school improvement. The author was surprised (although he should not have been) that every one of these schools had external partners assisting their development. The schools had developed partnerships that included intermediate units, businesses, nonprofit foundations, and national networks, but the most frequent partners were nearby colleges and universities. The connections between these dynamic schools and partnership could not be ignored, and the author became a believer in the power of partnership.

Let's begin our discussion of partnerships with one close to home: *parent–school partnership*. Price-Mitchell (2009) points out that what we used to refer to as "parent involvement" we now call parent–school partnership, implying "shared and equally valued roles in education"(p. 13). Auerbach (2010) calls the highest level of parent–school partnership "authentic partnership," which she defines as "mutually respectful alliances among educators, families, and community groups that value relationship building, dialogue, and power sharing as part of socially just, democratic schools"(p. 734).

We know that parents' participation in parent–school partnership improves their children's academic achievement (Anderson & Minke, 2007; Auerbach, 2010; DePlanty, Coulter-Kern, & Duchane, 2007; Toren, 2013; Wang & Sheikh-Khalil, 2014), but what conditions are necessary for an authentic partnership to form? Parents are more likely to become involved in partnership if the school invites and encourages parents to join; the partnership has a specific, clear purpose; and parents are directly involved in partnership activities (Auerbach, 2010; Evans & Radina, 2014; Green, Walker, Hoover-Dempsey, & Sandler, 2007; Mutsch & Collins, 2012). In the most productive parent–school partnerships, educators and parents develop reciprocal relationships, educators make parents aware of resources that can assist their children's learning, and educators learn from parents (Biggam, 2003). In short, parents become full members in a community of learners and leaders (Price-Mitchell, 2009).

School–community partnerships include but go beyond collaboration with parents, involving other stakeholders from the community. Sanders (2001) defines school–community partnerships as "connections between schools and community individuals, organizations, and businesses that are forged to promote students' social, emotional, physical, and intellectual development"(p. 20). There are three broad, often overlapping purposes of school–community collaboration, all connected to student learning: (1) school improvement; (2) student interaction with, service to, and learning from the community; and (3) community development. The latter purpose affects student learning, most obviously because students are members of the community, but also because community and school development (and thus student learning) are intimately related; one usually does not take place without the other.

A model for school–community partnership is described by Anderson-Butcher and associates (2010). The model calls for collaboration among educators, social workers, families, community service agencies, neighborhood groups, and other stakeholders to promote students' healthy development and academic learning, with an emphasis on resources and support outside of the school. Teams consisting of representatives from different groups analyze student achievement and other data, identify nonacademic barriers to school and student success, establish school improvement priorities, design and implement out-of-school programs and services, and engage in continuous data gathering to provide feedback on program progress. Authority and responsibility are distributed across the project teams as they manage after-school programs, service learning, family participation and support, health and social services, and other services. Additional examples of school–community partnership and collaboration are provided in Chapter 23.

The next type of partnership to discuss is the *district–school partnership*. It might seem strange to talk about a district–school partnership. Isn't the school a subdivision of the district, a box below the school board and central office on the organizational chart? This conception of the relationship between the district and the school just may be the problem. One of the great activist principals and public intellectuals of our time, Deborah Meier (2009), warns us, "the inequality of the power granted to the school's constituency and the power granted to the central system is too huge. Principals are, after all, far more 'accountable' to the officials 'downtown' than to their own constituents"(p. 24). The solution to this unequal power relationship is the development of district–school partnerships with a more balanced distribution of power and differentiated decision-making responsibilities. Glickman (1993) proposed the following roles for the school board and district:

> The school board's role is one of setting broad policies and providing resources that support schools' ability to accomplish this goal. . . . The job of both board and district is to define the district's core beliefs about teaching and learning; define the goals and objectives (outcomes) of an educated student; provide the money, technical services, and human consultation to allow schools to figure out how to get the job done and determine whether progress is being achieved. (p. 112)

The school board, district leaders, and representatives from individual schools (including educators, parents, and other community members) need to work out the details of district–school partnerships; to collaboratively decide what decision-making authority and responsibilities will be assigned to the district, assigned to the schools, and shared. However, it makes good organizational and pedagogical sense for schools to make their own decisions regarding:

- Curriculum, beyond the broad outcomes required by the district
- Organization of students
- Instructional program
- School schedule
- Student discipline policy
- Instructional resources and materials to be purchased and utilized within the parameters of funding negotiated with the district
- School-based professional development
- Student assessment
- The combination and balance of administrators, teachers, educational specialists, and support staff hired within the parameters of a personnel budget negotiated with the district
- Evaluation of teachers and other professionals

In an authentic partnership, of course, the degree of school autonomy is negotiated collaboratively between the district and school. Some schools might want and be ready for more autonomy, others less; however, the directionality of the partnership is toward increasing school autonomy, especially in the areas of curriculum, instruction, and student assessment. If it seems like the district gives up a great deal of power in the type of partnership we describe, it is only because the district has most of the power to start with. The advantage of a true school–district partnership is exactly the same for both the district and the school—that is, improved student learning.

School–university partnerships offer opportunities for both schools and universities to renew themselves. Universities should not be the "senior partners" in a school–university partnership; the university and school should be equal partners. Myran, Crum, and Clayton (2010) recommend four pillars for school–university partnerships:

- A developmental, iterative, and additive approach to school improvement focused on transformative growth
- A balance of theory and practice
- Clear, effective communication between partners
- A focus on instructional leadership

Based on their involvement in a school–university partnership, Kamler and associates (2009) describe lessons learned by partnership coordinators in three areas: collaboration, negotiations, and decision making. Lessons learned about collaboration include showing care by recognizing and addressing participants' needs and mediating when problems arise; maintaining momentum through planning by providing immediate responses to participants as well as following up; and creating opportunities for collaborative learning. Negotiation lessons include the need to reach compromise while maintaining the partnership's vision. Decision-making lessons use shared decision making to develop trust and to practice data-based flexibility.

The types of school–university partnerships are myriad. Teacher induction programs, collaborative action research, school improvement projects, and professional development programs are but a few examples. As with all partnerships, both partners should receive benefits from school–university collaboration. Often, the benefit to the university is that professors are provided opportunities to publish scholarly work based on their participation. In a true partnership, however, university research should never take precedence over school, teacher, or student development.

School–business partnerships can be mutually beneficial to both partners, but in these partnerships, especially, principles should be established to protect students, families, and communities. The first of these principles, we believe, should be that schools do not procure resources from business in exchange for commercialization of the school. Additional, pragmatic principles suggested by Engein (2003) include common values, support for the partnership at all levels of the business and school organization, goals that benefit both parties, specific intended outcomes and measures of success, clearly defined roles and responsibilities, and integrated activities at both the school and business site allowing for interaction and mutual cultural understanding.

Services rendered by the business partner should go beyond merely providing the school with resources. Services can include onsite business experiences for either teachers or students—such as shadowing workers, internships, or summer jobs focused on learning about the business; mentoring students; assisting students with out-of-school needs; and providing suggestions for the school curriculum (Pillay, Watters, Hoff, & Flynn, 2014; Sammon & Becton, 2001). A specific, creative example of a school–business partnership, *Science on the Shipyard,* is described by Harpole, Kerley, Silvernail, Kinard, and Brooks (2010). Teachers served as summer interns at a partner shipbuilder, receiving training on how to apply math, science, and technology to shipbuilding; hands-on practice in such jobs as electrical wiring, welding, and shipfitting; and producing ship-related products to take back to their classrooms. Teachers used the skills they developed in their internship to develop lessons enabling their students to learn and apply science, math, and technology to real-world projects.

Networks can be regional, national, or international. They have a clear, singular focus but usually promote a variety of activities related to that focus, with professional discourse an overarching priority. A network can be made up of schools or individual educators. Network organization and structures tend to be flexible and adaptable to a changing environment and changing membership. The focus of a network might be a particular academic subject, role (supervisor, teacher, parent), process (action research, professional development), concern (social justice, support for beginning teachers), or approach to learning (cooperative learning, student inquiry). A network could be entirely online, combine online discourse with an annual or semi-annual in-person meeting, or meet in person on a regular basis.

Networks promote individual professional growth as well as collaboration and collegiality as members share resources, experiences, and innovative ideas. Network members expand their perspective beyond their local educational setting, and often are provided regional, national, or international leadership opportunities within or through the network. This expansion of boundaries and opportunities can foster both educator and school empowerment.

Networks promote a common cause among members, and this common cause along with the power of numbers and collaboration can lead to positive educational change that would not happen without the network's support. Finally, networks recognize the achievements of their members and celebrate their collective accomplishments.

In our discussion of dynamic systems at the beginning of this chapter we said that the most complex dynamic systems interact and engage in mutual adaptation with their external environment. Partnerships and networks are excellent examples of how dynamic schools increase their capacity for continuous improvement through interaction and mutual adaptation with external stakeholders.

Beyond Newtonianism: The Quantum Paradigm and Dynamic Schools

Early in the 20th century, physicists began to discover behaviors of subatomic entities that could not be explained by Newtonian physics. As noted by Tang (2009), "Attempts to explain these anomalies led to the development of quantum theory, which is a totally new way of dealing with the problems of mechanics and electrodynamics in the atomic and subatomic world" (p. 3). Just as other fields had adopted the Newtonian view of reality in earlier times, so the ideas of quantum physics evolved into a broader paradigm for viewing the world. Eventually, the quantum paradigm was applied to organizations in general (Kilmann, 2001; Wheatley, 1994; Zohar, 1997) and schools in particular (Caine & Caine, 1997; Shaked & Schechter, 2013). Our discussion of dynamic schools has thus far been based on educational theory and research. As we delve into the quantum paradigm, we ask you to judge to what extent the dynamic school is related to, and perhaps even based on, the quantum paradigm. We will limit our discussion to those aspects of the quantum paradigm most relevant to schools.

Uncertainty and Potentiality

Two overlapping terms used in quantum theory are *uncertainty* and *potentiality*. Contrary to the principles of Newtonian physics, scientists studying subatomic particles have found that, although it is possible to measure the position or the momentum of a particle, it is impossible to measure both its position and momentum at the same time. The *uncertainty* principle thus means that it is impossible to accurately predict the trajectory of a particle. Electrons have no fixed paths around the nucleus of an atom but rather orbit the nucleus as "electron clouds." Quantum entities not only have no fixed paths, they have no independent identities: "Because they are indeterminate, quantum entities have no fully fixed identities until they are in relationship. This gives the quantum system maximum flexibility to define itself as it goes along. It co-creates with its environment" (Zohar, 1997, p. 50). Polkinghorne (2002) concludes, "If the study of quantum physics teaches us anything, it is that the world is full of surprises" (p. 87). Because the quantum world is indeterminate, the quantum paradigm is concerned with probabilities rather than Newtonian prediction and control.

If we accept the uncertainty principle as applicable to schools, it brings with it a number of implications. First, we cannot predict with certainty the effects of any instructional or school improvement effort. We should take the stance that improvement efforts and other aspects of the school community will co-evolve, probably in ways that we do not anticipate. The improvement *process* thus becomes more important than precise, predetermined goals and plans, first because the plans cannot provide for all of the unforeseen events that may unfold, but also because the predetermined goals may not meet the future needs of the evolving school community. Uncertainty means that even new, successful initiatives have an uncertain future because of the constantly changing school and community context, thus the improvement process must be ongoing, continuously seeking feedback, and making appropriate changes. Becoming comfortable with, or at least tolerant of, uncertainty becomes an essential disposition for both supervisors and teachers, and flexibility and responsiveness are important prerequisites for school renewal.

The concept of *potentiality,* related to the uncertainty principle, is based on the reality that subatomic particles do not have a definite position or momentum but have a potential for either of these. Quantum physics is thus concerned with possibilities rather than present reality. This concept has significant implications for schools. Taken seriously, potentiality means that supervisors and teachers, while not neglecting their current responsibilities, expend far more time and energy on imagining future possibilities such as:

- What would a curriculum that was relevant to students' real-world needs look like?
- How can teaching evolve so that it engages and excites all students?
- What types of assessment would authentically measure student growth and development in areas that really matter?

Potentiality calls for tapping teachers' imagination by encouraging them to share their dreams for the future. More concretely, supervisors honor potentiality by providing structures and time to engage in reflection and dialogue about possibilities for improving schools and classrooms. Reviewing and discussing a variety of outside literature and in-house data on future possibilities, visiting schools with successful innovations, and inviting the sharing of diverse points of view all can serve potentiality. Contributions to potentiality should not be limited to supervisors and teachers; parents, community members, and students can all make important contributions to a discussion of multiple possibilities and multiple potential paths for turning those possibilities into reality. *All* groups in the school community possess potentiality, and the potentiality of all groups and individuals should be honored, nourished, and drawn upon.

Complementarity

A subatomic entity may act as a particle or a wave, depending on how it is measured. If an experiment is designed to measure particles, then the entity will behave like a particle. If an experiment is designed to measure waves, then the entity will act like a wave. The entity has the potential to be a particle or a wave, but only *becomes* a particle or wave when it is observed! The famous physicist Neils Bohr (in Sokal, 1996) concludes, "A complete elucidation of one and the same object may require diverse points of view which defy a unique description"(p. 219). Another physicist, John Polkinghorne (2002), explains complementarity in somewhat different terms: "Quantum theory permits the mixing together of states that classically would be mutually exclusive of each other"(p. 21).

In applying complementarity to schools, one implication is that understanding what is going on in classrooms and schools requires multiple observers and observations, multiple types of data and types of data analysis, and multiple viewpoints from diverse stakeholders. Another implication is that many of the dichotomies we perceive in schools are only illusions. This realization is the first step in breaking down false dichotomies that harm teaching and learning, including perceived dichotomies such as organizational versus individual goals, the school versus the community, leaders versus teachers, affective versus academic learning, teachers' personal development versus professional development, students who are able versus students who are unable to engage in higher-level learning, and so forth.

Entanglement

Two particles, both in a spin-up and spin-down state, interact and then separate. When one of the particles is observed, it shifts to either a spin-up-only or a spin-down-only state. When this happens, the shift is communicated almost instantly to the second particle, which immediately shifts its spin. If the first particle has shifted to a spin-up-only state, then the second particle shifts to a spin-down-only state. If the first particle shifts to a spin-down-only state, then the second particle shifts to a spin-up-only state. The two particles are now *correlated* with each other. The communication between the first and second particle and the change in spin takes place almost instantly (faster than the speed of light) no matter how far the two particles have traveled from each other!

When applied to schools, entanglement means that events, experiences, or changes anywhere in the school can affect other aspects of the school. A change in the curriculum of one content area affects other content areas. One student being moved to a different ability group affects all students. A teacher changing her or his instructional strategies affects teaching and learning in other classrooms. Entanglement also means that what goes on in students' families affects the school, and what goes on in school affects families. An early-morning quarrel between a mother and father may impact the entire school day for several teachers and students. A student being bullied in school may impact the bullied student's family, and other families, for days after the bullying incident. On a broader scale, entanglement means that what goes on inside a school affects the community that the school serves (including community members that do not have children in school) and what goes on in the community affects the school. An obvious example of how the school affects the community relates to scores on the state's high-stakes achievement test, which can affect not only real estate values but also the community's overall image. Aspects of the community that affect the school include local economic conditions, community safety, the quality of housing, the types of community and health services available, and the cultural assets of the community. In short, school and community are "entangled."

One way that supervisors and teachers can address entanglement is to become more aware of the entanglements that affect teaching and learning. The principle of uncertainty means that it is impossible to understand all entanglements, but many of the more critical ones can be identified through communication among stakeholders. Supervisors and teachers need to engage in dialogue with each other and with students, parents, and community members about events, experiences, or changes that are affecting life in the classroom, school, and community. The quantum paradigm holds that prediction and control of all entanglements are impossible, but collaboration among stakeholders can impact certain leverage points for the benefit of teaching and learning. Supervision needs to establish structures and processes for teachers to get into each other's classrooms, to work together on group and schoolwide initiatives, and to work with parents and community members for both school and community development. Since parents and community members are already entangled with the school, they need to collaborate with educators on the "co-evolution" of the school and community.

Quantum Observation and Measurement

The quantum paradigm holds, first, that there are no such things as objective observation and measurement, and second, that an observation affects whatever is being measured. The subatomic entity, with potential to be either a particle or a wave, becomes a particle or a wave only when it is observed! The observation *causes* the entity to become a particle or wave. In the case of entanglement, it is the observation that causes the first particle to change its spin and communicate with the second entity, which then changes its spin. In both complementarity and entanglement, it is as though entities are responding to the observer by changing their state. The entity seems to change its state in order to give the observer what she or he is looking for! One conclusion to be drawn is that an observer cannot measure an entity or system without changing that entity or system. Another conclusion is that what we observe in any particular observation or measure in any single measurement is only part of a larger reality.

One implication for schools is that the educational measurements we use not only measure only a part of reality, but also affect the student or teacher behavior that is observed. The objectives of high-stakes achievement tests, for example, largely determine many schools' curriculum and teachers' instructional practice. Also, the school's teacher evaluation system often determines the teacher's behaviors, at least during the period when the teacher is observed for a summative evaluation. Unless we are cognizant of the fact that any single measurement reveals only part of reality, we may accept a very narrow view of student or teacher performance, overlooking other important aspects. Fleener (2002) brings home this point:

> What if Binet had developed the I.Q. emphasizing mechanical and artistic skill rather than analytic and verbal skills? Certainly many of us who have been privileged in school because we were "smart" would find ourselves in remedial classes! Where would mathematics and language arts be in this curriculum in a society that measured intelligence by artistic talent?"(p. 68)

A related implication is that schools should use a variety of measures to develop a more realistic picture of whatever it is that educators are seeking to learn about. Decisions about what to measure about student performance and how to measure it should involve students and teachers, and decisions about the measurement of teacher performance should be co-constructed by teachers and supervisors. Analysis of measurement outcomes should also be a collaborative process, as there usually are multiple interpretations of what data means, and multiple possibilities of why what was observed or measured took place. Finally, supervisors and teachers should consider observing and measuring aspects of teaching, learning, and schools that they perceive to be important but that are traditionally not observed or measured—we need to expand our notions of what should be measured and how it can be measured, while also recognizing that none of our measurements will be truly objective or provide a complete picture of reality.

Holism

In contrast to the Newtonian view of isolated objects traveling through a void, quantum physics views entities as connected through wavelike vibrations and invisible fields known only by their unifying effects. As simply stated by Rosado (2008), "everything is connected to everything else"(p. 2080). A system is an interactive whole, with the whole greater then the sum of its parts, and each part reflecting the whole. Not only are the parts of a system connected to each other, but the system also is intimately connected with the environment in which it exists.

If we apply holism to schools, then the relationships and interactions of members of the school community become more important than the adoption of prescribed programs or short-term efforts to solve isolated problems. The capacity for school renewal is based on relationships throughout the school, and the organizational energy for renewal comes from collaborative interactions. Wheatley (1994) concludes that a human organization's connecting fields are the values and vision that are developed through human interaction. Shared leadership characterizes a holistic school, which includes both collective decisions and different members of the school community stepping forward to provide leadership in particular situations. Shaked and Schechter (2013) suggest that holistic leadership includes (a) basing school renewal on a central, unifying school theme (values and vision) rather than discreet changes, (b) recognizing the interconnections and mutual influences of different aspects of the school environment, (c) considering multiple causes and aspects of school issues, and implementing multiple, coherent actions to address those issues, and (d) focusing on leverage points that, when acted upon, will impact the entire school community. Holistic school improvement involves interdisciplinary and vertical teams, joint school and community development efforts, and alliances with organizations and institutions outside the community that affect and are affected by the school.

Connecting the Quantum Paradigm with the Dynamic School

Let's return to our discussion of the dynamic school for a few moments and compare the characteristics of such a school to the quantum paradigm. The *shared leadership, collegiality, and collaboration* present in the dynamic school relate to the quantum notions of uncertainty and potentiality, in that it is difficult for the supervisor to predict where the shared leadership will take the school—prediction and control are sacrificed for the sake of potentiality. Shared leadership, collegiality, and collaboration also reflect complementarity in that they break down the false dichotomy of leadership and teaching. Finally, shared leadership, collegiality, and collaboration recognize the entanglement already present throughout the school and foster a holistic school culture.

The *cause beyond oneself* present in dynamic schools mirrors the invisible fields of quantum physics and connects people, structures, and processes throughout the school. The cause beyond oneself that includes the community served by the school recognizes the quantum entanglement of school and community. Successful *professional development* is based on the school's vision and values and thus supports holism, and is also job embedded and ongoing, preparing teachers for the continuously changing nature of their work (uncertainty principle) while honoring their potentiality.

The *positive learning climate* of the dynamic school can be viewed as a field that connects teachers, students, and learning and contributes to the quantum concept of holism. The moral tone and sense of empowerment present in positive learning environments acknowledges the potentiality of all members of the school community, and the inclusion of school-family and school-community relationships in the definition of a positive learning environment represents both a realization of entanglement of the school with outside stakeholders and complementarity that eliminates false dichotomies.

Authentic curriculum, instruction, and assessment relate to the quantum paradigm in multiple ways. First, although a school initiating authenticity cannot predict the future with certainty, the four principles of authenticity—higher-order thinking, deep knowledge, substantive conversation, and connection to the student's life beyond the school—offer tremendous potentiality. Authentic curriculum and instruction bring complementarity to mind, as they break down the false dichotomies of external mandates versus locally developed curriculum, students capable of learning higher-level versus those capable of learning only a "basic" curriculum, and "school learning" versus the student's world outside of the school. Authentic assessment is consistent with quantum observation and assessment, with its recognition that any one assessment does not measure all of the student's learning, and that what is learned, how it is learned, and how learning is measured are mutually influential. Authenticity is holistic, as authentic curriculum, instruction, and assessment are intimately connected.

Democracy, if it is deep, can become one of the invisible fields that connect the school community. Although democracy does not bring certainty about the future, it increases the potentiality for trust, collaboration, and learning. *Inquiry* is consistent with the uncertainty principle in that, rather than relying on externally generated programs and prescriptions, supervisors and teachers gather and reflect on data, articulate possible improvements, and test out those possibilities. Inquiry, if done well, mirrors quantum observation and measurement: Supervisors and teachers realize that they can never find out all there is to know about an issue through a single inquiry, and that as researchers they will affect the object of their research. Supervisors and teachers engaged in quantum observation and measurement collect multiple types of data, with multiple inquirers analyzing those data in multiple ways. Because no single inquiry is able to describe what is going on in schools and classrooms, and no action plan based on inquiry can resolve with certainty the problem being addressed, inquiry becomes an ongoing process involving repeated cycles of asking questions, gathering data, and taking action, with reflection during each phase of the cycle. Supervisor and teacher inquiry also involves complementarity, in that it includes researchers and practitioners as well as research and action within the same context. Finally, ongoing inquiry leads to a culture of inquiry that can serve as a field connecting different aspects of the school and thus supports holism.

Cultural responsiveness acknowledges the potentiality of students from all cultural groups. Responsiveness relates to complimentarity, first because it works against false dichotomies of learning ability, motivation, and behavior between groups, and also because it acknowledges different ways of learning and different ways of demonstrating that learning. Culturally responsive teachers' consideration of the strong connections between a student's learning and that student's cultural assets, and efforts to connect teaching to the student's home, community, and culture, relate to the quantum concept of entanglement. Responsive educators' efforts to develop personal relationships with students, promote positive relationships among students, and teach students cultural responsiveness represent a commitment to the interrelationships that characterize holism. In addition, the use of culturally sensitive, alternative, and multiple assessments of students from diverse groups is consistent with quantum observation and measurement.

Partnerships with the community, district, and nearby colleges or universities acknowledge existing relationships, of course, but also develop those relationships for the benefit of both the school and the partner. Multiple partnerships promote holism for the larger educational system, a holism that will be reflected in and benefit the school. Although business is not part of the educational system, the school and local businesses clearly are entangled in multiple ways, and harnessing that entanglement in appropriate ways can benefit both partners.

Networks involve complementarity by promoting both individual growth and regional, national, or international collaboration, and providing network members both the opportunity to benefit from membership and assist other network members. The effects that network members have on other members, often at a considerable distance, remind us of quantum entanglement, and the unifying power of networks reflects holism.

Closing Question

Is the quantum paradigm a subatomic reality that other fields use as metaphor for transitions needed to adapt to a changing world, or is there something deeper and broader at play here? Could it be that science, because of its cutting-edge nature, is often simply the first field to discover and articulate realities that also exist beyond the realm of science, that have universal application? In the tradition of the quantum paradigm, we have no definite answer to this question, but offer it to the reader as food for thought.

> ✔ **Check Your Understanding 3.0**   Click here to gauge your understanding of the key concepts presented in this chapter.

REFLECTIVE EXERCISE

Identify a schoolwide need at a school of your choice. What type of partnership, involving the school and at least two external partners, could assist the school to meet the need you have identified? Specifically,

- Who would be the partners?
- What would be the goals of the partnership?
- What would be the contributions of each partner?
- What structures would be established for communication and coordination among partners?
- What benefits would each partner receive?

chapter 4

Adult and Teacher Development Within the Context of the School

Learning Outcomes for This Chapter

After reading this chapter, you should be able to:

1. List the implications of any of the theories of adult learning discussed in this chapter for instructional supervision.
2. Explain why the notion of a universal model of adult development has been challenged.
3. Discuss what the authors mean by the "ebb and flow" of adult development.

Questions to Reflect On as You Read This Chapter

1. As you read the chapter, reflect on learning about each of the following concepts:
   - Andragogy
   - Transformative learning
   - Self-directed learning
   - Experiential learning
   - Situated cognition
   - Informal learning
2. How do you think adult thinking differs from that of younger learners? To what do you attribute these differences?
3. Two different teachers may approach the same teaching challenge in markedly different ways. In what ways do you think adult development may explain this?
4. As you read the various models of adult development, which resonate with your own experience?
5. What ways do you see that knowledge of adult development might be applied in supervision and professional development of teachers?

This chapter will serve as a core for thinking and practicing supervision in a developmental framework. So far, we have defined "a cause beyond oneself" as a demarcation between the collective, thoughtful, autonomous, and effective staffs of successful schools and the isolated, unreflective, and powerless staffs of unsuccessful schools. Knowledge of how teachers can grow as competent adults is the guiding principle for supervisors in finding ways to return wisdom, power, and control to both the individuals and the collective staff in order for them to become true professionals. With the understanding of how teachers change, the supervisor can plan direct assistance, evaluation of teaching, professional development, curriculum development, group development, and action research at an appropriate level to stimulate teacher growth and instructional improvement.

The research on adult learning and development has been prolific. We have attempted to distill the knowledge of adult and teacher development that has direct applications for supervision and supervisors. Readers who desire more detail should refer to the references cited. The use of such readily available and potentially rich knowledge about human growth can be extremely valuable to those who work with adults. If schools are to be successful, supervision must respond to teachers as changing adults.

Adults as Learners

Instructional improvement takes place when teachers improve their decision making about students, learning content, and teaching. The process of improving teacher decision making is largely a process of adult learning. Thus, research and theory on adult learning is an important component of the knowledge base for instructional supervision.

Intelligence and Wisdom

Two basic questions drove much of the early research on adult learning ability: Does ability to learn diminish with age? Are there differences between the learning process of adults and children? Thorndike (1928) was among the first to suggest that adult learning did not peak in youth and diminish steadily thereafter (a common belief of his day).

Horn and Cattell (1967) identified two categories of intelligence: fluid and crystallized. *Fluid intelligence,* which depends heavily on physiological and neurological capacities, peaks early and explains why youth excel on tasks requiring quick insight, short-term memorization, and complex interactions (Klauer & Phye, 2008; Merriam, Caffarella, & Baumgartner, 2007; Penta, Anghel, Talpos-Niculescu, Argesanu,

& Stanca Muntianu, (2015)). *Crystallized intelligence,* assessed by untimed measures calling for judgment, knowledge, and experience, is more heavily influenced by education and experience. Hence, older individuals show an advantage when it is measured. Research by Zimprich, Allenmand, and Dellenbach (2009) investigating the links between crystallized and fluid intelligence and components of the personality characteristic of Openness to Experience in middle-age and older adults revealed both (a) a strong connection between overall Openness to Experience and crystallized intelligence and (b) a strong connection between Interest in Intellectual Activities and both crystallized and fluid intelligence.

Contemporary theories of intelligence have extended the notion that intelligence consists of multiple components or factors. Most readers of this text will be familiar with Howard Gardner's theory of multiple intelligences (1999). Gardner initially posited seven types of intelligence (linguistic, logical-mathematical, musical, spatial, bodily-kinesthetic, intrapersonal, and interpersonal). He later added naturalistic intelligence and suggested there are likely other forms of intelligence. Gardner's ideas are also relevant to supervision. Supervisors can identify and utilize the learning strengths of individual teachers when assisting them with instructional improvement efforts. Supervisors can also assist teachers to gradually expand their repertoire of learning strategies.

Sternberg likewise has proposed a theory of intelligence that may be helpful in thinking about the cognition of teachers (Sternberg, 1988; Sternberg, Kaufman, & Grigorenko, 2008). It is called a *triarchic theory of intelligence* because it consists of three subtheories. The first subtheory is referred to as *componential;* it deals with cognitive processing. This part of the theory deals with what has traditionally been discussed in trying to understand intellectual ability. The second subtheory is *experiential,* which suggests that assessing intelligence requires consideration not only of the mental components but of the level of experience at which they are applied. Sternberg, intrigued by the differences between novices and experts, has suggested that experience promotes both the ability to respond automatically to routine situations and to deal effectively with novel situations. Thus, novice teachers can be expected to require different types of supervision than those who are more experienced.

Although the first two subtheories deal with processes said to be universal, Sternberg's third *contextual* subtheory deals with socially influenced abilities. Individuals are said to cope with life's challenges by adapting to the environment, shaping the environment, or selecting a different environment—all the while being influenced by what is considered appropriate and intelligent behavior within one's cultural milieu. This last contextual subtheory becomes important when one looks at how teachers deal with challenging situations. Some obviously have greater capacities than others to adapt to or change the classroom and school environment. Through appropriate supervision, teachers can be assisted in broadening their array of adaptation and change strategies. It is this kind of practical intelligence that intrigues Sternberg and other theorists who cite a lack of attention on the demonstration of adult intelligence through the identification and solution of real-world problems.

Sternberg (2001) and others have explored those particular forms of intelligence that have come to be referred to as *wisdom*. In his *balance theory of wisdom*, Sternberg posits that wisdom is a type of practical intelligence concerned with balancing intrapersonal interests (those of the individual), interpersonal interests (those of other people), and extrapersonal interests (aspects of environmental contexts, such as the community or city). For instance, according to this theory, the wise teacher considers his or her own interests and those of family in deciding whether to conform to an uncomfortable teaching environment, to seek to shape the environment, or to leave it. Johnson (2005) speculates that wisdom facilitates movement or growth in affective, spiritual, and relational domains, citing the work of Bassett (2005) in describing the characteristics of wisdom across these domains. Bassett engaged in a grounded theory study, drawing on literature across multiple disciplines as well as interviews with four people of "public distinction." He proposed a theory of *emergent wisdom*, pointing to four dimensions of wisdom: discerning (cognitive), respecting (affective), engaging (active), and transforming (reflective). More recently, Cooke and Carr (2014) have examined the construct of *practice wisdom* and its relationship to virtue in the context of professional decision making by teachers. Observing that teaching seems to "require flexible and adaptable context-specific judgment in complex and ever-changing circumstances"(p. 95), they compare this sort of practical deliberation to Aristotle's reference to practical wisdom (phronesis).

Theories of Adult Learning

As research increasingly put to rest the question of whether adults could continue to learn, attention focused on how their learning differed from that of children. The focus of the following overview of adult learning theories will be on those theories that have received particular attention over recent decades as adult educators sought to answer this question. A chronological review of the literature on adult learning would reveal in greater detail what this brief overview will suggest—a shift from a psychological orientation (Knowles, 1980; Tough, 1971) toward a sociocultural orientation (Hansman, 2008; Hayes & Flannery, 2000).

Andragogy.   The *theory of andragogy*, popularized in this country by Malcolm Knowles, has become one of the better-known theories of adult learning in recent years. Knowles (1980) proposed four basic assumptions of adult learning:

1. Adults have a psychological need to be self-directing.
2. Adults bring an expansive reservoir of experience that can and should be tapped in the learning situation.

3. Adults' readiness to learn is influenced by a need to solve real-life problems often related to adult developmental tasks.

4. Adults are performance centered in their orientation to learning—wanting to make immediate application of knowledge.

Later, Knowles added a fifth assumption—that adult learning is primarily intrinsically motivated (Knowles, 1984). The theory of andragogy no longer receives the uncritical acceptance that it once did, with questions raised about the extent to which these assumptions are exclusively true of adults (Tennant, 1986), the extent to which self-direction is an actual versus a desirable preference of adult learners (Brookfield, 2009), the conditions under which andragogy may or may not apply (Rachal, 2002), and the cultural nature of the assumptions (Sandlin, 2005). Knowles himself, before his death in 1997, came to acknowledge that differences between adults and children as learners may be a matter of degree and situation rather than a rigid dichotomy. Nevertheless, the theory of andragogy is still recognized by many for its foundational contribution to understanding about adults' learning (Merriam, 2008; Meyer & Murrell, 2014; Rose, Jeris, & Smith, 2005; Taylor & Laros, 2014).

Self-Directed Learning.   Even as self-direction in learning was emerging as one of the most challenged assumptions within andragogy, a distinct body of theory and research on adults' self-directed learning (SDL) was evolving. Allen Tough (1971) is generally credited with providing the first comprehensive description of self-directed learning—learning that adults engage in systematically as part of everyday life and without benefit of an instructor. A long-standing body of research on this topic has documented the ubiquitousness of adults' self-directed learning and led to the development of numerous models of self-directed learning as well as several instruments intended to measure it Eneau, 2008; Merriam, 2008). Lai (2011) utilized Guglielmino's (1997, 1997) *Self-Directed Learning Readiness Scale* (SDLRS) in a study of online learning effectiveness among civil servants engaged in professional learning in Taiwan. Study findings indicated the SDLRS significantly predicts online learning effectiveness scores, with the *active learning* subscale from the SDLRS serving as the strongest predictor. Four subscales of the SDLRS accounted for 26% of the variance in online learning effectiveness. An additional finding was that worker age was a strong predictor of *love of learning*, another SDLRS subscale, with older learners tending to exhibit greater love of learning.

The implications of the concept of self-directed learning are numerous for those who seek to foster teachers' growth and development through developmental supervision. Supervision should foster rather than inhibit self-directed learning by matching supervisory behaviors with teachers' readiness for self-direction. Just as Grow (1991) recommended that instructors match their teaching style to the estimated stage of self-direction of adult learners, so too the effective supervisor will adapt his or her supervisory style in response to the degree of self-directed readiness exhibited by the teacher in a given context. Additionally, as noted by Steinke (2012), efforts to foster SDL as a means of professional development for workers may be impacted by cultural influences. She cites Nah (1999) who argues that for workers from some backgrounds, including the Korean adults used as an example, the independence associated with SDL may be seen as contradictory to cultural norms favoring interdependence.

Heutogogy. Blaschke (2012) reviews a growing body of literature on *heutogogy*, first proposed by Hase and Kenyon (2000) as an extension of andragogy and self-directed learning theory, focused on increasing adult learner autonomy in *self-determined learning*. Hase and Kenyon (2000, 2007), originators of the construct, acknowledge Knowles's idea of self-directed learning as moving from a teacher-driven to a learner-centered model of adult teaching and learning. But in presenting heutogogy as a concept more suitable to 21st-century learning, they aim to shift the focus away from the *teacher* or mentor as a guide on the side to the *learner* who is genuinely self-determined, with the teacher or mentor serving more in the role of consultant. The goal of the supervisor or mentor in this context is to assist in the development of capability, since

> Capable people are more likely to be able to deal effectively with the turbulent environment in which they live by possessing an "all round" capacity centered on self-efficacy, knowing how to learn, creativity, the ability to use competencies in novel as well as familiar situations and working with others. (Hase & Kenyon, 2000, para 16)

The learner in this model seems similar in many ways to the autodidact described earlier by Candy (1991) in his lengthy tome on self-directed learning as the adult learner who maintains full control of his or her learning, while drawing on various people, media, and other resources as needed.

Transformational Learning. For some who question whether either andragogy or SDL theory represent a learning theory that is uniquely adult, transformative learning theory—proposed and revised most prominently by Jack Mezirow (2000)—offers an appealing alternative. Indeed, Taylor (2007) concludes that TL has replaced andragogy as the iconic adult learning theory of the field of adult education, to the point of being at similar risk of oversimplification and misapplication (Newman, 2012; Taylor & Laros, 2014). This theory grew out of Mezirow's research with reentry women in higher education. He has offered the following definition of transformative learning:

> Transformative learning refers to the process by which we transform our taken-for-granted frames of reference (meaning perspectives, habits of mind, mind-sets) to make them more inclusive, discriminating, open, emotionally capable of change, and reflective so that they may generate beliefs and opinions that will prove more true or justified to guide action. (Mezirow, 2000, pp. 7–8)

Kegan (2009) contrasts transformative learning (changes in *how* we know) with informative learning (changes in *what* we know), adding that we all experience potentially important kinds of change that do not bring about a fundamental shift in our frames of reference. Merriam (2004) argues that a relatively high level of cognitive development is a prerequisite of the critical reflection on experience, which is key to transformational learning. Erickson (2007), on the other hand, suggests that transformative learning is possible for adult learners of differing developmental levels, although the nature of the process may be influenced by their developmental level.

Perspective transformation often is described as triggered by a significant life event, originally referred to by Mezirow as a disorienting dilemma. Perspective transformation also can occur in response to minor events that create an opportunity for reflection and redirection or may occur when an accumulation of internal dilemmas creates a growing sense of disillusionment (English, 2005; Erickson, 2007; Howie & Bagnall, 2015; Mezirow, Taylor, et al., 2009). A teacher's trigger for transformative learning may occur in a situation as obvious as experiencing failure for the first time when she accepts a new position in an urban setting or as subtle as having a conversation with a gay student about the impact of other students' homophobic jokes on his learning.

Cranton (1994) recommended that the educator should critically reflect on his or her own meaning perspective of being an educator. She also described the processes by which the educator might accomplish this:

> The educator, in order to develop the meaning perspective of being an educator would: increase self awareness through consciousness-raising activities, make his or her assumptions about beliefs about practice explicit, engage in critical reflection on those assumptions and beliefs, engage in dialogue with others, and develop an informed theory of practice. (p. 214)

The strategies Cranton suggested that may be useful in this process are varied, including writing journals, visiting the classrooms of colleagues, conducting criteria analysis of incidents that epitomize their notions of success or failure in practice, experimenting with practice, eliciting feedback from learners, and consulting or engaging in dialogue with colleagues.

Situated Learning and Communities of Practice

At the heart of numerous conceptions of adult learning and education dating back to Dewey (1938) and Lindeman (1926) is the centrality of experience to learning. This concern with experience is reflected in Knowles's (1980) inclusion of the importance of adult experience as one of his original four assumptions about adult learning (Gorard & Selwyn, 2005). It is also reflected in Kolb's (1984) inclusion of two phases focusing on experience (concrete experience and active experimentation) as part of his four-phase model of the adult learning cycle.

The centrality of experience to learning takes on new dimensions when the emerging body of work on situated cognition is applied to consideration of adult learning. Many cite Brown, Collins, and Duguid (1989) as a seminal work in proposing a theory of *situated cognition*. Brown and colleagues (1989) and others emphasize the cognitive *apprenticeship* as a means for learners to acquire knowledge as participants in a community of practice (Cheng, 2014; Dennen, 2008; Hansman, 2008; Tilley & Callison, 2007). Wenger (2009) has described the role of *communities of practice* (CoP), or self-organized groups that share a common sense of purpose and a desire to learn from one another. Each of these strategies offers a valuable approach for fostering professional development of teachers, particularly those who are new to the field or to a particular school culture.

Although often framed within learning communities that are intentionally structured to promote professional learning rather than based on naturally forming communities, Lave and Wenger's (Lave & Wenger, 1991) concept of CoP has been frequently cited in recent years as a theoretical basis for collegial support and collaborative inquiry frameworks implemented as part of professional development efforts. For instance, Curry (2008), reported on a learning community of secondary level teachers. The high school in question had for several years organized teachers, initially on a voluntary basis, but later included all new teachers into critical friend groups (CFGs), with a 3-hour monthly meeting dedicated to their gatherings. The study analyzed four design features of CFGs: (1) diverse activities, (2) decentralized structure, (3) interdisciplinary membership, and (4) reliance on structured conversation tools called "protocols." Curry showed how each of these design features held advantages and disadvantages, as well as how the CFG approach enabled ongoing learning by teachers and administrators. Baek and Barab (2005) described a grounded theory study aimed at understanding the design dualities that emerged when teachers and designers worked together to build a Web-supported community of practice. The study looked at the efforts involved in creating an appropriate Web-based space for an online CoP called the Inquiry Learning Forum, intended to support the professional development of math and science teachers. Relying on multiple data sources, they identified five dualities between those who used the site and those who designed it—such as a duality of purpose (school reform versus daily support). They suggested that in uncovering these dualities, the findings from this case study might highlight challenges others confront in seeking to design Web-based structures that stimulate meaningful participation in communities of practice, and remind future designers to spend the upfront time needed to understand the culture of the participating teachers.

Recent work investigating the links between experience and adult learning in the workplace suggests that much of the meaningful learning that occurs in that context is of the informal and incidental variety rather than the highly structured learning traditionally associated with workplace training (Kerka, 1998; Uys, Gwele, McInerney, Rhyn, & Tanga, 2004). Marsick and Watkins (1990) originally presented a theory of informal and incidental learning in 1990. Later, incorporating the work of their doctoral students, Cseh and Lovin, as well as Wenger's (2009) theory of communities of practice, they revised the model to recognize the considerable importance of context (Cseh, Watkins, & Marsick, 1999) and later to pay greater attention to the roles of social interaction and social construction of knowledge (Marsick, Watkins, & Lovin, 2010). In the more recent conceptualization they view informal learning as interactive and less linear, describing it as an "amoeba-like process." *Informal learning* is usually intentional but less structured than formal learning. Examples include self-directed learning, networking, informal coaching, and mentoring. *Incidental learning*, on the other hand, is defined as a by-product of some other activity and is most often tacit or unconscious at the time. The model they proposed describes a progression of meaning-making that they warn is neither as linear nor as sequential as their model might suggest. Marsick and Watkins (1990) suggested that those wishing to help adults improve their informal learning (e.g., supervisors) might assist adults in identifying conditions in the sociocultural context that help them learn more effectively or that stand in the way of learning. Once such factors are identified, supervisors can help the learner deal with or change them.

> ▶ **Video Illustration**
>
> In this video, a new principal discusses how she and her staff met the challenge of improving student learning after the school became poorly rated. How does this video illustrate the value of situated learning utilizing existing communities of practice as an important component of school improvement?

Holistic Adult Learning

In recent years, a number of authors, eschewing the tendency in Western culture to equate learning with *only* the cognitive and rational dimensions of learning, have spoken of the need to study adult learning in a *holistic* fashion, including noncognitive dimensions such as somatic or embedded knowing, narrative learning, and spiritual learning. Merriam and colleagues (2007) dedicate an entire chapter to noncognitive dimensions of learning in the latest edition of *Learning in Adulthood*, including embodied, spiritual, and narrative learning. Clark (2001) attributes the growing attention to *somatic learning* (which includes an interest in kinesthetic learning and the role of emotions in learning) in part to the legitimization of the body as a source of knowledge. She cites Polanyi (1969) as arguing that knowledge actually starts in the body, and Michelson (1998) as criticizing the emphasis placed on the reflective (rational) components of experiential learning over the embodied experience that is the source of the learning.

Tolliver and Tisdell (2006) similarly invite those involved in the education of adults to look for ways to bring their own spirituality into the learning environment and to engage the spirituality of adult learners by introducing activities that activate meaning-making through imagery, symbol, metaphor, poetry, art, and music. Such activities, Tolliver and Tisdell (2006) maintain, can be used to promote transformative learning by engaging the whole person and assisting the learner in developing a more authentic identity without imposing a religious or spiritual agenda, even without any explicit discussion of spirituality.

Finally, Clark (2001) and more recently Rossiter and Clark (2010) have examined the place of *narrative* in adult learning. They stress the power of storytelling and particularly the creation of one's personal narrative as an aid for learning and intentional change. Clark (2001) also discusses the benefits of teachers of adults producing their own educational biographies as a tool for understanding how their own learning has shaped who they are.

In a qualitative study of eight experienced educators, Beattie, Dobson, Thornton, and Hegge (2007) integrated all the forms of noncognitive learning discussed here. In describing their study, they say:

> The research is grounded in a narrative tradition of research on teacher development where teacher learning is viewed as a creative, holistic, relational endeavor in which the personal and professional are intimately connected. It makes connections between narrative inquiry, holistic education and teacher development, and has the potential to make a contribution to the body of knowledge in teachers' knowledge/learning by exploring and describing the aesthetic and spiritual dimensions of educators' ways of knowing and being. (p. 119)

The authors' description of findings is generously sprinkled with excerpts from the narratives of teachers talking about the aesthetic and spiritual dimensions of their growth as professionals.

Critical Perspectives on Adult Learning

In recent decades, a number of philosophical and theoretical orientations have challenged dominant perspectives on adult learning, such as andragogy, self-directed learning, transformative learning, and experiential learning. These critical perspectives have included feminism (Carpenter, 2012), critical theory (Welton, 1995; Fleming, 2012; Habermas, 2001), critical race theory (Closson, 2010; Drayton, Rosser-Mims, Schwartz, & Guy, 2014), critical multiculturalism (Guo, 2013; Ross-Gordon, Brooks, Clunis, Parsells, & Parker, 2005), and postmodernism (Foucault, 1977; Lyotard, 1984; McArdle & Mansfield, 2013; Ostrom, Martin, & Zacharakis, 2008).

Kilgore (2001) has offered a brief synopsis of the critical and postmodern perspectives of adult learning, analyzing both their similarities and differences. As she notes, each of these perspectives challenges pillars of adult learning theory such as andragogy and self-directed learning as exclusionary and overly focused on the individual. Both critical and postmodern perspectives share assumptions that knowledge is socially constructed, along with an interest in power as a factor in learning. They differ, however, in other significant ways.

Critical theorists argue that *hegemony* (dominant influence or authority wielded by those in power) operates to preserve inequities linked to structures of privilege and oppression based on categories like race, ethnicity, gender, class, and age. In this view, learning involves reflecting on the hegemonic assumptions that often guide our practices and perhaps acting to change the practices as well as the assumptions. (Kilgore gives as an example the use and misuse of standardized tests.) Social justice is viewed as a core value. Postmodern theorists, on the other hand (Foucault, 1977; Lyotard, 1984), resist embracing *any* universal truth, emphasizing that knowledge is multifaceted and truths shift according to the experience and context of the knower. Even the same individual can hold multiple perspectives on a topic based on situational variables or in their multifaceted identities (what Sheared [1999] refers to as *polyrhythmic realities*).

Power is a consideration for each framework but in different ways. For instance, critical theories are interested in how the status quo (e.g., an individualistic focus on learning that research suggests may be culturally biased toward certain groups) can be interrupted to create more emancipatory knowledge (e.g., a greater emphasis on group learning, which research suggests is more culturally relevant for some groups of learners). Power is seen as held by some over others; for instance, the traditional role of principals invests them with greater power than teachers. From the postmodern perspective, power is present in every relationship and can be exercised by anyone to one degree or another. We must analyze (or deconstruct) the situation to know how power is being used (whether for repressive or liberating purposes) and by whom. In this view, teacher and parent participation in site-based management or participatory action research projects become tools both for producing knowledge collaboratively and for negotiating and rearranging power relationships.

Teachers as Adult Learners

Fullan (1991) pointed out that "educational change is a learning experience for the adults involved"(p. 66); and more recently that "student learning depends on every teacher learning all the time"(p. 35). Our knowledge of adult learning tells us that it is important to link learning about instructional innovations to teachers' past experiences and to allow them ample time to integrate innovations gradually into their teaching repertoire. Yet, in recent years, teachers have been bombarded with a plethora of innovations as part of the educational reform movement. Fullan (1991) concluded "many decisions about the kinds of educational innovations introduced in school districts are biased, poorly thought out, and unconnected to the stated purposes of education"(p. 8). This is no doubt why many innovations have failed. Other innovations potentially of significant value and technically sound have also failed. One reason for these failures may be that supervisors have not helped teachers to integrate the innovations with their past experiences or adapt the innovations to their current teaching practice. Moreover, teachers often simply are not provided sufficient time to learn about and adapt the innovation before a new innovation is given precedence by administrators and supervisors (Zepeda, 2004).

Sternberg's work on the experiential component of adult intelligence indicates that novice teachers need to be supervised differently than experienced teachers (Sternberg et al., 2008). One example of this need for differentiation is that many beginning teachers have more difficulty assessing and responding to novel teaching situations and problems than their experienced colleagues and thus are in need of more intensive support. Both Sternberg's (Sternberg, 1988; Sternberg et al., 2008) and Gardner's (2006) research on multiple intelligences takes us beyond differences between novice and experienced teachers and points to the need for identifying and utilizing different learning strengths of teachers at all levels of experience.

The need to individualize teacher learning, indicated by the literature on adult learning, stands in sharp contrast to the actual treatment of teachers. Many supervisors treat teachers as if they were all the same, rather than as individuals in various stages of adult growth. In most schools, teachers receive the same in-service workshops, the same observations, and the same assessments. It is as if teachers were stamped out of teacher training institutes as identical and thereafter have no further need to be viewed as individual learners. The research on adults shows the lack of wisdom of such assumptions.

The Sternberg et al. (2008) discussion of socially influenced abilities points to the need for teachers to engage in learning aimed at developing a variety of strategies for adapting to or changing their classroom and school environment. Both Mezirow's (2000) and Brookfield's (2009) work on adult learning indicates that in order to learn and grow, teachers need to participate in a continuous cycle of collaborative activity and reflection on that activity, and need to develop the powers of critical thinking. Finally, the writings of Knowles (1980, 1984), Mezirow (1981, 2000), and Brookfield (2009) have all supported the notion of the supervisor facilitating teacher growth toward empowerment and self-direction. Figure 4.1 reviews the knowledge on adult learning and its implications for instructional supervision.

Unfortunately, many schools do not foster collaborative action, reflection, critical thinking, or teacher empowerment. Rather, the hierarchical structure of many school systems—as well as the environmental problems of isolation, psychological dilemma, and lack of a shared technical culture discussed in Chapter 2—tends to work against the type of growth described in the adult learning literature. Conversely, Drago-Severson's (2007) qualitative study of principals as professional development leaders found

Knowledge about Adult Learning

Implications for Instructional Supervision

Intelligence

— Categories (Horn & Cattell)
  — Fluid
  — Crystallized

— Contemporary Theories
  — Multiple Intelligences (Gardner)
  — Triarchic Theory (Sternberg)

Theories of Adult Learning

— Andragogy (Knowles)

— Self-Directed Learning (Tough; Merriam; Grow)

— Transformational Learning (Mezirow; Kegan; Taylor; Cranton)

— Experience and Learning (Dewey; Lindeman; Knowles; Kolb)

— Situated Cognition (Brown et al.; Collins & Duguid; Hansman; Wenger)
  — Informal Learning (Marsick & Watkins)
  — Incidental Learning (Marsick & Watkins)

— Critical Theory (Habermas; Welton)

— Postmodern Theory (Foucault; Kilgore; Lyotard)

1. Differentiate supervision based on teachers' experience, learning strengths, and readiness level for self-directed learning.

2. Assist teachers to develop a variety of learning adaptations and change strategies.

3. Help teachers to identify, analyze, and solve classroom and school problems.

4. Link learning about instructional innovations to teachers' past learnings.

5. Allow ample time for teachers to gradually integrate innovations into their teaching repertoires.

6. Foster experiential learning, a continuous cycle of active experimentation and reflection on action.

7. Facilitate teacher empowerment and self-direction.

8. Support dialogue and collegial learning among teachers.

9. Help teachers take advantage of conditions supportive of learning and change nonsupportive conditions.

10. Foster teachers' critical thinking.

11. Help teachers' consider multiple perspectives on issues and problems.

figure **4.1** **Adults as Learners**

that those who successfully exercised their leadership to promote adult learning consistently employed four strategies, which she refers to as "pillar practices":

1. Encouraging various forms of teaming/partnering with colleagues within and outside school (e.g., teaching teams, curriculum teams, technology teams, diversity teams, developing partnerships with other organizations)

2. Providing opportunities for teachers to serve in leadership roles (e.g., mentoring graduate student interns, knowledge-based management, technology leaders, sharing decision making, leading accreditation teams)

3. Promoting collegial inquiry (e.g., reflection through writing and dialogue)

4. Mentoring

According to Drago-Severson, these pillar practices, particularly when adapted to teachers' developmental stages, foster transformative rather than informative learning (Drago-Severson, 2007; Drago-Severson, 2009).

Adult and Teacher Development

Literature on adult development can be seen as reflecting several distinct but related approaches. Just a few decades ago, the study of human development focused on children, and adulthood was either not a consideration or was thought to represent a period of stability. Theory and research on adult development for several decades emphasized development as an orderly progression. Because developmental psychologists did much of the work in this area, there was an emphasis on the change processes occurring in the individual with relatively little consideration of his or her interaction with the environment. Early approaches to adult development were rooted in such a tradition. Over time, alternative views of adult development evolved, with less concern for a universal progression and greater interest in the interaction between the individual and the social environment. Subsequent sections of this chapter will discuss adult development according to these five subtopics: (1) stage development, (2) life cycle development, (3) transition events, (4) role development, and (5) sociocultural influences on adult development.

Stage Theories of Adult and Teacher Development

We will begin discussion of adult development by focusing on developmental stage theories. Levine (1989) delineated the characteristics of stages:

> First and foremost is their structural nature. Each stage is a "structured whole," representing an underlying organization of thought or understanding. Stages are qualita-

tively different from one another. All emerge in sequence without variation; no stage can be skipped. Finally stages are "hierarchically integrated"; that is, progressive stages are increasingly complex and subsume earlier stages. Individuals always have access to the stages through which they have passed. Under ordinary circumstances or with proper supports, people will generally prefer to use the highest stages of which they are capable. (p. 86)

It may be helpful to look more closely at several specific stage theories.

Cognitive Development. Piaget described four stages of cognitive development: sensorimotor, preoperational, concrete operations, and formal operations (Blake & Pope, 2008). The person at the formal operations stage has already progressed beyond reasoning only for the "here and now" and can project into and relate time and space. A person at the formal operations stage uses hypothetical reasoning, understands complex symbols, and formulates abstract concepts.

Some researchers have found that formal thought is not demonstrated by all adults. There has also been considerable exploration of characteristic adult forms of thinking that go beyond Piaget's fourth stage to a postformal operations stage (Cartwright, Galupo, Tyree, & Jennings, 2009; Merriam & Bierema, 2014; Wynn, Mosholder, & Larsen, 2014). Terms like *postformal thought* (Sinnott, 2009), *integrative thought* (Kallio, 2011), and *epistemic understanding* (Baxter-Magolda, 2004) have been used to describe the highest stage of cognition observed in adults. Figure 4.2 represents the adult cognitive developmental continuum.

Ostorga (2006) provides insight into connections between teachers' cognitive development and their reflective thinking. Part of a larger study of student teachers, the two participants selected as the focus of this article were both adult learners, ages 28 and 35, who had previous experience in the classroom as paraprofessionals. Ostorga analyzed interview protocols and Measurement of Epistemological Reflection (MER) questionnaires developed by Baxter-Magolda (2004), as well as 15 weekly reflective journal entries. Neither participant exhibited epistemic stances at either end of the epistemological spectrum presented by Baxter-Magolda—absolute knowing and

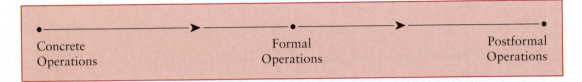

figure **4.2 Adult Cognitive Development Continuum**

Source: Adapted from Stephen P. Gordon (1990). *Assisting the entry-year teacher: A leadership resource.* Columbus, OH: Ohio Department of Education. Used with permission.

contextual knowing—rather, they exhibited adjacent stances in the middle of Baxter-Magolda's spectrum. Nonetheless observable differences were demonstrated in the nature of reflective statements made in their journals, coded according to Mezirow's (1981) taxonomy of reflectivity, developed as part of his work on transformational learning. Elena, the participant exhibiting a transitional epistemological stance, exhibited content level reflection in most of her journals, the most basic of Mezirow's levels of reflection, and only once engaged in a combination of content and process reflection. Shakira, the participant exhibiting an independent thinking epistemological stance, wrote at least one journal entry exhibiting premise reflection—the highest of Mezirow's levels of reflection—when she critiqued a response provided by her supervising teacher.

Moral Development.   Kohlberg & Kramer (2006) identified three broad categories of morality: the preconventional level, the conventional level, and the postconventional level. They further delineated two stages of development within each of these levels, with the second stage more advanced and organized than the first. Across the three levels, reasoning shifts from a self-centered perspective to one that increasingly considers the perspectives and rights of others. The individual at Level I makes decisions from a self-centered orientation. At Level II, individuals "do the right thing" because that is what is expected according to social norms. Finally, at Level III, moral decisions serve to recognize the social contract and to uphold individual rights. Although conflicts between these principles and legal mandates are recognized as problematic in the lower stage of Level III, moral principles come to take precedence by the time an individual reaches the highest stage of moral development. Kohlberg (Kohlberg & Armon, 1984; Kohlberg & Kramer, 2006) sees the higher stages as superior, and he sees enhancing development as an appropriate aim for education. Figure 4.3 represents the moral development continuum.

It is important here to also mention the work of Carol Gilligan (1982). Gilligan compared conclusions from Kohlberg's model of moral development with conclusions from her own research with women discussing personal decisions. People at the top of Kohlberg's stages worry about interfering with others' rights, whereas those at the top

Preconventional Level   Conventional Level   Postconventional Level

figure **4.3** **Moral Development Continuum**

Source: Adapted from Stephen P. Gordon (1990). *Assisting the entry-year teacher: A leadership resource.* Columbus, OH: Ohio Department of Education. Used with permission.

of Gilligan's stages worry about errors of omission, such as not helping others when possible. At Gilligan's highest stage, morality is conceived in terms of relationships, and goodness is equated with helping others. Gilligan (1979) proposed that a different conception of development emerges from the study of women's lives:

> The shift in women's judgment from an egocentric to a principled ethical understanding is articulated through their use of a distinct moral language, in which the terms "selfishness" and "responsibility" define the moral problem as one of care. Moral development then consists of the progressive reconstruction of this understanding toward a more adequate conception of care. (p. 442)

Several small-scale studies have investigated relationships between teachers' moral development and their understandings of teaching and learning. Johnson and Reiman (2007) explored the relationship between teacher dispositions in the moral/ethical domain and their actions in the classroom through a case study of three beginning teachers, all of whom were described as "lateral entry" teachers (entering without a teaching degree or specific training in education). All three teachers were found to operate primarily from a moral schema aimed at maintaining norms and emphasizing rules that are clear, consistent, and apply to everyone, which the authors reported is typical of beginning teachers. The three teachers varied, however, in the degree to which they also exhibited a personal interest schema (in which decisions are primarily based on the personal interest of the decision maker) or a postconventional schema (based on alterable social norms, with ideals that are open to justification and scrutiny). Using the Flanders Interaction Analysis System (also known as the Guided Analysis System, or GIAS) to document teacher actions, they found:

> When the teachers used more postconventional reasoning and less personal interest judgments, the percentage of direct instruction decreased. Teachers spent less time providing information and giving direction and more time prompting inquiry, accepting and using students' ideas and offering reinforcement. (Johnson & Reiman, 2007, p. 683)

Johnson and Reiman concluded that with increased percentages of postconventional reasoning teachers became more open to learner perspectives and engaged in more indirect interactions. They also found that in response to mentoring provided as part of the study, beginning teachers were able to move toward more complex levels of judgment, although they remained primarily at a below average level of complexity. In an earlier study, Reiman and Peace (2002) found an increase in moral/ethical development as well as a shift from self-concern to concern for the learners in eight teachers involved in peer coaching using a framework of social role-taking and guided reflection, as compared to a control group. Both these studies suggest that moral dispositions are linked to teaching practice, and that both dispositions and actions are amenable to tailored mentoring and coaching programs.

Levels of Consciousness.   Robert Kegan (1994, 2009), a self-acknowledged neo-Piagetian, is a more recent entrant on the scene of adult developmental psychology with his theory of levels of consciousness. As with the Piagetian shift from concrete to formal operations, the development of abstract thinking is a key characteristic of movement from Kegan's adolescent stage of durable category level to a more mature *cross-categorical* (or *third-order*) *consciousness*. The person functioning at the cross-categorical level is capable of thinking abstractly, reflecting on his or her own emotions, and being guided by beliefs and values that ensure loyalty to the larger community. At this stage the adult experiences a new construction of reality, with the needs, wants, and desires of others figuring as prominently as his or her own (Albertson, 2014; Bridwell, 2013; Taylor & Marienau, 1995).

Only with the transition from cross-categorical to *systems* (or *fourth-order*) *consciousness*, however, does the individual move beyond defining oneself in terms of those duties, devotions, and values to become a truly independent and autonomous person. At this level we can look objectively at our own perspective, compare it with that of others, and work to reconcile differences—a process associated with transformational learning (Bridwell, 2013; Kegan, 2009). It is the systems level of consciousness that is said to be necessary to meet the various demands of modern adult life (parenting, partnering, working, continued learning), but Kegan contends that many do not reach this stage until their 30s or 40s, if at all. Finally, as is common with stage theories, Kegan posits a level rarely achieved, *trans-systems* (or *fifth-order*) *consciousness*. Dialectical thinking is associated with this level of consciousness, said to be rare before midlife.

Kegan's model suggests that our expectations may be too high, both for ourselves and others. In the preface to his book *In Over Our Heads: The Mental Demands of Modern Life* (1994), he especially appeals to those who provide education, training, and supervision for other adults to be mindful of the mental demands we place on others. An example would be our expectation that teachers, even those recently graduated as traditional-age students, exhibit high levels of critical thinking and meta-cognitive skills, as he speculates these skills may not be fully evolved for many until their 30s and 40s. The emphasis Kegan places on continuing adult learning in the workplace, as well as in other domains of adult life, along with his suggestion that teaching/coaching can stimulate developmental growth, makes this a promising model for future examination with practicing teachers. It is this model upon which Drago-Severson (2009, 2012; Drago-Severson, Blum-DeStefano, & Asghar, 2013) bases her four-pillar model of leadership for adult growth. Kegan's model also provides a framework that is consistent with the principles of developmental supervision. Figure 4.4 depicts the continuum of adult consciousness.

Stages of Concern.   In the 1960s and early 1970s, Frances Fuller (1969) conducted pioneer studies of teacher concerns. In analyzing both her own studies and six others, she found that the responses by hundreds of teachers at various stages of experience showed different concerns.

figure 4.4 **Adult Consciousness Continuum**

Teachers at the *self-adequacy* stage focus on survival. They are concerned with doing well when a supervisor is present, getting favorable evaluations, and being accepted and respected by students and other teachers (Adams & Martray, 1981). Their primary concern is making it through the school day.

With survival and security assured, teachers think less of their own survival needs and begin to focus on *teaching tasks*. At this stage, teachers become more concerned with issues related to instructional and student discipline. They begin to think about altering or enriching the classroom schedule, the teaching materials, and their instructional methodology. Instructional concerns include the pressures of teaching, routinization and inflexibility of the teaching environment, student load, workload, and lack of academic freedom. Discipline concerns include class control, conflict between student and adult values and attitudes, and disruptive students (Adams & Martray, 1981). Concerns at this stage can be characterized as focused on the teaching environment and teaching responsibilities.

Superior teachers are at the highest stage of concern, referred to as the *teaching impact* stage. At this stage, teachers are most concerned with the impact on students' learning and students' well-being, even if it means departing from rules and norms. Academic concerns at this stage include diagnosing and meeting individual needs, sparking unmotivated students, and facilitating the intellectual and emotional development of students. The teacher with mature concerns also tends to be interested in the whole child, including interest in student health and nutrition, use of drugs by students, and dropout prevention (Adams & Martray, 1981). The unfolding of teachers' concerns evolves on a continuum reflecting a shifting perspective, from "I" concerns to concerns for "my group" to concerns for "all students." Figure 4.5 represents the continuum of teacher concerns. Although Fuller's initial studies linked stages

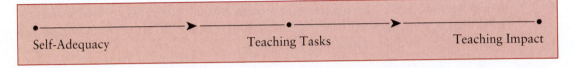

figure 4.5 **Teacher Concerns Continuum**

Source: Adapted from Stephen P. Gordon (1990). *Assisting the entry-year teacher: A leadership resource.* Columbus, OH: Ohio Department of Education. Used with permission.

of concern with stages of teacher experience, more recent studies indicate a complex relationship between teacher concerns and level of experience. Based on results of a six-month study of hopes and fears of intern teachers, Conway and Clark (2003) posit that with experience teacher concerns may shift both outward—from self to tasks and students as predicted by Fuller–and inward, as beginning teachers engage in a progression toward greater reflexivity and self-awareness of themselves as teachers. Basing his conclusions on a two-year longitudinal study of beginning teachers, Watzke (2007) takes a more critical stance toward Fuller's suggestion of a chronological progression in the development of teacher concerns. Findings from his study involving six repeated administrations of the Teachers Concerns Checklist over the span of the first two years of teaching showed that impact-related concerns were rated highest across all applications, while all categories of concerns related to self and selected categories of task level concerns (classroom conduct, instructional deterrents to teaching, and professional freedom) decreased as teachers progressed through their second year.

Integrating Stage Development Theories.   Investigators of adult and teacher development have postulated that the various developmental characteristics are related (Oja & Pine, 1984; Sullivan, McCullough, & Stager, 1970). Although still somewhat speculative, these findings suggest that many teachers at a given level (low, moderate, or high) in one developmental characteristic may operate at the same general level in another developmental characteristic. The probable relationship of various developmental characteristics allows one to make tentative composite descriptions of teachers of generally low, moderate, and high levels of stage development. Figure 4.6 reviews the four adult/teacher development continuums.

The majority of teachers appear to be in relatively moderate to low stages of cognitive or moral development or levels of consciousness—probably no different from the adult population at large (Oja & Pine, 1981). So what? What difference does it make that many teachers are not complex thinkers or autonomous? Perhaps one does not need higher-order thinking to teach. One could argue that if teaching were a simple enterprise with no need for decision making, then it would make little difference. In fact, if most teachers were autonomous and abstract, then trying to do a simple job would create great tension, resentment, and noncompliance. If teaching is a simple activity, schools need people who can reason simply. If teaching is complex and ever changing, however, then higher levels of reasoning are necessary. A simple thinker in a dynamic and difficult enterprise would be subjected to overwhelming pressures.

Sociologists have documented the environmental demands posed by making thousands of decisions daily, by constant psychological pressure, and by expectations that the teacher must do the job alone—unwatched and unaided. A teacher daily faces up to 150 students of various backgrounds, abilities, and interests, some of whom succeed while others fail. Concrete, rigid thinking on the part of the teacher cannot possibly improve instruction. As Madeline Hunter (1986) has noted, "Teaching . . . is a relativistic situational profession where *there are no absolutes*" (italics in original).

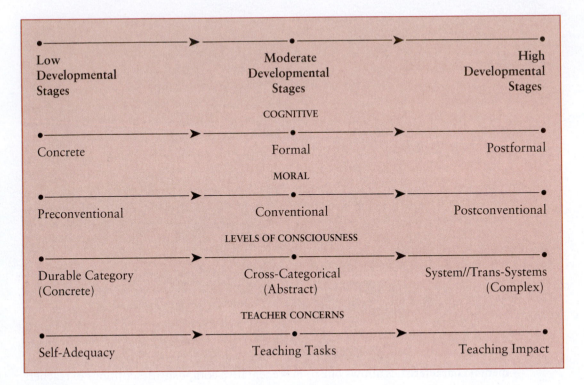

figure **4.6** **Teacher and Adult Stage Development**

Source: Adapted from Stephen P. Gordon (1990). *Assisting the entry-year teacher: A leadership resource.* Columbus, OH: Ohio Department of Education. Used with permission.

Teacher improvement can only come from abstract, multi-informational thought that can generate new responses toward new situations. Glassberg's (1979) review of research on teachers' stage development as related to instructional improvement concluded:

> In summary these studies suggest that high stage teachers tend to be adaptive in teaching style, flexible, and tolerant, and able to employ a wide range of teaching models. . . . Effective teaching in almost any view is a most complex form of human behaviour. Teachers at higher, more complex stages of human development appear as more effective in classrooms than their peers at lower stages.

The problem with the need for high-stage teachers is that, although the work by its nature demands autonomous and flexible thinking, teachers in most schools are not supported in ways to improve their thinking. The only alternative for a teacher in a complex environment who cannot adjust to multiple demands and is not being helped to acquire the abilities to think abstractly and autonomously is to *simplify and deaden the instructional environment*. Teachers make the environment less complex by disregarding differences among students and by establishing routines and instructional practices that remain the same day after day and year after year. Research on effective instruction (Biggers, Forbes, & Zangori, 2013; Davis & Smithey, 2009; Glatthorn, 2000; Hargreaves & Moore, 2000; Marzano, 2007; Tieso, 2001) indicates that it is based on adaptation of curriculum and materials to local settings and particular learning goals. In other words, effective teachers think about what they are currently doing, assess the results of their practice, explore with each other new possibilities for teaching students, and consider students' perspectives. Effective teaching has been misunderstood and misapplied as a set and sequence of certain teaching behaviors (review previous day's objectives, present objectives, explain, demonstrate, provide guided practice, check for understanding, etc.). This explanation of effectiveness is simply untrue. Rather, successful teachers are thoughtful teachers (Elliott & Schiff, 2001; Fairbanks et al., 2010; Ferraro, 2000).

Evidence of the relationship between high-stage attainment of teacher development and effective instructional practice can be found in several research studies. The works of Oja and Pine (1981), Phillips and Glickman (1991), and Thies-Sprinthall and Sprinthall (1987) are particularly important because they suggest that teachers, when provided with a stimulating and supportive environment, can reach higher stages of development. Yet, other research indicates that most teachers do not reach those higher stages.

Life Cycle Development, Teachers' Life Cycles, and the Teaching Career

The next area of adult development to be discussed is research on age-linked life cycle development. These theorists, too, have sought to define sequential and normative patterns of development. The pioneering theorists in this tradition tended to look at very broad age periods and the patterns or issues for resolution associated with them (Erikson, 1963), whereas later theorists have tended to posit a greater number of specific age periods (Levinson et al., 1978).

The study by Daniel Levinson and his colleagues (1978) of 40 men aged mid-30s to mid-40s is among the most frequently cited studies of life cycle development. This research described how individuals alternate through periods of stability and transition in a life structure whose critical components typically revolve around work and family. An occupational dream is said to be formed during young adulthood and nurtured, frequently with the assistance of the spouse and a mentor. Levinson's work is a coherent treatment of changes in a person's life but has limitations in that the subjects were all middle-class males from a limited set of occupations. A number of subsequent studies of women have substantiated the model in part, but differences have been found in the timing and quality of transitions and the ages associated with transitional periods among women (Levinson & Levinson, 1996).

Occupational development of teachers appears to run counter to the needs of teachers as they progress through the adult life cycle. The work of Levinson (1978) and Neugarten (1977) has pointed to early adulthood as a period of bravado, romance, and the pursuit of dreams. The young adult aged 20 to 35 is on an exciting search for status, comfort, and happiness in work, family, and friends. The middle years, ages 35 to 55, provide some disillusionment, reflection, and reordering of priorities according to a reassessment of one's capabilities and opportunities. In teaching, however, the young adulthood period, which should be one of romance, quickly becomes one of disillusionment. The person age 24 or 25 who has entered teaching to pursue his or her dreams often finds after 3 years that work life is going nowhere. The job does not excite; the advancements do not exist; and the variety of work is nonexistent. The result can be intense boredom, leading to resignation—either *from* the job or *on* the job. What does it mean to education when a young teacher's natural inclination toward excitement and idealism is bound by a straitjacket of repetition?

Let's ask the next question: What happens when the natural inclination of the middle-aged teacher to reflect and reorder his or her teaching priorities confronts the same six periods of 30 students that he or she has faced for the past 20 years? One might expect a further despair of any impulse to change and to improve. Finally, what about the older teacher who is perceived by many as an anomaly, a relic who has remained in teaching because of inability to advance into administration or supervision? The acquisition of 30 years of experience coincides with the natural time for consolidating achievements and identifying one's remaining career objectives. Instead, there is only the same job—the same job as that of the new teacher down the hall, who might be the age of the older teacher's grandchild. Where is the sense of responsibility, generativity, and accomplishment in seniority? Old and new teachers are treated the same, accorded the same status, and expected to conform to the same routines.

Teaching appears to be a topsy-turvy occupation, running against the natural adult life cycle. Those who continue to make lasting improvement and enhance their students' educational lives should have our utmost respect. If not fortunate enough to be in a school that responds to and supports phases of the adult life cycle, the effective teacher truly transcends the system and educates in spite of, not because of, the school.

A growing body of literature focuses on the links between teacher development and issues related to the adult lifespan. Levine (1987) encourages placing midlife teachers in situations permitting "a combination of teaching and administrative responsibilities that expands an adult's authority and mobility without sacrificing his or her expertise with children"(p. 16). Work on decision-making committees and mentorship of younger colleagues can provide such an outlet. Krupp (1987) argues that lack of career centrality and on-the-job retirement can be countered by bringing the older teachers' interests into the school. For instance, older teachers' interests in computers, photography, and gardening can be brought into the curriculum or extracurricular programs for students. Gehrke (1991) argues that we should more fully incorporate our understanding of adult development in developing programs for new teachers. This means both fostering the generative motivations of mature teachers and being sensitive to the fact that many young teachers are dealing with needs for intimacy. More recently, Drago-Severson, with several coauthors, has published a series of books linking adult learning and development theory, with a particular emphasis on Kegan's (1994, 2009) work on levels of consciousness and transformational learning, to a range of topics including teacher growth and development, models of professional development, and leadership development (Drago-Severson, 2009, 2012; Drago-Severson, Blum-DeStefano, & Asghar, 2013). Her work also points to ways in which the learning and growth of teachers at differing developmental stages can be best supported through varying support structures and strategies.

Transition Events

A third approach to adult development focuses more explicitly on the kinds of events associated with life transitions. Some theorists resist accepting the study of what are variably called *life events, critical events,* or *marker events* as part of the rubric of adult development because such a focus does not attempt to describe a universal, orderly sequence of development. However, Fiske and Chiriboga (1990) note that just as the assumption of adult stability gave way to models of adult development "as a progression of orderly transformations over time," more recent models have emphasized the role of transition events in our lives.

Life events have been typologized in a variety of ways. One typology, offered by Willis and Baltes (1980), seems to relate directly to the salience of the event for the individual. They talk about *normative age-graded events*—events that occur in many people's lives and that are anticipated around certain ages (such as marriage, birth of first child, and widowhood), *normative history-graded events*—those that affect large numbers of people in a given age cohort simultaneously (such as World War II and the Depression), and *nonnormative events*—those personal events that are not anticipated as part of the life course even though they may occur for many (such as divorce, unemployment, and unexpected illness). Events can be positive or negative, anticipated or unanticipated. Although events associated with expected transitions in adult lives are often the impetus for adult growth, it appears to be the unanticipated event, even if negative, that may provide the greatest opportunity for change and growth (Fiske & Chiriboga, 1990; Hogan, 2014; Napolitano, 2013).

Neugarten (1977, 1987) studied the timing of events such as childbearing, occupational advancement and peaking, children leaving home, retirement, personal illness, and death of a spouse or close friend. Many of these events are common to all or most adults, and the time of their occurrence, according to Neugarten, influences how the person responds and continues with life.

Neugarten's interpretation of these differential responses relates to the experience of the events as "on time" versus "off time"—that is, occurring at an age considered socially appropriate or not. Certainly, recent years have seen increasing variability in the timing of many common events, and perceptions regarding the correct timing of life transitions have been found to be influenced culturally by race, class, and gender (Setterson, 1996). As Merriam and colleagues (2007) observed, not having children, returning to school in later life, and beginning a new career in midlife are all more viable options today than decades ago. The growing number of teacher preparation programs aimed at adults choosing teaching as a second career gives testimony to her claim. Yet, the authors note that timing still matters when it comes to many life events, given the powerful influence age norms exert on our thinking.

Both personal transition events (marriage, birth of a child, divorce, death of a loved one) and professional transition events (entry into the profession, tenure, transferring schools, becoming a lead teacher or department chairperson) can have a significant impact on a teacher's career and teaching. Traditionally, personal and transitional events have been ignored and professional transitions have been given pro forma recognition by the school organization. Krupp (1987) has suggested that staff development programs providing an environment of trust and collegiality, as well as adult transition support networks within schools, can be an important means of assisting teachers as they prepare for anticipated change events, such as retirement, or cope with unanticipated changes, such as the sudden dependency of a parent. The support networks and professional development recommended by Krupp to assist teachers have been largely nonexistent in schools.

One exception in recent years has been the emergence of beginning teacher assistance programs, including the assignment of support teams and mentors to novice teachers. Hopefully, beginners' assistance programs will become the foundation on which career-long support for personal and professional transitions becomes available. Beyond formal support programs, schools need to become the type of collegial, caring, growth-oriented communities that sustain teachers in times of transition.

Role Development

Yet another strand of research has emphasized adult social roles, generally examining how adult lives are characterized by interacting roles related to work or career, family life, and personal development. Juhasz (1989) developed a model of adult roles that incorporates each of three major roles: family, work, and self. These roles are depicted as intertwining, sometimes in synchrony, sometimes with different momentum and force. This model emphasizes the active involvement of adults who take roles and choose which roles they will place emphasis on at given points in their lives, with self-esteem as the driving force "directing energies toward roles that will best enhance feelings of worth"(p. 307).

Merriam and Clark (1993) designed a questionnaire to study the relationship between life events in the domains of "work and love" (here broadly defined as the instrumental and expressive components of life) and adult learning. In essence, people graphed their life patterns, using two separate lines to show the ups and downs in these two domains of life. Respondents were asked next to list major events occurring in the last 20 years of their adult life (age 18 or older) and to describe learning experiences. From their analysis of 405 respondents, they found evidence for three different models used to characterize linkages between work and family life: (1) *segmentation*—when there is little or no connection, (2) *compensatory*—where individuals seek in one area the satisfaction or activities that are lacking in the other, and (3) *generalization*— where attitudes formed in the work setting spill over into family life or vice versa.

One of Merriam and Clark's most significant findings was the predominance of work-related learning for both men and women and the evidence that more learning occurs when things are going well in both arenas (work and family life). However, learning that led to a real perspective transformation most often was associated with coping with the difficult times in either work (e.g., being fired) or family life (e.g., losing a parent). Since much of the most significant adult learning appears to be from life experience, the role of the supervisor may be critical in helping teachers to experience growth as an outcome of unsettling life experiences in the professional, personal, or family domain. Although the supervisor need not and should not assume the role of therapist, one implication of the social role models of adult development is that a teacher's personal, family, and professional roles interact with and affect each other and need to be addressed holistically by supervision.

School systems and supervisors traditionally have been concerned only with teachers' professional roles, ignoring their personal and family roles. The few efforts intended to address the relationship of the three domains have been criticized as being beyond the scope of supervision, an inappropriate use of school resources, and superfluous to the improvement of teaching and learning. Yet, the literature on adult role development tells us that we cannot compartmentalize the personal, family, and professional aspects of a teacher's life. Put succinctly, teachers' other adult roles have direct effects on their instruction. Supervision, however, has largely failed to provide teachers with support to help them understand the interaction of their various adult roles, cope with role conflict and resulting stress, and develop the proper balance and synergy among alternative roles.

Beyond Universal Conceptions of Development: The Sociocultural Context of Adult Development

From the 1980s and through the present, a significant body of research has emerged examining the impact of social structural variables (e.g., race, class, gender, disability, or sexual orientation) on adult development, with greatest emphasis on the effects of gender and race/ethnicity. The intent of some researchers has been to develop more robust and inclusive theories, describing a broader range of people than earlier theories. In other cases, especially for researchers informed by the postmodern resistance to "grand" theories, there has been no such attempt at "umbrella" theories of adult development (Kilgore, 2001). The latter researchers have been interested in offering previously unavailable pictures of adult development for individuals from groups marginalized in the construction of knowledge about adult development, as well as in illustrating how structural variables like gender, race, and class intersect in the construction of our identities (Bridwell, 2013; Graue, 2005; McDermott & Schwartz, 2013; Sheared, 1999; Syed & Mitchell, 2013; Tisdell, 2000).

The Role of Gender in Adult Development.   Much of the literature examining the relationship of gender and adult development has looked specifically at women, in response to the initial claim that their lives and experiences were not accounted for in the early development of adult development theory. Emerging theory and research have taken two forms, in some cases extending or adapting earlier work based primarily on men and in other cases starting afresh with female or mixed gender samples.

In the first strand is the work of Gilligan (1982), challenging Kohlberg's model of moral development (Kohlberg & Turiel, 1971). Her work suggests men and women base their moral decisions on different criteria, with women using an ethic of care and men an ethic of justice. Similarly, Josselson (1987) reexamined Erikson's stage theory of psychosocial development, postulating four potential outcomes of Erikson's identity stage for women. Primary among her findings was that maintaining a sense of connectedness and affiliation with others is crucial for women.

The second strand of research consists of studies based specifically on the lives of women. One of the most cited sources in this strand is *Women's Ways of Knowing*, by Belenky, Clinchy, Goldberger, and Tarule (1986). Resisting the notion of hierarchical stages, Belenky and colleagues point to the development of voice as central to women's development and delineated five positions or categories in the development of women's knowledge: silence, received knowledge, subjective knowledge, procedural knowledge, and constructed knowledge. The developmental ideal is the integration of all five categories. Also representing this strand of research is the work of Peck (1986). She theorized women's lives as consisting of three contiguous layers, including an outermost core of sociohistorical context; a flexible, bidirectional "sphere of influence," consisting of the sum of multiple relationships; and a center core of self-definition. These spheres are presumed to be constantly interacting as women move through their lives.

Models of adult development, whether based on men's or women's lives, have been critiqued for their universalizing character, tending to ignore or discount diversity *among* men and women, and the degree to which individuals of each gender exhibit patterns described as typical of the opposite sex. For example, Anderson and Hayes (1996) found that both men and women value achievement as well as relationships, derive self-esteem from similar sources, and struggle with ongoing issues of holding on (connection) and letting go (separation). The tendency of these models to ignore diversity related to race, class, and culture has also been criticized. Harris (1996) examined how men from different subcultures viewed each of 24 cultural messages about masculinity and described differences related to class, race, sexual orientation, and community of origin (city, urban, rural). McDermott & Schwartz (2013) investigated *gender role journeys* among emerging adult men, examining the influence of differences in age, education, race, relational status, and sexual orientation. The construct of gender role journey has been developed to conceptualize how men construct and adapt to their gender role identities (O'Neil & Carroll, 1988). Four subgroups were identified: (1) men not questioning/accepting of traditional gender roles, (2) "pro-feminist activists," (3) men questioning with strong ambivalence, and (4) men questioning with weak ambivalence. The research findings suggest that men's gender role journeys differ by race, sexual orientation, relational status, and age. This literature may help to explain why some men are more willing to break mainstream cultural norms that discourage their entry into the elementary education teaching force.

The Role of Race and Ethnicity in Adult Development.   Just as early models of adult psychosocial development were critiqued by those who did not find them to be inclusive of women's experiences, so too concerns were raised about the applicability of supposedly universal models of adult development to members of racial and ethnic groups typically not included as participants in research exploring these models (Sneed, Schwartz, & Cross, 2006). Chavez and Guido-DiBrito (1999) provide an excellent overview of models of racial and ethnic identity, grounded in research exploring the impact of race and ethnicity on adult learners. Cross developed nigrescence theory, one of the earliest of these models (1971, 1995). According to early versions of this model, Blacks move from a pre-encounter stage of limited awareness of race or racial self-hatred through three stages (later revised to five stages) that reflect an increasingly positive Black identity (Sneed et al., 2006). The model was further revised and proposed as an expanded nigrescence model (NT-E), retaining the names of the initially proposed three stages, but reconceptualizing the stages as nonhierarchical frames of reference (Worrel, 2008). According to Worrell, the three frames of reference are seen as representing differentiated clusters of nine different racial attitudes that may be present to varying degrees in the same individual:

(a) three Pre-Encounter attitudes (Assimilation, Miseducation, and Self-Hatred), (b) two Immersion-Emersion attitudes (Intense Black Involvement and Anti-White), and (c) four Internationalization attitudes (Nationalist, Biculturalist, Multiculturalist Racial, and Multiculturalist Inclusive). (p. 158)

Chavez and Guido-DiBrito (1999), on the other hand, posited that immersion in one's own racial group acts as the primary trigger for such identity development. Similarly, they take issue with the focus on perceptions of other groups inherent in the most prominent model of White racial identity development, that of Helms (1993, 1995). Helms stresses interracial exposure as a powerful trigger for the development of a

White racial identity that moves beyond a dominant group assumption of White supe-riority toward a nonracist frame. Chavez and Guido-DiBrito argue that Helms's model places inordinate emphasis on the intersection of racial perceptions of others and racial perception of self. They are more intrigued by models of ethnic identity development.

A model of White ethnic identity by Katz (1989) identified values and perspectives of White American cultural identity. These values include autonomy, competitiveness, and a linear sense of time and can be contrasted with values such as harmony, balance, and respect for the wisdom of elders identified in Garrett and Walking Stick Garrett's (1994) model of Native American identity. Phinney (1990), on the other hand, devel-oped a model describing an ethnic identity process that can be applied more broadly. She emphasized two issues faced by members of nondominant group members: (1) dealing with stereotyping and prejudicial treatment by the dominant group and (2) resolving the clash between the value systems of their own ethnic culture and that of the dominant culture by negotiating a bicultural value system.

Several implications for adult learning can be drawn from these models. The mod-els generally suggest that although most individuals from White ethnic groups typically experience learning that is grounded in their own cultural norms, they may struggle with or resist learning in less familiar multicultural environments. This has implica-tions for efforts in the area of diversity training. On the other hand, persons from non-dominant cultural groups often have to learn to be at least bicultural in their learning if they are to succeed in mainstream learning environments. For instance, Alfred (2001) has pointed to the development of bicultural competence as a factor in the career development of successful (tenured) Black women faculty. She also has pointed to the assistive role that White male mentors played in some cases. Similarly, teachers from nondominant groups are likely to find that they must learn to successfully navigate two or more cultures, and their mentors need to remain sensitive to the challenges this presents. In the inverse, Alston (2014) examined cross-cultural mentoring relation-ships between White female doctoral student mentees and their Black female mentors. She found that these mentoring relationships provided a space for learning and self-reflection for the mentees with regard to the significance of their own Whiteness. She also discovered cultural points of connection were often shared around gender and motherhood, and that age differences (with mentors who were younger than mentees) sometimes provided an unanticipated challenge. Both mentors and mentees stressed the importance of trust while participating in cross-cultural mentoring relationships.

Current research on women's development and research on the place of race and ethnicity in identity development have challenged our thinking about the degree to which any single theory of adult development can adequately describe all adult lives. Yet, these models can still provide a useful heuristic for thinking about the many ways in which adults continue to change throughout the course of their lives and the myriad forces that come to influence these changes. For those who seek to provide assistance to teachers, familiarity with this literature serves as a reminder of the tremendous degree of difference that exists among the adult learners who constitute the teaching force.

t a b l e **4.1**   **Conceptual Models of Adult Development**

Universal, Orderly, Sequential		Interactive, Socially Contexted		
Hierarchical Stages	*Life Cycle Phases*	*Transition Events*	*Role Development*	*Sociocultural Variables*
Cognitive Piaget, Perry		*Critical Events* Brim and Ryff	*Family, Work, and Self* Juhasz	*Spheres of Influence* Peck
Moral Gilligan, Kohlberg	*Critical Issues* Erikson	*Stressful Events* Fiske et al.	*Love, Work, and Learning* Merriam and Clark	*Women's Ways of Knowing* Belenky et al.
	Stability vs. Transition Levinson	*On Time/Off Time* Neugarten		*Ethnic Identity Development* Cross, Helms, Phinney
Levels of Consciousness Kegan				
Concern Fuller				

Review of Adult/Teacher Development Models

Table 4.1 presents a schematic review of the five conceptual frameworks for adult development. One thing all five approaches have in common is the supposition that adult lives are characterized by change and adaptation. For teachers, as with all adult learners, the one thing we can be certain of is that things will not remain the same; thus, individuals will need to cope with changes as they arise. Supervision provides the opportunity for ascertaining the levels, stages, and issues of adult development in schools and assisting the teacher's professional development in the context of these realities.

Development: Ebb and Flow

Cognitive researchers have shown that stages of thinking vary according to the domain or topic Gardner, 2006; Sternberg, 1988). Fred loves to teach art to his second-grade youngsters. He's constantly looking for ideas, finding materials, and expending energy to improve his art program. Yet, when it comes to teaching mathematics, he puts in the required time, uses the worksheets, and muddles through the material. He never liked mathematics as a student and doesn't care to spend extra time on it. Suffice it to say that teachers, like all humans, are not static in their levels of thinking and commitment about all endeavors.

Furthermore, development can regress, recycle, or become blocked. Because one has reached a high level of development in one arena does not mean that level of development is consolidated eternally. *Experience* is a relative term—a teacher (or supervisor) with 30 years of teaching (or supervising) can still be inexperienced in many ways. Change the expectations of the job and/or change the clientele served, and suddenly there is an inexperienced person trying to figure out how to survive. Likewise, a first-year teacher may, after only a few months, be experienced and able to reason according to concerns beyond his or her own survival.

Alterations to a person's personal or professional situation can usher in regression in levels of thinking and levels of motivation. For instance, a highly committed and thoughtful faculty, who had made their school an exciting and successful place, were jolted when negotiations between the teachers' union and the school board resulted in a bitter strike. The immediate result on the school was that teachers retreated within their four walls, carrying out the letter of their contract and removing themselves from involvement in school curriculum and instruction issues. Most teachers retreated to a self-survival stage.

Teacher or adult development is not monolithic, linear, or eternal. The research on developmental stages provides lenses for viewing teachers individually and collectively as to their current levels of thinking and commitment. Through such lenses, we can explore possible interventions to assist teachers individually and collectively to move into higher stages of development.

> ✔ **Check Your Understanding 4.0**   Click here to gauge your understanding of the key concepts presented in this chapter.

REFLECTIVE EXERCISE

Assume that you have been assigned to design a professional development program to provide your school's mentor teachers with knowledge about adult learning and development that will be valuable in helping them assist other teachers in their schools. The program will begin with a day-long introduction of key topics. The program will include follow-up seminars and additional support continuing over a one-semester period.

- What critical topics regarding adult learning and development would you include in the day-long introductory workshop?
- What principles of adult learning would you consider in designing the day-long workshop?
- How would the follow-up seminars and support program be designed to maximize opportunities for the mentors' own continued learning individually and collaboratively as they work with other teachers during the remainder of the semester?

chapter 5

Reflections on Educational Beliefs, Teaching, and Supervision

Learning Outcomes for This Chapter

After reading this chapter, you should be able to:

1. Describe a supervision platform.
2. List different beliefs about the purpose of education described in this chapter.
3. Identify different beliefs about the purpose of supervision described in this chapter.
4. Describe the key elements of any of the superphilosophies presented in this chapter.
5. Explain in general terms any of the supervisory approaches presented in this chapter.
6. List three different broad combinations of decision-making power that might be present in supervisor–teacher interaction.
7. Discuss the effects of educators' cultural background on their educational beliefs and actions.

Questions to Reflect On as You Read This Chapter

1. What are the relationships among educational beliefs, teaching, and instructional supervision?
2. This chapter describes the educational platforms of three teachers: Joan Simpson, Bill Washington, and Pat Rogers. Which of these three teachers' platforms most closely reflects your own educational platform? If a group of educational experts observed you teaching for several days, which of the three teachers would the experts say you most resemble?
3. What are some beliefs you would include in your supervisory platform?
4. Which of the three superphilosophies discussed in this chapter most closely represents your own beliefs about education and supervision?
5. Which of the supervisory approaches introduced in this chapter would you be comfortable using as a supervisor working with individual teachers or groups?

As we seek ways to improve school and classroom instruction, we need to understand how present thinking, beliefs, and practices in the field of supervision interact with instruction and assumptions about students and teachers as learners. In this chapter we look at how one's supervisory beliefs are related to a particular educational philosophy or platform. An instrument will then be provided to help clarify each person's own supervisory beliefs, and we will examine how one's own supervisory beliefs fit along a control continuum. Finally, we will discuss how an educator's cultural background is an important factor in their beliefs about education.

How do we reconcile the uncertainties of supervision, teaching, and instructional improvement? How do we know whether we are progressing in the desired direction? Unless we reflect on our own beliefs, there is little to steer us.

Sergiovanni and Starratt (2007) note the importance of understanding one's own supervisory beliefs:

> What is needed is some firm footing in principle. Some have called our often unexpressed constellation of principles a platform. Just as a political party is supposed to base its decisions and actions on a party platform upon which it seeks election, so, too, supervisory personnel need a platform upon which, and in the light of which, they can carry on their work. With a clearly defined platform, they can begin to take a position relative to educational practices, looking beyond the surface behavior to probe for the real consequences of a variety of school practices. (pp. 243–244)

Knowing oneself as a supervisor is necessary before considering alternative practices and procedures. To move from a platform, we must first know where we are standing. Let's look at the human decisions that a supervisor must make about school improvement, teaching effectiveness, and one's purpose in working with teachers.

Beliefs, Goals, and Effective Teaching

Let's continue this reflection on practice by taking an innocuous statement about supervision that virtually no one would take issue with: The goal of supervision is to improve instruction. It sounds nice, until we ask for a definition of what type of instruction we wish to improve. Effective teaching, to a large extent, depends on what you believe should be taught. Different educational beliefs lead to different instructional goals that require different teaching strategies. Consider the following examples:

- If the goal is for students to master basic skills, then effective teaching might involve explanation, demonstration, practice, feedback, and more practice.

- If the goal is for students to learn classical culture, then effective teaching might consist of reading the great works, lecturing, and fostering Socratic discussion.

- If the goal is for students to become problem solvers, then effective teaching might call for exposing students to real-world problems and actively involving them in testing possible solutions and reaching resolutions.

- If the goal is social development, then effective teaching might consist of structuring cooperative learning and community-building activities.

- If the goal is personal development, then effective teaching might mean facilitating students' self-directed learning and self-assessment.

- If the goal is critical inquiry, then effective teaching might require the teacher to challenge students' current values and assumptions and to ask students to critique dominant belief systems, social structures, and power relationships.

In the final analysis, what constitutes instructional improvement and successful teaching can be defined only within the context of particular educational beliefs, instructional goals, local learning environments, and individual students. This means that the search for a single instructional model—effective for all learning content, students, and situations—is futile.

A more productive course of action is to identify various instructional strategies that are effective in relation to identified instructional goals and individual students. If this proposition is accepted, then the supervisor's role becomes one of assisting teachers to clarify school and classroom instructional goals, develop a variety of instructional strategies (e.g., direct instruction, constructivist teaching, cooperative learning, classroom dialogue, service learning), "mix and match" instructional strategies to learning goals and students, and assess the effects of instruction for the purpose of continuous improvement. With such a supervision emphasis, effective instruction is seen as the teacher's ability to use various ways of teaching according to the school's learning goals and students' learning styles.

 Video Illustration

In this video, four teachers discuss their beliefs about teaching and learning. As you watch the video, see if you can summarize each teacher's beliefs in a short phrase. As you review your summaries for each teacher, reflect on what might be going on in the teacher's class if you were to observe a full lesson taught by that teacher.

Beliefs About Education

Teachers' and supervisors' educational philosophies have a significant impact on instruction and instructional improvement efforts. The following are summaries of educational platforms of three teachers with different beliefs about education:

> Joan Simpson believes that the purpose of education should be to transmit a prescribed body of basic knowledge, skills, and cultural values to students. To do this effectively, the teacher must exercise control over the classroom, lesson content, and students. Content should be broken first into discrete academic areas and then into small elements, and learning should take place in a series of small, sequential steps. All students should be expected to master the same content. Grades and other types of external motivation are necessary to ensure student learning.
>
> Bill Washington believes that the purpose of education should be student growth, especially in inquiry and problem-solving skills. To promote such growth, the teacher conveys existing knowledge but also encourages students to experiment in order to test old ideas and find solutions to new problems. Bill believes that since inquiry is most successful in a democratic environment, the teacher should share control of the learning environment with students. Because problem solving often takes place within a social context, students should learn social skills as well as academic content.
>
> Pat Rogers believes that each child is unique and that the primary purpose of education should be to meet students' individual needs. The teacher should foster the development of each student toward his or her fullest potential. This means addressing students as whole persons by fostering their physical, emotional, cognitive, moral, and social development. Such holistic education includes facilitating student self-inquiry. Pat believes that students should have as much control over their own learning environment as their maturity level permits. Teachers should base lessons on students' experience, concerns, and interests. Students should be allowed to participate in assessing their own learning.

The three educational platforms just described do indeed represent contrasting beliefs. Based on their educational beliefs, Joan Simpson, Bill Washington, and Pat Rogers no doubt have quite different definitions of instructional improvement and effective teaching! Role Play 5.1 allows three members of a group to bring Joan, Bill, and Pat to life by assuming their identities in a teachers' lounge conversation.

You may view Joan, Bill, or Pat's platform as quite similar to your own, you may agree with parts of each, or you may have an entirely different set of beliefs. In any case, it is important for you to clarify your own educational beliefs. By reflecting on the following questions, you can begin to build your educational platform:

1. What should be the purpose of education?
2. What should be the content of the school curriculum?
3. Who should control the learning environment?
4. What should be the relationship between teacher and students?
5. Under what conditions is student learning most successful?

r o l e   p l a y   **5.1**

A Conversation in the Teachers' Lounge

Three participants agree to play the roles of Joan Simpson, Bill Washington, and Pat Rogers, and are provided time in advance of the role play to plan the details. The role play begins with the three teachers sitting at a table in the teachers' lounge. Each participant assumes the role of one of the three teachers, and each time they speak, what they say is consistent with the educational philosophy of the character they are playing as described in in this chapter. Topics that the three might discuss include:

1. A lesson they taught earlier that day
2. A student who is having difficulty in their class and how they plan to address that problem
3. How they assess student learning
4. The types of progress they are hoping their students make by the end of the school year
5. How they hope the new curriculum that the faculty is developing will be organized

6. What motivates students to do their best in school?
7. What is your definition of *effective teaching*?
8. What personal characteristics are possessed by a successful teacher?
9. How should the teacher assess student learning?
10. What is your definition of a *good school*?

Supervisory Beliefs

Most supervisors, of course, are former teachers. As a result, their views about learning, the nature of the learner, knowledge, and the role of the teacher in the classroom influence their view of supervision. After all, supervision is in many respects analogous to teaching. Teachers wish to improve students' behavior, achievement, and attitudes. Supervisors similarly wish to improve teachers' behavior, achievement, and attitudes.

The supervisory platforms of three supervisors are described next. As you read these platforms, note the relationship between the beliefs they contain and the teacher beliefs present in the three educational platforms discussed earlier in this chapter.

Bob Reynolds believes that the purpose of supervision is to monitor teachers to determine if their instruction includes the elements of effective instruction. If those elements are observed, the supervisor should provide positive reinforcement to ensure that they continue to be included in the teacher's lessons. Bob believes that if a teacher is not using or is incorrectly using the elements of effective instruction, the supervisor has a responsibility to provide remedial assistance by explaining and demonstrating correct instructional behaviors, setting standards of improvement, and monitoring and reinforcing the teacher's improvement efforts. In short, the supervisor should have primary responsibility for instructional improvement decisions.

Jan White believes that the purpose of supervision is to engage teachers in mutual inquiry aimed at the improvement of instruction. The supervisor and teacher should share perceptions of instructional problems, exchange suggestions for solving those problems, and negotiate an improvement plan. The improvement plan becomes a hypothesis to be tested by the teacher with the supervisor's assistance. Thus, Jan believes that supervisors and teachers should share the responsibility for instructional improvement.

Shawn Moore believes that the purpose of supervision should be to foster teacher reflection and autonomy and to facilitate teacher-driven instructional improvement. The supervisor should be concerned with the teacher's self-concept and personal development as well as the teacher's instructional performance. It is critical for the supervisor to establish a relationship with the teacher characterized by openness, trust, and acceptance. Shawn believes that the supervisor should allow the teacher to identify instructional problems, improvement plans, and criteria for success. The supervisor can assist the teacher's self-directed improvement through active listening, clarifying, encouraging, and reflecting. Thus, the teacher should have primary responsibility for instructional improvement decisions, with the supervisor serving as an active facilitator.

These descriptions show that supervisory platforms can be as varied as educational platforms. Role Play 5.2 allows three members of a group to bring to life supervisors Reynolds, White, and Moore as they are interviewed for a new supervisory position by the other members of the group, who assume the roles of teachers.

When we compare the educational platforms of Joan Simpson, Bill Washington, and Pat Rogers with the supervisory platforms of Bob Reynolds, Jan White, and Shawn Moore, we can see that both types of platforms reveal basic beliefs about knowledge, human nature, and control. By answering the following questions, you can begin the process of clarifying your own beliefs about instructional supervision. We suggest that you write responses to the questions, save your responses, and reassess your supervisory platform after you have finished reading this text.

1. What is your definition of *instructional supervision*?
2. What should be the ultimate purpose of supervision?
3. Who should supervise? Who should be supervised?
4. What knowledge, skills, attitudes, and values are possessed by successful supervisors?
5. What are the most important needs of teachers?
6. What makes for positive relationships between supervisors and teachers?
7. What types of activities should be part of instructional supervision?
8. What should be changed regarding the current practice of instructional supervision?

---

r o l e   p l a y **5.2**

Three Interviewees for a Supervisory Position

Three members of the group volunteer to play the roles of Bob Reynolds, Jan White, and Shawn Moore as they are interviewed for a supervisory position. The remaining members of the group assume the roles of teachers who have been asked by the administration to participate in separate question-and-answer sessions with each of the three candidates. The questions that the "teachers" ask should be those that will elicit information about various aspects of the candidate's supervisory platform. In providing answers to the questions they are asked, the group members playing the roles of Bob, Jan, and Shawn should strive to reflect the beliefs of the supervisor they are playing.

Supervisory Platform as Related to Educational Philosophy

Many educators view discussions of educational philosophy as overly abstract and irrelevant to the real world of supervisors and teachers. Yet, a supervisor's actions in working with teachers are based on supervisory beliefs, which in turn reflect a broader educational philosophy. Many different philosophies exist. Some, such as idealism and realism, date back to ancient times. Others, such as pragmatism and behaviorism, have been developed within the last century. Even more recent has been the emergence of progressivism, reconstructionism, and existentialism. Philosophies are numerous and overlapping, and many have historical roots in each other.

To unravel the major philosophical trends in education, one must decipher how philosophies differ from each other and then build overriding conceptual categories. Each conceptual category or superphilosophy is created by grouping various philosophies that have central agreement on the type and scope of education. In other words, there may be disagreement on the specific nature of knowledge, truth, and reality, yet they hang together as a general educational philosophy because they are in agreement on the purpose and treatment of education.*

With educational application in mind, divergent philosophies can be simplified and classified. Three major educational superphilosophies have direct relevance to supervision. These superphilosophies are essentialism, experimentalism, and existentialism.

---

*The descriptions of philosophy are taken from C. D. Glickman and J. P. Esposito, *Leadership Guide for Elementary School Improvement: Procedures for Assessment and Change* (Boston: Allyn & Bacon, 1979), p. 20.

Essentialism

Essentialism as a philosophy is derived from idealism and realism. *Idealism,* which dates back to Plato, espouses a belief in absolutes: The world we live in is merely a reflection of reality. Reality, truth, and standards of morality exist beyond our common ways of knowing. Only by training the mind do we glimpse the ultimates. Yet training the mind is not sufficient in itself; it only brings the mind nearer to grasping reality. Divine revelation, insight, and faith are the necessary elements for ultimate knowledge of what exists. Therefore, idealism emphasizes truth and reality existing outside of people. It is absolute and unchanging.

Realism, developed at the onset of the industrial age, places a similar emphasis on truth and reality being outside of people. Instead of humankind and the outer environment being separated from each other, realism maintains that humanity is part and parcel of that environment. The world is a preordained, mechanistic reality. All of existence operates according to scientific, cause-and-effect relations. It is as if existence is a clock that always runs according to mechanical principles governing levers, gauges, and gears. Humans have no existence apart from this clock; they are a part of the predetermined machine. Knowledge is learning how the machine works; truths are the scientific laws of regulation. Nothing exists outside the principles of nature. The purpose of education is to condition the mind to think in a natural, logical way. The mind should be trained to become consciously aware of the predetermined nature of the world.

Essentialism, created by William L. Bagley in 1938, encompasses the educational philosophies of idealism and realism. He took the ideas of knowledge being eternal and outside of humankind (idealism–absolutes; realism–natural laws) to form pedagogy. Essentialists emphasize that there is a body of timeless knowledge, both historical and contemporary, that is of value to the living (Gross, 2014; Parkay, Hass, & Anctil, 2010).

Essentialism in terms of supervision emphasizes the supervisor as the person who teaches truths about teaching to teachers. Supervisors are those most knowledgeable about those absolute standards. Teachers are then handled mechanistically to systematize and feed content to students. As teachers digest these teaching truths, they move closer to being good teachers.

Experimentalism

As Western society became more industrialized, optimism and confidence in human ability to control nature emerged. The philosophy of *pragmatism,* developed by Charles S. Peirce and William James, emphasized what people can do to nature rather than what nature does to humankind. John Dewey, circa 1920, further expanded on the writings of James by putting the individual squarely in the context of society. Humans can both reform and be reformed by society. Dewey's philosophy is, of course, the well-known school of progressive thought (Gross, 2014). *Reconstructionism* is a further offshoot of both pragmatism and progressivism. Richard Pratte (1971) cited the pamphlet *Dare the School Build a New Social Order?,* written by George S. Counts in 1932, as a guiding document for the then-radical notion that schools and students were the reformers of society.

Experimentalism emerges from the philosophies of pragmatism, progressivism, and reconstructionism. They hold in common a historical break from the more traditional philosophies of realism and idealism. The essentialist idea that knowledge, truth, and morality exist as absolute and outside humans was rejected. The emerging faith in the scientific method; the ability of humans to create their own laws, principles, and machines; and the fact that such human-made inventions would work for them demanded an accompanying philosophy. Experimentalism provided that philosophy: Reality was what worked.

If a person could form a hypothesis, test it, and find it to work, then it was regarded as tentatively true. On repeated experimentation with the same results, it became real. Yet experimentalists would never claim an absolute truth. The human environment was believed to be constantly changing, so that what one can do and prove today may not be probable tomorrow. A new situation and a different approach may alter yesterday's reality. Experimentalists point to the historical evidence of Newton's law of gravity as a past truth that has given way to Einstein's theory of relativity; they believe that in time, a new theory will replace Einstein's theory.

Morality is also viewed in relation to what works for humanity and human society. *Morality* is that behavior that promotes one's working with the group to achieve greater ends. To be wise is to understand how the environment (of things and people) affects oneself and how one might affect it. Whether action is moral or not is determined by the degree of progress that has been achieved by the group. The use of trial and error in a laboratory setting is the key to evaluating the outcome of action. Therefore, experimentalists do not view knowledge as absolute or external to human capabilities. Rather, knowledge is a result of the interaction between the scientific person and the environment.

The educational application of experimentalist thinking to supervision is well documented in the writing of Dewey. Teachers (as students) need to learn what are the truths of their time, but they should not rest content with that parcel of knowledge. Supervisors view schools as laboratories for working with teachers to test old hypotheses and to try new ones. Supervisors work democratically with teachers to achieve collective ends that will help everyone. Supervisors are not solely conveyors of age-old wisdom; they are both the conveyors of the rudimentary knowledge of the time and the guiders of trial-and-error, exploratory learning.

Existentialism

Existentialism as a school of thought is derived from the rejection of the other philosophies encompassed in essentialism and experimentalism. As such, it is a large category for many diverse philosophers. They have in common a scorn for rational, empirical, and systematic thinking as the way of knowing reality. As previously mentioned, the essentialists believe in rational thinking to help elevate the mind to uncover the absolutes of the universe. Experimentalists believe in rational, scientific thinking to explore and frame the relevant knowledge of the times; however, the existentialists believe that this same rational thinking restricts humans from discovering existence and therefore keeps them ignorant.

This philosophy has roots in the writings of Sören Kierkegaard in the mid-19th century. It has been popularized in drama and literature by such exponents as Albert Camus and Jean-Paul Sartre. The current popular cults of transcendental thinking, meditation, and introspection (knowing oneself) have a kinship with existentialism. The basic tenet of the philosophy is that the individual is the source of all reality. All that exists in the world is the meaning the individual puts on his or her own experiences. There is no absolute knowledge, no mechanical working of the universe, and no preordained logic. To believe in such inventions is merely the narrow, incorrect way humans interpret their own experiences.

Beyond the individual exists only chaos. The only reality that exists is one's own existence. Only by looking within oneself can one discern the truth of the outside disorder. Humanity is paramount. Human dignity and worth are of greatest importance; they are the source and dispenser of all truth. With this realization, one acquires a profound respect for all human beings and their uniqueness. Human relations become very important, affirming individual worth and protecting the individual's right to discover his or her own truth. Morality is the process of knowing oneself and allowing others the freedom to do likewise. Faith, intuition, mysticism, imagery, and transcendental experiences are all acceptable ways of discovery. Humans are totally free, not shaped by others or restricted by the flux of the times. They hold within themselves the capacity to form their own destiny (Duemer, 2012; Gross, 2014; Yue, 2011).

This philosophy of education, applied to supervision, means a full commitment to individual teacher choice. The supervisor provides an environment that enables the teacher to explore his or her own physical and mental capabilities. Teachers must learn for themselves (Kline & Abowitz, 2013). The supervisor does not dispense information, and shies away from intrusively guiding a teacher. Supervisors help when needed, protect the rights of others to self-discovery, and encounter the teacher as a person of full importance. Table 5.1 compares the three superphilosophies.

table **5.1** **Comparing Three Superphilosophies**

	Essentialism	**Experimentalism**	**Existentialism**
View of Reality (knowledge, truth, morality)	Exists outside humans, absolute, unchanging	Reality is what works; it is tentative, constantly changing	Individual is source of all reality; individual defines reality
How to Learn about Reality	Train the mind to think rationally	Interact with environment; experiment	Engage in self-discovery; create meaning
Application to Supervision	Supervisor is expert; mechanistically transmits instructional knowledge to teacher	Supervisor works democratically with teachers to test old hypotheses and try new ones	Supervisor facilitates teacher exploration and autonomous decision making

---

g r o u p   a c t i v i t y   **5.1**

Placing Yourself on the Educational Philosophy Continuum

Preparation

1. All group members complete the Educational Philosophy Q-Sort and review the "Characteristics of Philosophy Orientation" chart that follows the Q-sort (in Appendix A).

2. The instructor places small sheets of paper, each with the name of one of the philosophies, across the upper part of a wall, with an equal amount of space (3 to 4 feet) between all of the names. The names form a continuum in the following order: Perennialism–Essentialism–Progressivism–Reconstructionism–Critical Theory.

Activity

1. Based on the results of the Q-sort as well as their own reflection on their educational beliefs, students arrange themselves along the continuum. Some students may place themselves directly under one of the philosophies, others might place themselves between two different philosophies.

2. Students then each take a moment to explain why they placed themselves at that position on the continuum.

Appendix A presents the Educational Philosophy Q-Sort, developed by Bernard Badiali and based on five specific philosophical orientations rather than the three superphilosophies. Completing the Q-sort will allow you to determine with which of the five orientations your beliefs most closely align. Group Activity 5.1 is designed for group-member participation after completion of the Q-sort.

Checking Your Own Supervisory Beliefs

Let's step back and watch ourselves at work. First, we'll consider how we act with individual teachers, and then with groups. Read the Supervisory Interpersonal Behaviors Questionnaire for Working with Individuals (Box 5.1), and select the approach you most often take.

Next, take a look at the Supervisory Interpersonal Behaviors Questionnaire for Working with Groups (Box 5.2), and select the interpersonal behaviors you typically use when meeting with groups of teachers.

The supervisory approaches in these questionnaires correspond to the philosophies of essentialism, experimentalism, and existentialism and are labeled *directive* supervision, *collaborative* supervision, and *nondirective* supervision. Glickman and Tamashiro (1980) wrote:

Directive Supervision is an approach based on the belief that teaching consists of technical skills with known standards and competencies for all teachers to be effective. The supervisor's role is to inform, direct, model, and assess those competencies.

b o x 5.1

Supervisory Interpersonal Behaviors Questionnaire for Working with Individuals: A Scenario

The school day has just ended for students at Whichway School. Just as the teacher sits down at the desk, you (the supervisor) appear at the door and the teacher invites you in. "How is everything going?" you ask. Looking at the large stack of papers to correct, the teacher predicts a number of them will reflect that the students did not understand the work. "It's very frustrating working with this class. They have such a wide range of ability!" Then the teacher mentions another source of frustration: "Some of the students are discipline problems and their behavior results in class disruption."

After further discussion, the teacher and you agree that you will come into the classroom to observe what is going on, followed by a conference to discuss the classroom visit.

A few days later, after you have observed in the classroom and carefully analyzed the collected information, you begin to plan for the conference. You consider a number of approaches to use in the conference to help the teacher.

Approach A. Present what you saw in the classroom and ask for the teacher's perceptions. Listen to each other's responses. After clarifying the problem, each of you can propose ideas. Finally, you will agree on what is to be done in the classroom. You will mutually identify an objective and agree to an action plan that both of you will work together to carry out. The plan is for both of you to make.

Approach B. Listen to the teacher discuss what is going on in the classroom. Encourage the teacher to analyze the problem further, and ask questions to make sure the teacher is clear about his or her view of the problem. Finally, ask the teacher to determine and detail the actions he or she will take and

find out if you might be of further help. The plan is the teacher's to make.

Approach C. Share your observations with the teacher and tell the teacher what you believe to be the major focus for improvement. Ask the teacher for input into your observations and interpretations. Based on your own experience and knowledge, carefully delineate what you believe are alternative actions to improve the classroom and ask the teacher to consider and select from the options. The plan to follow is chosen by the teacher from the supervisor's suggestions.

Approach D. Present your beliefs about the situation and ask the teacher to confirm or revise the interpretation. After identifying the problem, offer directions to the teacher on what should be done and how to proceed. You can go into the classroom to demonstrate what you are telling the teacher to do, or tell the teacher to observe another teacher who does well in this particular area. Praise and reward the teacher for following the given assignment.

Response. Most often, I use Approach _____.

Interpretation.

Approach A: A cluster of *collaborative behaviors* in which the supervisor and teacher share the decision making about future improvement.

Approach B: A cluster of *nondirective behaviors* in which the supervisor helps the teacher formulate his or her own decisions about future improvement.

Approach C: A cluster of *directive informational behaviors* in which the supervisor frames the teacher's choices about future improvement.

Approach D: A cluster of *directive control behaviors* in which the supervisor makes the decision for the teacher.

Source: Adapted from an instrument developed by Katherine C. Ginkel (1983). "An Overview of a Study Which Examined the Relationship between Elementary School Teachers' Preference for Supervisory Conferencing Approach and Conceptual Level of Development," a paper presented at the annual meeting of the American Educational Research Association, Montreal, April. Used with permission of Katherine C. Ginkel.

b o x 5.2

Supervisory Interpersonal Behaviors Questionnaire for Working with Groups: A Scenario

You (the supervisor) have just called on the science teachers to decide on a policy for allowing students to use laboratory equipment outside of regular class time. Many students have complained about not having enough class time for doing their experiments. The issue is how and when to free up more laboratory time for students (before school, at lunchtime, during study hall, after school) under the supervision of certified teachers. How would you work with the science teachers to make a decision?

Approach A. Meet with the staff and explain that they need to decide what to do about this issue. Present the information you have about the problem and ask for clarification. Paraphrase what they say and, once the teachers verify your summary, ask them to decide among themselves what they are going to do. Remain in the meeting, helping to move the discussion along by calling on people, asking questions, and paraphrasing, but do not become involved in making your own position known or influencing the outcome in any conscious way.

Approach B. Meet with the staff by first explaining that you have to make a decision that will meet the needs of students, teachers, and supervisor. Either by consensus or, if not, then by majority vote, make a decision. You should listen, encourage, clarify, and reflect on each staff member's perception. Afterwards, ask each member, including yourself, to suggest possible solutions. Discuss each solution; prioritize the list; and, if no consensus emerges, call for a vote. Argue for your own solution, but go along with the group's decision.

Approach C. Meet with the staff and explain to them that there are several permissible actions that you have thought about that could remedy this situation. You would like them to discuss and agree on which of these actions or combinations of actions they would like to implement. Lay out the alternatives, explain the advantages and disadvantages of each, and then allow the group to discuss and decide among your alternatives.

Approach D. Meet with the staff and tell them you want their feedback before you make a decision about the issue. Make it clear that the staff's involvement is to be advisory. Ask for their suggestions, listen, encourage, clarify, and paraphrase their ideas. After everyone has had a chance to speak, decide what changes should be made. Tell them what you are going to do, when the changes will be made, and that you expect them to carry out the plan.

Response. Most often, I would use Approach _____.

Interpretation.

Approach A: A cluster of *nondirective behaviors* in which the supervisor assists the group to make its own decision.

Approach B: A cluster of *collaborative behaviors* in which the supervisor works as part of the group in making a group decision.

Approach C: A cluster of *directive informational behaviors* in which the supervisor works as the framer of choices among which the group is to decide.

Approach D: A cluster of *directive control behaviors* in which the supervisor makes the decision for the group.

Source: Adapted from an instrument developed by Katherine C. Ginkel (1983). "An Overview of a Study Which Examined the Relationship between Elementary School Teachers' Preference for Supervisory Conferencing Approach and Conceptual Level of Development," a paper presented at the annual meeting of the American Educational Research Association, Montreal, April. Used with permission of Katherine C. Ginkel.

Collaborative Supervision is based on the belief that teaching is primarily problem solving, whereby two or more persons jointly pose hypotheses to a problem, experiment, and implement those teaching strategies that appear to be most relevant in their own surroundings. The supervisor's role is to guide the problem-solving process, be an active member of the interaction, and keep the teachers focused on their common problems.

Non-Directive Supervision has as its premise that learning is primarily a private experience in which individuals must come up with their own solutions to improving the classroom experience for students. The supervisor's role is to listen, be nonjudgmental, and provide self-awareness and clarification experiences for teachers. (p. 76)

What Does Your Belief Mean in Terms of Supervisor and Teacher Responsibility?

Beliefs about supervision can be thought of in terms of decision-making responsibility (Table 5.2). An essentialist philosophy is premised on the supervisor being the expert on instruction and therefore having major decision-making responsibility. A situation of high supervisor responsibility and low teacher responsibility is labeled *directive supervision*. An experimentalist philosophy is premised on the supervisor and teachers being equal partners in instructional improvement; equal supervisor and teacher responsibility is labeled *collaborative supervision*. Existentialist philosophy is premised on teachers discovering their own capacities for instructional improvement. Low supervisor responsibility and high teacher responsibility is labeled *nondirective supervision*.

As we clarify our own educational philosophy and supervisory beliefs, we rarely find a pure ideological position. Therefore, Sergiovanni's idea of a supervisory platform becomes helpful. What combination of various philosophies and beliefs do we consider important? Perhaps our beliefs are mainly essentialist and directive yet contain parts of experimentalism and collaboration; or perhaps we have another combination of beliefs. A particular platform is not right or wrong; rather, it is an assessment of the beliefs we use to create the floor we stand on.

table 5.2 **Supervisory Belief and Decision-Making Responsibility**

Supervisory Belief	Decision-Making Responsibility
Directive	Supervisor high, teacher low
Collaborative	Supervisor and teacher equal
Nondirective	Supervisor low, teacher high

Educational Philosophy, Teachers, Supervisors, and Supervisory Approach

Thus far in this chapter we have discussed the beliefs of three teachers—Joan Simpson, Bill Washington, and Pat Rogers; the beliefs of three supervisors—Bob Reynolds, Jan White, and Shawn Moore; three superphilosophies—essentialism, experimentalism, and existentialism; and three supervisory approaches—directive, collaborative, and nondirective. Clearly there are some patterns present here, as summarized in Table 5.3. Teacher Joan Simpson and supervisor Bob Reynolds both embrace essentialism, teacher Bill Washington and supervisor Jan White's beliefs are based on experimentalism, and teacher Pat Rogers and supervisor Shawn Moore's beliefs reflect existentialism. As stated earlier, most supervisors were once teachers, and teachers tend to carry their most deeply held beliefs from the classroom to their supervisory roles. Many educators may have never articulated their beliefs in formal platforms, but they nonetheless possess those beliefs—and those beliefs are reflected in their everyday actions as teachers and supervisors, hence they are of vital importance to the students under their responsibility.

Where You Stand Depends on Where You Sit: Effects of Culture on Beliefs

A person's cultural background is an important aspect of what he or she believes about education. There is a natural tendency for members of the dominant culture to support curriculum and instruction that will transmit that culture to students. Students from minority cultures, however, may find it difficult to adapt to curriculum and instruction intended to convey the dominant culture and may resist (sometimes passively, sometimes actively) the transmission of that culture. This is not just a question of an unfortunate mismatch between dominant and minority cultures that eventually will be overcome as minority cultures are assimilated. Schools that marginalize the cultures of particular students marginalize those students as well. What is especially insidious about such marginalization is that educators may not realize they are partly responsible for its occurrence.

t a b l e **5.3** **Relating Philosophies, Teachers, Supervisors, and Supervisory Approaches**

Philosophy	Essentialism	Experimentalism	Existentialism
Teacher	Joan Simpson	Bill Washington	Pat Rogers
Supervisor	Bob Reynolds	Jan White	Shawn Moore
Supervisory Approach	Directive	Collaborative	Nondirective

> ▶ **Video Illustration**
>
> This video includes segments of a supervisor–teacher conference, with the supervisor discussing his supervisory beliefs, and teachers discussing the supervisor's style. Of the supervisory approaches discussed in this chapter, which approach or approaches do you believe the supervisor in the video has adopted?

Educators' beliefs about education often are influenced by cultural assumptions they may not be aware of because the assumptions are so deeply ingrained and taken for granted. These assumptions can influence the curriculum that educators design, their relationships with students and parents, the lessons they plan, how they assess students, and so forth. Because of the influences of our cultural assumptions and beliefs on students, it is not sufficient for us simply to articulate our beliefs and then base educational goals and practices on those beliefs. Rather, we should attempt to identify and critically examine our cultural assumptions. Such critique, often done in dialogue with others, can cause us to change assumptions that have negative effects on colleagues and students.

Identifying and critiquing cultural assumptions is not easy for individuals and schools to do. It usually is necessary to begin with an examination of our actions, cultural artifacts, and espoused beliefs and then to begin to search below the surface of those actions, artifacts, and beliefs for underlying assumptions. At the individual level, this might mean reflecting on questions such as the following:

- Do I have more difficulty working with some cultural groups than others? If so, why?
- How congruent are my espoused beliefs and actions when working with cultural groups different from my own?
- How does my cultural background influence my expectations of and interactions with parents?
- How does my cultural background contribute to my perceptions of effective teaching?
- How does my cultural background affect my expectations of students in general? My expectations of different student groups?

These questions provide entry points for critical reflection that can expand our understanding of cultural assumptions. Questions such as the following can assist groups to critically examine cultural effects on the school as an organization:

- How does the dominant culture inform our goals as a school? How do other cultures contribute to our goals?

- How is the dominant culture represented in our curriculum, including textbooks and curriculum materials? Are other cultures reflected positively in our curriculum?
- How do our cultural beliefs affect the way students are grouped and placed in various programs in our school?
- How do our cultural beliefs affect the school's disciplinary practices?
- How do our cultural beliefs affect the way we assess student learning?
- How do our cultural beliefs affect the way we interact with our students' families?

Another catalyst for changing beliefs is a better understanding of cultures different from our own. This can be done by reading literature about other cultures and about multicultural education, talking with students and colleagues from other cultures, interacting with parents and community members from different cultures in various community settings, and sharing educational and leadership roles within the school with representatives of various cultures. Better understanding of cultures, especially when achieved through interaction with those cultures, can overcome personal bias, change educational beliefs, and ultimately inform a different and more diverse educational practice.

✔ **Check Your Understanding 5.0**   Click here to gauge your understanding of the key concepts presented in this chapter.

REFLECTIVE EXERCISE

Several teachers from the math department at Lowell High School have complained to supervisor Sheryl Garcia that one of the math teachers, Rick Evans, is out of sync with the rest of the department. With the exception of Rick, the math teachers at Lowell have adopted an experimentalist approach to teaching math, including having students test alternative ways of solving math problems, applying math to real-world situations in their homes and communities, and collaborating with each other on math projects. Rick, who has 10 years of teaching experiences at another school, is in his second year at Lowell. Rick has an essentialist educational philosophy—he believes that math teachers need to "get back to the basics," by demonstrating to students how to solve math problems, providing them feedback as they practice solving problems, and assigning independent practice so students can perfect their problem-solving skills. The other math teachers have told Sheryl that their discussions with Rick urging him to make his teaching methods more congruent with the department's philosophy have been fruitless, and they have asked Sheryl to speak with Rick about the philosophical conflict. What steps would you advise Sheryl to take?

part 3

Interpersonal Skills

The organization of this book was outlined in Figure 1.1 in Chapter 1. The prerequisites for supervision as a developmental function are knowledge, interpersonal skills, and technical skills. Part 2 examined the critical knowledge base. Part 3 will describe interpersonal skills. Chapter 6 will introduce the supervisory behavior continuum, Chapter 7 will detail the use of directive control behaviors, Chapter 8 will detail the use of directive informational behaviors, Chapter 9 will detail the use of collaborative behaviors, Chapter 10 will detail the use of nondirective behaviors, and Chapter 11 will discuss in detail the theory and practice of developmental supervision.

Knowledge of what needs to be done for teacher growth and school success is the base of a triangle for supervisory action (see Figure III.1). Knowledge needs to be accompanied by interpersonal skills for communicating with teachers and technical skills for planning, assessing, observing, and evaluating instructional improvement. We will now turn to the interpersonal skill dimension.

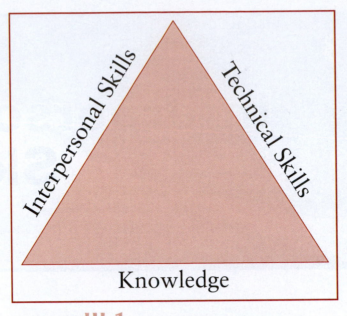

figure **III.1** **Prerequisite Dimensions for a Supervisor**

chapter 6

Supervisory Behavior Continuum: Know Thyself

Learning Outcomes for This Chapter

After reading this chapter, you should be able to:

1. Identify the outcome of each of the four supervisory approaches discussed in this chapter.
2. List the four windowpanes in the adaptation of the Johari Window presented in this chapter.
3. Elucidate the premise of cognitive dissonance.
4. Describe the Supervisor's Self-Assessment Tool.
5. Identify three methods for gathering data to compare with the supervisor's perceptions.
6. Summarize the 360-degree feedback strategy.

Questions to Reflect On as You Read This Chapter

1. Which of the four supervisory approaches discussed in this chapter have been used by supervisors you have worked with?
2. If a group of colleagues you work with or have worked with were asked to describe you as a professional, what aspects of your public self do you believe they would discuss? What are some professional attributes that you keep private and of which your colleagues are unaware?
3. Do you have a colleague who has had or now has difficulty working with others or achieving professional goals because of a particular aspect of the colleague's blind self? What is the colleague's "blind spot" and its negative effects?
4. Reflect on a time that you experienced major cognitive dissonance in your professional life. What were your initial feelings about this situation? How did you resolve the cognitive dissonance?
5. This chapter describes several ways in which a supervisor can gather feedback on his or her performance. As a supervisor, which of these strategies would you feel most comfortable trying out? Over time, which strategy do you believe would provide you with the most useful feedback?

This chapter looks at the range of interpersonal behaviors available to a supervisor who is working with individuals and groups of teachers. It will assess how supervisors typically behave with staff in school settings and then determine other behaviors that might be used skillfully and effectively. Later chapters will provide training in each of four clusters of interpersonal skills.

Broad categories of supervisory behaviors have been derived from many years of collecting supervisors' observations in meetings with individuals and groups of teachers for purposes of making classroom or school decisions (Glickman, 2002). These categories encompass almost all observed supervisory behaviors that are deemed purposeful. A *purposeful* behavior is defined as one that contributes to the decision being made at the conference or meeting. The derived categories of supervisory behaviors are listening, clarifying, encouraging, reflecting, presenting, problem solving, negotiating, directing, standardizing, and reinforcing. Definitions of each category are as follows:

- *Listening.* The supervisor sits and looks at the speaker and nods his or her head to show understanding. Guttural utterances ("uh-huh," "umm") also indicate listening.

- *Clarifying.* The supervisor asks questions and makes statements to clarify the speaker's point of view: "Do you mean that . . .?" "Would you explain this further?" "I'm confused about this." "I lost you on . . ."

- *Encouraging.* The supervisor provides acknowledgment responses that help the speaker continue to explain his or her positions: "Yes, I'm following you." "Continue on." "Ah, I see what you're saying; tell me more."

- *Reflecting.* The supervisor summarizes and paraphrases the speaker's message for verification of accuracy: "I understand that you mean . . ." "So, the issue is . . ." "I hear you saying . . ."

- *Presenting.* The supervisor gives his or her own ideas about the issue being discussed: "This is how I see it." "What can be done is . . ." "I'd like us to consider . . ." "I believe that . . ."

- *Problem solving.* The supervisor takes the initiative, usually after a preliminary discussion of the issue or problem, in pressing all those involved to generate a list of possible solutions. This is usually done through statements such as these: "Let's stop and each write down what can be done." "What ideas do we have to solve this problem?" "Let's think of all possible actions we can take."

- *Negotiating.* The supervisor moves the discussion from possible to probable solutions by discussing the consequences of each proposed action, exploring conflict or priorities, and narrowing down choices with questions such as these: "Where do we agree?" "How can we change that action to be acceptable to all?" "Can we find a compromise that will give each of us part of what we want?"

- *Directing.* The supervisor tells the participant(s) either what the choices are: "As I see it, these are the alternatives: You could do A. . ., B. . ., or C. . . Which of these makes the most sense to you and which will you use?" *Or* the supervisor tells the participants what is to be done: "I've decided that we will do . . ." "I want you to do . . ." "The policy will be . . ." "This is how it is going to be." "We will then proceed as follows."

- *Standardizing.* The supervisor sets the expected criteria and time for the decision to be implemented. Target objectives are set. Expectations are conveyed with words, such as: "By next Monday, we want to see . . ." "Report back to me on this change by . . ." "Have the first two activities carried out by . . ." "I want an improvement of 25 percent involvement by the next meeting." "We have agreed that all tasks will be done before the next observation."

- *Reinforcing.* The supervisor strengthens the directive and the criteria to be met by telling of possible consequences. Possible consequences can be positive, in the form of praise: "I know you can do it!" "I have confidence in your ability!" "I want to show others what you've done!" Consequences also can be negative: "If it's not done on time, we'll lose the support of . . ." "It must be understood that failure to get this done on time will result in . . ."

The foregoing categories of interpersonal supervisory behavior move participants toward a decision. Some supervisory behaviors place more responsibility on the teacher(s) to make the decision, others place more responsibility on the supervisor to make the decision, and still others indicate a shared responsibility for decision making. The categories of behaviors are listed in a sequence on the supervisory behavior continuum (Figure 6.1) to reflect the scale of control or power.

When a supervisor *listens* to the teacher, *clarifies* what the teacher says, *encourages* the teacher to speak more about the concern, and *reflects* by verifying the teacher's perceptions, then clearly it is the teacher who is in control. The supervisor's role is that of an active prober or sounding board for the teacher to make his or her own decision. The teacher has high control and the supervisor low control over the actual decision (in Figure 6.1, this is denoted by big *T*, small *s*). This is seen as a *nondirective interpersonal approach*.

When a supervisor uses nondirective behaviors to understand the teacher's point of view but then participates in the discussion by *presenting* his or her own ideas, *problem solving* by asking all parties to propose possible actions, and then *negotiating* to find a common course of action satisfactory to teacher and supervisor,

	1	2	3	4	5
	Listening	*Clarifying*	*Encouraging*	*Reflecting*	*Presenting*

T
_____
s

Clusters of behaviors: Nondirective

Key: T = Maximum teacher responsibility   S = Maximum supervisor responsibility
        t = Minimum teacher responsibility   s = Minimum supervisor responsibility

figure **6.1** **The Supervisory Behavior Continuum**

then the control over the decision is shared by all. This is viewed as a *collaborative interpersonal approach*.

When a supervisor *directs* the teacher in what the alternatives are from which the teacher might choose, and after the teacher selects, the supervisor *standardizes* the time and criteria of expected results, then the supervisor is the major source of information, providing the teacher with restricted choice (small *t*, big *S*). This is viewed as a *directive informational interpersonal approach*.

Finally, when a supervisor *directs* the teacher in what will be done, *standardizes* the time and criteria of expected results, and *reinforces* the consequences of action or inaction, then the supervisor has taken responsibility for the decision (small *t*, big *S*). The supervisor is clearly determining the actions for the teacher to follow. These behaviors are called a *directive control interpersonal approach*.

Outcomes of Conference

Another way of clarifying the distinctions among supervisory approaches is by looking at the outcomes of the conference and determining who controls the final decision for instructional improvement:

Approach	Outcome
Nondirective	Teacher self-plan
Collaborative	Mutual plan
Directive informational	Supervisor-suggested plan
Directive control	Supervisor-assigned plan

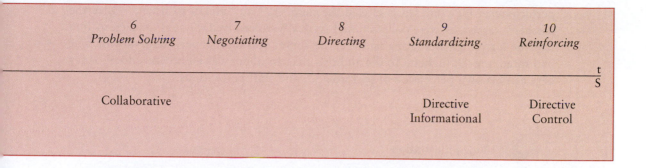

6 *Problem Solving*	7 *Negotiating*	8 *Directing*	9 *Standardizing*	10 *Reinforcing*

t
S

Collaborative   Directive   Directive
                                                   Informational   Control

In the nondirective approach, the supervisor facilitates the teacher's thinking in developing a self-plan. In the collaborative approach, both supervisor and teacher share information and possible practices as equals in arriving at a mutual plan. In the directive informational approach, the supervisor provides the focus and the parameters of possible actions, and the teacher is asked to choose from the supervisor's suggestions. In the directive control approach, the supervisor tells the teacher what is to be done. Nondirective provides maximum teacher choice; collaborative, mutual choice; directive informational, selected choice; and directive control, no choice in the outcome of the conference.

Valid Assessment of Self

We need to make sure that how we perceive ourselves is consistent with how others perceive us. As an example, let us give a personal instance of erroneous self-perception. As a school principal in New Hampshire, one of the authors regarded himself as operating a successful school and being accessible to teachers. He could document success by external evidence—state and national recognition the school had received and complimentary letters from numerous visitors. He documented his accessibility through casual discussions with teachers in the lounge and by having an open-office policy for every staff member who wished to speak with him. In his third year as a principal at this particular school, the superintendent asked all principals in the school system to allow teachers to evaluate principal performance. One item on the evaluation form was "Ability to Listen to Others," followed by a numerical scale of responses from 1 ("rarely listens") to 7 ("almost always listens"). Before giving the form to teachers, the author filled out the same evaluation form according to his own perception of his performance. He confidently circled the number 7 on "ability to listen." Once the teachers' responses were collected and results were received, he was amazed to find that the lowest teacher rating on the entire survey was on that very item, on which he had rated himself highest. To the author's chagrin, there was an obvious discrepancy between his own perception of performance and staff perceptions.

> ▶ **Video Illustration**
>
> This video tells the story of a first-year principal. Some questions to consider as you view the video follow: What was the major discrepancy between the principal's leadership style and faculty expectations? What did the principal learn because of that discrepancy? How did she adjust her behavior?

Johari Window

The Johari Window (Chang, Chen, & Yuan, 2012; Janas, 2001; Luft, 1970; Tombak, 2015) provides a graphic way to look at what we know and do not know about our behavior (Figure 6.2). Visualize a window with four windowpanes. In this scheme, there are four windowpanes of the self in which behaviors are either known or not known by self (the supervisor) and others (the teachers). In windowpane 1, there are behaviors that both supervisor and teachers know the supervisor uses. This is the *public self*. For example, the supervisor knows that when he or she is anxious, speech will become halting and hesitant; teachers are also aware of what such speech indicates.

In windowpane 2 is the *blind self*—behaviors the supervisor practices that are unknown to the self but are known to teachers. For example, as a school principal, one of the authors was displaying behaviors toward teachers that he thought were

	Known to Supervisor	Not Known to Supervisor
Known to Teachers	1. Public self	2. Blind self
Not Known to Teachers	3. Private self	4. Unknown self

figure **6.2** **Adaptation of Johari Window**

Source: Adapted from Joseph Luft (1970). *Group Processes: An Introduction to Group Dynamics*. New York: National Press Books.

listening behaviors, but teachers saw the same behaviors as a failure to listen. Of course, once one becomes aware of teachers' perceptions of those behaviors, the blind self becomes the public self.

In windowpane 3 is the *private self*—behaviors the supervisor has knowledge about but that teachers do not know. For instance, in new situations a supervisor might mask his or her insecurities by being extroverted in greeting others. Only the supervisor knows that this behavior is covering up insecurity. Once the supervisor discloses this perception to others, the private self becomes public.

Lastly, is windowpane 4, the *unknown self*. There are actions a supervisor takes of which both supervisors and teachers are unaware. From time to time, the supervisor might rapidly shift his legs while speaking behind a table. Neither supervisor nor teachers are aware of this leg movement. Perhaps a supervisor becomes irritated while a certain teacher is speaking. The supervisor may not know why he or she is irritated or even that such feeling exists, and the teacher may not know either. The unknown self is unconscious to all; it becomes private, blind, or public only by circumstances that create a new awareness.

What does the Johari Window have to do with supervision? We cannot become more effective as supervisors unless we know what we are doing. We may, at our discretion, decide to keep parts of ourselves private (e.g., we may not want teachers to know all the details of our life and personality). Yet we need to understand that by remaining largely private and not sharing the experiences that bind us as humans, we are creating a distance when we work with teachers. We may prefer formality and distance and may be able to document that such privateness accomplishes certain results. On the other hand, we must also accept that our privateness will be reciprocal and that staff may not easily discuss personal situations that may affect teaching performance. First, we must be aware of how private or public we are with our staff and determine if we desire teachers to be the same way with us. Second, as supervisors, we cannot afford to be blind to our own behaviors and the effect of those behaviors on others. We can improve only what we know; to believe only our own self-perceptions is to court disaster.

The author's perception of his listening behavior as a principal is a case in point. As long as he saw himself as a wonderful, accessible listener, it did not seem probable that teachers were not coming to him with instructional problems. However, he discovered that on two different occasions teachers had gone to the superintendent about instructional problems of which he was unaware. After the superintendent told him that teachers were going over his head, he angrily confronted the teachers with their "unprofessional" behavior. It did not occur to the author that he might have been the one at fault. After the staff evaluations, he could no longer delude himself. Many teachers were not telling him their concerns because they did not believe that he would really listen. The author had to face the fact that the staff did not see him as accessible. He might have avoided collecting such information, continued with his euphoric self-perception, and then been devastated as the school fell apart.

The Johari window is most useful to supervisors who use it as a framework to gather information and reflect on their performance in each of the four windowpanes:

1. Both the supervisor and teachers are aware of the supervisor's *public-self* behaviors, but the supervisor may not be aware of how those behaviors affect teachers or the underlying causes of public behaviors that have negative effects. With the help of a mentor or coach (like teachers, supervisors benefit from mentoring and coaching), supervisors can use anonymous surveys, observations, and informal conversations to decide what behaviors they wish to enhance and what behaviors they wish to change.

2. The supervisor can gather and reflect on data to become aware of behaviors of the *blind self* and make decisions about desired changes. For example, if the author in our earlier example of the blind self had used informal surveys, observations by neutral parties, and so forth to make himself aware of teacher perceptions of his leadership style, he could have become aware of the teachers' concerns and addressed the problem before the formal evaluation of his performance.

3. The supervisor can explore why some beliefs and behaviors are part of the *private self* and whether it would be better to keep private matters private or to share them with teachers. Reflective writing about important aspects of the private self is one strategy for exploring that windowpane. Also, a supervisor may be willing to discuss some otherwise private matters with a mentor or coach, and these confidential discussions might lead the supervisor to make some aspects of the private self public.

4. What about the *unknown self*? How can supervisors gather data and reflect on personal behaviors or assumptions they do not know about? The first step is self-awareness. For example, in a study by Diehl (2011), a small group of supervisors participating in a semester-long seminar used a combination of reflective writing and group dialogue to bring to the surface ways they reacted to accountability pressures they formerly were unaware of, as well as the effects of those blind behaviors on themselves, teachers, and students. The self-awareness resulting from the reflective writing and group dialogue was the first step in the supervisors changing some of their attitudes and behaviors in order to reduce their own stress and its adverse effects on other members of their school community.

Introductory Activity on the Johari Window

An introductory individual and group activity on the Johari window can help us get acquainted with three of its four panes. This activity is appropriate for group members who know each other well enough to make observations about one another. The steps for the activity are as follows:

1. Each member of the group is provided a copy of Activity Sheet 6.1. Reflecting on their own personal and professional characteristics, individuals list words or short phrases that they believe represent their public and private selves in the designated areas of the Johari window.

2. Each member of the group is given several copies of Activity Sheet 6.2. The number of copies each group member is provided equals the number of other group members. Each group member writes a list of positive characteristics about each of the other group members (each list should be on a separate page with the colleague's name at the top).

---

activity sheet **6.1**

My Public and Private Self

Directions: List words or short phrases that represent your public and private selves in the appropriate "windowpanes" below. Note: You will be sharing what you write with other members of the group.

My Public Self	My Blind Self
My Private Self	My Unknown Self

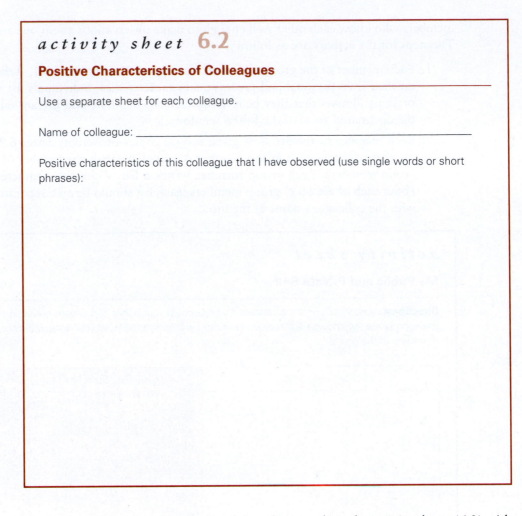

activity sheet **6.2**

Positive Characteristics of Colleagues

Use a separate sheet for each colleague.

Name of colleague: _____

Positive characteristics of this colleague that I have observed (use single words or short phrases):

3. Group members hand each of the other members the activity sheets (6.2) with the lists of positive characteristics (e.g., Mike gives the list he wrote about Maria to Maria, the list he wrote about Susie to Susie, and so forth).

4. Each member of the group reviews all of the sheets listing other members' perceptions of the reviewer's positive characteristics.

5. Each member of the group is given a copy of Activity Sheet 6.3. Based on their review of the comments made about them by others, each member lists words or short phrases in the public, private, and blind panes of the new Johari window. This may involve shifting some characteristics that were listed in the public pane on Activity Sheet 6.1 to the private pane on Activity Sheet 6.3, shifting some characteristics from the private pane to the public pane, or listing some characteristics as part of the (formerly) blind self.

activity sheet 6.3

My Public, Private Self, and Blind Self

Directions: After reviewing the comments others have made about you on Activity Sheet 6.2, revise the public- and private-self panes and make entries in the blind-self windowpane as appropriate.

My Public Self	My Blind Self
My Private Self	My Unknown Self

6. Group members engage in a discussion about changes they made in their partial Johari window as a result of reviewing the characteristics that other group members wrote about them.

This introductory activity, of course, does not provide participants with the full impact of the Johari window, because the unknown pane is not addressed and all of the perceptions received from others are positive. Gathering more critical data on all four selves within one's professional work setting can cause the supervisor to experience cognitive dissonance, which is often a prerequisite for change. Let's discuss what cognitive dissonance is all about next.

Cognitive Dissonance

Invalidity of perceptions creates *cognitive dissonance,* according to a model of motivation by psychologist Leon Festinger (1957) (see also Gorski, 2009; Weldeana & Abraham, 2014; Zepeda, 2006). The model is based on the premise that people cannot live with contradictory psychological evidence—that is, thinking of the self in one way while other sources of information indicate that they are different. When the author's perception of his listening abilities was contradicted by teacher perceptions, he experienced mental turmoil, or cognitive dissonance. We must wrestle with disparate perceptions and reconcile them. If not, the two differing sources of information will continue to bother us. This mental anguish drives us to resolve the question of what it is that we really do.

Cognitive dissonance by its nature is uncomfortable, but in the wider view it can be a catalyst for needed change. An example is provided in a study by Gordon and Brobeck (2010) that described cognitive dissonance experienced by a supervisor who was committed to using a nondirective approach with all teachers. As a result of listening to recordings of her postobservation conferences with teachers and engaging in dialogue about those conferences with a coach, the supervisor came to the uncomfortable realization that the nondirective approach worked well with expert teachers but not with struggling teachers. To resolve the cognitive dissonance caused by the supervisor's realization that her nondirective approach was inappropriate for some teachers, the supervisor made a commitment to use a variety of supervisory approaches, tailoring her approach to the developmental level of each teacher she worked with.

Comparing Self-Perceptions with Others' Perceptions

Box 6.1 provides an instrument that the supervisor uses to compare self-perceptions with teacher perceptions of supervisor performance. The Supervisor's Self-Assessment is divided into four sections—"Professional Characteristics," "Skills," "Individual Assistance," and "Schoolwide Assistance"—and yields a subscore for each section. The process of self-assessment begins with the supervisor completing and self-scoring the instrument. It is important for the supervisor to be totally open when completing the self-assessment, so as a general rule the supervisor should not be expected to share results with superiors or teachers. The supervisor next distributes the instrument to the teachers or a randomly selected sample of the teachers he or she supervises. It's important that the teachers complete and return the completed instruments anonymously. After calculating item, section, and overall means of teacher responses,

b o x **6.1**

Supervisor's Self-Assessment

Directions for Completing:

Place in the space before each item the number (1, 2, 3, or 4) of the response that most nearly indicates your level of agreement with the item:

1. Strongly disagree
2. Disagree
3. Agree
4. Strongly agree

Section A: Professional Characteristics

1. The supervisor is genuinely concerned with the growth and development of students.
2. The supervisor is genuinely concerned with the growth and development of teachers.
3. The supervisor is trustworthy.
4. The supervisor treats teachers fairly.
5. The supervisor is flexible.
6. The supervisor is ethical.

Section B: Skills

7. The supervisor displays communication skills.
8. The supervisor displays needs-assessment skills.
9. The supervisor displays planning skills.
10. The supervisor displays group-facilitation skills.
11. The supervisor displays problem-solving skills.
12. The supervisor displays change-agency skills.
13. The supervisor displays observation skills.
14. The supervisor displays conflict-resolution skills.

Section C: Individual Assistance

15. The supervisor effectively observes teaching and provides helpful feedback.
16. The supervisor provides useful instructional resources.
17. The supervisor fosters teacher reflection.
18. The supervisor demonstrates effective teaching.
19. The supervisor shares innovative instructional strategies.
20. The supervisor effectively assists beginning teachers.

21. The supervisor effectively assists teachers with instructional problems they are experiencing.
22. The supervisor effectively assists teachers to plan for instruction.
23. The supervisor effectively assists teachers to assess student learning.
24. The supervisor effectively assists teachers to individualize instruction.

Section D: Schoolwide Assistance

25. The supervisor effectively facilitates instructional dialogue among teachers.
26. The supervisor fosters a positive school culture.
27. The supervisor facilitates collective vision building.
28. The supervisor fosters teacher collaboration for schoolwide instructional improvement.
29. The supervisor fosters teacher empowerment.
30. The supervisor effectively facilitates teachers' professional development.
31. The supervisor effectively facilitates curriculum development.
32. The supervisor effectively facilitates program evaluation.

Directions for Scoring:

For the instrument completed by the supervisor, add the ratings for the items in each section to find subtotals. The range of possible subtotals for each section follows:

Section A: Professional Characteristics, from 6 to 24
Section B: Skills, from 8 to 32
Section C: Individual Assistance, from 10 to 40
Section D: Schoolwide Assistance, from 8 to 32

The overall rating (the sum of the four subtotals) ranges from 32 to 128.

For the instrument completed by teachers, calculate the mean scores for each item, section, and the overall rating. For example, if five teachers responded to the same item with ratings of 2, 3,

(continued)

4, 4, and 5, respectively, then the teachers' mean rating for that item would be 3.6. For an example at the section level, if the subtotals on Section A from five teachers were 16, 18, 19, 21, and 22, the mean ratings for Section A would be 19.2. For the overall mean, if individual overall ratings by five teachers were 83, 92, 100, 112, and 118, the overall mean for teacher ratings would be 101.

the supervisor can compare self-perceptions with teacher perceptions. When comparing self-ratings to teacher ratings on any particular item, the supervisor can reach a variety of conclusions:

1. Supervisor and teacher satisfaction with the supervisor's performance
2. Supervisor satisfaction and teacher dissatisfaction with the supervisor's performance
3. Supervisor dissatisfaction and teacher satisfaction with the supervisor's performance
4. Supervisor and teacher dissatisfaction with the supervisor's performance

Any of the last three conclusions can be the basis for supervisor-defined improvement objectives and supervisor-designed action plans for the improvement of instructional assistance.

Comparing Self-Perceptions to Recorded Behaviors

Another way to create cognitive dissonance as a catalyst for improvement of supervisory practice is for the supervisor to compare his or her perceptions to data gathered on the supervisor's actual behaviors. One of the key processes a supervisor is responsible for is gathering data on classroom behaviors to assist teachers to improve their instruction. It makes sense, then, for the supervisor to analyze data on her or his own performance for the purpose of improved supervision. Data gathering on supervision often takes place while the supervisor is interacting with individual teachers or groups. The data can be gathered in a number of ways. Another supervisor can observe a conference or meeting that the observed supervisor is conducting and gather requested data. The supervisor can electronically record a supervisory conference or meeting and review the recording. The supervisor can analyze documents that reflect supervisory behaviors, such as e-mails, memos, and observation reports that she or he has prepared.

The purpose of analyzing these types of data is to compare the supervisor's perceptions to recorded supervisory behaviors. Comparison of perceptions to data can create the same types of cognitive dissonance as the comparison of supervisor and teacher perceptions discussed in the previous section. In fact, comparing supervisor perceptions to hard data may bring about cognitive dissonance more easily than comparison of supervisor and teacher perceptions. The cognitive dissonance caused by self-analysis of data on supervisory behaviors can lead to changes in supervisory behaviors.

What types of data on supervisory performance should be gathered and analyzed? Data might be gathered on interpersonal behaviors in general. For example, when a supervisor attempts to use a collaborative approach, are collaborative behaviors in evidence, or does the supervisor slip into directive or nondirective behaviors? Data also can be used to compare the supervisor's behaviors with different groups. Does the supervisor treat men and women differently? Hispanics and Whites? Younger and older teachers? If so, why is one group treated differently from the other? If equity is an educational goal, then equitable treatment of teachers by supervisors should be a model for teachers and students. By recording and analyzing supervisory behaviors through the lens of equity, the supervisor can recognize problems in this area and begin to improve her or his own performance.

360-Degree Feedback

A comprehensive strategy for the supervisor to gather feedback on performance is 360-degree feedback (Bradley, Allen, Hamilton, & Filgo, 2006; Brutus & Derayeh, 2002; Dyer, 2001; Lepsinger & Lucia, 2009; Nieminen, Smerek, Kotrba, & Denison, 2013; Seyforth, 2008; Shinn, 2008), also known as multisource assessment or full-circle feedback. Initially used in business, 360-degree feedback is now applied in a variety of professions and organizations. The instructional supervisor using the strategy gathers feedback from all groups that she or he works with, including teachers, students, other supervisors, and central office administrators. The reason for gathering feedback from multiple groups is that different groups have different relationships with the supervisor and different perspectives on the supervisor's performance. Gathering data from each of the groups makes for a more comprehensive assessment. A coach or mentor without line authority over the supervisor assists the supervisor throughout the 360-degree assessment.

A number of principles guide the 360-degree feedback process. The feedback should be formative (used for the supervisor's professional development), not summative (used by the district to make administrative decisions about the supervisor). None of the supervisor's superiors should coordinate the process. The mentor or coach who assists the supervisor should be committed to the supervisor's growth and development, have data-gathering and analysis skills, and be willing to openly and honestly critique the supervisor's performance. In consultation with the mentor or coach, the supervisor should be allowed to select the groups that will participate in the assessment. The entire process should be confidential, with feedback reviewed only by the supervisor and mentor or coach.

The process begins with the supervisor collaborating with the mentor or coach to select particular areas of the supervisor's professional behavior to assess. Feedback instruments with generic areas to assess (e.g., communication, adaptability, relationships) have been developed (Profiles International, 2011), but if the supervisor establishes the areas for assessment, feedback can be tailored to the supervisor's specific role and school context. Before gathering feedback, the supervisor does a self-assessment so the supervisor's perceptions can later be compared to the feedback from others. In addition to multiple feedback groups, there often are multiple feedback-gathering methods. Teachers might be given a questionnaire, and the mentor or coach might interview other supervisors or conduct observations of the supervisor working with teachers. Once the feedback has been gathered, the mentor or coach assists the supervisor to review the feedback and identify both strengths and weaknesses in the supervisor's performance. The supervisor, in consultation with the mentor or coach, establishes goals aimed at enhancing strengths and improving in areas of weakness, and designs an action plan for meeting the improvement goals.

Whether data is gathered through asking teachers to complete a simple questionnaire, comparing self-perceptions to recorded behavior, or the more complex 360-degree feedback, supervisors need information about their performance in order to improve. Our beliefs guide our actions, and our beliefs provide us with the best guidance when they are informed by accurate knowledge about the effects of our behavior on those around us.

✔ **Check Your Understanding 6.0**   Click here to gauge your understanding of the key concepts presented in this chapter.

REFLECTIVE EXERCISE

Assume that you are a department chair with supervisory responsibilities and the principal of your school has asked you to pilot 360-degree feedback. The feedback is to be on your supervisory performance (not your teaching). The principal has offered to provide you and a coach of your choosing a stipend and released time to pilot the 360-degree process.

- What assurance would you seek from the principal before agreeing to pilot 360-degree feedback?
- What characteristics would you look for in a coach to assist you?
- On what aspects of your supervisory leadership would you gather feedback?
- From what groups would you gather feedback?

- What feedback-gathering tools (e.g., questionnaires, interviews, observations) would you use to gather data from each of the feedback groups you have identified?

- With what activities in the 360-degree process would you ask your coach for assistance? What activities would you carry out on your own?

chapter 7

Directive Control Behaviors

Learning Outcomes for this Chapter

After reading this chapter, you should be able to:

1. Summarize any of the characteristics described in this chapter of teachers best matched with directive control behaviors.

2. Explain any of the 10 categories of the supervisory behavior continuum as applied to the directive control supervisory approach.

3. Discuss what the authors mean by combining control and manipulation.

4. Recall three issues with directive control behaviors.

5. Give examples of situations where use of directive control is advisable.

6. Identify a specific way of moving from a directive control to a directive informational approach.

Questions to Reflect On as You Read This Chapter

1. As you read about the supervisory behaviors used in the directive control approach, which behaviors would you like to discuss or see demonstrated before you practice directive control behaviors in a role play?

2. When asked which supervisory approach they prefer to use, only a very small percentage of supervisors choose directive control (Thobega & Miller, 2007), yet this chapter tells us that many supervisors use directive control supervision on a regular basis. What are some possible reasons so many supervisors say they prefer to avoid directive control behaviors, yet actually use these behaviors frequently?

3. This chapter presents guidelines for when to use directive control supervision. With those guidelines in mind, think of a situation in which a supervisor's use of directive control was appropriate. What was

the teacher's or group's reaction? Think of a situation in which a supervisor's use of directive control was inappropriate. What was the teacher's or group's reaction?

4. If you have the opportunity to practice directive control behaviors in a role play, reflect on your feelings before, during, and after the role play. How well did you do in your effort to use directive control behaviors? After sufficient practice, would you feel comfortable using directive control supervision in an appropriate situation?

5. This chapter recommends that the supervisor move from directive control behaviors to directive informational behaviors as soon as possible. What are some indicators that a teacher initially best matched with a directive control approach is becoming ready for a shift toward directive informational supervisory behaviors? What are some ways that a supervisor can gradually shift from directive control to directive informational supervision?

The supervisor using directive control behaviors takes over the teacher's problem. The supervisor, who has identified the problem through observing the teacher and gathering other information on the teacher's performance, first describes the problem to the teacher. Next, the supervisor tells the teacher what to do to address the problem and explains how the required actions will help to solve the problem. The supervisor summarizes what is expected and describes a follow-up to determine if expectations are met. The teacher leaves the conference with a concrete plan for solving the problem. The supervisor using the directive control approach is assertive but not adversarial. (Regarding assertiveness, see Alberti & Emmons, 2008; Townsend, 2007. For more on the supervisor combining compassion and assertiveness, see Seco & Lopes, 2014.) Directive control supervision is not intended to humiliate or punish the teacher, but to provide straightforward, concrete assistance to a teacher who is experiencing serious difficulty.

Characteristics of Teachers Best Matched with Directive Control Behaviors

Based on the research on adult and teacher development reviewed in Chapter 4 as well as supervisors' descriptions of teachers at various developmental levels, we provide descriptions (in this chapter and the next three chapters) of dispositions and behaviors of teachers best matched with directive control, directive informational, collaborative, and nondirective supervision. Characteristics of the teacher best matched with directive control behaviors include the following:

- **Personality Profile:** Fearful, dependent, impulsive, defensive, with dichotomous thinking (sees things in "black and white").

- **Attitude Toward and Relationship with Students:** Does not recognize diversity among students; stereotypes students; maintains rigid relationships with students; believes students should work quietly; rewards student conformity.

- **Attitude Toward Rules:** Rule bound; becomes upset if school rules are not clear and strictly enforced; focused on the letter rather than the spirit of rules; presents classroom rules to students without explanation; takes a punitive approach to students who break the rules; despite the focus on rules, may apply rules inconsistently.

- **Teaching Style:** Believes that the purpose of teaching is to transmit knowledge; lessons are routinized, consisting of a limited number of instructional methods such as lecture, asking questions with short answers, and assigning worksheets.

- **Classroom Atmosphere:** An impersonal, rigid atmosphere characterized by passive learning leading to student boredom that may—despite the teacher's rule orientation—lead to student misbehavior, and eventually rebellion; considers the dominant culture as the appropriate classroom culture, which may lead to cultural clashes.

- **Decision Making:** Has a low tolerance for ambiguity; wishes to quickly arrive at the "one correct" answer; issues involved in the decision are viewed in black and white; individual decisions are made with limited information; when part of a group of teachers involved in decision making, may enlist an authority in order to quickly arrive at the correct decision.

- **Problem Solving:** Typically blames students or parents for the problem; continues to respond to the problem in the same way even though the response repeatedly fails; after repeated failures, may begin to ignore the problem and deny its negative effects; when asked to discuss the problem, becomes defensive; when asked to consider the underlying causes of the problem or alternative solutions, is unable to do so.

- **Response to Needed Change:** Denies the need for change, avoids involvement in the change process, and ignores the change as long as possible.

- **Relationship with Other Educators:** Avoids collaborative work as much as possible; generally rejects constructive feedback or offers of assistance from peers; may request assistance from a trusted colleague or the supervisor.

Directive Control Sequence of Behaviors

As we look at a typical sequence of behaviors along the supervisory behavior continuum (Figure 7.1), keep in mind that the sequence and frequency of behaviors will vary, especially in the beginning of the conference, but the directive control approach will end with the supervisor making the final decisions for the teacher.

1. **Presenting:** *Identifying the problem.* The supervisor begins with a general idea of what the needs and difficulties are. Having used observations and gathered information from other sources, the supervisor tells the teacher what seems to be the problem: "I understand that there is a problem with . . . "

2. **Clarifying:** *Asking the teacher for input into the problem.* The supervisor wants to gather direct information from the teacher about the problem prior to the solution stage. This is done by using the teacher in an advisory capacity, asking the teacher such questions as: "How do you see the problem?" "Why do you think these conditions exist?"

3. **Listening:** *Understanding the teacher's perception of the problem.* To gather maximum information in the shortest amount of time, the supervisor must attend carefully to what the teacher says. He or she listens both to the surface messages–"Computers are a waste of time"—and to underlying messages— "I don't know how to use the software"—in formulating a complete problem.

4. **Problem Solving:** *Mentally determining the best solution.* The supervisor processes the information and thinks, "What can be done?" After considering various possibilities, he or she selects the needed actions. The supervisor should be confident of having a good, manageable solution to the problem before conveying it to the teacher.

5. **Directing:** *Stating the solution.* The supervisor tells the teacher in a matter-of-fact way what needs to be done: "I want to see you do the following . . . " The phrasing of the directive is important. Avoid tentative suggestions: "Well, maybe you might consider doing . . . " "Don't you think it would be a good idea to . . . ?" The supervisor is not asking the teacher but *telling*. On the other hand, directing does not mean being vindictive, overbearing, condescending, or insulting. Avoid personal slights or paternalistic references: "I don't know why you can't figure out what needs to be done." "Why can't you get it right in the first place?" "Now listen, honey, I'm going to help you by . . . " A supervisor should state actions as *I* statements, not as what others think. Tell the teacher what *I* want to happen, not what parents, other teachers, or the superintendent would want to have happen. A statement such as, "If the superintendent saw this, he would tell you to do . . . ," is hiding behind someone else's authority. The supervisor needs to make statements based on his or her own position, credibility, and authority.

6. **Clarifying:** *Asking the teacher for input into the solution.* Possible difficulties with the supervisor's directive should be known before the teacher leaves the conference. For example, if circumstances exist that make teacher compliance with the directive impossible, it is better to adjust to those circumstances during the conference than to find out two weeks later why the plan failed. Therefore, after telling the teacher what is expected—"I want one-third of your students

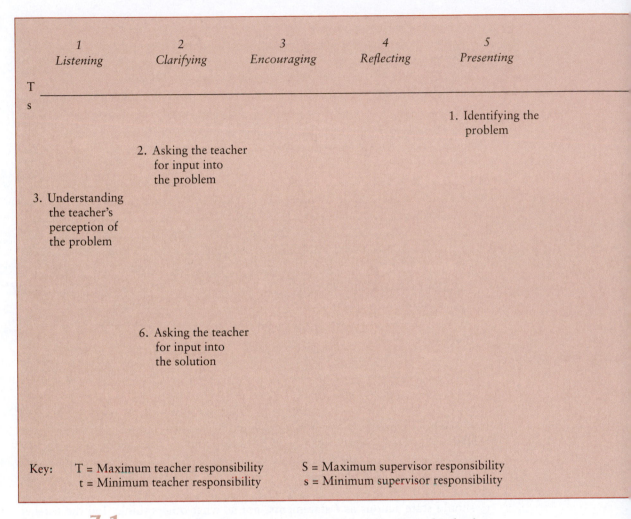

1	2	3	4	5
Listening	*Clarifying*	*Encouraging*	*Reflecting*	*Presenting*

T

s

1. Identifying the problem

2. Asking the teacher for input into the problem

3. Understanding the teacher's perception of the problem

6. Asking the teacher for input into the solution

Key: T = Maximum teacher responsibility   S = Maximum supervisor responsibility
        t = Minimum teacher responsibility   s = Minimum supervisor responsibility

f i g u r e **7.1** **The Supervisory Behavior Continuum: Directive Control Behaviors**

using the software program"—the supervisor needs to ask such questions as "What do you need to carry out this plan?" and "How can I help you carry out the plan?"

7. **Standardizing:** *Modifying and detailing expectations.* After considering the teacher's reactions to the directive, the supervisor solidifies the plan by building in the necessary assistance, resources, time lines, and criteria for expected success. The teacher is then told the revisions: "I can rearrange the visit time to . . . "

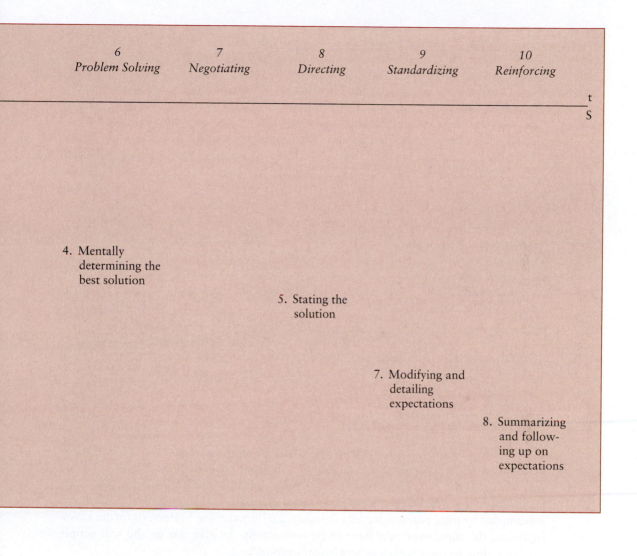

6	7	8	9	10
Problem Solving	*Negotiating*	*Directing*	*Standardizing*	*Reinforcing*

t

S

4. Mentally determining the best solution

5. Stating the solution

7. Modifying and detailing expectations

8. Summarizing and follow- ing up on expectations

"I will find those materials for you," "I will arrange for you to attend . . . " "I will change the time to three weeks."

8. **Reinforcing:** *Summarizing and following up on expectations.* The supervisor reviews the entire plan and establishes times for checking on progress. The supervisor closes the meeting by making sure the teacher clearly understands the plan: "Do you understand what you're to do?" "Tell me what it is you're now going to do."

A History of Overreliance on Control

Historically, control has been used by supervisors as a first rather than last resort. The tradition has been to rely on controlling behaviors with all teachers in all situations (Gordon, 1992; Harpaz, 2005). At times, this has been done by tying supervision to summative evaluation systems requiring certain teaching behaviors. At other times, social pressure has been applied to force teachers to conform to generic research-based teaching methods. (The research cited during such efforts often has been misinterpreted and oversimplified.) Even worse, some supervisors wishing to reduce teacher resistance have combined control and manipulation, hoping to convince teachers that they have participated in a decision when in fact the supervisor knew all along what the decision would be.

We strongly disagree with supervisors using directive control behaviors with all teachers and in all situations. We also oppose using directive control behaviors indefinitely. Finally, in all cases, we oppose control through *manipulation*. Although we admit that directive control is necessary with some teachers and groups in some situations, we believe that it should be used only when no other supervisory approach is feasible. When using a directive control approach with a teacher or group, the supervisor should be ready to move away from directive control toward noncontrolling behaviors as soon as possible.

Issues in Directive Control

Two of three major issues with using directive control behaviors have already been mentioned. One has to do with being forthright; the other, with control as a rare and temporary approach. The third issue is a consideration of time, which includes the need for directive control in response to emergencies. When the flow of school life is interrupted by irate parents, student defiance, malfunctioning heaters, or media investigations, the supervisor may have to be unilaterally decisive. He or she will simply not have time to meet with teachers before responding.

For example, a middle school principal was called at home by a newspaper reporter who sought her reaction to a fire marshal's report about unsafe cardboard partitions in a classroom of her school. The principal, totally unaware of the marshal's visit, refused comment and called the fire marshal to confirm the report. The marshal told her that all cardboard in classrooms was to be removed by the following morning. Deciding not to fight the fire marshal's orders and thus to avoid further newspaper attention, the principal told each teacher arriving at school the next morning of the fire marshal's report and told them to have their rooms cleared of all cardboard partitions before 10 a.m. She also informed them that they would meet later that afternoon to discuss the fire marshal's ruling and determine whether they wanted to appeal it. For the moment, she had used her own judgment. Later, when there was time to review the matter, she and the staff decided collaboratively to meet with the marshal about a proposal to reinstall cardboard partitions covered with fire-resistant plastic.

When to Use Directive Control Behaviors

Since directive behaviors raise issues of power, respect, expertise, and line and staff relationships, the following guidelines are given with caution. Directive control behaviors should be employed in these instances:

1. When the teacher is functioning at very low developmental level, as indicated by the characteristics described earlier, the directive control approach is appropriate.

2. When the teacher does not have awareness, knowledge, or inclination to act on an issue that a supervisor, who has organizational authority, thinks to be of critical importance to the students, the teacher, or the community, then the directive control approach should most likely be used.

3. When the teacher will have no involvement and the supervisor will be involved in carrying out the decision, and if the supervisor will be held totally accountable and the teacher will not, then the directive control approach should probably be used.

4. When the supervisor is committed to resolving the issue and the teacher is not, and when decisions do not concern the teacher, who prefers that the supervisor make the decision, the directive control approach should most likely be used.

5. In an emergency, when the supervisor does not have time to meet with the teacher, the directive control approach should be used.

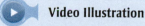 **Video Illustration**

This video is about a principal who took a directive control approach in her efforts to reform a school. As you watch the video, reflect on whether the directive control approach was necessary in the situation described.

---

role play **7.1**

Practicing Directive Control Behaviors

Directions: The class splits into groups of three. Using the teacher description and situation provided next, one member of each group assumes the role of the teacher, one member assumes the role of supervisor, and one member becomes the observer. The "supervisor" and "teacher" role play a conference in which the supervisor uses a directive control approach to address the teacher's instructional problem. The observer takes notes on the supervisor's performance during the conference and shares those notes with the other two group members after the role play. Finally, all three participants engage in reflective discussion of the role play and the directive control approach. (To assist in the role plays in Chapters 7 through 10, see Appendix B, which reviews and compares all four supervisory approaches.)

Teacher Description and Situation:
Middle school teacher Ben Crash has been overheard by the supervisor and other

teachers yelling at his students as he tries to gain control of his class. Each time he yells at his students to "quiet down" or "go to your seats," they seem to get more out of control. Even to those in other classrooms or walking down the hall, it is apparent that Ben frequently loses control over his classes. As he loses control, he becomes louder and louder and begins to use abusive language with his students, telling them to "shut up" or to "quit acting like morons." Teachers and parents have complained about the way Ben yells at his students. Teachers on Ben's instructional team have told the supervisor that they believe the root of his problem is that he gives students contradictory and confusing directions when he is trying to start a new learning activity. During a recent classroom observation, the supervisor observed that Ben did indeed give contradictory directions that confused and frustrated students.

Moving from Directive Control Toward Directive Informational Behaviors

In long-term supervisory situations and relationships, the supervisor should begin to shift from a directive control to a directive informational approach as soon as possible. Stabilizing an unstable situation or giving a teacher or group intensive support will tend to foster limited professional growth. Such growth is likely to continue only if the supervisor then begins to give the teacher or group limited opportunities to make decisions and assume some responsibility.

One way to do this is to begin to allow the teacher or the group *restricted choice*. For example, the supervisor might mandate an instructional improvement goal and then allow the teacher or group to choose from two or three clearly defined alternatives for meeting the goal. By doing this, the supervisor has begun movement toward directive informational supervision—an approach that is discussed in detail in the next chapter.

> ✔ **Check Your Understanding 7.0**   Click here to gauge your understanding of the key concepts presented in this chapter.

REFLECTIVE EXERCISE

Assume you have recently attended a seminar at which a visiting professor argued against instructional supervisors using the directive control approach with any teacher. The professor proposed that the supervisor should play the role of a helper, not attempt to control a teacher's behaviors. The speaker argued that successful change cannot be brought about unless the teacher perceives the need for change and has had a part in deciding how to bring about the needed change. He concluded that a directive control supervisory approach will only alienate teachers and make supervisors unwelcome in many classrooms. You have been asked to reply to the professor's argument at an upcoming seminar. What position will you take regarding the use of directive control supervision? What arguments will you use to support your position?

chapter 8

Directive Informational Behaviors

Learning Outcomes for This Chapter

After reading this chapter, you should be able to:

1. Summarize any of the characteristics of teachers best matched with a directive informational approach.
2. Explain any of the 10 categories of the supervisory behavior continuum as applied to the directive informational approach.
3. Recall the authors' analogies for directive control and directive informational statements.
4. List two issues in the directive informational approach.
5. Identify situations where use of the directive informational approach is advisable.
6. Describe a specific way to move from a directive informational to a collaborative approach.

Questions to Reflect On as You Read This Chapter

1. Directive informational supervision relies in large part on the supervisor providing information rather than prescription as the impetus for the teacher changing instructional behaviors. Do you believe that information without control can be a catalyst for teachers committing to change their instruction? If so, what are some types of information that could cause a teacher to commit to change?
2. Both directive control supervision and directive informational supervision use the same seven behaviors. Which behaviors are applied differently in the directive informational compared to the directive control approach, and how are they applied differently?
3. As you read about the supervisory behaviors used in the directive informational approach, which behaviors would you like to discuss or see demonstrated before you practice directive informational behaviors in a role play?

4. When teachers view videos of the same supervisor using the directive control approach in one post-observation conference and the directive informational approach in a different postobservation conference on the same lesson, they rate the directive informational supervision much higher. What do you believe is responsible for such results?

5. If you have the opportunity to practice directive informational behaviors in a role play, reflect on your feelings before, during, and after the role play. How well did you do in your effort to use directive informational behaviors? How does practicing directive informational behaviors compare to practicing directive control behaviors? After sufficient practice, would you feel comfortable using directive informational supervision in an appropriate situation?

The supervisor using a directive informational approach acts as the information source for the goal and activities of the improvement plan. The supervisor, based on observations, suggests a clear instructional improvement goal and discusses with the teacher alternative activities for reaching that goal. Through each step of the conference the supervisor remains the information source but always asks for and considers teacher perceptions.

In some situations, a teacher may not be experiencing any obvious problems with organizing or delivering lessons but may be teaching content or using methods that are inconsistent with the school's collective decisions about curriculum and instruction. In such cases, the supervisor shares information illustrating incongruence between the teacher's instruction and the school's vision, mission, core values, or curriculum (see Palandra, 2010; Sommers, 2009) and the goal of the conference becomes a plan for making the teacher's instruction consistent with schoolwide agreements.

> **▶ Video Illustration**
>
> The coach in this video is using a directive informational supervisory approach. Compare the approach the coach is using with the directive control approach that was described in the last chapter.

Characteristics of Teachers Best Matched with Directive Informational Behaviors

Characteristics of the teacher best matched with directive informational behaviors include the following:

Personality Profile: Beginning to emerge from dichotomous thinking and external control, but uncertain about how to improve and inconsistent in improvement efforts.

Attitude Toward and Relationship with Students: Beginning to move away from rigidity to understand that students are diverse and have diverse needs, but does not know how to differentiate instruction to meet those diverse needs.

Attitude Toward Rules: Less rule-bound than teachers of lowest developmental level, realizing that sometimes the situation should determine whether a rule should be followed, but sometimes has difficulty assessing the situation to determine whether a rule should be applied.

Teaching Style: Uses primarily teacher-centered methods but student learning is not entirely rote; for example, may allow the student to expand on an answer to a teacher question; open to new models of teaching but wants to be told how to implement those models; has trouble matching different models of teaching to learning outcomes; has difficulty applying new models to content and students.

Classroom Atmosphere: Not satisfied with passive or unengaged learners, but unable to articulate ways of changing the classroom atmosphere.

Decision Making: Willing to consider alternatives, but has difficulty envisioning those alternatives; can decide between two or three alternatives that are presented, but is overwhelmed when presented with a large number of alternatives.

Problem Solving: Blames a wide variety of external factors for classroom or student learning problems, such as the students, parents, computer games, television, previous teachers, poverty, a permissive society, and so on, but does not associate problems with her or his instruction; is willing to consider alternative solutions when initial efforts to solve a problem have failed, but has difficulty generating alternatives.

Change: Is concerned with personal effects of anticipated or recently initiated change (e.g., How will the change affect the teacher's time, work demands, instruction, and so on? What will be the teacher's responsibilities concerning the change? Does the teacher have the capacity to successfully adopt the change? Will the teacher be provided sufficient assistance to adopt the change?).

Relationships with Other Educators: Desires and accepts guidance from the supervisor and other teachers.

Directive Informational Sequence of Behaviors

In the directive informational approach, once the problem to be addressed has been presented and discussed, the supervisor provides a range of alternatives from which the teacher is asked to choose. The idea of choice is critical to the directive informational approach. The more self-determined teachers are, the greater their sense of accomplishment and the greater their students' self-determination (Roth, Assor, Kanat-Maymon, & Kaplan, 2007). Therefore, self-determination is to be fostered to the extent possible considering the teacher's level of development (Jasen in de Wal, den Brok, Hooijer, Martens, & van den Beemt, 2014) On the one hand, teachers best matched with a directive informational approach are not yet cognitively ready or motivated to solve complex instructional problems; on the other hand, teachers at this developmental level have the ability to choose from concrete alternatives for solving a clearly stated problem.

After the teacher chooses from alternative solutions, the supervisor and teacher establish the specifics of the action and follow-up plans. In each phase of the conference the supervisor provides information and offers viable options for the teacher to choose from. The sequence of directive informational behaviors (displayed in Figure 8.1) follows:

1. **Presenting:** *Identifying the problem.* Based on observations and previous experience the supervisor has with the teacher, the supervisor begins by reviewing his or her summarized observations.

2. **Clarifying:** *Asking the teacher for input into the problem.* The supervisor is careful not to move too quickly into a planning phase until checking to see what the teacher thinks of his or her interpretation of the problem.

3. **Listening:** *Understanding the teacher's perception of the problem.* The supervisor listens to determine if the teacher accepts the problem and improvement goal as important or if further explanation is required.

4. **Problem Solving:** *Mentally determining possible solutions.* The supervisor has given thought to some alternative solutions that might be considered by the teacher. When the teacher shares his or her perceptions of the problem, the supervisor mentally prepares to lay out the alternative solutions.

5. **Directing:** *Stating alternatives for the teacher to consider.* The supervisor carefully words the alternative solutions as possibilities, based on personal experience and knowledge, for the teacher to judge, consider, and respond to.

6. **Listening:** *Asking the teacher for input on the alternatives.* The supervisor asks the teacher to react to his or her suggestions. The teacher has the opportunity now to give the supervisor information to modify, eliminate, and revise before finalizing the choices.

7. **Directing:** *Framing the final choices.* In a straightforward manner, the supervisor lays out a final set of alternatives to choose from.

8. **Clarifying:** *Asking the teacher to choose.* The supervisor asks the teacher to decide and clarify which solutions or combinations he or she will use.

9. **Standardizing:** *Stating the specific actions to be taken.* At this juncture, the supervisor assists the teacher in developing a specific action plan to implement

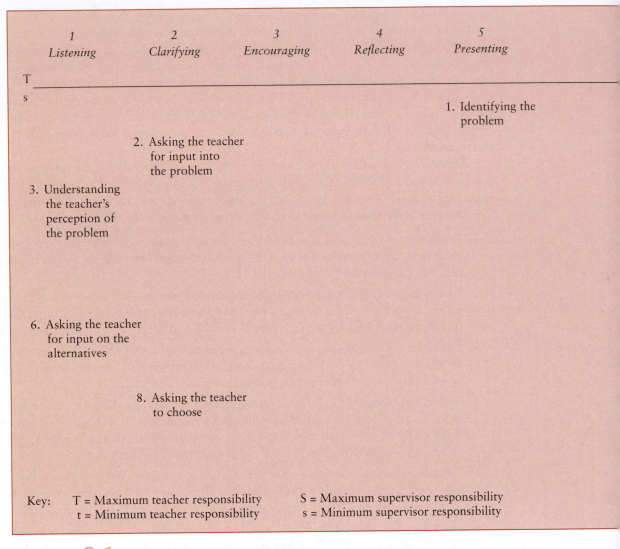

f i g u r e **8.1** **The Supervisory Behavior Continuum: Directive Informational Behaviors**

the chosen solution. The supervisor suggests alternative specific actions and criteria for success, and the teacher chooses from those alternatives.

10. **Reinforcing:** *Summarizing and following up on the plan.* The supervisor concludes the conference by restating the goal, the actions to be taken, the criteria for success, and the time for the next observation and/or conference.

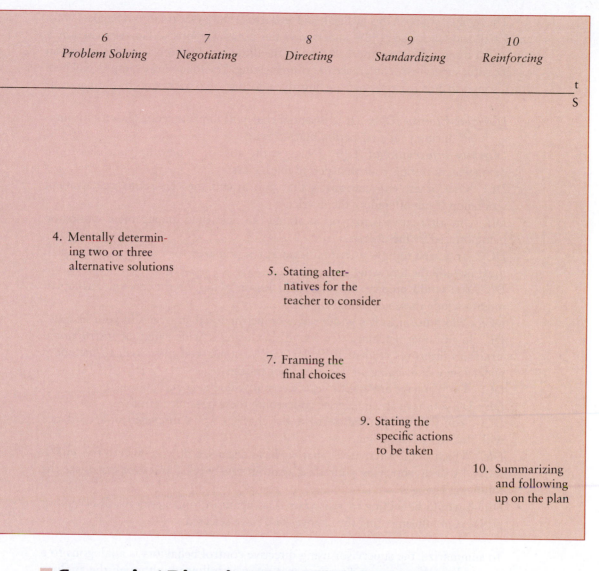

6	7	8	9	10
Problem Solving	*Negotiating*	*Directing*	*Standardizing*	*Reinforcing*

t

S

4. Mentally determin-
   ing two or three
   alternative solutions

5. Stating alter-
   natives for the
   teacher to consider

7. Framing the
   final choices

9. Stating the
   specific actions
   to be taken

10. Summarizing
    and following
    up on the plan

Comparing Directive Control and Directive Informational Statements

Students in supervision courses using this text often have difficulty distinguishing between directive control and directive informational behaviors, especially when practicing the different behaviors during role plays. This is not surprising, since there is often a thin line between controlling and informational language; and yet, that thin line is a critical one.

The seminal work on this by Pajak and Seyfarth (1983), Glickman and Pajak (1986), and Pajak and Glickman (1989) underscores this point. The precise language used by a supervisor using a directive approach can be the difference between a successful and an unsuccessful supervisory conference or group meeting. The following examples will help you distinguish directive control from directive informational statements by a supervisor:

Directive Control (DC): It is essential that you improve your classroom management during your first-period math class.

Directive Informational (DI): I suggest the goal of improving your classroom management during your first-period math class.

DC: One of my expectations is that you attend the classroom management workshop being offered by the district.

DI: One alternative is for you to attend the classroom management workshop being offered by the district.

DC: You need to have a written lesson plan prepared for each class. Each plan must include the following elements . . .

DI: You could prepare more detailed lesson plans for this group. Each plan might include these additional elements . . .

DC: You must include a wider range of instructional strategies in your lessons.

DI: In my own teaching, I've found that using a wide range of instructional strategies improves student behavior and learning. You may wish to include a wider range of teaching strategies in your lessons.

DC: Do you have any questions concerning these new expectations?

DI: Do you have any questions concerning these possible actions?

DC: You will be required to make the changes we've discussed in accordance with this written time line.

DI: Which of the alternatives that we have discussed do you wish to try out?

DC: I will be observing your class again in four weeks, and I expect to see the following changes . . .

DI: I would be willing to visit your class again in four weeks to observe your progress in implementing the changes you have selected.

To summarize, the supervisor using directive control behaviors is analogous to a judge or police officer giving directives that must be followed (although the analogy eventually breaks down because we know of no district where teachers go directly to jail for failing to follow a supervisor's suggestions for instructional improvement!). On the other hand, the supervisor using directive informational behaviors can be compared to a physician or attorney giving expert advice to a patient or client. The person receiving the advice does not have to follow it, but if he or she respects the expertise of the professional giving the advice, he or she will probably conclude that it is wise to act on the professional's suggestions (if you begin to compare the salaries of physicians or attorneys with instructional supervisors, once again our analogy falls apart, but we've made our point!).

Issues in the Directive Informational Approach

Anyone who uses a directive informational approach needs to be aware of his or her degree of expertise when delineating the choices available to others. Since the supervisor is placing oneself in the role of expert, the issues of confidence and credibility are crucial. The supervisor must be confident that he or she knows what practices will work in helping the teacher, because when the teacher chooses to use one or more of the supervisor's suggestions, the person ultimately responsible for the success or failure of the various practices will be the supervisor, not the teacher. After all, if I consider and select from your proposed actions, implement what you've suggested, and those actions don't work, I'm probably going to tell you the next time we meet, when we note that the goal is no closer to being achieved, "After all, I just did what you told me to do!"

The teacher is correct in holding the supervisor accountable for the results. Thus, the issue of credibility hovers above the directive informational approach. Not only must the supervisor be confident that her or his own knowledge and experience are superior to and different from those of the teacher, but the teacher must also believe that the supervisor possesses a source of wisdom that he or she does not have. When confidence and credibility in the supervisor's knowledge are shared by both parties and the teacher is either unaware, inexperienced, or stumped about what changes can be made, then the directive informational approach can be a most valuable set of behaviors to use.

When we begin on a path where we have not ventured before, we can learn a lot from a person who has explored that trail successfully many times in the past. This might be the reason why directive informational approaches are seen as most helpful to teachers when they are inexperienced, confused, unaware, or simply at a loss for what to do about a particular classroom or school goal. Finally, with a directive informational approach, it is imperative to remember that the teacher exercises some control in choosing which practice(s) to use. (This is not the case when we look at the directive control approach.)

When to Use Directive Informational Behaviors

Directive informational behaviors should be employed under the following circumstances:

1. When the teacher is functioning at a moderately low developmental level.
2. When the teacher does not possess the knowledge about an issue that the supervisor clearly possesses.
3. When the teacher feels confused, inexperienced, or is at a loss for what to do, and the supervisor knows of successful practices.
4. When the supervisor is willing to take responsibility for what the teacher chooses to try.

5. When the teacher believes that the supervisor is credible—a person who has the background and wisdom to know whereof he or she speaks.

6. When the time is short, the constraints are clear, and quick, concrete actions need to be taken.

Moving from Directive Informational Toward Collaborative Behaviors

In directive informational supervision, the teacher or group is given some choice but the supervisor still assumes *primary* decision-making responsibility. In the collaborative approach, the teacher and supervisor share decision-making responsibility

---

role play **8.1**

Practicing Directive Informational Behaviors

Directions: The class splits into groups of three. Using the teacher description and situation provided next, one member of each group assumes the role of the teacher, one member assumes the role of the supervisor, and one member assumes the role of observer. The "supervisor" and "teacher" role play a conference in which the supervisor uses a directive informational approach to address the teacher's instructional problem. The observer takes notes on the supervisor's performance during the conference and shares those notes with the other two group members after the role play. Finally, all three participants engage in reflective discussion of the role play and the directive informational approach. (To assist in the role plays in Chapters 7 through 10, see Appendix B, which reviews and compares all four supervisory approaches.)

Teacher Description and Situation: High school teacher Norma Watson, who is White, has seen the demographics of

her eleventh-grade social studies classes change dramatically over the last several years. The number of Latino students in the eleventh grade has gradually shifted from what used to be a small minority to 65%. Although Norma is well meaning, she has found it difficult to relate to a number of her Latino students. The same lectures that used to captivate most of her students no longer capture students' attention. Many of Norma's Latino students have complained to other teachers and to the principal that Norma's lectures are boring and never include a Latino perspective. For the first time in her career, Norma has drawn complaints from both Latino and other parents about her lack of classroom management. Norma realizes she has a problem. She wishes to make the lessons more relevant to her Latino students and to recapture the classroom management that she once had, but she is at a loss as to how to do these things.

equally. Movement from directive informational to collaborative is thus a matter of degree. The supervisor might begin that movement by suggesting an instructional improvement goal, asking the teacher or group to suggest one or two activities for moving toward the goal, and then suggesting a detailed action plan incorporating some of the teacher's proposed actions. Hopefully, the supervisor eventually will be able to enter a fully collaborative relationship with the teacher.

> ✔ **Check Your Understanding 8.0**   Click here to gauge your understanding of the key concepts presented in this chapter.

REFLECTIVE EXERCISE

Reflect on what you would do as a supervisor if you worked with a teacher who always wanted you to use the directive informational approach with him. This experienced teacher is quite comfortable in the classroom and when asked can clearly articulate concerns for his students and the school. Yet, unlike his peers, who prefer the collaborative or nondirective approach, this teacher favors being given a choice from your suggestions. Do you feel you should continue using the directive informational approach with this teacher or try to move the teacher toward collaborative supervision? What is the rationale for your decision?

chapter 9

Collaborative Behaviors

Learning Outcomes for this Chapter

After reading this chapter, you should be able to:

1. Summarize any of the characteristics of teachers best matched with a collaborative approach.
2. Explain any of the 10 categories of the supervisory behavior continuum as applied to the collaborative approach.
3. List two issues in the use of the collaborative approach.
4. Identify circumstances in which the collaborative approach is desirable.
5. Describe a specific way recommended in the chapter for moving from the collaborative to the nondirective approach.

Questions to Reflect On as You Read This Chapter

1. Both the teacher and supervisor participating in a collaborative conference discuss their perception of the problem, but the supervisor asks the teacher to share first. What are the advantages of the teacher sharing first?
2. Is it possible for a supervisor to implement the collaborative approach in a manner that is technically correct but still does not engage in authentic collaboration? If so, how might this occur?
3. As you read about the supervisory behaviors in the collaborative approach, which behaviors would you like to discuss or see demonstrated before you practice collaborative behaviors?
4. How could a new supervisor working with teachers who are best matched with a collaborative approach, but who have only experienced directive supervision, introduce collaborative supervision to those teachers?
5. If you have an opportunity to practice collaborative behaviors in a role play, reflect on your feelings before, during, and after the role play. How well did you do in your effort to use collaborative behaviors? Would you feel comfortable, after sufficient practice, using collaborative supervision in an appropriate situation?

The supervisor using collaborative behaviors wishes to resolve a problem that is shared equally with the teacher. The supervisor encourages the teacher to present his or her own perceptions and ideas. Yet the supervisor also honestly gives his or her own views. The result is a frank exchange of ideas. Both participants know they will have to agree on any course of action. In fact, when disagreement becomes obvious, the supervisor restates the disagreement and reassures the teacher that they will have to find a mutual solution. Disagreement is encouraged, not suppressed. As the conversation continues, when openings for possible agreements become apparent, the supervisor steers the conversation toward those ends. Finally, the teacher and supervisor either agree to an action or wind up stalemated. A stalemate will mean further negotiating, rethinking, and even the possible use of a third-party mediator or arbitrator.

Characteristics of Teachers Best Matched with Collaborative Behaviors

Characteristics of the teacher best matched with collaborative behaviors include the following:

Personality Profile: More objective than teachers at lower developmental levels; concerned with social relationships and social norms; moving toward independence.

Attitude Toward and Relationship with Students: Friendlier to students than teachers at lower developmental levels; accepts a wider range of student behaviors as acceptable; recognizes diverse student needs but requires assistance in addressing some needs.

Attitude Toward Rules: Believes that rules should be mutually agreed upon; believes in a distribution of internal and external control; explains reasons for rules to students; usually knows when to apply rules and when to ignore rules.

Teaching Style: Focused on doing a good job of teaching the required curriculum; able to use several different models of teaching effectively, but has not mastered the use of a wide range of models; more likely than teachers at lower developmental levels to differentiate between more and less important content; encourages students to express themselves, and adjusts teaching based on student reaction; willing to ask students higher-level questions, but may need assistance in formulating such questions.

Classroom Climate: More concerned with relationships between teacher and students and among students than teachers at lower developmental levels; beginning to acknowledge student inquisitiveness and creativity.

Decision Making: Becoming tolerant of ambiguity during the decision-making process; gathers a wider variety of information than teachers of lower developmental levels, but may have difficulty integrating that information; in group decision making, prefers a consensus and is willing to implement a group decision once it is made.

Problem Solving: More analytical than teachers at lower developmental levels; is able to recognize and define a classroom problem and identify some possible solutions, but is not able to identify the full range of alternative solutions; unlike teachers of lower developmental levels, accepts a fair amount of responsibility for classroom problems.

Change: Will accept the need for change if it is agreed upon by the group; is primarily concerned with the technical implementation of the change (skills needed, tasks to be accomplished); prefers formal professional development and assistance from colleagues in learning how to implement the change.

Relationships with Others: Wants positive relationships with supervisors and teachers; tends to be a "team player"; willing to listen to others' points of views and critiques, but also appreciates the opportunity to share own perspectives and ideas; believes in mutual responsibility for completing tasks and achieving goals.

Collaborative Sequence of Behaviors

Figure 9.1 shows a prototype of collaborative behaviors according to the supervisory behavior continuum. A conference between supervisor and teacher begins with an understanding of each other's identification of the problem and concludes with mutual agreement on the final plan. The reader should think of the supervisory behaviors as a piano keyboard, with the musician beginning by hitting the keys on the left, then playing the keys back and forth, and culminating by hitting the middle key—negotiating. Here are the 10 behaviors involved:

1. **Clarifying:** *Identifying the problem as seen by the teacher.* First, ask the teacher about the immediate problem or concern: "Please tell me what is bothering you." "Explain to me what you see as the greatest concern."
2. **Listening:** *Understanding the teacher's perception of the problem.* You (the supervisor) want to have as much information about the problem as possible before thinking about action. Therefore, when the teacher narrates his or her perceptions, the full range of nondirective behaviors should be used (eye contact, paraphrasing, asking probing questions, and being willing to allow the teacher to continue talking): "Tell me more." "Uh huh, I'm following you." "Do you mean . . . ?"

3. **Reflecting:** *Verifying the teacher's perception of the problem.* When the teacher has completed his or her description of the problem, check for accuracy by summarizing the teacher's statements and asking if the summary is accurate: "I understand that you see the problem as . . . Is this accurate?"

4. **Presenting:** *Providing the supervisor's perception of the problem.* Until this point, we have seen an abbreviated nondirective conference. Instead of asking the teacher to begin thinking of his or her own possible actions, however, you now move in and become part of the decision-making process. Give your own point of view about the current difficulty and fill in any information about the situation of which the teacher might be unaware: "I see the situation in this way." "The problem, as I see it, is . . . " (To minimize influencing the teacher's position, it is better for you to give your perceptions only after the teacher has given his or hers.)

5. **Clarifying:** *Seeking the teacher's understanding of the supervisor's perception of the problem.* In the same way that you paraphrased the teacher's statement of the problem and asked for verification, you now ask the teacher to do likewise: "Could you repeat what you think I'm trying to say?" Once you feel confident that the teacher understands your views, problem solving can begin.

6. **Problem Solving:** *Exchanging possible solutions.* If you and the teacher are familiar with each other and have worked collaboratively before, you can simply ask for a list of suggestions: "Let's both think about what might be done to improve this situation." Then listen to each other's ideas. If the teacher is not familiar with you or with the collaborative process, however, he or she may feel apprehensive about suggesting an idea that is different from the supervisor's. It might be better to stop the conference for a few minutes and have both supervisor and teacher write down possible actions before speaking: "So that we don't influence each other on possible solutions, let's take the next few minutes and write down what actions might be taken and then read each other's list." Obviously, once actions are in writing, they will not change according to what the other person has written. You the supervisor, therefore, have promoted a spectrum of personal ideas that are ready to be shared and discussed.

7. **Encouraging:** *Accepting conflict.* To keep the conference from turning into a competitive struggle, you need to reassure the teacher that disagreement is acceptable and that there will be no winners or losers: "It appears that we have some different ideas on how to handle this situation. By disagreeing we will find the best solution. Remember our agreement—we both have to agree with the solution before it will take place." You must genuinely believe that conflict between two caring professionals is productive for finding the best solution.

8. **Negotiating:** *Finding an acceptable solution.* After sharing and discussing, ask if there are suggestions common to both—"Where do we agree?"—and if there are suggestions markedly different—"Where do we differ?" If you find agreement,

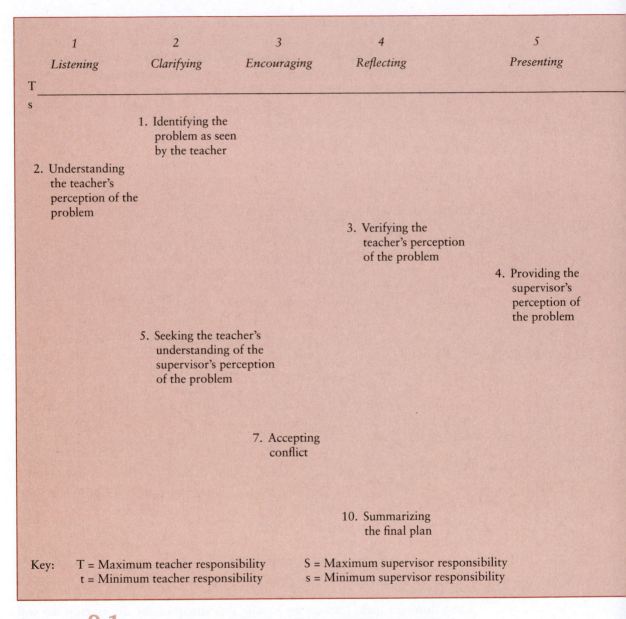

figure **9.1** **The Supervisory Behavior Continuum: Collaborative Behaviors**

then the conference proceeds. But if there is a vast difference in suggestions, then you can take four sequential actions. First, check to see whether the differences are as vast as they appear by having both yourself and the teacher explain

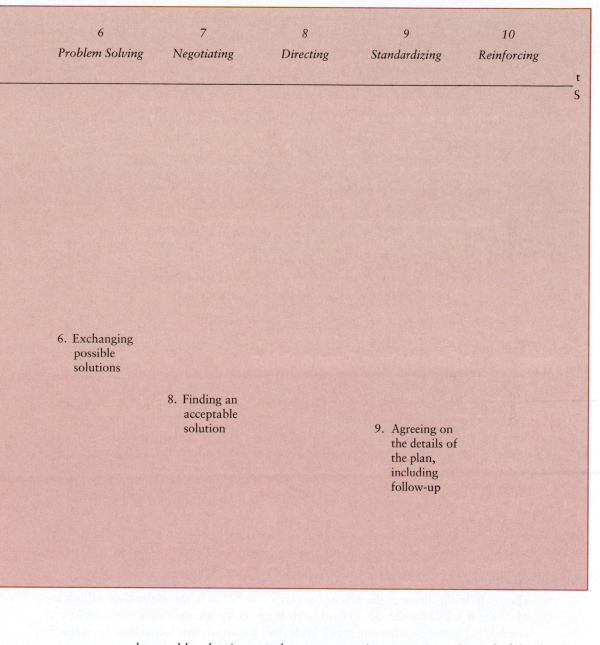

6	7	8	9	10
Problem Solving	*Negotiating*	*Directing*	*Standardizing*	*Reinforcing*

t

S

6. Exchanging
   possible
   solutions

8. Finding an
   acceptable
   solution

9. Agreeing on
   the details of
   the plan,
   including
   follow-up

thoroughly what is meant by your respective suggestions. Second, if the disagreement is still real, then find out how convinced each of you is that your suggestion be chosen: "How important is it to you that we do it your way?" If the importance of one person's suggestion is far greater than that of the other person's suggestion, then the question becomes whether one can give up his or her idea and live with the other's. Third, if grounds for agreement are not reached, you can consider a compromise: "How about if I give up this part of my suggestion and if you give up . . . " Or see if a totally new idea can be found: "Since we can't agree, let's drop our top choices for solutions and see if we can find another one."

9. **Standardizing:** *Agreeing on the details of the plan, including follow up.* Once agreement on an acceptable action has been reached, the supervisor needs to attend to the details of time, place, and follow-up. When will the plan be implemented? Where will it take place? Who will help? What resources are needed? Who will follow up? When? These details need to be discussed and agreed to so there will be a clarity and precision to the final plan.

10. **Reflecting:** *Summarizing the final plan.* The supervisor concludes the conference by checking that both parties agree to the action and details. The supervisor might do this verbally—"Could you repeat what you understand the plan to be and then I'll repeat my understanding"—or in writing—"Let's write this down together so that we are clear on what we've agreed to do."

Issues in Collaborative Supervision

Our work with collaboration has shown that it is a deceptively simple set of behaviors for supervisors to understand. The reason is that collaboration appears to be the democratic way of doing things. Most of us have been schooled in equality and democracy, and collaboration appears to be democracy in action. Therefore, it seems apparent that we should ask others for input and that decisions should be made by the majority. However, collaboration with an individual or a group involves more than the mechanical procedures of majority rule associated with a common (and incorrect) view of democracy.

One difficulty in working collaboratively occurs when the teacher (or group) believes a supervisor is manipulating the decision when in fact he or she is not. The teacher appears to concur with the supervisor's ideas and suggestions not because of their merit but because the teacher believes the supervisor is really giving a directive. The underlying message the teacher perceives is "This is my supervisor telling me what she thinks I should do. Even though she says we are making a joint decision, I know I had better do what she says." How does the supervisor know whether a teacher's agreement is sincere or mere compliance? The supervisor might confront the issue by asking the teacher whether he or she is agreeing or only pretending to agree with the supervisor's idea. Acknowledging that the supervisor suspects something is amiss brings the issue out into the open. A teacher who responds "I don't believe you really are going to let me have equal say" can be dealt with more easily than is possible when a supervisor guesses at the teacher's hidden feelings.

Teachers who refuse to disclose their feelings probably have a history of being mistreated by supervisors. Until the supervisor can demonstrate consistently that he or she really means to be collaborative, no progress will be made. The teacher is not going to believe the supervisor is being collaborative until there is proof (Rousmaniere & Ellis, 2013). True intent can be demonstrated by refusing to allow decisions to be made without teacher feedback. With nonresponsive and readily acquiescing teachers, a supervisor might say: "I don't know if you're agreeing with me because you like the idea or because of some power I hold over you. We won't carry out any action unless we both agree with that action. I want to be collaborative because I believe you have as much expertise on this matter as I do. Together we can make a better decision than separately. I'm uncertain why you are agreeing with me. Please tell me what you think."

A supervisor cannot find out what a teacher thinks without asking. As they continue to meet, the supervisor should begin by encouraging teachers to offer their own thoughts about the problem and suggestions for action. The supervisor should try to withhold any ideas of his or her own. Once the teacher's ideas are forthcoming, the supervisor can offer his or her ideas. When negotiating a final decision, the supervisor should let teachers take the lead. If teachers continue to be unresponsive or overly compliant with the supervisor after he or she has confronted the issue of perception and encouraged teacher initiative, then after several unsuccessful attempts, the supervisor might consider another approach.

When to Use Collaborative Behaviors

There are circumstances in which a supervisor definitely should use collaborative behaviors. Collaborative should be used in these instances:

1. When the teacher is functioning at a moderately high or mixed developmental level.

2. When the teacher and supervisor have approximately the same degree of expertise on the issue. (If the supervisor knows part of the problem and the teacher knows the other part, the collaborative approach should be used.)

3. When the teacher and supervisor will both be involved in carrying out the decision. (If the teacher and supervisor will be held accountable for showing results to someone else—say, parents or the superintendent—then the collaborative approach should be used.)

4. When the teacher and supervisor are both committed to solving the problem (If the teacher wants to be involved and if leaving the teacher out will lead to low morale and distrust, then the collaborative approach should be used).

Moving from Collaborative Toward Nondirective Behaviors

The developmental supervisor attempts gradually to move from collaborative toward nondirective interpersonal behaviors. As the teacher or group increases expertise, problem-solving capacity, and motivation, the supervisor hands over more and more decision-making responsibility. An example of a transitional phase between the

---

role play **9.1**

Practicing Collaborative Behaviors

Directions: The class splits into groups of three. Using the following teacher description and situation, one member of each group assumes the role of the teacher, one member assumes the role of the supervisor, and one member assumes the role of observer. The "supervisor" and "teacher" role play a conference in which the supervisor uses a collaborative approach to address the teacher's instructional problem. The observer takes notes on the supervisor's performance during the conference and shares those notes with the other two group members after the role play. Finally, all three participants engage in reflective discussion of the role play and the collaborative approach. (To assist in the role plays in Chapters 7 through 10, see Appendix B, which reviews and compares all four supervisory approaches.)

Teacher Description and Situation:
Marcus Johnson is a third-grade teacher at Hopewell Elementary School. Recently, Marcus's school district eliminated art as a separate subject at the elementary level, but the district also adopted a policy calling for art to be integrated across the elementary curriculum. Marcus has been teaching at Hopewell for five years. Although he did not major in art education in college, he has taught art in his self-contained classroom since coming to Hopewell and through self-directed professional development has become a fairly competent and creative art teacher. However, up until now he has focused his twice-a-week art periods purely on art; he has not been integrating the teaching of art with other content areas. In a recent hallway conversation with his supervisor, Marcus said that he has come up with some ideas for integrating art across the curriculum but could use some help in generating additional ideas.

collaborative and nondirective approach would be to use collaborative behaviors while assisting a teacher or group to decide on an instructional improvement goal and then shift to nondirective behaviors as the teacher or group decides on actions to reach the goal. Nondirective behaviors are discussed in the following chapter.

> ✔ **Check Your Understanding 9.0**   Click here to gauge your understanding of the key concepts presented in this chapter.

REFLECTIVE EXERCISE

Assume that supervisor Pat Ramirez has recently begun to use collaborative behaviors with a group of teachers who formerly had not experienced collaborative supervision, and Pat is trying to determine whether her efforts to be collaborative are "working" with these teachers. What advice would you give Pat concerning how she can gather information on each of the following concerns?

- Whether Pat is really giving the teachers decision-making power regarding the problem to be solved
- Whether the teachers perceive the decision-making process to be collaborative
- If the individual or group accepts—and understands that Pat accepts—disagreement and constructive conflict as part of the decision-making process
- If Pat's efforts at collaborative supervision are leading to solutions acceptable to the teachers

chapter 10

Nondirective Behaviors

Learning Outcomes for This Chapter

After reading this chapter, you should be able to:

1. Summarize any of the characteristics of teachers best matched with a nondirective approach.
2. Explain any of the 10 categories of the supervisory behavior continuum as applied to the nondirective approach.
3. Describe how to initiate nondirective supervision with a hesitant teacher or group.
4. Explain the difference between nondirective and laissez-faire supervision.
5. List four issues in the use of the nondirective approach.
6. Identify situations in which the nondirective approach is desirable.

Questions to Reflect On as You Read This Chapter

1. Do you know teachers who would respond well to the nondirective approach? If so, what characteristics of these teachers would make nondirective supervision a good match?
2. As you read about the supervisory behaviors in the nondirective approach, which behaviors would you like to discuss or see demonstrated before you practice nondirective behaviors?
3. The authors state that when a teacher asks for input from a supervisor using nondirective behaviors, "Ideally, it is better to refrain completely from giving one's ideas." Do you agree with this general guideline? Why or why not? Should there be exceptions to the general guideline? If so, what exceptions?
4. What are some reasons why a teacher would initially be reluctant to engage fully with a supervisor using nondirective behaviors? How should a supervisor respond to the teacher's reluctance?

5. If you have an opportunity to practice nondirective behaviors in a role play, reflect on your feelings before, during, and after the role play. How well did you do in your effort to use nondirective behaviors? Would you feel comfortable, after sufficient practice, using nondirective supervision in an appropriate situation?

Nondirective supervision is based on the assumption that an individual teacher knows best what instructional changes need to be made and has the ability to think and act on his or her own. The decision belongs to the teacher. The role of the supervisor is to assist the teacher in the process of thinking through his or her actions.

The supervisor behaves in ways that keep the teacher's thinking focused on observation, interpretation, problem identification, and problem solving. The supervisor helps the teacher to come to his or her own conclusions. The supervisor does not interject his or her own ideas into the discussion. All verbalizations by the supervisor are intended as feedback or to extend the teacher's thinking; they do not influence the actual design of the improvement plan.

Characteristics of Teachers Best Matched with Nondirective Behaviors

Characteristics of the teacher best matched with nondirective behaviors include the following:

Personality Profile: Autonomous; altruistic, behavior based on internal values; highly reflective; highly creative; copes well with stress; resilient.

Attitude Toward and Relationship with Students: Focused on the holistic, long-term development of students; culturally responsive; seeks information on how to identify and meet individual student needs; seeks and values student perspectives.

Attitude Toward Rules: Avoids the image of authority figure; interprets rules in light of the situation, students' perspective, and impact on individuals.

Teaching Style: Student-centered; develops own classroom curriculum that envelopes the school's curriculum; uses a wide variety of teaching models effectively; encourages and assists student self-expression; reflects in and on the practice of teaching; flexible and fluid; facilitates students as they ask questions, search for answers, develop theories, test ideas, and discover relationships; asks higher-level questions that stimulate higher-order thinking.

Classroom Climate: Warm and caring; supportive; challenging; cooperative; inquiring, reflective, engaged.

Decision Making: Highly tolerant of ambiguity; gathers and integrates a variety of relevant information before making a decision; open to others' suggestions but makes own decision on individual matters; in group decision making, supports the democratic process and works for consensus.

Problem Solving: Considers underlying causes before considering solutions; identifies and assesses a variety of possible solutions; relies on personal values to guide the problem-solving process; assumes full responsibility for individual decisions; in problems involving others, considers others' points of views and the effects of potential solutions on others; willing to compromise, but will not violate personal values.

Change: A leader in identifying and articulating the need for change; concerned about the impact of change on colleagues and students; assists others to implement change; helps to modify the change when necessary.

Relationships with Others: Provides leadership in the school, community, and profession; engages in reflective dialogue with other members of the school community; assists colleagues' growth and development; interested in others' perspectives; criticism from others is considered one source of information among others and is objectively assessed for its credibility; uses the supervisor as a "sounding board" for ideas about improving teaching.

Nondirective Sequence of Behaviors

Refer to the supervisory behavior continuum to understand how nondirective behaviors are used. Read carefully, because the misuse of listening, clarifying, encouraging, reflecting, problem solving, and presenting behaviors can result in a decision that is not really the teacher's choice.

Figure 10.1 shows a typical pattern of supervisory interpersonal behaviors used in a nondirective conference. They begin with listening and end with asking the teacher to present his or her decision. The sequence of behaviors between start and finish can vary, but the end should be the same—a noninfluenced teacher decision. Here are the 10 behaviors:

1. **Listening:** *Wait until the teacher's initial statement is made.* Face and look at the teacher; concentrate on what is being said. Avoid thinking about how you see the problem or what you think should be done. It is not easy to restrain your mind from galloping ahead, but your job is to understand what the teacher initially has said.

2. **Reflecting:** *Verbalize your understanding of the initial problem.* Include in your statement the teacher's feelings and perceived situation: "You're angry because students don't pay attention." Wait for an acknowledgment of accuracy from the teacher: "Yes, I am, but . . . " Do not offer your own opinion; your job is to capture what the teacher is saying.

3. **Clarifying:** *Probe for the underlying problem and/or additional information.* You now ask the teacher to look at the problem in some different ways and to consider new information concerning what might be contributing to the problem. Clarifying is done to help the teacher further identify, not solve, the problem. Avoid questions that are really solutions in disguise. Such questions as these: "Have you thought about taking up yoga to relax?" and "Maybe you could suspend that student for a few days—what do you think?" are inappropriate. Such leading or suggestive questions are attempts to influence the teacher's final decision.

4. **Encouraging:** *Show willingness to listen further as the teacher begins to identify the real problems.* Show that you will continue to assist and not leave the discussion incomplete. Statements such as these: "I'm following what you're saying; continue on," "Run that by me again," and "I'm following you" are correct. Saying "I like that idea," "Yes, that will work," "Ah, I agree with that," are, even unintentionally, influencing behaviors. A teacher, like any other person, cannot help but be influenced by the judgments a supervisor is making on what he or she says. Encouraging keeps the teacher thinking; praise, on the other hand, influences the final decision.

5. **Reflecting:** *Constantly paraphrase understanding of the teacher's message.* Throughout the discussion, check on the accuracy of what you understand the teacher to be saying. When the teacher adds more information to the perceived problem or explains different sources of the problem, considers the possible actions, and finally makes a decision, the supervisor should paraphrase. First, whenever you are uncertain of what the teacher is saying, you should paraphrase with a statement such as this: "I think you're saying . . . " or "I'm not sure, but do you mean . . . ?" Then you can sit back and allow the teacher to affirm or reject your understanding. Second, when the teacher has come to a halt in thinking about the problem, the paraphrase should be used to jog the teacher's mind to reflect on what has already been said and what more needs to be done. For example, after a considerable pause in the teacher's talk, the supervisor might say, "Well, let me see if I can summarize what has been said so far . . . " or "So this is where you are—you're angry because . . . " Comprehensive summarizing allows the teacher to rest, mentally stand off from oneself, and think about what has been said. Usually, such paraphrasing will stimulate the teacher to interject, add, and continue. Reflecting should not become mechanical or artificial, with the supervisor paraphrasing every teacher

	1 Listening	*2* Clarifying	*3* Encouraging	*4* Reflecting	*5* Presenting

T _____

s

1. Wait until the teacher's initial statement is made

2. Verbalize your understanding of the initial problem

3. Probe for the underlying problem and/or additional information

4. Show willingness to listen further

5. Constantly para-phrase understanding of the teacher's message

8. Ask the teacher for a commit-ment to a decision

10. Restate the teacher's plan

Key: T = Maximum teacher responsibility   S = Maximum supervisor responsibility
        t = Minimum teacher responsibility   s = Minimum supervisor responsibility

f i g u r e **10.1**   **The Supervisory Behavior Continuum: Nondirective Behaviors**

statement. Instead, it should be used judiciously when the supervisor is not completely clear about what has been said or when there is a long pause in the conversation. Incessant interjections of "I hear you saying . . . ," without aid or purpose, make teachers skeptical about the supervisor's concern.

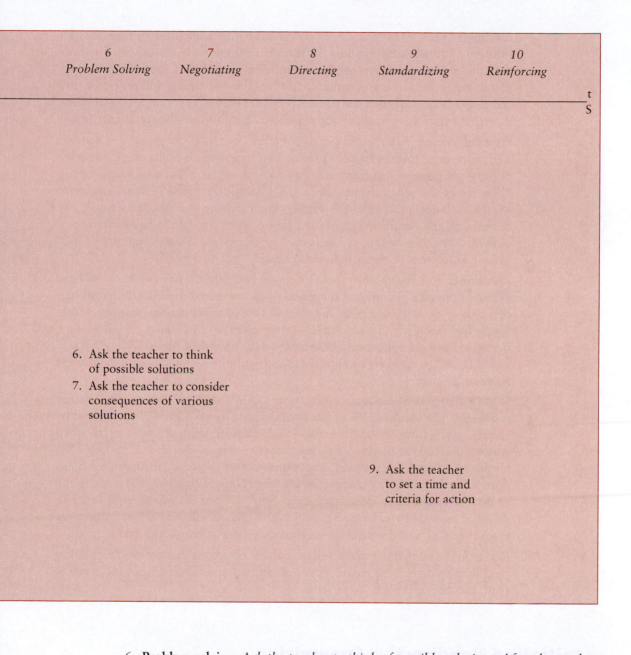

6	7	8	9	10
Problem Solving	*Negotiating*	*Directing*	*Standardizing*	*Reinforcing*

t

S

6. Ask the teacher to think
   of possible solutions
7. Ask the teacher to consider
   consequences of various
   solutions

9. Ask the teacher
   to set a time and
   criteria for action

6. **Problem solving:** *Ask the teacher to think of possible solutions.* After the teacher has finished identifying the problem and you are clear about his or her perception of the problem, your responsibility shifts to helping the teacher generate possible solutions. You can do this by asking straightforward questions: "What can you do about this?" "What else could be done?" "Think hard about actions

that might help." "Let me see if you can come up with three to four possible solutions." It is helpful to allow the teacher to think for a minute or two about possible actions before verbalizing them. After solutions have been proposed, you should reflect on the proposals, check on their accuracy, and probe for others. Regardless of whether the teacher proposes only a few or many possibilities, if further probing is not successful, then you should move the conference on.

7. **Problem solving:** *Ask the teacher to consider consequences of various actions.* The moment of truth is almost at hand. Your emphasis is on having the teacher move from possible to probable solutions. Taking each solution in order, ask: "What would happen if you did . . . ?" "Would it work?" "What problems would be associated with it?" Finally, after having the teacher explore the advantages and disadvantages of each action, he or she should be asked to compare the various actions: "Which would work best?" "Why do you think so?" "How would that be better than the others?"

8. **Presenting:** *Ask the teacher for a commitment to a decision.* After you have explored possible actions and the teacher has compared their likelihood of success, you must emphasize that the teacher should select actions that are within his or her resources *(do-able),* can be implemented in a short period of time *(feasible),* and are concrete *(accountable).* A simple question—"Well, what will you do now that is likely to improve the situation?"—should cut quickly to the heart of the matter.

9. **Standardizing:** *Ask the teacher to set a time and criteria for action.* The teacher is assisted in monitoring his or her own decision about future improvement by specifying the time period during which the action will be implemented, when various parts of the plan will be done, what resources are needed, and how the teacher will know the decision is working. A further series of supervisor questions to accomplish this purpose would be: "Now tell me what you are going to do." "What will be done first, next, last?" "What do you need in order to do it?" "How will you know it's working?" "When will it be done?" When the teacher can answer these questions, the conference is near completion.

10. **Reflecting:** *Restate the teacher's plan.* Before leaving, repeat the teacher's entire plan with "So you're going to do . . . " After the teacher verifies the restated plan, the session is over.

Initiating Nondirective Supervision

At a workshop facilitated by one of the authors, the author decided to illustrate the nondirective approach with an unstructured simulated conference, with the author taking the role of a supervisor and a volunteer participant assuming the role of a teacher. The focus of the conference was a real-world problem that the volunteer, a mentor-teacher, was experiencing. After a successful simulation in which the author used nondirective behaviors to facilitate the teacher's reflection on the problem, consideration of alternative solutions, and an action plan for solving the problem, the author congratulated the volunteer on a simulation well done. The teacher responded, "I don't feel as if I did a very good job. I didn't know what you were trying to get me to say. Was my solution the one you were looking for?" The author explained that there was no preconceived solution to the problem, that the "supervisor" in the role play was not trying to elicit any particular responses from the teacher. The teacher, who had been selected by his district as a mentor of other teachers because of his outstanding teaching and leadership, explained that he simply did not know how to respond to nondirective supervision because, in his many years of teaching, he had never been exposed to a nondirective approach.

This story illustrates the point that supervisors seldom use nondirective behaviors with teachers. Moreover, supervisors sometimes create the illusion of using nondirective behaviors when in fact they are manipulating a supervisory conference or group meeting toward a predetermined decision. When this happens often enough, teachers realize that the supervisor is attempting to manipulate them. Without any experience with authentic nondirective supervision, it's no wonder that teachers are leery of the supervisor who is trying to use that approach with them for the first time.

What's the solution when a teacher is perfectly capable of solving his or her own instructional problems but who, because of past experience, is likely to become confused or suspicious of the supervisor's first use of nondirective supervision? One technique is simply to explain to the teacher or group what nondirective supervision is, what specific behaviors are involved, and why the supervisor believes the teacher or group can benefit from the nondirective approach. Even when the supervisor has provided a rationale for nondirective supervision, some teachers may still be reluctant to identify problems, consider actions, commit to decisions, or establish criteria for success. When this happens, the supervisor should not automatically assume that the nondirective approach is inappropriate for the teacher or group. Rather, the supervisor should continue to build trust and rapport through active listening, probe for problems and related information, and encourage the teacher or group to describe situations and feelings. Eventually, the teacher or group should reach a stage of trust and self-confidence that will enable them to consider alternatives and generate an improvement plan. Supervisor commitment to teacher self-direction, along with the use of appropriate interpersonal behaviors, will ultimately lead to teacher-driven instructional improvement.

Nondirective, Not Laissez-Faire, Supervision

Some educators have criticized nondirective supervision by arguing that supervisors who use nondirective behaviors are abdicating their responsibility to assist teachers to improve their instructional performance. This is a valid argument against laissez-faire supervision, which advocates minimal supervisor involvement in the instructional improvement process. However, under our definition of nondirective supervision, the supervisor is actively involved in instructional improvement, clarifying, encouraging, reflecting, and facilitating teacher decision making at each stage of the improvement process.

Also, in developmental supervision, the nondirective approach is used only with those teachers who are operating at high levels of abstraction, motivation, and expertise. The developmental supervisor uses one of the other three supervisory approaches with teachers who are not ready to assume full decision-making responsibility.

Issues with Nondirective Supervision

Based on numerous skill-training sessions conducted with school leaders on employing nondirective behaviors, some common issues and practical questions have arisen:

1. Can a supervisor really remain nonjudgmental and not influence the teacher's or group's decision?
2. What happens if the teacher or group desires the supervisor's input?
3. What does a supervisor do with a teacher or group that is reluctant or not capable of generating solutions?
4. How exact or variable is the sequence of nondirective behaviors?

Whether a supervisor can really remain nonjudgmental is a legitimate concern. Even when one is consciously avoiding praise, not interjecting one's own ideas, and not offering solutions in the guise of questions, some influencing probably will take place. Any interaction between humans is bound to be influential. Frequency of eye contact, timing of questions, facial expressions, and ways of paraphrasing can always be interpreted by a teacher as approving or disapproving. There is no way to avoid influencing through unconscious supervisory responses. The best one can do is to minimize those behaviors that knowingly influence. One should not knowingly offer ideas, praise, or directions that will influence the teacher's decision.

What if the teacher or group asks for the supervisor's suggestions? Ideally, it is better to refrain completely from giving one's own ideas. If asked, the supervisor might respond, "I'm sorry, but I don't want to answer that. Instead, I want you to think through what can be done. Only you know your own situation. Therefore, what *I* think is not as important as what *you* think."

Being nondirective with an individual or group that is reluctant or not capable of generating solutions is tricky. If the teacher is reluctant but capable, the worst possible response would be for the supervisor to take over decision making for the teacher. Such a move might reinforce the teacher's reluctance to speak his or her own mind.

Reluctance usually stems from a disbelief that one will be listened to or allowed to act on one's own initiative. The supervisor must be patient, give constant encouragement, and be persistent. Patience is shown by listening and waiting, encouragement by accepting what the teacher says, and persistence by not allowing the teacher to rest without making a decision. A supervisor can be persistent by asking questions, by taking breaks from the conference, and by giving the teacher time for further reflection.

Capability is a different matter. What if a teacher or group is incapable of making a decision? If they continually insist they do not know what the problem is or have no ideas about what could be done, and if every supervisory prompt is met by vacant stares and shrugs of shoulders, then patience, encouragement, and persistence on the part of the supervisor will create further frustration and perhaps antagonism. If they simply don't know, no matter how nondirective the supervisor is, no decisions will be forthcoming. Obviously, if lack of capability is the source of nonresponsiveness, then the nondirective approach is an unwise choice of supervisory behaviors.

Finally, there is the question of sequence of nondirective behaviors. How precise is the order? The description of nondirective behaviors presented a prototype of 10 steps within the supervisory behavior continuum (Figure 10.1). One might visualize these steps as analogous to playing the left-hand side of a piano keyboard. The supervisor pianist begins the musical score with the farthest left-hand note (listening–waiting) and will end the score at note 10 (reflecting–restating). During the score (conference or meeting), the adept player will strike the notes (behaviors) back and forth between 1 and 10, pounding on some notes, lightly touching on others, returning, and swelling the underlying tone of the teacher or group voice. The score ends on note 10—reflecting and restating the teacher's or group's decision. The behaviors are not a prescription of fixed steps but rather a directionality of movements with a definite beginning and end.

When to Use Nondirective Behaviors

When and with whom should nondirective behaviors be used? A supervisor should consider using a nondirective approach in these situations:

1. When the teacher is functioning at a very high developmental level.
2. When the teacher possesses most of the knowledge and expertise about the issue and the supervisor's knowledge and expertise are minimal: "If you don't know anything about it and they do, let them solve it."
3. When the teacher has full responsibility for carrying out the decision and the supervisor has little involvement: "If they are going to be accountable for it and you aren't, let them solve it."

4. When the teacher is committed to solving the problem but the problem doesn't matter to the supervisor: "If they want to act and you couldn't care less, let them decide."

There are special circumstances in which initial use of nondirective behaviors is appropriate even if the preceding criteria are not met. Regardless of teacher developmental level, expertise, responsibility, or commitment, when a teacher or group has become extremely emotional over a problem, rational problem solving using any of the four supervisory approaches may be unproductive. What may be more beneficial in such situations is the initial use of the nondirective behaviors of listening, clarifying, encouraging, and reflecting as the teacher or group describes the problem and expresses the anger, frustration, fear, resentment, or other feelings the problem has generated. Once the teacher or group has had the opportunity to vent emotions in the presence of an empathetic listener, the supervisor can then shift to a problem-solving

---

role play **10.1**

Practicing Nondirective Behaviors

Directions: The class splits into groups of three. Using the following teacher description and situation, one member of each group assumes the role of the teacher, one member assumes the role of the supervisor, and one member assumes the role of observer. The "supervisor" and "teacher" role play a conference in which the supervisor uses a nondirective approach to address the teacher's instructional problem. The observer takes notes on the supervisor's performance during the conference and shares those notes with the other two group members after the role play. Finally, all three participants engage in reflective discussion of the role play and the nondirective approach. (To assist in the role plays in Chapters 7 through 10, see Appendix B, which reviews and compares all four supervisory approaches.)

Teacher Description and Situation: Martha Martinez, a teacher at Nelson Middle School, has won numerous teaching awards. Martha has provided professional development in educational technology at district workshops, serves on the school's technology committee, and has provided expert peer coaching to many of the other teachers at Nelson on integrating technology across the curriculum. Martha recently has agreed to have her classroom serve as a demonstration classroom for using technology to improve the teaching of language arts. In two weeks, Martha will teach her first demonstration lesson. She will teach the lesson to her own seventh-grade language arts students, and five other language arts teachers from Nelson will be on hand to observe. Martha has requested a conference with her supervisor to discuss how she can make her demonstration lesson valuable both to her students and to the teachers who will be observing.

mode, using the criteria of developmental level, expertise, responsibility, and commitment to select the appropriate supervisory approach for the problem-solving phase of the conference or meeting.

Although nondirective supervision can be a valuable means of assisting individual teacher development, we see its greatest potential in the supervisor facilitating expert teachers collaborating with each other for classroom and schoolwide instructional improvement. An example of nondirective supervision of teacher collaboration at the classroom level would be the supervisor facilitating a teacher-driven peer-coaching program. An example of nondirective supervision for schoolwide instructional improvement would be the supervisor assisting a group of teachers as the group plans, implements, and evaluates a series of integrated instructional units cutting across several content areas. The ultimate goal of developmental supervision is for the supervisor to be facilitating a self-actualized teaching staff engaged in collaborative and continuous instructional improvement.

> ✔ **Check Your Understanding 10.0**   Click here to gauge your understanding of the key concepts presented in this chapter.

REFLECTIVE EXERCISE

Critique the behaviors of a supervisor you know who believes he or she uses nondirective behaviors with teachers. Reflect on the following questions about the supervisor:

1. How do the teachers respond to the supervisor's efforts to use nondirective behaviors?

2. Does the supervisor ever use overt nondirective behaviors such as clarifying, encouraging, and reflecting while at the same time influencing teachers (intentionally or unintentionally) through subtle comments or nonverbal behaviors?

3. What does the supervisor do when he or she is attempting to use nondirective behaviors and a teacher asks for input?

4. Does the supervisor ever slip into laissez-faire supervision when attempting to use nondirective behaviors?

5. Based on your reflections concerning questions 1 through 4, is the supervisor authentic in his or her use of nondirective supervision, or are there changes the supervisor needs to make in order to be truly nondirective? If changes are necessary, what changes should the supervisor make?

chapter 11

Developmental Supervision

Learning Outcomes for This Chapter

After reading this chapter, you should be able to:

1. List the variables to consider when deciding which supervisory approach to use.
2. Identify two types of supervisor flexibility.
3. Discuss why teacher development should be a critical function of supervision.
4. Explain why it is not possible to develop an algorithm that determines the best supervisory approach to use with teachers.
5. Describe two ways in which developmental supervision is "developmental."

Questions to Reflect On as You Read This Chapter

1. Is matching the correct supervisory approach to a particular teacher or group more of a science or an art, or is it a balance of science and art?
2. Think about five or six teachers you have observed and with whom you have discussed teaching who represent a range of success. With what supervisory approach, in general, would each of these teachers be best matched?
3. Think of a teacher or group that, in a particular situation, would benefit most from one of the four supervisory approaches, but in a different situation would benefit most from a different approach. Why would the two different situations call for two different supervisory approaches with the same teacher or group?

4. Which of the four supervisory approaches would you be most comfortable using? Which approach would you be least comfortable using? As a supervisor, would you apply developmental supervision as it is described in this chapter? Would you use a modified version of developmental supervision? If so, what modifications would you make?

5. As you read about the three phases of developmental supervision, what does the chapter tell you about the developmental level and expertise required of a supervisor attempting to implement developmental supervision?

Thus far in Part 3, we have introduced the supervisory behavior continuum and explained each of the four supervisory approaches (directive control, directive informational, collaborative, and nondirective). This chapter provides an in-depth discussion of developmental supervision as an integrated model.

Developmental supervision has three phases:

1. Choosing the best entry-level approach
2. Applying the chosen approach
3. Fostering teacher development while gradually increasing teacher choice and decision-making responsibility

Our discussion of developmental supervision addresses each of these three phases.

Phase 1: Choosing the Best Approach

The teacher's levels of adult development, expertise, and commitment as well as responsibility for solving the problem and urgency of the situation all need to be considered when choosing which of four supervisory approaches—directive control, directive informational, collaborative, or nondirective—is the best match for the teacher.

Teachers at lower levels of adult developmental, expertise, and commitment seem well matched to directive supervision. They have difficulty defining problems, have few ways of responding to problems, and are unlikely to accept decision-making responsibility. They clearly are in need of the structure and intensive assistance provided by directive supervision. For most teachers in need of direction, a directive informational approach is appropriate. For teachers functioning at very low levels of development, expertise, and commitment and with serious instructional problems, a controlling directive approach might be necessary.

Teachers at moderately high levels of adult development, expertise, and commitment are usually best served by a collaborative supervisory approach. They can generate some possible solutions to an instructional problem but still need some assistance in examining all options and developing a comprehensive plan for instructional improvement. The brainstorming inherent in collaborative supervision allows the teacher or group to share perceptions and offer some possible alternatives for future action but also to receive the benefit of supervisor perceptions and proposals. Negotiated action plans made during collaborative supervision allow teachers to meet needs of emerging independence while receiving the moderate guidance needed to ensure that the plan will lead to instructional improvement.

Teachers or groups functioning at very high levels of adult development, expertise, and commitment are ready for the self-direction fostered by the nondirective supervisory approach. They are autonomous, explorative, and creative. They can think of a problem from many perspectives, generate a variety of alternative actions, think through each step of an action plan, and follow the plan through to completion. Table 11.1 provides an overview of factors to consider when selecting a supervisory approach.

The decision about which supervisory approach to use is straightforward if the measures for each variable in Table 11.1 line up under one of the four supervisory approaches. However, individual or group levels of adult development, expertise, and commitment, as well as responsibility for solving the problem and the urgency of the situation, can vary or fluctuate, which means that choosing the best approach can become more complicated than the broad guidelines just discussed might suggest. The following possibilities must be kept in mind:

1. Individual or group levels of development, expertise, and commitment may vary. For example, a teacher might be functioning at high levels of adult development in general, but at only moderate levels of expertise and commitment concerning a particular situation. In addition, a group might include teachers of low, moderate, and high developmental levels. Some general guidelines are to use a controlling directive approach if most characteristics of an individual or group indicate a very low decision-making capacity, informational directive supervision if most attributes point to a moderately low capacity, a collaborative approach if most characteristics indicate a moderately high capacity, and nondirective supervision if most attributes point to a very high capacity for decision making. When working with an individual or group with widely fluctuating characteristics, a collaborative approach would probably be most effective.

2. Characteristics of teachers and groups might change in certain situations. For example, a teacher who has successfully taught general science to middle school students for 10 years might regress to lower levels of development, expertise, or commitment after being transferred to a senior high school to teach chemistry and physics. In short, the developmental supervisor sometimes must change supervisory behaviors in order to adapt to a change in the teacher's or group's situation.

t a b l e **11.1** **Considerations for Selecting Supervisory Approach**

	Directive Control Approach	Directive Informational Approach	Collaborative Approach	Nondirective Approach
Teacher's Adult Developmental Level	Very Low	Moderately Low	Moderately High or Mixed	Very High
Teacher's Level of Instructional Expertise	Very Low	Moderately Low	Moderately High	Very High
Teacher's Level of Commitment	Very Low	Moderately Low	Moderately High	Very High
Teacher's Responsibility for Solving Problem	Very Low	Moderately Low	Same as Supervisor's	Very High
Supervisor's Responsibility for Solving Problem	Very High	Moderately High	Same as Teacher's	Very Low
Urgency of Situation	Very High	Moderately High	Moderately Low	Very Low

Research on adult and teacher development can suggest guidelines for determining the best supervisory approach. The tremendous variability of teacher characteristics, however, means that the supervisor must choose an approach on a case-by-case basis, relying on the knowledge base on teacher characteristics, recent observations of and interactions with the teacher or group, and analysis of the current situation. An important guideline is to provide teachers with as much initial choice as they are ready to assume and then foster teachers' decision-making capacity and expanded choice over time (Glickman, 2002).

Phase 2: Applying the Chosen Approach

Can a supervisor shift from one approach to another when working with teachers and groups at different developmental levels? Stated differently, can the same supervisor effectively use directive informational, directive control, collaborative, and nondirective behaviors with different teachers? Our own work with supervisors indicates that supervisors can demonstrate such flexibility, but only if the supervisors themselves are functioning at reasonably high levels of development, expertise, and commitment, and if they have had the opportunity to learn and practice the different supervisory approaches. We have found that the nondirective approach is the one that supervisors tend to have the most difficulty implementing, indicating that additional supervisor preparation for use of nondirective behaviors is warranted.

What if a supervisor in the early stages of working with a teacher or group—even after preliminary observation and discussion—is not sure which supervisory approach to use? A good rule of thumb in such cases is to *prepare to use a collaborative approach, but be ready to shift to a nondirective or directive approach if necessary.* When preparing to use a collaborative approach, a supervisor determines possible improvement goals, actions, and criteria to be considered and potentially integrated with goals, actions, and criteria suggested by the teacher or group. However, if during the early phases of the conference or meeting it becomes apparent that the teacher or group will be able to identify an appropriate goal and action plan on their own, then the supervisor can forget about his or her possible suggestions and shift to nondirective behaviors as a means of facilitating self-directed teacher planning. If, on the other hand, the teacher or group is unable to identify an obvious problem, any of its underlying causes, or any possible solutions, the supervisor can shift to a directive mode, mandating (directive control) or suggesting (directive informational) a goal, actions, and improvement criteria.

One type of supervisor flexibility is the ability to plan and implement different supervisory approaches with different teachers and groups. The ultimate supervisor flexibility, however, is the ability to "shift supervisory gears," so to speak, and effectively use an approach not originally planned because of new discoveries about a teacher or group, or the situation at hand. Like successful teachers, successful supervisors must be able to think on their feet and flex accordingly (Zellermayer & Margolin, 2005).

Phase 3: Fostering Teacher Development

The long-term goal of developmental supervision is teacher development toward a point where teachers, facilitated by supervisors, can assume full responsibility for instructional improvement. There are several reasons why we believe that teacher development should be a critical function of supervision:

- Teachers functioning at higher developmental levels tend to use a wide variety of instructional behaviors associated with successful teaching.

- Teachers who have themselves reached higher stages of consciousness and cognitive, moral, and ego development are more likely to foster their students' growth in those areas. In a democratic society, it is vital that students learn to think reflectively, function at high stages of moral reasoning, and be autonomous decision makers.

- Teachers at higher levels of adult development, expertise, and commitment are more likely to embrace "a cause beyond oneself" and participate in collective action toward schoolwide instructional improvement—a critical element found in the school improvement research.

Simply matching the best supervisory approach to the teacher's or group's current developmental levels can promote some degree of teacher development. And, as previous chapters in this text have discussed, the supervisor can facilitate teacher development by gradually decreasing supervisor control and increasing teacher control over the decision-making process. Beyond matching supervisory approach to teacher current developmental level, and gradually shifting approaches, there are additional strategies that supervisors can use to stimulate teacher development.

One method is to introduce teachers to new information about students and learning, innovative teaching strategies, and novel ways to frame and solve problems. Initially, new ways of thinking and acting that teachers are invited to explore should be linked to their existing knowledge, experience, and values. Gradually, teachers can be exposed to a broader spectrum of theory and practice.

Another method is to assign teachers to groups in which most of the other members are functioning at slightly higher developmental levels. Significant, ongoing professional interaction with teachers of somewhat higher development will tend to pull the teacher of lower development toward the group's functioning level.

Specific professional learning structures can foster teacher growth toward higher levels of development, provided they are offered on a long-term basis. Examples of these learning structures include:

- Mentoring beginning teachers on a day-to-day basis throughout the school year by experienced teachers who are at higher levels of development
- Programs incorporating role playing, simulations, and teaching of mini lessons using new practices, interspersed with guided reflection on those activities
- Classroom observations of colleagues' lessons, with reflective pre- and post-lesson discussions
- Co-teaching, with co-planning conferences before the lessons, and reflective post-lesson discussions
- Peer coaching (including preconferences, classroom observations, and postconferences); initially, teachers of lower developmental levels should receive expert coaching from teachers of higher developmental levels, but as teachers experience growth they can shift to participation in reciprocal coaching

Not Algorithms, but Guideposts for Decisions

Eventually, supervisors and teachers must discuss, question, and ask each other which supervisory approach has been most helpful in the past, which will be most helpful in the present, and which approach they should be striving for in the future. With the exception of emergency situations, this is the responsibility of both parties.

Life in the school world is ragged and complex. There are no algorithms to provide exactly correct responses to human behavior. Such formulas as "If individual X exhibits characteristics A, B, and C, then supervisor Y should do D, F, and G" do not and should not exist. Such algorithms are useful only in mechanically and technically controlled systems (such as computer operations, assembly production, or chemical alterations). Algorithms work in technical but not human endeavors, and it would be misleading to suggest that such supervision formulas are available. Instead, what is available is information about ourselves and others that can serve as guideposts to suggest what *might* be of use. Such developmental guideposts can help reduce some of the infinite complexity of the school world so that supervision can be a purposeful and thoughtful function for improving instruction.

Case Studies on Developmental Supervision

The following case studies provide examples of the four supervisory approaches—directive control, directive informational, collaborative, and nondirective—appropriately matched with the teachers and situations in the cases. Also, toward the end of each of the first three case studies, the supervisor makes initial efforts to move the teacher toward more choice and responsibility.

As you read the four case studies, compare them in relation to the following:

1. The teacher's levels of adult development, expertise, and commitment to solving the problem

2. The nature of the problem

3. The interpersonal behaviors of the supervisor, including any shifts in supervisory behavior that take place

Case Study One

After receiving complaints about Gerald Watson's teaching methods from students, parents, and other teachers, principal Martha Cozero observed Gerald's science class on several occasions. Regardless of lesson content or student population, all of the observed lessons followed the same pattern. First, seat by seat and row by row, students would take turns reading paragraphs from the science text. Next, Gerald would pass out a worksheet for students to complete independently. If students finished their worksheets before the end of class, they were told to begin their homework assignment, which always consisted of written exercises from the textbook. During independent seatwork, Gerald usually sat at his desk reading sports magazines, looking up only to give an "evil eye" to students who were talking to each other or getting out of their seats.

Martha was not surprised by Gerald's instructional routine. She *was* surprised that he made no attempt at more active teaching even during her classroom observations.

Martha used the first of several conferences with Gerald to try to find out more about his attitudes toward teaching science. He admitted that he rarely graded or returned the written assignments that he required students to complete. Gerald stated that he neither understood nor used the hands-on science program that the middle school science team had agreed to adopt the previous year. He had not attended the science team's after-school meetings that led to the decision to adopt the program. He had taken personal days rather than attend the all-day workshops during which science teachers developed skills necessary to implement the program. Gerald told Martha that he was six years away from retirement and saw no reason to learn new skills or use new teaching methods.

After reflecting on her classroom observations and conference with Gerald, Martha designed an improvement plan that she presented to him during their next conference. During that conference, she told Gerald that his current instructional strategies and failure to learn about or implement the school's science program were detrimental to student learning and that his approach to teaching science was unacceptable. She stated that Gerald's improvement goals would be to engage in more active teaching and make use of instructional strategies consistent with the science curriculum's goals. Martha mandated the following steps on Gerald's part:

1. End excessive reliance on students taking turns reading aloud from the science text.
2. Reduce the use of worksheets as a primary instructional strategy.
3. Review written assignments completed by students, and provide students with feedback on their performance.
4. Review the school district's written curriculum as well as teacher guides for the school's hands-on science program.
5. Visit other science teachers' classrooms to observe the science program in action.
6. Use more hands-on science activities consistent with the adopted science program.

The principal made it clear that the goals and activities she presented were not optional. Martha listened to Gerald's concerns and answered questions about the action plan. She promised to provide him with resources and materials necessary to implement the new science program. Martha scheduled a series of classroom observations that would allow her to monitor Gerald's progress with the plan and provide him with assistance and feedback on the new instructional strategies he would be trying out.

Gerald reluctantly began to implement the mandated improvement plan. Although progress was slow, his teaching methods did begin to change. Some of Gerald's attempts at hands-on learning worked well; others did not. Students were enjoying the hands-on activities and demonstrating levels of interest and learning that Gerald had not thought possible. Eventually, he admitted to Martha that missing the workshops on the new curriculum had been a mistake: There were many gaps in his knowledge of the new curriculum that his readings and observations had not filled.

Martha decided that Gerald needed formal training in how to implement the science program if he was going to continue to improve his teaching. She also decided that the effort and progress he had made warranted allowing Gerald some choice in how that training should be acquired. Martha offered Gerald three options for learning more about the program: attendance at two days of in-service education on the program offered by the program's publisher at a nearby intermediate unit, after-school workshops to be presented by the science supervisor at the district's other middle school, or individualized training by Jim Adams, the science coordinator at Gerald's middle school. Gerald had always liked Jim so he told Martha that he preferred to receive training from a colleague who was just down the hall and whom he could call on if he had problems implementing the curriculum. Jim agreed to work with Gerald, and Martha and Jim designed a plan to provide Gerald with several hours of individualized training and intensive classroom coaching.

Case Study Two

Veteran teacher Bill Levin was assigned as mentor to beginning teacher Janice Smith. Janice had joined the middle school teaching staff eager to try out a variety of innovative teaching strategies she had been introduced to during her teacher preparation program. Now, just two months into her teaching career, Janice was considering leaving the profession at the Thanksgiving break.

After a few observations of Janice's teaching, Bill was convinced that Janice had considerable potential as a teacher but that her classroom management problems might prevent her from reaching that potential. Although Janice had been exposed to brief discussions of student discipline problems in several of her teaching methods courses, she had never received systematic training in effective classroom management. Her lack of training and inexperience in dealing with middle school students was becoming increasingly apparent. On several visits to Janice's classroom, Bill observed considerable off-task behavior and numerous student disruptions. Rather than attempt to control the high noise level, Janice would first try to yell over the student conversations and then scream at disruptive students who had ignored her pleas to quiet down.

Janice knew she had classroom management problems but was not sure why the students behaved the way they did or what she could do to improve the situation. Based on his observations and discussions with Janice, Bill made the following suggestions to the novice teacher:

1. Establish a set of rules and procedures for classroom behavior, and determine natural consequences for students who fail to follow those rules and procedures.
2. Share the rules and procedures with the students, explaining the rationale for each rule, procedure, and natural consequence.

3. Give the students the opportunity to practice each rule and procedure under simulated conditions, and provide them with feedback on their performance.

4. Consistently enforce all rules and procedures, providing positive feedback for student compliance and carrying through on natural consequences for noncompliance.

Bill offered to help Janice develop her rules and procedures, rehearse her presentation and explanation to students, and plan opportunities for students to practice new guidelines and receive feedback on their performance. Bill also suggested that Janice try out a number of nonverbal and verbal interventions to correct minor student misbehaviors before they reached a disruptive stage. He explained how in his own classroom, he used nonverbal interventions such as eye contact, physical proximity, and touch control, as well as verbal interventions such as use of students' names, reminder of a rule or procedure, and explicit redirection. Bill invited Janice to visit his classroom and observe his classroom management techniques. He also offered to observe Janice's class as she implemented his suggested strategies and techniques and to provide her with feedback based on the observations.

Janice agreed to try out Bill's recommendations. With considerable assistance from her mentor, she implemented the suggested strategies and techniques. After several weeks, most of the students in Janice's class had increased their amount of time on task considerably and student disruptions had decreased. Janice had made it through to Thanksgiving and was willing to give teaching another chance, at least until the end of the school year.

Bill was pleased with the progress Janice had made but concerned about three students who seemed to be immune to his protégé's new classroom management strategies and techniques. He knew that even a few students could disrupt Janice's entire class if she was unable to help them change their behavior. The mentor offered two possibilities for dealing with the three disruptive students. One was for Janice to work individually with each of the problem students to develop a behavior contract. In the contract, teacher and student would negotiate specific behavioral improvement goals, a time period for meeting the goals, teacher and student actions, assessment of student progress, and rewards and consequences.

The second possibility suggested by Bill was that Janice keep daily logs of disruptive behaviors by each of the three students. The initial record keeping would last for a period of two weeks, with the students required to sign log entries each day. At the end of the two-week period, Janice could assign the three students individual improvement plans aimed at reducing the types of behaviors recorded in the logs. Once the plan was initiated, Janice could record both positive and disruptive student behaviors in the logs in order to document student progress toward improvement goals.

When Bill asked Janice to select one of the two options, she asked if it would be agreeable to use parts of both strategies by first logging student behaviors for two weeks and then negotiating a behavioral contract with each of the three students. Bill agreed that this would be an appropriate synthesis of the two strategies. He offered to assist Janice in reviewing the log entries and writing the three behavioral contracts—an offer that Janice readily accepted.

Case Study Three

Social studies teacher Mike Phillips had requested a conference with George Cantinni, his department chairperson. Mike was not satisfied with the quality of discussions in his current events class. George asked Mike to describe the type of class discussions he wanted to take place. Mike replied that he wanted to foster students' higher-level thinking and open dialogue concerning important social and political issues. When George asked Mike what was preventing such discussion, he replied that he probably hindered class discussions himself by asking too many simple recall questions rather than questions that would spark student interest and discussion. Another problem Mike discussed was that typically only a few students participated in class discussions, and he had done little to encourage those who did not participate to join in.

Based on Mike's description of the problem, George suggested that changes in the way Mike structured class discussions might be in order. He proposed that Mike and he take a few minutes to separately write down ideas for improvement. After both had reflected on and listed potential actions, George asked Mike to share his ideas. Mike's possible actions included asking students more open-ended questions, giving the entire class more time to think about a question before calling on one of the students to respond, and randomly calling on students in order to increase student participation. George responded that he agreed with the first two suggestions. He added that while randomly calling on students to respond was appropriate in some situations, he did not believe that it was a viable way to foster the open, reflective dialogue that Mike was hoping for.

George introduced additional possible actions by building on ideas already suggested by Mike. He suggested that Mike refer to the upper five categories of Bloom's taxonomy when planning discussion lessons, first to help determine the lesson's objectives and then to formulate relevant discussion questions. George reviewed Bloom's cognitive domain, which Mike vaguely recalled from his undergraduate years. To Mike's idea of giving the class time to think about questions before responding to them, George added the option of allowing students to discuss questions in small groups prior to whole-class discussion. Finally, George suggested that during whole-class discussions individual students as well as the class be provided adequate "wait time" to formulate their responses and that appropriate wait time also *follow* individual student responses.

Mike responded that he liked the idea of basing learning objectives and discussion questions on Bloom's taxonomy but thought he might have trouble formulating the different types of questions. He asked George if he would be willing to help develop some questions for Mike's next few lessons. George agreed and also offered to observe a few of Mike's lessons in order to record the number of questions asked within each category of Bloom's taxonomy. Mike replied that he would appreciate the feedback. Regarding George's suggestion of beginning discussions with small groups, Mike stated that for the time being he would prefer to lead whole-class discussions throughout his lessons. He said that he had a fairly good understanding of the different types of wait time but would like to have some feedback on how many seconds he was allowing for each type of wait time. George agreed to collect data on Mike's wait time during the observations they had already agreed to. Mike and George also agreed that in addition to types of questions and wait time, George would track the number of students who participated in each class discussion.

After considerably more discussion, Mike and George had worked out an action plan for instructional improvement. The plan was written as follows:

Goal. To increase student participation in open discussion requiring student interpretation, application, analysis, synthesis, and evaluation.

Mike Phillips's Responsibilities

1. Participate in the design of student learning objectives within each of Bloom's upper five categories of cognitive objectives (listed in goal statement).

2. Participate in the creation of open-ended discussion questions for each of the five types of learning objectives.

3. Allow at least five seconds after asking an open-ended question for a student to respond. Call on volunteers only.

4. Allow at least five seconds after calling on an individual student for the student to respond.

5. Wait at least five seconds after a student has responded to an open-ended question before continuing the discussion.

George Cantinni's Responsibilities

1. Assist Mr. Phillips in designing student learning objectives based on the upper five categories of Bloom's taxonomy.

2. Assist in creating open-ended discussion questions corresponding to stated objectives.

3. Periodically observe Mr. Phillips's class discussions. Collect data on the following:

   a. Frequency of teacher questions inviting student responses requiring interpretation, application, analysis, synthesis, and evaluation
   b. Duration of wait time after teacher questions, after calling on students to answer questions, and after student responses
   c. Frequency of each student's participation in open-ended discussions

Criteria for Success

1. In selected classes, open-ended questions will be asked and related discussions held at each of the five upper levels of Bloom's taxonomy.

2. When appropriate, at least five seconds of wait time will be provided after asking open-ended discussion questions, after calling on students to respond to questions, and after student responses.

3. Each student will make at least one contribution to each open-ended class discussion.

Working closely with George over a period of several weeks, Mike made steady progress toward his instructional improvement goal. Eventually, George suggested that Mike had developed sufficient skill at writing open-ended discussion questions that he no longer needed George's assistance during his lesson planning. Mike agreed but asked George if he would review Mike's discussion questions for a few weeks and give him feedback on their quality. George and Mike also decided that in lieu of additional classroom observations by George, Mike would electronically record his next few class discussions. He would review his own performance by analyzing the recording. George agreed to review the recording of any class discussion for which Mike requested expert feedback.

Case Study Four

Stella Simpson was assistant principal for instruction at Kennedy Elementary School. She had developed a professional development option for teachers wishing to participate in an individualized professional development program. Maria Sanchez had some tentative ideas for a program that would provide development opportunities for herself and others and requested a meeting with Stella to discuss the plan.

During their meeting, Stella listened, reflected, clarified, and encouraged as Maria discussed a problem she saw emerging at the school. With the growing popularity of cooperative learning, a number of teachers had decided to try out cooperative strategies in their classrooms. Unfortunately, few of the teachers had received in-depth training in cooperative learning. Most had attended only a 60-minute awareness session provided at a recent districtwide in-service education day.

Maria, who had received 30 hours of training in cooperative learning, was delighted that other teachers were taking an interest in cooperative learning. However, based on her classroom observations as part of the school's peer-coaching program, she was concerned that many teachers did not have a clear grasp of the basic elements of a cooperative learning lesson. Maria was concerned that if teachers did not develop sufficient expertise in cooperative learning, their use of it would be ineffective, and they would soon abandon it as an instructional strategy.

Stella paraphrased Maria's general concerns and then asked her to discuss specific problems teachers were having with cooperative learning. Maria replied that several teachers were attempting cooperative lessons without teaching students prerequisite social skills. She also stated that they were not building positive interdependence or individual accountability—two vital aspects of cooperative learning—into their lessons. Maria added that, based on her conversations with other teachers, these problems were not confined to teachers she had observed as a peer coach.

Stella agreed with Maria's observations. She had attended the same 30-hour training program as Maria, and her classroom observations verified Maria's concerns. Stella asked Maria for her perceptions of what could be done about the problem. As Maria presented her proposal, Stella continued to listen intently, sometimes paraphrasing Maria's statements, sometimes asking clarifying questions, other times encouraging Maria to elaborate. Maria proposed that she attend an advanced training program that would enable her to develop additional expertise in cooperative learning as well as skills necessary to deliver a training program to other teachers. After completing the advanced program, Maria would deliver a series of evening workshops providing 30 hours of basic training on cooperative learning to interested teachers. Maria also suggested that she provide classroom coaching to the teachers attending her workshops in order to assist them to transfer skills learned in the workshops to their classrooms.

Stella asked Maria if she had considered the difficulties she might encounter when attempting to provide instructional assistance to peers. Maria replied that she had considered the issue, but that since she would be working with volunteer teachers only, she did not see her peer status as a major problem. She reminded Stella that as a participant in the school's peer-coaching program she had successfully provided instructional assistance to many of the teachers who would attend the workshops. Also, she would not attempt to lead workshops for peers until she had received extensive leadership preparation.

Stella told Maria that if her plan was accepted, professional development funds could be used to pay for released time, the costs of Maria's leadership training, and the materials for the evening workshops that Maria would deliver. She told Maria that no funds were available to pay her for the considerable amount of personal time and energy Maria would have to spend to make the program a success. Stella asked Maria if she was willing to make the extensive commitment that her new leadership role would require. After receiving an affirmative response, Stella asked Maria to put together a detailed proposal, including goals, activities, needed resources, criteria for success, a time line, and a tentative budget.

Discussion of the Four Case Studies

We stated earlier that the ultimate aim of the supervisor should be reflective, autonomous teachers facilitated by nondirective supervision; however, the fact that many teachers are functioning at developmental levels or in situations in which self-direction is not feasible means that the supervisor often must initially use collaborative, directive informational, or, in rare cases, directive control behaviors. Each of the four case studies represents a different entry point for supervision. In each case, the supervisor based his or her initial supervisory approach on the teacher's levels of development, expertise, and commitment and the nature of the situation.

The case studies provide examples of three phases of developmental supervision. In Phase 1, the supervisor diagnoses the teacher's developmental levels, expertise, commitment, and educational situation and selects the interpersonal approach that creates the best supervisory match. In Phase 2, the supervisor uses the selected interpersonal approach to assist the teacher in instructional problem solving. In Phase 3 (illustrated in the first three case studies), the supervisor changes his or her interpersonal behavior in the direction of less supervisor control and more teacher control. Such a change in supervisory approach occurs only after the teacher has shown readiness to assume more decision-making responsibility.

In Case Study One, Martha Cozero determined that Gerald Watson was functioning at very low levels of development, expertise, and commitment. She was convinced that Gerald's purposeless instructional routine was a serious impediment to student learning. Martha decided to use directive control behaviors in her initial supervisory approach. She identified the problem, presented Gerald with the instructional improvement goal, and directed him to carry out actions to reach the goal. Martha followed up by monitoring and providing feedback on Gerald's progress. Once Gerald had shown some improvement in teaching behaviors and motivation, Martha took a first step away from complete control, asking Gerald to choose one of three training formats.

In Case Study Two, novice Janice Smith's lack of classroom management and problem-solving skills created a different type of instructional problem. Janice initially had been highly motivated. She realized she had classroom management problems. What she needed was intensive assistance in identifying causes and solutions. After observing and conferencing with Janice, mentor Bill Levin decided to use directive informational behaviors during his initial assistance to Janice. Bill identified a goal for Janice of improved classroom management. He suggested a number of actions that she and he could take to move toward that goal. It was up to Janice to accept or reject Bill's suggestions. After Janice had made considerable progress under his mentorship, Bill encouraged her to choose from two alternative strategies for working with three students who displayed chronic discipline problems. Janice and Bill's negotiation and mutual agreement to integrate the two strategies represent movement toward a more collaborative relationship between novice and mentor.

In Case Study Three, Mike Phillips was able to define the problem he was experiencing and identify some causes, but he needed assistance in thinking through a plan to solve the problem. Chairperson George Cantinni decided to use a collaborative approach with Mike. After listening to Mike's perceptions, George shared his own point of view and then suggested that he and Mike both develop and exchange options for solving the problem. During the negotiation process, both Mike and George accepted, rejected, and proposed modifications to ideas presented by the other. Eventually, Mike and George reached mutual agreement on an action plan. George's suggestion that Mike independently design his own discussion questions as well as record and review his class discussions was an attempt to move away from collaborative and toward nondirective supervision. Their agreement that George would be available to review Mike's discussion questions and recordings indicated a transitional phase between collaborative and nondirective supervision.

In Case Study Four, teacher Maria Sanchez was clearly functioning at very high levels of personal and professional development. Assistant principal Stella Simpson used nondirective interpersonal behaviors of listening, reflecting, clarifying, and encouraging as Maria discussed her concerns and proposal. Stella asked Maria to consider the consequences of her plan. Stella's request for a written proposal was made to encourage Maria to decide on details and standards and make a formal commitment to the plan.

Stella Simpson used noncontrolling interpersonal behaviors throughout Case Study Four, encouraging Maria Sanchez to assume full decision-making responsibility. Supervisors in the first three case studies used various levels of control, but *in each of the first three cases, the supervisor moved from more to less control and toward more decision-making responsibility on the part of the teacher*. Developmental supervision thus is developmental in two ways. First, the entry-level supervisory approach is matched with the teacher's current developmental level and the immediate situation. Second, supervisory behaviors are gradually modified to promote and accommodate long-range teacher development toward higher levels of reflection and problem-solving ability.

We purposefully provide case studies in this chapter demonstrating a clear match of the teacher's levels of adult development, expertise, and commitment with the supervisory approach. In the real world, other variables tend to enter the picture and interactions are more complex. The specific problem that the supervisor and teacher are dealing with also should be a determining factor. The past relationship of the teacher and supervisor is yet another variable to be considered. Even if we had a totally valid and reliable way of measuring a teacher's levels of adult development, expertise, and commitment (which we don't), it is impossible to predict in advance all of the other variables that might need to be considered when selecting the best supervisory approach. This is why deciding on the best approach is a human decision, not the result of a predetermined formula.

Group Activity 11.1 includes exercises for describing, providing initial assistance to, and fostering the long-term growth of teachers in need of different types of supervision.

✔ **Check Your Understanding 11.0**   Click here to gauge your understanding of the key concepts presented in this chapter.

group activity **11.1**

Writing and Reflecting on Teacher Cases

The group splits into small teams of three or four members who stay together throughout each part of the activity.

Part A.

Each team collaborates to write separate mini-cases (each no longer than one page in length) about:

- A teacher best matched with a directive control supervisory approach
- A teacher best matched with a directive informational supervisory approach
- A teacher best matched with a collaborative supervisory approach
- A teacher best matched with a nondirective supervisory approach

Each case should include (a) a description of the general professional characteristics of the teacher and (b) a description of a specific instructional problem that the teacher is experiencing.

Part B.

Each team shares copies of all four of its cases with one of the other teams. The team receiving cases from another team considers one of those cases at a time. For each case, the team discusses (a) ideas that the supervisor or teacher might bring forward (depending on the appropriate supervisory approach) in a conference to address the immediate problem, and (b) ongoing professional learning activities that would be appropriate for the teacher's long-term development.

Part C.

Each team reports to the whole group, briefly summarizing each of the four cases they worked on in Part B, and for each of those cases their suggestions for initial supervisory assistance and their recommendations for long-term teacher development.

REFLECTIVE EXERCISE

Consider the following scenario:

Megan Janson, a teacher at Lakeside High School, has come to instructional supervisor Jim Autry with a concern. Several female teachers have complained that Jim seems to be overly directive with them during conferences focused on instructional supervision. These same teachers have told Megan that they have heard from a number of male colleagues that Jim is nondirective when conferring with the male teachers.

Megan, a close friend of Jim, tells him she wanted him to know this so he could reflect on the situation and decide what, if anything, to do about it. Jim has been using different supervisory approaches with different teachers and groups lately, but has been trying to use collaborative supervision with most teachers and has been intentionally directive with only one female teacher and intentionally nondirective with only one male teacher. He is surprised and disturbed at the comments from female teachers reported by Megan.

What advice would you give Jim on each of the following issues?

1. How can Jim determine whether he is using directive behaviors with females better matched with a different approach, and/or being nondirective with males better matched with a different approach?

2. If Jim concludes that he really is using unintended interpersonal behaviors with some teachers, how can he explore possible reasons for such unintended behaviors?

3. If Jim eventually concludes that he has been engaging in unconscious gender bias in his supervisory conferences, what can he do to correct the situation? How can he verify improvement in this area?

Technical Skills

The supervisor who knows about characteristics of successful schools, the norms that mediate against success, and the ways teacher development contrasts with optimal adult development can begin to formulate a supervisory belief system that becomes a reality when interpersonal and technical skills of supervision are applied in practice.

The previous part matched directive control, directive informational, collaborative, and nondirective interpersonal skills in working with developmental levels of individuals and groups of teachers. Part 4 deals with the technical supervisory skills needed in working with teachers to observe, assess, plan, implement, and evaluate. Understanding schools and relating well to teachers are necessary components, but technical skills are equally important for accomplishing the tasks of supervision.

chapter 12

Observing Skills

Learning Outcomes for This Chapter

After reading this chapter, you should be able to:

1. Name at least five types of quantitative observations.
2. Identify at least three types of qualitative observations.
3. Describe tailored observation systems.
4. Summarize the purpose of a schoolwide classroom observation.
5. Explain why video recording is now a more practical tool for classroom observation than it was several years ago.

Questions to Reflect On as You Read This Chapter

1. This chapter stresses the distinction between observation and interpretation. What are some instances you have witnessed when an individual correctly described a situation or event but misinterpreted the meaning of the situation or event?
2. What are some teacher instructional concerns for which it would be more appropriate to gather quantitative data? Qualitative data?
3. How do the observation instruments presented in this chapter contrast with summative evaluation forms with which you are familiar?
4. What are some ways in which an observer's personal experiences and values could affect a classroom observation?

Consider the classroom shown in Figure 12.1. If you were an observer of this classroom, what would you say is happening? Of course, one illustration is not enough basis for an observation, but pretend you are seeing this episode for an entire class period. Could you say that the students have behavior problems, discipline is lax, the teacher is not responding to the students' interests, or the teacher is lecturing too much? If your observations are similar to those listed here, then you have fallen into the *interpretation trap*, which is the downfall of most attempts to help people improve their performance.

Observation is a two-part process—first *describing* what has been seen and then *interpreting* what it means. The mind almost simultaneously processes a visual image,

figure **12.1** **Classroom Picture**

integrates that image with previously stored images related to satisfactory and unsatisfactory experiences, and ascribes a value or meaning to that image. If a student yawns, our mind signals "boredom." If a teacher yells at students, our mind registers "losing control." A judgment derives from an image or a description of events. We must be aware of splitting that almost simultaneous process, of separating description from interpretation. When we lose the description of the event and retain only the interpretation, we create communication difficulties and obstacles to improvement. Sharing the description of events is the forerunner of professional improvement. Interpretation leads to resistance. When both parties can agree on what events occurred, they are more likely to agree on what needs to be changed.

Remember that if the goal of supervision is to enhance teachers' thought and commitment about improving classroom (and school) practice, observations should be used as a base of information to create an instructional dialogue between supervisor and teacher. Using description first when talking to a teacher about his or her classroom creates an instructional dialogue. Providing interpretations and evaluative statements first ushers in defensiveness, combativeness, or resentment in the teacher and stifles discussion.

Differentiating description from interpretation in observation is so crucial for instructional improvement that we need to refer back to our illustration of the classroom (Figure 12.1). Look at the picture again and tell what you now see going on. You might say that there are three students looking away from the teacher and talking to each other while the teacher stands in front of the room calling on a student in the front row. Can we agree that this is happening? Probably so, and thus we can *later* judge the rightness or wrongness of the event in regard to student learning. The teacher can more readily change the events of three students talking to each other and two others looking away than he or she can change being "a poor classroom manager."

Another distinction that needs to be made is the difference between formative and summative observation instruments. A *formative* observation instrument used to describe what is occurring in a classroom (consistent with what teacher and supervisor agreed to focus on and later discuss) is a means for professional growth and instructional improvement. Therefore, the use of a formative observation instrument is conditioned on prior agreement about what is most worthy of learning by that teacher in that classroom—whether the interest is derived from a desire to know more about himself or herself as a teacher, attempting a particular instructional model, experimenting with a new practice or strategy, or struggling with a problem or weakness. A *summative* evaluation instrument, on the other hand, is an externally imposed, uniformly applied measure, intended to judge all teachers on similar criteria to determine their worthiness, merit, and competence as employees. Distinctions between summative and formative evaluation are detailed in Chapter 16.

There are many ways to record descriptions. An observation instrument is a tool for organizing and recording different categories of classroom life. It can be as simple as a single category or as complex as a matrix of dozens of possible coded combinations. For example, an instrument can be used to count the displays on a classroom wall or to record the hundreds of students' and teachers' verbal and nonverbal interactions.

We will first look at quantitative observations, including categorical instruments, performance indicator instruments, visual diagramming, and space utilization. The second section will deal with qualitative observations, including verbatim, detached open-ended narrative, participant open-ended observation, focused questionnaire observation, and educational criticism. We will describe tailored observations—quantitative or qualitative observations designed to gather data on specific teacher concerns. Finally, we will discuss schoolwide classroom observation, used as one way of assessing or evaluating the school's overall instructional program.

Quantitative Observations

Quantitative observations are ways of measuring classroom events, behaviors, and objects. Definitions and categories must be precise. Eventually, the observations can be used for statistical operations.

Categorical Frequency Instrument

A categorical instrument is a form that defines certain events or behaviors that can be checked off at frequency intervals and then counted. Figure 12.2 is a categorical instrument that measures the frequency of different types of questions asked by the

Question Category	Tally	Total	Percent
Evaluation		0	0
Synthesis	I	1	5
Analysis	I	1	5
Application	II	2	10
Interpretation	III	3	15
Translation	IIII	4	20
Memory	̶T̶H̶L̶ IIII	9	45
Total of Questions Asked = 20			

figure **12.2** **Teacher Questions**

teacher. The seven categories of teacher questions are based on Bloom's taxonomy. (The taxonomy is explained in Chapter 19.) By dividing the number of questions in each category by the total number of questions asked by the teacher during the lesson, the observer can calculate the percent of total questions each category represents.

Other classroom topics can be observed with categorical instruments. For example, one can focus on on-task and off-task behaviors. To complete the instrument in Figure 12.3, the observer begins a sweep of the classroom every 5 minutes. During

Student	Time when Sweep Began							
	9:00	9:05	9:10	9:15	9:20	9:25	9:30	9:35
Andrew	A	C	D	E	E	A	B	B
Shawn G.	A	A	D	E	E	A	C	B
Maria	A	A	D	E	E	C	B	B
Sam	I	F	F	E	F	A	B	C
Barbara	H	F	D	E	E	F	F	B
Angie	C	G	G	C	E	G	G	G
Jeff	A	A	C	E	E	A	B	B
Jessica	F	F	D	E	E	A	B	E
Shawn L.	A	A	D	E	H	H	B	B
Chris	F	F	D	E	E	A	B	C
Michele	A	A	D	E	H	H	B	B
Mark	A	I	I	F	I	I	I	F
Melissa	C	A	D	E	E	C	H	B
John	J	A	J	I	J	J	J	J
Rolanda	A	C	D	E	E	A	B	F

Key

A = on task, listening/watching   F = off task, passive
B = on task, writing   G = off task, doing work for another class
C = on task, speaking   H = off task, listening to others
D = on task, reading   I = off task, disturbing others
E = on task, hands-on activity   J = off task, playing

figure **12.3** **Student On-Task and Off-Task Behaviors**

each sweep, the observer focuses on each student for approximately 20 seconds and then records that student's behavior. During a 40-minute lesson, the observer can make 8 sweeps. The instrument allows the observer to record specific on-task and off-task behaviors listed in the key at the bottom of the chart.

Performance Indicator Instruments

A performance indicator instrument records whether actions listed on the observation instrument have been observed. With some instruments, a third option—"not applicable" (N/A)—is included. Performance indicator instruments may also include space for the observer to add supplemental notes concerning the presence or absence of the action. Figure 12.4 is a performance indicator instrument used to record the presence

Elements	Response			Comments
Anticipatory set	Yes ___	No ___	N/A ___	_____
Statement of objective and purpose	Yes ___	No ___	N/A ___	_____
Input	Yes ___	No ___	N/A ___	_____
Modeling	Yes ___	No ___	N/A ___	_____
Checking for understanding	Yes ___	No ___	N/A ___	_____
Guided practice	Yes ___	No ___	N/A ___	_____
Independent practice	Yes ___	No ___	N/A ___	_____

figure **12.4** **Hunter Model Performance Indicators**

or absence of the elements in Madeline Hunter's lesson design model, a model well suited for direct instruction. Figure 12.5 is an instrument to assess whether each of the basic elements of a cooperative learning lesson is present.

The instrument in Figure 12.6 lists indicators of an authentic constructivist lesson, and that in Figure 12.7 lists indicators of culturally sensitive teaching. Because the indicators in Figures 12.6 and 12.7 are more open to interpretation than indicators in many instruments of this type, it is especially important for the observer to describe in the comments column specific classroom behaviors that are the basis for the observer's responses.

Remember that performance indicators used for observation purposes should not imply an absolute standard. The fact that a teacher does not perform all of the activities listed on the observation instrument may or may not be a cause of concern. Only after the supervisor and teacher have discussed the circumstances surrounding the teacher's instructional procedures can they be properly interpreted.

Elements	Response	Comments
Explanation of academic and social objectives	Yes ___ No ___ N/A ___	_____
Teaching of necessary social skills	Yes ___ No ___ N/A ___	_____
Face-to-face interaction	Yes ___ No ___ N/A ___	_____
Positive interdependence	Yes ___ No ___ N/A ___	_____
Individual accountability	Yes ___ No ___ N/A ___	_____
Group processing	Yes ___ No ___ N/A ___	_____

figure **12.5** **Cooperative Learning Performance Indicators**

Indicators	Response	Comments
Co-planned by teacher and students	Yes ___ No ___ N/A ___	_____ _____
In-depth explanation of big idea	Yes ___ No ___ N/A ___	_____ _____
Student initiated questions	Yes ___ No ___ N/A ___	_____ _____
Problem centered	Yes ___ No ___ N/A ___	_____ _____
Use of primary material	Yes ___ No ___ N/A ___	_____ _____
Students test own hypotheses	Yes ___ No ___ N/A ___	_____ _____
Dialogue fostered	Yes ___ No ___ N/A ___	_____ _____
Active learning	Yes ___ No ___ N/A ___	_____ _____
Collaborative learning	Yes ___ No ___ N/A ___	_____ _____
Students construct knowledge	Yes ___ No ___ N/A ___	_____ _____
Self- and group reflection on constructions	Yes ___ No ___ N/A ___	_____ _____
Learning assessed by teachers and students	Yes ___ No ___ N/A ___ Yes ___ No ___ N/A ___	_____
Assessment of process and product	Yes ___ No ___ N/A ___	_____

figure **12.6 Indicators of a Constructivist Lesson**

Visual Diagramming

Visual diagramming is another way to portray what is occurring in a classroom. A video recording of a classroom captures the closest representative picture of actual occurrences; however, there are other ways to portray observations, such as verbal

Indicators	Response	Comments
The Teacher		
Displays understanding of diverse cultures	Yes ___ No ___	_____
Displays personal regard for all students	Yes ___ No ___	_____
Uses instructional materials free of cultural bias	Yes ___ No ___	_____
Uses examples and materials that represent different cultures	Yes ___ No ___	_____
Promotes examination of concepts and issues from different cultural perspectives	Yes ___ No ___	_____
Facilitates higher-level learning for all students	Yes ___ No ___	_____
Adopts materials and instruction to different student learning styles	Yes ___ No ___	_____
Provides equitable opportunities for student participation	Yes ___ No ___	_____
Provides individual assistance, when necessary, for all students	Yes ___ No ___ N/A ___	_____
Intervenes to address acts of student intolerance	Yes ___ No ___ N/A ___	_____
Uses "teachable moments" to address cultural issues	Yes ___ No ___ N/A ___	_____
Reinforces student acts of respect for diverse cultures	Yes ___ No ___ N/A ___	_____

figure **12.7** **Indicators of Culturally Sensitive Teaching**

interactions among teachers and students and how a teacher uses space. After diagramming the occurrence, the supervisor and the teacher can view the picture and then analyze the events.

Classroom verbal interactions can be charted by drawing arrows symbolizing verbal statements between members in a classroom (Figure 12.8). The observer can use six separate sheets of this diagram and fill out one sheet for each time sample of

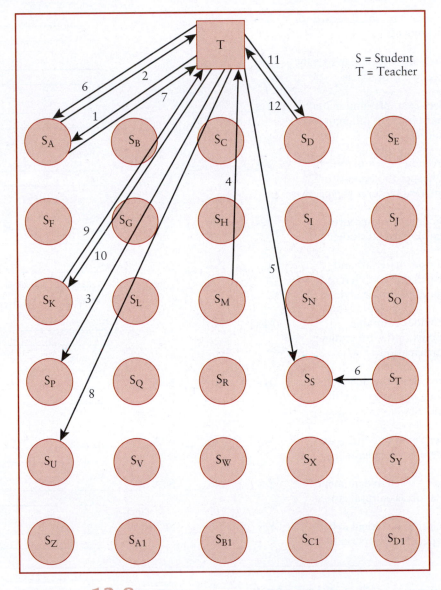

f i g u r e **12.8** **Diagram of Verbal Interaction, 9:10–9:15**

five minutes spaced throughout the hour. Each arrow drawn on the diagram would indicate a full statement directed to another person. The arrows are numbered in the sequence of statements. After diagramming, the observer would then have information on the frequency of individual student interaction, the amount of interaction with different areas of the room, which students triggered interactions among others, and which students were excluded.

For illustration purposes, if the diagram was a sample consistent with the other five samples of the classroom period, the observer would be able to state some of the following conclusions:

1. Interaction is mainly directed toward the left aisle and front row.
2. There is almost no attention to the last two rows in the back of the room or the two rows on the right.
3. Of 14 interactions, 12 included the teacher and 2 were between students.

Such diagramming is easier to follow with small groups and when students are not moving around the classroom. Class activities such as teacher lecturing interspersed with questions and answers or classroom discussions would be instructional sessions appropriate for diagramming. Another type of diagramming is flowcharting teacher space utilization, which follows the teacher's movement throughout the classroom. A sketch of the physical classroom is done first; then the observer follows the teacher by using arrows on the sketch (Figure 12.9).

Figure 12.9 illustrates a period of reading instruction. The arrow follows the teacher with each movement and is labeled with the time on the clock. After a class period, the observer and the teacher can see where the teacher has been and for how long. Such information might help make a teacher aware of the relationship of his or her space utilization to concerns of classroom management and instruction. For example, Figure 12.9 shows much physical presence in the front and on the left side of the classroom, with no presence at the rear learning centers or the middle work area.

Qualitative Observations

There are alternative means of observing based on not knowing exactly what is to be recorded. These are called *qualitative* or *descriptive* forms of observation. The observer goes into the classroom with a general focus or no focus at all and records events as they occur. The events are not made to fit into a specific category, nor are they measured. Only after the recording of events does the observer rearrange his or her observations into themes. Such recording of observations defies the use of an instrument. (An *instrument* is technically a measurement device.) Instead, qualitative observations record the complexity of classroom life.

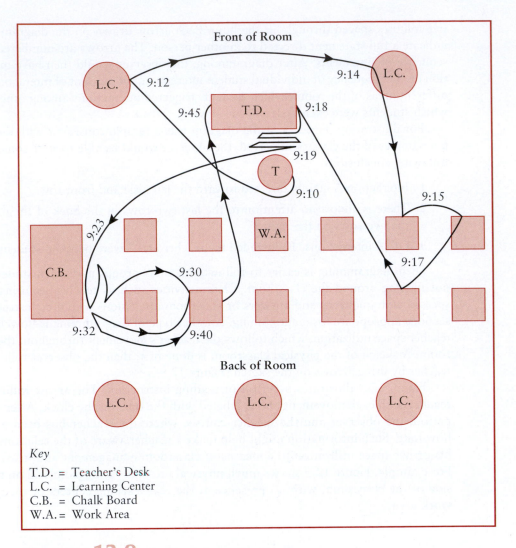

figure **12.9** **Teacher Space Utilization**

There are several types of qualitative observations. We will look at verbatim, detached open-ended narrative, participant open-ended observation, and focused questionnaire observation. These observations can be used by a supervisor to provide a broad and complex recording of classroom life.

Verbatim and Selected Verbatim

The observer taking verbatim notes (sometimes called *scripts*) records all verbal interaction taking place in the classroom. Verbatim notes allow the observer and teacher to identify patterns of interpersonal behavior during a lesson. Verbatim also provides specific examples of teacher–student or student–student interactions. For more efficient recording, the observer may abbreviate words and leave out words that add no meaning to the transcript.

Despite these timesavers, verbatim can be an arduous process requiring the observer to spend every moment taking notes, with no time for attention to anything else going on during the lesson. One alternative to verbatim is *selected verbatim,* in which the observer records only those interactions that relate to a particular focus agreed to by the observer and teacher prior to the observation. Figure 12.10 provides an excerpt from selective verbatim notes focused on teacher responses to students who initially gave incorrect or partially correct answers to teacher questions.

Detached Open-Ended Narrative

Detached open-ended narrative occurs when the supervisor steps into a classroom and records every person, event, or thing that attracts his or her attention. At the start,

C = Chris D.   10:20
T = Teacher
T. C, What are 3 branches of Fed. Govt.?
C. President, House, Senate
T. What branch Fed. Govt. is pres. head of?
C. Ah, I don't know
T. The president is Chief _____.
C. Executive! Executive branch!
T. The House and Senate are both part of what branch?
C. Legislative
T. Legislative branch, but both mean same thing. That's 2 branches,
    exec. and leg. What is the third branch?
C. The Courts.
T. What branch is made of Sup. Ct and other fed. cts.
C. Judicial
T. Right!

figure **12.10** **Excerpt from Selective Verbatim Notes**

the pages are empty, without questions, indicators, or categories. The heading might simply look like this:

Open-Ended Narrative

Observation Teacher: _____ Time: _____ Observer: _____

The recorder then has the task of writing, writing, and more writing. A sample of such an observation might read as follows:

> Students begin arriving at 10:13; the teacher is at his desk correcting papers. The bell rings at 10:15 to begin third period. Students keep arriving. Mr. X gets up from his desk to begin class at 10:25. In the meantime, students have put away their school bags and are awaiting instruction, except three girls in the back corner who are talking, combing their hair, and spreading the contents of their pocketbooks on their desks. Five minutes after Mr. X begins, he talks to them and they put away combs and pocketbooks. Mr. X describes the activities for the day but then cannot find his prepared handouts. After two minutes of looking, he finds the papers in his desk drawer.
>
> The intercom comes on at 10:30 with two announcements by the principal. Mr. X gives the assignments, and the class begins to read at 10:33. Two students are reprimanded for talking, and occasional student talk can be heard as Mr. X moves around and reviews yesterday's homework with students. He talks with 12 students before asking for class attention at 10:45. He then lectures on the classification of insects. The PowerPoint is difficult for students in the back to read. One student asks if he can darken the lights. . . .

With practice, the observer can write in shorthand to keep up with the flow of events. It is impossible to record all that could possibly be seen and heard in a classroom. The observer must constantly scan the entire classroom and decide what is significant.

Participant Open-Ended Observation

Participant open-ended observation occurs when the supervisor becomes a functioning part of the classroom (Marshall & Rossman, 2011). The supervisor assists in the instruction, helps students with questions, uses classroom materials, and talks with the teacher and students. Being involved in the classroom gives the supervisor an inside-out view of the classroom different from that of the detached observer who tries to be invisible and keep away from students and teachers. Obviously, events cannot be written down as they occur if the supervisor is engaged in talking, moving, and assisting. Instead, he or she must write between pauses in the action. The observation form can be carried on a clipboard so that notes can be taken on the run.

The participant observer takes sketchy notes (catchphrases and words) during classroom time so that afterward he or she can write in greater detail. These quick notes serve to remind the observer of the situation that will be described more fully after the observation period is over. The following is an example of such short notes:

> Teacher X directs students into study groups.
>
> John B. does not understand the assignment. I work with him on organizing the theme of a play.
>
> Sally T. and Ramona B. are wandering around. I ask them if they need help; they say no and leave the room (ask teacher about this).
>
> Sondra and her group are ready to role play their theme. I listen as they read through their parts.
>
> Steven's group is stuck; he doesn't know how to find materials on historic buildings. I suggest calling the town historic society.
>
> Susan is not participating at all—looking at *Teen Magazine*. The rest of the group just leaves her alone. (I wonder why?)
>
> The video shown has everyone's attention.
>
> Teacher X dismisses the class. I overhear a student say, "This class goes so quickly. I wish other classes were as much fun."

These are some notes from a 50-minute classroom period. Much more happened in the classroom than is noted, but the observer picks up insights from his or her involvement. The supervisor can later fill in details—the two girls leaving the classroom, the specifics of John's confusion about the theme, Susan's absorption in *Teen Magazine*, and so on.

Focused Questionnaire Observation

Qualitative observation can be done in a more focused manner by having general topics to use in recording events. An observer seeks information about specific questions.

For example, if a teacher was attempting to teach problem-solving skills, the observer might use the following questions to focus the observation:

Are students able to:

1. Distinguish between problems and their effects?
2. View a problem from the perspective of different groups and individuals?
3. Gather and analyze data to better understand the problem?

4. Identify various causes of the problem and how those causes relate or interact?

5. Generate alternative solutions and reflect on the potential effects of each alternative?

6. Develop a feasible plan for solving the problem?

7. Collaborate with each other in solving the problem?

8. Reflect on and assess their problem solving efforts and how they can improve problem solving in the future?

A focused questionnaire can revolve around a particular instructional model, such as direct instruction, cooperative learning, jurisprudence, advanced organizers, or indirect learning. It can be as narrow as looking at one or two questions within a particular model or as extensive as to include numerous questions about a model, or it can be generic in posing questions that would cross different teaching practices.

▶ Video Illustration

In the video, a peer coach completes a focused observation. After watching the video, think of an instructional model that is familiar to you. What might be three or four questions that a teacher and observer might wish to focus on during an observation using the instructional model that you have identified?

Tailored Observation Systems

Supervisors often observe lessons to collect data on unique instructional concerns or improvement efforts. If no observation system exists that is capable of gathering the desired data, the supervisor can design a tailored observation system. Tailored observation systems can be quantitative, qualitative, or a combination of both.

Figure 12.11 is a system designed to collect four specific types of data. The teacher in this example requested that the observer collect data on (1) how often the teacher called on each student; (2) whether each student's response was correct or incorrect; (3) whether the teacher drew out correct student responses through encouragement or prompting, especially after a student's initial response was incorrect; and (4) how often the teacher provided positive feedback to students making correct responses. In Figure 12.11, codes symbolize both student responses (−, +, ×) to teacher questions, and teacher reactions (→, O) to student responses. Several codes on the same line indicate verbal behaviors that were part of the same series of interactions. Codes on different lines indicate separate series of interactions.

In another example, teacher Simmons was concerned about the conduct of one of his students and asked the supervisor to collect data on the student's behaviors,

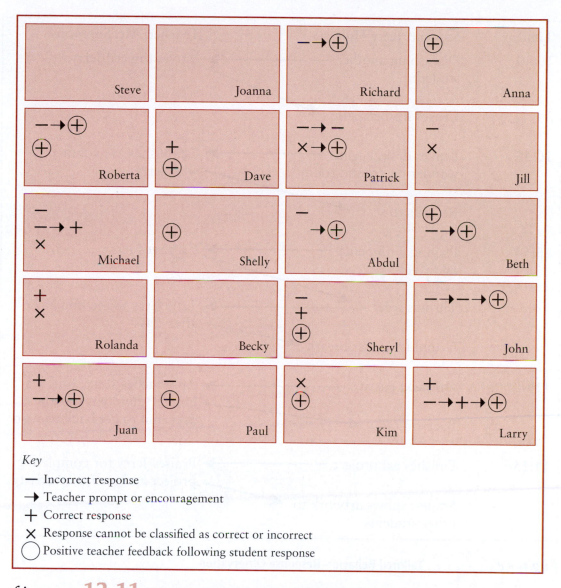

f i g u r e **12.11** **Tailored Question–Response Instrument**

Simmons's responses, and the effects of those responses on the student. Figure 12.12 is the observation chart completed by the supervisor. Arrows point to immediate responses of the teacher to selected student behaviors and immediate responses of the student to relevant teacher behaviors. Some of the most meaningful and helpful classroom observation data we have viewed have been collected with instruments designed by supervisors and teachers focused on specific teacher concerns.

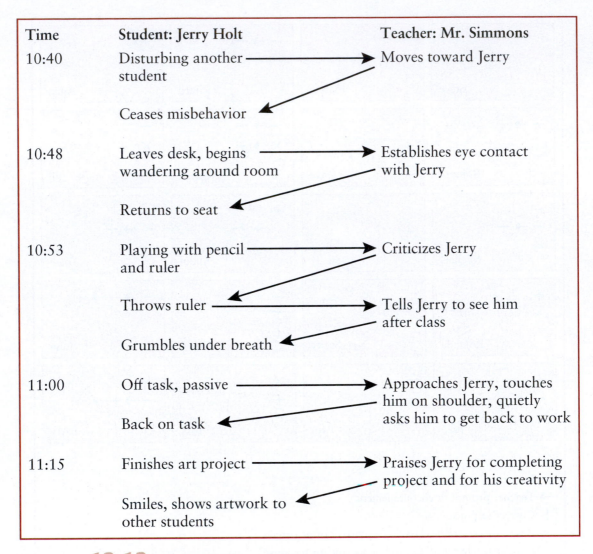

figure **12.12** **Tailored Behavior–Response Observation**

Schoolwide Classroom Observation

A school wishing to carry out a schoolwide instructional needs assessment or program evaluation may wish to gather data on teaching across the campus by conducting observations of all teachers engaged in classroom instruction. One of the authors consulted a school wishing to assess its overall instructional program, and to make schoolwide classroom observation part of that assessment. As one might expect, some of the teachers at the school were concerned about being observed as part of the needs assessment. One way the consultant and school leaders alleviated the teachers' concerns was by inviting them to help construct the observation system. During a faculty meeting, the consultant asked the teachers two questions: (1) What are some teaching methods a visitor to your classroom would typically observe? and (2) What student behaviors—either desired or undesired—would the visitor typically observe? The potential teacher and student behaviors listed by the faculty in response to these questions were used to construct the observation key presented in Figure 12.13. In addition to the behaviors suggested by the teachers, the observers added some blank lines to the key in case some teacher or student behaviors not anticipated by the faculty were displayed; the observers could simply add those behaviors to the teacher or student behavior list as they occurred during the observations. Because the teachers had been involved in deciding what behaviors would be observed, they were much more comfortable about being observed.

Teacher Behaviors	*Student Behaviors*
A. Lecturing	1. Read Aloud
B. Using Electronic Displays/Video	2. Taking Notes
C. Directing Students' Learning Activity	3. Listening
D. Reviewing Work with Students	4. Board Work
E. Reading to Students	5. Answering Questions Orally
F. Calling on Student Readers	6. Seat Work (Worksheets, Etc.)
H. Monitoring/Assisting Seat Work	7. Contributing to Open Discussion
I. Asking Students Short Questions	8. Cooperative Learning
J. Facilitating Open Discussion	10. Self-Directed Inquiry
K. Monitoring/Assisting Small Groups	11. Self-Directed Reading
M. Facilitating Student Inquiry	12. Disruptive
N. Praising	13. Passively Inattentive
O. Encouraging	14. Working on Inappropriate Task
P.	15. Inappropriate Movement
Q.	16.
R.	17.
S.	18.
T.	19.
U.	20.

figure **12.13** **Example of a Key for Schoolwide Classroom Observation**

Teacher's Name: _____

Subject: _____

Date of Observation: _____

Time of Observation: _____

Time 1st Scan Began: _____ Behaviors ⇩	Time 2nd Scan Began: _____ Behaviors ⇩	Time 3rd Scan Began: _____ Behaviors ⇩	Time 4th Scan Began: _____ Behaviors ⇩	Time 5th Scan Began: _____ Behaviors ⇩
T:	T:	T:	T:	T:
⇩	⇩	⇩	⇩	⇩
S 1:	S 1:	S 1:	S 1:	S 1:
S 2:	S 2:	S 2:	S 2:	S 2:
S 3:	S 3:	S 3:	S 3:	S 3:
S 4:	S 4:	S 4:	S 4:	S 4:
S 5:	S 5:	S 5:	S 5:	S 5:
S 6:	S 6:	S 6:	S 6:	S 6:
S 7:	S 7:	S 7:	S 7:	S 7:
S 8:	S 8:	S 8:	S 8:	S 8:
S 9:	S 9:	S 9:	S 9:	S 9:
S 10:	S 10:	S 10:	S 10:	S 10:
S 11:	S 11:	S 11:	S 11:	S 11:
S 12:	S 12:	S 12:	S 12:	S 12:
S 13:	S 13:	S 13:	S 13:	S 13:
S 14:	S 14:	S 14:	S 14:	S 14:
S 15:	S 15:	S 15:	S 15:	S 15:
S 16:	S 16:	S 16:	S 16:	S 16:
S 17:	S 17:	S 17:	S 17:	S 17:
S 18:	S 18:	S 18:	S 18:	S 18:
S 19:	S 19:	S 19:	S 19:	S 19:
S 20:	S 20:	S 20:	S 20:	S 20:

figure **12.14** **Example of an Observation Tool Used for Schoolwide Classroom Observation (see Figure 12.13 for observation key)**

The observers used an observation tool similar to the one shown in Figure 12.14 to record teacher and student behaviors during classroom observations (in order to save space, Figure 12.14 has fewer columns and rows then the actual observation tool). The observers scanned the classroom every five minutes, recording the teacher behavior observed at the beginning of the five-minute period by writing the letter that symbolized the teacher's behavior (see teacher behaviors A through O in Figure 12.13) after the T at the top of the appropriate column on the observation tool. During the remainder of the five-minute scan, the observer watched each student long enough to determine the student's behavior, then wrote the number representing that behavior (see student behaviors 1 through 15 in Figure 12.13) after the student's code (an S followed by a student number) on the observation tool.

Analysis of the data from the schoolwide classroom observation in our example provided the school's supervisors and teachers with a wealth of information about the teaching and learning going on across the campus. For example, as you review the teacher behaviors in Figure 12.13, note the shaded bar across that column. Those behaviors above the shaded bar can be called "teacher centered," and those below it are considered "student centered." Data from the observations allowed the educators to calculate the ratio of teacher-centered to student-centered instruction, not only in individual classrooms, but also throughout the school. Examining Figure 12.13 further, the first six student behaviors represent passive learning, behaviors 7 through 11 denote active learning, and behaviors 12 through 15 indicate a lack of student engagement. Thus, the assessment allowed calculation of the ratio of active to passive learning as well as the ratio of on-task to off-task behavior, again, for both individual classrooms and the entire school. The needs assessment allowed the school to identify a long-term professional development program for the faculty focused on the goals of increasing student-centered teaching and active student learning.

Here we have presented just one example of an observation system that can be used for schoolwide classroom observation and yield campus-wide data. There are many other data gathering systems that can be used for this purpose. Indeed, many of the observation tools provided in this chapter as tools for gathering individual classroom data can be adapted for campus-wide use. Just as the gathering of observation data in a single classroom should lead to dialogue between the supervisor and teacher about the meaning of the data and improvement goals based on that meaning, so schoolwide classroom observation should be the basis for dialogue across the campus on meaning and future collective action. Chapter 13 discusses assessment and planning for schoolwide instructional improvement, and campus-wide observation can help to identify schoolwide needs. Chapter 14 is focused on implementation and evaluation of schoolwide instructional improvement efforts, and campus-wide observation can help to monitor the implementation and evaluate the results of such efforts.

Review of Types and Purposes of Observation

Figure 12.15 illustrates the types of observation available to a supervisor. The purpose of the observation should determine the type, method, and role of observation:

- The *categorical frequency* observation is a quantitative method used by a detached observer for the purpose of counting, totaling, and statistically analyzing behaviors.

Type	Method		Role of Observer		Purpose
	Quantitative	*Qualitative*	*Detached*	*Participant*	
Categorical frequency	x		x		Count behaviors
Performance indicator	x		x		Evident or not
Visual diagramming	x		x		Picture verbal interaction
Space utilization	x		x		Picture movement
Verbatim		x	x		Script of verbal interaction
Detached open-ended narrative		x	x		Attention to unfolding event
Participant open-ended observation		x		x	Inside-out view
Focused questionnaire		x	x or	x	Focus on particular events
Tailored	x or	x	x or	x	Address unique concerns
Schoolwids classroom observation	x or	x	x		Gather data on teaching across the campus

figure **12.15 Observation Alternatives**

- The *performance indicator* observation is quantitatively used by a detached observer to record evidence of human behavior.

- *Visual diagramming* is a quantitative observation used by a detached observer for the purpose of depicting verbal interaction.

- Human *space utilization* observation is a quantitative measure used by a detached observer for the purpose of depicting the length and pattern of physical movement.

- *Verbatim* is a detached qualitative method in which the observer records all verbal interaction.

- The *detached open-ended narrative* is a qualitative observation used by a detached observer for recording events as they unfold.

- *Participant open-ended observation* is a qualitative technique used to record how people and events unfold to one involved in the classroom.

- The *focused questionnaire* is another qualitative method that can be used by a detached or participant observer for the purpose of gathering evidence according to general questions about classroom topics.

- *Tailored observation* systems cut across the different categories previously discussed. They are designed by the supervisor (or supervisor and teacher) to collect data on specific teacher concerns when there is no existing observation system for collecting such data. They may be quantitative or qualitative and may be used by a detached or participant observer.

- *Schoolwide classroom observation* can use either quantitative or qualitative methods to assess schoolwide instructional improvement needs as well as monitor the implementation and evaluate the results of campus-wide instructional improvement efforts.

Trends and Cautions Regarding Observation

Trends in classroom observation include the use of technology and collaborative walkthroughs. Technology can be used well or poorly, and walkthroughs can be more or less helpful to instructional improvement efforts. In this section we discuss how these innovations can be used in productive ways, and we provide some cautions about the need to combine observation of teaching with supervisor-teacher dialogue and co-interpretation.

Technology-Enhanced Observation

A wide range of technology now is available to assist supervisors with both quantitative and qualitative observations. This technology can be placed on a continuum from simple to complex. On the simple end of the continuum are *digital pens*. These pens initially are used to record data much as they have traditionally been gathered, but the digital pen is not your grandfather's writing instrument. Besides an ink cartridge, digital pens include a microphone, digital audio recorder, infrared camera, flash memory, and speaker. The observer uses the digital pen to write observation data—including words, symbols, and diagrams—on digital paper at the same time the pen is recording sound. Later, the observer can review audio from the lesson simply by tapping the observation notes from any part of the lesson. The observer analyzing data may have missed part of the verbal interaction or simply not recall what is meant by observation notes from part of the lesson. In such cases, the supervisor can immediately listen to the relevant part of the lesson for clarification. Also, the supervisor discussing written data with the teacher can play the audio from any part of the lesson for the teacher. The digitized, synchronized, written observation data and audio recording can be transferred to the observer's personal computer or sent directly to the observed teacher.

Video recording of teaching is another type of technology-enhanced observation. Observers have been using video cameras to gather classroom observation data for decades, but a number of factors have limited the use of video, including the obtrusiveness of large cameras and tripods, technical problems (lighting, acoustics, and so on), and the limited scope of teacher and student behaviors captured by standard lens cameras. Modern digital cameras, however, are small enough to be unobtrusive; wide-lens cameras can capture much more of what is going on in the classroom; and small wireless microphones clipped to teachers' clothing provide high-quality audio recordings (Johnson, Sullivan, & Williams, 2009). Additionally, we now have software that can convert audio recordings of classroom verbal interaction into transcripts that can be used for detailed analysis. The observer can use videos or transcripts of lessons to analyze data prior to a postconference, or analyze the video with the teacher during the postconference. Additionally, the ease with which videos now can be edited means that teachers can share and analyze each others' video clips in collaborative work for instructional improvement (Van Es, 2010).

A more complex type of observation technology is *webcam and bug-in-ear (BIE) technology* (Rock, Greg, Thead, Acker, Gable, & Zigmond, 2009; Scheeler, McKinnon, & Stout, 2012). Scholars studying the supervision of preservice teachers have done much of the research on this technology, but the technology can easily be adapted to the observation of in-service teachers. BIE technology allows the observer to provide immediate feedback to the teacher by electronic transmission to a battery-operated receiver (bug) placed inside the teacher's ear. BIE technology enables the observer to provide the teacher with real-time feedback on student behavior and teacher actions. The webcam allows the supervisor to observe the lesson from a distance, which, in addition to providing convenience and efficiency, removes the obvious awkwardness and disruption the observer would cause by communicating orally with the teacher while present in the classroom. The technology includes video recording of the lesson for later analysis and discussion. An important caution is necessary when considering webcam and BIE technology for the observation of in-service teachers. In teacher preparation programs, such technology often is associated with providing novices with immediate *corrective* feedback, reinforcement, and so on, which represent judgment by the observer. BIE feedback to in-service teachers, excepting an emergency situation, should consist of *observations* that can assist the teacher during the lesson, with more in-depth *interpretation* of those observations awaiting teacher-observer discussion in a postconference. The best use of BIE technology with in-service teachers is probably for assisting new teachers, teachers experiencing serious difficulty, or teachers trying out new instructional strategies who have requested real-time feedback.

How much technology is appropriate for classroom observations depends on a number of things, including the school's instructional improvement goals, types of data to be gathered, and available resources. We must keep in mind that for instructional supervision, the purpose of observation is not to measure every action that can be observed or produce impressive computer-generated data displays, but to improve teaching and learning.

Collaborative Walkthroughs

Administrator walkthroughs of classrooms have become popular ways to observe instruction. They are quick (a few minutes) and allow the administrator to have a visible presence in classrooms. Walkthroughs, if part of a teacher's summative evaluation, can provide the administrator with supplemental data to verify formal evaluations. Nonetheless, when it comes to the systematic observation and analysis needed to help teachers reflect deeply on their teaching and grow in teaching expertise, administrator walkthroughs have little to offer. In contrast, the *collaborative walkthrough* involving the supervisor facilitating 8 to 12 teachers visiting classrooms and gathering observation data has considerable potential for the improvement of teaching and learning.

In a collaborative walkthrough, different teachers can gather different types of data and consolidate those data after the observation, an advantage over the school administrator observing alone during a brief walkthrough. Additionally, the teachers doing the walkthrough have the opportunity to observe colleagues teaching, often to students whom the observers also teach, and to view teaching methods they may wish to try out in their own classrooms. Finally, collaborative walkthroughs can lead to collegiality and instructional dialogue—both among observers and between observers and host teachers—that we know is necessary for schoolwide instructional improvement.

Collaborative walkthroughs described by Madhlangobe and Gordon (2012) illustrate the power of this type of observation. The supervisor and approximately 12 high school teachers participate in each walkthrough. The supervisor and teachers meet before the walkthrough to discuss the observation. One teacher is asked to serve as group leader. The group of teachers is divided into three teams; one team is assigned to gather data on the classroom environment, a second team is asked to gather information on the teacher's behaviors, and a third team is assigned to gather data on student learning. The supervisor participates in the walkthrough with the teachers. During the walkthrough, teachers gather data they can use to improve their own teaching as well data to assist the host teacher.

The supervisor and teachers meet in the school library after the walkthrough to share observation data, discuss observed teaching methods they would like to try out in their own teaching, and decide on feedback to share with the host teacher. The supervisor attends the meeting, sharing ideas from other collaborative walkthroughs, and raising questions to enhance the discussion. The teacher assigned as the group leader takes notes on the group discussion, and later meets with the host teacher to share data and discuss the observed lesson. The supervisor who facilitates the collaborative walkthroughs reports that since the collaborative walkthroughs began teachers have improved their instruction, and collegiality and collaborative problem solving have increased throughout the school.

Video Illustration

Compare and contrast the collaborative walkthrough described in the three videos with the authors' description of collaborative walkthroughs.

Cautions Concerning Observation

Quantum physics informs us that a phenomenon cannot be measured without the measurement process interacting with the phenomenon and thus affecting the measurement (Rae, 2008). Closer to home for those of us who are educators, the constructivist epistemology holds that rather than identifying a fixed reality through objective observation, we construct knowledge by interacting with our environment and with others.

One implication for classroom observation is our need to realize that our observations are affected by our personal experiences and values, our presence in the classroom during the observation, the observation instrument we use, our skill at recording data, and so on. Another implication is that the interpretation of what the observation data mean is a construction and in most cases is best co-constructed with the teacher. Observation data, thus, should be an entry point for teacher-supervisor dialogue and co-interpretation during a postobservation conference. Clinical supervision, discussed in Chapter 15, provides a structure for teacher-supervisor dialogue on classroom observation.

> ✔ **Check Your Understanding 12.0** Click here to gauge your understanding of the key concepts presented in this chapter.

REFLECTIVE EXERCISE

Return to Figure 12.1 at the beginning of this chapter. Create two different interpretations of what is going on in the classroom depicted in the figure. In Interpretation 1, the teacher has lost control of the classroom. In Interpretation 2, all students are on task and engaged in meaningful learning activities. For each interpretation, explain what students who are out of their seats or facing each other are doing.

chapter 13

Assessing and Planning Skills

Learning Outcomes for This Chapter

After reading this chapter, you should be able to:

1. List the five parts of a plan for personal improvement.
2. Explain what the authors mean when they say that organizational instructional improvement efforts should be cyclical.
3. Enumerate at least six ways of assessing organizational instructional improvement needs.
4. Summarize the purpose of a Pareto chart.
5. Describe the information summarized in a process decision program chart.

Questions to Reflect On as You Read This Chapter

1. What are some areas of your worklife that would benefit from personal time assessment and planning for change in time allocations?
2. How does planning in an organization you work in or are familiar with compare with the ideas for planning presented in this chapter?
3. What ways of assessing needs and planning discussed in this chapter would benefit an organization you work in or are familiar with?
4. What are ways to involve stakeholders—teachers, staff, students, parents, and other members of the community served by the school—in applying ways of assessing and planning described in this chapter?
5. What are some situations you are familiar with in which assessing or planning processes are overly complex and need to be simplified in order to more accurately assess needs or develop better plans? How should these assessing or planning processes be changed?

Assessing and planning skills are useful to a supervisor in setting goals and activities for oneself as well as for others. This chapter begins with personal organization of time—assessing one's current use of professional time and then planning and managing the use of future time. It goes on to focus on techniques for organizational planning for the improvement of instruction.

Assessing and planning are two sides of the same coin. *Assessing* involves determining where you and your staff have been and where you and your staff currently are. *Planning* includes deciding where you want to go and choosing the path you and your staff hope to traverse in order to reach that destination. Until you are certain of the origination and destination of your travel, a map is useless. Once you are certain, a route can be created.

Personal Improvement

One of the authors visited a school system to meet with several first-year principals. The purpose of the consultation was for the new principals to talk to the consultant privately about their beginning experiences and to discuss possible changes that might improve their situations.

One principal stated that she was averaging three hours a day observing and participating in classrooms. Her major concern was with the amount of waiting time students were experiencing. Most of her teachers had divided their heterogeneous classrooms into numerous small groups. The principal wondered whether grouping certain classes homogeneously to begin with would result in fewer groups and less waiting time. The principal and consultant discussed the possible consequences of such a major change and whether less radical changes within the existing instructional program might be better. She left the session with a plan to discuss with the faculty the issue of waiting time and student grouping at the next school meeting.

The second beginning principal said that his major problem was getting out of his office to visit teachers. He wanted to be with his staff but found that paperwork, email, phone calls, and student discipline referrals kept him trapped in the office. He could find barely an hour a day to talk with staff and visit classrooms. Furthermore, the one-hour time outside the office was often interrupted by the school secretary calling him back with urgent business. The consultant and principal discussed why he was trapped in his office and what changes might be made.

After hearing about the second principal's situation, the consultant realized that the second principal had no more constraints on his time than did the first principal, who was averaging three hours a day visiting classrooms. Both had schools of comparable size in the same neighborhood. They worked for the same superintendent and had identical job responsibilities. Yet one principal was functioning as a supervisor attending to instructional improvement, while the other one was functioning only minimally in the realm of supervision. It seemed that the real difference between the two principals was not their intentions to function as supervisors but their ability to assess and plan professional time to correspond with professional intentions. Let's look at the use of professional time.

Assessing Time

To organize future time, one must assess one's current use of time. This can be done by keeping a daily log for 5 to 10 consecutive school days. Those supervisors who keep detailed appointment books might need only to return to their books at midday and at the end of the day to add notations on what actually transpired. Those who do not operate with such planned schedules can keep a daily log to be filled out at midday and at the end of the day. The log should be simple and should require only a few minutes to fill out. It might look like this:

Monday

8:00—8:50	Walked halls, visited teachers and custodians
8:50—9:20	Conference with parent
9:20—9:35	Email
9:35—10:30	Emergency—covered for sick teacher
10:30—12:00	Worked on class schedules, a few phone calls, several emails
12:00—12:30	Ate in cafeteria with teachers
12:30—12:35	Wrote morning log
12:35—12:55	Met with salesperson
12:55—1:30	Classroom visitation of Mr. Tadich
1:30—2:30	Meeting at superintendent's office
2:30—3:00	Helped supervise school dismissal
3:00—3:15	Talked with parents
3:15—4:00	Faculty meeting
4:00—4:15	Talked with teachers informally
4:15—5:30	A few phone calls, mostly email
5:30—5:40	Wrote afternoon log

After at least 5 days (preferably 10 days), the supervisor can analyze his or her current use of time by subsuming daily events in the log under large categories of time consumption. Figure 13.1 shows a sample categorical scheme.

Before transferring the daily log entries onto the time consumption chart, the supervisor should look at his or her job description and determine how his or her time *should* be spent according to job priorities. Which categories of supervisory involvement should receive the most attention? The supervisor can indicate approximate

	Monday	Tuesday	Wednesday	Thursday	Friday	Total	%
Paperwork							
Phone calls							
Email							
Assistant principals							
Parents and community							
Faculty							
Auxiliary personnel							
Central office							
Others							
Meetings							
Assistant principals							
Students							
Parents and community							
Faculty							
Auxiliary personnel							
Central office							
Others							
Classroom visits							
School hall and ground visits							
Private time for thinking							
Miscellaneous							

figure **13.1** **Supervisor Time Consumption Chart**

percentages according to this ideal use of time. After making a list of ideal time use, he or she can then write in actual time on the consumption charts, add up total time for each category, and then find the actual percentage of time being consumed for each category. He or she then has a comparison between preferred and actual consumption of time. The comparison might look like this:

Preferred Time	Actual Time
Paperwork—10%	25%
Phone calls—5%	6%
Email—15%	25%
Assistant principals—3%	10%
Parents—5%	5%
Faculty—4%	5%
Auxiliary—1%	1%
Central office—1%	1%
Others—1%	3%
Meetings—35%	28%
Assistant principals—6%	3%
Students—8%	5%
Parents and community—6%	2%
Faculty—12%	7%
Auxiliary—1%	5%
Central office—1%	5%
Others—1%	1%
Classroom visits—25%	10%
School hall and ground visits—5%	2%
Private time for thinking—3%	1%
Miscellaneous—2%	3%

This comparison of time was that of the second principal, who complained about the inability to get out of his office. The comparison showed that he was indeed spending much more time doing paperwork (10% preferred, 25% actual) and much less time on classroom visits (25% preferred, 10% actual). Further discrepancies were noted in considerably more time spent on email with assistant principals (3% preferred, 10% actual), as well as meetings with assistant principals (6% preferred, 3% actual), parents (6% preferred, 2% actual), faculty (12% preferred, 7% actual), auxiliary personnel (1% preferred, 5% actual), and central office personnel (1% preferred, 5% actual).

Changing Time Allocations: Planning

With this information on preferred and actual time use in front of the supervisor, he or she can decide what changes realistically can be made to attain the goal of increasing visitation time with teachers. The supervisor can consider a range of options to increase teacher visitation time. Some possibilities might include the following:

- *Paperwork*. Delegate more clerical work to administrative assistants, aides, or other assistants. Schedule paperwork for uninterrupted hours after school.
- *Email*. Develop a system for processing incoming email, including decision rules for when to respond to email and how to perform or delegate preresponse preparation when necessary.
- *Meetings*. See if meetings at central office and with auxiliary staff can be delegated, shortened, or scheduled after school hours. Use some of the time saved to increase the amount of time in individual and small-group meetings with assistant principals, faculty, students, parents, and other community members.
- *Classroom visits*. Increase classroom visits from one to two periods a day. Set up backup system with administrative assistant to cover all but real emergencies when in the classroom. Schedule visits for a set time each day.

Naturally, this supervisor cannot hope to achieve exact congruence between preferred and actual time use, but can come closer to his or her preference. Some time constraints, such as the time of central office meetings, probably are not under the principal's control. There are other factors over which he or she does have direct control: when to meet parents, accept phone calls, do paperwork, and respond to email. The key to future planning of time use is to accept the limitations that exist and work on those time periods that can be altered.

The first part of a plan to make actual use of time closer to preferred time use is to answer the question: What is the objective? A sample response might be: To double classroom visitation time. The second part of the plan is to answer the question: What actions need to be taken? A sample response might be (a) schedule set times each day for two classroom observations, (b) schedule uninterrupted time for paperwork and email in two two-hour blocks of time after school, and design an email processing system. The third part of the plan is to answer the question, When will these activities be done? Sample responses might be (a) classroom visits from 9 to 11 a.m. Monday and Wednesday and 1:00 to 2:30 p.m. Tuesday and Thursday, (b) paperwork scheduled for Monday and Friday 3:00 to 5:00 p.m. The fourth part of the plan is to answer the question, What resources will be needed to implement the activities? Sample responses might be (a) explain to secretary the need to protect uninterrupted times, (b) discuss with faculty the change and rationale behind my new schedule and arrange classroom visitation schedule. The fifth and final part of the plan is to answer the question, How will the success of the goal be evaluated? A sample response might be: Check whether the new schedule was followed and, after two weeks, review the daily log to see if time in classrooms has doubled.

A supervisor could illustrate the general plan in a flowchart (Figure 13.2). Other flowcharts could illustrate more specific planning. For example, Figure 13.3 shows a flowchart with a process for the supervisor to better deal with incoming email.

There are far more elaborate systems than the one depicted here for assessing and planning time. For example, the School Administration Management system (SAMs) (Turnbull et al., 2009)—designed to assist school leaders to find more time for instructional leadership—involves data collectors shadowing the supervisor for five days and tracking time the supervisor spends on various activities, a time manager or staff

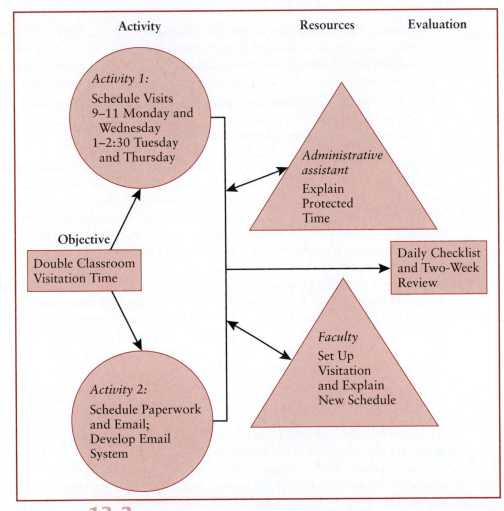

figure **13.2** **Flowchart for Increasing Classroom Visits**

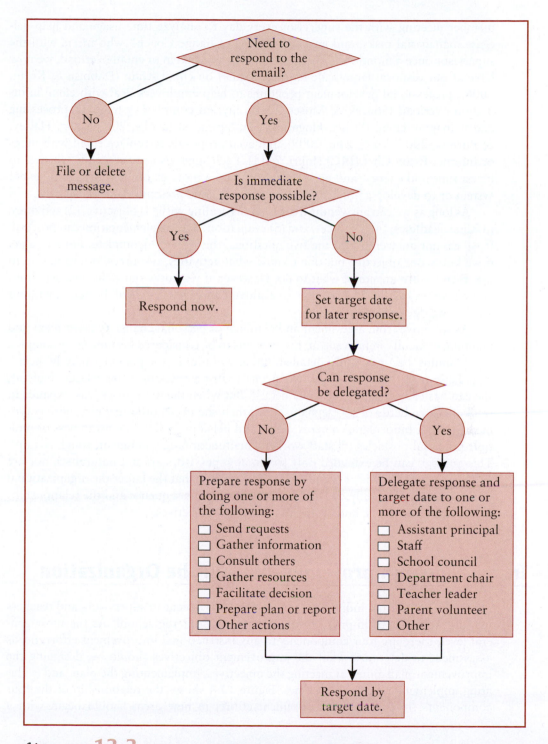

f i g u r e **13.3** **Process for Dealing with Incoming Email**

member meeting with the supervisor every day to analyze time usage and help del-egate managerial tasks, and an outside "Time Change Coach" who meets with the supervisor once a month. Regarding the universal problem of email overload, we now have at our disposal large-scale national studies on email strain (Dabbish & Kraut, 2006), professional development programs to help employees deal with email infor-mation overload (Soucek & Moser, 2010), myriad complex systems for processing and managing email (Fisher, Hogan, Brush, Smith, & Jacobs, 2006; Song, Halsey, & Burress, 2007; Yu & Zhu, 2009), and even proposals to replace email with blogs or Internet Relay Chat (IRC) (Johri, 2011). Each supervisor must decide whether to invest time and energy (and perhaps money) into a more elaborate time management system or to develop a homemade system like the one presented previously.

As long as we can answer the five questions dealing with (1) objective, (2) activities, (3) time deadlines, (4) resources, and (5) evaluation, then implementation can proceed. If we cannot answer any of the five questions, the plan is incomplete. For example, if we know our objective but don't know what activities, resources, or evaluation to use, then we are unsure of what to do. However, if we know our objective, activities, and resources but don't know how to evaluate our success, we will be acting without any knowledge of results.

As we move from assessment and planning of personal change to assessment and planning of faculty improvement, the elements to be considered become more complex and planning becomes more detailed. Other techniques for planning may be neces-sary. Let's use a "wild" analogy. When a naturalist is tracking a single large elephant, she can basically track the beast by herself. But when the naturalist's task expands to tracking three herds of 45 elephants each, then she needs other people, more equip-ment (radios, binoculars, cameras, jeeps, and helicopters), and an awareness of mul-tiple potential obstacles (ill staff workers, malfunctioning equipment, rough terrain). This analogy can be extended only so far, as supervisors are not naturalists, nor are teaching faculties herds of elephants. But the point is that the larger the organizational effort, the more carefully one needs to account for the sequence and the relationships of activities, resources, and evaluation to overall objectives.

Instructional Improvement Within the Organization

Let us shift now from individual supervisor improvement to supervisors and teachers working together to improve instruction throughout the school. At the most gen-eral level, there are four components to any instructional improvement effort: needs assessment to determine what the improvement objectives should be, designing the improvement plan aimed at meeting the objectives, implementing the plan, and evalu-ating implementation and outcomes. Figure 13.4 shows the relationship of the four components. Instructional improvement efforts in new areas should begin with a

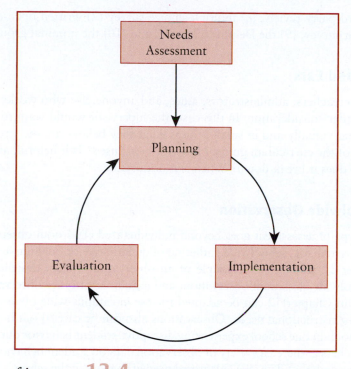

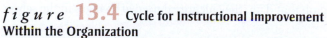

f i g u r e **13.4** **Cycle for Instructional Improvement Within the Organization**

needs assessment. As indicated in Figure 13.4, once the needs assessment has been completed, instructional improvement efforts should be cyclical in nature. The evaluation of implementation and outcomes should lead to renewed planning and the implementation of a revised plan. In the remainder of this chapter, we will discuss the needs assessment and planning components, and implementation and evaluation components will be addressed in Chapter 14.

Ways of Assessing Need

For purposes of illustration in our discussion of needs assessment, we will use an example of an elementary reading supervisor who is responsible for developing revised curriculum guides in reading. The first question for the reading supervisor is: What do we hope to accomplish with a new curriculum guide? To answer this question, we need to collect information about the past and present state of reading instruction. The supervisor can use multiple ways of assessing need: (1) eyes and ears, (2) schoolwide observations, (3) official records, (4) review of teacher and student work products,

(5) third-party review, (6) multiple-choice survey (7) written open-ended survey, (8) ranking survey, (9) the Delphi technique, and (10) the nominal group technique.

Eyes and Ears

Talk to teachers, administrators, aides, and anyone else who works directly with the task under consideration. In this case, the supervisor would want to ask teachers and aides individually and in small groups what they believe are the strengths and weaknesses of the curriculum guide. How is it being used? Is it helpful, and in what ways? Where does it break down? When is it not useful?

Schoolwide Observation

This type of assessment goes beyond individualized classroom observation. It consists of the systematic, schoolwide gathering of quantitative or qualitative observation data. Chapter 12 provides an example of an observation system designed specifically for a schoolwide classroom observation; and a number of other observation systems presented in Chapter 12 can be adapted for use in campus-wide observations to assess a school's instructional needs. Observations also can be carried out in common areas of the school. In one school experiencing disruptive student behavior during lunch periods, the teachers gathered a variety of observation data on student behaviors in the cafeteria, and based on that data, they identified needed changes in the school's lunch procedures.

Official Records

Look at any documents that indicate the current use and effect of the task under consideration. In this case, what do reading achievement test scores show? How about diagnostic reading tests? Are students mastering reading skills, or are there certain areas (comprehension, fluency, vocabulary) that are consistently out of line with others? What about the curriculum guide itself? When was it last revised? What recent knowledge about writing curriculum guides, instructional approaches to reading, and reading topics are not reflected in the current curriculum?

Review of Teacher and Student Work Products

Assessors can review teacher and student work products to assess need. Examples of teacher work products are unit and lesson plans, videos of teaching, and teacher portfolios. Examples of student work products include daily assignments, videos of student presentations, student projects, and student portfolios. Samples of work produced by several teachers or students can be reviewed to identify common instructional needs. In some schools, teachers build classroom and school portfolios that can be reviewed to analyze representative teacher and student work products.

Third-Party Review

Having a neutral outside person review the task area can be helpful. The supervisor might contact a university or central office consultant, a graduate doctoral student, or some other person with expertise to do an investigation and write a report. The third-party person should be given a clear description of the task (to look at the strengths and weaknesses of the reading curriculum guides), and care should be taken not to bias the third-party person's judgment. The report can then serve as an additional source of objective knowledge, not tied to any special interest in the forthcoming project.

Multiple-Choice Survey

This is perhaps the most common type of needs assessment survey. Multiple-choice surveys include the familiar Likert survey, with the possible responses to each item being strongly agree, agree, undecided, disagree, and strongly disagree. A multiple-choice survey can have as few as two possible responses. For example, the respondent can simply be asked to agree or disagree with each item in the survey.

> ▶ **Video Illustration**
>
> In this video, the supervisor is discussing the results of a student survey. As you watch the video, consider why it is important for the supervisor and teachers to engage in dialogue about the meaning of survey results.

Written Open-Ended Survey

To document and add to the information already received through the methods previously discussed, a written survey can be administered. Send out a brief questionnaire that asks teachers, aides, administrators, and parents what they think about the current reading curriculum. Keep the survey brief, and word the questions simply, without education jargon. An example of a survey is found in Figure 13.5.

Ranking Survey

After gathering ideas of the strengths and weaknesses of the task at hand from many sources, the supervisor can ask staff to rank the ideas. The supervisor can then compile a group frequency and numerical priority for each idea previously mentioned. For example, if—through eyes and ears, official documents, and open-ended surveys—the supervisor has collected a list of ideas about perceived weaknesses of the current

Explanation: As you may know, this year we are determining changes to be made in our reading curriculum. Would you please take a few minutes to respond to the following questions? Please be frank! We will use the information to rewrite our curriculum guides.

Question 1. What do you think about the current reading curriculum?

Question 2. What are the strengths of the current reading curriculum?

Question 3. What are the weaknesses of the current reading curriculum?

Question 4. What changes do you believe would improve the reading curriculum?

figure **13.5** **Survey of Reading Curriculum**

reading program, he or she then could disseminate the list back to teachers, aides, and others. The disseminated form might be as shown in Figure 13.6. The supervisor can meet with the staff and show the frequency of numbers assigned to each idea and the average score for each item. Those items receiving frequent low scores and/or with the lowest average scores would be the first to focus on when discussing curriculum revisions. The ranking survey can be further refined by having the participants do two separate rankings—first, to see how all the ideas rank, and second, to re-rank a shortened list of prioritized ideas.

Directions: The following are the ideas for possible changes that you have suggested. Please prioritize this list by placing the number 1 next to the idea needing the greatest attention, number 2 next to the item needing the next most attention, and so on until all items are ranked.

_____ Format of the guides
_____ Readability of the guides
_____ Activities to go with curriculum objectives
_____ Objectives and units dealing with reading newspapers
_____ Objectives and units dealing with reading in other subject areas
_____ More phonics and word recognition objectives
_____ Cross-reference units with materials in the classrooms
_____ Cross-reference objectives with fourth-grade competency-based reading test

figure **13.6** **Ranking Ideas for Improving Reading Curriculum**

Delphi Technique

Another written way to prioritize needs is the Delphi technique, developed by the Rand Corporation (Nworie, 2011). The technique, originally intended to forecast future trends, is often used for needs assessment. It is a combination of open-ended survey and ranking. The supervisor sends around a problem statement to staff: "We are looking at revisions in the reading curriculum. Write down what you believe needs to be done." The supervisor retrieves the written comments, reproduces everyone's comments, and returns all the comments to the participants. They read the comments and then individually write a synthesis of written comments, after which the supervisor reproduces everyone's comments, and returns all the comments to the participants. The participants rank the synthesized ideas. The supervisor collects and computes average and frequency of ratings and then returns the tallies to participants to re-rank. This procedure continues until clear priorities emerge.

Nominal Group Technique

The nominal group technique, made popular by Delbecq, Van de Ven, and Gustafson (1975), is an effective way to involve all individuals within large groups of stakeholders in needs assessment and goal setting (Kennedy & Clinton, 2009). The process is outlined here in eight steps:

1. The large group is divided into small groups. Each small group is assigned a facilitator to explain and coordinate the process.

2. Each individual within a small group silently generates and writes perceived needs.

3. In round-robin manner, participants orally share with their small group one perceived need at a time. The facilitator records each idea on a flip chart. At this point, there is no discussion—only a listing of perceived needs.

4. Small-group discussions of each perceived need are led by the facilitators. The purpose of the discussion is clarification of the perceived needs, not debate on their validity.

5. Individuals within each small group rate all of the perceived needs that were listed in step 3. This step usually takes the form of participants assigning each perceived need a numerical value. For example, the facilitator might instruct group members to rate each need from 1 to 5, with an item assigned a value of 1 considered to be unimportant and an item rated a 5 perceived to be an extremely important need.

6. Each small-group facilitator collects all group members' ratings and calculates a mean for each perceived need. The facilitator rewrites the perceived needs in rank order by mean and shares the results with the small group.

7. Each small group submits its list of ranked needs (without the means) for large-group consideration. By preagreement, each small group might submit only its top-ranked needs (perhaps its top five needs) to the large group.

8. A lead facilitator then takes the large group through steps 4 through 6. In the large-group version of step 4, any participant can ask for clarification of any perceived need, with the appropriate small-group facilitator providing the requested clarification. In the whole-group version of step 5, each participant rates all perceived needs presented to the large group. The product of the large-group version of step 6 is a list of organizational needs in rank order.

Analyzing Organizational Needs

Some organizational needs are easily understood and addressed by supervisors and teachers. Others are more complicated. They require analysis to determine their underlying causes before a plan can be formulated.

For decades, W. Edwards Deming (1986) argued for the use of data displays to examine factors that may contribute to organizational needs and problems. In this section we'll discuss a few types of charts suggested by Deming and his colleagues. We'll do this by applying each chart to a school situation. The words of Mary Walton (1986) should allay any anxiety concerning the use of such charts that the reader without expertise in complex data analysis might be experiencing:

> Some of the most useful statistical tools are neither difficult nor complicated to master. The level of mathematics necessary is no more than a seventh or eighth grader might learn. Several of the basic tools are merely ways of organizing and visually displaying data. In most cases, employees can collect the data and do much of the interpretation, and they are happy to do so because it gives them more responsibility. (p. 4)

Cause-and-Effect Diagrams

Figure 13.7 is an example of a cause-and-effect diagram, often referred to as a *fishbone diagram*. In our example, a newly formed staff-development committee has received feedback from teachers throughout the district that recent staff-development programs have been ineffective. Based on a series of interviews with representative groups of teachers, the committee constructed the cause-and-effect diagram in Figure 13.7.

Four general causes were identified for the ineffective professional development: (1) poor planning, (2) low-quality staff-development sessions, (3) inadequate support for the program, and (4) unsatisfactory program evaluation. Contributing causes within the poor planning category included failure to involve teachers in the planning process, the fact that the professional development plan was not based on teacher

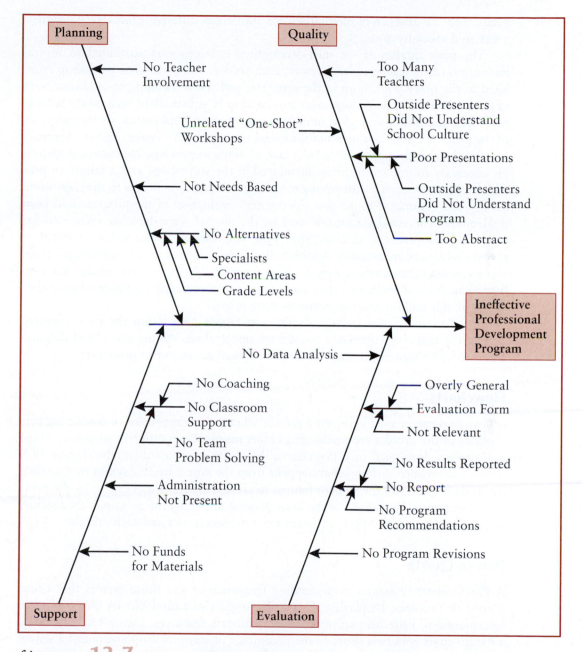

figure **13.7** **Cause-and-Effect Diagram**

needs, and the absence of alternatives for staff from different grade levels, content areas, and specialty areas.

The poor quality of the staff-development sessions was attributed to several issues: too many teachers were present, each session was a one-shot workshop unrelated to the other workshops in the program, and the workshop presentations were of poor quality. The workshops were perceived to be substandard because the outside presenters did not have a good understanding of the school culture or the purposes of the program, and their presentations were too abstract to evoke teacher interest.

Problems with support included a lack of funds to purchase instructional materials necessary to implement ideas introduced in the workshops and a failure to provide support for teachers attempting to transfer workshop concepts to the classroom. Finally, the committee found that the district's evaluation of the program had been inadequate. The evaluation forms used by the district were the same ones used for all staff-development workshops; they were not relevant to the specific content of the workshops being assessed. Additionally, the wording of the evaluation questions was so general that teachers were not sure what the questions were asking. Since no formal analysis of evaluation data took place, no information on program outcomes was available and no program revisions were made.

The "anatomy of a failure" depicted in Figure 13.7 is not the most pleasant project the planning committee could have undertaken. Yet the completed diagram was a valuable tool in planning future professional development programs.

Flowcharts

A flowchart can be used to review a process when either the process or conflicting perceptions of the process are resulting in unmet needs. When different parties involved in a process draw their own flowcharts, the charts often are dissimilar. Figure 13.8 shows a flowchart tracking what happens from the time a student is sent to the office for misbehavior until the student returns to class. This chart was drawn by the principal's secretary. Flowcharts of the same process drawn by the principal, the teacher, and the student might be very different from the secretary's and each other's!

Pareto Charts

A Pareto chart illustrates in descending frequency of size those factors that cause a need or problem. Displaying the relative impact of causal factors gives planners information to help them set priorities and allocate resources. Figure 13.9 illustrates a Pareto chart with bars showing the percentage of students dropping out of a senior high school for each of several reasons. Above the bars, a cumulative percentage line runs across the chart. These data would be valuable to a planning team designing a dropout prevention program.

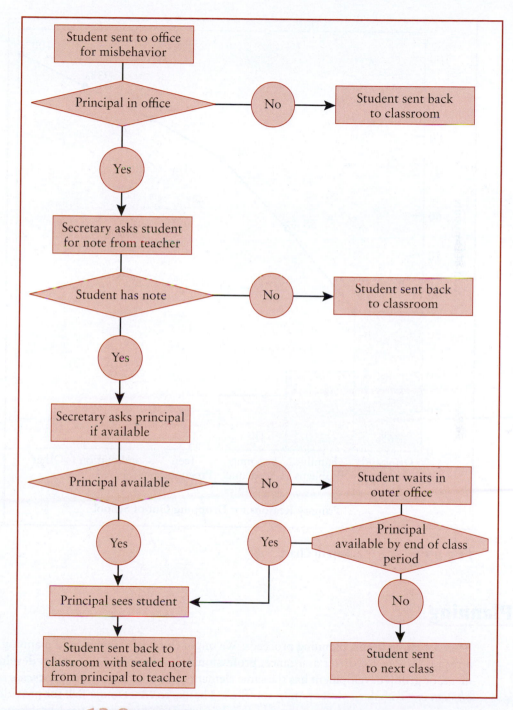

figure **13.8** **Flowchart**

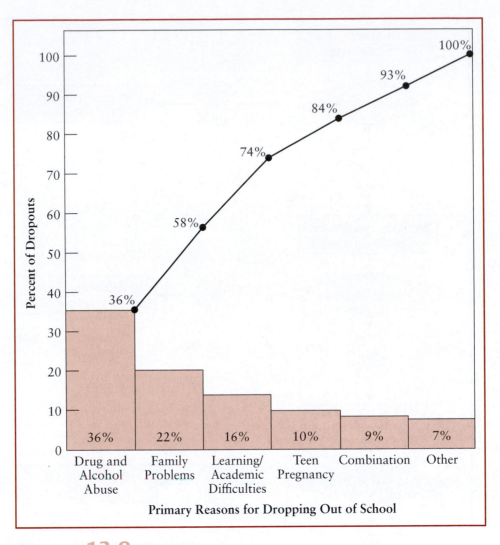

f i g u r e **13.9** **Pareto Chart**

Planning

After assessing needs, planning proceeds. We might think of assessing and planning as a recipe. A plan for direct assistance, professional development, curriculum develop-ment, or group development has the same elements as a cooking recipe. *We decide our objective:* "To bake a sweet potato soufflé." (Thanks to Ms. Donna Bell for providing this culinary example.) Knowing our family's previous history of food preferences, we are confident that if we cook the soufflé correctly, they will enjoy it and we will be held in positive regard for at least 10 minutes. Next, *we determine the activities and when they will take place:*

> *Activity 1:* Mash 6 cups of cooked sweet potatoes.
>
> *Activity 2:* Beat into the mashed potatoes: 4 eggs, 1 cup butter, 2 cups sugar, 1 cup milk, 1 teaspoon vanilla.
>
> *Activity 3:* Spread out in unbuttered pan.
>
> *Activity 4:* Mix in a separate bowl: 1 cup brown sugar, 2/3 cup flour, 1 cup butter, 1 cup chopped pecans.
>
> *Activity 5:* Spread this mix (Activity 4) evenly over the potatoes (Activity 3).
>
> *Activity 6:* Bake at 350° for 1 hour.

With the activities and times determined, *we need to identify resources.* Equipment resources are an oven, measuring cups, measuring spoons, a large bowl, a pan, a mixing fork, and a spreading knife. Food resources are potatoes, eggs, butter, sugar, vanilla, brown sugar, flour, pecans, and milk.

Finally, *we plan to evaluate the success* of our cooking endeavor by the following criteria: Everyone in our family will eat the sweet potato soufflé. At least two of the three members will ask for seconds. All of them will tell us we're wonderful cooks, and they will volunteer to wash the dishes.

If the supervisor tries acting as a gourmet of instructional cookery and planning recipes for success, all staff members will delight in the soufflé of instructional improvement. The food analogy has run its course (by now, you are probably heading for the refrigerator), and we can turn to assessing and planning within the school context. Techniques of planning discussed in this section include affinity diagrams, process decision program chart, and Gantt charts.

Affinity Diagrams

Let us assume that a needs assessment has identified a number of specific needs, with many of those needs appearing to be related to each other. An affinity diagram is a way of clustering needs and identifying broad goals that address a set of related needs. One way to begin the building of an affinity diagram is to list each identified need on a separate card or sticky note. Figure 13.10 displays results of a curriculum needs assessment. In the assessment, teachers, parents, and community members stated that students should attain each of the outcomes in Figure 13.10. The affinity diagram in Figure 13.11 clusters the curriculum needs and identifies a broad goal common to each cluster. Enfolding specific needs within larger categories enables the planning team to focus on a few broad goals, while retaining information on specific needs.

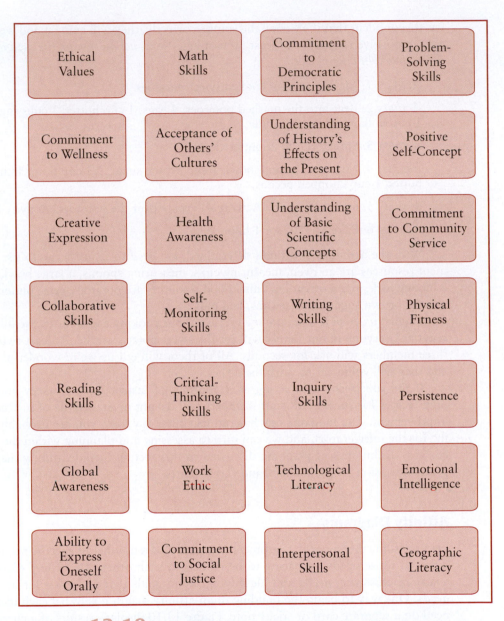

figure **13.10** Curriculum Needs, to Be Clustered in Affinity Diagram

Process Decision Program Chart

Members of the school community often anticipate problems with the implementation of instructional innovations. Sometimes these problems come to pass, and sometimes they don't, but it is wise to identify and be prepared to address potential landmines.

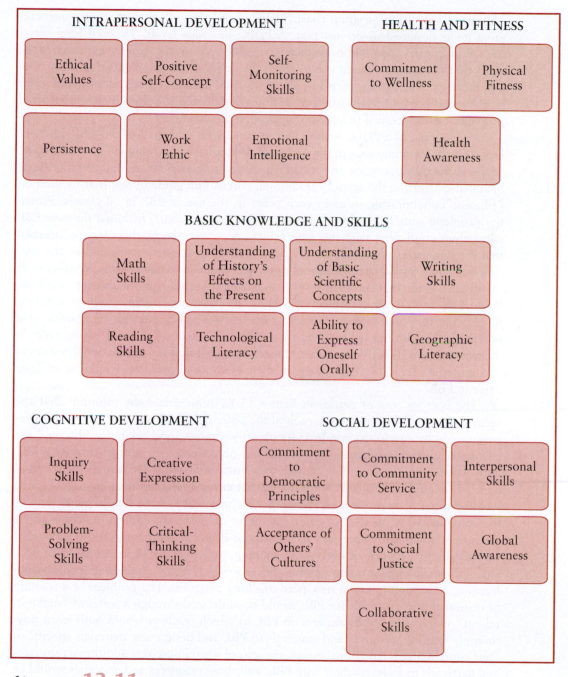

figure **13.11** **Affinity Diagram**

The process decision program chart (PDPC)—and the reflection that goes into creating it—is designed to do just that. A PDPC has four levels. The first level states the school's instructional improvement goal. The second level briefly summarizes the tasks that need to be carried out to reach the goal (which are detailed in a separate and more extensive program plan). The third level describes potential problems with implementation; and the fourth level outlines anticipated solutions for each potential problem (again, detailed in a separate planning document).

An example of a PDPC is shown in Figure 13.12. The goal of the school (top of chart) in the example was to implement problem-based learning (PBL) schoolwide. Major tasks the supervisor and teachers planned to complete (second row on chart) included converting the school's traditional curriculum guide to one that focused on PBL, and collaborating to assist each other in the use of PBL in all classes. Potential problems anticipated by the faculty (third row on chart) included the new PBL curriculum conflicting with the state achievement test; the teachers were concerned that the new curriculum would not "cover" all of the content measured by the test. Another concern was that the school's planned curriculum guide would conflict with the district guide that the central office expected all schools in the district to follow. Regarding the task of implementing PBL in all classrooms, many teachers reported that, while they had been provided an overview of PBL and saw its considerable potential, they did not believe they possessed the skills to implement it effectively in their classrooms. Finally, a number of teachers noted that the instructional resources and materials they had been using in their traditional teaching would be of little value in PBL.

The bottom row of entries in Figure 13.12 summarizes the solutions that the faculty identified with respect to each of the potential problems. The state test objectives would be enveloped into broader objectives more appropriate for PBL, and the new curriculum guide would show which test objectives were addressed by each PBL unit. A liaison group would work with the central office to make sure the new school curriculum guide was aligned with the district curriculum, and the new school guide would consist of two columns, showing the congruence of the school guide (one of the columns) with the district guide (the other column). To address concerns about the instructional skills necessary to implement PBL, the teachers would be provided several all-day sessions of initial skill training, and ongoing support would be provided through collaboration within the school's already established professional learning communities and a new peer coaching program. The problem of a scarcity of resources and materials for PBL would be addressed through a series of "make-it, take-it" workshops led by experts on PBL in which teachers would both learn how to apply existing resources and materials to PBL and design new materials specific to their content areas. Also, if necessary, the school would purchase additional resources and materials to assist teachers with PBL, and those resources and materials would be available for teachers to check out from the teachers' resource room.

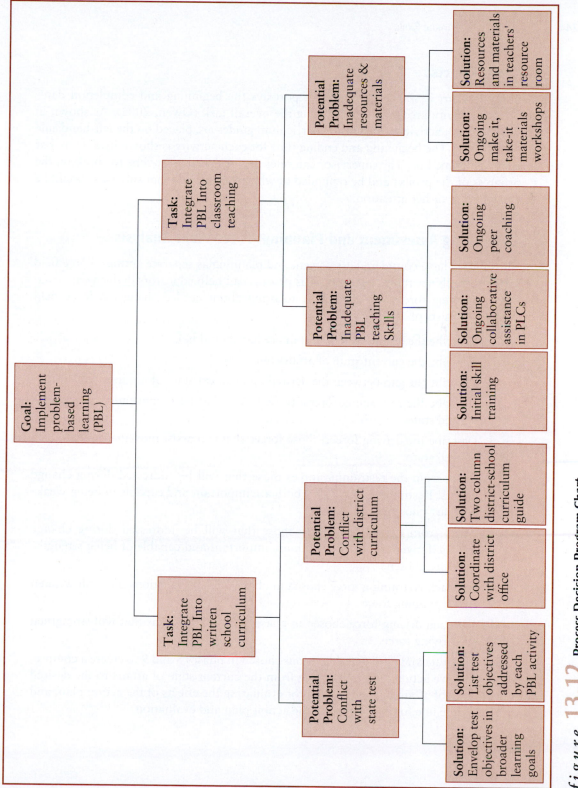

figure **13.12** Process Decision Program Chart

243

Gantt Charts

A Gantt chart is simply a graph that portrays the beginning and completion dates of each activity involved in completing the overall task (Owen, 2002). As shown in Figure 13.13, activities for revising curriculum guides are placed on the left-hand side of the chart. The beginning and ending time for each activity is shown by a white bar across the time line. The supervisor can refer to the chart at any time to check on the progress of the project and be reminded of what groups and what subtasks should be receiving his or her attention.

Combining Assessment and Planning: Force Field Analysis

Thus far we have considered assessment and planning as separate entities. Force field analysis combines these functions. This process can help educators define goals, analyze competing forces, and plan how to bring about needed change. A force field analysis consists of 10 phases:

1. Describe the desired state of affairs (what should be).
2. Describe the current state of affairs (what is).
3. Describe the gap between the desired and current state of affairs.
4. Describe the restraining forces: those forces that resist movement toward the desired state.
5. Describe the driving forces: those forces that can assist movement toward the desired state.
6. Select from the restraining forces those that will be addressed during change efforts. Restraining forces that both are important and capable of being weakened are chosen.
7. Select from the driving forces those that will be addressed during change efforts. Driving forces that both are important and capable of being strengthened are chosen.
8. For each restraining force chosen in phase 6, identify actions that will weaken the restraining force.
9. For each driving force chosen in phase 7, identify actions that will strengthen the driving force.
10. Integrate and sequence the actions chosen in phases 8 and 9 to create a comprehensive action plan for moving from the current state of affairs to the desired state of affairs. Include a plan for evaluating the effects of the action plan, and a time line for implementing the action plan and evaluation.

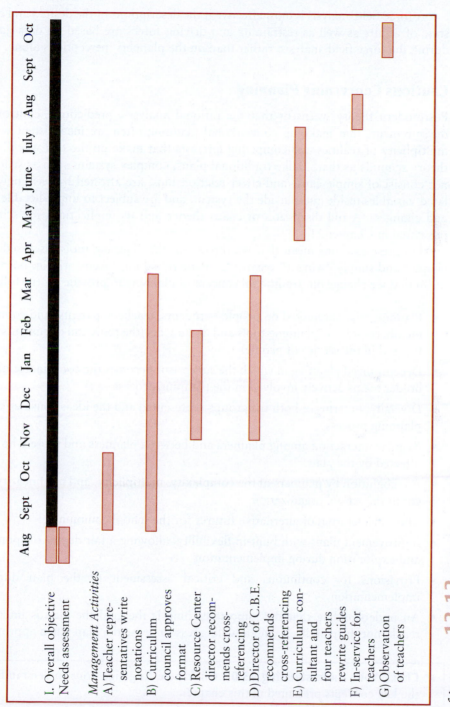

	Aug	Sept	Oct	Nov	Dec	Jan	Feb	Mar	Apr	May	June	July	Aug	Sept	Oct
I. Overall objective															
Needs assessment															
Management Activities															
A) Teacher representatives write notations															
B) Curriculum council approves format															
C) Resource Center director recommends cross-referencing															
D) Director of C.B.E. recommends cross-referencing															
E) Curriculum consultant and four teachers rewrite guides															
F) In-service for teachers															
G) Observation of teachers															

f i g u r e **13.13** Gantt Chart

A force field analysis is most effective if the descriptions of the desired and current state of affairs as well as restraining and driving forces are based on data gathered during the force field analysis, rather than on the planners' perceptions alone.

Cautions Concerning Planning

Postmodern theory warns us that the rational analyses, predictions, controls, and measurements that make up conventional planning often are inconsistent with the multiplicity of realities and competing interests that make up the real world. Chaos theory reminds us that, unlike traditional plans, complex systems such as schools do not consist of simple cause-and-effect relationships, are affected by seemingly unrelated variables inside and outside the system, and are subject to unpredictable events and changes. (A full discussion of chaos theory and its implications for schools is presented in Chapter 21.)

Do these cautions mean that we throw out the planning tools discussed in this chapter and simply "wing it" regarding instructional improvement? No, but they do mean that we change our traditional concept of planning to provide for the following:

- Planning that is centered on people—students, teachers, parents, and community members—not on planning tools and documents (the tools and documents should be used in the service of people)
- Decentralized planning in which the supervisor becomes the coordinator of stakeholder teams actively involved in the planning process
- Diversity, in terms of both the groups represented and the ideas considered in the planning process
- Regular interaction among planners and between planners and those who will be affected by the plan
- A recognition by planners of the complexity, multiplicity, and nonlinearity inherent in the school organization
- The consideration of alternative futures for the school community
- Improvement plans with built-in flexibility, allowing a fair degree of spontaneity and exploration during implementation
- Provisions for continuous and critical assessment of the plan during its implementation
- An understanding that the important thing is the goal the plan is intended to reach, not the plan itself, and a willingness to revise the plan when appropriate

> ✔ **Check Your Understanding 13.0**   Click here to gauge your understanding of the key concepts presented in this chapter.

REFLECTIVE EXERCISE

Western High School serves a community that includes both low- and middle-income neighborhoods. Approximately 20% of the students at Western are African American, 5% are Asian, 30% are Latino, and 45% are White. The teacher staff at Western is 70% White, 20% Latino, and 10% African American, with a blend of beginning, mid-career, and late-career teachers. Lucinda Murphy, principal at Western, has decided to assess the school's climate. She wants to include the teachers, staff, students, and parents in the assessment. Lucinda also wishes to use a variety of needs assessment methods in order to develop a full picture of the school's climate and changes needed to improve the climate. What ways of assessing described in this chapter would you recommend that Lucinda use in the assessment? With which group(s) of stakeholders and for what specific purpose would you suggest that each selected method be used?

chapter 14

Implementation and Evaluation Skills

Learning Outcomes for This Chapter

After reading this chapter, you should be able to:

1. List, in order, the five stages of implementation.
2. Identify five factors that affect implementation.
3. Classify given stages of concern at the self, task, or impact level.
4. Discuss why teachers should be involved in program evaluation.
5. Describe the difference between formative and summative program evaluation.
6. Explain the purpose of empowerment evaluation.

Questions to Reflect On as You Read This Chapter

1. Think of an innovation that was attempted at a school you work in or are familiar with. Did the innovation go through each of the five stages of implementation described in this chapter? If so, what was taking place at each stage, and how did moving through that stage affect the innovation? If the innovation did not move through each stage, which stage or stages were left out, and how, if at all, did omitting the missing stage or stages affect the innovation?

2. Reflect on the implementation of an innovation currently taking place in a school you work in or are familiar with. How are the five factors that affect implementation discussed in this chapter impacting implementation, either positively or negatively?

3. This chapter reviews Wolfe's five typical methods of program evaluation. Although Wolfe presents the methods in a humorous light, many schools actually use methods approximating Wolfe's. What program evaluations have you participated in or observed that have relied on one or more of Wolfe's methods? Which method or methods were used?

4. Consider an instructional program you are familiar with for which a summative evaluation is warranted. What questions about the program should the evaluation focus on? From what data sources (persons, places, things, events, or processes) should data needed to answer your evaluation questions be collected? What data gathering methods (observing, testing, surveying, interviewing, and so on) should be used to collect data from the sources you have identified?

5. In what ways would a school that you work at or are familiar with benefit from empowerment evaluation? What concerns would you have about bringing empowerment evaluation to the school?

In Chapter 13 we dealt with the first two components of instructional improvement at the school level, needs assessment and planning. In this chapter we discuss the third and fourth components, implementation and evaluation. Our treatment of the third component will focus on the implementation of an innovation: a new curriculum, instructional strategy, model of teaching, or instructional program. In Chapter 21 we will discuss the broader topic of school culture and change. Here we describe the stages of implementing an innovation, factors affecting the quality of implementation, and implementation at the individual level. In the second part of this chapter we discuss formative and summative evaluation as well as empowerment evaluation.

Stages of Implementation

Assuming that a needs assessment has been carried out and a plan developed, major innovations still need to proceed through several stages of implementation if they are to have a reasonable chance of success. A number of scholars have described the stages of implementation (Fixsen et al., 2005; Stiegelbauer, 2008; Swain-Bradway, Pinkney, & Flannery, 2015; Wood, McQuarrie, & Thompson, 1982), and although they do not all agree on the number of stages or names of each stage, there is enough consistency among the scholars to identify five broad stages: (1) readiness, (2) installation, (3) initiation, (4) full operation, and (5) continuation and renewal. Depending on the innovation, it may take 2 to 4 years to reach the continuation and renewal stage.

Readiness

Although all teachers should be involved in the needs assessment that identifies the need for the innovation and should have contributed to the general plan for making the innovation a reality, this does not mean that all teachers are ready to implement the innovation. Wood et al. (1982) provided a classic definition of readiness: "faculty members study, select, and make a commitment to new behaviors and programs that focus on improving professional practice and student achievement" (p. 28).Gordon (1999) identified five types of readiness. If these characteristics are not present, it is best for the school to delay the innovation until they can be developed. *Cultural readiness* requires the school to have sufficient levels of "open communication, trust, collaboration, and collegiality" (p. 48) to give the innovation a reasonable chance of success. *Conceptual readiness* means that the faculty, as a group, has conceptualized the changes in teaching and learning they want the innovation to bring about. *Personal readiness* calls for those who will be involved in implementation to have at least a general idea of what will be expected of them in terms of time, energy, and activity as well as the benefits of the innovation for themselves and their students. *Political readiness* is present when the parents, the community, and the district support the innovation, and when the innovation is congruent with applicable state and federal policy. *Resource readiness* means that the school has either recommitted existing resources or procured new resources necessary to initiate the innovation and to keep the innovation in operation long enough to assess its effects on teaching and learning. Readiness does not guarantee that an innovation will succeed, but the innovation's survival is in doubt if readiness is absent.

Installation

During this stage, resources and startup materials are procured, implementation teams are created, and leaders are assigned and prepared for their leadership roles. Guide-lines, schedules, instructional materials, tracking forms, logs, reflective journals, and other tools associated with the innovation are distributed and explained. Support structures such as professional development days, demonstration lessons, mentoring, peer coaching, co-teaching, professional learning communities, critical friends, released time, and so forth, are organized around the innovation. In short, the elements necessary to initiate the innovation move from the planning documents to concrete reality.

Initiation

With most innovations, the initiation stage includes initial skill training. At this stage, teachers make their first efforts to apply the innovation, assisted by the aforementioned support structures. Volunteers may try out the innovation before others, and then assist others in their early application. For example, on a campus implementing new forms of technology-enhanced instruction, teachers who have become comfortable with the new technology may be given released time to visit the classrooms of teachers just starting to use the technology to assist them with implementation. At this stage, implementation is most likely to be incremental. For instance, if the innovation is interdisciplinary curriculum, a group of teachers may pilot one or two interdisciplin-ary units a semester during the initiation phase. In a school moving toward construc-tivist teaching, teachers accustomed to more traditional teaching may teach just a few constructivist lessons a week.

Full Operation

At this stage, the innovation has become standard practice. Most teachers have become proficient at using the innovation, and with the exception of new teachers, support structures have shifted from skill development to assisting teachers in sharing variations of the innovation and ideas for applying the innovation to new content or novel situations. By this point, teachers have orchestrated mutual adaptations between the innovation and the rest of the educational environment. The innovation has been integrated into the overall instructional program. By this stage, teachers have developed firm opinions of the innovation's strengths and weaknesses.

Continuation and Renewal

No matter how successful an innovation has been, time and energy must be expended to sustain it. Formal and informal leaders who assisted with implementation eventually leave the school. Resources and materials become depleted and must be replaced. New teachers must learn the rationale for the innovation and skills to continue its implementation. Also, changes in the district, the community served by the school, and the student population mean that the innovation must be renewed if it is to remain congruent with the educational environment. Renewal should be based on data gathered on the effects of the innovation, including feedback from stakeholders.

Factors that Affect Implementation

Fixsen et al. (2005) describe three degrees of implementation:

1. Paper implementation: the policy calling for the innovation and procedures for implementation are in print and available.
2. Process implementation: training on the innovation is provided, manuals on implementation are distributed, coaches are assigned to assist with implementation, and so forth.
3. Performance implementation: the innovation is actually being applied in a way that benefits those who it is intended to benefit.

The problem with innovations in schools (and other organizations as well) is that many innovations never progress beyond the first or second degree of implementation. To illustrate, one of the authors once attended a state-level meeting of educators at which a school district was given an award for an innovative beginning teacher support program. A few days later, the author, who knew teachers in the district, congratulated them on the award. The teachers responded that they had never heard of the support program in question, and that new teachers in their schools were not receiving any new types of support. The award-winning support program was in fact a "paper program" that, at least at that point in time, had never been implemented at the school level.

As major innovations proceed through the previously discussed stages of implementation, a variety of other factors affect the quality of implementation (Durlak & DuPre, 2008; Fixsen et al., 2005; Stiegelbauer, 2008). These factors can be grouped under five broad categories:

External Factors: These include any factors outside of the school that impact implementation, including parents and community, the district office and other schools in the district, and state and federal policies.

The School Organization: The school culture, including its levels of collegiality, collaboration, and openness to change, is one important factor within this category. School leadership is also critical, especially the leaders' change-facilitation skills and commitment to the innovation. The innovation, if it is to be successful, must also have support from teachers who are trusted and respected by their colleagues. The school's level of shared decision making is an important factor, including the extent to which the decision to adopt the innovation was a shared one.

Teachers: Important factors regarding teachers include whether they have a clear understanding of the innovation and if they see benefits of the innovation for themselves and their students. The motivation and capacity of teachers to develop the skills necessary to implement the innovation are also key factors.

The Innovation: Stiegelbauer (2008) notes that the size and complexity of an innovation are salient factors in whether implementation will be successful. If the innovation is too small or too simple, teachers are not likely to take it seriously. If the change is too large and complex, teachers may resist it. Another crucial factor is whether the innovation is consistent with the school's vision and mission, and whether it is compatible with school and classroom practices valued by the school community. The flexibility of the innovation is another relevant factor: Is the innovation capable of mutual adaptation with current school structures, processes, and practices?

Support: Initial training in how to implement a major innovation is usually necessary but never sufficient. With most innovations, several support structures increase the probability of success. Early on, teachers benefit from seeing the innovation modeled in visits to other schools, workshops, or demonstration lessons. As they begin to apply a new curriculum or teaching model in their own classrooms, teachers can receive classroom assistance through co-teaching, peer coaching, or collaborative walkthroughs. Problems with implementation are bound to occur, and problem solving can take place in professional learning groups or conversations with critical friends. The presence and quality of support structures are significant factors in all stages of implementation.

Our discussion of factors that affect implementation is closely related to the concept of *fidelity*, which simply means that the innovation is implemented as the designed. On the one hand, Lendrum and Humphrey (2012) report that the lower fidelity, the greater the risk that the innovation will fail to bring about the intended outcomes. On the other hand, the same authors state, "local changes are inevitable and surface-level adaptations may contribute to the effectiveness and sustainability of an intervention" (p. 643). The key to the fidelity–adaptation debate, according to Lendrum and Humphrey, is to strike a balance between the two, maintaining the core features of the innovation, while allowing teachers to adapt other aspects of the innovation to their own students and teaching environment.

The desire for fidelity also needs to be tempered with flexibility in the support structures provided during implementation. For example, a peer coach's assistance should not be focused entirely at ensuring fidelity. Rather, the coach and teacher receiving assistance should engage in reflective inquiry about how the innovation can be adapted to the teacher's strengths, students' needs, and content being taught without losing the core qualities of the innovation.

> ▶ **Video Illustration**
>
> In this video, the supervisor and teachers are discussing data on a new curriculum being implemented at their school. As you watch the video, reflect on how the discussion in the video relates to the fidelity–adaptation debate discussed in this section of the chapter.

Implementation at the Individual Level

Teachers have different concerns about innovations and go through the implementation process at different rates as their concerns are addressed. Hall and Hord (2006) state, "Even when the change is introduced to every member of the organization at the same time, the rate of making the change and of developing skill and competence in using it will vary individually" (p. 7). In short, teachers and others need individualized assistance when implementing an innovation. Hall and Hord (2006) have identified seven stages (0–6) of concern about the innovation. Figure 14.1 describes the seven stages.

Individuals may have concerns at several stages at any given time, but their most intense concerns often are at a particular stage. The stages of concern are developmental, moving from stage 0 (lowest stage) to stage 6 (highest stage). Individuals need to have their intense concerns at a particular stage met before they can concentrate on the next highest stage. The specific concerns of a teacher result not just from the innovation in isolation, but from the interplay of the innovation, the teacher's personal and professional characteristics, and the educational context (Kwok, 2014).

Impact			
6	Refocusing	The focus is on exploration of more universal benefits from the innovation, including the possibility of major changes or replacement with a more powerful alternative. Individual has definite ideas about alternatives to the proposed or existing form of the innovation.
5	Collaboration	The focus is on coordination and cooperation with others regarding use of the innovation.
4	Consequence	Attention focuses on impact of the innovation on students in his or her immediate sphere of influence. The focus is on relevance of the innovation for students, evaluation of student outcomes, including performance and competencies, and changes needed to increase student outcomes.
Task			
3	Management	Attention is focused on the processes and tasks of using the innovation and the best use of information and resources. Issues related to efficiency, organizing, managing, scheduling, and time demands are utmost.
Self			
2	Personal	Individual is uncertain about the demands of the innovation, his or her inadequacy to meet those demands, and his or her role with the innovation. This includes analysis of his or her role in relation to the reward structure of the organization, decision making, and consideration of potential conflicts with existing structures or personal commitment. Financial or status implications of the program for self and colleagues may also be reflected.
1	Informational	A general awareness of the innovation and interest in learning more detail about it is indicated. The person seems to be unworried about himself or herself in relation to the innovation. She or he is interested in substantive aspects of the innovation in a selfless manner such as general characteristics, effects, and requirements for use.
Unrelated			
0	Awareness	Little concern about or involvement with the innovation is indicated.

figure **14.1** **Stages of Concern About the Innovation**

Source: Adapted from Hall, Gene E.; Hord, Shirley M., *Implementing Change: Patterns, Principles, and Potholes*, 3rd Ed., © 2011. Reprinted and Electronically reproduced by permission of Pearson Education, Inc., Upper Saddle River, New Jersey.

Stages of Concern		Expressions of Concern
Impact		
6	Refocusing	I have some ideas about something that would work even better.
5	Collaboration	I am concerned about relating what I am doing with what other instructors are doing.
4	Consequence	How is my use affecting kids?
Task		
3	Management	I seem to be spending all my time getting material ready.
Self		
2	Personal	How will using it affect me?
1	Informational	I would like to know more about it.
Unrelated		
0	Awareness	I am not concerned about it (the innovation).

f i g u r e **14.2** **Stages of Concern: Typical Expressions of Concern About the Innovation**

Source: Adapted from Hall, Gene E.; Hord, Shirley M., *Implementing Change: Patterns, Principles, and Potholes,* 3rd Ed., © 2011. Reprinted and Electronically reproduced by permission of Pearson Education, Inc., Upper Saddle River, New Jersey. p. 140.

Hall and Hord (2006) describe three ways supervisors and other change leaders can assess educators' stages of concern about an innovation: (1) informal conversations, (2) an open-ended question asking educators to write about their concerns, and (3) the 35-item *Stages of Concern Questionnaire*. Figure 14.2 describes expressions voiced at each stage of concern.

Once teachers' stages of concern have been identified, supervisors and other change leaders can assist change by addressing those concerns and fostering teacher development toward higher stages of concern. The innovation will have a much greater chance for success once a critical mass of teachers reaches the *impact* stages of concern (*consequence, collaboration,* and *refocusing*). Teachers with these higher stages of concern are a worthwhile innovation's best friend!

Evaluation of Instructional Improvement Efforts

Perhaps no area in education has gone through such a dramatic expansion in knowledge, techniques, and attention than the field of educational evaluation. What once seemed the province of experts, consultants, and "university types" has now become a part of day-to-day operations in schools. The national accountability and testing movement has certainly been a contributing cause. More important has been the role of the literature on successful schools, which has made clear that decisions about instructional changes should be made from a base of comprehensive and credible data about students, and that those affected most directly by instructional change (i.e., teachers) should be involved in defining, implementing, and interpreting the evaluation agenda.

In schools and districts that do improve instruction, evaluation is not a perfunctory paper assignment done by a particular person or division to fulfill district or state requirements. Rather, evaluation is seen as the basis for determining professional actions as to the "what and how" of improving learning for students. Knowledgeable decision making about instruction comes from intense and critical study of the consequences of the common work of teachers: *teaching*. Including teachers in determining the criteria, procedures, and use of evaluative data in schools is not simply a nice thing to do—*it is essential to do*. If teachers are to extend their own thinking and commitment about collective instruction, they have to be part of the evaluation process. Without their involvement, policy makers have denied teachers the intellectual engagement of viewing teaching as a collective activity—"a cause beyond oneself."

The Intersection of Instructional Supervision and Program Evaluation

What types of program evaluation are within the arena of instructional supervision? The criterion for answering this question is whether the program directly affects teaching and learning. For example, a district's transportation, facilities maintenance, and athletic programs all are important, but evaluating these programs is an administrative responsibility, not a function of instructional supervision. Traditional programs that directly affect teaching and learning include curricula, instructional programs, professional development, student assessment, and so on. Additionally, in recent years, instructional supervision has expanded to include programs in areas like teacher leadership, action research, social justice, and community building, as the relationship of these areas with teaching and learning has been acknowledged.

Because program evaluation within the arena of instructional supervision relates directly to teaching and learning, it makes sense for teachers to be involved in instructional program evaluation: They are the professionals who have the responsibility for implementing instructional programs, have a firsthand view of how the programs are working, and are in the best position to gather and analyze relevant evaluation data. Later in this chapter we will discuss empowerment evaluation as a vehicle for teacher participation in program evaluation.

Judgments

How do we know our instructional programs are successful? Should we continue with the same curriculum, instructional methods, scheduling, and grouping practices, or should changes be made? Evaluating is the act of making such a judgment. How do we decide whether something is good or bad? Frequently, we make judgments with statements such as: "What a great reading program," "What a lousy classroom," and "What wonderful students." How do we really know if something is great, lousy, or wonderful? Wolfe (1969) has offered a tongue-in-cheek classification of five typical methods by which we make such judgments:

Cosmetic method: You examine the program, and if it looks good it is good. Does everybody look busy? The key is attractive and full bulletin boards covered with projects emanating from the program.

Cardiac method: No matter what the data say, you know in your heart that the program was a success. This is similar to the use in medical research of subclinical findings.

Colloquial method: After a brief meeting, preferably at a local watering hole, a group of project staff members conclude that success was achieved. No one can refute a group decision.

Curricular method: A successful program is one that can be installed with the least disruption of the ongoing school program. Programs that are truly different are to be eschewed at all costs.

Computational method: If you have to have data, analyze them to death. Whatever the nature of the statistics, use the most sophisticated multivariate regression discontinuity procedures known to humans.

Wolfe's humor aside, let's look at reasonable, valid ways of evaluating. In the turbulence of instructional change, it is useful to know whether the new practice is going to be any better than the old. If not, then we may be investing large amounts of energy without a justifiable increase in instructional benefits to students. If we are to make a commitment to instructional change, we must also make a commitment to evaluating that instructional change. If not, then we truly do not know what we are doing.

Two Types of Program Evaluation: Formative and Summative

There are two broad purposes of educational evaluation. *Formative evaluation* is intended to improve a program. It is carried out while the program is in progress and can be ongoing throughout the life of the program. *Summative evaluation* results in a definitive judgment about the value of a program. It is carried out after a program has been in existence for a period of time. A summative evaluation is usually the basis for a decision about whether the program will continue, undergo major revisions, or be terminated. Formative and summative program evaluations are not always mutually exclusive. For instance, data gathered for formative evaluations might be reanalyzed later as part of a summative evaluation.

Formative Program Evaluation

Formative evaluation is appropriate at any stage of implementation, but is best initiated at the earliest stage. Evaluation data can be gathered both on how well the program is being implemented and on the effects of the program. Several of the ways of assessing need presented in Chapter 13 can be adapted for formative evaluation. These include:

- Schoolwide classroom observation
- Review of student work products
- Review of official records
- Third-party review
- Multiple-choice survey
- Open-ended survey

The two groups that tend to be most involved in instructional programs are teachers and students, so it makes sense to gather data from those populations. In some cases, it is also wise to gather data from parents and community members. In addition to the data collection methods just listed, interviews or informal discussions with small, representative groups of stakeholders can also be very helpful.

The best types of formative assessments are ongoing, enabling periodic adjustments to the program. Two methods for informal and continuous data gathering are the feedback window (also called the parking lot) and the progress board. Although both of these tools, as originally conceived, were wall charts in locations where educators visited on a regular basis (e.g., the teachers' lounge, the teachers' workroom), electronic versions of both can be used. The feedback window, shown in Figure 14.3, allows any stakeholder to provide feedback on any or all of four areas, each area represented by a "window pane."

What aspects of the program are working well?	What questions do you have about the program?
What types of assistance do you need to better implement the program?	What suggestions do you have for improving the program?

figure 14.3 **Feedback Window**

The progress board is completed at the end of each month, individually or in a group meeting. The collaborative dialogue that takes place when the entries are made in a group meeting makes that our preferred option. A portion of a progress board (for January through May) is illustrated in Figure 14.4. The top two entries in the left-hand column of the board ask the teachers to evaluate the program over the previous month. The middle three entries call for an assessment of the major

	January	February	March	April	May
What went well this month					
Problems identified this month					
Effects thus far on teachers					
Effects thus far on school culture					
Effects thus far on students					
Improve-ment goals for next month					
New resources & support needed					

figure 14.4 **Portion of a Progress Board**

effects of the program since its inception, allowing any changes in effects to be tracked from month to month. The bottom two entries request that teachers set goals for the next month aimed at improving the program, and identify resources and other types of support they will need to meet those goals. The project board provides for short-term formative evaluations of the program as well as a long-term record of positive and negative aspects of program implementation, effects, and modifications.

Summative Program Evaluation

As we noted earlier, the purpose of summative program evaluation is to decide whether a program will be continued, restructured, or eliminated. The stakes are higher in summative program evaluation, so it tends to be more formal, comprehensive, and rigorous than formative evaluation. A number of key decisions must be made in a summative program evaluation. We examine each of these decisions next.

Who Will Evaluate?   Whether the supervisor, a team of faculty members, central office personnel, or private consultants should be responsible for coordinating an evaluation depends on the particular school's resources and the purpose of the evaluation. However, it is critical that teachers be involved in evaluation of instructional programs. All stakeholders should be not only subjects of study but co-investigators of the study as well. As Greene (1986) has noted, there exists a "consensus on the need for stakeholder participation" (p. 1), and such participation is defined as "shared decision making, rather than just advising or providing input" (p. 9).

What Questions Need to Be Answered?   Evaluation questions will depend on the nature of the program and what members of the evaluation's audience wish to learn about the program. Let's say that a new social studies curriculum is to be evaluated. An *implementation* question might be: To what extent has the new curriculum been implemented at the classroom level? An *outcomes* question might be: What changes in students' knowledge, skills, and attitudes have resulted from the new curriculum? Once the evaluation questions have been formulated, they become the basis for the remainder of the evaluation.

What Data Will Be Gathered and How?   *Data sources* are persons, places, things, events, or processes from which data needed to answer evaluation questions can be gathered. Examples of data sources are students, teachers, principals, parents, teaching episodes, student products, and school records. *Data-gathering methods* are ways to collect data from sources. Examples include testing, observations, content analysis, case studies, review of records, administration of rating scales and surveys, and interviewing. Our bias is toward using multiple sources of data and multiple data-collection methods for each evaluation question. Multiple sources and methods increase the likelihood that the evaluation results will be valid (Llosa & Slayton, 2009).

How Will the Data Be Analyzed? Data analysis is largely determined by the evaluation questions and types of data. Decisions to be made include how to organize, summarize, and display data, and how to reach conclusions based on the data. Central office, university, or private experts may be necessary to assist with complex quantitative or qualitative analysis. Stakeholders, however, can make valuable contributions to data analysis, especially by reviewing results and suggesting explanations, implications, and conclusions.

How Will the Evaluation Be Reported? After collecting and analyzing the results of tests, observations, surveys, interviews, and testimonials, how should the evaluation be reported? The answer is largely determined by the audience. Most school board members and superintendents will not read a 200-page technical report on the raw data, statistical treatments, and evaluation methodologies. They are interested in the results and conclusions. The technical report should be available to decision makers and referenced in an executive summary. Any reader of the executive summary who is confused or desires more information about certain parts of the paper can check the complete technical report. On the other hand, if the audience for the evaluation report consists of people with sophisticated evaluation skills, a complete technical report would be in order.

Regardless of the audience, certain types of information are included in most evaluation reports. (Again, these components will vary in length and technical sophistication depending on the audience.) Typical evaluation reports include discussions of the following:

1. The purpose of the evaluation
2. A description of the program being evaluated
3. Evaluation questions or objectives
4. Methodology, including data sources, data gathering methods, and data analysis methods
5. Results and conclusions, including strengths and weaknesses of the program
6. Recommendations for the future

As we said earlier, the evaluation questions are the basis for decisions regarding other components of the evaluation. Figure 14.5 provides an evaluation-planning matrix with a column for writing evaluation questions. For each question, there are cells on the matrix for identifying the coordinator, evaluation team, data sources, data gathering methods, data analysis methods, timeline, and resources needed for addressing the question.

Evaluation Question	Coordinator	Evaluation Team Members	Data Sources	Data-Gathering Methods	Data Analysis Methods	Evaluation Time Line	Resources Needed
1)							
2)							
3)							
4)							
5)							
6)							

figure **14.5** **Chart for Planning Data Gathering and Analysis**

Program Evaluation and Teacher Empowerment

David Fetterman and Abraham Wandersman (2007), leading proponents of *empowerment evaluation* (EE), define it as "the use of evaluation concepts, techniques, and findings to foster improvement and self-determination" (p. 186). EE has been used in health care, community development, business, government, and education (Fetterman & Wandersman, 2005). Applied to instructional supervision, EE involves supervisors facilitating teachers as they perform program evaluations. Herein, we describe the purposes of EE, necessary supervisory support, and the EE process.

Purposes

EE seeks to improve the program being evaluated, while also improving the school culture. The premise is that inviting teachers to work together evaluating a program they are part of will improve communication, increase collaboration, and foster collegiality. The process seeks to increase teachers' understanding of program evaluation and their confidence as evaluators. EE also attempts to free teachers from narrow views of their professional roles and help them become more self-directed. A final purpose of EE is to build both individual and school capacity to carry out future program evaluations.

Support

Supervisory support for empowerment evaluation begins with professional development to provide teachers with an understanding of EE and the skills to gather and analyze evaluation data. Teachers need to learn how to develop and administer simple classroom observation instruments, surveys, and interviews; how to mine existing data from school archives; and how to perform basic data analysis. The supervisor must also provide teachers with the resources to carry out EE, including time, space, and material resources.

A supervisor cannot simply assign teachers to start doing EE, even after professional development on the EE process. Teachers engaged in program evaluation need technical and moral support in each phase of the evaluation process. Teacher-evaluators need technical support in deciding on evaluation questions, choosing or creating data collection instruments, organizing and analyzing data, and planning for change. Teachers also need moral support to gain confidence in performing evaluations, as well as assurance that their conclusions and recommendations make sense. Most importantly, teachers need to know they will be supported in carrying the evaluation through to completion and implementing program improvement. Nothing can destroy teachers' commitment to EE as quickly as the supervisor suspending EE to focus on other initiatives or failing to support follow-up for program improvement.

Process

The steps in EE are deceptively simple: (1) decide on the evaluation team's mission, (2) evaluate the current program, and (3) plan for the future (Fetterman & Wandersman, 2007). Underlying the three-step process are a number of principles of EE that not only increase its complexity, but also make it a powerful vehicle for both program and teacher development.

We take the liberty here of adapting EE's principles (Fetterman & Wandersman, 2005) to teachers evaluating instructional programs. One principle is that the school's professional community should take ownership of the evaluation. The evaluation should include all members of the professional community who wish to be involved, but the idea of inclusion here also means that all other stakeholders—including students, parents, and community members—should be consulted and kept informed throughout the evaluation.

The evaluation should reflect teachers' knowledge of (1) their students, (2) the students' culture, and (3) how the program has been adapted to the local context. The teacher-evaluators, in turn, should seek out other stakeholders' perspectives on the program. EE is a democratic process characterized by transparency, collaboration, and shared decision making. Although decisions are democratic, they are informed by data gathered by the teachers from the school and community, and from outside sources like research literature and comparable schools with similar programs.

EE is not just about making judgments on the current program, but also includes planning for improvement. The EE improvement plan includes both an intervention and a strategy for assessing the intervention. EE is cyclical: program evaluation leads to an improvement plan that leads to an intervention that leads to a new evaluation. Finally, EE includes internal accountability. The teacher-evaluators hold themselves accountable to all of the school's stakeholders, seeking feedback from stakeholders on the quality of their evaluation, plan, and intervention.

> ✔ **Check Your Understanding 14.0** Click here to gauge your understanding of the key concepts presented in this chapter.

REFLECTIVE EXERCISE

Think of a specific schoolwide instructional innovation you believe would improve student learning if implemented in PK-12 education. Figure 14.1 describes six levels of concern about an innovation and Figure 14.2 lists six corresponding expressions of concern about an innovation. Beginning with stage 1 and ending with stage 6, what types of professional development would you recommend for teachers at each stage of concern about the innovation you have identified?

part 5

Technical Tasks of Supervision

If one has responsibility for the improvement of instruction, what does one do? We've accounted for what the supervisor needs to possess in terms of knowledge, interpersonal skills, and technical skills. What are the technical tasks of supervision that can bring about improved instruction? They are direct assistance to teachers, evaluation of teaching, group development, professional development, curriculum development, and action research. How does instruction improve?

- *Direct assistance.* The supervisor can provide or facilitate one-to-one support to teachers to improve instruction.
- *Evaluation of teaching.* The supervisor can provide or coordinate assessment of instruction at the individual teacher, team, or school level.
- *Group development.* The supervisor can provide for instructional problem-solving meetings among teachers to improve instruction.
- *Professional development.* The supervisor can provide learning opportunities for teachers to improve instruction.

- *Curriculum development.* The supervisor can provide for changes in teaching content and instructional materials to improve instruction.
- *Action research.* The supervisor can assist teachers in planning, implementing, and assessing their own instructional improvement projects.

Each of these tasks is directly related to improving instruction. A supervisor needs to take responsibility for these tasks if a school is to become increasingly effective. Part 5 will detail how these tasks can be performed so that teachers take individual and collective responsibility for instructional improvement.

chapter 15

Direct Assistance to Teachers

Learning Outcomes for This Chapter

After reading this chapter, you should be able to:

1. Name the five steps in clinical supervision.
2. Identify supervisory approaches appropriate for clinical supervision.
3. Distinguish between reciprocal and expert peer coaching.
4. List at least four strategies a mentor can use to assist a beginning teacher.
5. Describe how a teacher can foster a democratic and moral society.

Questions to Reflect On as You Read This Chapter

1. Reflect on the 12 principles of clinical supervision discussed in this chapter. In a school district where clinical supervision was being introduced, which of the principles would be most appealing to teachers? Which principles would it be most difficult for supervisors to apply in the current era of accountability? Which principles would be the most important ones to emphasize during the phase-in of clinical supervision?

2. Many summative evaluation programs use the same structure as clinical supervision. What are key differences between summative evaluation and clinical supervision in (a) the preconference, (b) observation, and (c) postconference?

3. One concern about clinical supervision expressed by some supervisors is the extensive time required to provide clinical supervision to large numbers of teachers on a regular basis. Is peer coaching the solution to the supervisor's time problem? In other words, would it be beneficial for supervisors to shift roles from providing clinical supervision to coordinating peer coaching programs?

4. Some peer coaching programs are successful, but others experience problems and are short lived. If, as a supervisor, you wished to establish a successful peer coaching program, what actions would you take to increase the program's chances of success?

5. Compare this chapter's recommendations for selecting, preparing, and supporting mentors; matching mentors with beginning teachers; and mentor support for beginning teachers with a teacher mentoring program with which you are familiar.

Direct assistance to help teachers improve instruction can come from different sources. This book has contended that someone needs to take responsibility for the supervisory function of direct assistance to ensure that teachers receive feedback, are not left alone, and are involved as part of a collective staff.

Teachers who receive regular classroom feedback are also most satisfied with teaching (Saphier, 2011; Silva & Contreras, 2011). Direct assistance to teachers is one of the crucial elements of a successful school (Glickman, 2002; Nidus & Sadder, 2011). Keeping the frequency and source of direct assistance in mind, we will look at three established structures for providing direct assistance: clinical supervision, peer coaching, and mentoring.

Clinical Supervision

Although there are multiple ways of observing, the clinical supervision model for conducting observations with teachers is relatively standard and accepted. The model is derived from the pioneering work of Morris Cogan with supervisors of intern teachers at Harvard University. Cogan's *Clinical Supervision* (Cogan, 1973) and Robert Goldhammer's book, also entitled *Clinical Supervision* (Goldhammer, 1969), are publications resulting from this pioneer work. Since then, numerous refinements and alterations of clinical supervision have been made (Pajak, 2008).

Clinical supervision consists of both a set of principles and a structure. The language used to describe the principles may vary from model to model of clinical supervision, but there is widespread agreement on 12 principles. Clinical supervision:

1. is classroom based.

2. has as its purpose both the improvement of instruction and the teacher's long-term professional development.

3. is separate from summative evaluation.

4. requires the supervisor's understanding of child development, pedagogy, and teacher development.

5. requires that the supervisor possess interpersonal, observation, and problem-solving skills.

6. is nonjudgmental.

7. is based on mutual trust.

8. requires a collegial relationship in which the teacher and supervisor are considered equals and co-contributors to the improvement process.

9. is data-based.

10. gathers data based on the teacher's concerns or curiosities about the lesson to be observed.

11. involves the teacher and supervisor in reflective dialogue.

12. is cyclical: the five-step clinical cycle is repeated on a regular basis.

The structure of clinical supervision can be simplified into five steps:

1. Preconference with teacher

2. Observation of classroom

3. Analysis of observation data and planning for postconference

4. Postconference with teacher

5. Critique of previous four steps

Step 1: Preconference

At the *preconference,* the supervisor sits with the teacher and determines (1) the reason and purpose for the observation, (2) the focus of the observation, and (3) the method and form of observation to be used. These determinations are made before the actual observation, so that both supervisor and teacher are clear about what will transpire. The purpose of the observation, as mentioned in Chapter 12, should provide the criteria for making the remaining decisions on focus, method, and time of observation.

Step 2: Observation

The next step, *observation,* is the time to follow through with the understandings of the preconference. The observer might use any one observation method or a combination of methods. Examples of observation methods include categorical frequencies, performance indicators, visual diagramming, space utilization, verbatim, detached open-ended narratives, participant observation, focused questionnaire, and tailored observation systems. The observer should keep in mind the difference between *descriptions* of events and *interpretations.* The purpose of observation is description.

Step 3: Analysis and Planning

The *analysis* of the observation and planning for the postconference are now possible. The supervisor leaves the classroom with his or her observations and seeks solitude. He or she lays out the recorded pages of observations and studies the information. The task might be counting up frequencies, looking for recurring patterns, isolating a major occurrence, or discovering which performance indicators were present and which were not. Regardless of the instrument, questionnaire, or open-ended form used, the supervisor must make sense out of a large mass of information.

A case study might help to clarify data analysis. Supervisor A has completed a verbal interaction instrument for students and teacher. She reviews the 10 sheets, tallies the columns, and records the analysis on the worksheet.

1. The teacher asked 27 questions and received 42 answers.
2. Out of 276 total verbal moves, 6 were student to student; the other 270 were teacher to student or student to teacher.
3. The teacher asks 21 of the 25 students in the class at least 1 question.

Let's examine one more case, this time of Supervisor B doing a participant observation. The supervisor reads through his brief classroom notes, picks out the most significant events, and writes the following analysis.

1. James, Tyrone, Felix, and Sondra asked me about the assignment they were supposed to be doing.
2. Kirk and Felipe were talking with each other about sports the three times I overheard them.
3. Kim looked across the aisle at Jose's work six times.

The supervisor no doubt will have tentative interpretations of the observation data, but final interpretations will await teacher–supervisor discussion of the data in the postconference.

The last determination for the supervisor to make in step 3 of the clinical structure is to choose what interpersonal approach to use with the teacher in the postconference. The directive informational, collaborative, and nondirective approaches to supervision were explained in Chapter 8, 9, and 10, respectively. Should the supervisor use a directive informational approach by presenting his or her observations and interpretations, asking for teacher input, setting a goal, and providing teachers with alternative actions to choose from? Should the supervisor be collaborative by sharing the observation, allowing the teacher to present his or her own interpretations, and negotiating a mutual contract for future improvement? Should the supervisor be nondirective by explaining his or her observations and encouraging the teacher to analyze, interpret, and make his or her own plan?

The supervisor must consider the individual teacher's level of development, expertise, and commitment when choosing the supervisory approach. When working with a teacher who is best matched with a collaborative or nondirective approach and who has experience with clinical supervision, some supervisors provide the teacher with the observation data prior to the postconference. This allows the teacher to review the data in advance and bring his or her preliminary interpretations to the postconference.

Step 4: Postconference

With the completed observation form, completed analysis, and the chosen interpersonal approach, the supervisor is ready to meet with the teacher in a *postconference*. The postconference is held to share the observation data and analysis, interpret the meaning of the data, and produce a plan for instructional improvement.

The first order of business is to let the teacher in on the observation—to reflect back to the teacher what was seen. Then the supervisor can follow the chosen approach—directive informational, collaborative, or nondirective. The conference ends with a plan for further improvement. Figure 15.1 can be used to develop such a plan.

The *objective* is a statement of what the teacher will attain for the next observation: "I will improve student-to-student interaction by 50 percent in group discussions." *Activities* are the listed preparation points to accomplish the objective: (1) Practice pausing at least three seconds before answering a student response; (2) practice using open-ended questions; (3) set up ongoing mini-debates. *Resources* are the materials and/or people needed to do the activities: (1) Read a book on leading

---

Postconference Date _____   Observed Teacher _____

Time _____   Peer Supervisor _____

Objective to be worked on:

Activities to be undertaken to achieve objectives:

Resources needed:

Time and date for next preconference:

---

figure **15.1** **Plan for Instructional Improvement**

discussion groups; (2) attend a workshop on "Involving Students"; (3) observe Mr. Filler when he holds a science discussion. *Date* and *time* specify when the teacher will be ready to display his or her improvement. Such a plan—whether designed by the teacher, the supervisor, or both—should be clearly understood by both parties before they leave the postconference.

Step 5: Critique

The *critique* of the previous four steps is a time for reviewing whether the format and procedures from preconference through postconference were satisfactory and whether revisions might be needed before repeating the sequence. The critique can be held at the end of the postconference. It need not be a formal session but can be a brief

table **15.1**   **Activities for Each Step of Clinical Supervision**

Step	Specific Activities
Preconference	Begin conference on positive note Discuss teacher's lesson plan Discuss teacher's concerns about lesson Discuss behaviors to be observed Select or design an observation instrument Discuss logistics of observation Review conference decisions End conference on positive note
Observation	Gather data agreed upon in preconference Focus on description; avoid interpretation
Analysis and Planning	Analyze data Summarize data in preparation for postconference Choose interpersonal approach for postconference Plan postconference
Postconference	Begin conference on positive note Review preconference decisions Share and explain observation data Discuss and interpret observation data Identify improvement objective Plan improvement activities and discuss needed resources Discuss criteria and follow-up to assess plan Review conference decisions End conference on positive note
Critique	Critique preconference Critique observation process Critique observation data provided to teacher Critique postconference Discuss ways to improve clinical supervision

discussion, consisting of questions such as: What was valuable in what we have been doing? What was of little value? What changes could be suggested?

The critique has both symbolic and functional value. It indicates that the supervisor is involved in an improvement effort in the same way as the supervisee. Furthermore, the feedback from the teacher gives the supervisor a chance to decide on what practices to continue, revise, or change when working with the teacher in the future.

The five steps are now complete, and a tangible plan of future action is in the hands of the teacher. The supervisor is prepared to review the plan in the next preconference and reestablish focus and method of observation. Specific actions for each step in clinical supervision are shown in Table 15.1.

The Relationship of Clinical Supervision with Other Processes

Because clinical supervision involves classroom observation and conferral, it is only natural for evaluation of classroom teaching to come to mind when reading about the clinical model. Also, since Part 3 of this book was all about developmental supervision, including alternative interpersonal approaches that can be used when conferring with teachers, the reader may already be considering use of the various interpersonal approaches in clinical supervision. Let's take a few moments to discuss the relationship of clinical supervision to both evaluation of teaching and developmental supervision.

Comparing Clinical Supervision with Evaluation of Teaching

In Chapter 16 we will discuss the differences between summative and formative evaluation of teaching in detail. For now, let us simply state that clinical supervision is consistent with *formative* evaluation, but not *summative* evaluation, of teaching. Clinical supervision provides nonjudgmental assistance aimed at improving the teacher's instruction, and because of that, it has been equated by some with formative evaluation. Clinical supervision actually includes but goes beyond formative evaluation by helping the teacher to design and implement an action plan to meet instructional improvement goals.

Clinical supervision is *not* consistent with summative evaluation; it is not intended to gather data to make judgments about whether teachers are meeting performance criteria for continued employment. Some school districts have confused the two processes by calling their summative evaluation cycle *clinical supervision*. At one level, this is understandable. Both clinical supervision and summative evaluation can take place within similar structures, including a preconference, classroom visit, and postconference. To understand the difference between the two concepts we must look beyond the structure to the purpose and principles of clinical supervision, which clearly are not consistent with those of summative evaluation. The two processes need to be separate, for the same reasons that formative and summative evaluation of teaching should be separate (again, we will elaborate on the distinction between formative and summative evaluation of teaching in Chapter 16).

Integrating Clinical Supervision and Developmental Supervision

As discussed in Part 3, developmental supervision calls for the supervisor to match one of four interpersonal approaches—directive control, directive informational, collaborative, or nondirective—with teachers' developmental levels, expertise, and commitment. Are all four of these interpersonal approaches consistent with clinical supervision? Our view is that directive informational, collaborative, and nondirective supervisory approaches are all consistent with the clinical model.

Using a directive informational approach, the supervisor can suggest and explain two or three alternative observation foci and data collection methods in the preconference and ask the teacher to select from the options provided. In the directive informational postconference, the supervisor can help the teacher to interpret observation data and ask the teacher to choose from a limited range of possible improvement objectives, activities, and follow-ups.

The supervisor and teacher engaged in a collaborative preconference can consider observation alternatives and select a mutually agreeable observation focus and data collection method. In the collaborative postconference, the supervisor and teacher can share decision-making responsibility as they build an action plan for instructional improvement.

The supervisor using nondirective behaviors in a preconference can ask the teacher to choose the focus of the observation and facilitate the teacher as he or she chooses or creates an observation system that the supervisor would feel comfortable using. In the nondirective postconference, the supervisor clarifies, encourages, and reflects as the teacher designs his or her own improvement plan.

Although directive control behaviors are necessary in rare situations, over the long term, we do not consider those behaviors to be consistent with the purpose and principles of clinical supervision. Directive control should be used only in short-term, crisis situations, not as part of a normal clinical cycle.

Peer Coaching

Since teachers naturally turn to each other for help more often than to a supervisor, and since supervision is concerned primarily with improving instruction rather than with summative evaluation (renewal of contracts), teachers helping teachers has become a formalized and well-received way of ensuring direct assistance to every staff member. With the advent of extended responsibilities for career-ladder teachers, mentor teachers, master teachers, grade-level chairpersons, team leaders, and department heads, the time and resources for peer assistance have increased.

If teachers become proficient in observation skills and the format of clinical supervision, the supervisor can take on the role of clarifier, trainer, scheduler, and troubleshooter—clarifier by determining the purpose; trainer by preparing the teachers for the task; scheduler by forming teams or trios of teachers who take responsibility for preconferencing, observing, and postconferencing with each other; and troubleshooter by consulting with teams of teachers who are experiencing difficulties and with individual teachers who need more specialized attention. The use of teachers helping teachers through clinical supervision has been labeled *peer coaching*.

Obviously, the way to begin such a program is not to call a staff meeting and announce, "Since I can't see each of you as much as I would like, why don't you start to visit each other? Go to it!" Without planning and resources, disaster is inevitable. To be successful, peer coaching needs components addressing purpose, preparation, scheduling, and troubleshooting. Let's take each in turn.

Purpose

Before beginning a peer-coaching program, clarifying purpose and goals is necessary (Zwart, Wubbels, Bergen, & Bolhuis, 2009). First, will the program consist of *reciprocal coaching*, with teachers observing and conferring with each other, or *expert coaching*, in which better trained or more experienced teachers assist lesser trained or less experienced teachers? Second, in a peer program, who is to be the recipient of assistance? Should a teacher who is the observer take from the observation some ideas to use, or should the teacher who is the observed take from the observation some actions to use? Third, will the observations and feedback focus on common instructional skills that each teacher is attempting to learn and implement, or will the observations and feedback focus on the teacher's own idiosyncratic concern with his or her teaching? Fourth, should the observations and feedback focus on the teacher's teaching or on students' behaviors? Fifth, is the goal of coaching to be greater awareness and more reflective decision making, or the implementation of particular teaching skills? Ultimately, how does the coaching goal fit into the larger school goal of improving instruction for students?

These are not idle questions. A peer-coaching program void of articulated definition and purpose has no rudder for steering and selecting the training, scheduling, and troubleshooting essential for success (Hooker, 2013). Instead, it becomes another fad, exciting in that it's on the "cutting edge" of school change but lacking substance in terms of what is to be accomplished. If there is a lack of direction in peer coaching programs, well-intentioned teachers will have a vague sense of having done something pleasant but little sense of accomplishment.

Therefore, the first step is to meet with teachers to discuss how a proposed peer coaching program would fit into a school's or district's instructional goals and then to decide on the specific purposes of the program. For example, if the purpose is simply to acquaint teachers with each other's teaching strategies, less preparation is needed than if the purpose is to provide teachers with feedback on their teaching and assist them with developing action plans for instructional improvement. The next subsection provides some training guidelines for proceeding with a peer coaching program that is focused on the purpose of reflective decision making.

> ### ▶ Video Illustration
>
> As you watch this video, ask yourself: How are the behaviors of the expert coach in the video similar to the behaviors you would expect reciprocal coaches to exhibit? How are the behaviors of the expert coach different than the behaviors you would expect reciprocal coaches to exhibit?

Preparation

Before implementation, preparation of teachers would include training on (1) understanding the purpose and procedures of peer coaching, (2) conducting a preconference for determining the focus of observations, (3) conducting and analyzing an observation to distinguish between observing and interpreting classroom events, and (4) conducting two postconferences with different approaches for developing action plans—one using a nondirective approach, the other using a collaborative approach.

A standard form for writing instructional improvement plans in the postconference should be reviewed. The form should be simple and easy to fill out. Each peer member should understand that a completed plan is the object of the first four clinical steps and the basis for beginning the next round of supervision. For purposes of training, you may use the Figure 15.1 form and the forms found in Chapter 12.

Training sessions of about six hours should provide the minimum knowledge and skills to begin peer coaching. After peers have gained some familiarity with the process through demonstrations, modeling, and practice in the workshop setting, they will be anxious but ready to begin a coaching cycle. For the initial attempts, perfection is not expected, of course.

After the first cycle of implementation, a follow-up meeting should be held to discuss what has occurred and what revisions need to be made before beginning the second cycle. It is often convenient to review the past cycle and conduct the preconference for the next cycle during the same meeting. This gives participants a sense of sharing and learning from each other, enables the trainer to answer questions, allows for observation schedules to be arranged, and eliminates the need to meet another time to hold the preconference. From this point on, follow-up meetings concluding and beginning further cycles can be held every two to three weeks until the agreed-on number of peer cycles have been finished. For the first year, it is recommended that at least four cycles be conducted—two times being the coach and two times being coached.

Toward the end of the year, a culminating meeting should be held to summarize the advantages and disadvantages of using peer coaching and to make a recommendation on whether to continue the program for the following year.

Let's emphasize that the program should be based on *agreement* and *volunteerism*. If an entire staff is willing to be involved, that's fine, but if only three teachers are willing, it is still a beginning and a previously unavailable source of help for those three teachers.

> ▶ **Video Illustration**
>
> As you watch this video, think about how the discussion will prepare the teacher who will be the coach. Will the teacher who will be observed have a more successful experience with peer coaching?

Scheduling

A teacher will have a more difficult time becoming enthusiastic about a project if it means increasing the amount of personal time and energy expended beyond an already full day. Because peer coaching will require additional time, the program should be voluntary, at least in the beginning. Greater participation of teachers is likely if the supervisor can schedule time for peer coaching during the school day.

For example, placing teachers together in teams that share the same planning or lunch periods would allow for pre- and postconferences during the school day. Hiring a few substitutes for two days, twice a semester, would allow teachers to be relieved of class duties so that they can observe their peers. One substitute could relieve six classroom teachers for one period at a time. Relief could also be found by having the supervisor (we mean you!) occasionally substitute for a teacher for one class period. This would enable the teacher to observe and would also give the supervisor a glimpse into the operating world of the classroom. Another way of freeing time for peer observations is for teachers to release each other by periodically scheduling a video, lecture, or some other large-group instruction so that two classes can be taught by one teacher. Whatever the actual schedule used to release teachers for peer coaching, preplanning by supervisor and teachers is needed to ensure that teachers can participate without extreme personal sacrifice. Research on lasting classroom change has shown that scheduling released time for teachers during the school day is critical (Zwart et al., 2009).

Another issue is arranging teams of teachers. As in most issues in education, there are no hard-and-fast rules. Generally, teachers should be grouped with each other so that they are comfortable together but not necessarily at identical levels of experience and/or competence. It may be useful to put experienced teachers with new ones, superior teachers with adequate ones, or adequate teachers with struggling ones.

Troubleshooting

The third component of establishing a peer coaching program is the close monitoring of peer progress (Zwart et al., 2009). The supervisor should be available to peer teams as a resource person. For example, what happens when the preconference concludes with an agreement to observe a teacher's verbal interaction in the classroom and the peer coach is at a loss about where to find such an observation instrument? The training program should answer such questions, but orientation meetings cannot cover all possible needs. The supervisor must therefore monitor the needs of peer teams and be able to step in to help.

An elaborate monitoring device is not necessary. The supervisor might simply wander around the halls and check with peer coaches every few weeks. At periodic faculty meetings, he or she might ask peer coaches to write a note on their team progress. The supervisor should be sure that books, videos, and methods/instruments for observations are catalogued and available to teachers in the professional library.

Now that the supervisor can attend to *purpose, training, scheduling,* and *troubleshooting,* a peer coaching program can be implemented. The initial implementation of such a program undoubtedly will create more work for the supervisor. However, the initial work is less than would be necessary for providing clinical supervision to every teacher two or three times a year. If it is important enough to supervisor and staff, the time spent at the start in preparing for the program will pay off with ongoing instructional improvement of teachers.

Mentoring

As discussed in Chapter 2, inadequate induction of beginning teachers as a characteristic of the work environment of traditional schools is a real problem. Beginning teacher assistance programs can go a long way toward solving this problem, and the mentoring of new teachers typically is at the center of such support programs. Most schools with mentoring programs for beginning teachers assign a single mentor to each new teacher; some schools assign a team of mentors to the novice. In the case of mentoring teams, it is best to assign one of the mentors as the lead mentor, so that mentor can coordinate team support for the beginner.

Mentor Selection, Preparation, and Support

In the best of all worlds, experienced teachers would informally match up with each beginning teacher and provide that teacher with the support necessary for a successful induction to the school and profession. In many schools, however, this simply does not happen, and it is necessary to assign mentors to new teachers. Some teachers have more potential to be effective mentors, and those are the teachers who should fill that role. A selection process for mentors should be in place, one that not only chooses well-qualified teachers but also conveys to all members of the school community that it is an honor to be chosen as a mentor. Mentors should be chosen from volunteers who have been provided a clear description of a mentor's role and responsibilities.

We know that successful mentors have particular characteristics, thus such characteristics should be considered in the selection process. Successful mentors are student centered, possess both content knowledge and pedagogical skills, are trustworthy, have good communication skills, seek input before making decisions, collaborate with others, and are supportive of colleagues (Gilles, Carrillo, Wang, Stegall, & Bumgarner, 2013; Kissau & King, 2014; Maor & McConney, 2015). Although teachers at various career stages can be successful mentors, if part of the mentor's role is to introduce the beginning teacher to the school organization and culture, then the mentor will need to have sufficient experience to understand and assist the beginner to navigate that organization and culture.

It is best for the supervisor to establish a mentor selection committee including teachers and other stakeholders to plan and implement the selection process and choose a pool of mentors from which matches with beginners can be made. Many of the attributes of successful mentors listed previously are difficult to measure, thus the decision should be based on a variety of indicators. Aspiring mentors can document previous instructional leadership activities in written applications, write short philosophies of mentoring, respond to scenarios of beginning teachers experiencing problems, interview with the selection committee, and so forth.

The general characteristics associated with successful mentoring are good starting points, but once mentors are selected, they need initial professional development to develop knowledge and skills for mentoring. Depending on skills that they already possess from previous instructional leadership, mentors may need to learn about problems of beginning teachers, adult learning theory, observation skills, conferencing skills, providing psychological support, and so on. Once mentors begin working with beginning teachers, they need ongoing support in the form of released time, common meeting time with beginners, and support seminars in which they can share experiences and receive assistance in addressing problems encountered in mentoring.

Matching Mentors with Beginners

Not all mentor–mentee relationships work, and one of the primary reasons for failure is a poor initial matching of mentor and mentee (Klinge, 2015). There is no foolproof formula for a successful match, but there are several provisions that can increase the chances for success. The relationship tends to be more successful if both parties teach in the same content area and at the same grade level (LoCasale-Crouch, Davis, Wiens, & Pianta, 2012). It is preferable that the mentor and mentee teach in classrooms that are in physical proximity, which enables more continuous interaction and opportunities for immediate assistance when necessary. Perhaps the most important mentor–mentee matches, however, are those of personal style and teaching philosophy.

Mentor Support for the Beginning Teacher

Successful mentors treat their mentees as equals and see their primary role as fostering their mentee's growth and development. The single most important thing the mentor can do is to develop a trusting, supportive relationship with the mentee. To develop a positive relationship, the mentor and mentee must meet on a regular basis. Good mentors provide mentees with feedback and advice, but also ask mentees for input into the mentoring process. As Kissau & King (2014) state, "Mentees should be given opportunities to ask questions, share experiences, and reflect on their decision-making process"(p. 146).

Although support provided to mentees needs to be individualized (LoCasale-Crouch et al., 2012), there are a number of types of assistance that most mentees need. It is best for the mentor and mentee to meet before the beginning of the mentee's first year of teaching so the mentor can orient the beginner to the school, the community the school serves, and the students. Also, the mentor can introduce the mentee to the curriculum, help the beginner to organize the classroom, and plan the first few days of teaching in detail. Once the school year is underway, most beginners will need continued assistance with planning instructional units and daily lessons, classroom management, differentiated instruction, and working with struggling students. Throughout the school year, beginning teachers may need some level of consultation on each task they carry out for the first time—requesting instructional materials, referring a student, assigning grades, meeting with parents, and so forth.

Strategies the mentor can use to assist the mentee include demonstration teaching; team teaching; making arrangements for the beginner to observe effective teachers; peer coaching; and regular meetings in which the mentee can reflect on teaching, request assistance, and engage in mutual problem solving with the mentor (Bullough, 2012). Although this is a discussion of mentoring, we would be remiss if we did not point out that mentoring is not the only part of beginning teacher assistance programs. New teachers should also receive regular assistance from supervisors and other colleagues, and can benefit from professional development targeted at areas of need and regular support sessions provided to groups of beginning teachers.

Benefits of Mentoring

The benefits of effective mentoring for beginning teachers include deeper reflection on teaching, clarification of educational beliefs, increased self-confidence, improved motivation, enhanced problem-solving skills, better classroom management, improved teaching skills, an understanding of the school's culture and norms, and a sense of belonging to and acceptance by the school community (Gilles et al., 2013; Klinge, 2015; Kissau & King, 2014; LoCasale-Crouch et al., 2012). Mentors also receive benefits from their work with beginning teachers. Like the mentees they work with, successful mentors improve their reflection, problem-solving skills, and self-confidence. Additionally, mentors develop feelings of self-satisfaction from observing their mentees' improved teaching. Mentoring can rejuvenate experienced teachers' careers and help prepare them for other leadership roles (Klinge, 2015; Kissau & King, 2014; Maor & McConney, 2015). The school also benefits from mentoring; the beginner is acculturated into the school community, teacher retention is increased, and the success of new teachers enhances the school's reputation and teacher recruitment. The most important benefits of mentoring beginning teachers are for students—successful mentoring can foster a year of growth and development for students being taught by a beginning teacher, and ensure that students will not be subjected to constant teacher turnover and being taught by a steady stream of unsupported novices.

Reciprocal Mentoring

Up to this point our discussion of mentoring has focused on experienced teachers mentoring beginning teachers. Let's turn our attention now to reciprocal mentoring, which usually involves experienced teachers mentoring each other. For example, one experienced science teacher may have recently received professional development, gaining expertise in a number of new labs, but may be having difficulty with classroom management while using the labs. Another experienced science teacher, with excellent classroom management skills, may be interested in using the labs with her students but lacks knowledge about how to utilize the labs. The two teachers can mentor each other in their respective areas of need as they implement the labs. Many of the same strategies used for mentoring beginners—demonstration lessons, peer teaching, peer coaching, meetings for reflective problem solving, and so forth—can be used in reciprocal mentoring by experienced teachers. Another promising type of reciprocal mentoring is among beginning teachers. For example, in a study by Forbes (2004), as a result of mentoring each other, beginning teachers developed insights into instructional planning, classroom management, new instructional strategies, and professional relationships. Our view on reciprocal mentoring by beginning teachers is that, while it can be very beneficial for the new teachers, it is best used as a supplement to mentoring by experienced teachers. While beginning teachers can be tremendous sources of both emotional and instructional support to one another, most beginners have not reached the stage of teaching expertise or the knowledge of school culture possessed by experienced, successful teachers, thus the latter need to assume leading roles in the mentoring of new teachers.

Reverse Mentoring

Reverse mentoring, in which new or younger members of an organization serve as mentors to older, experienced members, has been used in business since the turn of the century (Biss & DuFrene, 2006). One area in which reverse mentoring may prove useful in PK-12 schools is technology. Technology is constantly changing, with each new generation quickly outpacing previous generations in the use of technology innovations. Many beginning teachers can mentor their more experienced colleagues in the use of the latest educational technology. Additionally, many new teachers are in their early 20s and find it easier to understand and relate to the interests, concerns, and learning needs of their students than older teachers. Younger teachers thus can serve as mentors to their older colleagues on current youth culture and how knowledge of that culture can be incorporated into classroom teaching and learning. Although we see potential for reverse mentoring in PK-12 schools, we do not believe it should replace the mentoring of beginning teachers by experienced teachers. The assistance that beginners can provide to experienced teachers is meaningful, but this does not alter the fact that new teachers have a host of support needs that can and should be addressed by their experienced colleagues.

Using Direct Assistance to Improve Classroom Culture

A great deal of direct assistance is for the purpose of improving teachers' instructional skills or solving immediate instructional problems. As important as these goals are, direct assistance can help teachers reach deeper goals based on democratic and moral purposes. The classroom can be viewed as both a microcosm of the larger culture and as a vehicle for transforming that culture. By modeling and encouraging adherence to democratic and moral values in the classroom, the teacher fosters a democratic and moral society (Silva Dias & Menezes, 2013).

Supervisors and teachers can begin the process of improving classroom culture by asking such questions as the following:

1. Are students treated equitably by the teacher and by each other?
2. Do the teacher and students follow democratic principles appropriate to the students' ages and maturity levels?
3. Do the teacher and students demonstrate compassion to those in need?
4. Do students feel physically and emotionally safe?
5. Are all cultures respected, valued, and celebrated?

Processes such as clinical supervision, peer coaching, and mentoring can be used to answer questions such as these. Quantitative observation data can be gathered in this area (e.g., data can be gathered on whether the teacher gives students response opportunities, assistance, or praise in an equitable manner), but often, rich narrative is needed to adequately describe classroom culture. The teacher and supervisor, coach, or mentor can work together to interpret the meaning of data on classroom culture, and to develop action plans for cultural improvement. Because classroom culture is so complex, conferral and action planning for cultural improvement will be more complicated than conferral and planning for technical improvement, and cultural improvement will take much longer than implementing a new teaching skill. However, if a critical goal of education is a more democratic society, then the increased complexity and longer duration of cultural improvement efforts are well justified.

> ✔ **Check Your Understanding 15.0**   Click here to gauge your understanding of the key concepts presented in this chapter.

REFLECTIVE EXERCISE

Assume that you have been contacted by a principal who recently began using clinical supervision with an invitation to visit the principal's school to assess and provide feedback on the principal's performance as a clinical supervisor. During your assessment, what questions about the principal's approach to clinical supervision would you ask the principal? The teachers? What would you look for if you shadowed the principal as she or he went through a clinical supervision cycle with a teacher? What would you look for as you reviewed several samples of data the principal had collected during classroom observations?

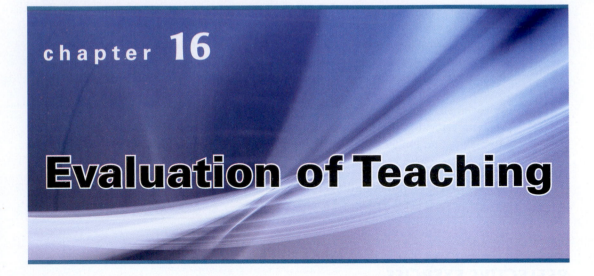

chapter 16

Evaluation of Teaching

Learning Outcomes for This Chapter

After reading this chapter, you should be able to:

1. Recount the authors' rationale for their stance that the results of high-stakes achievement tests should not be a measure used in the evaluation of teaching.

2. Explain three ways to separate summative and formative evaluation of teaching.

3. Identify the first priority for dealing with the low-performing teacher.

4. List at least five methods for assisting with the formative evaluation of teaching.

5. Describe what is assessed in schoolwide evaluation of teaching.

Questions to Reflect On as You Read This Chapter

1. Consider a school you are familiar with where student achievement is part of the evaluation of teaching. What have been the effects of this policy on teachers and teaching? On students?

2. If you had a choice, would you prefer to be an educator at a school that combines summative and formative evaluation of teaching, or a school where they are separate? What are the reasons for your preference?

3. Choose any of the domains of teaching in Figure 16.2. What specific types of teaching performance within the chosen domain should be the subject of summative evaluation of teaching?

4. Which of the methods for assisting with the formative evaluation of teaching that you have *not* been involved with would you like to try out at some point in the future? Why do you believe the chosen structure is promising?

5. A teacher portfolio can be used either for formative (improvement) or summative (decision on future employment) teacher evaluation. How would the development and contents of a portfolio used for summative teacher evaluation differ from the development and contents of a portfolio used for formative evaluation?

6. Think of a team of teachers who you are familiar with that would benefit from team evaluation of teaching. What, specifically, would the team evaluate? What types of data would be gathered? What types of assistance would the team need during the evaluation?

There is considerable support among experts on the evaluation of teaching for the proposition that, historically, things have not gone well in this area (Danielson, 2010/2011; Kowalski & Dolph, 2015; Marshall, 2006; Marzano, 2012; Maslow & Kelley, 2012; Toch, 2008). One problem with traditional evaluation systems is that their expectations for teachers have not been clear. Customarily, evaluation of teaching has centered on checklists with overly general performance categories such as "satisfactory" and "unsatisfactory," or "excellent," "acceptable," and "needs improvement." Also, many of the criteria in conventional evaluation systems have nothing to do with teaching.

Another problem with traditional evaluation is a lack of evaluator preparation for using the system. Consequently, evaluators may lack understanding of the overall evaluation process or how to use the evaluation tools. Evaluators who are not properly prepared are more likely to perform biased evaluations. The evaluator may be biased in terms of what constitutes quality teaching, or worse yet, in regard to a teacher's age, race, ethnicity, or gender. A long-standing problem for principals and assistant principals who are assigned to evaluate teachers across the curriculum is that they are likely to lack knowledge in some content areas.

School administrators are usually pressed for time, which means that they may not be able to do as many evaluations as necessary to properly evaluate teaching. Marshall (2006) notes that even a principal who makes frequent visits to a teacher's classroom observes less than 1% of that teacher's instruction. This means that what the administrator observes may not be a fair representation of the teacher's instruction from day to day. Although having more evaluators would go a long way toward addressing the problem of time, multiple evaluators represent a different (but not a new) problem: a lack of consistency among evaluators. The lack of clarity in traditional evaluation systems combined with inadequate preparation of evaluators means that one evaluator may well interpret the evaluation criteria differently than another; two teachers in the same school who demonstrate the same quality of instruction may be assigned different ratings. When we move beyond the individual school, the disparity in teacher ratings is likely to become worse.

All of the problems with traditional evaluation have left a sour taste in the mouths of teachers and school administrators. In a national survey of teachers, only 26% of the respondents believed that their last evaluation had been "useful and effective" (Duffett, Farkas, Rotherham, & Silva, 2008, (pp. 3). Kim Marshall (2006), a former principal, reflects on conversations with fellow principals:

> We ruefully observed that the whole process is often a meaningless ritual. Administrators observe; we do our write-ups and fill out the evaluation forms; teachers sign them, sometimes with pro forma objections; occasionally we use evaluations to make serious criticism, which may or may not be heeded; very occasionally we use them to make a case for firing a chronically ineffective teacher; but most of the time, our evaluations are accepted with a shrug and have virtually no impact on student learning. (p. 3)

The New Wave of Evaluation Systems: From the Frying Pan to the Fire?

In the 1980s, Thomas McGreal stated, "One of the few enduring initiatives in education is the often strident call for 'new and improved' teacher evaluation systems" (McGreal 1988, (p. 1). McGreal's words ring as true today as when he wrote them. Spurred on by the promise of federal dollars, over the last several years states have mandated evaluation systems intended as "levers" for improved teaching and student achievement. These new accountability systems typically include standards for effective teaching, state or district rubrics to assess compliance with the standards, and multiple classroom observations to rate teaching performance based on the rubrics. Many of the new state evaluation systems also include what they refer to as a "value added" component, meaning that part of a teacher's evaluation is based on student performance, often measured by the state's high-stakes achievement test. Teachers who are rated poorly on the rubric or whose students do poorly on performance measures usually are placed on an individual growth plan, and ultimately can be fired for not meeting standards (Behrent, 2016; Bolyard, 2015; Derrington & Campbell, 2015; Dodson, 2015; Morgan, Hodge, Trepinski, & Anderson, 2014; Schachter, 2012).

Research on the new evaluation systems, and especially on tying student test scores to individual teacher evaluations, has not been positive. Test scores of students taught by the same teacher tend to be unstable, meaning they change from group to group in the same subject in the same year, and from year to year as new groups of students taught by the same teacher take different versions of the same test (Darling-Hammond, Amrein-Beardsley, Haertel, & Rothstein, 2011; Morgan et al., 2014; Murphy, Hallinger, & Heck, 2013). Another problem with linking student test scores to teacher evaluation is that, as important as the individual teacher is, there are many other things that influence student achievement. Some of these factors include past learning, other teachers, class size, other students, the school environment, the curriculum, instructional resources, and a host of social and economic factors. Moreover, attempts to separate a teacher's effects on student learning from other factors have been unsuccessful (Behrent, 2016; Darling-Hammond et al., 2011; Noddings, 2007; Murphy et al., 2013; Toch, 2008).

Evaluators' ratings of teachers also tend to be unstable over time, and the ratings of the same teacher by different evaluators often are inconsistent (Morgan et al., 2014; Murphy et al., 2013). The type of observation most often conducted by evaluators is the classroom walkthrough, found in one study to be inversely related to student achievement (Grissom, Loeb, & Master, 2013). Murphy and associates (2013) review the evidence on the new wave of teacher evaluation systems and conclude that it raises serious questions about the stability of value-added measures, the validity of administrator evaluations, and the capacity of teacher evaluation to improve teaching.

In most districts, school administrators are the ones who must implement the new evaluation system, and for the most part principals' reports on the systems are negative. School leaders report they did not have sufficient time to put the new system in place, and that neither they nor the teachers in their school received adequate training on the system. Principals complain that it takes too much time to carry out the tasks associated with the new evaluation system, including multiple observations, working with teachers on individual growth plans, and all of the paperwork they must complete. In some states principals report problems with the technology used to submit evaluation reports. Many school administrators report dissatisfaction with the use of student test scores as part of teacher evaluation, and difficulty converting teacher performance described in complex rubrics to one- or two-word ratings. Numerous principals do not believe that the new evaluation systems are accurately measuring teacher performance or improving teaching and learning, and they are concerned that the new systems are damaging their relationships with teachers (Dodson, 2015; Kowalski & Dolph, 2015).

Beyond the research on the new wave of evaluation systems there are philosophical and moral issues to be considered. Croft, Roberts, and Stenhouse (2016) argue that high-stakes testing and the new wave of teacher evaluation systems "represent a confluence of systematic and orchestrated education reform efforts" that together "comprise a perfect storm that is eroding the bedrock of public education in the United States" (p. 70). Murphy, Hallinger, and Heck (2013) maintain that teacher evaluation in its current state is "an instrument of industrial-age management" that "privileges organizational architecture (bureaucracy, hierarchy, and institutionalism) under a very thin layer of professionalism" (p. 352).

If we reflect for a moment on some of the language used by proponents to describe the new wave of evaluation systems, it does give us cause for concern. Advocates talk about the need for "levers" or "drivers" for improving schools. One applies pressure at one end of a lever to force something at the other end to move. One definition of a driver is "a tool, such as a screwdriver or hammer, that is used for imparting forceful pressure on another object" (The Free Dictionary, n.d.). This language is definitely not the language of partnership or collaboration. Noddings (2007) examines the term *accountability,* the foundation for the new evaluation systems. She notes that the term comes from the corporate world, and that people are accountable to those above them. Noddings suggests that a more appropriate word for teachers would be *responsible*, as teachers are responsible for their students. Whether teachers carry out their myriad responsibilities to their students is far too complex a question to be answered by a single achievement test or a set of one-word performance ratings.

Noddings (2007) points out the dangers of using student test scores as a measure of accountability. A teacher who teaches different subjects and is faced with the prospect of an evaluation based on test results is likely to focus more on the tested subjects than the other subjects. A teacher teaching a tested subject is more likely to focus on the content in that subject that will tested at the expense of other, sometimes important content within the subject. Teaching to the test means that students will not develop an understanding of the broader meaning and value of the subject. Moreover, teachers evaluated on content-area test results are less likely to teach important concepts that cut across content areas and are not measured by any of the subject-area tests.

As Behrent (2016) points out, a focus on individual teacher performance ratings fosters competition rather than the collegiality and collaboration associated with improving schools. More broadly, when the focus is exclusively on teacher ratings, "issues in education are individualized and removed from the broader social, economic and political context in which education takes place" (p. 51). Champ (2015) concludes that when a new-wave evaluation system contradicts what teachers know about teaching and learning, and teachers realize that an evaluation system is inconsistent, unreliable, and does not improve student achievement, one result is resistance and conflict. The results of the new wave of evaluation systems can lead educators to drastic career decisions. Dodson (2015) reports that many principals are considering retiring early because of their dissatisfaction with the evaluation systems, and that, "[a]cross the country, teachers are retiring, quitting, or getting fired in districts where new teacher evaluation instruments include student test scores" (p. 54).

In the final analysis, all of the money, time, and effort invested in new-wave evaluation is probably not worth it. Murphy et al. (2013) conclude,

> . . . if school improvement is the goal, school leaders would be advised to spend their time and energy in areas other than teacher evaluation. . . . school administrators will be more likely to positively impact instructional quality if they allocate their direct efforts with teachers into facilitative channels. (p. 352)

Summative and Formative Evaluation

Summative and formative are two broad categories of teacher evaluation. Summative teacher evaluation is an administrative function intended to meet the organizational need for teacher accountability. It involves decisions about whether a teacher should be granted tenure, placed on probation or terminated, and in some cases, whether a teacher should receive a bonus or salary increase for outstanding performance. Summative evaluation is based on policies that mandate its purpose, frequency, and procedures. Teacher performance is usually documented on an evaluation form. On the form, an administrator completes checklists, rating scales, or narratives indicating the extent to which the teacher has met performance criteria. Evaluation forms usually are standard (same criteria for all teachers) and global (general enough to apply to teachers with different responsibilities). Summative evaluations typically judge teachers on the quality of their instruction as well as other areas, such as compliance with school regulations, cooperation with administration and colleagues, completion of extracurricular assignments, and so on.

Formative teacher evaluation is a supervisory function intended to assist and support teachers in professional growth and the improvement of teaching. It is focused on the needs of teachers rather than on the organization's need for accountability. While summative evaluation is concerned with a summary of performance over a specific time period, formative evaluation is ongoing and concerned with continuous improvement. Rather than relying on standardized evaluation instruments that gather data on all essential performance criteria, formative evaluation is usually based on a selected focus for instructional improvement (e.g., questioning techniques, student participation, classroom movement, implementing a new instructional model), with the focus changing over time. Thus, the observation systems described in Chapter 12 are well suited for formative evaluation.

Table 16.1 summarizes our comparison of summative and formative teacher evaluation.

table **16.1** Comparison of Summative and Formative Teacher Evaluation

	Summative	Formative
Function	Administrative	Supervisory
Purpose	Accountability; judgment on teacher performance; employment decisions	Assistance; professional development; improvement of teaching
Scope	Instruction; compliance with regulations; extracurricular responsibilities; personal qualities	Instruction
Focus	Written standards and standardized rubric or evaluation form	Any classroom data (e.g., observation, artifacts, etc.) relevant to the teacher's instructional concerns and needs
Duration	Set period (usually one academic year)	Ongoing (aimed at continuous improvement)
Concerns	Standardization, validity, reliability, due process	Building trust, rapport, and collegiality; understanding context; understanding and addressing teacher concerns and needs
Evaluator	Usually an administrator; final decision by administrator	Administrator, supervisor, self, peers, students, and sometimes parents

One historical issue in the field of instructional supervision is whether summative and formative evaluation of teaching should be integrated or kept separate. Indeed, many on the "keep-them-separate" side of the argument say that summative evaluation of teaching should not even be considered part of the field of supervision—that it is a "management" or "administrative" function. Those in favor of integrating formative and summative evaluation say that integration is necessary for a coherent evaluation system, and that the professionals conducting formative evaluation need to also possess summative power in order to have the "clout" necessary for teachers to take their recommendations seriously. We take a different view, that we explain in detail in the next section. First, allow us to provide an overview on our stance on the summative–formative issue. We hold that:

1. both summative and formative evaluation of teaching are necessary.
2. summative and formative evaluation of teaching should be separate.
3. the primary emphasis should be placed on formative evaluation of teaching.

Why Summative and Formative Evaluation of Teaching Should Be Separate

Most school districts have a single evaluation system and maintain that their system meets both summative and formative needs. However, when schools attempt to carry out summative and formative evaluation simultaneously, they tend to place primary emphasis on summative goals, and formative evaluation is reduced to secondary status. Indeed, when we closely examine the evaluation of teaching in districts and schools that purport to have combined systems that emphasize formative evaluation, in most cases the structures, processes, and time commitments in those systems actually focus on summative evaluation.

Evaluation systems that attempt to combine summative and formative evaluation while relying on rating scales alone are particularly suspect. "A school system that relies solely on periodic evaluations of teacher performance through rating scales *may* capture data suited for in-system summative purposes but will be handicapped in pursuing formative/developmental objectives" (Allison, 1981, p. 15 emphasis in original). One reason for this is that summative rating scales are designed to be standardized, global, legally defensible, efficiently completed and processed, and often include many noninstructional criteria. Also, although most would agree that the context of teaching (the school environment, students' prior learning, instructional time, and so on) should be considered in evaluation, the need to use standardized, global instruments means that context cannot be fully considered in summative evaluation. On the other hand, context is an important aspect of formative evaluation. In short, much of the meaningful data for formative assessment are precluded when only summative instruments are used in the evaluation system, but such data can be gathered and utilized in a separate formative process.

It is widely recognized by principals and teachers that summative evaluation, while necessary to make employment decisions, does not lead to instructional improvement for most teachers. Successful formative evaluation depends on trust and open communication between the teacher and evaluator. Yet summative evaluation is potentially punitive. The possibility of a bad performance rating is always lurking in the background. It is human nature to avoid being totally open with an evaluator about problems one is experiencing when the evaluation might lead to a poor performance rating—and possible termination. Many principals believe that they are exceptions to the rule and can successfully integrate summative and formative evaluation. One of the foremost experts on evaluation, James Popham (1988) disagrees: "Many administrators who have been thrust into the formative-summative evaluator role will protest that they can, having 'earned the trust' of their teachers, carry out both teacher evaluation functions simultaneously. They are deluding themselves" (p. 59).

We're not arguing that summative evaluation should be eliminated in favor of formative evaluation. Both types of evaluation are necessary. Like Popham (1988), we maintain that since they have entirely different purposes, they need to be kept separate. With McGreal (1982), we argue that the likelihood that either type of evaluation system will succeed is greater if both systems are internally consistent, which can be accomplished only by the two systems being kept separate. If separated, can the two systems coexist? Yes, but only if the purposes of both systems are clearly defined, the systems are perceived by teachers as distinct, and the integrity of both systems is protected (Allison, 1981).

Most scholars and practitioners agree that the evaluation of teaching by itself is not likely to improve instruction; the evaluation must be tied to professional development. However, as Smylie (2014) points out, the linkage between the evaluation of teaching and professional development is weak in most schools. Although the emphasis in most schools is on summative evaluation, formative evaluation better informs and improves the professional development that is necessary for improved teaching (Young, Range, Hvidston, & Mette, 2015), thus it makes sense to place the emphasis on formative evaluation, while maintaining summative evaluation as a necessary but separate component of the overall evaluation system.

How to Separate Summative and Formative Evaluation

One way to separate the two types of evaluation is to use different evaluators. For example, first-year teachers (who clearly need to have both types of evaluation) could have their summative evaluation carried out by an administrator and formative evaluation by an experienced teacher assigned as their mentor. Experienced teachers could receive summative evaluation from the principal and formative evaluation from an assistant principal for instruction, lead teacher, or peer coach. Also, there are successful evaluation systems in place in which teacher leaders carry out summative evaluations of beginning (Young et al., 2015) and even experienced (Darling-Hammond et al., 2011) teachers, thus administrators doing formative evaluation and teachers doing summative evaluation, while unusual, is a viable option. There are many different ways for summative and formative evaluation to be done by different evaluators. The important things are to make clear to everyone who is responsible for each type of evaluation, to provide both types of evaluators with adequate preparation, and to have evaluators with different roles carry out their evaluations separately.

Another way to separate summative and formative evaluation relates to the time period when each is carried out. For example, all summative evaluations of returning teachers could be carried out in the fall of each school year, leaving the remainder of the year for formative assessment. When this strategy is used, the same person or persons can perform both types of evaluation. This strategy does not work as well if formative evaluation is carried out in the fall and summative evaluation takes place throughout the rest of the year, because the teacher involved in formative evaluation during the fall realizes that summative evaluation is looming on the horizon. That knowledge may affect the willingness of the teacher to engage in open and honest communication about his or her need for instructional improvement. It's better to get the summative evaluation out of the way early in the year, give the teacher his or her "seal of approval," and then allow the teacher and supervisor to engage in nonjudgmental assessment for the remainder of the school year. A long-term variation of the "separate time periods" strategy is to conduct summative evaluation throughout the first year of a multiyear cycle and then focus on formative evaluation for the next two to three years, returning to a summative year at the beginning of the next three- to four-year cycle. Should serious problems with a teacher's performance develop during a formative assessment year, that teacher could be shifted back to a summative evaluation-remediation track until the problem is resolved.

A third way of separating summative and formative evaluation (that admittedly runs counter to the current heavy emphasis on summative evaluation) has been suggested by Thomas McGreal (1983). Under McGreal's model, a clear and visible set of minimum performance expectations would be developed, including administrative, personal, and instructional expectations. Teacher performance regarding these minimal expectations would be continuously, informally monitored, but no special procedures or evaluation instruments would be established. If a problem occurred with a teacher's performance, the administrator would remind the teacher of minimum expectations. If the problem continued to occur, the administrator would issue to the teacher a written notice of the teacher's deficiency, with a copy placed in the teacher's file. If serious violations continued even after the formal notice, the administrator would recommend more serious administrative action. Beyond these contingencies, there would be no standard summative evaluation process or annual write-up. This would take care of summative evaluation. Most of the time and energy spent on evaluation would be for formative assessment, including goal setting, a focus on teaching, systematic classroom observation, and collecting and analyzing additional classroom data. These additional data could include peer, parent, student, and self-evaluation, as well as student performance and classroom artifacts.

Which strategy for separating summative and formative evaluation is the best for a district or school will depend on state and district policies as well the level of administrative and supervisory expertise, the size of the staff, teacher preference, and available resources. The important thing is that they be kept separate. Doing so will mean that both summative and formative evaluations are carried out more effectively.

> ▶ **Video Illustration**
>
> As you watch this video, consider whether the evaluation taking place is summative, formative, or a combination of summative and formative.

Suggestions for Summative Evaluation

How much flexibility districts and schools have in designing summative evaluation systems, of course, depends on state laws and policies. If given the leeway to do so, the first step is to identify the domains of teaching in which teachers are expected to demonstrate knowledge, skills, and behaviors. Wheeler and Scriven (2006), Marshall (2006), the National Institute for Excellence in Teaching (2012), and Danielson (2015) have each suggested several domains that we have listed in Table 16.2, with similar domains listed across the same rows in the table (Danielson's domain of instructional purpose and accuracy of content cuts across the first two rows). As you can see from reviewing Table 16.2, there is a great deal of similarity across the four sets of proposed domains.

Simply identifying broad domains, of course, is not sufficient. Specific types of expected knowledge, skills, and behaviors must be identified within each domain, and ratings must be established to indicate the extent to which the teacher is displaying those expectations. In the Danielson (2015) framework, for example, each domain is broken down into "components," which in turn are broken down into "elements." Many school districts have adopted or modified rubrics such as the one developed by Danielson, which includes performance levels (unsatisfactory, basic, proficient, or distinguished) and observable criteria indicating the teacher's performance level for each element. Finally, teacher ratings (based on performance levels) and evidence supporting those ratings must be summarized in a written evaluation report. The identification of domains of teaching; expected knowledge, skills, and behaviors within

t a b l e **16.2** **Examples of Domains of Teaching**

Wheeler & Scriven, (2006, p. 37)	Marshall (2006, p. 6)	National Institute for Excellence in Teaching (2012, p. 2)	Danielson (2015, pp. 40–41)
Knowledge of Subject Matter			Clarity of Instructional Purpose and Accuracy of Content
	Planning and Preparation for Learning	Designing and Planning Instruction	
		The Learning Environment	Safe, Respectful, Supportive, and Challenging Learning Environment
	Classroom Management		Classroom Management
Instructional Competence	Delivery of Instruction	Instruction	Student Intellectual Engagement
Assessment Competence	Monitoring, Assessment, and Follow-up		Successful Learning for All Students
Professionalism	Professional Responsibilities	Professionalism Responsibilities	Professionalism
Other Duties to the School and Community	Faculty and Community Outreach		

those domains; performance levels; and performance criteria all contribute to a more valid and reliable summative evaluation only if those doing the evaluation have a clear understanding of the system and the skills to use it. Teachers being evaluated also need to understand the system, including performance expectations and performance levels as defined by the system.

Other key components of effective summative evaluation include the data to be gathered and data gathering methods. Nearly all experts agree on the need to gather multiple types of evaluation data. Any data gathered should be directly related to one or more of the performance indicators established within the selected domains of teaching. Systematic classroom observations; discussions with the teacher about observed lessons; written teacher self-evaluations; review of teaching artifacts like unit plans and student work products; examination of evidence of student growth over time; and collaboration with colleagues, parents, and the community for the improvement of student learning all may be appropriate, depending on performance expectations and indicators. In some districts, teachers submit performance portfolios including artifacts and reports as evidence of meeting criteria in each teaching domain. For reasons discussed earlier in this chapter, we do not recommend that the use of students' performance on high-stakes achievement tests be part of the summative evaluation of teaching.

Whatever data gathering methods are used in summative evaluation of teaching, it is essential that evaluators be well trained in those methods. Teachers also need to be provided information on what data will be gathered, who will gather the data, how the data will be gathered, and how often the data will be gathered (Tucker & DeSander, 2006). Evaluators need to give frequent and timely feedback to teachers on the results of evaluation activities (Darling- Hammond et al., 2011).

This brings us to the topic of working with the low-performing teacher. The first priority in such cases, which are far more rare than detractors of our schools would have us believe, should be to assist the teacher to raise her or his performance to a satisfactory level. If the teacher continues to perform poorly, the possibility of a mismatch between a teacher with unfulfilled promise and the school should be considered. No incompetent or uncommitted teacher should be transferred to another school to "get rid" of the teacher, but we know a number of teachers who were poor matches for one school who then became successes in other schools with contexts more congruent with their abilities.

Teachers who are not improving and are not open to career counseling must be notified of deficiencies and the evidence of those deficiencies. The teacher should be given the opportunity to respond in writing to that notice. The teacher must be provided a remediation plan including improvement goals, assistance that will be provided, how progress toward improvement goals will be measured, and how feedback on improvement efforts will be provided (McGrath, 2006). The remediation plan should be viewed and treated by the administration as a real effort to assist the teacher, not merely as steps in the termination process. For an in-depth discussion of this topic, we recommend Sally Zepeda's (2016) book, *The Leader's Guide to Working with Underperforming Teachers.*

Suggestions for Formative Evaluation

In this section we discuss several different methods that can be used for the formative evaluation of teaching. Actually, one expert or another has recommended each of these methods as a way of gathering summative evaluation data; however, each method is used in a very different way for formative evaluation. Also, provided they are different from the evaluators doing summative evaluation, evaluators using any of these methods for formative evaluation are in a different relationship with the teacher than evaluators engaged in summative evaluation. In summative evaluation, like it or not, the evaluator has a level of power over the teacher; in effective formative evaluation the evaluator and teacher are coequals in the evaluation process. Indeed, in the remainder of this discussion we will refer to the professional assisting the teacher in the formative evaluation process as the "facilitator" rather than the "evaluator."

Using Rubrics

It might surprise readers that we recommend rubrics as a part of formative evaluation after discussing them as a part of summative evaluation in many schools. However, rubrics like those designed by Danielson (2013) can be used selectively in formative evaluation. In summative evaluation the teacher is judged on all performance indicators on the rubric; in formative evaluation the teacher and facilitator can cooperatively choose particular domains and components, and assess teacher performance within those domains and components with an eye toward improvement.

Classroom Observations

Observation and conferral in clinical supervision and peer coaching (Chapter 15) are forms of formative evaluation. In formative observation, the observer does not need to gather data on all instructional performance indicators in the summative evaluation system, nor does the teacher necessarily need to be assigned performance ratings. Observation can focus on a particular area of instruction that the teacher is concerned about and be the basis for conferral on how the teacher can improve practice in that area.

> **Video Illustration**
>
> As you watch this video, consider whether the conference will help the teacher improve his instruction. On what do you base your prediction?

Videos

In most summative evaluations that include video recordings of teachers' lessons, the primary reason the teacher submits the videos is to provide evidence of satisfactory teaching. In formative evaluation, the purposes of recording lessons are to reflect on the videos, identify areas for improvement, and engage in dialogue about how to achieve that improvement. The facilitator can assist the teacher in video recording lessons, but with modern video cameras, that will not always be necessary. The observer and facilitator can view the video together or separately, but it is important for them to meet to confer on the video and how what was learned from the video can improve the teacher's instruction.

Review of Student Work

Teachers submitting student work as part of summative evaluation, if they have good self-preservation instincts, will submit work that the students did well on. In formative evaluation, the teachers benefit the most when they and their facilitators review student work reflecting a range of student performance. The teacher and facilitator can analyze student work to identify underlying causes of problems students are experiencing, and discuss ways of addressing those problems.

Peer, Student, and Parent Feedback

Peers can observe the teacher teaching, examine teaching artifacts, and review measures of student achievement, then give feedback to the teacher and facilitator. In formative peer review, the teacher should be allowed to request teachers who they respect and trust to provide peer feedback.

> ### ▶ Video Illustration
>
> As you watch this video, reflect on the advantages of having a teacher conducting a formative evaluation of a colleague.

Some principals and teachers are reluctant to gather student feedback, especially from younger students; however, educators who know that feedback will not be part of a summative evaluation or be placed in teachers' files are more likely to consider student perceptions, and age-appropriate methods of gathering student feedback can be built into the data collection process.

Even parents who do not regularly visit schools and classrooms can provide selective feedback to their children's teachers. Parents can inform teachers if their children feel welcome at school, understand how to do their homework, and so forth. The teacher and facilitator can review feedback from peers, students, and parents, and identify relevant feedback that can be the basis for instructional improvement efforts.

Visits to Other Teachers' Classrooms

Facilitators can arrange for teachers being evaluated to visit the classrooms of expert teachers in order to (1) compare their teaching to the expert teaching they are observing as a way of assessing their own performance, and (2) identify expert teaching behaviors that they may wish to incorporate into their own teaching. Visits to classrooms where the same students, grade levels, or content areas are being taught are typically the most helpful. After observing a peer's instruction, the teacher should meet with the facilitator to discuss what was learned and how the teacher can use that learning to improve her or his own instruction.

Individualized Improvement Plans

A facilitator can assist a teacher with an individualized instructional improvement plan that is not part of the school's summative evaluation system. Such a plan calls for three types of formative assessment. First, the teacher completes an initial self-assessment that can include the analysis and synthesis of data gathered through several of the methods already discussed. The self-assessment is the basis for the teacher's plan for instructional improvement (often a year-long plan). Second, the teacher and facilitator gather and analyze data as the plan is being implemented to assess progress. Third, at the completion of implementation (usually at the end of the school year), outcome data is gathered.

Self-Reflection

As a method of formative assessment, self-reflection can contribute to all of the methods previously discussed as well as stand on its own as a method for assessing and improving teaching. There are several aids to self-reflection, including reflective logs, reflective journals, and audio journals. The teacher can use a reflective log to record observations on student learning, describe instructional problems, and track improvement efforts, and also discuss log entries with the facilitator. Reflective journals can be used for more personal and deeper reflections, with the teacher selecting which journal entries to share with the facilitator. Despite the significant potential of reflective writing, keeping reflective logs and journals does not appeal to some teachers; an alternative for those teachers is audio recording of oral reflections.

Portfolio Development

Teacher portfolios can be used for either summative or formative evaluation, but each type of evaluation requires a different type of portfolio. Teachers who are developing a portfolio that will be used as part of their summative evaluation are concerned with providing evidence of effective teaching tied to the school's expectations, and ultimately tied to the performance ratings they will receive from whomever completes their evaluation report. Teachers developing formative portfolios can identify problems they wish to work on or new teaching strategies they wish to explore; use portfolios as vehicles for developing, recording, and reflecting upon self-directed improvement efforts; and share their portfolios with colleagues. Teachers can incorporate ideas from each other's portfolios into their own professional development.

One type of annual portfolio recommended for formative evaluation is divided into four sections. Section 1 includes the teacher's self-assessment of teaching during the first several weeks of the school year. The content of this section includes data from peer observations, student work products and achievement records, student surveys, and so on. Teacher reflections on the meaning of the data and implications for instructional improvement also are displayed in section 1.

Section 2 of the portfolio includes a plan for individual improvement to be implemented throughout the remainder of the school year. The plan includes instructional improvement goals and actions intended to meet the goals. Planned actions might be attending professional development workshops, joining a study group, trying out new teaching strategies, and so on. Section 2 also contains a plan for evaluating the results of the improvement activities. Reflections on why the planned actions were chosen and anticipated results also can be included in section 2.

Section 3 of the portfolio is developed over the remainder of the school year. Entries in this section include illustrations of and reflections on improvement activities. Agendas from professional development programs attended, feedback from coaches who observed new teaching strategies, samples of student performance over time, and myriad other entries document improvement efforts and measures of growth. Artifacts and reflections in section 3 tell the story of the teacher's improvement journey.

Although measures of progress toward improvement goals are present throughout section 3 of the portfolio, it is section 4 where the teacher enters year-end summary data on progress toward improvement goals. Final reflections on the school year and judgments about the success of improvement activities are entered. General reflections on personal and professional growth also may be included. The teacher probably will have new students the following school year and may even be teaching different courses, so the end of the school year is not the appropriate time for developing a detailed improvement plan for the next year; however, the teacher may wish to conclude section 4 of the portfolio with a general discussion of some potential new improvement goals.

Although summative and formative portfolios both can include artifacts and reflections on professional growth, the different purposes of the two types of portfolios make both the overall spirit and many specific entries in one type of portfolio very different from the other. The time and effort needed to develop either type of portfolio necessitate that districts and schools wishing to use portfolios choose between the two types. Either type of portfolio is appropriate, but if the primary purpose is to improve teaching and learning, our bet is on the formative portfolio.

Contextualizing and Personalizing Formative Evaluation

One complaint that educators make about state and district summative evaluation systems is that they do not consider the teaching context, including factors like community socioeconomic factors, the school's resources, and students' prior learning. Since formative evaluation is free of the legal requirements attached to summative evaluation, it can consider and even be tailored to the school and classroom context. In formative evaluation, schools and teachers can be allowed a great deal of flexibility in choosing what aspects of instruction to assess, the methods of evaluation, and improvement goals. Indeed, formative evaluation can be individualized to match each teacher's professional context and needs.

Beyond Evaluation of Individual Teaching

A core proposition of the National Board for Professional Teaching Standards (NBPTS) is, "Teachers are members of professional learning communities" (2014, n.p.). In its seminal document *What Teachers Should Know and Be Able to Do*, NBPTS states, "Teachers contribute to school effectiveness by collaborating with other professionals" (1989, p. 18). If we are going to take seriously the premise that teachers need to work together in teams and schoolwide for the improvement of teaching and learning, then it makes sense to evaluate teaching at the team and school levels.

Team Evaluation of Teaching

There are a variety of instructional teams in schools, including grade-level, looping, multi-age, content-area, inclusion, and interdisciplinary teams, to name a few. Formative, self-evaluation by team members facilitated by a supervisor or teacher leader is the most meaningful approach to team evaluation. The focus of the evaluation will depend on the purpose of the team and students the team is responsible for, but many of the same data collection methods used for formative evaluation of individual teachers can be used by the team. The difference here is that the evaluation is focused on the *team's* instructional performance and effects on student learning. Teachers on the team can observe each other and the students they are responsible for in each other's classrooms, develop common rubrics for assessing student progress, and meet together to analyze students' work. Collaborative data gathering and analysis should lead to collaborative design and implementation of an improvement plan, and continued evaluation to assess and modify improvement efforts.

Schoolwide Evaluation of Teaching

In Chapter 2 we talked about dynamic schools having a "cause beyond oneself." Such a cause is centered on teaching and learning, and schools have a responsibility to evaluate the teaching going on throughout the school to determine if it is consistent with the school's vision and mission. The evaluation we are talking about goes beyond student performance on the state's high-stakes achievement test; it includes examining the school's learning environment, instructional programs, classroom instruction, and a variety of student outcomes. This is such a major endeavor it should not be left to a "one-shot" visit by an external evaluation team. Rather, schoolwide evaluation of teaching should be an ongoing process with educators collecting school data through curriculum mapping, collaborative learning walks, and review of a variety of student achievement measures. The school also should seek continuous input from parents, community members, and critical friends. Collective analysis of data and discussion of improvement needs should alternate between small-group and whole-faculty meetings.

Schoolwide evaluation of teaching can inform instructional improvement efforts built around professional development (Chapter 18), curriculum development (Chapter 19), action research (Chapter 20), changing the school culture (Chapter 21), addressing diversity (Chapter 22), and building community (Chapter 23).

> ✔ **Check Your Understanding 16.0**   Click here to gauge your understanding of the key concepts presented in this chapter.

REFLECTIVE EXERCISE

Imagine you are part of a three-member panel sitting on a stage in front of a group of educators at a public forum on teacher evaluation. The topic of the panel discussion is whether formative and summative teacher evaluation should be integrated or kept separate. The first panel member argues that if a school district is to have a coherent and consistent teacher evaluation program, formative and summative teacher evaluation must be integrated within a single process. The second panel member proposes that, because of the need for trust and openness between the teacher and the supervisor who is providing formative evaluation, formative and summative teacher evaluation needs to be separate. It is now your turn to speak to the audience. What position will you take? What arguments will you use to support your position?

chapter 17

Group Development

Learning Outcomes for This Chapter

After reading this chapter, you should be able to:

1. List the five stages of group development.
2. Specify the collaborative skills of a successful group.
3. Identify the three broad categories of roles observed in groups.
4. Relate at least three ways a supervisor can assist a group toward higher levels of development, expertise, and commitment.
5. Explain why conflict within groups should be encouraged and supported.
6. Enumerate important aspects of preparing for a meeting.

Questions to Reflect On as You Read This Chapter

1. Think about a group that you were a member of that has completed its work. Did the group go through all five stages of development that the authors describe in this chapter? Did the group get "stuck" in one of the stages? If the group did not go through the stages described by the authors, did it go through other stages? If so, what would you label each of those stages, and what was going on with the group during each stage?

2. As you read about task, person, and dysfunctional behaviors, reflect on a group that you have been part of or observed that did not work well together. Why do you believe the group did not function well? Was it because of missing task roles? Missing person roles? The presence of dysfunctional roles? Would adding either task or personal roles have helped the group work together? If so, what specific task or person roles would have helped?

3. Reflect on a dysfunctional member of a group you have been part of or observed. Why do you think the group member assumed a dysfunctional role? Was the dysfunctional behavior due solely to the group member's personality, or could there have been other factors, such as the group's mission, membership, leader, discussions, and so forth, or factors present in the larger organization? Did the leader and group address the dysfunctional behavior appropriately? Could the leader or group have better addressed the dysfunctional behavior? If so, how?

4. The authors state in this chapter that successful groups frequently experience conflict. Reflect on a highly successful group that you were part of or observed that experienced considerable conflict. Was the nature of this conflict different from the conflict you have experienced or observed in less successful groups? If so, how was it different? Did the group leader and other group members in the successful group deal with the conflict differently than leaders and members of less successful groups? If so, how?

5. What elements from the meeting checklist would you like to see included in planning for future meetings that you lead or participate in?

Avertical team at Highlands Elementary School is using action research to improve student literacy. The Level Six team at M. L. King Middle School is developing a new interdisciplinary curriculum. A teacher task force at Edwards High School is examining strategies for assisting students with special needs.

These teams are different in terms of school level and purpose, but they also have much in common. Each of the groups is expected to complete a task that will involve making a number of decisions along the way. Each group needs to be concerned about maintaining positive interpersonal relationships, and each group is almost certain to face some level of conflict and some types of dysfunctional behavior along the way. There are myriad teams with myriad purposes operating at schools across the nation, but they all possess some common developmental phases, roles, and challenges. This chapter discusses the stages of group development, characteristics of successful groups, group roles, applying developmental supervision to groups, resolving conflict, and preparing for meetings.

Stages of Group Development

Scholars have identified five stages of group development: forming, storming, norming, performing, and adjourning (Bonebright, 2010; Levi, 2014; Necsoi, 2015; Tuckman & Jensen, 1977; Wheelan, 2016). Some groups journey through all five stages, others become arrested in a lower stage and either continue functioning at less than full capacity or disband because of their inability to fulfill their mission. Let's review group members' concerns and behaviors as well as the group leader's responsibilities at each stage.

Forming

In the forming stage, group members are uncertain and anxious. They wonder how they will be expected to behave, whether they will be accepted, what they will be asked to do, whether they will be able to perform satisfactorily, and if group membership will be rewarding. Group members at this stage are fairly passive and reliant on the group leader. Those who do not know each other may be very quiet, and those who know each other may engage in conversations about outside experiences that take the group off task. Early interaction tends to be more focused on people either getting to know each other or renewing friendships than on accomplishing tasks. Due to the anxiety, uncertainty, and absence of established trusting relationships, groups in the forming stage tend to make little progress on the group's mission. One of the group leader's responsibilities at this stage is to foster a positive climate for group meetings. The leader should focus on developing positive relationships with group members and leading activities and conversations that assist the group members to develop positive relationships with each other. The leader also needs to assist group members to understand the group's mission and member roles.

Storming

In the storming stage, the conformity of the norming stage is replaced by conflict. Some of this conflict may result from anxiety about the organization's expectations, some from power struggles within the group, and some from differences of opinion about group goals, roles, and procedures. This conflict should not be viewed as a negative thing; it is necessary for the group to move to the next stage of development; however, if the conflict is not managed properly, the group can become stuck in the storming stage and fail to complete its mission. The group leader should invite discussion of issues causing conflict, seek diverse perspectives on those issues, and make it clear that all perspectives have value. The leader should foster an open and trusting group ethos during these discussions, one that will carry forward into the future stages of the group's development. The leader's goal is to convince the group to direct the conflict toward the forging of common values, goals, norms, and procedures. For the leader, this process becomes a balancing act: The leader must balance the need to promote—and sometimes restore—positive interpersonal relationships with the need to address the task at hand, and to balance attention to individual, group, and organizational needs in the creation of a unified purpose.

Norming

In the norming stage, through discussion and negotiation, the group develops ground rules for social interaction, goals, and procedures for achieving the goals. The group becomes more organized. Conflict is reduced, and interpersonal relationships improve. Group members begin to trust each other more, and as a result, members become both more willing to freely express themselves and more willing to consider the ideas of others. As members of the group increase their trust in each other, they also increase their trust in the group as a whole. Increased commitment to the group and its mission leads to group cohesion and group identity. The group is now able to focus on its mission, and is becoming productive. The leader's role in this phase is to facilitate the group as it establishes its norms (not to dictate those norms), and to foster group consensus on goals, roles, and procedures that will assist the group in achieving its mission. Throughout the norming stage, it is important for the leader to provide the group with feedback on its journey from conflict to collaboration.

Performing

At this stage, the group has reached full maturity and optimal performance. Although members of the group maintain positive interpersonal relationships, their primary focus is meeting the group's goals. Members shift roles and tasks as necessary for group success. Group members are conscious of each other's assets and call on those assets as needed. Tasks are differentiated, but coordinated and tied to group goals. Individuals openly share needed information and resources. The group has become expert at identifying, analyzing, and solving problems. In short, the group is highly effective and highly productive. For a team at the performing stage, the leader's responsibilities are to encourage continuous improvement, provide challenging new tasks, and recognize both individual and team performance.

Adjourning

If a group discontinues its activities because it has completed its mission, celebration is in order. Members of successful teams may regret the team is disbanding, because they will no longer be involved in the team activities or the close interpersonal relationships that the team has fostered. Other teams adjourn because of conflict or a realization that the team's goals cannot be met. Members of failed teams may focus on making excuses for the failure. In schools, there are many standing teams that may temporarily adjourn because they have completed a long-term project or an academic year; the next team project may involve very different goals, with some old members leaving the team and new members joining. One task of the team leader is to honor the team for its efforts. For successful teams, the leader can provide structures allowing team members who wish to continue communicating and providing mutual support to do so. Whether the team has concluded its work in success or failure, or simply adjourned for the summer, the team leader should gather and share data on team performance. For both the successful and failed team, the data can be used to assist other teams in the future. For the team that has adjourned temporarily, the data becomes feedback for improved performance in the future.

Characteristics of Effective Groups

The scholarship on group development includes a number of characteristics of successful groups (Beebe & Masterson, 2015; Biech, 2008; Johnson & Johnson, 2013; Levi, 2014; Mickan & Rodger, 2000; Sheard & Kakabadse, 2002; Wheelan, 2016). The seeds for these characteristics are planted in the forming and storming stages. The characteristics then develop in the norming stage and reach full fruition in the performing stage. A brief review of the characteristics follows:

- The group has clear goals that challenge and unify the group. The group's goals are congruent with the organization's goals. Group members' roles and responsibilities as well as group structures and processes are built around the group's goals.

- Although the leader may need to rely on a directive approach in the forming and norming stages, as the group—and individual members—develop, a collaborative approach may be more appropriate for the forming stage and a nondirective approach for the performing stage (we'll discuss applying developmental supervision to groups later in this chapter). In the fully functioning group, major decisions that affect the entire group and its mission are made by consensus. Leadership for specific tasks is distributed throughout the group, with different members assuming leadership for tasks that are well matched with their knowledge and abilities. Members are flexible and willing to assume different leadership roles as the group's needs change.

- The group ethos is collegial, collaborative, and cohesive. Members understand, agree with, and follow group norms. The group values the diversity of its membership as well as diverse ideas offered by its members. Participation is balanced, with all members rather than just a few contributing to group conversations. Group members trust and support each other.

- The group has developed collaborative skills, including communication, decision making, conflict management, planning, and problem solving skills. During group meetings, task and personal roles are present as needed, and dysfunctional roles are minimized (see the discussion of group member roles later in the chapter).

- The group is supported by the organization with the time, information, and other resources necessary to complete its mission. The organization recognizes and honors the group for its accomplishments and individual members for their contributions.

- The group continuously gathers data on its process and progress. The group makes adjustments in its goals and activities based on the ongoing assessment. The organization holds the group accountable for carrying out its mission, and the group holds itself and its members responsible for accomplishing that mission.

Group Member Roles

Regarding member roles, there are two dimensions of an effective group (Levi, 2014): the task dimension and the person dimension. The *task* dimension represents the content and purpose of the group meeting. The task is what is to be accomplished by the end of the meetings. Typical tasks of professional groups might be deciding on a new textbook, writing a new instructional schedule, coordinating a particular curriculum, or preparing a professional development plan. An effective group, obviously, accomplishes what it sets out to do. The *person* dimension of an effective group comprises the interpersonal process and the satisfaction participants derive from working with each other. Concern and sensitivity to participants' feelings create a climate of desiring to meet with each other from week to week to accomplish and implement the group task.

Let's explain these two dimensions in a different way. Specific task behaviors are clarifying the group's purpose, keeping discussions focused, setting time limits, and appraising group progress toward the goal. A leader who says, "We're getting off the track; let's get back to discussing textbooks," is exhibiting a task behavior. Specific person behaviors seen in a group include recognizing people for their contributions, smiling, injecting humor, and listening attentively. A leader who says, "Fred, I'm following what you've been saying; it's a point worth considering," would be demonstrating a person behavior.

Imagine a group that exhibits only task behaviors. The meeting would be formal, cold, and tense. People would not receive feedback, would not be encouraged, and probably would swallow hard before addressing the unsmiling, staring faces. Such a group would accomplish its task quickly, with little mutual support. The decision would be quick because participants would wish to remove themselves from the tense environment as soon as possible. The formality of the sessions would prevent in-depth discussions of feelings, attitudes, and differences of opinion. Decisions would be made on the basis of incomplete information and commitment from group members. The implementation of the decision would be problematic at best.

Next, imagine a group that exhibits only person behaviors. There would be much personal chatter, humorous storytelling, and frequent backslapping and touching. People would be smiling and laughing. The image of a raucous cocktail party might characterize a group with all person behaviors and no task behaviors, and the morning-after hangover is also analogous to the sense of accomplishment after a meeting devoid of task behaviors. People would enjoy each other's company for its own sake; everyone would have a wonderful time, but little would be done.

The leader wishing to ensure that all necessary roles are present first needs to determine what behaviors are indicative of roles already in existence. Are some members displaying task roles and/or person roles? What roles are ongoing? Are certain roles lacking? Remember that both task and person roles are functional to group performance. Another set of roles and behaviors, called *dysfunctional,* distracts a group from task and person relations. Dysfunctional roles, unlike functional roles, are a concern when present. After listing and briefly describing the most common functional member roles, we will examine dysfunctional roles.

Task Roles

The following descriptions are adapted from those listed by Benne and Sheats (1948):

Initiator–contributor. Contributes new ideas or different perspectives on topic. Initiates discussion on different aspects of topic being discussed or a new topic.

Information seeker. Seeks to verify accuracy of information being considered. Requests new information from expert sources.

Opinion seeker. Asks others to state their beliefs and feelings concerning an issue or a position concerning a proposal under discussion.

Information giver. Shares factual knowledge, observations, or experiences concerning the topic being discussed.

Opinion giver. Shares beliefs or suggestions concerning the issue at hand.

Elaborator. Builds on others' ideas by providing additional information, examples, or potential effects.

Coordinator. Describes connections among different ideas. Seeks to synthesize alternative proposals.

Orienter. Sums up the discussion thus far and reviews consensus or differing views to that point. Alerts the group when its discussion has strayed from its purpose and prompts the group to refocus its discussion on that purpose.

Evaluator-critic. Assesses group process for effectiveness and fairness, and appraises group proposals for adequacy, practicality, and feasibility.

Energizer. Keeps the group focused on considering alternatives, making decisions, and completing its task.

Procedural technician. Provides materials and resources (handouts, flipchart, markers, technology, and so forth) the group needs to complete its task.

Recorder. Takes notes on issues discussed, proposals, and decisions.

A group needs these member roles to keep moving toward accomplishing its task. A leader can use these descriptions to figure out what roles are missing. Additional roles might need to be assigned to group members or incorporated by the leader. For example, a group might contain most of the task roles except for a procedural technician or recorder. Such a group probably would converse easily but would bog down on recalling what has been said. The leader who knows what roles are needed can ask for a volunteer to be a recorder and summarizer. Knowledge of task roles and behaviors enables a leader to assess what roles are evident and what further roles need to be assigned. The leader might take on some of the missing roles, assign them to others, or add particular persons to a group.

Person Roles

The knowledge of person roles and behaviors provides a guide to the group leader. Consider the following descriptions:

Encourager. Affirms, supports, and accepts the contribution of other members. Shows warmth and a positive attitude toward others.

Harmonizer. Conciliates differences between individuals. Looks for ways to reduce tension between members through nonthreatening explanations and humor.

Compromiser. Offers to change his or her proposals for the good of the group. Willing to yield position or to acknowledge own errors by meeting other opposing ideas halfway.

Gatekeeper or expediter. Regulates flow of communication by seeing that all members have a chance to talk. Encourages quiet persons to speak and puts limits on those who dominate the conversation. Proposes new regulations for discussions when participation becomes unbalanced.

Standard setter: Ego ideal. Appeals to group's pride by not letting group members give up when trouble occurs. Exudes confidence that the group is a good one and can make sound decisions.

Observer and commentator. Monitors the working of the group. Records who speaks to whom, where and when most roadblocks occur, and the frequency and length of individual members' participation. Provides feedback when the group wishes to evaluate its procedures and processes.

Follower. Is willing to accept the decisions of the group and follow them even though he or she has not been active or influential in those decisions. Serves as a listener to group discussion.

The seven person roles provide human satisfaction and group cohesiveness. People feel positive about meeting and talking with each other and comfortable enough to express their ideas. As a result, meetings are seen as pleasant times to continue the group's work. When person roles are missing, a group may face severe difficulties in making acceptable and committed decisions. Without person behaviors and roles, only the strongest, most assured, and vocal members will speak. Decisions might be made that more timid persons strongly reject but the group may not know that such strong disapproval exists.

Again, it is the group leader's responsibility to see if people roles are evident. If roles are missing, then he or she can confront the group with their absence, pick up the role(s) himself or herself, quietly suggest particular roles to existing members, or add to the group other individuals who more naturally play such roles. *Both task and person roles, when not already in existence, need to be added.*

Dysfunctional Roles

Dysfunctional roles and behaviors are those that are conspicuous in their presence. Such roles and behaviors disrupt the progress toward a group goal and weaken group cohesiveness. Consider the following:

Aggressor. Personally attacks the worth of other members. Belittles and deflates the status, wisdom, and motivation of others. Examples of such verbal attacks are: "That's the most ridiculous thing I've ever heard," "You must be crazy to suggest. . . ."

Blocker. Sees all opinions and suggestions by group members as negative. Opposes any decision being made and stubbornly refuses to propose alternatives. Examples of such blocking statements are: "That's a terrible idea," "I don't want to do that," "It's futile to do anything."

Recognition seeker. Uses the group setting to receive personal attention. Examples of such behaviors are dropping books, scattering papers, coughing incessantly, pretending to be asleep, raising hand and then forgetting what one was going to say.

Self-confessor. Uses the group to ventilate personal feelings not related to the group's tasks. Talks about personal problems or feelings of inadequacy whenever he or she can see ways to slip such confessions into the group discussion. Examples of self-confessing statements are: "This discussion reminds me of when I was a little child and the weight problem I had," or when the group is talking about differences of opinion, "You should hear my son and me fight; I don't know what to do about him."

Playboy or playgirl. Lacks interest and involvement by using the group setting to have a merry time. Distracts other members from the group's purpose. Tells private jokes, passes notes, makes faces at others, plays cards, and so on.

Dominator. Asserts superiority in controlling group discussion and dictates what certain members should do. Claims to know more about the issue under discussion and have better solutions than anyone else. Has elaborate answers to almost every question and monopolizes the discussion.

Help seeker. Tries to gain group's sympathy by expressing feelings of inadequacy or personal confusion. Uses such self-derogation as reason for not contributing: "This is all too confusing for me," "I can't make a decision on my own," "Why ask me? I can't help."

Special-interest pleader. Has no opinion or suggestions of his or her own but instead speaks for what others would say or do. Cloaks own bias by using an outside group: "We couldn't do that. Do you know what the school board would think?" "If those parents down in the local restaurant ever heard that we were going to change. . . ."

Dysfunctional roles are fairly self-evident in a group. The leader's responsibility is to reduce or eliminate such dysfunctional roles before they severely harm the morale and efficiency of the group. He or she might try to understand the dysfunctional member's reason for acting as an aggressor, playboy, special interest pleader, and so on and then either confront the person privately or provide changes within the group to satisfy the unmet needs that are leading to the dysfunctional behavior.

Dealing with Dysfunctional Members

The fact that a group is made up of individuals with varying temperaments and motivations is important when thinking about ways to work with groups. Dealing with individuals, particularly those who display dysfunctional behaviors, is an additional responsibility of a group leader.

If the leader has observed the group at work and has determined that his or her own leader behaviors are appropriate for most members of the group, yet there continue to be a few dysfunctional members, then individual treatment might be in order. The procedure for treating a dysfunctional member is: (1) observe the member, (2) try to understand why the member is acting unproductively, (3) communicate with the member about the behavior, (4) establish some rules for future behavior, and (5) redirect the unfavorable behavior (Corey & Corey, 1982; Eckstein, 2005; Kemp, 1970). Each step of this procedure will be amplified:

1. *Observe the member.* When and with whom does the dysfunctional behavior occur? What does the group member do, and how do others respond? For example, a dominator might start monopolizing the conversation as soon as he or she walks into the meeting. Other people might be interested in the dominator's talk for the first few minutes of the meeting but become increasingly annoyed as the dominator continues. They might roll their eyes, yawn, fidget, or make comments to each other.

2. *Try to understand the member.* Why does the member persist with dysfunctional behavior? Does he or she know the behavior is unproductive? Is the behavior being used to mask some underlying emotion? For example, a playboy might be insecure about his own worth and pretend not to care rather than exposing inner thoughts to the scrutiny of the group.

3. *Communicate with the member.* What can you communicate about the group member's behavior and the situation? Describe the situation and the behavior to the member without denigration. Instead of saying, "You're being an aggressive

son of a gun," say, "I've noticed that you speak loudly and angrily to Sara. At the last meeting, you told her to keep her mouth shut." Tell the dysfunctional member the effect of the behavior on you as group leader: "When you tell Sara to shut up and tell Bob that he's stupid, it starts an argument that takes time away from the meeting. I can't complete the agenda on time when those arguments take place."

4. *Establish some rules for future behaviors.* Either ask the member to suggest some rules that he or she can abide by in the future, or tell the member your future rules, or establish them jointly. Regardless of which tactic is chosen, the leader should think of rules that would minimize further disruptions to the group. For example, the leader might say to a self-confessor, "The next time you have a personal problem, come speak to me privately about it," or to a dominator, "I'm going to enforce a two-minute limit on every member's participation," or to a blocker, "If you don't think we're on the right course, tell us your objection once and only once."

role play 17.1
Task and Dysfunctional Roles

Preparation. This role play can involve 8 to 16 participants, sitting around a large meeting table, with the other students sitting outside of the space occupied by the table and role players. The instructor assigns an equal number of task and dysfunctional roles (four to eight of each). Each role player is provided a sign with the name of his or her specific role printed on it, and the signs are displayed on the table in a manner allowing each of the other role players and the observers to see what role each participant is playing. Role players are asked to review the chapter's description of their assigned task or dysfunctional role before the role play begins.

Scene. The role players are all teachers at an elementary school. Each spring students, teachers, and parent volunteers participate in an all-day field day. The field day is at a different location and involves different activities each year. The field day is to be a learning experience, not just fun and games. The teachers are all part of a leaderless

group that has been asked by the school principal to plan next spring's field day. Specifically, the principal has asked the group to identify a learning theme and destination as well as a schedule of activities for the field day. The role players are to set aside their "real-life" meeting behaviors and play the role they are assigned at every opportunity during the role play. The observers are asked to take open-ended notes on what they see happening during the role play. The role play should last 5–10 minutes, with the instructor deciding when to end it.

Whole-Group Processing. After the role play, the instructor asks the observers to share what they observed during the role play and their reactions. Next, the instructor asks the role players to share their observations and feelings during the role play. Finally, the instructor asks for a few individuals in the whole group to summarize, in five words or less, the overall effect on the group of having task and dysfunctional roles only.

5. *Redirect the unfavorable behavior.* Pick up on the group member's dysfunctional behavior, and try to make it functional. A dominator can be assigned the role of recorder, summarizer, or timekeeper. A playboy can be given an opening time for sharing a funny story to relax the group before starting official business. An aggressor can be asked to play devil's advocate and argue the position of an adversary.

The five steps outlined here will help the meeting leader understand and deal with individual dysfunctional behavior. The steps are predicated on the leader confronting the dysfunctional member in private. Dysfunctional behaviors that occur infrequently and in isolated situations might simply be ignored. The leader can respond to infrequent misbehaviors or make light of them: "Sara, I guess you really got wound up today; perhaps we might hear from someone else now." Only incessant behaviors that distract the entire group need to be dealt with via direct confrontation. Confrontation is not easy but is necessary at times for the sake of the group. (Role Play 17.4 provides a demonstration of how to deal with a dysfunctional group member.)

---

role play 17.2

Person and Dysfunctional Roles

Preparation. This role play can involve 8 to 14 participants sitting around a large meeting table, with the other students sitting outside of the space occupied by the table and role players. The instructor assigns an equal number of person and dysfunctional roles (four to seven of each). Each role player is provided a sign with the name of his or her specific role printed on it, and signs are displayed on the table in a manner allowing each of the other role players and the observers to see what role each participant is playing. Role players are asked to review the chapter's description of their assigned person or dysfunctional role before the role play begins.

Scene. The role players are all high school teachers in a leaderless group charged by the principal to make some decisions about what a service learning program the school has committed to should look like. The principal has asked the group, with representatives from all academic departments, to determine the program's goals, which departments will participate in the program, and some potential service learning projects to share with the rest of the faculty. The role players are to set aside their "real-life" meeting behaviors and play the role they are assigned at every opportunity during the role play. The observers are asked to take open-ended notes on what they see happening during the role play. The role play should last 5 to 10 minutes, with the instructor deciding when to end it.

Whole-Group Processing. After the role play, the instructor asks the observers to share what they observed during the role play and their reactions. Next, the instructor asks the role players to share their observations and feelings during the role play. Finally, the instructor asks for a few individuals in the whole group to summarize, in five words or less, the overall effect on the group of having person and dysfunctional roles only.

role play **17.3**

Task and Person Roles

Preparation.   This role play can involve 8 to 14 participants sitting around a meeting table, with the other students sitting outside of the space occupied by the table and role players. The instructor assigns an equal number of task and person roles (four to seven of each). Each role player is provided a sign with the name of his or her specific role printed on it, and the signs are displayed on the table in a manner allowing each of the other role players and the observers to see what role each participant is playing. Role players are asked to review the chapter's description of their assigned task or person role before the role play begins.

Scene.   The role players are all middle school teachers in a leaderless group that has been asked by the principal to come up with a proposed plan for using a professional development grant of $50,000 given to the school by a benefactor. The only

stipulation in the grant is that the funds be used for the improvement of teaching and learning. The role players are to set aside their "real-life" meeting behaviors and play the role they are assigned at every opportunity during the role play. The observers are asked to take open-ended notes on what they see happening during the role play. The role play should last 5 to 10 minutes, with the instructor deciding when to end it.

Whole-Group Processing.   After the role play, the instructor asks the observers to share what they observed during the role play and their reactions. Next, the instructor asks the role players to share their observations and feelings during the role play. Finally, the instructor asks for a few individuals in the whole group to summarize, in five words or less, the overall effect on the group of having a balance of task and person roles but no dysfunctional roles.

Applying Developmental Supervision to Groups

Since it has been a while since we discussed developmental supervision, let's briefly return to that topic, this time to explain how developmental supervision is used with groups. The developmental supervisor first matches one of the four supervisory approaches to the group's characteristics:

- *Directive control behaviors* are used with a group functioning at very low developmental levels, lacking the expertise needed to act on the problem, and without any commitment to its resolution, or in an emergency situation. In group meetings, a supervisor uses directive control behaviors to give a clear message about what changes are expected. The supervisor *presents* by stating his or her understanding of the problem, *clarifies* by asking group members if they have any perceptions to add, *listens* to input, and then *problem solves* by reassessing the problem and possible solutions. She or he then *directs* by stating what is to be done, *clarifies* by asking for additional input, *standardizes* by laying out a specific timeline and

role play 17.4

Dealing with a Dysfunctional Group Member

Context.   The purpose of this role play is for a subgroup of four to provide a demonstration to the remainder of the group on how to effectively deal with a dysfunctional group member. Participants will need approximately 20 minutes of preparation time away from the rest of the group. In the role play, a "supervisor" and three "teachers" are members of a committee meeting to discuss a school-wide instructional issue. In their preparation for the role play, the role players may choose the school level (elementary, middle, or high school), the issue to be discussed, and any other details of the fictional situation that they need to agree on to perform an effective role play. The group is assigned or chooses a dysfunctional role that one member of the group will assume during the role play. The role play is presented in three scenes.

Scene 1 (5 minutes).   The supervisor and three teachers begin the meeting. Throughout the scene, one of the teachers assumes a dysfunctional role that is clearly impeding the rest of the group's efforts to resolve the issue. The supervisor observes the teacher's dysfunctional behaviors. This scene ends with a break in the meeting, with the issue unresolved. During the break the other two teachers leave to get a cup of coffee, and the supervisor and the dysfunctional teacher are left alone.

Scene 2 (5 minutes).   In a private discussion with the dysfunctional teacher during the break, the supervisor uses techniques suggested under this chapter's heading, "Dealing with Dysfunctional Members" to address the teacher's behaviors. The specific discussion will depend on the dysfunctional role that the teacher has been playing. The discussion culminates with an agreed-on plan for minimizing future disruptions.

Scene 3 (5 minutes).   The other teachers return and the meeting resumes. Due to the agreements worked out during the break and the supervisor's support during the second part of the group meeting, the teacher's dysfunctional behaviors are greatly reduced. The group is able to resolve the issue under discussion.

Whole-Group Processing

(5 minutes).   The entire group discusses what the dysfunctional role was, specific behaviors that indicated the dysfunctional role, and effects of the dysfunctional role on the group in Scene 1. Next, the group discusses the techniques used by the supervisor in Scenes 2 and 3 to deal with the dysfunctional role and the effects of those techniques on the teacher and group.

expectations, and *reinforces* by monitoring the expected group performance. The supervisor moves away from directive control and toward directive informational behaviors as soon as possible.

- *Directive informational behaviors* are used with a group functioning at moderately low levels of development, expertise, and commitment. The supervisor *presents* by stating his or her understanding of the problem, *clarifies* by asking group members for input, *listens* to their perceptions of the problem, and *problem solves* by formulating two or three alternative solutions. He or she *directs* by stating the alternatives, *listens* after asking the group for input, and *directs* by reformulating and stating final choices. The supervisor *clarifies* by asking the group to choose from alternatives, *standardizes* by suggesting a timeline and criteria for success, and *reinforces* by suggesting ways to follow up.

- *Collaborative behaviors* are used when the group is functioning at moderately high or mixed levels of development, the supervisor and group have the same degree of expertise concerning the problem, and both the supervisor and group are committed to solving the problem. The supervisor *clarifies* by asking group members for their perceptions of the problem, *listens* to group perceptions, and *reflects* by verifying group perceptions. The supervisor *presents* by adding his or her perceptions, *clarifies* by determining if the group understands supervisor perceptions, *problem solves* by exchanging suggested solutions, *encourages* by accepting conflict, and *negotiates* a mutually acceptable solution. Finally, the supervisor *reflects* by summarizing the collaborative plan.

- *Nondirective behaviors* are used when the group is functioning at very high developmental levels, possesses extensive expertise, and is highly committed to solving the problem. The supervisor *listens* as group members provide their perceptions of the problem, *reflects* by paraphrasing group members' perceptions and feelings, *probes* the group for additional information on the problem's underlying causes, *listens* further to teacher perceptions, and *reflects* further by continuing to paraphrase group members' comments. The supervisor *problem solves* by asking the group to think of possible actions and to consider the consequences of potential actions, *presents* by asking the group to commit to a plan of action, *standardizes* by asking the group to establish a timeline and criteria for success, and *reflects* by restating the group's plan.

The long-term goal of the developmental supervisor is to assist the group toward higher levels of development, expertise, and commitment. This can be accomplished through arranging for professional development on collaborative skills, providing observer feedback on group behaviors, encouraging self-study, facilitating reflection on group process, and using a variety of other strategies for group development. As the group develops, the supervisor gradually shifts from directive to collaborative or from collaborative to nondirective behaviors.

Resolving Conflict

The key to a productive group is the way ongoing conflict is resolved. Conflicts are particular disagreements that occur between two or more members at a particular time. *Conflict is not necessarily dysfunctional.* In fact, research has shown that successful groups exhibit much conflict (Fullan, 2000; Thistlethwaite & Jackson, 2014).

A group can make wise decisions only when there is a wealth of information and ideas to consider. Information and ideas are generated through conflict. To suppress conflict is to limit the group's decision-making capacity (Levi, 2014; Woods, 2012). Therefore, the leader should encourage conflict, not stifle it. Of course, conflict, if not handled correctly, can degenerate into adversarial and harmful relations. It is not conflict that is bad; it is the way the leader deals with it that determines its value (Chen, 2006; Fairchild & Hunter, 2014; Franz, 2012; Tekleab, Quigley, & Tesluk, 2009).

Conflict occurs when there is a disagreement over ideas. The leader should keep the disagreement focused on the ideas rather than on the personalities of the members. The following procedure for handling conflict serves as a ready reference for the group leader:

1. Ask each member to state his or her conflicting position.
2. Ask each member to restate the other's position.
3. Ask each member if conflict still exists.
4. Ask for underlying value positions: Why do they still stick to their positions?
5. Ask other members of the group if there is a third position that synthesizes, compromises, or transcends the conflict. If not, reclarify the various positions. Acknowledge that there exists no apparent reconciliation, and move the discussion to other matters.

The following is an application of conflict resolution procedures to a high school meeting.

The supervisor from the central office has called a meeting of the English high school department heads to discuss possible changes in the tenth-grade English curriculum. The topic of composition writing comes up, and two department heads begin to argue. Mrs. Strick of Toofarback High School says,

> We need to require three formal compositions each semester from each 10th-grader. Each composition should be graded according to spelling, punctuation, and format. I'm sick and tired of seeing kids coming into the 11th grade without being able to put a sentence together!

Mr. Ease of Space High School objects: "Are you serious? Six technical compositions a year should just about kill any remaining interest that tenth graders have in writing. That is a ridiculous idea!"

The language supervisor, Mr. Cool, is now aware of a conflict and wants to capitalize on these varying points of view in providing information to the group. At the same time, he is aware of emotional intensity in this conflict (words such as *sick and tired* and *ridiculous*) and wishes to soften the emotion and promote the ideas. So he uses step 1 and asks the two members to state their conflicting positions:

> Mrs. Strick and Mr. Ease, you both have definite ideas about the requirements of technical compositions. We are interested in fully understanding what you think. Would you each take a few minutes and further explain your positions?

After Mrs. Strick and Mr. Ease have stated their positions, the supervisor moves to step 2 by asking each member to restate the other's position:

"Now that you have stated your position, I want to make sure that you fully understand each other. Mrs. Strick, would you please paraphrase Mr. Ease's position, and Mr. Ease, would you repeat Mrs. Strick's position?" Mrs. Strick says, "Mr. Ease thinks that technical writing assignments are a waste of time and students lose interest." Mr. Ease replies, "No, I didn't say they are a waste of time; but if such assignments are frequent, students learn to hate English class." Mr. Ease then restates Mrs. Strick's position: "You're saying that tenth graders need skills in the basics of writing. Required compositions would ensure proper spelling, grammar, and format." Mrs. Strick replies, "Yes, that's what I'm saying."

Now that both positions have been made and paraphrased, Supervisor Cool goes to step 3 and asks if conflict still exists:

He asks Mrs. Strick and Mr. Ease: "Are you both still far apart about composition requirements for tenth-grade English?" Mrs. Strick nods, but Mr. Ease says, "Well, not as far apart as at the beginning. I'm not against some technical writing requirements. It's the number, three for each semester, that hangs me up. I could accept one per semester." Mrs. Strick replies, "Well, I can't. If they are going to write correctly, they must do it frequently. Three compositions a semester is just the minimum!"

Mr. Cool, knowing that Mrs. Strick is adamant about her position, goes to step 4, asking for the underlying value:

Mr. Cool asks Mrs. Strick: "Could you explain why technical composition writing is important to you?" Mrs. Strick says, "Kids today don't get any basics in writing. Everything is creativity, expression, write it like you speak it in the streets! I was taught standards of good manners and proper English. If these kids are to succeed in later life, they have to know how to write according to accepted business and professional standards. I'm not being hardnosed for my own sake. It's them I'm concerned about!" Mr. Cool turns to Mr. Ease and asks, "What about you? Why do you disagree?" Mr. Ease replies, "I don't completely disagree, but I'm against making tenth-grade English class a technical writing drill. Writing should be a vehicle for expression and students should love, not dread, it. They should be able to write personal thoughts, juggle words and formats, and not worry about every comma and dotted *i*. Let them play with words before pushing standards at them. I don't write letters with one-and-a-half-inch margins to my friends or in my diary—why should kids have to? Sure, there is a need for them to learn to write formally, but not at the expense of hating to write!"

Mr. Cool restates the conflict to the group: "We have an obvious disagreement between Mrs. Strick and Mr. Ease. Mrs. Strick believes there should be at least three technical compositions per semester in the tenth grade. Mr. Ease believes there should be less emphasis on technical writing and more on expressive writing."

Supervisor Cool goes to step 5: *Asking other members of the group if there is a third position that can be taken.* Some members might side with one over the other, suggest a compromise (one technical composition in the first semester, two in the second semester), or offer a new alternative (let's require a 3-week mini-course of technical writing and let each school decide the type of work and assignments). If the conflict between Mrs. Strick and Mr. Ease does not resolve itself, the supervisor acknowledges that the conflict remains: "We understand the difference of opinion that you both have, and we can't find a ready solution." Then he moves to other matters: "Eventually the committee will have to decide or vote on what to do about required assignments. For now, we'll leave this particular issue and discuss the 10th-grade testing program."

Conflict cannot and should not be avoided. Conflict, if encouraged and supported, will enable a group to make better decisions. It is the group leader's handling of conflict that makes the difference. The group should have the feeling that it is all right to disagree and that anyone who does disagree will be able to make his or her full position known. Role Play 17.5 provides for demonstrations of the right way and the wrong way to deal with conflict within a group.

role play 17.5
Resolving Conflict

Context. The purpose of this role play is for a subgroup of five to provide a demonstration to the remainder of the group on how to effectively resolve conflict within a group. Participants will need approximately 20 minutes of preparation time away from the rest of the group. In the role play, a "supervisor" and four "teachers" are members of a committee meeting to discuss a schoolwide instructional issue. In their preparation for the role play, the role players may choose the school level, the issue to be discussed, and any other details of the fictional situation that they need to agree on to perform an effective role play. The group is assigned or chooses a conflict to be played out between two members of the group during the meeting. The role play is presented in two scenes.

Scene 1: Wrong Way (5 minutes). Soon after the beginning of the meeting, a conflict breaks out between two of the teachers. The supervisor and the other teachers in the group deal with the conflict poorly, and the meeting deteriorates rapidly. The meeting breaks up with neither the interpersonal conflict nor the original issue resolved.

Scene 2: Right Way (10 minutes). This scene involves the same group, the same setting, and the same issue. The same conflict breaks out between the same two teachers. This time, however, the supervisor and teachers in the group use procedures discussed under this chapter's topic, "Resolving Conflict," to facilitate a resolution of the conflict and the original issue by the end of the meeting.

Whole-Group Processing (5 minutes). The entire group discusses the nature of the conflict, the failed efforts to resolve it, and effects of the conflict on the group in Scene 1. Also discussed are the techniques used to resolve the conflict and the effects of the conflict resolution process in Scene 2.

▶ **Video Illustration**

After you watch the video, assess the value of role playing difficult situations as a tool for increasing a group's capacity to resolve conflict.

Preparing for Group Meetings

A group can proceed more easily with its task if the leader has made certain preparations. Some especially important aspects of preparing for a meeting include planning an agenda, establishing ground rules, and writing guided discussion questions.

Agendas

A group has to be clear on its task and purpose. Why are they meeting? What are they to accomplish? Is there to be a product? An agenda distributed several days before the actual meeting will inform members of the reasons for the meeting and what will be accomplished. The agenda need not be elaborate. See Figure 17.1 as a sample agenda. Notice how the agenda includes a brief explanation and a breakdown of items. Time

To: All physical education teachers
From: Morris Bailey, athletic director
Subject: Agenda for the meeting of February 23 in Room 253, 3:30–5:00

Next Thursday will be the last meeting before voting on the revisions of our student progress forms. Remember, bring any progress forms you have collected from other school systems. Sally and Bruce are to report on the forms provided by the State Department. At the conclusion of the meeting, we are to make specific recommendations of changes.

Agenda

I.	Review purpose of meeting	3:30–3:40
II.	Report from Sally and Bruce on State Department forms	3:40–4:00
III.	Report on other school system forms	4:00–4:20
IV.	Discussion of possible revisions	4:20–4:40
V.	Recommendations	4:40–5:00

See you Thursday. Please be on time!

figure **17.1** **Sample Agenda**

limits for each item provide members with a sense of priorities as well as the assurance that the leader plans to end on time. Keeping to starting and ending times displays respect for group members' personal schedules.

Establishing Ground Rules

Participants will need to know not only agenda items like the meeting's purpose, place, time, and topics but also behaviors that are expected of them at the meeting (Allen & Rogelberg, 2013). Ground rules can be established in advance concerning any of the following:

- Type of participation expected (sharing of information, professional dialogue, choosing from established alternatives, brainstorming, problem solving, conflict resolution, and so on)
- Roles to be assigned (coordinator, time keeper, information giver, recorder, and so on)
- Interpersonal expectations (everyone contributes, use active listening, criticize ideas but not people, consider each person's views, use agreed-on conflict management strategies, and so on)
- Decision-making method (decision by averaging individuals' opinions, majority vote, consensus, and so on)
- Type of follow-up expected (assigned tasks, continued dialogue, classroom implementation, follow-up meeting, and so on)

Guided Discussion

When meeting with a small group to discuss an issue, it is helpful to have in mind the type of questions to ask. Typically, questions to be asked will shift during a meeting. At the beginning of the meeting, the leader usually spends time clarifying the topic for discussion. During the meeting, the leader uses open-ended questions that allow for the seeking, elaborating, and coordinating of ideas, opinions, and information. At the conclusion of the meeting, the leader asks questions that summarize what has been accomplished and what remains to be done.

Some discussion questions that might help as a reference are presented in Figure 17.2. Prior to a meeting, the leader might review the questions and write down specific questions concerning the topic to have as references. When the discussion stalls, the leader can review these and ask one of the preselected questions. A discussion guide helps the leader ensure that the topic will be thoroughly examined.

Facilitating successful meetings, as indicated by the foregoing discussion, is more complicated than one might assume. Figure 17.3 provides a checklist of suggestions for preparation, conducting the meeting, and follow-up.

Questions Designed to Open Up Discussion

1. What do you think about the problem as stated?
2. What has been your experience in dealing with this problem?
3. Would anyone care to offer suggestions on facts we need to better our understanding of the problem?

Questions Designed to Broaden Participation

1. Now that we have heard from a number of our members, would others who have not spoken like to add their ideas?
2. How do the ideas presented so far sound to those of you who have been thinking about them?
3. What other phases of the problem should be explored?

Questions Designed to Limit Participation

1. To the overactive participant: We appreciate your contributions. However, it might be well to hear from some of the others. Would some of you who have not spoken care to add your ideas to those already expressed?
2. You have made several good statements, and I am wondering if someone else might like to make some remarks?
3. Since all our group members have not yet had an opportunity to speak, I wonder if you would hold your comments until a little later?

Questions Designed to Focus Discussion

1. Where are we now in relation to our goal for this discussion?
2. Would you like to have me review my understanding of the things we have said and the progress we have made in this direction?
3. Your comment is interesting, but I wonder if it is germane to the chief problem that is before us.

Questions Designed to Help the Group Move Along

1. I wonder if we have spent enough time on this phase of the problem. Should we move to another aspect of it?
2. Have we gone into this part of the problem far enough so that we might now shift our attention and consider this additional area?
3. In view of the time we have set for ourselves, would it be appropriate to look at the next question before us?

Questions Designed to Help the Group Evaluate Itself

1. I wonder if any of you have a feeling that we are blocked on this particular question? Why are we tending to slow down?
2. Should we take a look at our original objective for this discussion and see where we are in relation to it?
3. Now that we are nearing the conclusion of our meeting, would anyone like to offer suggestions on how we might improve our next meeting?

Questions Designed to Help the Group Reach a Decision

1. Am I right in sensing agreement at these points? (Leader then gives brief summary.)
2. Since we seem to be tending to move in the direction of a decision, should we consider what it will mean for our group if we decide the matter this way?
3. What have we accomplished in our discussion up to this point?

Questions Designed to Lend Continuity to the Discussion

1. Since we had time for partial consideration of the problem at the last meeting, would someone care to review what we covered then?
2. Since we cannot reach a decision at this meeting, what are some of the points we should take up at the next one?
3. Would someone care to suggest points on which we need further preparation before we convene again?

figure **17.2 Questions for Use in Leadership Discussion**

Before the Meeting

- Define the goal of the meeting. Make sure it's realistic.
- Decide what to accomplish at the meeting.
- Make sure the goal can be accomplished in one meeting.
- Develop a list of questions and problems to start group discussion

Prepare the following in advance:

- Facilities (e.g., seating, audio visual equipment, lighting, temperature)
- List of participants (keep numbers in line with meeting purpose)
- Agenda with time frames
- Discussion outline

Conducting a Meeting

- Start on time.
- Group members should introduce themselves.
- Discuss "housekeeping" items (e.g., breaks, restroom locations, refreshments).
- Follow the agenda to accomplish the desired purpose.
- Make sure everyone participates.
- Stimulate, guide, and control discussion.
- Strive to achieve consensus (at best) or majority decision (at worst).
- Accurately capture minutes.

Before you adjourn:

- Firm up decision.
- Make assignments for pending work items.
- Set up next meeting times, dates, and purpose, if needed.

Follow-up

- Have action items, tasks, people, and times clearly identified.
- Prepare report/minutes of the meeting.
- Periodically evaluate the effectiveness of the meeting.
- Decide how subsequent meetings can be improved.
- Leader should periodically check on progress of work items.

figure **17.3** **Effective Meeting Checklist**

Source: U.S. Department of Agriculture, *People, Partnerships, and Communities,* Issue 5, March 2005. Retrieved from http://www.nrcs.usda.wps/portal/nrccs/detailfull/nationall people/outreach!oel?cid=stelprdb1045637

> ✔ **Check Your Understanding 17.0**   Click here to gauge your understanding of the key concepts presented in this chapter.

REFLECTIVE EXERCISE

This chapter offers possible questions for the leader to ask during group discussion, including potential questions to (1) open up discussion, (2) broaden interpretation, (3) limit participation, (4) focus discussion, (5) help the group move along, (6) help the group evaluate itself, (7) reach a decision, and (8) lend continuity to the discussion. For each of these eight purposes, create at least one additional question the leader might ask.

chapter 18

Professional Development

Learning Outcomes for This Chapter

After reading this chapter, you should be able to:

1. Identify the focus of successful professional development.
2. Explain how a school can integrate schoolwide, group, and individual professional development.
3. Enumerate the steps in individually-planned professional development.
4. Name the three stages of learning in professional development.
5. List the five evaluation levels in Guskey's system for evaluating professional development programs.
6. Recall the two dimensions upon which the authors maintain commitment to a professional development program is premised.

Questions to Reflect On as You Read This Chapter

1. Professional development in K-12 schools has a poor reputation among teachers. Why do you believe this is so? Do you believe that the ideas presented in this chapter, if implemented, would change teachers' attitudes about professional development? Which ideas in this chapter do you believe would have the greatest positive impact on professional development and teachers' attitudes about professional development?

2. One characteristic of successful professional development is the integration of schoolwide, group, and individual goals. Why do you think this is the case?

3. This chapter describes several alternative professional development formats. Think of a schoolwide professional development goal. How could several professional development formats be connected in a program designed to meet the goal you have identified?

4. This chapter describes three stages of professional development: (1) orientation, (2) integration, and (3) refinement. The authors maintain that many professional development programs never move beyond the orientation stage. As you read about the three stages, think of a professional development program you participated in that never got past the orientation stage. What were the results of the program moving through the orientation stage only? If the program would have continued through all these stages of professional development, what activities could have been carried out at the integration stage? At the refinement stage? How might have the effects of the program been more positive if all three stages had been addressed?

5. Why do you think teachers historically have not been more involved in planning, delivering, and assessing their own professional development? What needs to change to make teachers authentic agents in professional development? How would professional development change if teachers played the primary role in its planning, delivery, and assessment?

Bob Jeffries, director of professional development, calls six school principals into his office to plan for the upcoming in-service day. He begins by explaining that the in-service program will start with a morning session, attended by the entire school system faculty, in the high school auditorium. The afternoon will consist of individual school activities, with the principal being responsible for whatever transpires. Mr. Jeffries asks the principals, "What might we do for the morning session?" One principal suggests that at this time of year teachers could use an emotional lift and that an inspirational speaker would be good. Another principal adds that she had heard a Dr. Zweibach give a great talk, entitled "The Thrill of Teaching," at a national principals' conference last summer. She thinks he would be a terrific speaker. Bob Jeffries likes these suggestions and tells the principals he will call Dr. Zweibach and make arrangements for his appearance.

On the in-service day, 238 teachers file into the auditorium and fill all but the first eight rows of seats. Mr. Jeffries makes a few introductory remarks about how fortunate "we" are to have Dr. Zweibach with "us" and then turns the session over to Dr. Zweibach. A rumpled, middle-aged university professor walks to the microphone and launches into his talk on the thrill of teaching. Within 10 minutes, signs of restlessness, boredom, and bitterness are evident throughout the audience. It seems that 12 of the teachers are sitting through a talk they had heard Dr. Zweibach deliver verbatim two years earlier at a teacher convention; 15 others are thinking about the classroom work they could be doing to prepare for next semester and wondering, "Why in the world are we sitting through this talk?" Another 22 teachers have become impatient with Dr. Zweibach's continual reference to the academic high school settings where he found teaching thrills. Their own work settings are vocational, special education, and elementary; they can't relate what he is saying about high schools to their world. Eventually, some teachers begin to correct papers, read, or knit; a few appear to fall asleep. On the other hand, nearly half the members of the audience remain attentive and give Dr. Zweibach a rousing ovation when he concludes. The other half appear relieved that the talk is finally over and they can return to their own schools. Upon leaving the auditorium, one can overhear such remarks as, "What a great talk!" and "Why do we have to put up with all this staff development crap?"

This depiction of an in-service day is typical of many school systems. Some teachers find it valuable, but many do not. Professional development is often viewed by supervisors, administrators, and teachers as a number of days contracted for in the school calendar that simply need to be endured.

Professional development, if properly planned and implemented, *can* be a powerful force for teacher development and the improvement of teaching and learning. In this chapter we will discuss what good professional development looks like, how to evaluate professional development, and why teachers should be agents in professional development.

Characteristics of Successful Professional Development Programs

Reviews of research on professional development (Comas & Barufaldi, 2011; Gordon, 2004; Guskey, 2003; Reeves, 2012) identify a number of characteristics associated with successful professional development programs. These characteristics include the following:

1. Involvement of teachers in planning, implementing, and evaluating their own professional development
2. A focus on teaching and learning
3. Integration of professional development goals with school improvement goals
4. Coherence of individual, group, and schoolwide professional development
5. Administrative support, including provision of time and other resources
6. Relevant, job-embedded professional development
7. Collegiality and collaboration among teachers and between teachers and administrators
8. Active learning
9. Inquiry
10. Self-reflection
11. Inclusion of content on diversity and cultural responsiveness
12. Follow-up to support application of learning

13. Ongoing, data-based program assessment

14. Continuous professional development that becomes part of the school culture

15. Development of leadership capacity

As you review these characteristics, reflect on a professional development program with which you are familiar. How many of the 15 characteristics are present in the program?

Integrating Schoolwide, Group, and Individual Professional Development

One characteristic of effective professional development is the integration of schoolwide, group, and individual goals. How does a school go about doing this? To begin, it is critical that all members of the school community provide input into schoolwide professional development goals. The schoolwide goals should be broad enough to allow groups and individuals to set their own goals, consistent with school goals.

For an example of integrating schoolwide and group professional development, let us assume that a middle school has identified improved student discipline as a schoolwide professional development goal. Different grade-level or instructional teams, all committed to improved discipline, might identify different group goals relative to the school goal. One group might decide that they need to focus their professional development on improving students' respect for others. Another group might determine that their primary need is to improve students' on-task behavior during class. A third group may wish to focus on finding ways to encourage self-discipline so that students take more responsibility for completing their homework, studying for tests, and asking for assistance.

Different groups also may decide that they prefer different professional development formats. One group may decide that they prefer to form a study group that will share readings, visit other schools to see how they address student discipline, and discuss how exemplary practices can be adapted to their students. The second group may decide that they wish to attend a training program on effective discipline, followed up by peer coaching at the classroom level. The third group might prefer to follow an action research format, gathering classroom data to find out more about the problem, designing an action plan, implementing the plan, and gathering evaluation data to determine effects. Although it is important that various groups within the school be allowed to adapt schoolwide goals to group needs, it also is important that each group show how its particular goals relate to and support the schoolwide goals.

A faculty is made up of individuals, and schoolwide professional development cannot take place without individual development. Thus, it is important to integrate individual professional development goals with group and schoolwide goals. Let us return to our example of the schoolwide goal of improved student discipline. You will recall that one possible group goal was improving students' respect for others. Even this more focused goal would have different meanings to different teachers within the group that chose the goal. For one teacher it might mean helping students work together in cooperative groups. For another teacher it could mean students respecting other students from different cultures. For a third teacher it might mean working with students who are disrespectful to authority figures. Thus, even within the group goal of increased respect for others, there should be opportunities for teachers to identify individual goals consistent with group and school goals.

Since adults, like students, have different experiences and learning styles, teachers within the study group might pursue different learning activities and make different contributions to the group. One teacher might bring to the group reports from visits to other schools, another teacher might share journal articles related to the topic of student respect for others, and so forth. The individual teacher can connect individual goals to group and schoolwide goals in a manner that allows individual professional development activities to serve all three types of goals.

Alternative Professional Development Formats

We are rapidly moving away from the era when professional development usually means either a 60-minute speech by an outside consultant or a "one-shot" workshop. A variety of new formats for professional development have emerged over the last several years. Some examples follow:

- *Beginning teacher assistance programs.* The new teacher is provided ongoing, intensive assistance throughout at least the first year of teaching. This support includes such things as an assigned mentor; an orientation to the school and community; assistance from a support team including the mentor, other teachers, and a supervisor; training in classroom management and effective teaching; and support seminars focused on beginning teachers' concerns (Bullough, 2012; Lambeth, 2012).

- *Skill development programs.* This consists of several workshops over a period of months, and classroom coaching between workshops to assist teachers in transforming new skills to their daily teaching.

- *Teacher centers.* Teachers can meet at a central location to engage in professional dialogue, develop skills, plan innovations, and gather or create instructional materials.

- *Teacher institutes.* Teachers participate in intensive learning experiences on single, complex topics over a period of consecutive days or weeks.

- *Professional learning communities.* Groups of teachers develop a set of common beliefs, share leadership, engage in collective learning, and collaborate on curriculum and instructional improvement efforts, with all of these activities focused on the improvement of student learning. We provide a more detailed discussion of professional learning communities in Chapter 23.

- *Lesson study*. A group of teachers identify a long-term goal for improved student learning, review research on how to best achieve that goal, and use the research as a basis for a collaboratively-planned unit of instruction. The teachers select a single lesson from the unit of instruction and create a detailed lesson plan that exemplifies teaching consistent with the long-term goal. One member of the group teaches the lesson while the other teachers in the group observe and gather data on various aspects of the lesson. After the lesson, the teachers meet to share and analyze data and discuss how the lesson could be improved. Another teacher in the group may use the improved lesson plan to teach the lesson a second time to a different class, with the group again observing and holding a post-lesson discussion (Howell & Saye, 2016; Lewis, 2009; Lieberman, 2009).

- *Networks*. Teachers from different schools share information, concerns, and accomplishments and engage in common learning through computer links, newsletters, and occasional seminars and conferences.

- *Teacher leadership*. Teachers participate in leadership preparation programs and assist other teachers by assuming one or more leadership roles (workshop presenter, cooperating teacher, mentor, expert coach, instructional team leader, curriculum developer). The teacher-leader not only assists other teachers but also experiences professional growth as a result of being involved in leadership activities (Poekert, 2012).

- *Teacher as writer*. This increasingly popular format has teachers reflect on and write about their students, teaching, and professional growth. Such writing can be in the form of private journals, essays, or reaction papers to share with colleagues, or formal articles for publication in educational journals.

- *Individually planned professional development*. Teachers assess their own professional needs, set individual goals and objectives, plan and carry out activities, and assess results.

- *School visits*. Teachers from schools that are considering adopting an instructional innovation can visit other schools where the innovation has been implemented successfully, to both observe the innovation being applied in classrooms and discuss the innovation with teachers who have developed expertise in its use.

- *Partnerships*. Partnerships are affiliations between schools and universities, community agencies, or businesses, in which both partners are considered equal, have mutual rights and responsibilities, make contributions, and receive benefits (Holen & Yunk, 2014). Partnerships can take myriad forms. For example, a school and community agencies might collaborate on a needs assessment of community educational needs, with data gathered from the assessment informing both the school curriculum and community services. Or, a corporation might offer summer internships to teachers, who then incorporate what they have learned over the summer into their teaching.

There can be considerable overlap between various professional development formats (not to mention between professional development and the other four tasks of supervision!). Our own experience as staff developers and researchers has led us to conclude that many of the most successful professional development programs combine multiple formats.

> ▶ **Video Illustration**
>
> As you watch this video, consider how the professional development in the video differs from traditional professional development.

Stages of Professional Development

Professional development typically involves three stages of learning: (1) orientation, (2) integration, and (3) refinement. To illustrate these three stages, we will relate them to staff development on the cooperative learning instructional model.

In the *orientation stage*, benefits, responsibilities, and personal concerns about involvement in staff development are addressed. Next, participants engage in learning necessary for initial real-world application. In our cooperative learning example, orientation topics might include the following:*

- Differences among cooperative, competitive, and individual learning
- Differences between cooperative learning and traditional group work
- Research on cooperative learning
- Basic elements of cooperative learning (teaching social skills, positive interdependence, face-to-face interaction, individual accountability, group processing)
- Forming cooperative groups
- Standard cooperative learning structures (think–pair–share, jigsaw, student teams achievement divisions [STAD], teams–games–tournaments [TGT], group investigation, and so on)
- Planning cooperative lessons

Failure to take teachers beyond the orientation stage is one reason why many staff development programs are ineffective: Teachers are given rudimentary knowledge or skills and then are left to fend for themselves.

---

*Outlining a complete professional development program on cooperative learning is beyond the scope of this text. Some critical topics are listed to provide examples of the types of learning in each stage of professional development. Sources of cooperative learning professional development topics are Johnson (2009) and Kagan and Kagan (2009).

In the *integration stage*, teachers are assisted as they apply previous learning in their classrooms and schools. One aspect of integration is learning to adapt general learning to specific situations. In the cooperative learning example, this would mean learning to alter cooperative teaching strategies to make them appropriate for different learning content and students. A related aspect of integration is regular and effective use of the new learning. This would mean, for example, that the teacher develops enough competence and confidence in cooperative learning methods to make them part of his or her standard repertoire of instructional strategies.

In the *refinement stage*, teachers move from basic competence to expertness through continuous experimentation and reflection. In the refinement stage of staff development on cooperative learning, teachers would become experts at a wide range of cooperative learning strategies and at mixing and matching those strategies for optimal student learning. Teachers in the refinement stage synthesize different types of previous learning in order to create new learning. In our cooperative learning example, a teacher at this stage might combine aspects of two or more standard cooperative learning structures to create a more complex structure. For another example, a teacher at the refinement stage might synthesize whole language and cooperative learning strategies to create an entirely new teaching strategy. Perhaps the best thing that a supervisor can do when teachers have reached this stage is to sign them up as teacher–staff developers!

Evaluating Professional Development

The evaluation form in Figure 18.1 is intended to evaluate a single professional development session. A more complex system is needed to evaluate the overall professional development program. Guskey (2002) has proposed a system designed specifically to evaluate professional development that is consistent with our discussion of the evaluation of instructional improvement efforts in Chapter 14. Guskey's system includes gathering data on five different levels: participants' reactions, participants' learning, organization support and change, participants' use of new knowledge and skills, and student learning outcomes. For each level, Guskey proposes questions to be addressed, methods of data gathering, what should be measured, and how information gathered at that level should be used. Table 18.1 summarizes Guskey's system.

> **▶ Video Illustration**
>
> As you watch this video, consider how the informal evaluation of professional development depicted can supplement the formal evaluation tools presented in this chapter.

Teachers as Objects or Agents in Professional Development

A superintendent remarked that he had been at a national conference and attended a presentation on "Elements of Effective Instruction." He decided that this was exactly what the teachers needed. As a result, the district was off and running with a three-year commitment to training all principals and teachers in "elements." Highly paid national consultants were brought in; personnel were identified for advanced training and traveled during the summer to faraway sites; and virtually all contracted in-service time and school supervision was devoted to "elements."

It was not long before a new evaluation instrument was established to check that every teacher was using the training in effective instruction in the same prescribed manner. Over the three years, expenditures by the school district exceeded $300,000, not including the cost of human time. What have been the results? No appreciable gain in student achievement, considerable grumbling by a core of "malcontent" teachers, enthusiasm by the chosen core of teachers who received special training and compensation, and a firm claim by the superintendent that "We now have focused long-term professional development on scientifically derived principles, and our teaching is more effective."

In recent years, education has been bombarded by packaged programs on "effective teaching," "effective schools," "effective supervision," and "effective discipline." All claim to be derived from research and to have documented success, and all use the components and sequence of transfer of training that have been sorely lacking in traditional professional development programs. The programs provide for explanation, demonstration, modeling, role playing, practice, and coaching. They are not one-shot programs—they are focused and they are classroom based.

The only problem is that the people who think these programs are worth the cost and effort are the same people who have a personal investment and commitment to use them. If the programs are not as successful as predicted, the decision makers do not blame the program but rather the lack of enough training to ensure that teachers "do it right." Schools, districts, and states that have committed themselves to such programs come to the ludicrous conclusion that they need more training, more money, and greater enforcement to see that all teachers will finally learn to teach as prescribed more frequently and correctly. This is an incredible rationalization by policy makers that their initial decision was right, regardless of the effect that the program is having on teachers.

This rationale underscores the point that commitment is premised on two dimensions: one is choice and the other is responsibility to make knowledgeable decisions about one's work. That's why the superintendent wants so badly to see this program on "effective elements" work. The superintendent had the choice and took responsibility for making the decision. The selected core of teachers also want to see this program work, because they were given choice and responsibility in making decisions

We would like your feedback to plan future professional development sessions. For each item, please circle the response that most closely describes your level of agreement with the statement, and provide comments in the space provided. If you need more space, feel free to use the back of the sheet.

Professional Development Topic _____

Date _____

The Session:	Strongly Disagree	Disagree	Agree	Strongly Agree
1. Was well-organized	1	2	3	4
2. Was relevant to my work	1	2	3	4
3. Was consistent with our school improvement goals	1	2	3	4
4. Contributes to our overall professional development program	1	2	3	4
5. Allowed for active participation	1	2	3	4
6. Provided opportunities for collaboration	1	2	3	4

figure **18.1** **Professional Development Session Evaluation**

7. Promoted reflection	1	2	3	4

_____
_____
_____

8. Included plans for continuation of learning	1	2	3	4

_____
_____
_____

9. Has improved my leadership capacity	1	2	3	4

_____
_____
_____

10. Is likely to ultimately improve our students' learning	1	2	3	4

_____
_____
_____

Suggestions for future meetings: _____
_____
_____

on how to train others. Yet most teachers and principals were not given any choice or responsibility in these decisions about the needs of their students and themselves. Instead, they were treated as objects rather than as agents of professional development, without due regard for their capacity to make wise decisions in the interest of students and teaching. Without choice or responsibility to make knowledgeable decisions about their work, they have little motivation or commitment to somebody else's program.

To use knowledge about characteristics, formats, and stages of professional development, without an awareness of the need to truly involve teachers as decision makers in professional development, will leave us where we currently are. We will be more sophisticated in teaching teachers how to follow someone else's program, but we will find little commitment on the part of teachers or little stimulation to increase teachers' own collective and critical capacities to make lasting changes.

t a b l e **18.1** **Five Levels of Professional Development Evaluation**

Evaluation Level	What Questions Are Addressed?
1. Participants' Reactions	Did they like it? Was their time well spent? Did the material make sense? Will it be useful? Was the leader knowledgeable and helpful? Were the refreshments fresh and tasty? Was the room the right temperature? Were the chairs comfortable?
2. Participants' Learning	Did participants acquire the intended knowledge and skills?
3. Organization Support & Change	Was implementation advocated, facilitated, and supported? Was the support public and overt? Were problems addressed quickly and efficiently? Were sufficient resources made available? Were successes recognized and shared? What was the impact on the organization? Did it affect the organization's climate and procedures?
4. Participants' Use of New Knowledge and Skills	Did participants effectively apply the new knowledge and skills?
5. Student Learning Outcomes	What was the impact on students? Did it affect student performance or achievement? Did it influence students' physical or emotional well-being? Are students more confident as learners? Is student attendance improving? Are dropouts decreasing?

Source: Thomas R. Guskey. (2002). "Does It Make a Difference? Evaluating Professional Development." *Educational Leadership, 59*(6), 48–49. Copyright 2002 Thomas R. Guskey. Permission granted by author.

▶ **Video Illustration**

As you watch this video, think about how the principal's approach to professional development changes between the beginning and the end of the video clip. How do the teachers appear to react to that change?

How Will Information Be Gathered?	What Is Measured or Assessed?	How Will Information Be Used?
Questionnaires administered at the end of the session	Initial satisfaction with the experience	To improve program design and delivery
Paper-and-pencil instruments Simulations Demonstrations Participants' reflections (oral and/or written) Participant portfolios	New knowledge and skills of participants	To improve program content, format, and organization
District and school records Minutes from follow-up meetings Questionnaires Structured interviews with participants and district or school administrators Participant portfolios	The organization's advocacy, support, accommodation, facilitation, and recognition	To document and improve organization support To inform future change efforts
Questionnaires Structured interviews with participants and their supervisors Participant reflections (oral and/or written) Participant portfolios Direct observations Video or audio tapes	Degree and quality of implementation	To document and improve the implementation of program content
Student records School records Questionnaires Structured interviews with students, parents, teachers, and/or administrators Participant portfolios	Student learning outcomes: Cognitive (Performance & Achievement) Affective (Attitudes & Dispositions) Psychomotor (Skills & Behaviors)	To focus and improve all aspects of program design, implementation, and follow-up To demonstrate the overall impact of professional development

> ✔ **Check Your Understanding 18.0**   Click here to gauge your understanding of the key concepts presented in this chapter.

REFLECTIVE EXERCISE

Think of a professional development session you have recently attended. Assess the session by completing the evaluation form in Figure 18.1. Assume you have been asked to modify the session for delivery to a new group. How would you change the lower-rated aspects of the session to improve professional learning?

chapter 19

Curriculum Development

Learning Outcomes for This Chapter

After reading this chapter, you should be able to:

1. Summarize the authors' response to the argument that teachers don't need to have a say in the curriculum because they can use their professional expertise and creativity when they plan how to teach the curriculum in their classrooms.

2. Enumerate five issues concerning teacher involvement in curriculum development that need to be addressed.

3. Define the transformation approach to integrating multicultural and ethnic content into the curriculum.

4. Explain the authors' position on how curriculum maps should be used.

5. List Wiggins and McTighe's six facets of understanding.

Questions to Reflect On as You Read This Chapter

1. This chapter lists five sources of curriculum development. Rank the five sources from 1 to 5, with 1 having the most influence over PK-12 curriculum and 5 having the least influence. Next, rank the five sources from 1 to 5 according to what you believe the order of influence should be. Is there a discrepancy between your first and second ranking? If so, why do you believe this discrepancy exists? If there was a discrepancy between your first and second ranking, how might curriculum, teaching, and learning change if the order of influence was what you said it should be rather than what it is?

2. Which of the three meta-orientations to curriculum described in this chapter do you most agree with? Why?

3. Identify your position on how much curriculum choice should be given to teachers by choosing a location between no choice and "total choice" on the curriculum cone in Figure 19.5. Why did you select your chosen position on the curriculum cone?

4. What are some examples of learning activities that represent a transformation approach to multicultural curriculum reform? What are some examples of learning activities that represent a social action approach?

5. What types of preparation would teachers need before participating in the curriculum mapping described in this chapter?

6. Compare Wiggins and McTighe's understanding by design to curriculum development at a school you are familiar with. What, if any, components of understanding by design would you like to see incorporated (or, if your school is already using understanding by design, better implemented) in curriculum development at the school you selected?

"In addition to the student relationship, teaching is a moral activity because, in designing curriculum, teachers select certain objectives and pieces of content over others with the intention of changing the behaviors of students in order to achieve desirable educational ends" (Johnson, 2010, p. 97). Moral activity is explicitly expressed in a school's curriculum. To be an effective school is of little matter unless the personnel within an organization first have defined what is meant by a *good school*— what should students learn in order to be well educated? The institutional job then becomes one of effectively achieving that definition of goodness. As Sergiovanni (1987) remarked, "It's not important to do things right, unless we are doing the right things!" Curriculum is the moral deliberation on what is "right" for students to be taught.

Ultimately, decisions about a good school, appropriate curriculum, and needs of students should be made by those closest to students. After considering the available experts, research, readings, and articulated conflicts, it is the people in the schools, districts, and local communities who should ultimately decide what is worthy to teach. However, by default, pressure, and abdication, curriculum decisions have generally been made by those farthest from the classroom action.

Curriculum can be developed at many levels—by outside specialists, school district specialists, school curriculum teams, and teachers alone. At the national level, commercial materials such as textbooks, learning kits, and audiovisual materials are developed mainly by outside specialists. Earlier in the century, No Child Left Behind (NCLB) and Race to the Top (RTTT) introduced unprecedented federal controls over K-12 school curriculum in the 50 states. Although the Common Core State Standards (CCSS) were adopted state by state, adopting CCSS made states eligible for millions of dollars in federal grants. At the state level, departments of education have become increasingly active in curriculum development. States have legislated statewide competency tests for student promotion and graduation and have developed statewide curriculum guides for local schools to ensure the teaching of those competencies. At the local level, many school systems have written their own curriculum guides for coordinating instruction across grade levels. This is done either by having curriculum specialists at the district level write the guides themselves or by having such specialists work with

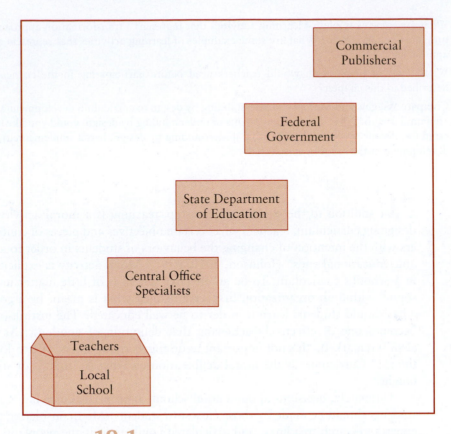

f i g u r e **19.1** **Illustration of Sources of Curriculum Development**

representative teams of teachers (perhaps with community and student representation). Rarely do local schools turn curriculum development entirely over to teachers.

We can think about sources of curriculum development according to Figure 19.1 (see Oliva, 2008). Much curriculum is developed at the state, federal, and commercial levels. In other words, most curricula are produced far away from the local teacher and the local schools.

Legislated Learning

It is a shame that most educators experience curriculum as something given that they must follow. Why is it that curriculum is no longer a province for school inquiry and action but rather a matter of complying with external mandates? The reason is that in the era of legislated learning, teachers and school leaders are seen as incapable of knowing what their students should be taught (Fitzharris, 2005).

State-Mandated Curriculum

By 2010, most states had adopted the Common Core, but in recent years several states have withdrawn their support for that curriculum (Crowder, 2014). Critics of the Common Core have criticized its exclusive focus on preparing students for college or employment; the lack of field testing preceding its adoption; its one-size-fits-all content; and the restrictions that Common Core, in combination with corresponding high-stakes achievement tests, places on local decision making (Crowder, 2014; Eppley, 2015; Kern, 2014; Knoester & Parkison, 2015). A study by Murphy and Torff (2016) supports the critics; teachers responding to a survey on Common Core perceived that it reduced their capacity for effective teaching.

Whether or not they remain tied to Common Core, most states still control what is taught in public PK-12 schools through a combination of state standards and high-stakes achievement tests intended to enforce those standards. The purpose of the mandated curriculum is to transmit knowledge and skills deemed essential by the state legislature or educational bureaucracy. The required curriculum is often presented as a laundry list of required objectives in each subject area (or at least each basic subject area) at each grade level. Objectives tend to be within the lower categories of Bloom's taxonomy, at the knowledge or comprehension level. (See Table 19.1 later in this chapter.) There are seldom any connections made between the objectives in different content areas. Even the objectives within a given content area are usually discrete from one another. In short, in terms of purpose, content, organization, and format, state-mandated curriculum tends to be at the lowest level of curriculum development. It is therefore very difficult for teachers in states with mandated curricula to function beyond the imitative maintenance level of involvement in curriculum development (Crocco & Costigan, 2007; National Council of Teachers of English, 2014).

One argument often made by state officials discussing this reality is that teachers don't need to have a say in the curriculum because they can use their professional expertise and creativity when they plan how to teach the curriculum in their classrooms. These policy makers fail to understand that *the curriculum, if rigidly enforced, has a significant impact on how teachers teach*. For example, teachers working under a highly prescribed curriculum with long lists of required objectives will approach instruction quite differently than teachers with a webbed curriculum that they have designed themselves. In short, *what* gets taught (curriculum) has a strong impact on *how* it gets taught (instruction). Noddings (2007) suggests several dangers of teaching driven by detailed external standards applied to all students:

1. Narrowing learning
2. Failing to introduce potentially interesting topics (exposure)
3. Failing to identify individual students' varying motivations
4. Missing chances to connect with other subjects

5. Missing chances for collateral learning
6. Making life dull for teachers (p. 54)

High-Stakes Tests and the Curriculum

One way the federal government and states have attempted to control curriculum in schools is through the use of high-stakes tests intended to measure whether the state curriculum is being taught effectively. In states without a mandated curriculum but with high-stakes tests, the test itself becomes the curriculum. "In many instances, teachers find themselves compromising their educational visions, engaging in practices such as 'teaching to the test,' constricting the curriculum, devoting precious resources to test preparation materials, and drilling students on practice tests" (Gunzenhauser, 2006, p. 244).

We don't want to imply that learning standards and assessment are by their very nature bad. Standards and assessment that have been constructed with wide participation and are thoughtful and reasonable can be a way to address class, race/ethnicity, and gender inequities of expectations, resources, and targeted assistance. The issues here are: Who should define such standards? What should be multiple ways of assessing such learning? What should be the consequences for students, teachers, and schools? What flexibility, freedom, and authority should be given to classrooms and schools to be accountable? After all, it is hard to be accountable for what one has no control over (Pace, 2015; Valli & Buese, 2007).

Curriculum Development as a Vehicle for Enhancing Collective Thinking about Instruction

The tragedy of district and school curriculum being simply a mirror image of the state curriculum or state test is the loss of a powerful vehicle for creating a broader instructional dialogue in a school or district, which could enhance teachers' individual and collective thinking about these questions: What is worth teaching, how shall we teach, and how shall we assess? Most teachers—when trusted, when given time and money, and when given the assistance, choice, and responsibility to develop curricula—will make extraordinarily sound decisions about what students should be taught. Often, their decisions will be far superior to those made in central offices, state departments, or commercial publishing firms (Boote, 2006).

Teachers who are involved in making decisions about school curriculum go through changes in their own thinking about teaching. To discuss, debate, and finally come to an agreement with peers about what is important for students to know is an intellectually challenging experience.

The issue of whether teachers should be involved in curriculum development also has implications for school improvement. Part of the capacity for school improvement, according to Gordon and Boone (2012), is "the capacity to make wise value decisions about the goals of the educational process" (p. 46). Curricular decisions are perfect examples of the value decisions Gordon and Boone reference. School improvement is highly contextual (Hallinger & Heck, 2010; Mongon & Chapman, 2012) and thus requires local decision making (Coe, 2009; Massell, Goertz, & Barnes, 2015). Curriculum development is an essential part of school improvement, is itself highly contextual, and thus also requires local decision making. Local decisions about curriculum are best made by the teachers who deliver that curriculum, with assistance from supervisors and input from curriculum experts as well as students, parents, and the community served by the school.

> **Video Illustration**
>
> As you watch this video, think about what you find commendable about the teacher activity displayed. What do you find concerning about the activity?

It is clear that in order for schools to be successful, teachers need to be involved in curriculum development. The issues that remain are these:

1. What should be the purpose of the curriculum?
2. What should be the content of the curriculum?
3. How should the curriculum be organized?
4. In what format should the curriculum be written?
5. At what level of curriculum development should teachers be involved?

Forthcoming sections will discuss each of these issues.

What Should Be the Purpose of the Curriculum?

Alternative beliefs about the purpose of the curriculum are described by Miller and Seller (1985) as orientations to curriculum. They describe three *meta-orientations*, or positions:

- In the *transmission position* the function of education is to transmit facts, skills, and values to students. Specifically, this orientation stresses mastery of traditional school subjects through traditional teaching methodologies. (pp. 5–6) (emphasis supplied).
- In the *transaction position* the individual is seen as rational and capable of intelligent problem solving. Education is viewed as a dialogue between the student and the curriculum in which the student reconstructs knowledge through the dialogue process. The central elements in the transaction position are an emphasis on curriculum strategies that

promote problem solving, . . . application of problem solving skills within social contexts in general and within the context of the democratic process, . . . and development of cognitive skills within the academic disciplines. (pp. 6–7) (emphasis supplied)

- The *transformation position* focuses on personal and social change. It encompasses . . . teaching students skills that promote personal and social transformation . . . [and] a vision of social change as movement toward harmony with the environment rather than an effort to exert control over it. (p. 8) (emphasis supplied)

If Miller and Seller's three orientations to curriculum sound vaguely familiar, it may be due to the discussion of educational philosophies in Chapter 5. The transmission curriculum orientation is related to the educational philosophy of essentialism. The transactional curriculum orientation is based largely on the philosophy of experimentalism. Aspects of the transformation orientation are related to the philosophy of existentialism. In Chapter 5, we found that our educational beliefs help to shape our definition of effective teaching and instructional improvement. Similarly, curriculum orientations drive the curriculum development process and affect the curriculum's purpose, content, organization, and format.

Therefore, it is important that early in the curriculum design process the curriculum development team examines alternative curriculum orientations and clarifies its own orientation. The most basic decision the team needs to make (with input from all stakeholders) is whether the purpose of the curriculum will be to transmit, transact, transform, or accomplish some combination thereof.

What Should Be the Content of the Curriculum?

Curriculum, for purposes of this text, is the *what* of instruction—that is, what is intentionally taught to students in a district, school, or classroom. The elements of curriculum are sequence and continuity, scope, and balance (Ornstein & Hunkins, 2012). *Sequence* is the ordering of learning experiences, and *continuity* is the length or duration of such experiences. *Scope* is the range of learning experiences to be offered. *Balance* is the degree and number of topics, subjects, and learning experiences that adequately prepare students. A curriculum is developed by deciding: (1) What should students learn? (2) What is the order of content for the student to follow? (3) How is the learning to be evaluated? (Handler, 2012; Oliva, 2008; Ornstein & Hunkins, 2012).

Decisions about curriculum content are influenced by priorities of state and federal governments, values of professional educators and the local community, knowledge of student development, current economics (Bigham & Riney, 2014), and future societal conditions. Underlying all decisions about curriculum content are curriculum orientations (transmission, transaction, or transformation), which ultimately are derived from educational philosophies (essentialism, experimentalism, or existentialism).

Benjamin Bloom's taxonomy of learning might serve as a guide for determining types of learning within or across content areas (see Table 19.1). Bloom's lower levels of learning—(1) knowledge and (2) comprehension—are based on students recalling and demonstrating known answers. Curriculum objectives calling for knowledge and comprehension tend to dominate a curriculum with the purpose of transmission. Bloom's intermediate levels of learning—(3) application and (4) analysis—are based on students using logic to solve problems and reflect on their own thought process. Curriculum objectives at the application and analysis levels are emphasized in a curriculum with the purpose of transaction. Bloom's higher levels of learning—(5) synthesis and (6) evaluation—are based on combining various knowledge, facts, skills, and logic to make unique personal judgments. Curriculum objectives at the synthesis and evaluation levels are prevalent in a curriculum with the purpose of transformation. By examining a written curriculum, then, we can ascertain whether its purpose (and the curriculum developers' underlying orientation) is transmission, transaction, or transformation.

How Should the Curriculum Be Organized?

Three broad approaches to organizing curriculum content are discipline based, interdisciplinary, and transdisciplinary. A *discipline-based curriculum* is described by Jacobs (1989):

> The discipline-based content design option focuses on a strict interpretation of the disciplines with separate subjects in separate time blocks during the school day. No attempt for integration is made, in fact, it is avoided. Traditional approaches to subjects such as language arts, mathematics, science, social studies, music, art, and physical education are the usual fare. In secondary programs, these general academic and arts areas break down into more specific fields, such as algebra under mathematics or American history under social studies. There are some variations of block scheduling and the way the week or cycle is programmed. Nevertheless, knowledge is presented in separate fields without a deliberate attempt to show the relationships among them. (p. 14)

Because of its emphasis on breaking learning down into discrete segments of traditional content to be learned in specified blocks of time, the discipline-based approach

table **19.1** **Bloom's Taxonomy**

Level of Thinking	Description
1. Knowledge	Student recalls or recognizes information.
2. Comprehension	Student demonstrates understanding of information.
3. Application	Student uses the learned information to solve a problem.
4. Analysis	Student classifies or breaks down the learned information to draw
5. Synthesis	conclusions or make generalizations.
6. Evaluation	Student applies the learned information to create a new, original product. Student judges the value of the learned information based on his or her values and beliefs.

Source: Based on Benjamin Bloom (1956). *Taxonomy of Educational Objectives. Handbook I: The Cognitive Domain.* New York: David McKay.

is best suited to a curriculum with the purpose of transmission. This approach clearly has been the dominant curriculum organization pattern in the United States.

In an *interdisciplinary curriculum,* common themes connect traditional content areas. For instance, different aspects of an instructional unit on transportation might be taught in science, math, social studies, language arts, art, music, and physical education, or a set of common concepts or skills (e.g., technology or problem-solving skills) might connect different subject areas throughout the year. Figure 19.2 illustrates an interdisciplinary curriculum. A curriculum organization of this type requires extensive team planning. Since the interdisciplinary approach encourages students to discover relationships and make applications across existing content areas, it is most appropriate for a curriculum with the purpose of transactional learning (Jenkins, 2005).

In a *transdisciplinary curriculum,* traditional disciplines do not exist. The entire curriculum is organized around common themes, skills, or problems. Daily learning activities are built around the topic being studied rather than conforming to academic

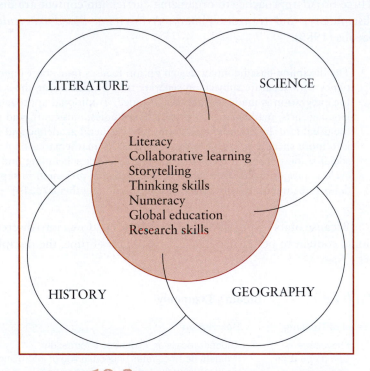

figure **19.2** **Illustration of an Interdisciplinary Curriculum**

Source: S. M. Drake, J. Bebbington, S. Laksman, P. Mackie, N. Maynes, & L. Wayne (1992). *Developing an Integrated Curriculum Using the Story Model,* p. 4. Ontario: The Ontario Institute for Studies in Education Press. Reprinted with permission of University of Toronto Press.

disciplines or class schedules. For example, while studying the concept of commerce, students could spend all of their school time developing, managing, and analyzing their own in-school "marketplace." Students might study selected content from economics, math, sociology, communication, politics, ethics, history, and other academic disciplines but only as such content became relevant to the commercial community they were developing.

Transdisciplinary curricula usually begin with very broad intended learning outcomes. The integration into the curriculum of contemporary problems from the real world and students' interests and concerns become part of an ongoing curriculum development process. This type of curriculum organization can be successful only if teachers are willing to totally reconceptualize their concept of the school curriculum. A transdisciplinary curriculum organization requires students to synthesize knowledge and skills from various content areas and encourages student creativity and self-direction. Such an organizational pattern is most consistent with a curriculum with the purpose of transforming teaching and learning.

In What Format Should the Curriculum Be Written?

This section will discuss various formats used in writing curriculum. Behavioral-objective, webbing, and results-only formats will be described. Like the content and organization of curriculum, its format reflects a curriculum orientation. Behavioral-objective formats reflect a transmission orientation. Webbing formats reflect a transaction orientation. Results-only formats reflect a transformation orientation.

Behavioral-objective format.   Predetermined knowledge, facts, and skills are written in curriculum guides in a linear cause-and-effect format. The curriculum developers determine what is to be learned, state the learning as a behavioral objective, specify the teaching/learning activities, and conclude with a posttest to see if the objective has been achieved.

Figure 19.3 is an example of a behavioral-objective guide written for a fifth-grade social studies class. Curriculum developers break their unit into the most important facts or skills that cover the subject. They write behavioral objectives for each fact or skill. Each behavioral objective is the basis for a sequence of activities and evaluation. The teacher who uses such a curriculum guide is expected to follow the sequence of activities and administer the evaluation. Recycling activities might be included in the guide for those students who do not pass the evaluation. Each behavioral-objective plan is tightly sequenced so that one objective is mastered before a student moves to the next. (For example, after identifying and spelling the original 13 American colonies, the next objective might be identifying and spelling those states that came into the Union from 1776 to 1810.)

Behavioral objective: At the end of the week, students will recall and spell the original 13 colonies at a 100 percent level of mastery.

Activities:

1. Lecture on 13 colonies.
2. Students fill in map of 13 colonies.
3. Students read pp. 113–118 of text and do assignments on p. 119 as homework.
4. Call on students at random to spell the various colonies.

Evaluation: Ask students to recall the names and spell correctly each of the 13 original colonies on a sheet of paper.

f i g u r e **19.3** **Behavioral-Objective Format**

Most school curricula that have been written in the last several decades follow a behavioral-objective format. It is particularly easy to use in subjects such as mathematics and physical sciences, where skills are obvious and facts are clear (2 plus 2 is always 4, for example, but is war always justifiable?). So prevalent has been the behavioral-objective format in curriculum writing in recent years that many educators know of no other way to write curricula.

Webbing.   Curriculum can be written in a format that shows relationships of activities around a central theme. William Kilpatrick popularized this type of curriculum in writing about the work unit (Kilpatrick, 1925). Instead of predetermining the knowledge or skills, the curriculum developer determines the major theme, related themes, and then possible student activities.

The webbing format can be conceived of in this way:

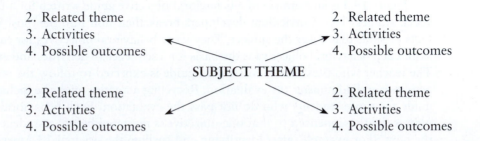

After the activities have been written, the curriculum developers write possible learning outcomes: "Students will be able to identify four major environmental issues," "Students will be able to argue and give evidence for both the pro and con sides of each issue," "Students will take a personal stance on each issue." In planning activities, developers consider multiple modes of learning via reading, writing, listening, and constructing and then integrate many fields of knowledge around a central theme. In Figure 19.4, notice how the theme of environmental issues integrates activities in sociology, mathematics, economics, history, journalism, physics, and biology.

A webbing curriculum guide would contain a blueprint of the web followed by sections for each related theme with activities, possible outcomes, and resources needed. Notice that the webbed curriculum includes possible outcomes and allows for the possibility of others. In a behavioral-objective curriculum, activities are controlled

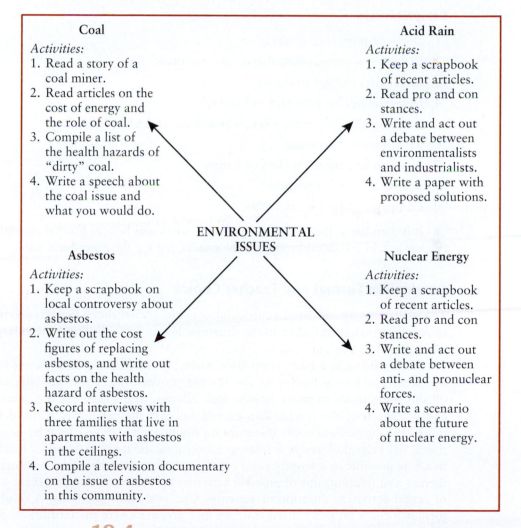

Coal

Activities:
1. Read a story of a coal miner.
2. Read articles on the cost of energy and the role of coal.
3. Compile a list of the health hazards of "dirty" coal.
4. Write a speech about the coal issue and what you would do.

Acid Rain

Activities:
1. Keep a scrapbook of recent articles.
2. Read pro and con stances.
3. Write and act out a debate between environmentalists and industrialists.
4. Write a paper with proposed solutions.

ENVIRONMENTAL ISSUES

Asbestos

Activities:
1. Keep a scrapbook on local controversy about asbestos.
2. Write out the cost figures of replacing asbestos, and write out facts on the health hazard of asbestos.
3. Record interviews with three families that live in apartments with asbestos in the ceilings.
4. Compile a television documentary on the issue of asbestos in this community.

Nuclear Energy

Activities:
1. Keep a scrapbook of recent articles.
2. Read pro and con stances.
3. Write and act out a debate between anti- and pronuclear forces.
4. Write a scenario about the future of nuclear energy.

figure **19.4** **Webbing Format**

toward predetermined ends. In a webbed curriculum, activities lead to possible and unanticipated learning.

Results-only format.   A results-only format for curriculum provides teachers with the widest latitude for using materials, activities, and methods. Such a curriculum specifies the goals and general learning about a subject, theme unit, or course. The guide might include ways to evaluate the learning.

For example, a results-only guide in elementary reading might specify the following skills to be learned:

Comprehension

1. Develops powers of observation
2. Classifies by name, color, shape, size, positions, use
3. Anticipates endings to stories
4. Discriminates between fact and fantasy
5. Understands who, what, when, where, how, and why phrases
6. Recalls a story sequence
7. Reads to find the main ideas of a story
8. Reads to draw a conclusion
9. Compares and contrasts stories

It is then left to the teacher to determine when and how to teach these skills. The teacher is held accountable only for the results, not for the procedures used.

Curriculum Format and Teacher Choice

The less specificity and detail a curriculum has, the greater the choice given to teachers to vary instruction according to the situation. Figure 19.5 illustrates the enlargement of teacher choice by curriculum.

Picture being in a curriculum cone where, at the behavioral-objective bottom, a teacher can barely budge. As the teacher moves toward the webbing area, he or she finds room to move hands, feet, elbows, and knees. At the results-only end of the cone, the teacher can extend fully. If the teacher is allowed to step out of the curriculum cone, there are no limits on where and how he or she can move. Behavioral-objective formats predetermine the *what* and *how* of teaching as much as possible in a loosely coupled organization. A webbing format focuses on themes and relationships of possible activities for teachers but gives them a choice of actual activities, duration of activities, and evaluation methods. A results-only format focuses on generalized learning and gives teachers the latitude to proceed as they wish.

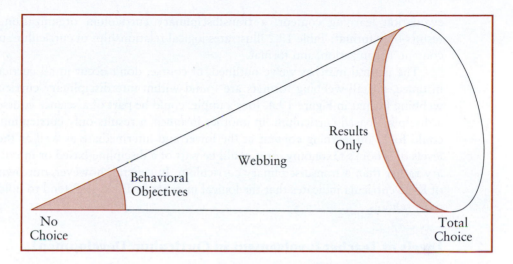

f i g u r e **19.5** **Curriculum Format as a Reflection of Teacher Choice: The Curriculum Cone**

It would appear relatively easy to match teacher stages of development to curriculum formats. It is not so easy, however; further examination of type and degree of involvement in curriculum development is necessary.

If a school has decided to use a behavioral-objective format, that does not necessarily mean that classroom teachers have little choice about how to teach. Perhaps the teachers have chosen to use that format; perhaps they wrote the curriculum themselves. Also, an elaborately detailed behavioral-objective curriculum could be presented to teachers as a reference guide to use as they wish. Simply knowing the format of the curriculum will not tell us how much choice was given to teachers. Although behavioral curricula usually are used as prescriptive teaching and equated with limiting choice, this is not always so. Therefore, before completing the picture of curriculum and teacher choice, it is necessary to consider how curricula are developed, interpreted, and implemented.

Relationship of Curriculum Purpose, Content, Organization, and Format

In previous sections we have proposed logical links among curriculum purpose, content, organization, and format. To review, a curriculum with the purpose of transmission is logically matched with knowledge and comprehension learning content, discipline-based curriculum organization, and behavioral-objective format. A curriculum with the purpose of transaction is well matched with application and analysis learning content, interdisciplinary curriculum organization, and webbing format. A curriculum with the purpose of transformation is consistent with synthesis and evaluation learning content, a transdisciplinary curriculum organization, and a results-only format. Table 19.2 illustrates logical relationships of curriculum purpose, content, organization, and format.

The natural matches we've outlined, of course, don't occur in all curricula. For instance, not all webbing formats are found within interdisciplinary curricula. The webbing format in Figure 19.4, for example, could be part of a science course within a discipline-based curriculum. In another instance, a results-only curriculum format could focus on learning content at the lower and intermediate as well as the higher levels of Bloom's taxonomy, or it could be part of a discipline-based or interdisciplinary rather than a transdisciplinary curriculum. In general, however, our own review of K-12 curricula indicates that the logical matches in Table 19.2 tend to hold true in most schools.

Levels of Teacher Involvement in Curriculum Development

Tanner and Tanner (2007) wrote of teachers and local schools functioning in curriculum development at one of three levels: (1) imitative maintenance, (2) mediative, or (3) creative-generative. Teachers at Level 1 are concerned with maintaining and following the existing curriculum. Teachers at Level 2 look at development as refining the existing curriculum. Teachers at Level 3 are concerned with improving and changing the curriculum according to the most current knowledge about learning and societal conditions. Tanner and Tanner explained these three levels as follows:

Level 1: Imitative maintenance.   Teachers operating at Level I rely on textbooks, workbooks, and routine activities, subject by subject. Skills are treated as dead ends rather than as means of generating further learning. Ready-made materials are used without critical evaluation, resulting in a multiplicity of isolated skill-development activities. (The already segmental curriculum is further fragmented.) The imagination of the teacher does not go beyond maintaining the status quo. This teacher would like to think that he or she has less freedom than may actually exist for curriculum improvement. In the secondary school, concern for curriculum development is largely confined to each departmental domain.

When change is made, it is made on the adoption level, without adaptation to local needs. Curriculum development at this level consists of plugging in the package to the

t a b l e **19.2** **Logical Relationships of Curriculum Purpose, Content, Organization, and Format**

Curriculum Purpose	Transmission	Transaction	Transformation
Curriculum Content	Knowledge Comprehension	Application Analysis	Synthesis Evaluation
Curriculum Organization	Discipline Based	Interdisciplinary	Transdisciplinary
Curriculum Format	Behavioral Objective	Webbing	Results Only

existing situation without attention to the resulting interactions. Teachers at this level tend to be left alone to struggle with innovations that are handed to them from above. Schools are turned inward, with the principal as the sole resource for classroom assistance.

Level 2: Mediative. Teachers at Level 2 are aware of the need to integrate curriculum content and deal with emergent conditions. (Societal problems such as the energy crisis and children's questions about things that interest and concern them are examples of emergent conditions.) Although teachers at this level may have an aggregate conception of curriculum, implementation does not go beyond the occasional correlation of certain subjects. The focus of curriculum remains segmental; theory remains divorced from practice; curriculum improvement remains at the level of refining existing practice.

Yet teachers at the second level of curriculum development do not blindly plug in an innovation or curriculum package to the existing situation. The necessary adaptations, accommodations, and adjustments are made and capitalize on a range of resources for curriculum improvement, including pupils, parents, and peers; and they utilize resources beyond the local school. Teachers are consumers of professional literature on approved practices and tap the resources of the university through inservice courses. The mediative level is a level of awareness and accommodation. Teachers are attracted to, and can articulate, new ideas but their efforts to improve the curriculum fall short of the necessary reconstruction for substantive problem solving.

Level 3: Creative-generative. Teachers at Level 3 take an aggregate approach to curriculum development. Ideally, the curriculum is examined in its entirety by the teacher and the entire school staff, and questions of priority and relationship are asked. While individual teachers can and should be at the creative-generative level, a macrocurricular approach requires cooperative planning for vertical and horizontal articulation.

Granted that teachers as individuals usually cannot create new schoolwide curricula, an individual teacher can establish continuities and relationships in his or her own teaching and with other teachers. Teachers at Level 3 use generalizations and problems as centers of curriculum organization. They stress the broad concepts that specialized subjects share in common, and they use and develop courses of study that cross subject fields. These are aggregate treatments.

Teachers at the third level of curriculum development think about what they are doing and try to find more effective ways of working. They are able to diagnose their problems and formulate hypotheses for solutions. They experiment in their classrooms and communicate their insights to other teachers.

Teachers at this level are consumers of research and seek greater responsibility for curriculum decisions at the school and classroom levels. They exercise independent judgment in selecting curriculum materials and adapt them to local needs. They regard themselves as professionals and, as such, are continually involved in the problems of making decisions regarding learning experiences. To this end, their antennae are turned outward to a wide range of resources.*

---

*Excerpt from Daniel Tanner and Laurel N. Tanner, *Curriculum Development: Theory into Practice*, 4th ed., pp. 413–414. Copyright © 2007 by Pearson Prentice Hall Upper Saddle River, NJ. Reprinted by permission.

Integrating Curriculum Format with Developers and Levels of Development

To integrate what has been said about curriculum format, developers, and development, refer to Figure 19.6. When the developers are either outside the school system or from the district level and the curriculum is in a tightly prescribed format, development will be primarily *imitative,* characterized by teachers following the course of study. When the developers are intermediate teams of teachers led by district specialists and the curriculum is written with objectives and suggested activities, development will be primarily *mediative,* characterized by teachers revising and adapting the course of study to their immediate situation. When curriculum developers are teams of teachers using specialists as resource persons or individual teachers with a results-only curriculum format that identifies what students should learn and leaves activities to the teacher, then development is *creative-generative,* characterized by ongoing creativity.

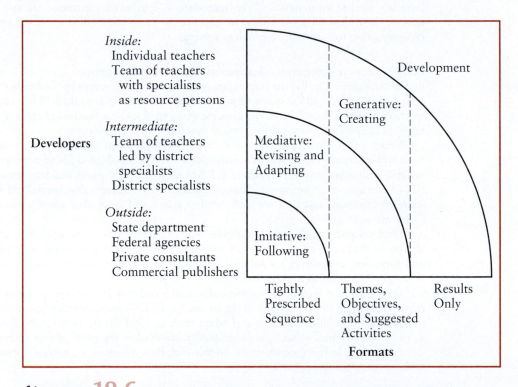

f i g u r e **19.6** **Integrating Curriculum Format with Developers and Levels of Development**

Matching Curriculum Development with Teacher Development

A progression of curriculum development matched with teacher development might look like Table 19.3. The supervisor might think of his or her staff in terms of the commitment, thinking, and expertise they currently bring to curriculum and then determine whether the current curriculum is appropriately matched with the teachers' level of curriculum functioning. If the present curriculum is inappropriate to teachers' development, readjustments to the curriculum would be in order.

A staff that has a low level of curriculum functioning—as displayed by little commitment to change, little ability to suggest possible changes, and little curriculum expertise—initially would be matched with an outside-developed, behavioral-objective, and imitative curriculum. They should be allowed to make minor revisions in adapting the curriculum to their classrooms. On the other hand, a staff that has a moderate level of curriculum functioning (as displayed by a desire to change, ability to think of possible changes, but a lack of expertise in writing curriculum) would be appropriately matched with a curriculum originally developed by outside experts but substantially revised by an internal team of teachers led by a curriculum specialist. The format of the curriculum might be eclectic in its use of behavioral objectives and webbing. Throughout the development and implementation, teachers should have

t a b l e **19.3** **Progression of Curriculum Matched with Characteristics of Staff**

	Stage 1	Stage 2	Stage 3
Staff Characteristics			
Commitment to curriculum change	Low commitment to change	Would like to make change	Eager to make change
Level of thinking about curriculum	Low ability to think about possible changes	Can think of some possible changes	Has many suggestions
Expertise in curriculum procedures	Low expertise in how to proceed	Does not know how to write curriculum	Knows how to proceed
Curriculum Characteristics			
Developers	Outside developers	Externally developed but substantially revised by team of teachers led by specialists	Internally developed by team of teachers with specialists as resource
Format	Behavioral-objective, highly structured	Eclectic format using behavior objectives, webbing	Results-only, with suggested activities
Development	Imitative, with allowance for minor revisions	To be mutually adapted	To be discussed and changed continually

problem-solving meetings for purposes of curriculum adaptation. Finally, a staff that is at a high level of curriculum functioning (as displayed by initiating and suggesting ways to change and knowing how to proceed in creating curriculum) would be appropriately matched with an internally developed curriculum. The format should emphasize results only with *suggested* activities and should be continuously open to revision.

The supervisor should keep in mind the question, How does one increase teacher control over curriculum making? If a staff has been appropriately matched—for example, low-functioning staff with an imitative curriculum—and successful implementation is occurring, then the supervisor should plan for the next cycle of curriculum development to give teachers additional responsibilities by serving on decision-making teams under the leadership of a curriculum specialist. This would lead to more mutually adaptive curriculum and at the same time continue to stimulate and increase teacher commitment, development, and expertise.

The supervisor wishing to facilitate changes in curriculum purpose, content, organization, and format must remember that successful change will be based on teachers changing their conceptions of curriculum and their level of involvement in curriculum development. Change in teachers *and* curriculum is more likely to be successful if done in an incremental manner. For example, rather than announcing that the school will be moving from a discipline-based to interdisciplinary curriculum organization, the supervisor could initially encourage small teams of teachers functioning at moderate to high levels of development, expertise, and commitment to plan and teach a few interdisciplinary units of instruction throughout the school year.

In another school, already operating at an interdisciplinary level, movement toward a transdisciplinary curriculum could begin with a group of teachers operating at high levels of development, expertise, and commitment forming a "broad field." A *broad field* results from the fusion of two or more separate disciplines. Courses or subjects (rather than departments) with titles like "humanities," "social science," and "natural science" usually reflect a broad-field approach. The formation of one or more broad fields involving a subset of faculty and curricula would not represent a fully transdisciplinary curriculum, but it would be a major step in that direction.

Large-scale teacher-driven changes in curriculum content, organization, and format will not take place unless teachers change their curriculum orientations or beliefs about the purpose of curriculum. Yet, teachers are not likely to change their orientations unless their levels of understanding of and involvement in curriculum development gradually increase. Supervisor openness and trust building, staff development in curriculum design, and time, support, and rewards for teacher involvement can all foster teacher *and* curriculum development. Throughout the curriculum development process, the supervisor must remember that if he or she has a curriculum orientation or favors a curriculum content, organization, or format different from teachers, then the supervisor is not necessarily right and the teachers wrong. Government mandates, the community, the school's mission and culture, parents, teachers, and students must all be considered when deciding which direction curriculum development should take and at what rate it should proceed.

The Curriculum and Cultural Diversity

There are a variety of reasons why the curriculum should be culturally diverse. First, students from nondominant cultures are not likely to reach their learning potential if the curriculum ignores their culture. Second, a society cannot offer democracy, equal opportunity, and justice for all unless it experiences, understands, and respects the variety of cultures that make up the society (Ford, 2014). Third, communities and societies that recognize the value of diversity and invite citizens from different cultures to participate in their development experience more educational, economic, and social success: The quality of life for all citizens improves (Bloemraad & Wright, 2014). A culturally diverse curriculum, then, benefits all students, as well as the community and society (Ukpokodu, 2010).

How do schools integrate multicultural and ethnic content into their curriculum? James Banks (2014) has described four approaches to integration. Banks presented the approaches as four levels of integration, with Level 1 the least effective and Level 4 the most effective.

Level 1, the *contributions approach,* calls for inserting minority culture heroes, holidays, and elements (food, dances, music, art) into the curriculum alongside mainstream content. This is the easiest approach to implement, but it leaves the curriculum virtually unchanged.

Level 2, the *additive approach,* adds concepts and perspectives from other cultures to the mainstream curriculum without changing the curriculum's basic structure. This approach might include adding books by minority authors, a few units of instruction, or a single course to the curriculum.

Level 3, the *transformation approach,* changes the fundamental structure of the curriculum by enabling students to consider concepts, issues, and problems from several different cultural perspectives rather than from only the dominant culture's perspective.

Level 4, the *social action approach,* includes all aspects of the transformation approach but also requires students to engage in critical inquiry about cultural issues and problems and to take action for social change.

Figure 19.7 summarizes the four approaches.

Unfortunately, many school curricula have not gone beyond the contributions approach. Why the gap between scholarship on multicultural curriculum and practice? Geneva Gay (2005) has offered an explanation:

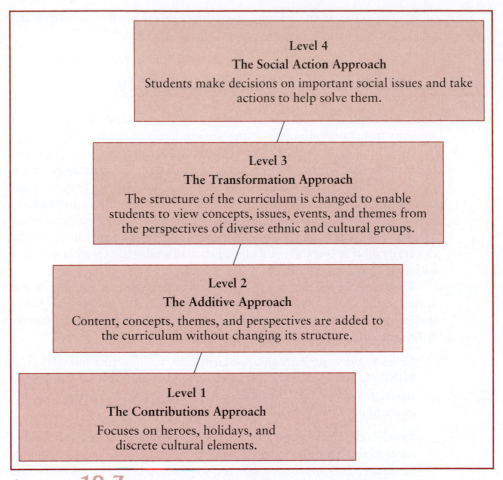

figure **19.7** **Banks's Approaches to Multicultural Curriculum Reform**

Source: Reprinted with permission of the author from: James A. Banks, *An Introduction to Multicultural Education* (5th edition). Boston: Pearson, 2014, page 54.

Most school teachers and administrators have good intentions about implementing the ideas and proposals suggested in the scholarship on multicultural education. Unfortunately, many do not have the knowledge base and pedagogical skills needed. Others are still struggling with how to resolve what they see as inherent tensions between the national ideals of the United States embedded in the motto *E Pluribus Unum* and recognizing, accepting, and promoting diversity in schools and society. Confusion is still rampant over calls for diversity, equity, and excellence in education. Too many educators continue to believe that to treat students differently based on their cultural heritages, ethnic identities, and background experiences is synonymous to discrimination, and to promote diversity is to compromise high-quality performance and standards of excellence. This confusion drives some educators to question the merits of education for diversity, to judge it divisive and counterproductive, and to redefine it in ways that reaffirm their comfort levels and serve their own purposes. These reactions have different consequences on efforts to implement multicultural education, but in general they produce distortions, inaccuracies, and misconceptions that are not consistent with the thinking, research, and writing of multicultural education scholars. (pp. 109–110)

Gay (2005) has proposed that we begin to close the gap between scholarship and practice by developing well-articulated guidelines for translating theoretical principles into practice, establishing performance standards for educators, and providing professional development to help educators meet those standards. The professional development Gay has proposed would be long term, assisting educators to develop self-understanding, cultural knowledge, and multicultural education skills.

Curriculum Mapping—and Remapping

Over the last several decades, different versions of curriculum mapping have been used for different purposes. Curriculum mapping was developed in the 1980s by Fenwick English (1980) as a form of curriculum audit; it was used to document what teachers taught and how much time they spent on each topic so the taught curriculum could be compared with the district's curriculum guide and testing program. English's model was not immediately concerned with curriculum development; he stated, "Curriculum mapping invents or creates no 'new' curriculum. Rather, it attempts to describe the curriculum that currently exists" (p. 559). According to English, after the curriculum audit, the curriculum developer could decide to use the curriculum map to make the taught and written curriculum more consistent with each other.

In the 1990s, Heidi Hayes Jacobs (1997) introduced a different version of curriculum mapping, one that involves teachers throughout the process, and includes mapping not only knowledge and skills taught but also the assessments made by teachers. Jacobs' model also engages teachers in reviewing each other's curriculum maps and collectively revising the overall curriculum based on that review. In the present age of accountability, many districts have moved away from Jacobs' participatory model of curriculum mapping, back to curriculum mapping as audit, tracking what teachers teach in order to make sure it is in line with state standards and achievement tests (Shilling, 2013).

Our view is that curriculum mapping should be used not as an auditing tool but as a way to involve teachers in reflection on what and how they teach and in teacher-driven curriculum development. We also believe that curriculum mapping should include analysis and improvement of *content, instruction, and assessment*. The model we present is intended for curriculum mapping at the school level. Curriculum mapping using the model can be either horizontal or vertical. For example, elementary teachers using the model could be teaching the same content to different groups of students at the same grade level, or teaching different grade levels (e.g., fourth, fifth, and sixth grades). Secondary teachers using the model could be teaching different sections of the same course, or a sequence of courses (e.g., English I, II, and III).

Table 19.4 represents the first phase of the model. For each curriculum unit, the teacher keeps a log of each specific type of content taught within the unit. For example, in a civics unit on the election of U.S. presidents, specific content might include campaign finance, the primary process, the party conventions, great debates in presidential elections, election night, and the Electoral College. For each specific area of content taught within a unit, the teacher summarizes not only that content but also the dates the content was taught, the teaching methods used, and the assessment methods. For elementary and middle school, the individual mapping goes on for a year. For high schools, the mapping of a single course can be done in one semester, but if a group of teachers is mapping a set of courses that are taught in sequence, it may take longer to map each course in the sequence.

The next component of the mapping model is reflective review and comparison of the maps created by participating teachers. Preliminary review and comparison can take place during the semester or school year, but full review must await the completion of the semester, year, or course sequence. Teachers participating in the mapping share their individual maps with each other. Teachers review all individual maps, and then convene to develop a comparison map. A simple version of a matrix for comparison mapping is shown in Table 19.5. In addition to the headings for unit topics, specific content, and dates shown in Table 19.5, more complex maps can be constructed allowing comparison of teaching and assessment methods as well as other aspects of the curriculum the teachers wish to compare. And, of course, there would be a "Teacher" section of the comparison map for each teacher in the group who has taught one of the classes, grade levels, or courses being compared.

t a b l e 19.4 **Individual Teacher Curriculum Log**

Teacher: _____				
Grade Level/Content Area or Course: _____				
Unit Topic	**Specific Content Taught**	**Dates Specific Content Taught**	**Teaching Method(s)**	**Assessment Method(s)**

t a b l e **19.5 Comparing Curriculum Maps**

Teacher: _____			Teacher: _____			Teacher: _____		
Grade Level/Content Area or Course: _____			Grade Level/Content Area or Course: _____			Grade Level/Content Area or Course: _____		
Unit Topic	Specific Content Taught	Dates Specific Content Taught	Unit Topic	Specific Content Taught	Dates Specific Content Taught	Unit Topic	Specific Content Taught	Dates Specific Content Taught

After the teachers have constructed the comparison map, it is time to review and reflect with the aid of prompts like those shown in Table 19.6. First, teachers review the comparison map individually, considering issues raised by the map and preparing questions or discussion points. Next, the teachers meet as a group to discuss issues and potential revisions. Several questions teachers need to consider concern gaps in the curriculum. Is there content required by the state standards that is not being taught? If there is a mandated district curriculum, are there gaps between the district and taught curriculum? There are a variety of national educational associations that recommend curriculum in various content areas. The curriculum suggested by the professional associations tends to represent higher-level, more holistic learning than the curriculum mandated by policy makers, hence it is important to consider the relevant associations' recommendations.

Teachers also need to look at redundancies in the curriculum, with an eye toward eliminating unnecessary repetition. Some content may be out of scope, meaning it is not related to any of the school's curriculum goals. Out-of-scope content should be removed from the curriculum, providing more space for necessary content. The sequence of content—both in individual courses and across the curriculum—needs to be examined in order to be sure that learning later in sequence builds upon earlier learning. Appraising the amount of time spent on particular content is important, both because spending more than optimal time on one topic decreases the amount of time available for other important content, and because there is a need for a reasonable level of consistency among teachers who teach the same grade level or course.

The level of difficulty of particular content should be analyzed to determine if it is appropriate for the developmental level of students to whom it is taught. The same content often can be taught at different levels of difficulty, thus when level of difficulty

t a b l e **19.6** **Prompts for Individual-Review and Group-Discussion Notes**

Gaps Compared to State Standards:	Gaps Compared to District Curriculum:	Gaps Compared to Professional Association's Suggested Curriculum:	Gaps Compared to Unique Local Needs:
Redundancies:	Issues with Scope:	Issues with Sequence:	Issues with Time Spent on Unit(s) or Specific Content:
Issues with Level of Difficulty of Specified Content:	Teaching Methods:	Assessment Methods:	Resources:

for some content is found to be too high or low for students in a particular grade level or course, teachers can discuss whether to move the content to another part of the curriculum or leave it where it is and adjust the level of difficulty. Curriculum cannot really be separated from the teaching that delivers it, thus review of the curriculum map should include analyzing teaching methods associated with different types of content. Discussing the methods used by different teachers will allow the group to decide which methods have worked well and which have not. The idea here is not to decide the one best way to teach a unit or parts of a unit. Different teachers may well have had success teaching the same content with different teaching methods, and there is no reason why successful methods cannot be listed in the new curriculum map as alternatives from which teachers may choose. Of course, there is always the possibility that teacher dialogue will result in new and exciting teaching methods being identified and incorporated into the curriculum. Assessment methods listed on the map also should be appraised, again, with the purpose of choosing the most promising methods

t a b l e **19.7** **New Curriculum Map**

1	2	3	4	5	6	7	8	9
Unit Topic	Specific Content	No. of Days for Specific Content	State Req. to be Met	Dist. Req. to be Met	Ass. Req. to be met	Potential Teaching Methods	Potential Assessment Methods	Resources Available

Grade Level/Content Area or Course: _____

as alternatives for the teacher to choose from, and with the possibility that new assessment methods will emerge from teacher discourse. Finally, the "resources" prompt in Table 19.6 can lead to teachers reviewing existing instructional resources to determine which ones should be included in the new curriculum map, as well as new resources the group may wish to request, and once procured, add to the map.

After constructing and sharing individual maps, collectively developing a comparison map, and using the prompts in Table 19.6 to analyze the comparison map and consider potential revisions, the teachers are ready to collaboratively develop revised, articulated curriculum maps with headings like those in Table 19.7. The teachers revise unit topics for each grade level/content area or course (column 1), specific content for each unit (column 2), and the number of days to be spent on each part of each unit (column 3). The teachers briefly note on the map state and district mandates that are addressed in each part of each unit (columns 4 and 5), and how each part of the unit relates to one or more professional organizations' curriculum guidelines (column 6). Potential teaching and assessment methods are listed (columns 7 and 8), and available instructional resources are identified (column 9).

Developing Curriculum Units: Understanding by Design

Another curriculum development model, *Understanding by Design* (UbD), was developed by Grant Wiggins and Joy McTighe (2005, 2011). Two goals of UbD are to help students develop meaningful understandings and to transfer their learning to new contexts. "Understanding is revealed when students autonomously make sense of and transfer their learning through authentic performance. Six facets of understanding—the capacities to *explain, interpret, apply, shift perspective, empathize,* and *self assess*—serve as indicators of understanding" (2011, p. 4). UbD uses *backward design,* in which curriculum developers (1) identify desired results, (2) determine what evidence will show that students have achieved the desired results, and (3) develop a learning plan for students. Backward design, according to Wiggins and McTighe, prevents two typical, ineffective ways of curriculum development: planning the curriculum around engaging activities, or around the content of an external source such as a textbook. UbD does not prescribe particular content—it is, rather, a framework used first to develop curriculum units and then to design daily lesson plans. Let's take a closer look at the three stages of UbD as proposed by Wiggins and McTighe (2005, 2011).

Stage 1: Identify desired results.   The curriculum developers identify long-term goals, including *meaning goals* (the understanding of "big ideas") and *transfer goals* (the application of understandings in new contexts). The developers also create *essential questions* that students will consider throughout the unit to stay focused on the meaning goals. Short-term goals, called *acquisition goals,* also are identified; they consist of desired knowledge and skills encompassed by the broader meaning and transfer goals. Already established standards and goals (required by the state, district, and so forth) related to the desired results are listed in the Stage 1 document to remind teachers of the relationship between the established standards or goals and the curriculum unit's desired results.

Stage 2: Determine evidence.   Curriculum developers identify two general types of evidence to determine whether desired results are met: performance tasks and other evidence. *Performance tasks* are used to assess student learning for all meaning and transfer goals; they can be real world or simulated tasks. *Other evidence* is used to help determine if students have achieved meaning and transfer goals as well as to determine if students have achieved acquisition goals (short-term knowledge and skills). Other evidence consists of more traditional assessment methods such as demonstration of discrete skills, quizzes, tests, and so forth. Evaluation criteria to indicate the level of learning are identified for each type of performance and for other evidence. Students are given multiple opportunities to show they have achieved Stage 1 goals.

Stage 3: Develop learning plan.   The learning plan includes preassessments to determine the student's prior knowledge, skills, and understandings. Educators may need to adjust the unit's learning activities for the class or some individuals based on the results of the preassessment. The plan includes learning events designed for students to meet acquisition, meaning, and transfer goals. Another component of the learning plan is progress monitoring, including strategies for ongoing assessment of student learning and providing students with feedback. As with the preassessment, teachers using the learning plan may need to adjust the plan based on information gathered through monitoring of student progress.

Keys to success of learning by design.   Figure 19.8 provides an overview of all three stages of UbD. Wiggins and McTighe (2005, 2011) stress the need for all three stages

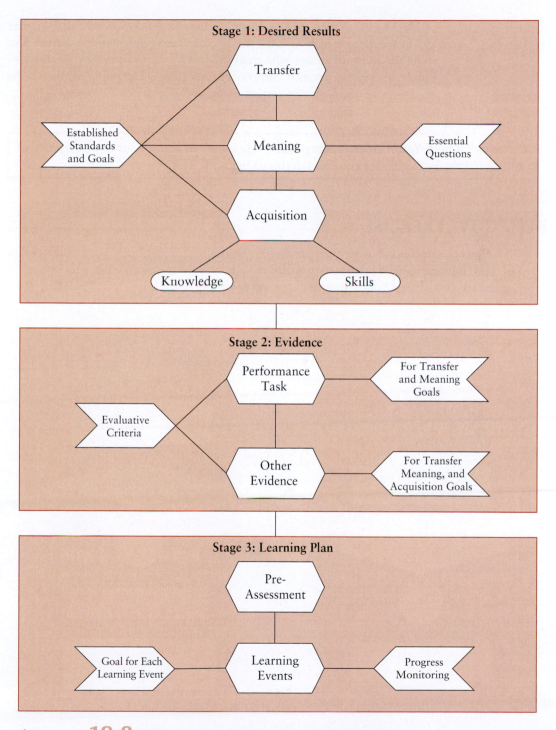

figure **19.8** Wiggins and McTighe's Understanding by Design

of UbD to be aligned for the design process to work as intended. Another key to success, we believe, is for the teachers who implement the curriculum to be the same educators who used the UbD process to design the curriculum, with varying levels of supervisory assistance depending on the teachers' levels of development, commitment, and expertise.

✔ **Check Your Understanding 19.0**   Click here to gauge your understanding of the key concepts presented in this chapter.

REFLECTIVE EXERCISE

Draw a conceptual map that illustrates the important concepts about curriculum development you have learned from this chapter and relationships among the concepts. Share and discuss your conceptual map with colleagues.

chapter 20

Action Research: The School as the Center of Inquiry

Learning Outcomes for This Chapter

After reading this chapter, you should be able to:

1. List the five phases of traditional action research.
2. Describe general outcomes of successful schoolwide action research.
3. Enumerate the four phases of appreciative inquiry.
4. State the principles of shared governance for instructional improvement.
5. Summarize the authors' suggestions for assisting action research.

Questions to Reflect On as You Read This Chapter

1. How would you discuss action research with a teacher who was leery of becoming involved in research?
2. Why do you think the authors present action research as "the core of related supervisory activities"?
3. Which type of action research—traditional (problem-based), interpretive, critical, or appreciative—is most intriguing to you? Why?
4. This chapter addresses both action research and democratic governance. Why are these two topics naturally related to each other?
5. Assume that a school you are familiar with has decided to institute shared governance for action research. What are some ways that the model for shared governance presented by the authors in this chapter could be modified to adapt the model to the school you have in mind?

> *Why should our schools not be staffed, gradually if you will, by scholar-teachers in command of the conceptual tools and methods of inquiry requisite to investigating the learning process as it operates in their own classrooms? Why should our schools not nurture the continuing wisdom and power of such scholar-teachers?*
>
> (Schaefer, 1967, p. 5)

The famous social scientist Kurt Lewin devoted his career to studying democracy and the relationships among individuals within groups. His contributions ushered in the school of gestalt psychology, group dynamics, and the concept of action research. He argued that social research should be based on the actions groups take to improve their conditions. Social research should not focus on controlled experiments, removed from real conditions. As people plan changes and engage in real activities, fact finding should determine whether success is being achieved and whether further planning and action are necessary (Lewin, 1948, p. 206).

Stephen Corey (1953) applied Lewin's concept of action research to education. He argued that traditional research is done mainly by researchers outside the public school and has little influence on school practice. Corey wrote:

> Learning that changes behavior substantially is most likely to result when a person himself tries to improve a situation that makes a difference to him. . . . When he defines the problem, hypothesizes actions that may help him cope with it, engages in these actions, studies the consequences, and generalizes from them, he will more frequently internalize the experience than when all this is done for him by somebody else, and he reads about it. . . . The value of action research . . . is determined primarily by the extent to which findings lead to improvement in the practices of the people engaged in the research. (p. 9)

Thus, action research in education is study conducted by colleagues in a school setting of the results of their activities to improve instruction. Although an individual teacher can conduct action research, in most cases it is best done as a cooperative endeavor by faculty attempting to improve on a common instructional concern (Allen & Calhoun, 2009; Calhoun, 2009; Castro Garcés & Granada, 2016; Clauset, Lick, & Murphy, 2008; Gordon, 2008; Kapachtsi & Kakana, 2012; Pine, 2009; Sagor, 2009).

As Richard Sagor (1993) wrote, "By turning to *collaborative* action research . . . we can renew our commitment to thoughtful teaching and also begin developing an active community of professionals" (p. 10). Action research implies that the practitioners are the researchers. The objectivity and rigor of research methodology can be questioned by classical researchers, but the benefits of the process for students and teachers seem to outweigh the loss of experimental purity (López-Pastor, Monjas, & Manrique, 2011).

In addressing the power of teacher-led research, Hubbard and Power (1993, p. xiii) wrote: "Teachers throughout the world are developing professionally by becoming teacher-researchers, a wonderful new breed of artists-in-residence. Using our own classrooms as laboratories and our students as collaborators, we are changing the way we work with students as we look at our classrooms systematically through research." More recently, Pine (2009) stated:

> Teachers are privileged through the action research process to produce knowledge and consequently experience that "knowledge is power." As knowledge and action are joined in changing practice, there is growing recognition of the power of teachers to change and reform education from the inside rather than having change and reform imposed top down from the outside. (p. 31)

Table 20.1 compares traditional research with action research.

Video Illustration

The teacher in these videos is discussing classroom-based action research that she has conducted. How would schoolwide action research be similar to classroom-based action research? What challenges would schoolwide action research present that are not present with classroom-based action research? What advantages would schoolwide action research provide that classroom-based action research does not? How could classroom-based action research compliment schoolwide action research?

t a b l e **20.1** **Comparison of Traditional Research and Action Research**

	Traditional Research	Action Research
Usually led by	Outside expert	Practitioners
Purpose	Develop new knowledge	Solve practical problem; improve practice
Types of data gathered	Quantitative or qualitative	Quantitative or qualitative
Purpose of gathering and analyzing data	Gain better understanding of phenomenon; develop or test hypotheses	Explore practical problem; guide action planning; evaluate results
Standard for quality research	Peer review of methods and results	Research results in desired change
Primary audience(s)	Other researchers, the profession, government, or private agencies	Members of the school community

How Is Action Research Conducted?

In the first phase of action research, a focus area is selected—an area of teaching and learning in need of improvement. Second, a needs assessment gathers data on the focus area. The purposes of data gathering at this stage are to understand the problem and how it might be solved and to gather baseline data to help with the evaluation of improvement efforts. The third phase of action research is to design an action plan for solving the problem. The plan includes activities for evaluating the success of improvement efforts. The fourth phase is the implementation of the plan. The fifth phase of action research is the evaluation: data on the action plan's effects are gathered and analyzed. Based on the evaluation, action plan objectives and activities may be continued, expanded, revised, or discontinued.

If these five phases sound suspiciously similar to the development of action plans with individual teachers in Chapter 15 (direct assistance), then you have won the first round of the supervision concentration game. The aim of direct assistance to teachers is to promote increased thought, choice, and responsibility in individual teachers. Action research can promote increased thought, choice and responsibility at the individual, small-group, or school level. The supervisor's role is to determine what type of assistance teachers need (directive informational, collaborative, or nondirective), depending on the developmental levels of the teachers with respect to the focus area of the action research. Figure 20.1 depicts the five phases of action research.

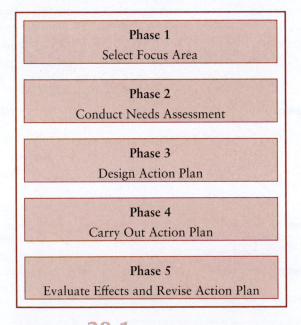

Phase 1
Select Focus Area

Phase 2
Conduct Needs Assessment

Phase 3
Design Action Plan

Phase 4
Carry Out Action Plan

Phase 5
Evaluate Effects and Revise Action Plan

figure **20.1** **Five Phases of Action Research**

Collective action research can integrate direct assistance, evaluation of teaching, group development, professional development, and curriculum development. First, the team conducts a needs assessment of faculty and collects baseline data to determine common goals for improvement of instruction. Observations can be used as part of a needs assessment, with any of the following types of observation chosen:

- Categorical frequency
- Performance indicator
- Visual diagramming
- Verbatim or selective verbatim
- Detached open-ended narrative
- Participant open-ended observation
- Focused questionnaire
- Tailored observation systems
- Schoolwide classroom observations

Use of these types of observations is explained in Chapter 12.

Broader techniques for needs assessment can be chosen from the following list:

- Eyes and ears
- Official records
- Review of teacher and student work products
- Third-party review
- Multiple-choice survey
- Written open-ended survey
- Check and ranking survey
- Delphi technique
- Nominal group technique
- Cause-and-effect diagrams
- Flowcharts
- Pareto charts

Explanations of these assessment techniques can be found in Chapter 13.

Second, the team brainstorms activities that will cut across supervision tasks. The team can respond to these five questions corresponding to technical supervisory tasks:

1. What type and frequency of direct assistance must be provided to teachers to reach our instructional goals?

2. What types of formative evaluation of teaching should be included in the action plan?

3. What meetings and discussions need to be arranged as part of group development for faculty to share and reach our instructional goals?

4. What professional development opportunities, such as lectures, workshops, demonstrations, courses, and visits, need to be provided for faculty to reach our instructional goals?

5. What is the necessary curriculum development in terms of course content, curriculum guides, lesson plans, and instructional materials to reach our instructional goals?

These technical tasks of supervision are explained in Chapters 15, 16, 17, 18, and 19.

Third, the team makes a plan relating activities to goals. Techniques for writing plans are as follows:

- Affinity diagrams
- Process decision program chart
- Gantt charts
- Force field analysis

A description of each planning device can be found in Chapter 13.

Fourth, the team implements the plan, moving through the stages of readiness, installation, initiation, full operations, and continuation and renewal discussed in Chapter 14. Parallel with implementation, the team conducts ongoing formative evaluation of the action research and its effects, choosing observations from Chapter 12 and formative evaluation methods from Chapter 14 to do so. Based on formative assessment, ongoing modifications in the action research are made as appropriate.

Fifth, the team chooses a summative program evaluation design that will enable them to analyze data, determine whether objectives have been met, and decide what further actions need to be taken. The summative evaluation is often carried out toward the end of the school year. The design can be quantitative, qualitative, or a combination of both. Questions to be asked in the evaluation include the following:

- What is the purpose of the evaluation?
- Who will evaluate?
- What questions need to be answered?
- What data will be gathered and how?
- How will the data be analyzed?
- How will the evaluation be reported?

To understand the components of a summative program evaluation, refer to Chapter 14. As with needs assessment and formative evaluation, observation tools found in Chapter 12 can be used to gather some of the summative evaluation data.

Previously, each technical task of supervision (direct assistance, evaluation of teaching, group development, professional development, and curriculum development) was discussed separately. In reality, any effort to improve instruction must relate each task to the others. It is time to soften the boundaries between the tasks and show how action research can be the vehicle for their integration.

Action research is focused on the need to improve instruction, as perceived by the faculty. As instructional improvements are identified, faculty and supervisor plan related activities to be implemented in each of the technical tasks of supervision (see Figure 20.2).

Think of action research as a huge meteor falling into the middle of the supervision ocean. As it hits, it causes a rippling of water that activates the four seas of direct assistance, professional development, curriculum development, and group development. The rippling of water continues to increase in force until a giant wave gathers and crashes onto all instructional shores, sweeping away the old sand of past instructional failures and replacing it with the new sand of instructional improvement. Stepping away from the beach, let's look at the characteristics of successful action research.

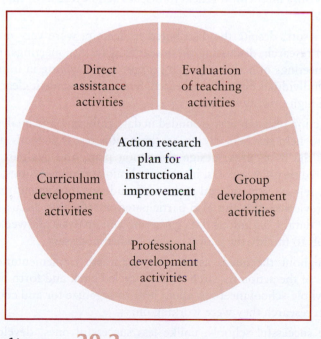

figure **20.2** **Action Research as the Core of Related Supervisory Activities**

Characteristics of Successful Action Research

Not all action research is successful. Sometimes action research never gets off the ground because teachers do not realize how much work is involved, never fully commit to the process, or are unable to organize for action research because of a lack of time, resources, or supervisory support. Some schools get off to a great start with action research but discontinue it after a year or so because key players leave the school, competing priorities and programs displace the action research, or the action research was viewed as a short-term project rather than an ongoing process of reflective inquiry and instructional improvement. A study by Gordon, Stiegelbauer, and Diehl (2008) compared more and less successful action research programs and found that more successful action research possessed certain characteristics that were not present in less successful programs. In the more successful programs:

- Supervisors distributed leadership for action research throughout the school. Principals asked teachers to join action research study groups, planning groups, evaluation teams, and so forth, and invited teachers to assume leadership roles like curriculum developer, demonstration teacher, peer coach, and so on. When supervisors met with teachers to discuss action research, they treated teachers as equals.

- Supervisors, despite the distributed leadership, were very much involved in the action research, discussing the research at faculty meetings, participating in formal meetings of action research groups, and engaging in informal conversations with individuals about the research. Supervisors made it clear the action research was a high priority to them.

- The action research was grounded in data gathering and analysis. Data were gathered to help teachers decide on the action research focus area, find out more about the focus area, design the action plan, and evaluate results. Data were gathered through surveys, interviews, brainstorming sessions, classroom observations, self-assessment, and reviews of student achievement records. Teachers not only reviewed data but also participated in reflective discussion on the meaning of the data. Continuous data gathering and analysis allowed the more successful schools to modify the action research when necessary.

- Throughout the needs assessment, planning, implementation, and evaluation stages of the action research teachers cycled back and forth between small-group and whole-school meetings about how to organize for and coordinate the stage of action research they were working on.

- More successful schools, unlike less successful ones, developed fairly detailed written action plans for their research and maintained written records of implementation and evaluation activities. This ongoing documentation may be an indicator of a more organized approach to action research.

- Extensive collaboration was in evidence at the more successful schools. The principal, members of the action research leadership team, and teachers throughout the school who were participating in the action research all reported extensive collaboration with each other. Collaboration led to increased trust and respect among members of the school community, which, in turn, led to increased collaboration.

- The more successful schools provided extensive support for teachers engaged in action research, including on-site professional development, funding for travel to conferences and workshops, instructional materials, and—most importantly—time to work on the action research. The successful schools also took full advantage of external resources, such as assistance from university experts, small grants to help fund the action research, and the use of critical friends from outside the school community who visited the school regularly to provide technical assistance and share feedback.

- The schools with more successful action research took an incremental, steady approach to action research, gradually expanding improvement activities and the number of teachers involved in action research. Less successful schools either went back and forth on their commitment to action research—sometimes restarting the research several times before it faded away—or spent considerable time and energy on action research during the first year only to sharply diminish commitment and activity during the second year.

- Schools with more successful action research not only met their improvement goals but experienced other positive outcomes not reported by less successful schools. Teachers at more successful schools reported increased collegiality, more experimentation and risk taking, and improved teaching and learning as a result of participating in action research. Teachers at the more successful schools also reported that action research had made reflective inquiry part of their school's culture.

Expanding Boundaries: Alternative Approaches to Action Research

The approach to action research emphasized in this book, as well as in most schools that use action research, is a problem-solving approach. A problem is identified, needs assessment data are gathered to find out more about the problem, an action plan is designed to solve the problem, the plan is implemented, and evaluation data are gathered to determine what progress was made and what revisions in the action plan might be needed. There are alternative approaches to action research that schools may wish to consider. Three such alternatives include interpretive action research, critical action research, and appreciative inquiry.

Interpretive Action Research

Teachers doing interpretive research are attempting to understand phenomena in schools and the meaning that participants make of those phenomena. Examples of phenomena that might be studied include a school's culture, classroom implementation of a new curriculum, and interactions between teachers and students during classroom discussions of controversial issues (Shapiro, 2014).

For a more detailed example, let us say a group of teachers decided to carry out an interpretive study on the use of a new inquiry-based science program. Research questions might include the following:

1. What does the teacher experience during inquiry learning?
2. What does the student experience during inquiry learning?
3. How does the teacher describe learning that results from inquiry learning?
4. How does the student describe learning that results from inquiry learning?

To gather data on these questions, interpretive researchers might observe inquiry lessons and take extensive field notes on class activities, interactions between teachers and students and among students, and so on. Additionally, the teacher-researchers might conduct interviews with teachers and students on their experiences with inquiry learning and their interpretation of learning resulting from inquiry lessons. The researchers probably would find that different participants experience the same learning activities differently and construct different interpretations of inquiry learning. Through dialogue on alternative perspectives and interpretations identified in the action research, teachers can gain a more holistic understanding of the phenomena being studied. The dialogue and increased understanding that results can be the foundation for improved practice. For instance, based on the results of their interpretive research, teachers in our inquiry-learning example might modify the way they present science problems to students.

Critical Action Research

Critical research examines and challenges established, taken-for-granted ways of doing things that support inequity, with an eye toward changing practice to increase equity (Hadfield, 2012; Keen Wong, 2014). In particular, critical research examines power relations that lead to inequity. External social, economic, and political forces that cause inequity also are examined, and ways to overcome those forces' negative effects are considered. An important process used by critical researchers is *praxis*, which denotes an interactive cycle of practice and theory building. In critical action research, praxis takes the form of an ongoing cycle of action and reflection aimed at emancipating groups and individuals from inequitable treatment.

Teachers engaged in critical action research on a high school's tracking system could begin the research by formulating a set of critical questions such as the following:

- Whose interests are served by the existence of the tracking system?
- What cultural values are reinforced by the tracking system? What cultural values are delegitimized?
- What power relations are present in the current tracking system?
- How does the tracking system reflect socioeconomic realities in the community that the school serves?
- How does the tracking system reflect ethnic and racial issues present in society?
- Who decides which students are placed in the various tracks?
- Who is placed at an advantage by the tracking system? Who is placed at a disadvantage?

Teachers who are engaged in critical action research find answers to these questions through repeated cycles of data gathering and dialogue on the meaning of the data. Eventually, the researchers begin to focus on a series of questions about changing the system to increase equity:

- How can we include parents and students in decisions about how best to meet student learning needs?
- How can the diverse learning needs of students be met in an emancipatory way?
- What ways of grouping students will benefit the least advantaged students?
- How can student grouping promote democracy and social justice?
- How can the growth and development of all students be placed in the center of the decision-making process at this school?

Again, teachers would go about finding answers to these questions through repeated cycles of data gathering and dialogue. In time, teachers and other members of the school community would use research results as the basis for changes in decision making, student grouping, curriculum, and instruction. The test for the effectiveness of critical action research is whether equity has been increased in a meaningful way.

Appreciative Inquiry

Appreciative inquiry, a model of action research developed outside of education, is becoming a powerful form of practitioner research in PK-12 schools. The original developers, Cooperrider and Srivastva (1987), proposed their appreciative approach as an alternative to the traditional problem-solving model; they believed that a group or organization is more likely to move forward if it builds on what is already positive about the group or organization, not by dwelling on existing problems. Appreciative inquiry departs from traditional models of action research in that it is focused on "how people think rather than what people do" and a commitment "to let go of control in planned change efforts and nurture a more improvisational approach to the action phase" (Bushe & Kassam, 2005, p. 176). Appreciative inquiry is based on five underlying principles and has five phases. Let's discuss the principles first, applying them to schools. Keep in mind that this approach also can be used by a small group of educators with common responsibilities within the school.

The constructionist principle: Members of a school community have socially constructed the present reality of school life, thus they can co-construct a better reality for the future.

The principle of simultaneity: Inquiry about a school situation cannot really be separated from intervention—inquiry and intervention are really two sides of the same coin.

The poetic principle: Members of the school community can best appreciate the positive aspects of the school by recollecting and telling stories about those positive aspects. Such positive stories can be the foundation for future growth.

The anticipatory principle: When members of a school community have co-constructed a positive vision of the future, describe that future in vivid detail, and believe they can make that vision a reality, they tend to naturally move toward that vision.

The positive principle: Positive images of the past, present, and future are accompanied by hope and confidence, celebration of accomplishments as the school moves forward, and positive energy propelling the school toward its vision.

The original model of appreciative inquiry included four phases—*discovery, dream, design,* and *destiny* (Ludema, Cooperrider, & Barrett, 2001). A more recent model has added a "fifth D" at the beginning of the process—*define* (Tschannen-Moran & Tschannen-Moran, 2011). Let's briefly describe each of the five phases in the 5-D Cycle.

Define: Consistent with the principles of appreciative inquiry, a research topic is stated in positive terms. For school groups that have not previously used appreciative inquiry, prior to topic selection introductory exercises and discussions may be necessary to move participants away from the traditional problem-solving mindset and toward the appreciative approach.

Discovery: Educators discuss what they value most about their school, their work, and their colleagues. Typically, this is done by the educators breaking into pairs and interviewing each other, then reporting interview results to the entire group, with the group then identifying positive themes that cut across the interview data. These positive themes become the foundation for the dream phase.

Dream: In the dream phase the educators focus on the research topic and envision a better future in the topic area. Part of the dreaming is about how the positive aspects of the school described in the discover phase can be utilized in addressing the research topic. Another part of the dream phase consists of envisioning a better future relative to the research topic. The educators develop a rich, detailed image of where they want to be by the end of the research.

Design: In the design phase, the educators develop a tentative plan for how they are going to achieve the dream articulated in the previous stage. This phase begins with brainstorming possible ways to make the dream a reality; the emphasis here is on generating creative ideas, not judging the merit of those ideas. After brainstorming, the educators reach consensus on the ideas that are the most consistent with the school's positive attributes and most exciting to them, and then integrate those strategies in an action plan. The design process includes commitments from educators to assist with carrying out the agreed-upon strategies.

Destiny: In the destiny phase the educators construct the new reality envisioned in the dream phase by carrying out the strategies identified in the design phase. This phase is more about continued exploration then typical program implementation. The destiny phase is characterized by a great deal of flexibility; the strategies developed in the design phase are modified as necessary based on their effects and changing conditions. Not every educator in the school may have been involved in the previous phases, but during the destiny phase more and more members of the school community are invited to join the process, and are drawn into the research because of its appreciative stance and positive effects.

Appreciative inquiry is cyclical. For example, a school might go through all five phases during a school year and then start a new cycle the following year with either a revised or a new research topic. Although appreciative inquiry is not yet widely used in PK-12 education, in cases where the authors have facilitated or observed it in schools, teachers have responded very positively. The only difficulty has been the "mind shift" required to transition from the problem-solving view that dominates education to the appreciative view. Once this shift is made, however, we find that educators embrace appreciative inquiry and use it successfully.

Shared Governance for Action Research

> As a paradigm of collaborative, participatory, and democratic inquiry, teacher action research is the intellectual and affective heart and soul of a knowledge democracy.
>
> (Pine, 2009, p. 27)

A shortcoming of earlier studies of school improvement and action research has been the lack of descriptions of how individual schools or districts went about the process of change. Achieving "a cause beyond oneself" in pursuing collaborative and collective instructional goals for students sounds admirable, but how does a supervisor initiate and sustain such efforts?

What follows is one explanation using case studies from the public schools that are part of the League of Professional Schools (Allen & Calhoun, 2009). The model of shared governance and schoolwide instructional change has been adapted and used in elementary, middle, and secondary schools in Georgia, South Carolina, Vermont, Michigan, and the United States Department of Defense Dependent Schools in Europe.

---

small-group exercise **20.1**

Planning a Schoolwide Action Research Project

Your small group will first describe a school context and then develop a skeletal action plan for a schoolwide action research project at the school. The focus of the action research should be one of common interest to all group members. The action plan will be for the first year of the action research.

1. School information
   - What is the school level (high school, middle school, elementary school)?
   - What type of community does the school serve (urban, suburban, or rural)?
   - How many students are in the school?
   - What is the school's student ethnic/racial and SES breakdown?
2. What is the general focus area for the action research? (Assume the focus area has been identified through a schoolwide needs assessment.)
3. What is the specific goal of the action research?
4. What are the different groups that will be involved in the action research?

5. What professional development activities will be provided to help teachers move toward the action research goal?
6. What types of curriculum development will take place to help the school move toward the action research goal?
7. What types of direct assistance will be provided to individual teachers to help them implement the action research?
8. What types of formative teacher evaluation will assist the action research?
9. How will the action research be evaluated?
   - What will formative evaluation (to make sure the action plan is being implemented as planned and to improve the action research as it is being implemented) consist of?
   - What will summative evaluation (to make decisions about the success level of the first year of the action research and necessary revisions for the second year) consist of?

Premises

Three declarative premises underlie shared governance:

1. Every professional in the school who so desires can be involved in making decisions about schoolwide instructional improvements.

2. Any professional in the school who does not desire to is not obligated to be involved in making decisions about schoolwide instructional improvements.

3. Once a decision is made about schoolwide instructional improvements, all staff must implement the decision.

Thus, an individual can choose to be or not to be part of the decision-making process. However, once decisions are made, all individuals must implement the agreed-upon actions. Operationalizing these premises allows a school to move forward with people who are interested in participating, without forcing any individual who is not interested into a corner. Afterward, an individual who did not wish to participate in making decisions has no grounds for complaint about decisions regarding schoolwide instructional actions. Perhaps when the next issue, concern, or topic is brought up for schoolwide action, nonparticipants who have been disgruntled with previous decisions will have a renewed interest in participating.

Principles

The principles in operating shared governance for instructional improvement are as follows:

1. **One person, one vote.** Each representative has the same rights, responsibilities, and voting power as any other representative. Each teacher who sits on the representative schoolwide council has the same vote as the school principal or any other administrator or formal supervisor.

2. **Limit decisions to schoolwide instruction within the control and sphere of responsibility of the school.** Action research and shared governance involves the core of a school's existence: curriculum, teaching, and learning. Areas for decision making should be schoolwide and instructional. Issues of day-to-day administration, contracts, school board policies, other schools, and personnel are not the concerns of shared governance for schoolwide action research. The scope of concerns for deliberations, decisions, and actions is always grounded in the question: What should *we* be doing *here* with *our* school to improve learning for *our* students?

3. **Authentic feedback necessitates small groups.** Large meetings result in input from the most confident, the loudest, and the most powerful persons—who are not necessarily the wisest, most insightful, or most interested persons. A true forum for intellectual discourse is a small group (ideally, 7 to 11 members); so, shared governance in large schools must include small groups.

Operational Model

The work of Schmuck and Runkel (1994) has provided the basis for an operational model for shared governance, action research, and school improvement that uses the premises of individual choice of involvement and implementation by all and the principles of one person, one vote; focus on teaching; and small groups. The model discussed here is a compilation of various models used by schools in the League of Professional Schools (Allen & Calhoun, 2009). Many schools use comparable models of operation and have their own specific versions. The goal is not to advocate a particular model of shared governance but to achieve the premises and principles of shared governance and action research, leading to a purposeful, collective, and thoughtful school—a school that is the center of inquiry.

The Formal Groups. Shared governance in this model involves three groups (see Figure 20.3). The *executive council* is a 7- to 11-member body, consisting of a majority of teachers with administrators. Parent and student representatives can serve as well. (For more details about representation of other groups, see Glickman, 1993.) Teachers could be democratically chosen from liaison groups (described in the following paragraph) or from among grade-level heads, team leaders, department heads, and union representatives. They could be elected at large from the faculty, or some combination of election and appointment could be used. They hold a term of at least three years and move off the council at staggered times. Teachers serve as chairperson and co-chairperson of the executive council. The principal is a member of the committee with the same rights and responsibilities as any other member. The executive council's responsibility is solely to act on and monitor schoolwide instructional improvement recommendations. *The council does not make recommendations;* it is an approving board. Recommendations must come from task force groups within the school. The

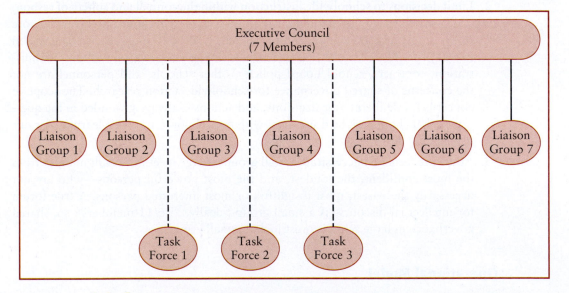

figure 20.3 **Groups Involved in Shared Governance for Action Research**

executive council does not involve itself in administrative matters, community relations, school board policies, personnel matters, or issues that are departmental in nature. It acts on instructional improvement recommendations that the faculty has the legal power to carry out. This differentiation between instructional and administrative responsibilities helps avoid problems that can arise from delving into matters beyond the school's own control.

Liaison groups are formal groups set up as communication links between the faculty and executive council concerning needs, reactions, opinions, and ideas about schoolwide instruction. Liaison groups are an important unit for considering the faculty's ideas and opinions about assessing instructional goals and responding to proposed recommendations. For example, in the case of a school with 50 teachers, there could be seven liaison groups consisting of approximately seven faculty members each. An alphabetized list of all faculty names is gathered and each person is assigned a number from 1 to 7. All 1s go to liaison group 1, all 2s go to liaison group 2, and so forth. This assignment procedure ensures that members in each liaison group come from various departments and grade levels. Each liaison group is a microcosm of the entire school. Each group elects a representative to the council. The executive council member can (a) call the liaison group together from time to time for a brief meeting to review a specific recommendation under executive council consideration, (b) gather written opinions about a particular proposal, or (c) simply drop by and talk to the various liaison group members.

Task forces are the last type of group shown in Figure 20.3. These ad hoc task groups of volunteers are formed after the executive council has solicited feedback from all the liaison groups about perceived schoolwide instructional needs and reviewed any existing data on schoolwide instruction. The executive council then targets priority instructional areas for the next one to three years. Schoolwide priorities might be such matters as increasing instructional time, coordinating curriculum, improving student attitudes, teaching higher-order thinking, increasing student success rates, improving school discipline, improving school and classroom climate, improving the quality of feedback to students, or improving test scores.

Once the needs for improvement have been selected by the executive council, ad hoc task force groups are formed by recruiting volunteers who have an interest in and a commitment to the particular topic. At least one executive council member serves on each task force, but this person normally does not serve as chair of the task force. The task force volunteers meet, review their task, select their own chairperson, schedule meetings, and set a timeline for making a final recommendation for schoolwide action to the executive council. Depending on the topic, one task force might meet three times over three weeks to make a recommendation, whereas another task force might meet every other week for five months before making a recommendation.

Decision-Making Procedures. When the task force is ready to make a recommendation, it makes its report in three parts: (1) goals and objectives, (2) action plan

(What will be done, by whom, and when?), and (3) evaluation (How will the success of actions be known?). The executive council discusses the recommendations and either makes an immediate decision to approve (most councils use a consensus vote to approve a first-time recommendation) or, without the required vote, tables the recommendation until the next meeting. During the interim, the executive council members can discuss the recommendation and check with their respective liaison groups to gather input from the entire faculty. At the next meeting, a second vote can be taken. (Most councils use a two-thirds vote to approve a tabled recommendation.) By the second vote, the council will have a good sense of total faculty receptivity and the chances of successful implementation. Some issues are deemed so important by the council that the final decision is made by going back to the entire faculty, parents, and students.

Implementation. After a decision has been made, the executive council (with the task force) announces the approved plan to the school. The task force then disbands, and the executive council implements the plan. It becomes the responsibility of the executive council (including the principal) to enforce the schoolwide decisions and to oversee action research that monitors and evaluates the results.

Suggestions for Assisting Action Research

Our work with schools using action research leads to additional suggestions for increasing the quality of teacher research. First, it is important that teachers receive basic preparation in gathering and analyzing data. Here we are not talking about making every teacher an expert in research design and statistical analysis. Rather, teachers should be introduced to a variety of simple data-gathering methods, both quantitative and qualitative. Also, teachers need to learn simple methods for reviewing and summarizing data and drawing data-based conclusions.

Second, to ensure that no teachers or students are placed at academic, social, or emotional risk, the school governance body should establish a set of ethical guidelines for action research, along with a process for reviewing research proposals to make sure they comply with the guidelines.

Third, resources need to be provided for action research teams. The most important resource needed by teacher-researchers is *time* to plan action research, gather and analyze data, and implement action plans.

Finally, teachers should be provided opportunities to share action research with the school community, and even with teachers from other schools. Sharing action research gives recognition to the teacher-researchers, serves as a basis for reflective dialogue among teachers, and provides other teachers with ideas for improving instruction in their own classrooms and schools (Congreve, 2015).

Supervision provides a focus, structure, and time for teachers to be engaged in dialogue, debate, research, decisions, and actions about instruction. Without focus, teachers will not discuss teaching, because it has not been an accepted norm for discussion in most schools. Without structure, there are no clear apparatuses, procedures, and rules for how decisions are made and implemented. Without time, there is no functional or symbolic expression that teachers have the capacity to make collective and wise instructional decisions on behalf of students.

> ✔ **Check Your Understanding 20.0**   Click here to gauge your understanding of the key concepts presented in this chapter.

REFLECTIVE EXERCISE

The example of critical action research provided in this chapter was centered on a school's tracking system. Identify a situation in a school you are familiar with that would be a worthy focus for critical action research. Develop a set of critical questions to be addressed in the research. For each question you create, what types of data could be gathered in order to answer that question? How would an action research team go about gathering each type of data?

part 6

Cultural Tasks of Supervision

The chapters in Part 6 address cultural tasks of supervision that both transcend and utilize the technical tasks. Chapter 21 explores alternative theories of change, describes school cultures of continuous improvement, and recommends changes in the conditions of teaching. Chapter 22 discusses achievement gaps among diverse groups, societal problems and cultural clashes that cause inequity, and how culturally responsive schools and teaching can increase equity for diverse socioeconomic, racial, and ethnic groups; females; sexual minorities; and students with disabilities. Finally, Chapter 23 compares schools as organizations to schools as communities, describes attributes of authentic school communities, and urges schools to engage with the communities they serve.

chapter 21

Facilitating Change

Learning Outcomes for This Chapter

After reading this chapter, you should be able to:

1. Summarize the foci of chaos theory.

2. Explain meta-narratives, and the position of postmodern theory regarding the meta-narrative.

3. List eight key concepts in educational change theory.

4. State what chaos theory, postmodernism, and education change theory have in common regarding the predictability of change within complex systems.

5. Summarize what types of policies the authors maintain are needed as part of changing the conditions of teaching.

Questions to Reflect On as You Read This Chapter

1. Reflect for a few moments on a failed change effort at a school with which you are familiar, then reflect for a few moments on a successful change effort. What were the differences between the two change efforts that led one of them to fail and the other one to succeed?

2. The authors discuss seven aspects of chaos theory they believe can be applied to school change. As you read about each aspect, reflect on whether you have observed its presence in schools.

3. Which beliefs of postmodernism described in this chapter do you agree with? Which postmodern beliefs do you disagree with? Which postmodern beliefs do you need to reflect on further?

4. Reflect on a school that you are familiar with. Which of the 12 cultural norms of continuous improvement are present in the school? What do you believe are the affects of the presence or absence of each of the norms?

5. In the last section of this chapter, the authors recommend seven changes in the conditions of teachers. Which of those recommendations do you agree with, and why? Which of those recommendations do you disagree with, and why?

The imagery of educational reform says more about hope and good intentions than it does about anything else. That the road to hell is indeed paved with good intentions is an adage quite appropriate to the history of educational reform.

(Sarason, 1990, p. 129)

The need for educational change is as apparent as the fact that our world is continuously changing—changing at an ever-increasing rate. Changes in U.S. demographics, culture, environment, science, technology, and economy mean that our schools must change if they are to prepare students to be successful and contributing members of society and if society is going to offer all of its citizens life, liberty, and the pursuit of happiness.

Unfortunately, most efforts at school change fail to improve schools or student learning, and many make things worse. Why do we continue to experience what Sarason (1990) calls "the predictable failure of educational reform"? Sarason argues that one reason is that those attempting to bring about change (including those inside and outside schools) have only a superficial understanding of school culture, including the power relationships within that culture. Fullan (1997) believes that the complexity of educational change is a big part of its difficulty:

Take any educational policy or problem and start listing all of the forces that could figure in the solution and that would need to be influenced to make for productive change. Then, take the idea that unplanned factors are inevitable—government policy changes or gets constantly redefined. Key leaders leave, important contact people are shifted to another role, new technology is invented, immigration increases, recession reduces available resources, a bitter conflict erupts, and so on. Finally, realize that every new variable that enters the equation—those unpredictable but inevitable noise factors—produce ten other ramifications, which in turn produce tens of other reactions and on and on. (p. 33)

Evans (1996) proposes that the traditional model used for most change efforts in schools, the *rational–structural model,* is the reason that most change efforts fail. This model assumes that the organization and surrounding environment are stable and predictable and that planning for change is a rational, objective, and linear process that leads to a detailed blueprint for change. As described by Evans:

Whether the blueprint calls for new outputs or for greater efficiency in current outputs it focuses on changes in the organization's structure and in its tasks, roles, and rules.

The methodology for innovation is almost entirely top-down in nature, a combination of dissemination and pressure. There may be much lip service paid to "participation," but this usually means getting people to "go along," to have a "sense of ownership." The implementation goal is to have staff adopt the expert plan as is. This requires explanation, persuasion, training, and incentives; if these fail to produce the proper results, it requires mandates, requirements, and policies. (p. 8)

Evans argues that change efforts based on the rational–structural model have a high failure rate. Typically, Evans notes, teachers are blamed for the failure, when in fact the designers and the change model they use are responsible. Repeated failures at change can severely reduce a school's capacity for change in the future. Again, according to Evans:

Most attempts at collective change in education seem to fail, and failure means frustration, wasted time, feelings of incompetence and lack of support, and disillusionment. . . . The more that teachers or others have had negative experiences with previous implementation attempts in the district or elsewhere, the more cynical or apathetic they will be about the next change presented regardless of the merit of the new idea or proposal. (pp. 73–74)

Repeated failures can create a reflexive resistance to change, with teachers and others sabotaging new change efforts in their early stages.

Given the facts that (1) schools need to change if they are going to meet the needs of today's students and society and (2) most change efforts fail, what are we to do? Change experts have been urging us for years to consider alternative theories on change that go beyond the rational–structural approach. Sarason (1990) warns, "If you start by accepting the present structure, if you insist that those who seek to change it must guarantee ahead of time that it will work, you guarantee one thing: nothing will change" (p. 173). Fullan (1997) argues, "There are fundamental reasons why controlling strategies don't work. . . . The solution lies in better ways of thinking about, and dealing with, inherently unpredictable processes" (p. 33). In the next three sections of this chapter, we will introduce new ways of thinking about change. We will discuss chaos theory and postmodern theory as well as a number of innovative change theories from within the field of education.

Video Illustration

Watch the following video about Fenway High School. What characteristics make the campus different from a conventional school?

Chaos Theory

Chaos theory cuts across a wide number of disciplines, including biology, chemistry, mathematics, meteorology, and physics. The "new science" of chaos has two foci: (1) the exploration of the hidden order that exists within a chaotic system and (2) the study of how self-organization emerges from chaos (Akmansoy & Kartal, 2014; Hayles, 1990; Larsson & Dahlin, 2012; Mason, 2008; Murphy, 2011; Reigeluth, 2004). Chaos theory involves a number of related concepts, not all of which are relevant to change in schools and classrooms. Those aspects of chaos theory that are relevant to educational change are reviewed here, along with potential applications for school change.

Nonlinearity

In a linear system, simple cause-and-effect relationships exist: *A* causes *B*, which causes *C*, and so on. A linear system is analogous to a line of dominoes. When the first domino is knocked down, it knocks down the second, the second knocks down the third, and so on.

A chaotic system is *nonlinear* (Krishnamurthy, 2015). A nonlinear system is analogous to bowling. When the ball is rolled toward a set of pins, myriad variables come into play and interact with each other. The slightest variation in how the bowling ball is released may result in a strike in one frame and a split or a gutter ball in the next.

School improvement efforts traditionally have treated the change process as linear, with each step in the change effort affecting the next step in a simple cause-and-effect relationship. But despite linear organization charts and improvement plans, schools are not linear systems; they are nonlinear, chaotic systems. An implication for this reality is that a change effort should be viewed as an organic process, not as a blueprint to be drawn and followed:

> Here the metaphor for change is the growth and development of a complex organism (for example, a human being) rather than the operation of a simple machine. A complex organism begins life at a relatively small stage. Its development is not completely predictable. Its health requires interdependence, consistency, and balance among its various subsystems. Finally, organisms that flourish tend to be adaptable to changing environments. In fact, they are themselves in a constant state of change or "becoming." (Gordon, 1992, p. 73)

The fact that schools are nonlinear systems means that change cannot be controlled from above. It can only be nurtured by promoting a culture for change. The supervisor attempting to nurture such a culture needs to remember Fullan's (2009) admonition not to believe that the change the supervisor envisions is the one that should or even could be implemented. Rather, it is the interaction of the supervisor's ideas about change with ideas from other members of the school community—and the interaction of the change process with many other variables within the school culture—that will determine the direction of change.

Complexity

Chaotic systems take complex forms, making their precise measurement difficult if not impossible (Gleick, 2008).

The complexity of schools means that improvement needs and the level of success of improvement efforts cannot be precisely measured solely by external research on effective schools, legislated standards, or the results of standardized achievement tests. Keedy and Achilles (1997) argue that *local* educators must ask these questions:

1. Why they want to change
2. What they want to achieve
3. How to go about the change process (p. 116)

We would argue that local educators need to ask a fourth question as well: How can we measure success? Keedy and Achilles recommend that supervisors and teachers reach consensus on answers to these questions through collaborative, critical inquiry informed by awareness of the change process.

Butterfly Effect

Theoretical meteorologist Edward Lorenz made the term *butterfly effect* famous when he argued that a butterfly stirring its wings in Beijing today could unleash powerful storms in New York City next month. In technical terms, this phenomenon is known as *sensitive dependence on initial conditions*. It means that a small and seemingly unrelated event in one part of a system can have enormous effects on other parts of the system.

One implication of sensitive dependence on initial conditions is the impossibility of predicting the long-term future of any chaotic system. In this respect, the butterfly effect applies to school change: It is impossible to predict the long-term effects of school improvement efforts. This does not mean that formal planning for school change should not take place. Rather, a different type of planning is needed. Planning in a chaotic system like a school should be medium range (1 to 2 years) rather than long range (5 to 10 years). It should emphasize general goals, broad guidelines, and built-in flexibility (Gordon, 1992). Formal planning in an unpredictable system needs to focus on process rather than product, with the goal of producing "a stream of wise decisions designed to achieve the mission of the organization" (Patterson, Purkey, & Parker, 1986, p. 19).

Fractals

A *fractal* is a geometric shape that is similar to itself at different scales (Ambika, 2015; Gleick, 2008). Midsized branches of a tree are remarkably similar in shape to the larger branches from which they come. Smaller branches, in turn, are the same shape as the midsized branches from which they come, and so on. Other examples of fractals include coastlines, mountains, clouds, rivers, weather patterns, and the human vascular system. Complex social systems can also reveal self-similarity on different scales: At each level of the system, specific patterns of organization and culture reappear.

Like fractals in nature, schools reveal self-similarity in different scales. For example, a schoolwide staff-development day, a department meeting, a classroom lesson, and a hallway interaction between a teacher and a student might all reveal the same cultural characteristics. Thus, reflective inquiry at the school, team, classroom, and individual level can help educators better understand their school culture, needed change, and pathways to improvement.

Feedback Mechanisms

Chaotic systems contain *feedback loops* that allow outputs to feed back into the system as inputs (Chatterjee, 2013). Feedback can bring stability or turbulence to a system. For example, a thermostat is a feedback mechanism that causes stability in the temperature. Conversely, when the sound from a loudspeaker feeds back through a microphone, it is rapidly magnified to create a disruptive shriek (Gleick, 2008). Feedback can also cause a system to move toward greater levels of complexity. Physicist Joseph Ford, for example, has referred to evolution as "chaos with feedback" (cited in Gleick, 1987, p. 314).

Once school improvement efforts are underway, feedback becomes essential for monitoring and assessing change (Beabout, 2010). Feedback mechanisms need to be created and maintained. Feedback can take the form of student performance data, survey results, quality circles, third-party reviews, and so forth. The important thing is that meaningful data on the results of change efforts be made available to teachers and that they be given opportunities to reflect on the data and redirect their change efforts accordingly.

Turbulence

Turbulence can be caused from disturbances inside or outside a system. Consider a river, flowing smoothly until it runs through a bed of rocks. The water is then disturbed and becomes unstable. Turbulence can also be caused by a heavy rain that greatly increases the volume of water flowing through the riverbed. The more complex a system is, the more subject it is to instability due to turbulence. If the instability becomes great enough, a point of phase transition is reached; sudden, radical change takes place, resulting in either reorganization or disintegration.

All complex systems experience turbulence, but efforts at change tend to increase its frequency and intensity. Turbulence is not always negative, however. Without some disturbance, the system would remain in a steady state and improvement would not be possible (Gleick, 2008). However, too much turbulence (from outside or inside the school) can cause school improvement efforts to disintegrate (Johnson, 2013). Keedy and Achilles (1997, p. 115) have written that supervisors and teachers should construct a *normative consensus,* "a collective, critically-examined, and contextually-based agreement" of essential school norms that they can hold fast to during times of turbulence. The authors have maintained that it is this normative consensus (referred to earlier in this text as "a cause beyond oneself") that can hold a school together during the change process.

Strange Attractors

Chaotic systems are not truly random. Rather, they possess patterns that are extremely complex and unpredictable but stay within certain parameters (Gleick, 2008). *Strange attractors* are "deeply encoded structures" within chaotic systems. According to Hayles (1990):

> The discovery that chaos possesses deep structures of order is all the more remarkable because of the wide range of systems that demonstrate this behavior. They range from lynx fur returns to outbreaks of measles epidemics, from the rise and fall of the Nile River to eye movements in schizophrenics. (p. 10)

Chaos theory informs us that order and chaos are not opposites. Rather, in the words of Wheatley (1992), they are "mirror images, one containing the other" (p. 11).

Is it possible for supervisors and teachers to create strange attractors within schools that will, albeit in unpredictable ways, create permanent patterns leading to school improvement? Policy makers have attempted to do just that, mandating such structures as site-based management, shared decision making, and parent choice; however, such external mandates have all failed to lead to patterns of improvement. According to Keedy (1995), the design that should be embedded throughout the social fabric of schools—for our purpose, a strange attractor—is student-centered learning.

Postmodern Theory

Postmodernism is a broad theory that cuts across a variety of fields, including philosophy, epistemology, theology, language studies, psychology, ethics, art, architecture, and feminist studies. Atkinson (2002) summarizes the characteristics of postmodernism as follows:

- Resistance to certainty and resolution
- Rejection of fixed notions of reality, knowledge, or method
- Acceptance of complexity, of lack of clarity, and of multiplicity
- Acknowledgment of subjectivity, contradiction, and irony
- Irreverence for traditions of philosophy or morality
- Deliberate intent to unsettle assumptions and presuppositions
- Refusal to accept boundaries or hierarchies in ways of thinking
- Disruption of binaries that define things as either/or (p. 74)

With this overview, let us delve deeper into the meaning of postmodernism and its implications for school change.

The theory of postmodernism is perhaps best understood by discussing what it is *against*. First and foremost, it is opposed to *metanarratives*. Hart (2004) defines a metanarrative as "something that overarches all human activities and seeks to guide them: the natural primacy of human consciousness, the fair distribution of wealth in society, and the steady march of moral progress" (p. 2). Postmodernism is antimodernism, which means it stands against many of the "-isms" that are part of that broad category. Postmodernism includes the following:

- *Antiessentialism,* which argues there is no natural human nature. All that we are has been formed by our history and culture.
- *Antirealism,* which means there is no reality external to what the human mind conceives as reality. Human language does not represent reality.
- *Antifoundationalism,* which holds there is no basic knowledge or belief that cannot be challenged.
- *Antireductionism,* which argues the whole cannot be understood or explained by analyzing its parts.

Postmodernism holds that although individuals and groups are greatly influenced by the cultures to which they belong, cultures are not homogeneous. Rather, individuals and groups within particular cultures have diverse perspectives, beliefs, values, interests, and needs. There is little value in making generalizations within particular cultures, let alone across cultures. Differences among individuals and groups must be recognized and honored. Postmodernism argues that knowledge is socially constructed within a particular context at a particular time; hence, knowledge changes from one context to another and over time. Since individuals and groups exist within different perspectives, there is no single truth about any complex phenomenon; rather there are multiple truths. Like knowledge, truth can change with changing conditions (Uzun, 2014). Cilliers (1998) warns us that all of this does not mean that individuals and groups are totally isolated with nothing in common. Rather, as social beings, individuals and groups form social networks and engage in dialogue, and thus broad commonalities do exist, although these commonalities may be expressed in different ways and may change over time.

Power is another concept addressed by postmodernists. Power relations within a culture are highly important. Significant change efforts are likely to challenge existing power relations; thus, it is important for these relations to be recognized and addressed. Despite appearances, power is not really possessed by any one individual or group; any member of a culture can exercise power.

Postmodernism asserts that there are multiple ways of framing problems and many ways of developing solutions. The problem-solving process should respect alternative perspectives and take an eclectic approach, synthesizing ideas of different groups and individuals. Postmodernism rejects the notion of the internal or external expert identifying and solving problems. Contexts, players, and circumstances vary greatly from culture to culture and even among different situations within a single culture. Thus, the expertise needed to frame and solve problems is unique to particular cultures and situations.

Postmodernists believe that neither individual nor collaborative efforts are the best path to change. Rather, combined individual and collaborative efforts are most likely to result in change. However, change is always unpredictable; it may or may not lead to real progress. Progress, when it does occur, will be at the local level, ungeneralizable to other cultures or even to future change efforts within the local culture. Moreover, the value of change is always relative. Change that is perceived as progress in one culture may not be perceived as progress in another. Indeed, different perceptions of change may be held within the same culture.

Many critics of postmodernism consider it to be ill defined, overly cynical, and sometimes self-contradictory. Others consider it a natural and authentic reaction to the excesses of modernity. We do not agree with all that is proposed under the banner of postmodernism (neither do most postmodernists!), but we do believe that many postmodern observations can be applied to educational change. For instance, postmodernism calls into question metanarratives long associated with educational change, such as the rational–structural approach discussed earlier in this chapter. Postmodernism warns us that grand schemes for improving schools (No Child Left Behind, state-mandated curricula, and popular commercial programs) are by themselves not likely to bring about desired change.

Under the postmodern view, school change efforts are greatly influenced by the local context, including the community the school serves, the school culture, and varied perspectives within that culture. Thus, an early part of the change process might involve collaboratively studying the community and school culture, including existing power relations and their effects. Doing so would require gathering and analyzing data on the school and community and engaging in reflective dialogue on implications for school change.

Postmodernism reminds educators that knowledge gained from self-study is socially constructed knowledge and best developed by inviting and synthesizing multiple perspectives, values, and experiences. The postmodern view assumes that even when general agreement on needed change is reached, different groups and individuals within the school will conceptualize that change in different ways—thus, the need for ongoing dialogue, analyzing the change process from multiple perspectives along the way. The supervisor and other change leaders should realize that different groups and individuals will require different types of assistance during implementation, that implementation will occur in different ways in different classrooms, and that perceptions of progress will vary. The progress and effects of the change effort will be unpredictable, therefore requiring continuous feedback from teachers and others and, in all likelihood, ongoing modification of the change process.

Education Change Theory

Over the last several years, a growing body of new theory on school change has emerged in the educational literature (examples include Bain, 2007; Day, Gu, & Sammons, 2016; Evans, 1996; Fullan, 1997, 2002, 2003, 2005, 2006, 2007, 2009; Gordon, 2008; Hall & Hord, 2006; Hargreaves & Goodson, 2006; Hargreaves, Lieberman, Fullan, & Hopkins, 1998; Hopkins, 2007; Levin & Fullan, 2008; Senge et al., 2000; Zmuda, Kuklis, & Kline, 2004). Much of this recent theory is based on the study of actual efforts at school change. As one might expect, the experts who present theories on school change do not agree completely, but they do agree in large part on key concepts. We will present several of those concepts in the following sections. As you review them, note how different this emergent change theory is from traditional theories on how to change schools. Also, compare recent education change theory to the chaos and postmodern theories described earlier. We think you will conclude that there is a fair amount of consistency across these more recent theories, despite their widely different sources.

Capacity

Many schools lack the capacity to initiate significant improvement efforts with a reasonable chance of success. Poor communication, low trust levels, and the absence of collaboration are all typical reasons cited for low readiness. All of these problems are part of the school's *culture,* which is a complex system of relationships, norms, practices, beliefs, and assumptions.

A good first step toward improving a school's capacity for change is for members of the school community to study and critique their own school culture. What are the school's common instructional practices? What beliefs, values, and assumptions underlie these practices? How do these practices affect teachers and students?

Another focus for self-study is how past or current change efforts have interacted with various aspects of the school's culture. Determining this will help educators to understand just how complex school change is. As Stiegelbauer (2008) notes, "Change in practice requires change in behaviors, skills, attitudes, beliefs, and, frequently, ways that people work with one another. Each of these is a kind of innovation in itself and a reason that change is always complex" (p. 122). Boyd (1992) argues that any significant change affects the entire school:

> A school is a complex organism. It is not just a building with people inside. To change schools it is necessary to consider the effects of change on all parts of the organism. Each part is dependent upon the other parts and all parts react to changes in any other part. (p. 1)

The complexity of change described by Stiegelbauer and Boyd can be best understood by teachers when they engage in reflective inquiry and dialogue on the interactive effects of change and culture in their own school.

Beyond developing a better understanding of the complexities of school culture and change efforts, a school can increase its capacity for change in a number of ways. One critical process is trust building. Allen and Glickman (1998) remind us that "trust is built by actions, not words" (p. 514). Teachers trust supervisors when they are allowed to share in decision making about change, when their opinions are respected, when the commitments made to them are consistently kept, and when they are supported during the change process. Supervisors trust teachers "when they observe that, given adequate information and opportunities to interact with each other, teachers are capable of making decisions that reflect a school wide perspective and concern for all children" (Allen & Glickman, 1998, p. 514).

Another way to develop readiness is to create opportunities for regular dialogue across the school community. Gordon, Stiegelbauer, and Diehl (2008) found that schools with a high capacity for change provided for cycles of small-group and whole-school dialogue. At the small-group level, dialogue took place in a variety of groups: leadership, grade level, content area, task force, and so on. At the whole-school level, dialogue involved small groups reporting to the large group and the large group holding general discussions of how information and ideas shared by small groups could be integrated within the schoolwide change effort. Bain (2007) recommends that schools establish communication networks:

> Networks make collaboration possible. They disperse control in self-organizing schools because they permit the ready flow of feedback to all levels in the school. . . . [In different areas of the network,] teachers work together in teaching and learning teams, instead of working alone. Teams are employed to capture the potential of small-world relationships by making it possible for individual teachers to engage in constant formal and informal professional communication. (p. 55)

Traditional change models call for the organization to develop a vision before proceeding with change. However, Fullan (1997) argues that, although a shared vision is necessary for success, the vision should not be established prior to initiating change. "Vision emerges from, more than it precedes, action" (p. 42). Fullan's rationale for this statement is that a truly *shared vision* must emerge from the joint work of leaders and teachers over time as they engage in the change process. Fullan also argues that, because of the complexity of schools and change, even after a school vision has emerged, it must be redefined over time to evolve with changing conditions.

An alternative to creating a vision prior to initiating change is for the school community to develop a broad set of principles that will direct the change process. Some examples of agreed-on principles include the following:

- Change will be the result of collaborative efforts among leaders, teachers, and representatives of the community that the school serves.
- Change will be informed by both external research and by data gathered within the school and community.
- Change will take place within a framework of democratic governance.
- Change efforts will consider the diversity among students and adults in the school community.
- Change efforts will consider the need to reduce the achievement gap between different student groups.

Of course, each school needs to develop its own set of change principles, and consensus even on broad principles like those just listed will require considerable study, reflection, and dialogue. Once principles are agreed upon, however, they should be embedded deeply in future change efforts.

Studying the school's culture and the change process, building trust, engaging in dialogue, and establishing change principles all can help the school develop a capacity for *initiating* change. Developing that capacity, however, is only the beginning of the change process.

▶ Video Illustration

As you view this video, assess the principal's efforts to build capacity in the school where she has recently assumed leadership. What do you think of her strategies?

Commitment

How do teachers develop a commitment to change? On the one hand, merely mandating change does not work. On the other hand, one cannot expect teachers to take ownership of change at the beginning of the change process—before they have worked with the change over time, before they understand all of the implications of the change, and before the change has shown positive effects (Fullan, 2007; Lukacs, 2015). Nolan (2007) suggests that one way to build commitment for change is to ask teachers to "interrogate the status quo":

> Questioning concerning why we do things the way we do and how effective those strategies are should be the starting point. Action research and data-driven decision-making can be powerful tools for raising questions about the status quo and examining the efficiency of current policies and procedures. (p. 6)

Evans (1996) agrees with Nolan, noting that "to even begin to be open to change, people must first be unhappy with the status quo in some way and must then find the change relevant to their concerns" (p. 80).

Fullan (2005) believes that engaging teachers' moral purpose is a pathway to commitment: "In education, moral purpose involves committing to raise the bar and close the gap in student achievement—for example, increasing literacy for all, with special attention to those most disadvantaged" (p. 54). Nolan (2007) advises, "Do not ask teachers to commit themselves to innovations per se; rather focus on the potential impact that the initiative will have on their students" (p. 5).

Although teachers cannot know in advance how an innovation will play out or whether it will be successful, they can be helped to know as much about the innovation as possible, including the theory underlying it, the responsibilities they will assume if they commit to it, and the potential advantages it offers to students. Finally, if teachers are going to commit to change, they must be shown that the change is *feasible*. According to Evans (1996):

> Teachers must not only want to implement a change, they must feel that they can achieve it. They need to see change not only as appropriate for students and as promising better learning but also as something practical that they and their school can manage. (p. 85)

The path to commitment includes many of the same processes as capacity building: inquiry, reflection, and dialogue. On the path to commitment, those processes are used to better understand the proposed change and to decide whether it is in the best interest of the school community.

Leadership

In matters of school change, traditional top-down leadership is a recipe for failure. "Leadership, to be effective, must spread throughout the organization" (Fullan, 2005, p. 57). One way to begin the distribution of leadership for change is to appoint a core leadership team that includes a majority of teachers. This team can coordinate the change effort, and members can serve as liaisons to other teachers (Gordon et al., 2008). Over time, other teachers throughout the school can assume various leadership roles in the change effort. Teachers can be leaders of action research teams, study groups, curriculum development teams, instructional support teams, community relations teams, and so on, with all of these leadership roles related to the change effort.

Successful change leaders continuously search for teachers who are ready to provide leadership in order to assign those teachers leadership roles (Gordon et al., 2008). Allen and Glickman (1998) reported that the school leaders they worked with in change efforts "came to realize that the heart of the decision-making process was not the leadership team, but the quality of involvement of everyone in the decision-making process" (p. 519). In the successful schools that Allen and Glickman studied,

> Leadership team members stopped defining themselves as decision makers and became coordinators of the involvement of all. . . . Small groups, formal and ad hoc, gave anyone who wanted the opportunity to participate in defining the issues, structuring courses of actions, and monitoring the effects of actions. (p. 520)

▶ Video Illustration

Watch the following video. In what ways is the leadership in the video consistent with the discussion of leadership in this section? What might be some "next steps" the principal and teacher leaders could take to further distribute leadership?

Evolutionary Planning

Fullan's (1997) admonition that change is a journey, not a blueprint, applies here. Significant change is a *long* journey along a winding, uneven path, with inevitable but unpredictable barriers along the way. The complexity of schools and nonlinear nature of change calls for planning that is continuously evolving. The essential component of evolutionary planning is *feedback*—feedback on how well the innovation is understood, how many are participating in the change process, the level of implementation, its effects on students, and so on. Ongoing data gathering, reflection, and dialogue all are critical here, as supervisors and teachers collaborate to make informed decisions during each phase of the change journey.

Although evolutionary planning requires a great deal of collaboration, it also requires individual teachers to make a steady stream of decisions on how to apply the innovation at the classroom level. Individual teachers need to work out what schoolwide change will mean to them and their students (Fullan, 2007); they need to integrate innovations with their own practices, beliefs, and teaching styles. Teachers also need to gather data on the effects of the innovation on their students, reflect on that data, and make appropriate modifications to the innovation. Supervisors, in turn, need to be flexible and supportive as teachers engage in evolutionary planning at the classroom level.

Problem Solving

Given the complexity and unpredictability of change at the school level, problems will arise. Fullan (1997) tells us that "problems are our friends":

> It seems perverse to say that problems are our friends, but we cannot develop effective responses to complex situations unless we actively seek and confront the real problems which are in fact difficult to solve. Problems are our friends because it is only through immersing ourselves in problems that we can come up with creative solutions. Problems are the route to deeper change and deeper satisfaction. In this sense effective organizations "embrace problems" rather than avoid them. (p. 40)

Like problems, conflicts are necessary to the success of the change process. In fact, supervisors should worry about an absence of conflict, which could signal either apathy about the innovation or opponents working behind the scenes to sabotage the innovation. As we said in Chapter 17, conflict generates information, ideas, and alternatives, all of which lead to better decision making.

Resistance to change typically is viewed as a problem to be overcome; however, Fullan (2002) urges change leaders to "redefine resistance." Resisters sometimes raise important issues, and addressing such issues can improve the innovation.

> The wise change leader will encourage resisters to make their objections public and attend carefully to the potential negatives that are identified. Once deficiencies or unintended negatives have been identified, it is possible to rethink the initiative or to find ways to minimize the potential problems. Using the work of resisters to your advantage can lead to imaginative solutions for overcoming potential problems. (Nolan, 2007, p. 7)

Support

Educational change theory suggests the need for both external and internal support. Networks of schools involved in change efforts, often sponsored by universities, can provide multiple types of external support (Gordon, 2008). Such support might include the following:

- Regional professional development and planning meetings
- Critical friends from outside the school who provide on-site assistance

- Material resources to which individual schools may not have access
- Assistance with data gathering and data analysis
- Opportunities for schools to share ideas, data, successes, problems, and solutions with each other
- Opportunities for educators with experience and expertise in the change process to mentor less-experienced educators from other schools
- Electronic information retrieval and networking systems
- Regional conferences where network schools can share their change efforts and results with educators from outside the network

Internal support includes providing all members of the school community with adequate information about the innovation. Educators almost always need resources to bring about change, and in most cases, the most critical resource is time to work on the change. Change efforts go through different phases—readiness, installation, initiation, full operation, and continuation—and different types of support are needed during each phase.

The most powerful type of support, according to Stiegelbauer (2008), comes from the learning relationships that develop during the change process: "An implementation process needs models, teachers, coaches, mentors, and evaluators to address all phases. Further, such personnel need to be able to work together positively according to their strengths" (p. 127).

Change theory tells us that support for change must be accompanied by a certain amount of pressure, even when educators are committed to the innovation (Fullan, 2007). Nelson (2008) found that pressure and support best stimulate change when they are applied simultaneously.

Coherence

Two enemies of coherent change are overload and fragmentation. *Overload* means that a school is involved in too many change initiatives. *Fragmentation* means that different change initiatives are disjointed or even at cross purposes (Fullan, 2002). Some obvious ways to move toward coherence are to be selective about the number of change efforts and to make sure that change efforts are consistent. Bain (2007) proposes several strategies for building coherence:

1. *School-level schema.* This is a commonly held body of knowledge, beliefs, and strategies concerning the innovation. It includes all members of the school community being familiar with the underlying theory and research on the innovation, along with development of a common language associated with it.

For example, if the innovation was cooperative learning, all teachers would be able to discuss concepts like *positive interdependence, individual accountability,* and *group processing.*

2. *Embedded design.* The design features of the innovation are embedded within each major subsystem of the school organization: professional development, school support systems, curriculum, teaching, assessment, technology, and so on. In our cooperative learning example, professional development would be about cooperative learning and use cooperative learning strategies, the curriculum would foster cooperative learning, student evaluation would include assessment of cooperative skills, and so on.

3. *Similarity of scale.* The school-level schema for the innovation is applied at each level of the organization. For example, just as students would use the principles of cooperative learning to solve a problem they were assigned, so teams of teachers would use the same principles to solve problems at the grade level or department level, and school leadership teams would use these same principles to solve schoolwide problems.

Bain's (2007) strategies, all of which are work intensive and long term, support the suggestion that schools should carefully select a limited number of innovations rather than embrace every interesting innovation that appears on the horizon.

Norms of Continuous Improvement

As Stiegelbauer (2008) reminds us, "The broader agenda of change is the development of an organizational capacity to adapt to changing needs and conditions. . . . The goal is not mastery of a single innovation but ongoing learning and the development of collaborative work cultures" (p. 125). Schools that reach the cultural stage that Stiegelbauer refers to have been called different things by different change theorists: "self-renewing schools," "schools that learn," "self-organizing schools," and so on. Whatever we call these schools, we should recognize that they all have developed the capacity to continuously assess themselves in light of changing external and internal conditions, to identify needed change, and to move toward that change. It is not that these schools have reached a state of perfection. To borrow from the language Abraham Maslow used to identify high-performing individuals, they are "self-actualizing" (but never "self-actualized") schools.

A number of change theorists have identified cultural norms held by continuously improving schools (see, for example, Barnett & O'Mahony, 2006; Eilers & Camacho, 2007; Gordon et al., 2008; Louis, 2007; Mitchell, 1995; Saphier & King, 1985; Senge et al., 2000). Figure 21.1 provides a composite list of cultural norms for continuous improvement.

1. *Distributed, supportive leadership:* The leader involves the entire school community in decision making, promotes teacher leadership, provides direct support, and coordinates external and peer support. Different types of support are provided during different phases of the change process.

2. *Professional dialogue:* Communication is open and honest, information is shared, sensitive issues are raised when necessary, and attempts are made to understand others' points of view.

3. *Trust and confidence:* Individuals keep their commitments and trust others to do the same. Individuals show professional respect for each other. Trust building and mutual respect lead to confidence in oneself and others.

4. *Critique:* Current practices, beliefs, values, and assumptions are analyzed critically. Power relationships and imbalances are critiqued. Cultural bias is identified and addressed.

5. *Reflective inquiry:* The external knowledge base is explored. Internal data on the school culture and student learning are gathered, analyzed, and discussed. Cycles of action and reflection are used at the individual, team, and school levels.

6. *Productive conflict:* Conflict is expected, acknowledged, and used to improve the change process. Conflict is resolved through communication, inquiry, and problem-solving processes.

7. *Unity of purpose:* Members of the school community are concerned with all students in the school, not just those they work with. Educators agree on a common focus for change and on principles that will be followed during the change process. Change efforts are coordinated and coherent.

8. *Incremental approach:* The school community "thinks big and starts small." Incremental steps are taken toward long-term goals. Evolutionary planning is used to adapt the change effort to changing conditions. Change is viewed as an ongoing, never-ending process.

9. *Professional development:* A variety of coordinated professional development formats are used to assist the change effort—study groups, skill development, mentoring, peer coaching, institutes, and so on.

10. *Collegiality and collaboration:* Teaching is deprivatized; teachers share strategies, materials, problems, and possible solutions. Teachers observe each other to learn new ways of teaching, gather classroom data, and provide feedback. Collegial groups analyze common problems, plan common solutions, and assess results of improvement efforts. Professional relationships are powerful sources of support for change.

figure **21.1**   **Norms Present in School Cultures of Continuous Improvement**

11. *Experimentation and risk taking:* Teachers are open to new ways of teaching, encouraged to experiment with new practices, and supported if experiments do not succeed. Risk taking is encouraged in the classroom and in group efforts to improve the school environment, curriculum, instructional program, and so forth. Teachers are encouraged to engage in new forms of professional development and new leadership roles.

12. *Recognition, sharing, and celebration:* Teachers and others are recognized for participation and success in change efforts. Teachers and groups share their work on change with each other. The school shares its change efforts and results with parents, the community, and outside educators. The school celebrates the change process with special events and ceremonies and establishes new traditions consistent with new practices.

f i g u r e **21.1** **Continued**

▶ **Video Illustration**

Watch the following video. Which of the 12 cultural norms for continuous improvement are in evidence in the faculty meeting shown in this video? Which, if any, of the 12 norms for continuous improvement are not in evidence?

Making Connections

Chaos theory, postmodern theory, and educational change theory were each developed in entirely different disciplines for entirely different reasons, yet it is difficult to ignore patterns that appear across all three. Although they obviously are not interchangeable, the three areas of study all have implications for educational communities, and in many areas they seem to confirm one another. Table 21.1 reviews some key elements of each theory. As you review Table 21.1, note the similarities of elements across each row. Could it be that there are realities that run deeper than any one field of study, realities that apply to any change process in our world? We'll let the reader ponder this question and decide.

Changing the Conditions of Teaching

Any discussion on change in education would be incomplete if it did not address the conditions of teaching across the nation over the last several years. To say the least, these conditions have not been optimal. All of the research on change now available

t a b l e **21.1** **Comparing Chaos Theory, Postmodernism, and Educational Change Theory**

Chaos Theory	Postmodernism	Educational Change Theory
Nonlinearity: change is organic; cannot control from above; multiple interactions affect change; effects of change on system not highly predictable	Rejects boundaries and hierarchies; grand, universal schemes do not work; rejects "expert" solutions; multiple ways to frame and solve problems; change affected by local context; rejects rational–structural approach	Evolutionary planning; change is a journey; incremental approach; variety of professional development options; experimentation and risk taking; change affected by school and community context
Complexity: measurement of complex systems difficult; external measurement standards insufficient	Rejects certainty; recognizes multiplicity and lack of clarity; context, players, and circumstances vary greatly from setting to setting; cannot understand whole by analyzing parts; little value in generalizations	Develop understanding by exploring the complexity and uniqueness of the school's culture; build capacity for dealing with complex school issues through dialogue, trust building, and development of guiding principles
Butterfly effect: complex systems are highly interdependent; long-term prediction is difficult	Change is unpredictable	Evolutionary planning; learning relationships; incremental approach; continuous, wise decisions; outcomes of change efforts are not fully predictable
Fractals: self-similarity on different scale	Networking and dialogue lead to some broad commonalities, but with many variations within and across groups; anyone has power	Distributed leadership and responsibility; coherence (school-level schema and embedded design) with flexibility for group and individual adaptation
Feedback mechanisms: feedback loops bring stability or disturbance; necessary for both equilibrium and growth toward greater complexity	Multiple perspectives, values, and experiences are present; change process needs to be analyzed through multiple views; since progress and effects of change are unpredictable, need continuous feedback and modification during the change process	Evolutionary planning and implementation; data-informed reflective inquiry and professional dialogue to address problems, resistance, and conflict
Turbulence: from disturbances inside or outside system; complex systems more subject to instability due to turbulence; system needs some turbulence for growth; too much disturbance leads to disintegration	Deliberately attempts to create turbulence by questioning assumptions, challenging binaries, confronting existing power structures	Educators invited to embrace moral purpose; challenge the status quo; critique current practices, beliefs, values, and assumptions; productive conflict encouraged; leadership provides balance of pressure and support for change
Strange attractors: deeply encoded structures; complex and unpredictable patterns that stay within certain parameters	Invite input from multiple groups and individuals; synthesize multiple perspectives, values, and experiences	Constants might include things like a focus on student learning; trust and confidence; unity of purpose (a cause beyond oneself); collegiality and collaboration; and recognition, sharing, and celebration

will be of little value if changing the conditions of teaching is not a central goal of both external and internal school improvement efforts:

- Change is needed *away from* treating teachers as technicians expected to transmit curriculum developed by bureaucrats, using canned methods published by commercial interests, and measuring student learning through one-size-fits-all tests mandated by policy makers and *toward* treating teachers as professionals invited to make professional decisions about curriculum, instruction, and student assessment.

- Change is needed *away from* overloading teachers to the extent that they are unable to develop the teacher–student relationships, engage in the reflective planning, and perform the critical self-assessment required for effective teaching and *toward* the manageable class and student load that are prerequisites for quality teaching.

- Change is needed *away from* the physical and psychological isolation caused by outmoded school structures and norms of individualism and *toward* structures and norms that provide opportunities for professional dialogue and collaborative work.

- Change is needed *away from* bureaucratic organizations in which teachers are overwhelmed by regulations and paperwork or—worse yet—mistreated by authoritarian organizations more representative of old-style dictatorships than modern democracies and *toward* democratic school communities in which supervisors promote shared decision making, collegiality, and teacher leadership.

- Change is needed *away from* policies that treat teachers as part of the problem and consider education a low priority in the allocation of resources and *toward* policies that value teachers as part of the solution and provide the human and material resources teachers need to improve schools and provide all students with a quality education.

- Change is needed *away from* teaching as an unstaged career with minimal extrinsic rewards and *toward* teaching as a career in which teachers are properly inducted into the profession and provided new responsibilities, appropriate support, increased recognition, and significantly increased salary at each career stage.

- Change is needed *away from* diversity as a combination of colors and symbols and *toward* a vision of practice that values and honors respect and dignity as well as shared power and decision making.

Many teachers today are facing negative conditions, but there are also efforts to improve the conditions of teaching. Many members of the business community, concerned citizens' groups, and policy makers are working to improve external conditions, and many supervisors are working from the inside to make schools centers of democracy, inquiry, and dialogue. The door for improving external and internal conditions will never close; it's simply a matter of whether or not we care to step in and make a difference.

✔ **Check Your Understanding 21.0**   Click here to gauge your understanding of the key concepts presented in this chapter.

REFLECTIVE EXERCISE

Draw a concept map (web) with three main nodes labeled: "Chaos Theory," "Post-modernism," and "Educational Change Research." Draw line segments out from each node to terms you write that represent what you consider to be key elements of each of the three theories. Draw additional line segments that represent connections between the various elements within and across the three theories. Be prepared to explain your concept map to colleagues.

chapter 22

Addressing Diversity

Learning Outcomes for This Chapter

After reading this chapter, you should be able to:

1. Describe the assets-based approach to teaching low-socioeconomic and racial/ethnic minority students.
2. Provide examples of gender inequity.
3. Define heteronormative.
4. State the four disability rights goals summarized by McLaughlin (2010).
5. List overarching causes of the inequity experienced by the four broad cultural groups discussed in this chapter.
6. Explain how the technical tasks of supervision relate to diversity.

Questions to Reflect On as You Read This Chapter

1. Kirsch and associates predict that if we do not act to close the widening gaps in skill levels among different cultural groups there are "a number of predictable and dire implications for future generations" (Kirsch, Braun, Yamamoto, & Sum, 2007, p. 7). What do you believe some of these implications are?

2. As you read this chapter, contemplate what needs to be done at the school level, school-community level, and societal level to close the achievement gaps among diverse groups of students.

3. Reflect on cultural clashes in PK-12 education that you have been part of or observed. Based on your experiences and observations, does this chapter's discussion of the reasons for and effects of cultural clashes ring true?

4. What can culturally responsive supervisors and teachers do to help colleagues become more culturally responsive? To develop culturally responsive *schools*?

5. If a school was going to develop public statements centered on (1) the treatment of students from diverse racial and ethnic cultures, (2) gender equity, (3) the treatment of LGBT students, and (4) students with disabilities, what critical elements should be included in each of the four public statements?

> *A major problem facing the nation-state is how to recognize and legitimize differences and yet construct an overarching national identity that incorporates the voices, experiences, and hopes of the diverse groups that compose it. What groups will participate in constructing a new national identity, and what factors will be used to motivate powerful groups to share power with marginalized groups, are also issues that have to be addressed. Power sharing is an essential characteristic of a nation-state that reflects the culture of its diverse population.*
>
> *(Banks, 2000, p. 28)*

Given the growing diversity in the United States, and the continuing achievement gap between different student groups, addressing diversity in our schools is an increasingly critical need. People are not born with the prejudice and bias that contribute to the achievement gap. These attitudes are taught, and schools can teach future citizens different attitudes about those who belong to different cultures. Also, students from diverse cultures do not underachieve because they are less intelligent or less interested in learning than students from the dominant culture, but because of the incompatibility between their culture and traditional schooling in U.S. society. If we need to change schools and the way we teach to close the achievement gap, then addressing diversity should be a task of instructional supervision.

In this chapter, we will examine teaching and learning in relation to marginalized economic, racial, and ethnic groups; gender; sexual and gender minorities; and students with disabilities. We will examine how the conventional school culture and conventional teaching practices impede the learning of students who are not members of the dominant culture, and we will discuss strategies for making schools and teaching more responsive to diverse cultures.

Achievement Gaps Among Economic, Racial, and Ethnic Groups

Despite the espoused commitment in the United States to equal opportunity for all, there exists a wide gap in educational outcomes among various economic, racial, and ethnic groups. Table 22.1 shows percentages of students in selected economic, racial, and ethnic groups that demonstrated at least basic skill levels in reading, writing, math, and science on the National Assessment of Educational Progress (NAEP). Compared to students below the poverty level, far more students above the poverty level demonstrated basic skills across the various grade levels and content areas. Much higher percentages of Whites than African Americans and Latinos scored at a basic level or higher (National Center for Education Statistics, n.d.).

Less than 60% of students starting high school in high-poverty districts are likely to graduate, compared to over 75% of students in low-poverty districts (Swanson, 2004a, 2004b). Between 70% and 80% of Whites who start high school graduate in 4 years, compared to between 50% and 60% of African American and Latino students (Amos, 2008; Hoff, 2008; Swanson, 2004a, 2004b). The negative effects of not completing high school in the United States are serious. High school dropouts not only have less earning power than graduates, but they are also more likely to live in poverty and become involved in criminal behavior (Boisjoly, Harris, & Duncan, 1998; Kim, Chang, Singh, & Allen, 2015; Neild, Balfanz, & Herzog, 2007).

We all should ponder the reality that it is our society, our institutions, and our schools that have let so many lower-socioeconomic and racial/ethnic minority students down—that have failed to address the learning needs of so many bright young people with so much potential—in large part because of their family income, their ethnicity or race, or their first language. National shame is in order here. Rather than dwell on that shame, we need to transform it into an urgent moral imperative to change the way we educate low-income and racial/ethnic minority students.

t a b l e **22.1** Percentages of Selected Student Groups At or Above Basic Skill Level

Subject Area	Year of Test	Grade Level	All Students	Students Above Poverty Level	Students Below Poverty Level	Whites	African Americans	Latinos
Reading	2015	4	69	83	56	79	52	55
	2015	8	76	87	64	85	58	66
	2013	12	75	NA	NA	83	56	64
Writing	2011	8	80	90	68	87	65	69
	2011	12	79	NA	NA	87	61	65
Math	2015	4	82	92	72	90	65	73
	2015	8	71	84	58	82	48	60
	2013	12	65	NA	NA	75	38	50
Science	2009	4	72	86	56	87	47	53
	2011	8	65	80	48	80	37	48
	2009	12	60	68	39	72	29	42

NA=Not Available.
Source: National Center for Educational Statistics. NAEP Data Explorer, http://nces.ed.gove/nationsreport/NDE

As the educational and economic gaps between the haves and have-nots in our society increase, the United States is becoming increasingly diverse. Demographers suggest that by the year 2050, non-Hispanic Whites will be a minority in the United States, comprising about 47% of the population (Passel & Cohn, 2008). Kirsch and associates (2007) warn that our nation's increasing diversity, the widening gaps in skill levels among different groups, and changes in the economy due to technology and globalization are all combining to create what they call "the perfect storm":

> We are in the midst of a perfect storm in which these three powerful forces are combining to generate waves that already have had a considerable impact on our nation. Unlike the perfect storm chronicled in the novel written by Sebastian Junger, the forces behind this storm continue to gain strength, and calm seas are nowhere in sight. We can't hope to ride this one out. If we continue on our present heading and fail to take effective action, the storm will have a number of predictable and dire implications for future generations. with consequences that extend well beyond the economic realm to the ethos of our society. (Kirsch et al., 2007, p. 7)

The aforementioned moral imperative to correct the inequalities in education should be the primary reason that supervisors and teachers respond to diversity as they work to close achievement gaps between student groups. The storm on the horizon, a storm whose winds we already feel, provides additional impetus for addressing issues of diversity.

A Societal or a School Problem?

Classism and racism have negative effects on the quality of life for many of our nation's poor and racial/ethnic minorities, and these negative effects extend to the quality of education for these groups. Rothstein (2004) has shown how inadequate wages, substandard housing, and poor health care create living conditions that place many poor and racial/ethnic minority students at a disadvantage right from the beginning of their formal education. Moreover, many lower-socioeconomic children have fewer out-of-school educational opportunities than middle- and upper-class students. For example, middle- and upper-class students are more likely to have access to a variety of books, go to summer camps or on family vacations, visit museums and zoos, take dance or music lessons, and so on. Rothstein (2004) argues that half or more of the variation in student achievement between lower-socioeconomic students and other students is due to nonschool factors such as family income, housing conditions, health care, and out-of-school educational opportunities.

Educational policy in the United States—at the federal, state, and local levels—tends to reinforce the inequities present in society at large. For instance, the federal courts have ended many of the nation's most successful desegregation plans (Goldring, Cohen-Vogel, Smrekar, & Taylor, 2006; Wells, Duran, & White, 2008). There are now, once again, many public schools in the United States that have virtually

100% racial/ethnic minority students (Frankenberg, Lee, & Orfield, 2003; Orfield & Frankenberg, 2014). On average across the nation, if local and state expenditures are combined, states spend less money on their highest-poverty districts than their lowest-poverty districts (Adamson & Darling-Hammond, 2012; Wiener & Pristoop, 2006). Funding inequities also exist at the federal level. Because the federal government's Title I formula factors in the state's average per-student expenditure, high-spending states get more Title I money per poor child than low-spending states. "The net effect is that Title I does not reduce, but rather reinforces, inequality among states" (Liu, 2006, p. 2). Additionally, schools with many students who are poor or racial/ethnic minorities have higher percentages of out-of-field teachers (teachers without a major or minor in the subject they teach), are more likely to be assigned novice teachers, and have teachers with lower salaries than schools that serve wealthier students and lower numbers of racial/ethnic minority students (Peske & Haycock, 2006).

How are educators to respond to the systemic problems in U.S. society, as reflected in educational policy, that place lower-socioeconomic and racial/ethnic minority children at such a disadvantage? Some analysts say that unless our society addresses problems such as inadequate housing, poor health care, segregation, and inequitable school funding, schools will never be able to bridge the achievement gap. These experts admit that schools can make some difference but argue that many of the conditions that cause the gap are beyond the schools' control. Other analysts believe that schools *can* bridge the achievement gap. They point to the effective schools and school improvement research and say that if some schools serving low-socioeconomic and racial/ethnic minority students can do it, then all schools can. These experts tell educators to forget about social conditions they cannot control and focus on increasing the achievement of poor and racial/ethnic minority students and on preparing them to overcome the barriers of poverty, classism, and racism present in U.S. society.

Our own position is that PK-12 educators need to take a two-tiered approach to the issue of inequitable treatment of diverse groups. First, supervisors and teachers need to examine their own cultural identities, develop competencies for working with cultures different from their own, and create culturally responsive classrooms and schools. Second, supervisors and teachers need to become directly involved in efforts to change public policy that works against lower-socioeconomic and racial/ethnic minority children. Educators in PK-12 should become involved in local and national efforts to ensure that all families have access to living wages, adequate housing, and basic health care. Moreover, supervisors and teachers need to work to end segregation, inequitable school funding, and state and national educational policies that hurt lower-socioeconomic and racial/ethnic minority children. Supervisors and teachers will not be able to do it alone; rather, they will need to become part of a coalition of PK-12 educators, university educators, parents, businesspersons, and policy makers who recognize the critical need for change. Members of this coalition will need to help educate the general public, the corporate world, and politicians on the need for change and to push for new legislation at the state and federal levels.

Now that we have considered issues of equity through a wide lens, the rest of this chapter will focus more narrowly on the classroom and school, including the cultural clashes that lead to inequitable treatment of some students and how culturally responsive teachers and schools can address diversity.

Cultural Clashes

Lower-socioeconomic and racial/ethnic minority students often have low levels of academic achievement because of clashes between their culture and the dominant culture's values and interests. The organizational structures, norms, values, curricula, instructional strategies, and student assessment methods in most schools support the dominant culture. Moreover, despite the increase in the number of students from diverse cultures, the number of White teachers and principals remains disproportionately high (Chamberlain, 2005; Saifer & Barton, 2007).

Part of the problem is caused by blatant stereotypes of lower-socioeconomic and racial/ethnic minority students: this or that group is "less academic" or "less motivated" or has parents who are "less concerned" about their children's education (Castro, 2014; Kumar & Hamer, 2013). However, much of the damage done to lower-socioeconomic and racial/ethnic minority students is more subtle, and is often done by well-meaning educators who are not even aware of what they are doing (Carlisle, Jackson, & George, 2006). Often, the real problem is educators not understanding a group's cultural norms. For example, Valenzuela (1999) points out that the concept of *educación* is an important part of Mexican American culture:

> *Educación* is a conceptually broader term than its English language cognate. It refers to the family's role of inculcating in children a sense of moral, social, and personal responsibility and serves as the foundation for all other learning. Though inclusive of formal academic training, *educación* additionally refers to competence in the social world, wherein one respects the dignity and individuality of others. (p. 23)

One implication of *educación* for teaching Mexican American students is the need for the teacher to develop caring, reciprocal relationships with students and to promote such relationships among students. A teacher who remains distant from Mexican American students, isolates them from each other, and emphasizes academic competition does a disservice to them. According to Valenzuela (1999):

> When teachers deny their students the opportunity to engage in reciprocal relationships, they simultaneously invalidate the definition of education that most of these young people embrace. And since that definition is thoroughly grounded in Mexican culture, its rejection constitutes a dismissal of their culture as well. (p. 23)

Delpit (2006) provides another example of teachers not understanding students' cultures in her story of a White teacher's reaction to a story written and read aloud by Marti, a second-grade African American student:

Marti: "Once upon a time, there was an old lady, and this old lady ain't had no sense."

Teacher (interrupting): "Marti, that sounds like the beginning of a wonderful story, but could you tell me how you would say it in Standard English?"

Marti (head down, thinking for a minute, softly said): "There was an old lady who didn't have any sense."

Marti (hand on hip, raised voice): "But this lady ain't had no sense!" (p. 169)

The teacher in the story did not realize that the second-grade student understood Standard English but wanted to stray from this form to better articulate and assert her point. Not understanding cultural norms can cause teachers to underestimate the ability of poor and racial/ethnic minority students and thus "teach down" to them, focusing on basic skills, conducting drill and practice, and depriving students of developing the higher-level skills they are perfectly capable of learning (Bae, Halloway, Li, & Bempechat, 2008).

Another type of cultural clash consists of misinterpretation by the dominant culture of lower-socioeconomic and racial/ethnic minority students' behaviors. Students from lower-socioeconomic and minority groups often are viewed as not caring about education (Amatea, Cholewa, & Mixon, 2012) But as Valenzuela (1999) points out, the school is sending the message to these students that their culture has no value and is asking them to reject their culture in favor of the dominant culture. Valenzuela argues that it is not *education* that many minority students don't care for; it is the *type of schooling* they are receiving. Thus, lower-socioeconomic and racial/ethnic minority students' behaviors can be viewed as a way of coping with how they are treated (Bensimon, 2007; Garcia & Dominguez, 1997) or of resisting the destruction of their culture by the dominant culture (Valenzuela, 1999).

Different communication styles often cause cultural clashes. Students from *high-context cultures* tend to take time to describe the context of a situation, often in the form of a story. Teachers from the dominant culture, on the other hand, tend to be *low context;* they prefer direct, explicit messages and often consider messages from members of high-context cultures to be rambling and confused. Students from high-context cultures may be corrected by teachers, come to believe that their communication style is inferior, and withdraw from classroom interaction (Chamberlain, 2005; Milner & Ford, 2007). European Americans tend to value written communication more than other forms of literacy, while people from many other cultures place a greater value on oral language. Also, European Americans tend to favor topic-centered, linear narratives, while people from some minority cultures prefer episodic narratives that shift from setting to setting and are nonlinear (Chamberlain, 2005; Delpit, 2006). Problems occur when European American teachers perceive narratives written in episodic style to be inferior to their own topic-centered preference.

Cultural differences are also responsible for the misdiagnosis of many lower socioeconomic and racial/ethnic minority students as special education students, resulting in their overreferral to special programs. Conversely, the failure to identify lower-socioeconomic and racial/ethnic minority students as gifted results in their underreferral to gifted programs (De Valenzuela, Copeland, Qi, & Park, 2006; Fiedler et al., 2008; Milner & Ford, 2007; Tyson, 2011). Banks (2000) argues that some concepts underlying special education placement are socially constructed by the dominant culture: "When establishing categories for race, mental retardation, and giftedness, individuals and groups with power construct categories and characteristics and distribute rewards and privileges that benefit the existing hierarchies" (p. 38). Banks (2000) maintains that individuals who are judged competent within their own cultures and communities often are labeled as mentally retarded in schools. And to reiterate, lower-socioeconomic and racial/ethnic minority students are severely underrepresented in gifted and talented programs.

Banks (2000) believes that middle-class White parents use their knowledge of the system and political power to help get their children admitted to gifted and talented programs, which usually have better teachers, smaller classes, and more intellectual content. At the same time, many lower-socioeconomic and racial/ethnic minority students are placed in lower-track programs that lack intellectual engagement. As described by Banks (2000), "Classes for lower-track students tend to be characterized by low-level instruction, drill exercises, and a lack of higher-level content" (p. 37).

According to Chamberlain (2005), many teachers from the dominant culture are unable to distinguish between underachievement due to a disability and underachievement due to cultural clashes. Chamberlain also describes how educational diagnosticians misidentify diverse students for special education or lower-track programs because of biased tests, inadequate opportunities for students to learn tested material, students' poor test-taking skills, culturally inappropriate test norms, failure to gather adequate data, and incorrect interpretation of data.

The curriculum in many schools clashes with diverse cultures because it is primarily a Eurocentric, middle-class curriculum. If other cultures are not represented in the curriculum, then students from nondominant cultures must ignore their own cultures and learn Eurocentric content to be successful.

The cultural conflict inherent in being forced to learn a Eurocentric curriculum puts children from other cultures at a tremendous disadvantage. Lower-socioeconomic and racial/ethnic minority students come to school with extensive funds of knowledge from their own culture—knowledge that is accessed through interacting with individuals and drawing on resources from supportive networks within the culture (Dworin, 2006; Moll, Amanti, Neff, & González, 1992; Rios-Aguilar, 2010; Risko & Walker-Dalhouse, 2007; Stritikus, 2006). However, if the only curriculum to be learned is a Eurocentric one, then the funds of knowledge within the student's culture become irrelevant to his or her schooling. Moreover, in schools with a Eurocentric curriculum, individuals and groups who look like students from non-European cultures are absent from or misrepresented in the curriculum, thus students from non-European cultures find it difficult to relate to the curriculum. Quoting Valenzuela (1999), "The extant curriculum fails to build on students' skills, knowledge, and cultural background" (p. 175).

Everything that we have been discussing—stereotypes, misunderstanding of cultural norms, misinterpretation of student behaviors, different communication styles, overreferral and misdiagnosis, and the Eurocentric middle-class curriculum—contribute to a deficit model for educating lower-socioeconomic and racial/ethnic minority students. The dominant culture views the cultures of lower-socioeconomic and racial/ethnic minority students as deficits to be overcome, rather than assets to build on. Many schools thus engage in what Valenzuela (1999) refers to as "subtractive schooling"; they take away lower-socioeconomic and racial/ethnic minority students' cultures as well as the social capital that is part of those cultures.

One example of subtractive schooling is the goal of many schools to transition English as a second language (ESL) students to English-speaking rather than bilingual students. These students are classified as *limited English proficient*. Their Spanish language is viewed as a deficit to be replaced by English (Chigeza, 2011; Stritikus, 2006). Another example of subtractive schooling is separating low-socioeconomic and racial/ethnic minority groups into separate tracks or ability groups. Higher-achieving low-socioeconomic and racial/ethnic minority students have cultural capital and learning strategies to share with lower-achieving students from the same cultures; however, if higher- and lower-achieving students are separated by tracking or grouping, peer relationships cannot be established and social capital cannot be shared.

Why have so many educators from the dominant culture failed to develop a better understanding of lower-socioeconomic and racial/ethnic minority cultures and not learned how to be more culturally responsive? One reason is that most teacher and leadership preparation programs, as well as most in-service professional development programs, do not adequately address cultural understanding (Batt, 2008). Another reason is the low level of interaction between educators from the dominant culture and the families and communities of students from low-socioeconomic and racial/ethnic minority groups. Teachers from the dominant culture often do not live in the same communities or visit their students' families outside of school. Teachers of marginalized students often communicate with those students' parents only when serious behavioral or academic problems arise.

There is typically little collaboration with parents and community members about how to make the school's curriculum and instruction more culturally responsive. Although educators often criticize low-socioeconomic and racial/ethnic minority parents for not being involved in their children's education, in fact, schools often set up barriers to parent involvement by scheduling impractical times and places for meetings, assuming a remedial approach, and manipulating communication through power tactics and the use of technical jargon. Because of such barriers, low-socioeconomic and racial/ethnic minority parents who try to become involved with their children's schools can soon become disillusioned and inactive (De Gaetano, 2007; Garcia & Dominguez, 1997).

Culturally Responsive Teaching

Successful teaching of diverse students is *culturally responsive*. Ladson-Billings (2009) notes that culturally responsive teaching begins with a set of beliefs:

Teachers who practice culturally relevant methods can be identified by the way they see themselves and others. They see their teaching as an art rather than a technical skill. They believe that all of their students can succeed rather than that failure is inevitable for some. They see themselves as part of the community and they see teaching as giving back to the community. They help students make connections between their local, national, racial, cultural, and global identities . . . . They believe that knowledge is continuously re-created, and shared by teachers and students alike. They view the content of the curriculum critically and are passionate about it. (p. 28)

Culturally responsive teachers accept all students as they are, but they also accept responsibility for helping all students learn. Here, *learning* means developing basic knowledge and skills but also critical and creative thinking. Responsive teachers help students *choose* academic success. How does a teacher do this? The key is to build relationships that are based on genuine care for all students. Caring leads to concern, which leads to an effort to develop relationships (Howard, 2002). A big part of relationship building is personal attention, including attention to nonacademic matters beyond the classroom. Relationship building also includes treating diverse students as individuals *and* as members of a particular culture (Brown, 2004; Brown, 2007; Cartledge & Kourea, 2008; Delpit, 2006; Kidd, Sanchez, & Thorp, 2007; Ladson-Billings, 2009; Richards, Brown, & Forde, 2007).

The classrooms of culturally responsive teachers are multicultural. Linguistic diversity is accepted and incorporated into lessons, but language codes used by the dominant culture also are taught (Bernhard, Diaz, & Allgood, 2005). In the case of students with a dominant language other than English, linguistic diversity means bilingual education, with students learning the curriculum in their dominant language as they develop English-speaking skills. The goal is to develop bilingual students, rather than to replace students' dominant languages with English. More broadly speaking, culturally responsive teachers validate knowledge that is not valued by the dominant culture while teaching standard knowledge as well; they strive to maintain the integrity of each student's culture while fostering academic excellence (Ladson-Billings, 2009).

Culturally responsive teachers learn as much as they can about their students and their students' families and communities and use what they learn in their teaching (Hudiburg, Mascher, Sagehorn, & Stidham, 2015; Saifer & Barton, 2007; Villegas & Lucas, 2007). Part of this learning comes from engaging in dialogue with adult members of the school community. Again, according to Delpit (2006):

Appropriate education for poor children and children of color can only be devised in consultation with adults who share their culture. Black parents, teachers of color, and members of poor communities must be allowed to participate fully in the discussion of what kind of instruction is in their children's best interest. (p. 45)

Responsive teachers also learn from their students as students share knowledge about themselves, their families, and their communities. Teachers then use this knowledge to become part of the students' world (Ladson-Billings, 2009; Michael & Young, 2005).

Culturally responsive teachers take an *assets-based* approach to teaching low-socioeconomic and racial/ethnic minority students—the polar opposite of the deficit approach described earlier. An assets-based approach bases teaching and learning on strengths students already possess, including knowledge that they bring with them to the classroom. Since many of a low-socioeconomic and racial/ethnic minority student's assets have been acquired from his or her culture, teaching and learning are intentionally integrated with that culture; the student's heritage and real-life experiences become part of the curriculum (Ladson-Billings, 2009). Learning is connected to the student's culture at the classroom, school, home, and community levels (Saifer & Barton, 2007). Ladson-Billings (1995a) provides an example of making such connections in her description of one teacher's "artist or craftsperson-in-residence" program, designed to highlight parents as knowledgeable resources and to affirm African American culture. Parents visited the classroom to conduct seminars on areas in which they possessed expertise. Students followed up on these seminars by conducting research to extend their knowledge on the topic.

Another part of assets-based education is helping students to realize that they have the potential for academic success. If students are treated as if they have potential, then they will be more likely to realize that potential (Michael & Young, 2005). Culturally responsive teachers make it clear that they are working with smart, capable students. Ladson-Billings (1995b) shares techniques used by responsive teachers she has observed. In one example, each student was asked to identify an area of expertise, become a "classroom expert" on that area, and deliver a presentation about it or assist other students who were having difficulty in that area. In another example, teachers assisted students whose futures were most tenuous (as indicated by a history of "misbehavior") to become their classrooms' intellectual leaders. These students were invited to lead discussions, inquiry, and student critique of the status quo. The purpose of strategies like these is to disrupt the denigration of lower-socioeconomic and racial/ethnic minority students and thwart self-fulfilling prophesies of failure, thus giving students an opportunity to choose academic success (Ladson-Billings, 2009).

Another characteristic of culturally responsive teaching is the creation of a classroom environment that is caring and collaborative and that reflects the beliefs and values of students' families and communities (Michael & Young, 2005). Students in the classrooms of responsive teachers are made to feel they are part of an extended caring family, where the teacher cares for students and students are taught to take care of each other (Brown, 2004). This caring environment includes a great deal of collaborative learning, as described by Ladson-Billings (1995b):

> To solidify the social relationships in their classes, the teachers encouraged the students to learn collaboratively, teach each other, and be responsible for the academic success of others. These collaborative arrangements were not necessarily structured like those of cooperative learning. Instead, the teachers used a combination of formal and informal peer collaborations. One teacher used a buddy system, where each student was paired

with another. The buddies checked each other's homework and class assignments. Buddies quizzed each other for tests, and, if one buddy was absent, it was the responsibility of the other to call to see why and to help with makeup work. The teachers used this ethos of reciprocity and mutuality to insist that one person's success was the success of all and one person's failure was the failure of all. These feelings were exemplified by the teacher who insisted, "We're a family. We have to care for one another as if our very survival depended on it." (p. 481)

Culturally responsive teachers combine extensive support with assertiveness. Responsive teachers collaborate with their students to develop clear behavioral and academic guidelines and to firmly enforce those guidelines (Saifer & Barton, 2007). Students are held accountable for meeting expectations but are treated with respect and dignity (Howard, 2002). Responsive teachers avoid power struggles with students by refusing to engage in arguments and providing students with "escape routes" so they are not embarrassed in front of their peers (Brown, 2004). Responsive teachers use a variety of techniques to convince students to choose success, while never using deficit language.

Ladson-Billings (1995b) describes how culturally responsive teachers hold students accountable for success:

> Students were not permitted to choose failure in their classrooms. They cajoled, nagged, pestered, and bribed the students to work at high intellectual levels. Absent from their discourse about students was the "language of lacking." Students were never referred to as being from a single-parent household, being on AFDC [welfare], or needing psychological evaluation. Instead, teachers talked about their own shortcomings and limitations and ways they needed to change to ensure student success. (p. 479)

A final characteristic of culturally responsive teachers is the transformational nature of their teaching. Responsive teachers do not ignore issues of race and culture but rather engage students in critiquing the status quo, in learning how to cope with prejudice and discrimination, and in working to bring about change (Codrington, 2014; Ladson-Billings, 2009). The focus of this work could be inside or outside the classroom. At the classroom level, the students and teacher might collaboratively critique the school curriculum, the textbooks they use, or the way their learning is assessed and then work together for curriculum and instructional change. Outside the classroom, the teacher and students could work collectively to identify and solve problems in the community—or even the larger society—caused by prejudice or discrimination. Following a transformational approach does not mean that the teacher ignores the codes used by the dominant culture or the power realities present in society. Culturally responsive teachers realize that low-socioeconomic and racial/ethnic minority students need to learn the codes of the dominant culture to be successful and need to understand power relations so they can work to change those realities (Delpit, 2006).

> ▶ **Video Illustration**
>
> After you watch this video, think about how you would introduce the concepts of subtractive schooling and assets-based education to a faculty that was not familiar with these concepts.

Culturally Responsive Schools

Having a few culturally responsive teachers in a school that serves diverse groups is simply not enough. The aim should be to create a culturally responsive *school*. Here, we will discuss three important processes needed to move toward creating a culturally responsive school: teacher development, school development, and collaboration with families and the community.

Teacher Development.   One goal of a school that aims to become culturally responsive is to move more and more members of the school community toward intercultural sensitivity. Sensitivity is not something that teachers do or don't have; teachers actually move through developmental stages of sensitivity. Cushner, McClelland, and Safford (2009) describe six stages of intercultural sensitivity, which were originally identified by Bennett (1993):

1. *Denial.* Individuals in the denial stage are unable to see authentic cultural differences, isolate themselves within their own cultures, and stereotype and discriminate against members of other cultures, sometimes considering others to be mentally and socially deficient.

2. *Defense.* At this stage, individuals recognize some cultural differences but consider them negative attributes of the other culture. These individuals are unable to deal with cultural differences and become defensive, adopting an us-versus-them attitude. Persons at this stage consider their culture to be superior and denigrate other cultures.

3. *Minimization.* This is the "colorblind" stage, the stage where most teachers are. Individuals at this stage recognize and accept surface cultural differences, such as traditional foods, music, and recreational activities, but they continue to believe that everyone is basically alike. They believe that everyone has the same basic values, needs, and motivations—that "we all want the same things out of life."

4. *Acceptance.* Persons at this stage accept the fact that different cultures have different values and behaviors and do not consider values and behaviors different from their own as bad. Cultural differences are seen as viable alternatives to the dominant culture. Individuals at this stage accept other cultures but still have not developed the skills necessary to work effectively with them.

5. *Adaptation.* Persons at this stage are able to shift from their own culture's frame of reference to other frames; they can view persons and situations through the worldview of other cultures. This enables them to better empathize with people from other cultures and to better communicate across cultures. Teachers at this stage are able to modify their teaching so that their expectations, interactions, and responses to students from different cultures vary in appropriate ways.

6. *Integration.* Individuals at this stage have internalized multiple frames of reference. They are bicultural or multicultural; their identity is not tied to any one culture. They feel equally comfortable with any of the multiple cultures with which they identify, and they are able to mediate between different cultural groups. Teachers who have reached the integration stage should be enlisted to build bridges between cultures.

The lower three stages on intercultural sensitivity (denial, defense, and minimization) are classified as *ethnocentric* stages, and the higher three stages (acceptance, adaptation, and integration) are considered *ethnorelative* stages. As we mentioned earlier, most teachers are at the minimization stage and thus are ethnocentric. Teacher development, therefore, needs to move teachers toward the ethnorelative stages of cultural sensitivity.

Guerra and Nelson (2008) have presented a four-phase model for developing culturally proficient teachers. In phase 1, teachers analyze a variety of student data disaggregated by race, ethnicity, and socioeconomic status. The data examined include test scores, discipline referrals, placement in special education and gifted programs, course grades, retention rates, parent involvement, and college acceptance. The teachers' data analysis typically reveals patterns of inequity, showing that low-socioeconomic and racial/ethnic minority students have been ill served by the status quo. The data are reviewed without the names of students or teachers so teachers do not become defensive. Guerra and Nelson warn that teachers will react differently during discussion of the patterns found in the data. Some will recognize inequity in schooling as the cause of achievement gaps, but some will blame the students and parents. In phase 1, teachers also become aware of strategies to address inequities by reading about and discussing how culturally responsive teachers overcome such inequities. Some teachers will be motivated by the success stories; others will dismiss them (Guerra & Nelson, 2008).

In phase 2, teachers' readiness for change is assessed by having them engage in simulations intended to demonstrate culture's influences and cultural clashes. After the simulations, teachers discuss the experience in debriefing sessions. Facilitators observe the teachers' behaviors closely to see which teachers recognize and accept cultural differences. Based on the teachers' reactions to the student data and success stories in phase 1 and the simulations in phase 2, those who are ready for more advanced work on cultural proficiency are invited to participate in phases 3 and 4. Those who are not ready for advanced work are provided with additional phase 1 and phase 2 activities to help them develop readiness and participate in phases 3 and 4 at a later time (Guerra & Nelson, 2008).

In phase 3, teachers learn how the culture they belong to includes a set of values, beliefs, and expectations, which in turn influences the way they teach. Teachers also learn about the cultures of their students, that conventional schools attempt to transmit the dominant culture to all students, and that the resulting cultural clashes have negative effects on low-socioeconomic and racial/ethnic minority students. Learning activities in phase 3 include book studies, video analyses, simulations, and participation in community events. The focus at this stage is on the practices of teachers in general, rather than those of individual participants (Guerra & Nelson, 2008).

Phase 4 involves teachers analyzing the same student data examined in phase 1, but this time, in addition to remaining disaggregated by ethnicity and socioeconomic status, the data are broken down by individual teachers, grade levels, and departments. Teachers thus become aware of patterns of inequity in their own classrooms and instructional teams. Teachers may also survey or interview students and parents to shed light on inequitable practices. Along with data gathering and analysis, teachers continue book study and video analysis to learn more about the negative effects of cultural clashes and deficit teaching on low-socioeconomic and racial/ethnic minority students. The activities in phase 4 often cause teachers cognitive dissonance (see Chapter 6), which can lead teachers to reframe their views of diverse cultures and begin to shift from a deficit approach to an assets-based approach to teaching and learning (Guerra & Nelson, 2008).

School Development.   Culturally responsive teachers are the heart and soul of a culturally responsive school, but the school as a community also has a vital role to play in addressing diversity. Some suggestions for school development follow:

- A schoolwide commitment to cultural responsiveness should be made by creating what Madsen and Mabokela (2005) call an *organizational identity* that addresses the complexity of diversity and is inclusive of and responsive to diverse cultures. According to these authors, "Organizational identity is defined as the organization members' collective understanding of the features that are presumed to be central and permanent and that distinguish the organization from other organizations" (p. 120). A school with an organizational identity as a culturally responsive school has not necessarily achieved that status. However, it is suggesting to everyone inside and outside the organization that cultural responsiveness is its goal, and it is inviting all stakeholders to critique its progress toward that goal.

- Schools need to hire more racial/ethnic minority teachers in general but specifically more African American teachers for schools with African American students, more Latino teachers for schools with Latino students, and more bilingual and multilingual teachers for schools with ESL students.

- Schools with large low-socioeconomic and racial/ethnic minority student populations should hire more teachers from teacher education programs that teach cultural responsiveness, more teachers with majors in the subjects they are going to teach, and more highly qualified teachers in general.

- In schools with lower-socioeconomic and racial/ethnic minority students, all members of the school community need to become immersed in the school's diverse cultures, continuously learning about their students and the students' families and communities (Michael & Young, 2005). This learning process can be facilitated by a network of adults (supervisors, teachers, parents, other community members) who are members of or knowledgeable about diverse cultures.

- The school should develop an inclusive curriculum that incorporates diverse students' languages and cultural backgrounds (Chamberlain, 2005). The curriculum should reflect both transformation and social action approaches (Banks, 2010). In the *transformational approach,* students view curriculum content from the perspectives of diverse groups. In the *social action approach,* students examine and act on social issues related to diversity (see Chapter 19). Basic skills are integrated into the rich content provided in the transformation and social action curriculum.

- All members of the school community need to work at developing a nurturing school environment, with relationships between adults and students and among students based on authentic caring. This nurturing environment should be accompanied by high expectations for all students (Valenzuela, 1999).

- Tracking and ability grouping should be eliminated. This will enable access for *all* lower-socioeconomic and racial/ethnic minority students to higher-level learning that traditionally is not provided to students in lower-level tracks and groups. Also, eliminating tracking and ability grouping will allow higher-achieving poor and racial/ethnic minority students to network and share their funds of knowledge and learning strategies with lower-achieving poor and racial/ethnic minority students.

- Schools need to establish infrastructures that allow adults (supervisors, teachers, parents) from different cultural groups to communicate on a regular basis and to collaborate on how to make schools more culturally responsive. Various groups can collaborate on school policies, curriculum development, instructional practices, and student assessment methods.

- Methods for student assessment must become more culturally responsive. Educators who conduct assessment need to learn to avoid culturally biased assessments, to distinguish between underachievement due to disability and underachievement due to cultural incongruence, and to use a variety of culturally sensitive assessment methods, rather than rely exclusively on norm-referenced tests. Student assessment needs to shift from a diagnostic-prescriptive focus to one of student advocacy (Chamberlain, 2005).

- The school's ultimate goal should be to integrate cultural knowledge throughout *all* school operations. Cultural responsiveness needs to become institutionalized as part of the school culture (Lindsey, Roberts, & Campbell Jones, 2005). New members of the school community need to be socialized into the school's commitment to diversity and culturally responsive practices.

Collaboration with Families and the Community. The third leg that supports a culturally responsive school is collaboration with students' families and the community. First and foremost, supervisors and teachers should accept parents as essential partners in their children's education. Parents should be welcome at school, not just as visitors but as part of the school community. Schools should be organized so that supervisors and teachers are available to meet with parents to discuss their concerns. For both individual and group meetings, strategies should be developed to help overcome barriers to parents meeting with educators, such as work schedules, transportation problems, and child-care issues (Griner & Stewart, 2013; Lee & Bowen, 2006). During meetings, parents should always be treated as equals who have much to contribute. Parents' communication styles, cultural values, and childrearing practices should be respected.

Parents should be part of the school leadership. They can be given roles on the school leadership council and on important committees and task forces. Parents in leadership roles can serve as liaisons to other parents. Parents can also be invited to assume a variety of other educational roles based on their experience, interest, and available time.

An interesting concept with much promise is the school-based parent center, which is managed by parents for the benefit of other parents, the school, and the community. A center usually is provided its own space on campus and an operating budget, with parent volunteers doing most of the work. The center might provide parent education classes, forums for school–parent dialogue, services to students, or cultural events for the community. Parent centers can serve as a bridge between the school, the parents, and the community.

Schools serving diverse students need to collaborate not just with students' families but also with other members of the community the school serves. Diverse community members can sit on school advisory groups, be guest teachers, and serve as role models for students. Through service learning and social action, students can become directly involved in community development. The school can become a center of community assistance, providing a variety of human services to community members. In addition, the school can enter into partnerships with community agencies and programs, becoming part of a larger network of education and human support (see Chapter 23).

In our earlier discussion of school development, we discussed Madsen and Mabokela's (2005) idea of the school establishing an organizational identity as a culturally responsive school. These authors argue that work on organizational identity should be an interactive process, with the school projecting what type of organization it wishes to be, the community providing feedback on the school's actual performance, and the school modifying its performance accordingly. Through this process, the school continuously responds to a diverse community.

> ▶ **Video Illustration**
>
> As you watch this video, identify specific ways that the principal and/or faculty in the video have strengthened relationships with families and the community.

Gender Equity

Conventional schools tend to foster *gender inequity*, in which female students are subject to considerable sexual harassment and discrimination. In many textbooks and other curriculum materials, females are depicted as needy, passive, and subordinate to males. In conventional classrooms, teachers interact more with boys than with girls, and boys tend to control the classroom discussion. Girls are made to believe they are unable to solve problems on their own, yet they are less likely to receive helpful feedback. Thus, girls often become "invisible students" in the classroom (Bauer, 2000). The vast majority of females experience some form of sexual harassment at school and often find it difficult to get assistance if they report the harassment (Fry, 2003; Ormerod, Collinsworth, & Perry, 2008).

The inequitable treatment of females in schools can have devastating effects. Gruber and Fineran (2007) found that the chief effects of sexual harassment on both middle and high school girls were lower self-esteem, poorer mental health, worse physical health, and higher levels of trauma symptoms, with high school girls having more severe effects than middle school girls in each category. Girls' self-confidence often drops dramatically during early adolescence (Mullen & Tuten, 2004; Kommer, 2006). Mullen and Tuten (2004) note that "resiliency, optimism, curiosity, and risk-taking all seem to take a nosedive. . . . Those teenagers who live such disablement have been viewed as passive, self-conscious, low in self-esteem, preoccupied with looking attractive and appearing unintelligent, and non–goal oriented" (p. 294). To make matters worse, teachers in conventional schools who attempt to address gender inequities often encounter hostility from colleagues and parents (Fry, 2003).

Although girls suffer the most from gender inequity, boys are affected as well. For example, boys are more likely to need supplemental reading instruction, receive a discipline referral, be identified as a special education student, be suspended or expelled, and drop out of school (Taylor & Lorimer, 2003; Kommer, 2006). "The fact that boys lag behind girls with respect to a variety of important educational outcomes has been called the 'Silent gender gap'" (Dee, 2007, p. 531). Moreover, we are beginning to realize that boys have many of the same problems with self-esteem as girls, although they are socialized to hide their feelings of inadequacy (Kommer, 2006). Boys, too, then, have been mistreated by traditional schooling (Kommer, 2006).

The goal of efforts to address gender issues in schools "is not to treat boys and girls equally, but to create equity by purposely addressing the particular needs of each gender" (Kommer, 2006, p. 250). A good place for supervisors to start efforts toward gender equity is to open a dialogue on the effects of such inequity on students. Research and other readings on gender issues can inform that dialogue. Fry (2003) suggests that schools develop a gender equity plan that has goals, guidelines, and benchmarks. Although such a plan would vary from school to school, some nonnegotiables would be in order. For example, one goal for all schools should be eliminating from the school all forms of sexual harassment.

Sanders and Cotton Nelson (2004) describe a process that involves teachers in working for gender equity. During an all-day workshop at the beginning of the process, teachers are presented data on girls' underachievement and discuss gender-related problems they observe in their classrooms. After the initial workshop, participants meet periodically for half-day workshops focused on topics such as gender stereotypes and teacher expectations, interpersonal dynamics among different groups, gender bias in the curriculum, and so on. Between workshops, teachers engage in a variety of learning activities. They observe gender issues being played out in public places and popular media and search for gender bias in their own schools and classrooms. They also do gender experiments, such as having colleagues observe their teaching for bias and trying out new strategies to make their classrooms more equitable. At the next workshop, teachers bring data they have gathered and share their learning experiences. Sanders and Cotton Nelson have found that this process helps teachers to realize that gender bias does exist—in society, in schools, and even in their own classrooms. In the workshops, teachers also develop knowledge and skills to promote gender equity.

Kommer (2006) suggests additional strategies that teachers can use to create gender equity, including balancing competitive and cooperative activities, considering gender when forming student groups, providing equal response opportunities, inviting gender role models to the classroom, and providing a gender-neutral learning environment. Another important thing teachers can do to promote gender equity is to facilitate dialogue among girls and boys in which they talk about inequity, its effects on them and their peers, and how students can work together with teachers to develop equitable classrooms and schools.

▶ Video Illustration

After you watch this video, reflect on how the results of the study shared by the teacher could be used as part of a professional development program on gender equity.

> ▶ **Video Illustration**
>
> After you watch this video, reflect on the types of teasing and bullying in a school you are familiar with that relate to gender issues. What are ways that supervisors and teachers could effectively confront these behaviors as well as the underlying gender issues?

Equity for Sexual and Gender Minorities

Consider the following statistics:

- An estimated 10% of students in U.S. schools are gay or lesbian (Weiler, 2003).
- Over 80% of gay and lesbian students have been verbally abused. Ninety percent have heard antigay remarks, and 25% of those remarks have been voiced by school staff (Glimps, 2005; Whelan, 2006).
- Twenty percent of gay and lesbian youth have been physically assaulted at school (Whelan, 2006).
- In a third or more of the incidents in which gay and lesbian students have been harassed at school, adults witnessed the abuse and did nothing to help (Birkett, Espelage, & Koenig, 2009; Weiler, 2003).
- Nearly two out of three gays and lesbian youth have reported that they felt unsafe at school (Birkett et al., 2009; Weiler, 2003; Goodenow, Szalacha, & Westheimer, 2006).
- The grade-point averages of students reporting frequent harassment are over 10% lower than those of other students (Whelan, 2006).
- Gay and lesbian youth commit suicide at a rate two to three times that of other youth. Issues of sexual identity play a role in 30% of youth suicides (Hansen, 2007; van Wormer & McKinney, 2003).

Payne (2007) reminds us that most schools are *heteronormative,* which means popularity and group membership are equated with heterosexuality. Youth who do not conform to the expectations of heterosexuality are subject to ridicule, gossip, and isolation. Moreover, Payne notes, "Current school practices are invested in preserving the heterosexist structure of schools and continuing to reinforce heterosexuality as the norm" (p. 77). Payne cites school rituals like electing cheerleaders, prom kings and queens, and "cutest couple" as examples of the institutional support for heterosexual popularity and power. Many educators support the heteronormative nature of schools by ignoring the harassment of lesbian, gay, bisexual, and transgender (LGBT) students or even by joining the ridicule of these minorities. Even sexual minority teachers often remain silent as LGBT students are abused (van Wormer & McKinney, 2003).

How sexual and gender minority students are treated in schools creates a serious dilemma for these students:

> The instinct for many is to hide their identity, which deepens their sense of confusion, isolation, and self-doubt. On the other hand, LGBT youth who do come out face the very real risk of violence, harassment, prejudice, discrimination, and stigmatization. (Weiler, 2003, p. 11)

The stress and lack of support eventually take their toll on many LGBT students:

> The stressors related to either hiding or revealing one's sexual identity place sexual minority students at a higher risk for developing mental health, physical, and educational problems. Because survival at school is the priority, many LGBT students experience academic and learning problems. (Weiler, 2003, p. 11)

Such problems include more frequent absences, less involvement in school activities, worse grades, and a higher dropout rate than heterosexual students (Birkett et al., 2009; Glimps, 2005; Hansen, 2007; Walls, Kane, & Wisneski, 2010; Weiler, 2003; Whelan, 2006).

Problems resulting from the abuse of sexual and gender minority students go beyond academics. LGBT students are more likely to engage in high-risk behaviors such as drinking, drug abuse, and unsafe sex (Espelage, Aragon, Birkett, & Koenig, 2008; Glimps 2005; van Wormer & McKinney, 2003). It is not the fact that they are sexual and gender minorities but the abuse they receive that leads LGBT students to engage in such risky behaviors (Glimps, 2005). Many LGBT students are homeless, having been thrown out of their homes by their parents because of their sexual orientation or gender identity (van Wormer & McKinney, 2003; Weiler, 2003). And as noted earlier, the suicide rate of lesbian and gay students is far higher than that of heterosexual students (Hansen, 2007; van Wormer & McKinney, 2003; Goodenow et al., 2006).

The fact that many schools do nothing about prejudice and discrimination against LGBT students—indeed, that they contribute to the prejudice and discrimination—means that they are miseducating both sexual and gender minority *and* heterosexual students. Grayson (1987) discusses this reality:

> The failure of school officials to provide protection from peer harassment and violence reflects only a portion of the harm caused by the hatred of gay males and lesbians in schools. Homophobia hinders the development of all school children from growing into tolerant and compassionate members of a harmonious and cohesive pluralistic society. Acceptance of prejudice against lesbians and gay males contributes to the authority of privileged groups, validating prejudice and discrimination against others. It reinforces rigid sex role behavior and the imposed silence and misinformation keeps people ignorant of accurate information and facts. (p. 136)

Schools can begin to promote equity for LGBT students by establishing a school policy that protects and supports those students (Goodenow et al., 2006; Hansen, 2007; Mayberry, 2006; Walls et al., 2010). The policy should not only rule out harassment of LGBT students but also affirm their right to be respected members of the school community. The policy should be disseminated to students, teachers, parents, and the community. This can be accomplished through public meetings in which information on the need for such a policy is shared and misinformation about LGBT students is dispelled.

As with professional development to promote equity for other marginalized student groups, developing self-awareness is a critical part of helping teachers to work with LGBT students. Supervisors can help teachers develop self-awareness by facilitating a process proposed by Van Den Bergh and Crisp (2004). The process includes five phases:

1. Self-reflect on one's own sexual orientation, in terms of its development, influences, and experiences.

2. Reflect upon one's previous contact with GLBT individuals, both personally and professionally.

3. Evaluate one's reaction to GLBT individuals, both in terms of positive and negative experiences.

4. Self-evaluate the cognitive, affective, and behavioral components of one's responses to GLBT individuals in order to develop awareness of potential heterosexism or homophobia.

5. Participate in personal and professional activities that foster a greater understanding of GLBT individuals and culture. (p. 227)

In addition to engaging in personal development, supervisors and teachers need to collaboratively examine different aspects of schooling that might contribute to inequity, including (1) school policies that might conflict with the school's nondiscrimination policy, (2) the school climate, (3) student discipline, (4) the curriculum, (5) teaching practices, (6) interactions in classrooms and common areas, and (7) student achievement. Teachers can gather and analyze data in any of these areas, identifying foci for improvement.

Once problem areas have been identified, a variety of strategies can be used to foster equity for LGBT students. Depending on the needs of the particular school, any of the following strategies can promote equity:

- School safety and antibullying programs are a trend in public education. If a school initiates one of these programs, protection of LGBT students should be a key feature. Both teachers and parents should be involved in designing and carrying out the program. The program should address educating students on the need to treat LGBT students with respect and include monitoring of student and adult behaviors toward sexual minority and transgender students. When abuse of an LGBT student occurs, adults need to intervene promptly to work with both the abused and the abuser.

- Reform the curriculum. A curriculum that promotes heterosexuals as superior and LGBT as inferior needs to be changed. One way to do so is to introduce literature that promotes LGBT persons in a positive light. The work and lives of sexual minority and transgender persons who have made significant contributions in various fields can also be integrated into appropriate subjects. Case studies of prejudice and discrimination can be used to critique the dominant culture's treatment of LGBT persons. Advanced courses could focus on gay studies or involve students in social action against the abuse of sexual minorities.

- Teachers can work together to change their teaching practices so their classrooms are more inclusive of LGBT students and they do a better job of preventing prejudice and discrimination against those students. This collaboration can include joint planning of inclusive lessons, observations of each other's teaching, and collegial dialogue on how to better support sexual and gender minority students.

- The school can appoint an adult advocate or team of advocates for LGBT students. The advocate or team can work directly with sexual and gender minority students, refer those students to external resources and outside support groups, be the liaison between LGBT students and adults in the school community, and press for changes in policy and practice that will make life at school better for sexual and gender minority students (Goodenow et al., 2006).

- The school can create an in-school support group for LGBT students. Gay–straight alliance clubs, for example, not only provide group support for sexual minority and transgender students but also help to improve intercultural understanding between LGBT students and those from the dominant culture (Goodenow et al., 2006; Walls et al., 2010).

Equity for Students with Disabilities

Although concern for educating children with special needs in America's public schools can be traced back to the early 1800s, the modern era of special education began with the passage of the Education for All Handicapped Children Act (EAHCA, Public Law 94–142) in 1975 (Spaulding & Pratt, 2015). This legislation, now known as the Individuals with Disabilities Education Act (IDEA) (2004), requires all schools receiving federal funding to provide disabled students with free, appropriate public education (FAPE) in the least restrictive environment (LRE) possible. More specifically, the purposes of IDEA relative to K-12 education are

- to ensure that all children with disabilities have available to them a free appropriate public education that emphasizes special education and related services designed to meet their unique needs and prepare them for further education, employment and independent living

- to ensure that the rights of children with disabilities and parents of such children are protected
- to assist states, localities, educational service agencies and federal agencies to provide for the education of all children with disabilities
- to ensure that educators and parents have the necessary tools to improve educational results for children with disabilities...
- to assess, and ensure the effectiveness of efforts to educate children with disabilities (Individuals with Disabilities Education Improvement Act of 2004, Sec. 601).

As of the 2012-2013 school year, 6.4 million, approximately 13% of all U.S. public school students, were receiving special education services (National Center for Educational Statistics, 2015). The percentage of students with disabilities in each of 13 disability types is shown in Figure 22.1.

Despite federal legislation, and the approximately $100 billion per year spent by public schools to educate students with special needs (IDEA Funding Coalition, n.d.), these students' academic achievement lags behind their peers. Schifier (2011) found that, on average, special needs students take 5 years to complete high school; 72.4% graduated within 8 years of beginning high school, and 25% dropped out before earning a diploma. Additionally, McLaughlin (2010) reports that special needs students are significantly less likely to attend postsecondary schools than the population

Highest Percentages

Specific disability (such as dyslexia or dysgraphia)—35%
Speech or language impairment —21%
Other health impairment (such as asthma or epilepsy) —12%

Lower Percentages

Autism— 8%
Intellectual disability—7%
Developmental delay—6%
Emotional disturbance (such as depression or schizophrenia)—6%

Lowest Percentages

Multiple disabilities—2%
Hearing impairment—1%
Orthopedic impairment (such as those caused by cerebral palsy)—1%
Deaf-blindness—less than 0.5%
Traumatic brain injury—less than 0.5%
Visual impairments—less than 0.5%

figure **22.1** **Percentage of Students in Each Disability Type**

Source: National Center for Educational Statistics. Retrieved from http://nces.ed.gov/programs/coe/indicator_cgg.asp

at large; those who do make the leap to higher education are much more likely to attend 2-year or vocational schools, as opposed to 4-year or professional schools. McLaughlin also cites studies showing that only 37% of disabled adults are gainfully employed, and 22% of those adults claim that the cause for their unemployment is a lack of job training. Furthermore, the work typically done by this population consists of part-time, low-wage jobs that provide few, if any, benefits such as health insurance.

Given federal law mandating equitable treatment of students with disabilities, why does the achievement gap continue? Some blame inadequate funding by the federal government to carry out federal mandates. Others lament that there is an ongoing shortage of certified special education teachers in this nation, and that both general and special education teachers are not consistently receiving the training necessary to adequately meet the needs of special education students (Smith, Robb, West, & Tyler, 2010). Some authors speak of the lack of specific skills, such as collaboration, as particular areas of concern, pointing to studies that suggest that teacher education programs that teach such skills produce teachers who feel better prepared to address the complexities involved in educating students with special needs and are less likely to leave the profession (Hamilton-Jones & Vail, 2014).

Another problem, one that relates directly to our earlier discussion of equity for racial and ethnic minorities, is the disproportionate representation of students from racial and ethnic minorities in special education. For example, a disproportionate number of African Americans are identified as having intellectual disabilities and emotional disabilities, and English language learners are disproportionately represented in groups identified as learning disabled and intellectually disabled (Zhang, Katsiyannis, Ju, & Roberts, 2014). Skiba et al. (2008) point out: "Disproportionate representation is greater in the judgmental or 'soft' disability categories of MR, ED, or LD than in the nonjudgmental or 'hard' disability categories, such as hearing impairment, visual impairment, or orthopedic impairment" (p. 269).

We have already discussed many of the factors responsible for disproportionality—lack of cultural responsiveness, cultural conflicts, bias in referral and identification, and so forth. Another, self-perpetuating, factor is that when minority students are inappropriately placed in special education classes it limits their access to instruction that truly meets their needs. Disproportionality conflates issues of disability and social equity; many students who currently receive special education services would be better served by correcting the inequitable conditions in which they live.

What can teachers and supervisors do to address the problems we have been discussing and ensure equity for students with disabilities? McLaughlin (2010) summarizes four disability rights goals that are the basis for IDEA and the individualized improvement plan that it requires:

> . . . a student with a disability who is being treated equitably is being considered as an individual, is given full access to those aspects of life available to persons without disabilities, has opportunities to make decisions about both mundane and important life events, and has opportunities to become independent and self sustaining. (p. 269)

How does a school move toward the achievement of these equity goals? McLeskey and Waldron (2002) discuss a number of lessons they have learned from assisting teachers and supervisors to develop inclusive schools. First, while any educator in the school can initiate school change, eventually both teachers and supervisors must support the change effort if it is to be successful. Because the types, severity, and conditions that cause inequity are different from school to school, each school must be empowered to establish its own inclusive program—there are no external, generic models that can simply be "adopted." Changes in one aspect of the school's program, or even in an individual classroom, affect the entire school, thus change for the equitable treatment of students with disabilities is whole-school change, not simply an add-on to the school's instructional program. Ultimately we are concerned with changing the school culture. As we discussed more generally in Chapter 21, change efforts are almost sure to meet resistance, and McLeskey and Waldron urge leaders to honor that resistance and use it to improve the program. Professional development is a key ingredient in assisting teachers to address inequity. An important goal of the program should be to expand what McLeskey and Waldron call the "circle of tolerance," with increasing numbers of formerly perceived differences considered normal. The school can move toward this goal through co-teaching, para-educators, peer tutoring, and differentiated teaching. Finally, McLeskey and Waldron point out that because of the complexity and ever-changing nature of disabilities, a program to develop an inclusive school can never really be complete, but rather must be ongoing and focused on continuous improvement.

Inclusive practices for middle and secondary schools (which we believe could be adapted for elementary students as well) suggested by Villa, Thousand, Nevin, and Liston (2005) include the following:

- Differentiated instruction
- An interdisciplinary approach to curriculum and instruction
- Use of technology to empower students and address individual student needs
- Collaborative learning and peer assistance
- Curricular modifications such as different instructional materials, modified expectations for the same learning activity, and integration of life or social skills with academic content
- Teaching students to accept responsibility, resolve conflict, and practice self-determination
- Authentic assessment

At the organizational level, Villa and colleagues recommend block scheduling, heterogeneous grouping of students (de-tracking), and collaborative teaching involving regular teachers, special education teachers, and paraprofessionals.

The problem of disproportionality also needs to be addressed by teachers and supervisors. Because the reasons for disproportionality are complex and vary from school to school, Skiba et al. (2008) recommend that each school begin to address the problem with a needs assessment to identify the types of disproportionality that might be present and their underlying causes. Skiba et al. also make general recommendations for reducing disproportionality, including professional development in culturally responsive teaching, culturally responsive classroom management, improvement of assessment techniques so that cultural differences can be separated from learning disabilities, teaching focused on preventing learning difficulties and early intervention when such difficulties are identified, and the involvement of community and family in the assessment and intervention process. Finally, Skiba et al. make recommendations at the policy level for reform in such areas as school finance, state testing, and teacher preparation.

Overarching Patterns

Although our discussions of (1) economic, racial, and ethnic minorities, (2) gender inequity, (3) sexual and gender minorities, and (4) students with disabilities in our schools are based on different bodies of literature, overarching patterns can be identified. Many of the problems faced by students in diverse groups are the result of cultural clashes between their culture and the dominant culture. These cultural clashes, in turn, result from a lack of understanding or an inability to respond to cultural differences.

To move forward, it is necessary for members of the dominant culture to learn about their own culture, other cultures, cultural clashes, and the negative effects of cultural clashes on diverse groups. This learning, especially if it involves teachers, seems to happen as a result of being confronted with data that are incongruent with one's beliefs about other cultures, reflecting on the data, engaging in dialogue with colleagues on the meaning of the data, and making a commitment to change the way diverse groups are treated. New knowledge gained through experiential learning leads to forming new attitudes, which leads to taking action on behalf of diverse groups.

Connecting the Technical Tasks of Supervision to Cultural Responsiveness

Our discussion on responding to diversity provides a good opportunity to show how the technical tasks of supervision cannot really be separated from the cultural tasks. Rather, the technical tasks can be used as vehicles to complete the cultural tasks. All six technical tasks (direct assistance, evaluation of teaching, group development, professional development, curriculum development, and action research) can be integrated in responding to diversity.

Action research can be a framework for integrating the other technical tasks of supervision into a comprehensive program to address diversity. Early in the action research process, teachers can gather data on the achievement gap between various student groups, cultural clashes, and the negative effects of cultural clashes on diverse student groups. The task of *group development* is carried out through each phase of action research but is especially vital in the early phases of action research for addressing diversity. Early in the process, teachers are involved in critical discussions of the negative effects of schooling on students from marginalized groups and confronting their own role in maintaining the status quo. These group discussions require balancing task and personal roles, dealing with some dysfunctional behaviors, managing conflict in constructive ways, and facilitating small- and large-group decision making.

Once teachers have made a commitment to addressing diversity and selected a focus within that broad area, it is time for action planning. The remaining technical tasks of supervision all can be included in the action plan. *Professional development* can provide teachers with the knowledge, skills, and strategies to address the needs of diverse students. *Curriculum development* can enable teachers to critique the status quo and to develop a curriculum that is culturally responsive and informs social action. *Direct assistance* can help teachers to apply culturally responsive teaching through clinical supervision, peer coaching, demonstration teaching, mentoring, and so on. And formative evaluation of teaching (more appropriate for this purpose than summative evaluation), can provide individual teachers and instructional teams feedback on their progress toward becoming more culturally responsive.

After implementing the action plan for a period of time, teachers can continue action research by gathering data to assess the effects of the action plan on the school and its diverse groups and to plan future actions to increase the school's cultural responsiveness. In summary, the technical tasks of supervision—powerful processes for improving instruction by themselves—can also contribute to broader cultural tasks such as addressing diversity.

✔ **Check Your Understanding 22.0**   Click here to gauge your understanding of the key concepts presented in this chapter.

REFLECTIVE EXERCISE

Base this exercise on a school you are familiar with. What are the "top 10" actions the school can take to better address cultural diversity? Different cultural categories you might consider addressing as you complete this exercise include race, ethnicity, socioeconomic status, gender, sexual orientation, students with disabilities, and so forth. Your top 10 actions could relate to establishing policies, creating structures, developing processes, providing professional development, designing curriculum, assessing students, grouping students, changing teaching practices, working with parents, collaborating with the community, and so forth. Be specific in describing each of your top 10 actions.

chapter 23

Building Community

Learning Outcomes for This Chapter

After reading this chapter, you should be able to:

1. Summarize the authors' three reasons why schools should be democratic communities.

2. Recall Noddings's three components of teaching care.

3. List six characteristics of a professional learning community.

4. Explain what the authors mean with their statement that, when schools are communities of inquiry, classrooms become their own centers of inquiry.

5. Enumerate three specific learning models that connect students to the community and the larger society.

6. Describe the relationship of the five attributes of a school community.

Questions to Reflect On as You Read This Chapter

1. Do you consider PK-12 schools to be more like the typical conception of an *organization* or a *community*? How can schools become less like organizations and more like communities?

2. Consider the differences between education *for* democracy and education *through* democracy.

3. The section on moral community in this chapter describes nine principles of a moral community. How would increasing the presence of each of these principles improve the lives and learning of students in PK-12 schools?

4. Many schools across the nation have what they refer to as professional learning communities (PLCs). If you are familiar with one of those schools, to what degree do you believe it has embraced the six characteristics of PLCs discussed in this chapter? What indicators of the presence or absence of the characteristics are present in the school you are considering?

5. As you read the section "Engagement with the Larger Community" in this chapter, identify connections of the three types of engagement described (school-based and school-linked community service, community development, and the community as a learning environment) with student learning.

Sergiovanni (1994a, 1994b, 1999, 2004) and others have proposed viewing schools as *communities* rather than *organizations*. Organizations are known for their "linear lines of communication, chain-of-command decision making, differentiation of tasks, hierarchical supervision, and formal rules and regulations" (Scribner, Cockrell, Cockrell, & Valentine, 1999, p. 135). In an organization, the leader decides what needs to be done and bargains with workers to gain their cooperation, offering them something they want in exchange for doing what the leader wants. Rewards are provided for compliance and punishments for noncompliance. Individuals thus are bound together by bartering and self-interest (Sergiovanni, 1999). Classical organization theory is tied to the factory model, with its emphasis on efficiency and productivity:

> The adoption of this bureaucratic theory using the Carnegie units of grades and specializations adopted by the modern school system has resulted in the modern factory schools where the product is the student prepared for the work force to fuel the economy. The problem with this organizational theory for schools is that students are not products and don't usually respond positively to a culture that adds to them as if they were a car on an assembly line. Many students fall by the wayside in this factory model as rejects or seconds off the assembly line. (Martin & MacNeil, 2007, para. 1)

In contrast to organizations, relationships in communities are based on shared identity, beliefs, values, and goals. Members of a community are mutually committed to each other and the community (Hord, 2008). Sergiovanni (1999) makes this comparison of communities and organizations:

> Life in organizations and life in communities are different in both quality and kind. In communities we create our social lives with others who have intentions similar to ours. In organizations relationships are constructed for us by others and become codified into a system of hierarchies, roles, and role expectations. Communities too are confronted with issues of control. But instead of relying on external control measures communities rely more on norms, purposes, values, professional socialization, collegiality, and natural independence. (p. 119)

Merely agreeing to view schools as communities rather than organizations, of course, is not a magic elixir for all of our schools' problems. For one thing, not all communities are good communities. A community can be insular, myopic, or prejudiced. Over time, communities can develop internal conflicts, become dysfunctional, and deteriorate. Shields and Seltzer (1997) note, "many schools may be just as accurately described as microcosms of the conflicts and disparities in the wider community than as examples of Sergiovanni's emotional and normative relationships" (p. 415). These authors believe that this reality can be addressed by educators committing to community development as a moral endeavor in which they explore differences and commonalities; work to create democratic, inclusive communities; and achieve unity *within* diversity in order to build what Sergiovanni (1994a) refers to as an *authentic community*. Table 23.1 compares terms associated with classic organizations with those describing authentic communities.

Most educators who compare classic organizations to authentic communities readily conclude that they would rather work in a school that exemplifies an authentic community. However, we should also consider that students benefit greatly from attending a school that possesses the characteristics of a true community. Osterman (2000) reports that students who perceive themselves as belonging to and accepted

t a b l e **23.1** Classic Organizations and Authentic Communities Compared

	Classic Organizations	Authentic Communities
Leadership	• Transactional leadership • Technical-rational approach • Management • Hierarchy • Top-down communication • Leader "sells" and members "buy into" vision • Bureaucracy • Control • Monitoring • Evaluation	• Transformational leadership • Democracy • Dialogue • Collectively developed vision • Mutual influence • Consensus making • Horizontal communication • Leadership networks • Personal agency
Motivation	• Individualism • Competition • Self-interest • External rewards and sanctions	• Moral principles • Shared beliefs, values, and goals • Safety • Members' needs met • Intrinsic rewards • Faith in one another • Hope for the future
Relationships	• Relationships based on defined roles and responsibilities • Contractual relationships and resulting obligations • Bargaining • Bartering	• Sense of belonging and acceptance • Mutual caring and concern • Mutual trust • Collegiality and collaboration • Positive interdependence
Priorities	• Policies, procedures, and regulations • Prescribed expectations • Outputs/products • Skills and competencies • Measurement	• Commitment to the common good • Balancing individual rights and social responsibilities • Unity within diversity • Holistic growth and development

by a school that functions as an authentic community are more motivated to learn and more engaged in the learning process, and in turn experience a higher quality of learning. Moreover, students who are supported by teachers and other students in a communal environment develop interpersonal skills that will assist them to develop positive interpersonal relationships outside of school and in adulthood. Finally, Osterman concludes that schools that serve as authentic communities foster the emotional and personal development of students.

In Table 23.1 we list the characteristics of any authentic community, but what exactly makes a *school* a true community? Strike (2000) offers some general requisites. First, there must be what he calls "a shared view of human flourishing" (p. 619)—how do we prepare students for moral, productive, and happy lives in community with others? Second, a vision of the good life must lead to shared educational goals that, when met, will assist students to live the envisioned good life. Third, members of the school community must collaborate to work toward the realization of the agreed-upon goals. And fourth, the collaboration and resulting educational activities "must generate the goods of community such as a sense of belonging, loyalty, trust, mutual attachment and concern" (p. 619).

Based on our work with many schools and our research on successful schools, we suggest five attributes of a fully functioning school community: (1) democracy, (2) moral principles, (3) professional learning, (4) inquiry, and (5) engagement with the wider community. We will explore each of these attributes in this chapter.

Democratic Community

There are at least three powerful reasons that schools should be democratic communities. First, the most important reason that U.S. public schools exist is to sustain democracy by preparing students to be informed and responsible citizens (Isac, Maslowski, Creemers, & van der Werf, 2014; Martin & Chiodo, 2007; Schultz, 2007). Second, with democratic governance, schools work better and are more likely to improve. Third, in a democratic community, students experience higher-level learning and higher levels of achievement than in conventional schools (Flanagan, Cumsille, Gill, & Gallay, 2007).

Goodlad (2004) argues that educating students in democracy is essential to sustaining a democratic society:

> In a democracy, schooling is vitally important and very different from schooling in other societies. No other institution in our society is as suited as the public schools for introducing the young to both the ideas inherent in a social and political democracy as well as the ideals from which democracy is derived. That is why thoughtful men and women dating back to the very origins of our country have consistently envisioned a prominent and essential role for public schooling in the creating and sustaining of a democratic republic. (p. 19)

John Dewey is one of those thoughtful men and women to whom Goodlad refers. Dewey (1916) wrote, "A democracy is more than a form of government; it is primarily a mode of associated living, of conjoint communicated experience" (p. 93). In other words, democracy is about the social relationships of community members. Citizens need to understand how others' actions affect them and how their actions affect others. In an authentic democracy, citizens seek to understand the experiences, values, and needs of others and balance their interests with those of others (Bleazby, 2006; Rhoads, 1998). Dewey believed not only that schools need to prepare students for democratic life but also that the way to do so is for students to *experience* democracy within the school community.

If schools are to promote democracy, then, they should do the following:

- Value and respect each individual and promote the well-being of all members of the school community.
- Work to understand, be responsive to, and ensure equitable treatment of all minority groups.
- Involve all members of the school community—including teachers, students, and parents—in decision making, and expand the areas of decision making in which they are involved.
- Encourage two-way communication, the free flow of ideas, and open discussion of controversial issues.
- Foster critical reflection on and critique of power relations, school structures, the curriculum, and instructional practices, and be open to change for the common good.
- Engage in collaborative work and collective leadership.
- Allow freedom of choice.
- Embrace norms of civic participation and service to others.

In addition to preserving our democratic society, democratic schools work better and improve more than conventional schools. Indeed, Mallory and Reavis (2007) conclude that "a school culture based on democracy-centered principles is essential to continuous school improvement" (p. 10). School improvement has been associated with a number of variables, including teacher empowerment, teacher leadership, collaboration, collegiality, reflective dialogue, and teacher choice (Gordon, Stiegelbauer, & Diehl, 2008). If you examine these variables, you will find that they are all far more likely to occur in a democratic community than a school in which decisions are made by the principal or a small leadership team.

Our concepts of democracy and community are compatible with recent scholarship that indicates true leadership does not consist of a single person in a leadership role making decisions but results from relationships and interactions among many individuals, including formal and informal leaders (Harris, 2008; Scribner, Sawyer,

Watson, & Myers, 2007; Spillane, 2005). Scribner and colleagues (2007) suggest that "decisions emerge from collaborative dialogues between many individuals, engaged in mutually dependent activities" (p. 70). This description of leadership sounds a lot like leadership in the communities described by Sergiovanni (1999) as well as the relational democracy espoused by Dewey (1916).

Democracy is not only a way of governing and relating to one another but also a theory of how students learn. In schools practicing a democratic pedagogy, students do these things:

- Work actively with problems, ideas, materials, and other people as they learn skills and content
- Have escalating degrees of choices, both as individuals and groups, within the parameters provided by the teacher
- Are responsible to their peers, teachers, parents, and school community, using educational time purposefully, intelligently, and productively
- Share their learning with one another, teachers, parents, and other community members
- Decide how to make their learning a contribution to their community
- Assume escalating responsibilities for securing resources (of people and materials outside of school) and finding places where they can apply and further their learning
- Demonstrate what they know and can do in public settings and receive public feedback, and
- Work together and learn from one another, individually and in groups, at a pace that challenges all (Glickman, 1998, p. 18)

A long line of research shows that students taught in a democratic community using the pedagogy just described—regardless of their socioeconomic, racial, or ethnic status—perform at a higher level than other students on a variety of achievement measures (Bleazby, 2006; Darling-Hammond, 1997; Flanagan et al., 2007; Joyce, Wolf, & Calhoun, 1993; Meier, 1995; Newmann, Marks, & Gamoran, 1995).

Moral Community*

A moral school community is committed to the overall well-being, growth, and development of each community member. Moral communities are built around moral principles that, when taken together and taken seriously, foster the development of a school that enables students to develop as moral persons prepared to contribute to a better society. Several of those moral principles are suggested here.

---

*Portions of this section originally were published in Stephen P. Gordon (2001), "The Good School." *Florida Educational Leadership, 1*(2), 13–15.

Care

In caring schools, adults are open and receptive to students. They engage students in informal conversations, listen to students attentively, and are aware of what is going on in students' lives inside and outside of school. Adults try to place themselves in students' shoes to understand their experiences, concerns, and actions and put forth time and energy to respond to students' needs, to bring out the best in students, and to promote students' success. Care is reciprocal; it is not complete unless the student receiving the care recognizes it, accepts it, and responds to it (Noddings, 2005, 2010). Schussler and Collins (2006) found that students felt cared for when they were provided opportunities to succeed, were treated with respect, and felt they belonged in school because of positive relationships with teachers and other students, and when the school showed flexibility in accommodating them and provided a family atmosphere.

Noddings (2005, 2010) reminds us that teachers need not only to care for students but also to help them develop the capacity to care for others. This begins with *modeling*. Teachers can't just tell students to care for others; they need to show them by developing caring relationships. Another component of teaching care is *dialogue*—open-ended, two-way conversation in which the outcome cannot be predicted. Engaging in dialogue develops students' capacity to communicate, to share decision making, and to support each other in problem solving. A third part of teaching students to care is providing opportunities to *practice* caregiving in order to develop skills and attitudes associated with care. Finally, teachers should use *confirmation* to teach care, identifying students' "better selves" and encouraging them to develop those better, caring selves (Noddings, 2005, 2010).

Although teachers caring for students and teaching students to care for others is at the heart of a caring school community, the principle of care applies to everyone associated with the school. In a community of care, school leaders, teachers, students, and parents are all caregivers and care receivers.

Video Illustration

As you watch this video, reflect on suggestions you would make to the principal and teachers on how to continue to develop a culture of care throughout the school.

Wholeness

Authentic care for students leads to the realization that one cannot separate different aspects of student growth. The moral school is committed to students' cognitive, physical, emotional, creative, social, and moral development (Oser, Althof, &

Higgins-D'Alessandro, 2008). Not only is growth in all of these areas necessary for the development of the whole person, but the different domains of learning are interactive and interdependent; growth in one domain is enhanced by growth in the others. The principle of wholeness applies to adult members of the school community as well. For example, the school needs to concern itself with teachers' pedagogical growth; their physical and emotional well-being; and their creative, social, and moral development.

Connectedness

Schools have an obligation to break down artificial barriers to natural relationships in students' lives and learning. For example, the education provided to students must be relevant to both their present and their future, not focused on one at the expense of the other. Connections between different content areas must be made, and the world of the classroom needs to be connected to life outside the school, including the local, national, and world communities (National Commission on Service Learning, 2002; Simons & Cleary, 2006). The principle of connectedness also means that members of the school community should not be restricted to single roles (Biag, 2016). Administrators, teachers, and students should all engage in leadership, teaching, and learning, albeit at different levels and with different emphases.

 Video Illustration

What ideas are presented in this video for:

- Connecting students to each other?
- Connecting students' social and academic development?
- Connecting teachers to each other?
- Connecting parents to the school?

Inclusion

Inclusion, as a moral principle, combines the beliefs in equality and equity. It begins with equality. All students are of equal worth as human beings and as members of the school community. A belief in equality leads to a commitment to equity. Those who have physical, cognitive, emotional, or social challenges should be provided the necessary assistance, including extraordinary measures if necessary, to enable them to remain members of the community and to lead fulfilling lives first as students and later as adults. The moral school responds to all cultures and all students—low-socio-economic students, racial and ethnic minorities, immigrants, non-English-speaking students, gay and lesbian students, and so on (Flanagan et al., 2007; Glanz, 2010).

> **Video Illustration**
>
> The educator in this video describes how she fosters inclusion by pairing students with each other. After watching the video, reflect on other things that teachers could do to create a climate of inclusion in their classrooms.

> **Video Illustration**
>
> After you watch this video, think about the physical or social conditions at a school you are familiar with that might keep disabled students from feeling fully included in the school community. What can the school do to remove those barriers?

Justice

Teaching about social justice is part of this principle, as is providing justice as a means of facilitating teaching and learning. Justice includes holding teachers accountable for effective instruction and holding students accountable for learning. In an educational context, however, accountability should mean providing feedback on one's performance and assistance for improving future performance, not issuing rewards and punishments.

At its core, justice means treating members of the school community in a fair and consistent manner. By being just with students, educators can to some extent counter the injustice that students may face in society. By modeling justice, educators can teach students to treat others justly (Molinari, Speltini, & Passini, 2013; Schultz, 2008). Such justice, repeated daily, can facilitate student learning in all areas and eventually lead to a more just society. Justice must also be provided to all adults in the school community. Adults who are treated justly learn better how to treat students justly. A school will very likely provide its students no more justice than it provides its staff.

Peace

Student misbehavior is one of the major school problems reported by supervisors and teachers. Especially troublesome is misbehavior that interferes with the right of other students to learn. Worse yet, in recent years, there has been a frightening increase in student violence (Akiba, 2008). Perhaps one way to approach this problem is to change from a school characterized by "effective student discipline" to a school of "peace." Moving toward this vision will require supervisors, teachers, and students to develop or enhance communication, collaboration, and conflict management skills. Doing so will also require supervisors, teachers, and students to develop a new self-concept, viewing themselves not just as leaders or teachers or students but as healers and peacemakers. For those who argue that we cannot afford to spend school time learning about healing and peacemaking, our response is that considering the growing incivility in our communities and schools, we can no longer afford *not* to engage in such learning.

Freedom

Learning and freedom—freedom to dream, to explore, to take risks, and to learn from failures—go hand in hand. Educators need freedom to grow professionally, and likewise, students need freedom to develop to their full potential (Nash-Ditzel & Brown, 2012). Granted, students and adults function at varying stages of development and thus possess varying capacities for responding to freedom. For some, freedom may need to be introduced gradually, initially presented as restricted choice. Regardless, it is the *directionality* of the school's efforts that is important. All members of the school community should be moving toward increased freedom of choice in what they learn, how they learn, and how they demonstrate learning (Dooner, Mandzuk, & Clifton, 2008). Those who equate school reform with external control find this principle particularly difficult to accept.

Trust

Consistent efforts on behalf of care, wholeness, connectedness, inclusion, justice, peace, and freedom can lead to trusting relationships among members of the school community. Trust is both a product of adhering to the other principles and a requirement for those principles to flourish over the long run. Authentic learning is based not merely on the transmission of knowledge and skills but primarily on personal relationships, and trust is the ground on which those relationships are built (Hord, 2008; Huddy, 2015). For all its importance, however, personal trust is not the only type of trust present in a good school. There is also trust in the moral principles to which the school is committed—trust that these principles, if adhered to, will result in a better education and more fulfilling lives for students and a better future for society.

Empowerment

As a moral principle, empowerment certainly includes involving members of the school community in making decisions about matters that affect them, but it also goes beyond this standard definition. Empowerment also means changing assumptions, norms, roles, and relationships that act as barriers to educators' and students' growth toward self-reliance and self-actualization. It includes not only an invitation to become involved in decisions concerning leadership, teaching, and learning but also to acquire the information and skills necessary to engage in effective decision making in each of these areas. Finally, empowerment means instilling in educators and students a commitment to facilitate the empowerment of *other* members of the school community.

Professional Learning Community

Hord and Sommers (2008) define *professional learning communities (PLCs)* as "communities of professionals working to improve student learning together, by engaging in continuous collective learning of their own" (p. ix). Descriptions of specific characteristics of PLCs vary (Cranston, 2011; DuFour, 2005; DuFour, Eaker, & DuFour, 2005; Hipp, Huffman, Pankake, & Olivier, 2008; Hord & Sommers, 2008; Louis, Kruse, & Marks, 1996; Servage, 2008; Stoll, Bolam, McMahon, Wallace, & Thomas, 2006), but most descriptions include these six characteristics:

1. *Shared beliefs, values, and norms.* Educators reach consensus on a clear set of views about the purpose of school, about children and how they learn, and the role of school leaders, teachers, students, and parents in the learning process (Hipp et al., 2008). "Clear shared values and norms, collectively reinforced, increase the likelihood of teachers' success" (Louis et al., 1996, p. 181).

2. *Distributed, supportive leadership.* It is not surprising that the same type of leadership discussed in Chapter 21 as needed to facilitate change also fosters PLCs. Hord and Sommers (2008) describe two types of support provided to PLCs: (a) structural support (time to meet, a place to work, material resources) and (b) relational support (the fostering of openness, honesty, respect, and caring among educators). The supervisor shares decision making with teachers and other members of the school community and distributes leadership throughout the school with the goal of "developing the leadership potential of all staff members" (DuFour et al., 2005, p. 23).

3. *Collective learning.* The rationale of collective learning is that individual teachers learning new knowledge and skills in isolation is not enough to improve student learning schoolwide (Hord, 2008). Collective learning is job embedded and involves educators in the same school learning together (DuFour et al., 2005; Giles & Hargreaves, 2006; Hipp et al., 2007). The process begins with conversations among educators about students, teaching, and learning. The school community chooses an area for improvement, decides what it needs to learn to make the improvement, and plans collective learning experiences. Part of the learning process is trying out new skills and strategies, discussing the effects of the new practice, and deciding how the new practice can be improved (Hord & Sommers, 2008).

4. *Deprivatization of teaching.* One of the traditional norms of teaching is that teaching is a private act; the teacher's classroom is not open to other teachers. This privatization of teaching has kept teachers from providing each other instructional assistance. In a deprivatized school, teachers visit each other's classrooms for various reasons: to observe, gather data, and provide feedback; to pick up new ideas from each other; to team teach; and so on. Another part of deprivatization is the open discussion among teachers of problems and concerns about teaching and the sharing of ideas about how to address those problems and concerns.

5. *Focus on student learning.* DuFour and Reeves (2016) suggests that PLCs focus on four critical questions:
   • What do we want students to learn?
   • How will we know if they have learned it?
   • What will we do if they have not learned it?
   • How will we provide extended learning opportunities for students who have mastered the content? (p. 70)

   In PLCs, the focus of attention is on students' intellectual development, not merely on techniques or activities that seem interesting and are likely to keep students engaged (Louis et al., 1996). The focus of student assessment in PLCs is ongoing formative assessment to identify student learning needs, to provide feedback to help teachers adjust their teaching, and to track student progress over time. Student assessments "are easily accessible and openly shared between teachers who then assist each other in addressing areas of concern" (DuFour et al., 2005, p. 22).

6. *Collaboration.* In Chapter 2, we described how the legacy of the one-room school and the "egg crate" structure of traditional schools has kept teachers in their classrooms and out of contact with other adults for most of the school day. PLCs free teachers from isolation and provide peer support as they share information and expertise; work together to develop curriculum, create instructional materials, assess student learning; and engage in joint problem solving (Giles & Hargreaves, 2006; Hipp et al., 2008; Louis et al., 1996; Teague & Anfara, 2012).

The research on the effects of PLCs is promising. In a review of that research, Vescio, Ross, and Adams (2008) found that PLCs make teachers more student centered, improve the teaching culture, and improve student achievement. Some researchers, however, advise caution regarding PLCs. Scribner, Hager, and Warne (2002), for example, conclude that, in addition to the shared identity of the PLC, teachers should be allowed to maintain an individual identity and some level of professional autonomy. According to the authors, "This autonomy does not preclude them from participating in and belonging to the professional community" (p. 70). The idea here is to create a balance, addressing both the school community's goals and the individual teacher's needs.

▶ **Video Illustration**

As you watch this video, which of the six characteristics of PLCs appear to be present at the school?

Community of Inquiry

Although some scholars equate a community of inquiry with reflective dialogue alone, we take a broader view, as illustrated in Figure 23.1. If you are thinking that the process shown in the figure looks a lot like a generalized version of action research, as described in Chapter 20, you are correct! However, the cycle of inquiry can be used in many ways other than in action research. For instance, the inquiry cycle is used on a small scale in clinical supervision or peer coaching (see Chapter 15) when participants select a focus during the preconference and use data gathered during the classroom observation to inform reflective dialogue in the postconference, culminating in an action plan to improve teaching. The cycle of inquiry can be used in a broader scale in curriculum development (see Chapter 19) when teachers gather data on the effects of a curriculum on students, engage in reflective dialogue on the meaning of the data, and take action by designing new curriculum units. Examples of the cycle of inquiry integrated into a cultural task of supervision can be found in programs to increase equity (see Chapter 22), in which teachers analyze data on achievement gaps, participate in reflective dialogue on how the school's culture and their own teaching contribute to the gaps, and take action to become more culturally responsive. In short, the cycle of inquiry is not just applied in the supervision task of action research; it can be integrated with any technical or cultural task of supervision.

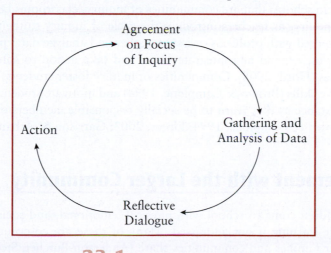

figure **23.1** **The Cycle of Inquiry**

Data gathering and analysis are essential to systematic inquiry, but the word *data* evokes a negative response from many teachers. Earl and Katz (2006) encourage educators to become more comfortable with using data as part of their everyday efforts to improve practice:

> Using data does not have to be a mechanical or technical process that denigrates educators' intuition, teaching philosophy, and personal experience. In fact using data wisely is a human thinking activity that draws on personal views but also on capturing and organizing ideas in some systematic way, turning the information into meaningful actions. . . . Data are a necessary part of an ongoing process of analysis, insight, new learning, and changes in practice. (pp. 14–15)

Earl and Katz (2006) also suggest ways schools can promote the use of data, including structuring opportunities for teachers to engage with data, using data to foster a sense of moral urgency to work for change, providing time for inquiry, and enlisting the services of outside critical friends to critique and support data-based improvement of practice.

Data and data analysis provide a basis for *reflective dialogue* among teachers: dialogue about student learning, student assessment, equity, school–community relations, and so on. The dialogue can center on teachers helping teachers to examine their classroom practice or on a collective critique of the school as a learning community. Over time, reflective dialogue creates a network of knowledge and support for all members of the school community (Gordon, 2008; Hipp et al., 2008; Smith-Maddox, 1999).

The final phase in the cycle of inquiry is *action* to improve teaching and learning. In a community of inquiry, this action is informed by data gathering and analysis and reflective dialogue, and the action itself becomes the subject of a new cycle of inquiry, using new data and continued dialogue to assess and modify improvement efforts.

In schools that are communities of inquiry, classrooms become their own centers of inquiry, as teachers introduce the cycle of inquiry to their students. Students are presented with problems or issues, gather and analyze data, present and defend alternatives, expand and integrate ideas, and take action to solve problems or address issues (Hord, 2008). Communities of inquiry foster students' cognitive and metacognitive skills (Brown & Campione, 1994) and motivate students to receive and provide assistance as they learn to be socially responsible members of a learning community (Brown & Campione, 1994; Elbers, 2003; Garrison & Arbaugh, 2007).

Engagement with the Larger Community

Children come to school with physical, emotional, and social needs that will affect their learning if not addressed. Many of these are co-occurring needs—needs that their families and communities share (Anderson-Butcher, Stetler, & Midle, 2006). It makes sense, then, for schools to work with families and communities to meet these needs. Also, communities are valuable sources of knowledge and rich learning environments that teachers can tap to make learning more relevant and meaningful. Historically, instructional supervision has paid little attention to the relationship among community development, school development, and student learning, or to the enormous potential of community-based learning. In recent years, the scope of supervision has expanded beyond the classroom in recognition of the need for schoolwide, collaborative efforts to enhance teaching and learning. The scope of supervision needs to expand still further, to include school–community collaboration. Here, we will discuss three aspects of engagement with the wider community: school-based and school-linked community service, community development, and the community as a learning environment.

School-Based and School-Linked Community Service

Dryfoos (1994) defines the full-service school as one that "integrates educational, medical, social and/or human services that are beneficial to meeting the needs of children and youth and their families on school grounds or in locations which are easily accessible" (p. 142). The services provided to students, families, and community members might include the following:

- Welcoming and orientation for new members of the community
- Providing basic needs such as food, clothing, and school supplies free or at reduced cost
- Providing meals on weekends and holidays and during vacations
- Health screening and basic health services
- Dental services
- Vision services
- Mental health services
- Substance abuse treatment
- Parental care
- Adult education
- Parent education
- Community empowerment programs
- Social services
- Early childhood/preschool education
- Child care
- Family support programs

Lawson (1999) advocates a wide range of services like those just listed but believes that a variety of community organizations should work with schools to provide them: "Collaboration is required. It both reflects and promotes interdependent relationships. Schools, community agencies, neighborhood organizations, and religious institutions depend on each other. When one succeeds, the others' results often improve. When one fails, others may follow" (p. 19). Lawson maintains that the various community organizations are motivated to collaborate in community service because of enlightened self-interest (also see Santiago, Ferrara, & Blank, 2010).

Community Development

The community development approach begins with the idea that the school is part of a much larger ecosystem that is responsible for the growth and development of all its members (Hiatt-Michael, 2006). Since the school is continuously affecting and affected by other parts of the larger educational environment (the community), it should integrate its educational efforts with other community efforts to assist all members of the ecosystem to grow and develop. As described by Timpane and Reich (1997):

> Community development changes the core identity of schools from isolated, independent agencies to institutions enmeshed with other community agencies in an interconnected landscape of support for the well-being of students and learners. It beckons schools to consider and respond to learning needs throughout the community, not just to those of children within the school building. (p. 466)

Because the community's overall health affects school development and student learning, it is appropriate for supervisors, teachers, and, in many cases, students (Lawson, Claiborne, Hardiman, Austin, & Surko, 2007) to participate in community development, defined as a process to improve the "economic, social, cultural, and/or environmental situation" (Christenson, Fendley, & Robinson, 1989, p. 14). Two guidelines for schools to participate in community development are (1) to connect the community development process directly to school development and student learning, and (2) to coordinate participation in community development with other community agencies and organizations.

The Community as a Learning Environment

According to Arrington and Moore (2001), "When we purposefully involve students in learning experiences that stretch far beyond the school walls into the community and the world, we provide motivation and relevance that can make a difference in children achieving school success" (p. 56). Learning models that connect students to the community and larger society include service learning, place-based learning, and democratic learning.

Service Learning.   The service learning model integrates the curriculum with community service and occurs only when service is accompanied by academic learning. In service learning, students analyze community issues, choose a service project, plan activities, perform the service, and engage in individual and group reflection on the project (Arrington & Moore, 2001; Flanagan et al., 2007). Service learning can take place within any content area and often cuts across several content areas.

Place-Based Learning.   The place-based learning model uses social, cultural, and natural aspects of the students' local environment as the context for learning (Smith, 2007). A snapshot of place-based learning is shared by Smith (2002):

> When Environment Middle School students go to Brookside Wetlands, . . . their water samples and inventories of macro invertebrates, collected and compiled over the course of the year, become part of a report to Portland's Bureau of Environmental Services. The project allows for a direct rather than mediated experience of the world. The water is cold—the mud, slippery. And when the class spots two geese threatening with outstretched necks a third who tries to cross the invisible boundary that marks their territory, everyone watches in silence. (p. 31)

In place-based learning, students produce rather than consume knowledge, teachers are co-learners and guides rather than instructors, and students solve real-world problems rather than fictitious ones (Powers, 2004; Smith, 2002).

Democratic Learning.   The democratic learning model asks students to integrate their personal concerns with concerns about the larger world and the common good. Students decide on a common theme, often dealing with race, ethnicity, class, gender, or another issue of diversity. Within the common theme, small groups and individuals develop their own questions and projects. The questions that students ask in democratic learning tend to focus on serious social issues, such as war and peace, the environment, and the family. As students explore issues, they engage in rigorous academic work, display high-level cognitive skills, show mutual respect, and build community (Beane, 2002; Marri, 2005).

Five Attributes, One Community

The relationship of the five attributes of a school community is shown in Figure 23.2. Although each attribute is different from the others, there is considerable overlap and interaction among the five attributes. Let us consider for a moment one of the attributes, democracy, in relationship to the others. Historically, democracy

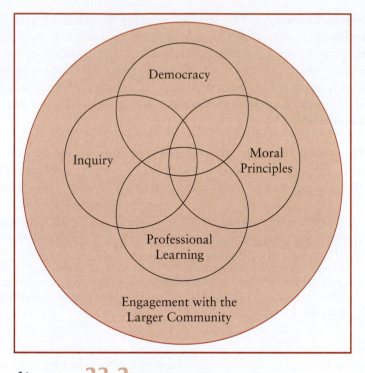

figure **23.2** **Relationship of Attributes of an Authentic School Community**

has never been defined merely as majority rule; rather, it has been considered a way of life based on underlying moral principles (the second attribute). Also, professional learning (the third attribute) works best if supported by democratic leadership and conducted by teachers in a democratic manner. Inquiry (the fourth attribute) requires the openness and freedom of a democratic environment. Finally, school–community engagement (the fifth attribute) works best if school and community participants use a democratic process for making decisions about school and community development. We could go through this same process with any of the attributes of community. Each attribute of an authentic community flows into and supports each of the other attributes.

Conclusion

This book, *SuperVision and Instructional Leadership,* is first and foremost about the ideas of purpose, hope, and growth and development for all of our students.

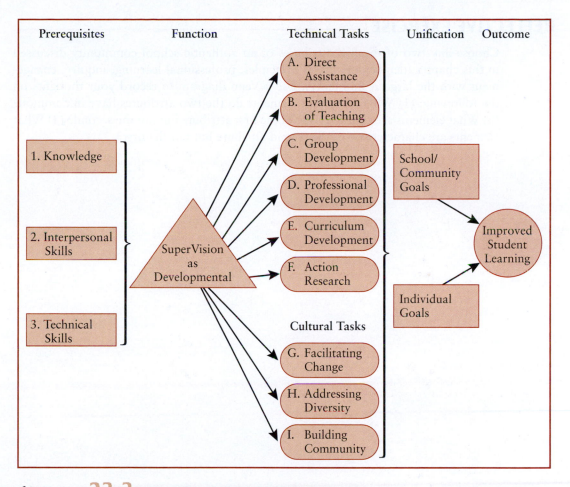

figure **23.3** **SuperVision and Successful Schools**

Figure 23.3 reviews the knowledge, skills, technical tasks, and cultural tasks for achieving a purposeful school dedicated to the continuing enhancement of teaching and learning.

Please remember that competence without a clear purpose results in direction-less change, and purpose without competence provides inefficiency and frustration. We hope that you, the reader, in whatever role of instructional leadership, will add coherence and congruence to the education of all students in your own school and community. After all, this is the primary reason we chose to be educators—to practice what we believe.

✔ **Check Your Understanding 23.0**   Click here to gauge your understanding of the key concepts presented in this chapter.

REFLECTIVE EXERCISE

Choose any two of the five attributes of an authentic school community discussed in this chapter (democracy, moral principles, professional learning, inquiry, engagement with the larger community). Use a Venn diagram to record your thoughts on the following: (1) What important elements do the two attributes have in common? (2) What elements are characteristic of the first attribute but not the second? (3) What elements are characteristic of the second attribute but not the first?

appendix A

Educational Philosophy Q Sort*

Below you will find 20 statements describing our public system of education. These statements are arranged in four categories. They address the aims of education, the nature of knowledge, the role of the teacher, and the purpose of the curriculum. Your task is to prioritize these statements by numbering them from 1 to 5 in each category. Assign the number 5 to the statement you believe best represents your beliefs, 4 to the statement you believe represents your belief next, and so on until you have assigned a number to all five statements in each category. When you have completed this task, follow the directions in the rating guide to summarize your responses.

Aims

___ A. To improve and reconstruct society; education for change

___ B. To promote democratic, social living; to foster creative self-learning

___ C. To educate the rational person; to cultivate the intellect through transmitting worthwhile knowledge that has been gathered, organized, and systematized

___ D. To provide for the construction of active citizens; to nourish civic literacy, citizen participation and political responsibility

___ E. To promote the intellectual growth of the individual; to educate the competent person for the benefit of humanity

Knowledge

___ A. Focus on skills and subjects needed to identify and ameliorate problems of society; active concern with contemporary and future society

___ B. Focus on past permanent studies, mastery of facts and universal truths
___ C. Focus on reconstructing a visionary language and public philosophy that puts equality, liberty, and human life at the center of the notions of democracy and citizenship
___ D. Focus on growth and development; a living–learning process; active and relevant learning
___ E. Focus on essential skills and academic subjects; mastery of concepts and principles of subject matter

Teacher's Role

___ A. Teachers are critical intellectuals who create democratic sites for social transformation. They empower students to question how knowledge is produced and distributed
___ B. Teachers serve as change agents for reform; they help students become aware of problems confronting humankind
___ C. Teachers should help students think rationally, based on the Socratic method and oral exposition; explicitly teach traditional values
___ D. Teachers are guides for problem solving and scientific inquiry
___ E. Teachers should act as authority figures who have expertise in subject field or content areas

Curriculum

___ A. Curriculum centers on classical subjects and literary analysis; it is constant
___ B. Curriculum centers on social critique and social change dedicated to both self- and social empowerment
___ C. Curriculum centers around essential skills (the three Rs) and major content subjects (English, science, history, math, and foreign language)
___ D. Curriculum centers on examining social, economic, and political problems, present and future, on a national as well as international level
___ E. Curriculum centers on student interest; involves the application of human problems; subject matter is interdisciplinary

Rating Guide for the Educational Philosophy Q-Sort

When you have completed the Q-Sort, go back and look at each category. Place the number that you assigned to each statement in the space provided in the rating guide. Add the columns to determine the educational philosophy with which you most agree. Grouped together, these statements represent the major tenets of each philosophy.

	Perennialism	Essentialism	Progressivism	Reconstructionism	Critical Theory
Aims	C	E	B	A	D
Knowledge	B	E	D	A	C
Teacher's Role	C	E	D	B	A
Curriculum	A	C	E	D	B
Total					

Making Sense of Your Ratings

The chart on the next page will help you determine which philosophy your beliefs most closely align with. It is rare when ratings indicate a strong alignment with only one philosophy. Usually ratings indicate an eclectic mix with one or two ratings emerging as a preference.

Characteristics of Philosophical Orientations

Orientation	Philosophical Base	Instructional Objective	Knowledge
Perennialism	Realism	To educate the rational person; to cultivate intellect	Focus on past and permanent studies; mastery of facts and timeless knowledge
Essentialism	Idealism; Realism	To promote the intellectual growth of the individual; to educate the competent person	Essential skills and academic subjects; mastery of concepts and principles of subject matter
Progressivism	Pragmatism	To promote democratic, social living	Knowledge leads to growth and development; a living–learning process; focus on active and interesting learning
Social Reconstructionism	Pragmatism	To improve and reconstruct society and education for change and social reform	Skills and subjects needed to identify and ameliorate problems of society; learning is active, concerned with contemporary and future society
Critical Theory	Marxism	To challenge and deconstruct society, the status quo, and powerful oppressors; to teach citizens to act politically for social justice	Focus on how the world works to privilege some and not others; awareness of race, class, gender, sexuality, and (dis)ability politics

*All components of the Educational Philosophy Q Sort adapted from Bernard Badiali (2005), Standards for Supervision of Curriculum Development. In S. P. Gordon (Ed.), *Standards for Instructional Supervision* (pp. 171–190). Larchmont, NY: Eye on Education.

Role of Teacher	Curriculum Focus	Related Curriculum Trends
Teacher helps students think rationally; based on the Socratic method and oral exposition; explicit teaching of traditional values	Classical subject; literary analysis; constant curriculum	Great books; Paideia proposal (Hutchins, Adler)
Teacher is authority in his or her field; explicit teaching of traditional values	Essential skills (the three Rs) and essential subjects (English, math, science, history, foreign language)	Back to basics; Excellence in education (Bagley, Bestor, Bennett)
Teacher is a guide for problem solving and scientific inquiry	Based on students' interests; involves the application of human problems and affairs; interdisciplinary subject matter; activities and projects	Relevant curriculum; humanistic education; alternative and free schooling (Dewey, Beane)
Teacher serves as an agent of change and reform; acts as a project director and research leader, helps students become aware of problems confronting humanity	Emphasis on social science and social research; examining social, economic, and political problems; focus on present and future trends	Equality of education; cultural pluralism, international education; futurism (Counts, Grants, & Sleeter)
Teacher acts with conscience and resolve as a social agent of change in the world with students	Teacher opens up societal norms to criticism and action	Some forms of service learning; socially active, alternative education programs (Freire, Apple, Giroux)

appendix **B**

Review of Interpersonal Behavior in the Four Supervisory Approaches

The four supervisory approaches used in developmental supervision are briefly summarized and compared on the next page. We suggest that graduate students and practitioners practicing the different approaches during role plays have the summaries at hand for use as a quick reference during practice sessions.

Directive Control

1. Present problem.
2. Ask teacher for input into problem.
3. Listen to understand teacher's perception of problem.
4. Mentally determine solution.
5. State solution to teacher.
6. Ask teacher for input into solution.
7. Modify and detail expected actions.
8. Summarize expected actions and describe follow-up.

Directive Informational

1. Identify problem.
2. Ask teacher for input into problem.
3. Listen to understand teacher's perception of problem.
4. Mentally determine two or three alternative solutions.
5. State alternative solutions to teacher.
6. Ask teacher for views on each alternative solution.
7. Modify alternative solutions and frame final choices.
8. Ask teacher to choose one of the alternative solutions.
9. State specific actions to be taken and follow-up.
10. Summarize expected actions and follow-up.

Collaborative

1. Ask for teacher's perception of problem.
2. Listen to understand teacher's perception of problem.
3. Verify teacher's perception of problem.
4. Present your perception of problem by building on teacher's perception when possible.
5. Check for teacher's understanding of your perception of problem.
6. Exchange possible solutions (allow teacher to first offer solutions; build on teacher solutions when possible) and jointly consider consequences of each alternative.
7. Accept conflict that may arise.
8. Negotiate a mutually acceptable solution.
9. Agree on specific actions to be taken, including follow-up.
10. Summarize final plan.

Nondirective

1. Listen while teacher identifies problem.
2. Verbalize teacher's initial description of problem.
3. Probe for additional information.
4. Encourage teacher to reflect on various aspects of problem.
5. Continuously paraphrase teacher's message.
6. Ask teacher to think of possible solutions.
7. For each possible solution, ask teacher to consider consequences.
8. Ask teacher to decide on solution and specific actions.
9. Ask teacher to set times for actions and criteria for plan.
10. Summarize teacher's plan.

References

Chapter 1

Bogotch, I. E. (2002). Educational leadership and social justice: Practice into theory. *Journal of School Leadership, 12*, 138–156.

Fallon, G., & Barnett, J. (2009). Impacts of school organizational restructuring into a collaborative setting on the nature of emerging forms of collegiality. *International Journal of Education Policy and Leadership, 4*(9), 1–13.

Furman, G. C. (2004). The ethic of community. *Journal of Educational Administration 42*, 215–235.

Glickman, C. D. (1993). Renewing America's schools: A guide for school-based action. San Francisco: Jossey-Bass

Glickman, C. D. (1998). *Revolutionizing America's schools*. San Francisco: Jossey-Bass.

Glickman, C. D. (2003). *Holding sacred ground: Courageous leadership for democratic schools*. San Francisco: Jossey-Bass.

Gordon, S. P. (Ed.). (1995, April). *Newsletter of the Instructional Supervision Special Interest Group of the American Educational Research Association.*

Gordon, S. P. (1997). Has the field of supervision evolved to a point that it should be called something else? *Yes.* In J. Glanz & R. F. Neville (Eds.), *Educational supervision: Perspectives, issues, and controversies* (pp. 114–123). Norwood, MA: Christopher-Gordon.

Gordon, S. P., Jacobs, J., & Solis, R. (2013, April-May). *Critical issues in teacher leadership: Phase I of a national study.* Paper presented at the annual meeting of the American Educational Research Association, San Francisco, CA.

Hart, A. W. I. (1995). Reconceiving school leadership: Emergent views. *The Elementary School Journal, 96*(1), 9–28.

Jacobs, J., Gordon, S. P., & Solis, R. (2013, October). *Critical issues in teacher leadership: A national look at teacher leader perceptions.* Paper presented at the annual meeting of the Council of Professors of Instructional Supervision, University Park, PA.

Kohm, B., & Nance, B. (2009). Creating collaborative cultures. *Educational Leadership, 67*(2), 67–72.

Laviè, J. M. (2006). Academic discourses on school-based teacher collaboration: Revisiting the arguments. *Educational Administration Quarterly, 42*(5), 773–805.

Nolan, J., & Hoover, L. A. (2010). *Teacher supervision and evaluation: Theory into practice.* (3rd ed.) New York: Wiley.

Printy, S. M., Marks, H. M., & Bowers, A. J. (2009). Integrated leadership: How principals and teachers share transformational and instructional influence. *Journal of School Leadership, 19*, 504–532.

Sergiovanni, T. J. (2006). Getting practical: Enhancing collegiality and intrinsic motivation. In T. J. Sergiovanni (Ed.), *Rethinking leadership: A collection of articles* (pp. 120–144). Thousand Oaks, CA: Corwin Press.

Snow-Gerono, J. L. (2008). Locating supervision– A reflective framework for negotiating tensions within conceptual and procedural foci for teacher development. *Teaching and Teacher Education, 24*, 1502–1515.

Sullivan, S., & Glanz, J. (2009). *Supervision that improves teaching and learning: Strategies and techniques.* Thousand Oaks, CA: Corwin Press.

Zepeda, S. J. (2005). Standards of collegiality and collaboration. In S. P. Gordon (Ed.), *Standards for instructional supervision: Enhancing teaching and learning* (pp. 63–75). Larchmont, NY: Eye on Education.

Chapter 2

Achinstein, B., Ogawa, R., & Speiglman, A. (2004). Are we creating separate and unequal tracks of teachers? The effects of state policy, local conditions, and teacher characteristics on new teacher socialization. *American Educational Research Journal, 41*(3), 557–603.

Angelle, P. (2006). Instructional leadership and monitoring: Increasing teacher intent to stay through socialization. *NASSP Bulletin, 90*, 318–334.

Anhorn, R. (2008). The profession that eats its young. *Delta Kappa Gamma Bulletin, 16*, 15–26.

Bass, L., & Gerstl-Pepin, C. (2011). Declaring bankruptcy on educational inequity. *Educational Policy*, 25(6), 908–934.

Birkeland, S., & Johnson, S. M. (2002). What keeps new teachers in the swim? *Journal of Staff Development*, 23(4), 18–21.

Bolman, L. G., & Deal, T. E. (2002). Leading with soul and spirit. *School Administrator*, 59(2), 21–26.

Brooks, J., Hughes, R., & Brooks, M. (2008). Fear and trembling in the American high school: Educational reform and teacher alienation. *Educational Policy*, 22(1), 45–62.

Buchanan, J., Prescott, A., Schuck, S., Aubusson, P., & Burke, P. (2013). Teacher retention and attrition: Views of early career teachers. *Australian Journal of Teacher Education*, 38(3), 112–129.

Chang, M. L. (2009). An appraisal perspective of teacher burnout: Examining the emotional work of teachers. *Educational Psychology Review*, 21(3), 193–218.

Cherubini, L. (2009). Reconciling the tensions of new teachers' socialisation into school culture: A review of the research. *Issues in Educational Research*, 19(2), 83–99.

Chubbuck, S. M., Clift, R. T., & Alland, J. (2001). Playing it safe as a novice teacher: Implications for programs for new teachers. *Journal of Teacher Education*, 52(5), 365–376.

Colley, A. C. (2002). What can principals do about new teacher attrition? *Principal*, 81(4), 22–24.

Collie, R., Shapka, J., & Perry, N. (2012). School climate and social-emotional learning: Predicting teacher stress, job satisfaction, and teaching efficacy. *Journal of Educational Psychology*, 104(4), 1189–1204.

Craig, C. (2013). From stories of staying to stories of leaving: A US beginning teacher's experience. *Journal of Curriculum Studies*, 46(1), 81–115.

Darling-Hammond, L. (2006). Constructing 21st century teacher education. *Journal of Teacher Education*, 57(3), 300–314.

David, J. (2009). Collaborative inquiry. *Educational Leadership*, 66(4).

DeAngelis, K., & Presley, J. (2011). Toward a more nuanced understanding of new teacher attrition. *Education and Urban Society*, 43(5), 598–626.

Desimone, L., & Long, D. (2010). Teacher effects and the achievement gap: Do teacher and teaching quality influence the achievement gap

between black and white and high- and low-SES students in the early grades? *Teachers College Record*, 112(12), 3024–3073.

DuFour, R. (2011). Work together, but only if you want to. *Phi Delta Kappan*, 92(5), 57–61.

Fantilli, R. D., & McDougall, D. E. (2009). A study of novice teachers: Challenges and supports in the first years. *Teaching and Teacher Education*, 25(6), 814–825.

Feiman-Nemser, S. (2003). What new teachers need to learn. *Educational Leadership*, 60(8), 25–29.

Gallant, A., & Riley, P. (2014). Early career teacher attrition: New thoughts on an intractable problem. *Teacher Development: An International Journal of Teachers' Professional Development*, 18(4), 562–580.

Garrett, J. L. (2006). Across the threshold. *Kappa Delta Pi Record*, 43(1), 12–13.

Gomez, J., & Futrell, M. H. (2008). How tracking creates a poverty of learning. *Educational Leadership*, 65(8), 74–78.

Gordon, S. P., & Maxey, S. (2000). *How to help beginning teachers succeed*. Alexandria, VA: Association for Supervision and Curriculum Development.

Grayson, J. L., & Alvarez, H. K. (2008). School climate factors relating to teacher burnout: A mediator model. *Teaching and Teacher Education*, 24(5), 1349–1363.

Haycock, K., & Hanushek, E. (2010). An effective teacher in every classroom. *Education Next*, 10(3), 46–52.

Henry, G., Fortner, K., & Bastian, K. (2012). The effects of experience and attrition for novice high-school science and mathematics teachers. *Science*, 335, 1118–1121.

Hoigaard, R., Giske, R., & Sundsli, K. (2012). Newly qualified teacher's work engagement and teacher efficacy influences on job satisfaction, burnout, and the intention to quit. *European Journal of Teacher Education*, 35(3), 347–357.

Hoy, A. W., & Spero, R. B. (2005). Changes in teacher efficacy during the early years of teaching: A comparison of four measures. *Teaching and Teacher Education*, 21(4), 343–356.

Imig, D. G., & Imig, S. R. (2006). What do beginning teachers need to know? An essay. *Journal of Teacher Education*, 57(3), 286–291.

Ingersoll, R., & Smith, T. (2003). The wrong solution to the teacher shortage. *Educational Leadership*, 60, 30–33.

Ingersoll, R. M. (2002). Deprofessionalizing the teaching profession: The problem of out-of-field teaching. *Educational Horizons, 80*(1), 28–31.

Johnson, H. R. (2001). Administrators and mentors: Keys in the success of beginning teachers. *Journal of Instructional Psychology, 28*(1), 44–49.

Johnson, S. M., & Kardos, S. M. (2002). Keeping new teachers in mind. *Educational Leadership, 59*(6), 12–16.

Kaiser, A. (2011). *Beginning teacher attrition and mobility: Results from the first through third waves of the 2007–2008 beginning teacher longitudinal study* (NCES Report 2011-318). Retrieved from National Center for Education Statistics website: http://nces.ed.gov/pubs2011/2011318.pdf

Kilmann, R. H. (2001). *Quantum organizations: A new paradigm for achieving organizational success and personal meaning.* Newport Coast, CA: Kilmann Diagnostics.

Kohm, B., & Nance, B. (2009). Creating collaborative cultures. *Educational Leadership, 67*(2).

Kuhn, T.S. (1970). *The structure of scientific revolutions* (2nd ed.). Chicago, IL: University of Chicago Press.

Lleras, C. (2008). Race, racial concentration, and the dynamics of educational inequality across urban and suburban schools. *American Educational Research Journal, 45*(4), 886–912.

Maistre, C. L., & Paré, A. (2010). Whatever it takes: How beginning teachers learn to survive. *Teaching and Teacher Education, 26*(3), 559–564.

McCann, T. M., & Johannesen, L. (2004). Why do teachers cry? *Clearing House, 77,* 138–145.

McMillan, S., & Price, M. A. (2005). A representative journey of teachers perceptions of self: A readers' theater. In J. Brophy & S. Pinnegar (Eds.)., *Learning from research on teaching: Perspective, methodology, and representation* (Volume 11, pp. 137–169). Bingley, UK: Emerald Group Publishing Limited.

Mitchell, S. N., Reilly, R. C., & Logue, M. E. (2009). Benefits of collaborative action research for the beginning teacher. *Teaching and Teacher Education, 25*(2), 344–349.

Morrison, C. (2013). Teacher identity in the early career phase: Trajectories that explain and influence development. *Australian Journal of Teacher Education, 38*(4), 91–107.

Pietarinen, J., Pyhalto, K., Soini, T., & Salmela-Aro, K. (2013). Reducing teacher burnout: A socio-contextual approach. *Teaching and Teacher Education, 35,* 62–72.

Price, H., & Collett, J. (2012). The role of exchange and emotion on commitment: A study of teachers. *Social Science Research, 41*(6), 1469–1479.

Rios, F., Bath, D., Foster, A., Maaka, M., Michelli, N., & Urban, E. (2009). *Inequities in public education.* Seattle, WA: Institute for Education Inquiry.

Schaefer, L. (2013). Beginning teacher attrition: A question of identity making and identity shifting. *Teachers and Teaching: Theory and Practice, 19*(3), 260–274.

Scherff, L., Ollis, J., & Rosencrans, L. (2006). Starting the journey together: A teacher educator and her "students" navigate their first semester in the secondary English classroom. *Issues in Teacher Education, 15*(2), 43–59.

Schuck, S., Aubusson, P., Buchanan, J., Prescott, A., Louviere, J., & Burke, P. (2011). *Retaining effective early career teachers in NSW schools* (UTS: Center for Research in Learning and Change and Center for Study of Choice). Retrieved from University Technology of Sydney website: http://www.uts.edu.au/sites/default/files/Beginning_Teacher_Retention_Report_0.pdf

Stansbury, K. (2001). What new teachers need. *Leadership, 30*(3), 18–21.

Tang, C. L. (2009). *Fundamentals of quantum mechanics: For solid state electronics and optics.* New York, NY: Cambridge University Press.

Van Droogenbroeck, F., Spruyt, B., & Vanroelen, C. (2014). Burnout among senior teachers: Investigating the role of workload and interpersonal relationships at work. *Teaching and Teacher Education, 43,* 99–109.

Veenman, S. (1984). Perceived problems of beginning teachers. *Review of Educational Research, 54*(2), 143–178.

Welton, A. (2013). Even more racially isolated than before: Problematizing the vision for "diversity" in a racially mixed high school. *Teachers College Record, 115*(11), 1–42.

Wheatley, M. J. (1994). *Leadership and the new science: Learning about organizations from an orderly universe.* San Francisco, CA: Barrett-Koehler.

Zohar, D. (1997). Rewiring the corporate brain: Using the new science to rethink how we structure and lead organizations. San Francisco: Barrett-Koehler.

Chapter 3

Allodi, M. W. (2010). Goals and values in school: A model developed for describing, evaluating, and changing the social climate of learning environments. *Social Psychology of Education, 13*, 207–235.

Anderson, K. J., & Minke, K. M. (2007). Parent involvement in education: Toward an understanding of parents' decision making. *Journal of Educational Research, 100*, 311–323.

Anderson-Butcher, D., Lawson, H. A., Iachini, A., Flaspohler, P., Bean, J., & Wade-Mdivanian, R. (2010). Emergent evidence in support of a common collaboration model for school improvement. *Children & Schools, 32*, 160–171.

Auerbach, S. (2010). Beyond coffee with the principal: Toward leadership for authentic school–family partnerships. *Journal of School Leadership, 20*, 728–757.

Balan, R., Manko, T., & Phillips, K. (2011). Instructional improvement through professional development. *Dialogues: Teaching & Learning Journal, 5*(2), 1–18.

Biggam, S. (2003). Making the most of parent partnerships to strengthen literacy development: Lessons from John and Janet Poeton and recent research. *New England Reading Association Journal, 39*(3), 24–27.

Caine, R. N., & Caine, G. (1997). *Education on the edge of possibility.* Alexandria, VA: Association for Supervision and Curriculum Development.

Carr, J. F., Herman, N., & Harris, D. E. (2005). *Creating dynamic schools through mentoring, coaching, and collaboration.* Alexandria, VA: Association for Supervision and Curriculum Development.

Cohen, J. (2007). Evaluating and improving school improvement: Creating a climate for learning. *Independent School, 67*(1), 18–26.

Cohen, J., McCabe, E., Michelli, N. M., & Pickeral, T. (2009). School climate: Research, policy, practice, and teacher education. *Teacher College Record, 111*(1), 180–213.

Dennis, J., & O'Hair, M. J. (2010). Overcoming obstacles in using authentic instruction: A comparative case study of high school math & science teachers. *American Secondary Education, 38*(2), 4–22.

DePlanty, J., Coulter-Kern, R., & Duchane, K. A. (2007). Perceptions of parent involvement in academic achievement. *Journal of Educational Research, 100*, 361–368.

Doll, B. (2010). Positive school climate. *Principal Leadership, 11*(4), 12–16.

Earl, L. M., & Katz, S. (2006). *Leading schools in a data-rich world.* Thousand Oaks, CA: Corwin Press.

Edwards, S. W., & Chapman, P. E. (2009). *Six pillars of dynamic schools.* Alexandria, VA: Educational Research Service.

Engein, J. T. (2003). The funding challenge. *Principal Leadership, 3*(5). Retrieved from http://www.nassp.org/tabid/3788/default.aspx?topic=46778

Evans, M., & Radina, R. (2014). Great expectations? Critical discourse analysis of Title I school-family compacts. *School Community Journal, 24*(2), 107–126.

Fairman, J., & Mackenzie, S. (2015). How teacher leaders influence others and understand their leadership. *International Journal of Leadership in Education: Theory and Practice, 18*(1), 61–87.

Fleener M. J. (2002). *Curriculum dynamics: Recreating heart.* New York, NY: Peter Lang.

Fullan, M. (2000). The three stories of educational reform. *Phi Delta Kappan, 81*, 581–584.

Furman, G. C., & Starratt, R. J. (2002). Leadership for democratic community in schools. In J. Murphy (Ed.), *The educational leadership challenge: Redefining leadership for the 21st century: 101st yearbook of the National Society for the Study of Education* (pp. 105–133). Chicago, IL: University of Chicago Press.

Gajda, R., & Koliba, C. J. (2008). Evaluating and improving the quality of teacher collaboration: A field-tested framework for secondary school leaders. *NASSP Bulletin, 92*(2), 133–153.

Gillen, A., Wright, A., & Spink, L. (2011). Student perceptions of a positive climate for learning: A case study. *Educational Psychology in Practice, 27*(1), 65–82.

Gilles, C., Carrillo, L., Wang, Y., Stegall, J., & Bumgarner, B. (2013). "Working with my mentor is like having a second brain/hands/feet/eyes": Perceptions of novice teachers. *English Journal, 102*(3), 78–86.

Glickman, C. D. (1993). *Renewing America's schools: A guide for school-based action.* San Francisco: CA: Jossey-Bass.

Glickman, C. D. (1998). Revolution, education, and the practice of democracy. *The Educational Forum, 63*(1), 16–22.

Goddard, Y. L., Goddard, R. D., & Tschannen-Moran, M. (2007). A theoretical and empirical investigation of teacher collaboration for school improvement and student achievement in public elementary schools. *Teacher's College Record, 109*(4), 877–896.

Gordon, S. P. (2004). *Professional development for school improvement: Empowering learning communities*. Boston, MA: Allyn & Bacon.

Gordon, S. P. (2008). Introduction: The power of collaborative action research. In S. P. Gordon (Ed.), *Collaborative action research: Developing professional learning communities* (pp. 1–12). New York: Teachers College Press.

Gordon, S. P., & Boone, M. (2012, August). Conflicting models and the future of leadership preparation: A call for integration. A paper presented at the annual meeting of the National Council of Professors of Educational Administration, Kansas City, MO.

Green, C. L., Walker, J. M. T., Hoover-Dempsey, K. V., & Sandler, H. (2007). Parents' motivations for involvement in children's education: An empirical test of a theoretical model of parental involvement. *Journal of Educational Psychology, 99*, 532–544.

Hansen-Thomas, H., Casey, P., & Grosso, L. (2013). Multiplying the effect of professional development: Teachers training teachers. *TESOL Journal, 4*(1), 129–150.

Harpole, S. H., Kerley, L. H., Silvernail, D. L., Kinard, F., & Brooks, P. (2010). Science on the shipyard. *Science Teacher, 77*(4) 48–52.

Heck, R., & Hallinger, P. (2014). Modeling the longitudinal effects of school leadership on teaching and learning. *Journal of Educational Administration, 52*(5), 653–681.

Ingersoll, R. M., & Strong, M. (2011). The impact of induction and mentoring programs for beginning teachers: A critical review of the research. *Review of Educational Research, 81*(2), 201–233.

Kamler, E., Szpara, M., Dornisch, M., Goubeaud, K., Levine, G., & Brechtel, S. (2009). Realities of a school-university partnership: Focus on leadership. *Journal of School Leadership, 19*(1), 81–117.

Kensler, L. W., Caskie, G. I. L., Barber, M. E., & White, G. P. (2009). The ecology of democratic learning communities: Faculty trust and continuous learning in public middle schools. *Journal of School Leadership, 19*, 697–735.

Kilmann, R. H. (2001). Quantum organizations: A new paradigm for achieving organizational success and personal meaning. Newport Coast, CA: Kilmann Diagnostics.

Kohm, B., & Nance, B. (2009). Creating collaborative cultures. *Educational Leadership, 67*(2), 67–72.

Larsen, C., & Rieckhoff, B. (2014). Distributed leadership: Principals describe shared roles in a PDS. *International Journal of Leadership in Education: Theory and Practice, 17*(3), 304–326.

LoCasale-Crouch, J., Davis, E., Wiens, P., & Pianta, R. (2012). The role of the mentor in supporting new teachers: Associations with self-efficacy, reflection, and quality. *Mentoring & Tutoring: Partnership in Learning, 20*(3), 303–323.

Mallory, B. J., & Reavis, C. (2007). Planning for school improvement: Closing the gap of culture with democratic principles. *Educational Planning, 16*(2), 8–18.

Marshall, M. L. (2004). *Examining school climate: Defining factors and educational influence.* Georgia State University Center for School Safety, School Climate, and Classroom Management. Retrieved from http://education.gsu.edu/schoolsafety/

Meier, D. (2009). What I've learned. In C. D. Glickman (Ed.), *Those who dared* (pp. 9–19). New York: Teachers College Press.

Mutsch, C., & Collins, S. (2012). Partners in learning: Schools' engagement with parents, families and communities in New Zealand. *School Community Journal, 22*(1), 167–187.

Myran, S., Crum, K. S., & Clayton, J. (2010). Four pillars of effective university-school partnerships: Implications for educational planning. *Educational Planning, 19*(2), 46–60.

Newmann, F. M., & Associates. (1996). *Authentic achievement: Restructuring schools for intellectual quality*. San Francisco, CA: Jossey-Bass.

Pillay, H., Watters, J., Hoff, L., & Flynn, M. (2014). Dimensions of effectiveness and efficiency: A case study on industry-school partnerships. *Journal of Vocational Education & Traning, 66*(4), 537–553.

Polkinghorne, J. (2002). *Quantum theory: A short introduction.* New York, NY: Oxford University Press.

Preble, B., & Taylor, L. (2009). School climate through students' eyes. *Educational Leadership, 66*(4), 35–40.

Preus, B. (2012). Authentic instruction for 21st century learning: Higher order thinking in an inclusive school. *American Secondary Education, 40*(3), 59–79.

Price-Mitchell, M. (2009). Boundary dynamics: Implications for building parent–school partnerships. *The School Community Journal, 19*(2), 9–26.

Printy, S. M., Marks, G. H. M., & Bowers, A. J. (2009). Integrated leadership: How principals and teachers share transformational and instructional influence. *Journal of School Leadership, 19*(5), 504–532.

Rallis, S. F., & Goldring, E. G. (2000). *Principals of dynamic schools: Taking charge of change.* Thousand Oaks, CA; Corwin Press.

Rallis, S. F., Rossman, G. B., Cobb, C. D., Reagan., T. G., & Kuntz, A. (2008). *Leading dynamic schools: How to create and implement ethical policies.* Thousand Oaks, CA: Corwin Press.

Rosado, C. (2008). Context determines content: Quantum physics as a framework for 'wholeness' in urban transformation. *Urban Studies, 45,* 2075–2097.

Sammon, G., & Becton, M. (2001, February). Principles of partnerships. *Principal Leadership,* 1(6). Retrieved from http://massp.org/Content .aspx? Topic=48923

Sanders, M. G. (2001). The role of "community" in comprehensive school, family, and community programmes. *The Elementary School Journal, 102,* 19–34.

Skaked, H., & Schechter, C. (2013). Seeing wholes: The concept of systems thinking and its implementation in school leadership. *International Review of Education, 59,* 771–791.

Sokal, A. D. (1996). Transgressing the boundaries: Toward a transformative hermeneutics of quantum gravity. *Social Text, 14*(1&2), 217–252.

Starratt, R. J. (2007). Leading a community of learners: Learning to be moral by engaging the morality of learning. *Educational Management Administration & Leadership, 35,* 165–183.

Tang, C. L. (2009). *Fundamentals of quantum mechanics: For solid state electronics and optics.* New York, NY: Cambridge University Press.

Toren, N. (2013). Multiple dimensions of parental involvement and its links to young adolescent self-evaluation and academic achievement. *Psychology in the Schools, 50*(6), 634–649.

Wahlstrom, K. L., & Louis, K. S. (2008). How teachers experience principal leadership: The roles of professional community, trust, efficacy, and shared responsibility. *Educational Administration Quarterly, 44*(4), 548–495.

Wang, J., Odell, S. J., & Schwille, S. A. (2008). Effects of teacher induction on beginning teachers' teaching: A critical review of the literature. *Journal of Teacher Education, 59*(2), 132–152.

Wang, M.T., & Sheikh-Khalil, S. (2014). Does parental involvement matter for student achievement and mental health in high school? *Child Development, 85*(2), 610–625.

Watson, S. T., & Scribner, J. P. (2007). Beyond distributed leadership: Collaborating, interaction, and emergent reciprocal influence. *Journal of School Leadership, 17,* 443–468.

Wheatley, M. J. (1994). *Leadership and the new science: Learning about organizations from an orderly universe.* San Francisco, CA: Barrett-Koehler.

Youngs, H. (2014). Moving beyond distributed leadership to distributed forms: A contextual and socio-cultural analysis of two New Zealand secondary schools. *Leading & Managing, 20*(2), 89-104.

Zohar, D. (1997). *Rewiring the corporate brain: Using the new science to rethink how we structure and lead organizations.* San Francisco: Barrett-Koehler.

Chapter 4

Adams, R. D., & Martray, C. (1981, April). *Teacher development: A study of factors related to teacher concerns for pre, beginning, and experienced teachers.* Paper presented at the annual meeting of the American Educational Research Association, Los Angeles.

Albertson, S. (2014). Deconstruction toward reconstruction: A constructive-developmental consideration of deconstructive necessities in transitions. *Behavioral Developmental Bulletin, 19*(4), 76–82.

Alfred, M. V. (2001). Expanding theories of career development: Adding the voices of African American women in the White academy. *Adult Education Quarterly, 51,* 108–127.

Alston, G. (2014). *Cross-cultural mentoring relationship in higher education: A feminist grounded theory study.* (Doctoral dissertation).

Available from ProQuest Dissertations and Theses Global (UMI No. 3629151)

Anderson, D. Y., & Hayes, C. L. (1996). *Gender, identity and self-esteem: A new look at adult development.* New York: Springer.

Baek, E.-O., & Barab, S. A. (2005). A Study of dynamic design dualities in a web-supported community of practice for teachers. *Educational Technology & Society, 8*(4), 161–177.

Bassett, C. (2005). Emergent wisdom: Living a life in widening circles. *ReVision, 27*(4), 6–11.

Baxter-Magolda, M. (2004). Evolution of a constructivist conceptualization of epistemological reflection. *Educational Psychologist, 39*(1), 31–42.

Beattie, M., Dobson, D., Thornton, G., & Hegge, L. (2007). Interacting narratives: Creating and re-creating the self. *International Journal of Lifelong Education, 26*(2), 119–141.

Belenky, M. F., Clinchy, B. M., Goldberger, N. R., & Tarule, J. M. (1986). *Women's ways of knowing: The development of self, voice, and mind.* New York: Basic Books.

Biggers, M., Forbes, C., & Zangori, L. (2013). Elementary teachers' curriculum design and pedagogical reasoning for supporting students' comparison and evaluation of evidence-based explanations. *Elementary School Journal, 114*(1), 48–72.

Blake, B., & Pope, T. (2008). Developmental psychology: Incorporating Piaget's and Vygotsky's theories in classrooms. *Journal of Cross-Disciplinary Perspectives in Education, 1*(1), 59–67.

Blaschke, L. (2012). Heutagogy and lifelong learning: A review of heutagogical practice and self-determined learning. *The International Review of Research in Open and Distance Learning, 13*(1), 56–71.

Bridwell, S. (2013). A constructive-developmental perspective on the transformative learning of adults marginalized by race, class, and gender. *Adult Education Quarterly, 63*(2), 127–146.

Brookfield, S. D. (2009). Self-directed learning. In R. Maclean & D. Wilson (Eds.), *International handbook of education for the changing world of work* (pp. 2615–2627). Netherlands, UK: Springer.

Brown, J. S., Collins, A., & Duguid, P. (1989). Situated cognition and the culture of learning. *Educational Researcher, 18*(1), 32–42.

Candy, P. C. (1991). *Self-direction for lifelong learning: A comprehensive guide to theory and practice.* San Francisco: Jossey-Bass.

Carpenter, S. (2012). Centering Marxist-feminist theory in adult learning. *Adult Education Quarterly, 62*(1), 19–35.

Cartwright, K. B., Galupo, M. P., Tyree, S. D., & Jennings, J. G. (2009). Reliability and validity of the complex postformal thought questionnaire: Assessing adults' cognitive development. *Journal of Adult Development, 16*, 183–189.

Chavez, A. F., & Guido-DiBrito, F. (1999). Racial and ethnic identity and development. In M. C. Clark & R. S. Caffarella (Eds.), *An update on adult development theory: New ways of thinking about the life course (New Directions for Adult and Continuing Education,* no. 84). San Francisco: Jossey-Bass.

Cheng, C. C. (2014). Situated learning and professional development: A case study of applying cognitive apprenticeship and community of practices in a kindergarten. *Problems of Education in the 21st Century, 59*, 15–24.

Clark, M. C. (2001). Off the beaten path: Some creative approaches to adult learning. In S. Merriam (Ed.), *An update on adult learning (New Directions for Adult and Continuing Education,* no. 89) (pp. 83–91). San Francisco: Jossey-Bass.

Closson, R. (2010). Critical race theory and adult education. *Adult Education Quarterly, 60*, 261–283.

Conway, P. F., & Clark, C. (2003). The journey inward and outward: A re-examination of Fuller's concerns-based model of teacher development. *Teaching and Teacher Education 19*, 465–482.

Cooke, S., & Carr, D. (2014). Virtue, practical wisdom and character in teaching. *British Journal of Educational Studies, 62*(2), 91–110.

Cranton, P. (1994). *Understanding and promoting transformative learning.* San Francisco: Jossey-Bass.

Cross, W. E. (1995). The psychology of nigrescence: Revising the Cross model. In J. G. Ponterott, J. M. Casa, L. A. Suzuki, & C. M. Alexander (Eds.), *Handbook of multicultural counseling.* Thousand Oaks, CA: Sage.

Cross, W. E., (1971). Toward a psychology of Black liberation: The Negro-to-Black conversion experience. *Black World, 20*(9), 13–27.

Cseh, M., Watkins, K. E., & Marsick, V. J. (1999). Reconceptualizing Marsick and Watkins' model of informal and incidental learning in the workplace. In K. Kuchinke (Ed.), *1999 Proceedings of the*

Academy of HRD (pp. 349–355). Baton Rouge, LA: Academy of Human Resource Development.

Curry, M. (2008). Critical friends groups: The possibilities and limitations embedded in teacher professional communities aimed at instructional improvement and school reform. *Teachers College Record, 110*, 733–774.

Davis, E. A., & Smithey, J. (2009). Beginning teachers moving toward effective elementary science teaching. *Science Education, 93*, 745–770.

Dennen, V. P. (2008). Cognitive apprenticeship in educational practice: Research on scaffolding, modeling, mentoring, and coaching as instructional strategies. In M. Spector (Ed.), *Handbook of research on educational communications and technology*. New York: Erlbaum.

Dewey, J. (1938). *Experience and education*. New York: Collier.

Drago-Severson, E. (2007). Helping adults learn: Principals as professional development leaders. *Teachers College Record, 109*(1), 70–125.

Drago-Severson, E. (2009). *Leading adult learning: Supporting adult development in our schools*. Thousand Oaks, CA: Corwin.

Drago-Severson, E. (2012). *Helping educators grow: Strategies and practices for leadership development*. Cambridge, MA: Harvard Press.

Drago-Severson, E., Blum-DeStefano, J., & Asghar, A. (2013). *Learning for leadership: Developmental strategies for building capacity in our schools*. Thousand Oaks, CA: Corwin/Sage.

Drayton, B., Rosser-Mims, D., Schwartz, J., & Guy, T. (2014). Black males and adult education: A call to action. *New Directions for Adult & Continuing Education, 144*, 89–92.

Elliott, V., & Schiff, S. (2001). A look within. *Journal of Staff Development, 22*(2), 39–42.

Eneau, J. (2008). From autonomy to reciprocity, or vice versa? French personalism's contribution to a new perspective on self-directed learning. *Adult Education Quarterly, 59*(3), 229–248.

English, L. M. (2005). Historical and contemporary explorations of the social change and spiritual directions of adult education. *Teachers College Record, 107*(6), 1169–1192.

Erickson, D. M. (2007). A developmental reforming of the phases of meaning in transformational learning. *Adult Education Quarterly, 58*(1), 61–80.

Erikson, E. H. (1963). *Childhood and society* (2nd ed.). New York: Norton.

Fairbanks, C. M., Duffy, G. G., Faircloth, B. S., He, Y., Levin, B., Rogh, J., & Stein, C. (2010).

Beyond knowledge: Exploring why some teachers are more thoughtfully adaptive than others. *Journal of Teacher Education, 1*(1–2), 161–171.

Ferraro, J. M. (2000). *Reflective practice and professional development*. Washington, DC: ERIC Clearinghouse on Teaching and Teacher Education. (ERIC ED 449 120)

Fiske, M., & Chiriboga, D. A. (1990). *Change and continuity in adult life*. San Francisco: Jossey-Bass.

Fleming, T. (2012). Fromm and Habermas: Allies for adult education and democracy. *Studies in Philosophy & Education, 31*(2), 123–136.

Foucault, M. (1977). *Power/knowledge*. New York: Pantheon Books.

Fullan, M. G. (1991). *The new meaning of educational change* (2nd ed.). New York: Teachers College Press.

Fuller, F. F. (1969). Concerns of teachers: A developmental conceptualization. *American Educational Research Journal, 6*(2), 207–266.

Gardner, H. (1999). *Intelligence reframed: Multiple intelligences for the 21st century*. New York: Basic Books.

Gardner, H. (2006). *Multiple intelligences: New horizons in theory and practice*. New York: Basic Books.

Garrett, J. T., & Walking Stick Garrett, M. (1994). The path of good medicine: Understanding and counseling Native American Indians. *Journal of Multicultural Counseling and Development, 22*, 134–144.

Gehrke, N. J. (1991). Seeing our way to better helping of beginning teachers. *Educational Forum, 55*(3), 233–242.

Gilligan, C. (1979). Woman's place in man's life cycle. *Harvard Educational Review, 49*(4), 431–446.

Gilligan, C. (1982). *In a different voice*. Cambridge, MA: Harvard University Press.

Glassberg, S. (1979). *Developing models of teacher development*. (ERIC ED 171 685)

Glatthorn, A. A. (2000). *The principal as curriculum leader: Shaping what is taught and tested* (2nd ed.). Thousand Oaks, CA: Corwin Press.

Gorard, S., & Selwyn, N. (2005). What makes a life-long learner? *Teachers College Record, 107*(6), 1193–1216.

Graue, E. (2005). Theorizing and describing preservice teachers' images of families and schooling. *Teachers College Record, 107*(1), 157–185.

Grow, G. (1991). Teaching learners to be self-directed: A stage approach. *Adult Education Quarterly, 41*(3), 125–149.

Guglielmino, L. M. (1977). *Development of the self-directed learning readiness scale* (Doctoral dissertation, University of Georgia, 1977). Dissertation Abstracts International, 38, 6467A.

Guglielmino, L. M. (1997). Reliability and validity of the self-directed learning readiness scale and the learning preference assessment. In H. B. Long & Associates, *Expanding horizons in self-directed learning* (pp. 209-222). Norman, OK: University of Oklahoma.

Guo, Y. (2013). Language policies and programs for adult immigrants in Canada: A critical analysis. *Canadian Ethnic Studies Journal, 45*(1), 23–41.

Habermas, J. (2001). *On the pragmatics of social interaction. Preliminary studies in the theory of communicative action.* Cambridge, MA: MIT Press.

Hansman, C. A. (2008). Adult learning in communities of practice. In C. Kimble, P. M. Hildreth, & I. Bourdon (Eds.), *Communities of practice: Creating learning environments for educators* (Vol. 1, pp. 293–310). Charlotte, NC: Information Age.

Hargreaves, A., & Moore, S. (2000). Curriculum integration and classroom relevance: A study of teachers' practice. *Journal of Curriculum and Supervision, 15*(2), 89–112.

Harris, I. (1996). *Messages men hear: Constructing masculinities.* London, UK: Taylor.

Hase, S., & Kenyon, C. (2000). *From andragogy to heutagogy.* Ultibase. Retrieved from http://www.psy.gla.ac.uk/~steve/pr/Heutagogy.html

Hase, S., & Kenyon, C. (2007). Heutagogy: A child of complexity theory. *Complicity: An International Journal of Complexity and Education, 4*(1), 111–118.

Hayes, E., & Flannery, D. D. (2000). *Women as learners: The significance of gender in adult learning.* San Francisco: Jossey-Bass.

Helms, J. E. (1993). Introduction: Review of racial identity terminology. In J. E. Helms (Ed.), *Black and White racial identity: Theory, research and practice.* Westport, CT: Praeger.

Helms, J. E. (1995). An update of Helms' White and People of Color racial identity models. In J. G. Ponterott, J. M. Casas, L. A. Suzuki, & C. M. Alexander (Eds.), *Handbook of multicultural counseling.* Thousand Oaks, CA: Sage.

Hogan, C. (2014). Transformative learning through conceptual metaphors. *Adult Learning, 25*(4), 134–141.

Horn, J. L., & Cattell, R. B. (1967). Age differences in fluid and crystallized intelligence. *Acta Psychological, 26*, 107–129.

Howie, P., & Bagnall, R. (2015). A critical comparison of transformation and deep approach theories of learning. *International Journal of Lifelong Education, 34*(3), 348–365.

Hunter, M. (1986). To be or not to be—Hunterized. *Tennessee Educational Leadership, 12*, 70.

Johnson, A. J. (2005). Reflections on wisdom as movement in the life space. *ReVision, 28*(1), 24–28.

Johnson, L. E., & Reiman, A. J. (2007). Beginning teacher disposition: Examining the moral/ethical domain. *Teaching and Teacher Education, 23*, 676–687.

Josselson, R. (1987). *Finding herself: Pathways to identity development in women.* San Francisco: Jossey-Bass.

Juhasz, A. M. (1989). A role-based approach to adult development: The triple helix model. *International Journal of Aging and Human Development, 29*(4), 301–315.

Kallio, E. (2011). Integrative thinking is the key: An evaluation of current research into the development of thinking in adults. *Theory & Psychology, 2*, 785–801.

Katz, J. H. (1989). The challenge of diversity. In C. Woolbright (Ed.), *College unions at work* (Monograph No. 11, 1–17). Bloomington, IN: Association of College Unions-International.

Kegan, R. (1994). *In over our heads: The mental demands of modern life.* Cambridge, MA: Harvard University Press.

Kegan, R. (2009). A constructive-developmental approach to transformative learning. In K. Illeris (Ed.), *Contemporary theories of learning: Learning theorists . . . in their own words* (pp. 35–52). New York: Routledge.

Kerka, S. (1998). *New perspectives on mentoring.* ERIC Digest No. 194. (ERIC ED 418 249)

Kilgore, D. W. (2001). Critical and postmodern perspectives on adult learning. In S. B. Merriam (Ed.), *The new update on adult learning theory* (New Directions for Adult and Continuing Education, no. 89). San Francisco: Jossey-Bass.

Klauer, K. J., & Phye, G. D. (2008). Inductive reasoning: A training approach. *Review of Educational Research, 78*(1), 85–123.

Knowles, M. S. (1980). *The modern practice of adult education: From pedagogy to andragogy* (2nd ed.). Chicago: Association/Follett.

Knowles, M. S. (1984). *Andragogy in action: Applying modern principles of adult learning.* San Francisco: Jossey-Bass.

Kohlberg, L., & Armon, C. (1984). Three types of stage models used in the study of adult development. In M. Commons, F. A. Richards, & C. A. Armon (Eds.), *Beyond formal operations: Late adolescent and adult cognitive development.* New York: Praeger.

Kohlberg, L., & Kramer, R. (2006). Continuities and discontinuities in childhood and adult moral development. In B. A. Marlowe & A. S. Canestrari (Eds.), *Educational psychology in context: Readings for future teachers* (pp. 117–118). Thousand Oaks, CA: Sage.

Kohlberg, L., & Turiel, E. (1971). Moral development and moral education. In G. Lessor (Ed.), *Psychology and educational practice.* Chicago: Scott, Foresman.

Kolb, D. A. (1984). *Experiential learning.* Englewood Cliffs, NJ: Prentice Hall.

Krupp, J. (1987). Understanding and motivating personnel in the second half of life. *Journal of Education, 169*(1), 20–47.

Lai, H-J. (2011). The influence of adult learners' self-directed learning readiness and network literacy on online learning effectiveness: A study of civil servants in Taiwan. *Educational Technology & Society, 14*(2), 98–106.

Lave, J., & Wenger, E. (1991). Situated learning: legitimate peripheral participation. Cambridge, England: Cambridge University Press.

Levine, S. L. (1987). Understanding life cycle issues: A resource for school leaders. *Journal of Education, 169*(1), 7–19.

Levine, S. L. (1989). *Promoting adult growth in schools.* Boston: Allyn & Bacon.

Levinson, D. J., & Levinson, J. D. (1996). *The seasons of a woman's life.* New York: Knopf.

Levinson, D. J., et al. (1978). *The seasons in a man's life.* New York: Knopf.

Lindeman, E. (1926). *The meaning of adult education.* New York: New Republic.

Lyotard, J. F. (1984). *The postmodern condition: A report on knowledge.* Minneapolis: University of Minnesota Press.

Marsick, V. J., & Watkins, K. (1990). *Informal and incidental learning in the workplace.* New York: Routledge.

Marsick, V. J., Watkins, K. E., & Lovin, B. (2010). Revisiting informal and incidental learning as a vehicle for professional learning and development. *Elaborating Professionalism, 5,* 59–76.

Marzano, R. J. (2007). *The art and science of teaching: A comprehensive framework for effective instruction.* Alexandria, VA: Association for Supervision and Curriculum Development.

McArdle, K., & Mansfield, S. (2013). Developing a discourse of the postmodern community development professional. *Discourse: Studies in the Cultural Politics of Education, 34*(1), 107–117.

McDermott, R., & Schwartz, J. (2013). Toward a better understanding of emerging adult men's gender role journeys: Differences in age, education, race, relationship status, and sexual orientation. *Psychology of Men & Masculinity, 14*(2), 202–210. San Francisco.

Merriam, S. B. (2004). The role of cognitive development in Mezirow's transformational learning theory. *Adult Education Quarterly, 55*(1), 60–68.

Merriam, S. B. (Ed.). (2008). *Third update on adult learning theory (New Directions for Adult and Continuing Education,* no. 119). San Francisco: Jossey-Bass.

Merriam, S. & Bierema. L. (2014). Adult learning: Linking theory and practice. San Francisco: CA: Jossey-Bass.

Merriam, S. B., & Clark, M. C. (1993). Learning from experience: What makes it significant? *International Journal of Lifelong Education, 12*(2), 129–138.

Merriam, S. B., Caffarella, R., & Baumgartner, L. (2007). *Learning in adulthood: A comprehensive guide* (3rd ed.). San Francisco: Jossey-Bass.

Meyer, K., & Murrell, V. (2014). A national study of theories and their importance for faculty development for online teaching. *Online Journal of Distance Learning Administration, 17*(2).

Mezirow, J. (1981). A critical theory of adult learning and education. *Adult Education Quarterly, 32*(1), 3–24.

Mezirow, J., & Associates. (1990). *Fostering critical reflection in adulthood. A guide to transformative and emancipatory learning.* San Francisco: Jossey-Bass.

Mezirow, J. (2000). Learning to think like an adult: Core concepts of transformation theory. In J. M. Mezirow & Associates (Eds.), *Learning as transformation: Critical perspectives on a theory in progress.* San Francisco: Jossey-Bass.

Mezirow, J. Taylor, E. W., & Associates. (2009). *Transformative learning in practice: Insights from community, workplace, and higher education.* San Francisco: Jossey-Bass.

Michelson, E. (1998). Remembering: The return of the body to experiential learning. *Studies in Continuing Education, 20,* 217–233.

Nah, Y. (1999). Can a self-directed learner be independent, autonomous and interdependent?: Implications for practice. *Adult Learning, 11*(1), 18

Napolitano, C. M. (2013). More than just a simple twist of fate: Serendipitous relations in developmental science. *Human Development, 55*(5), 291–318.

Neugarten, B. L. (1977). Personality and aging. In J. E. Birren & K. W. Schaie (Eds.), *Handbook of the psychology of aging.* New York: Van Nostrand Reinhold.

Neugarten, B., & Neugarten, D. (1987). The changing meaning of age. *Psychology Today, 21*(5), 29–33.

Newman, M. (2012). Calling transformative learning into question: Some mutinous thoughts. *Adult Education Quarterly, 62*(1), 36–55.

Oja, S. N., & Pine, G. J. (1981, April). *Toward a theory of staff development.* Paper presented at the annual meeting of the American Educational Research Association, Los Angeles.

Oja, S. N., & Pine, G. J. (1984). *Collaborative action research: A two-year study of teachers' stages of development and school contexts.* Durham: University of New Hampshire.

O'Neil, J. M., & Caroll, M. R. (1988). A gender role workshop focused on sexism, gender role conflict, and the gender role journey. *Journal of Counseling and Development, 67,* 193–197.

Ostorga, A. N. (2006). Developing teachers who are reflective practitioners: A complex process. *Issues in Teacher Education, 15*(2), 5–20.

Ostrom, C. S., Martin, W. J., & Zacharakis, J. (2008). Autopoiesis and the cosmology of postmodern adult education. *Adult Education Quarterly, 58,* 299–317.

Peck, T. A. (1986). Women's self-definition in adulthood: From a different model? *Psychology of Women Quarterly, 10*(3), 274–284.

Penta, S., Anghel, M., Talpos-Niculescu, C., Argesanu, V., & Stanca Muntianu, L. (2015).

Enhancing task solving efficiency by the stimulation of crystallized and/or fluid intelligence using environmental factors. *Romanian Journal of Medical Practice, 10*(1), 36–40.

Phillips, M. D., & Glickman, C. D. (1991). Peer coaching: Developmental approach to enhance teacher thinking. *Journal of Staff Development, 12*(2), 20–25.

Phinney, J. S. (1990). Ethnic identity in adolescents and adults: Review of the research. *Psychological Bulletin, 108,* 499–514.

Polanyi, M. (1969). *Knowing and being.* Chicago: University of Chicago Press.

Rachal, J. R. (2002). Andragogy's detectives: A critique of the present and a proposal for the future. *Adult Education Quarterly, 52*(3), 210–227.

Reiman, A. J., & Peace, S. D. (2002). Promoting teachers' moral reasoning and collaborative inquiry performance: A developmental roletaking and guided inquiry study. *Journal of Moral Education, 31*(1), 61–66.

Rose, A. D., Jeris, L., & Smith, R. (2005). Is adult education a calling? Shaping identity and practice in steel mill learning centers. *Teachers College Record, 107*(6), 1305–1334.

Ross-Gordon, J., Brooks, A. K., Clunis, T., Parsells, R., & Parker, U. (2005). An analysis of work-related literature focusing on race and ethnicity. In R. J. Hill & R. Kiely (Eds.), *Proceedings of the 46th Annual Adult Education Research Conference* (pp. 375–380). Athens: University of Georgia.

Rossiter, M., & Clark, M. C. (Eds.). (2010). *Narrative perspectives on adult education (New Directions for Adult and Continuing Education, no. 126).* San Francisco: Jossey-Bass.

Sandlin, J. A. (2005). Andragogy and its discontents: An analysis of andragogy from three critical perspectives. *PAACE Journal of Lifelong Learning, 14,* 25–42.

Settersten, R. A. (1996). What's the latest: Cultural age deadlines for educational and work transitions. *The Gerontologist, 36*(5), 602–13.

Sheared, V. (1999). Giving voice: Inclusion of African American students' polyrhythmic realities in adult basic education. In T. C. Guy (Ed.), *Providing culturally relevant adult education: A challenge for the twenty-first century (New Directions for Adult and Continuing Education, no. 82).* San Francisco: Jossey-Bass.

Sinnott, J. D. (2009). Cognitive development as the dance of adaptive transformation: NeoPiagetian perspectives on adult cognitive development. In M. C. Smith with N. DeFrates-Densch (Eds.), *Handbook of research on adult learning and development*. New York: Routledge.

Sneed, J. R., Schwartz, S. J., & Cross, W. E. (2006). A multicultural critique of identity status theory and research: A call for integration. *Identity: An International Journal of Theory and Research*, 6(1), 61–84.

Steinke, K. (2012). Implementing SDL as professional development in K-12. *International Forum of Teaching and Studies*, 8(1), 54–63.

Sternberg, R. J. (1988). *Triarchic mind: A new theory of human intelligence*. New York: Viking.

Sternberg, R. J. (2001). Why schools should teach for wisdom: The balance theory of wisdom in educational settings. *Educational Psychologies*, 36(4), 227–245.

Sternberg, R. J., Kaufman, J. C., & Grigorenko, E. L. (2008). *Applied intelligence*. New York: Cambridge University Press.

Sullivan, E. V., McCullough, G., & Stager, M. A. (1970). Developmental study of the relationship between conceptual, ego, and moral development. *Child Development*, 41, 399–411.

Syed, M., & Mitchell, L. (2013). Race, ethnicity, and emerging adulthood: Retrospect and prospects. *Emerging Adulthood*, 1(2), 83–95.

Taylor, E. (2007). An update on transformative learning theory: A critical review of the empirical research (1999–2005). *International Journal of Lifelong Education*, 26(2), 173–191.

Taylor, E., & Laros, A. (2014). Researching the practice of fostering transformative learning: Lessons learned from the study of andragogy. *Journal of Transformative Education*, 12(2), 134–147.

Taylor, K., & Marienau, C. (1995). Bridging practice and theory for women's adult development. In K. Taylor & C. Marienau (Eds.), *Learning environments for women's adult development: Building toward change (New Directions for Adult and Continuing Education, no. 65)*. San Francisco: Jossey-Bass.

Tennant, M. (1986). An evaluation of Knowles' theory of adult learning. *International Journal of Lifelong Education*, 5(2), 113–122.

Thies-Sprinthall, L., & Sprinthall, N. A. (1987). Experienced teachers: Agents for revitalization and renewal as mentors and teacher educators. *Journal of Education*, 169(1), 65–79.

Thorndike, E. L., Bergman, E. O., Tilton, J., & Woodyard, E. (1928). *Adult learning*. New York: Macmillan.

Tieso, C. (2001). Curriculum: Broad brushstrokes or paint-by-the-numbers? *The Teacher Educator*, 36(3), 199–213.

Tilley, C. L., & Callison, D. (2007). New mentors for new media: Harnessing the instructional potential of cognitive apprenticeships. *Knowledge Quest*, 35(5), 26–31.

Tisdell, E. (2000). Feminist pedagogies. In E. Hayes & D. Flannery (Eds.), *Women as learners: The significance of gender in adult learning*. San Francisco: Jossey-Bass.

Tolliver, D. E., & Tisdell, E. J. (2006). Engaging spirituality in the transformative higher education classroom. In E. Taylor (Ed.), *Teaching for change: Fostering transformational learning (New Directions for Adult and Continuing Education, no. 109, pp. 37–47)*. San Francisco: Jossey-Bass.

Tough, A. (1971). *The adult's learning projects: A fresh approach to theory and practice in adult learning*. Toronto, Canada: Ontario Institute for Studies in Education.

Uys, L. R., Gwele, N. S., McInerney, P., Rhyn, L., & Tanga, T. (2004). The competence of nursing graduates from problem-based programs in South Africa. *Journal of Nursing Education*, 43(8), 352–361.

Watzke, J. L. (2007). Longitudinal research on beginning teacher development: Complexity as a challenge to concerns-based stage theory. *Teaching and Teacher Education*, 23, 106–122.

Welton, M. R. (1995). The critical turn in adult education theory. In M. R. Welton (Ed.),. *In defense of the lifeworld* (pp. 11–38). Albany: State University of New York Press.

Wenger, E. (2009). A social theory of learning. In K. Illeris (Ed.), *Contemporary theories of learning: Learning theorists . . . in their own words* (pp. 200–208). New York: Routledge.

Willis, S. L., & Baltes, P. B. (1980). Intelligence in adulthood and aging: Contemporary issues. In L. W. Poon (Ed.), *Aging in the 1980s: Psychological issues*. Washington, DC: American Psychological Association.

Worrell, F. C. (2008). Nigrescence attitudes in adolescence, emerging adulthood, and adulthood. *Journal of Black Psychology*, 34, 156–178.

Wynn, C., Mosholder, R., & Larsen, C. (2014). Measuring the effects of problem-based learning on the development of postformal thinking skills and engagement of first-year learning community students. *Learning Communities Research and Practice*, 2(2). Retrieved from http://washington-center.evergreen.edu/lcrpjournal/vol2/iss2/4

Zepeda, S. J. (2004). Leadership to build learning communities. *The Educational Forum*, 68(2), 144–151.

Zimprich, D., Allemand, M., & Dellenbach, M. (2009). Openness to experience, fluid intelligence, and crystallized intelligence in middle-aged and old adults. *Journal of Research in Personality*, 43, 444–454.

Chapter 5

Duemer, L. (2012). Existentialism as a framework for qualitative research: Understanding freedom and choice in educational organizations. *Journal of Philosophy & History of Education*, 62(1), 171–179.

Ginkel, K. C. (1983, April). *An overview of a study which examined the relationship between elementary school teachers' preference for supervisory conferencing approach and conceptual level of development.* Paper presented at the American Educational Research Association, Montreal, Canada.

Glickman, C. D., & Tamashiro, R. T. (1980). Determining one's beliefs regarding teacher supervision. *Bulletin*, 64(440), 74–81.

Gross, S. (2014). Where's Houdini when you need him? Breaking out of the U.S. educational reform straightjacket to reclaim our democracy. *Journal of School Leadership*, 24(6), 1099–1124.

Kline, K., & Abowitz, K. K. (2013). Moving out of the cellar: A new (?) existentialism for a future without teachers. *Critical Questions in Education*, 4(2), 156–167.

Parkay, F. W., Hass, G., & Anctil, E. J. (2010). *Curriculum leadership: Readings for developing quality educational programs* (9th ed.). Boston: Allyn & Bacon.

Pratte, R. (1971). *Contemporary theories of education*. Scranton, PA: T. Y. Crowell.

Sergiovanni, T. J., & Starratt, R. J. (2007). *Supervision: A redefinition* (8th ed.). New York: McGraw-Hill.

Yue, A. R. (2011). An existentialist in Iqaluit: Existentialism and reflexivity informing pedagogy in the Canadian North. *Journal of Management Education*, 35, 119–137.

Chapter 6

Bradley, T. P., Allen, J. M., Hamilton, S., & Filgo, S. K. (2006). Leadership perception: Analysis of 360-degree feedback. *Performance Improvement Quarterly*, 19(1) 7–24.

Brutus, S., & Derayeh, M. (2002). Multisource assessment programs in organizations: An insider's perspective. *Human Resource Development Quarterly*, 13, 187–202.

Chang, W. W., Chen, C-H. L., & Yuan, Y-H. (2012). Exploring the unknown. International service and individual transformation. *Adult Education Quarterly*. 62, 230–251. doi:10.1177/0741613611402049

Diehl, J. N. (2011). *Collaborative autobiography: A vehicle for administrator reflection on multiple accountability pressures.* (Doctoral dissertation). San Marcos: Texas State University.

Dyer, K. M. (2001). The power of 360-degree feedback. *Educational leadership*, 58(5), 35–38.

Festinger, L. (1957). *A theory of cognitive dissonance*. Stanford, CA: Stanford University Press.

Glickman, C. D. (2002). *Leadership for learning: How to help teachers succeed*. Alexandria, VA: Association for Supervision and Curriculum Development.

Gordon, S. P., & Brobeck, S. R. (2010). Coaching the mentor: Facilitating reflection and change. *Mentoring and tutoring: Partnerships in Learning*, 18(4), 427–447.

Gorski, P. C. (2009). Cognitive dissonance as a strategy in social justice teaching. *Multicultural Education*, 17(1), 54–57.

Janas, M. (2001). Getting a clear view. *Journal of Staff Development*, 22(2), 32–34.

Lepsinger, R., & Lucia, A. (2009). *The art and science of 360-degree feedback*. San Francisco: Wiley.

Luft, J. (1970). *Group processes: An introduction to group dynamics*. New York: National Press Books.

Nieminen, L., Smerek, R., Kotrba, L., & Denison, D. (2013). What does an executive coaching intervention add beyond facilitated multisource feedback? Effects on leader self-ratings and perceived effectiveness. *Human Resource Development Quarterly*, 24(2), 145–176.

Profiles International. (2011). *Profiles CheckPoint 360° Competency Feedback System™. History, development and research information.* Waco, TX: Author.

Seyforth, J. (2008). *Human resource leadership for effective schools*. Richmond, VA: Pearson.

Shinn, S. (2008). Leadership in the round. *BizEd*, 7(2), 32–38.

Tombak, A. (2015). Self-knowledge skills of educational administrators (Kyrenia example). *The Proceedings of 5th World Conference on Learning, Teaching, and Educational Leadership, Procedia – Social and Behavioral Sciences, 186*, 820–824.

Weldeana, H., & Abraham, S. (2014). The effect of an historical perspective on prospective teachers' beliefs in learning mathematics. *Journal of Mathematics TeacherEducation, 17*(4), 303–330.

Zepeda, S. J. (2006). Cognitive dissonance, supervision, and administrative team conflict. *International Journal of Educational Management, 20*(3), 224–232.

Chapter 7

Alberti, R. E., & Emmons, M. L. (2008). *Your perfect right: Assertiveness and equality in your life and relationships* (9th ed.). Manassas Park, VA: Impact.

Gordon, S. P. (1992). Paradigms, transitions, and the new supervision. *Journal of Curriculum and Supervision, 8*(1), 62–76.

Harpaz, Y. (2005). Teaching and learning in a community of thinking. *Journal of Curriculum and Supervision, 20*(2), 136–157.

Seco, V., & Lopes, M. (2014). Between compassionateness and assertiveness: A trust matrix for leaders. *Journal of Industrial Engineering & Management, 7*(3), 622–644.

Thobega, M., & Miller, G. (2007). Supervisory behaviors of cooperating agricultural education teachers. *Journal of Agricultural Education, 48*(1), 64–74.

Townsend, A. (2007). *Assertiveness and diversity*. Basingstoke, UK: Palgrave Macmillan.

Chapter 8

Jasen in de Wal, J., den Brok, P.J. Hooijer, J.G., Martens, R.L., & van den Beemt, A. (2014). Teachers engagement in professional learning : Exploring motivational profiles. *Learning and Individual Differences, 36*, 27–36.

Glickman, C. D., & Pajak, E. F. (1986). Supervisors' discrimination among three types of supervisory scripts. *Educational and Psychological Research, 6*(4), 279–289.

Pajak, E. F., & Glickman, C. D. (1989). Informational and controlling language in simulated supervisory conferences. *American Educational Research Journal, 26*(1), 93–106.

Pajak, E. F., & Seyfarth, J. J. (1983). Authentic supervision reconciles the irreconcilables. *Educational Leadership, 40*(8), 20–23.

Palandra, M. (2010). The role of instructional supervision in district-wide reform. *International Journal of Leadership in Education, 13*(2), 221–234.

Roth, G., Assor, A., Kanat-Maymon, Y., & Kaplan, H. (2007). Autonomous motivation for teaching: How self-determined teaching may lead to self-determined learning. *Journal of Educational Psychology, 99*, 761–774.

Sommers, D. (2009). Informational leadership: Leading with the end in mind. *Techniques 84*(4), 42–45. Retrieved from www.acteonline.org

Rousmaniere, T. G., & Ellis, M.V. (2013). Developing the construct and measure of collaborative clinical supervision: The supervisee's perspective. *Training and Education in Professional Psychology, 7*(4), 300–308.

Chapter 9

Rousmaniere, T. G., & Ellis, M.V. (2013). Developing the construct and measure of collaborative clinical supervision: The supervisee's perspective. *Training and Education in Professional Psychology, 7*(4), 300–308.

Chapter 11

Glickman, C. D. (2002). *Leadership for learning: How to help teachers succeed*. Alexandria, VA: Association for Supervision and Curriculum Development.

Gordon, S. P. (1990). Developmental supervision: An exploratory study of a promising model. *Journal of Curriculum and Supervision, 5*, 293–307.

Phillips, M., & Glickman, C. D. (1991). Peer coaching: Developmental approach to enhancing teacher thinking. *Journal of Staff Development, 12*(2), 20–25.

Siens, C., & Ebmeier, H. (1996). Developmental supervision and the reflective thinking of teachers. *Journal of Curriculum and Supervision, 11*(4), 299–319.

Zellermayer, M., & Margolin, I. (2005). Teacher educators' professional learning described through the lens of complexity theory. *Teachers College Record, 107*(6), 1275–1304.

Chapter 12

Johnson, B., Sullivan, A. M., & Williams, D. (2009). A one-eyed look at classroom life: Using new technologies to enrich classroom-based research. *Issues in Educational Research, 19*(1), 34–47.

Madhlangobe, L., & Gordon, S. P. (2012). Culturally responsive leadership in a diverse school: A case study of a high school leader. *NASSP Bulletin, 96*(3), 177–202.

Marshall, C., & Rossman, G. B. (2011). *Designing qualitative research* (5th ed.). Los Angeles, CA: Sage.

Rae, A. I. M. (2008). *Quantum physics: A beginner's guide*. Oxford, England: OneWorld Publications.

Rock, M. L., Gregg, M., Thead, B. K., Acker, S. E., Gable, R. A., & Zigmond, N. P. (2009). Can you hear me now?: Evaluation of an online wireless technology to provide real-time feedback to special education teachers-in-training. *Teacher Education and Special Education, 32*(1), 64–82.

Scheeler, M. C., McKinnon, K., & Stout, J. (2012). Effects of immediate feedback delivered via Webcam and bug-in-ear technology on preservice teacher performance. *Teacher Education and Special Education, 35*(1), 77–90.

Van Es, E. (2010). Videodiscussion is advised. *Journal of Staff Development, 31*(1), 54–58.

Chapter 13

Dabbish, L., & Kraut, R. (2006). *Email overload at work: An analysis of factors associated with email strain*. Paper presented at the Conference on Computer Supported Collaborative Work, ACM. Retrieved from http://dl.acm.org.libproxy.txstate.edu/citation.cfm?id1180941

Delbecq, A. L., Van de Ven, A. H., & Gustafson, D. H. (1975). *Group techniques for program planning*. Glenview, IL: Scott Foresman.

Deming, W. E. (1986). *Out of the crisis*. Cambridge, MA: Massachusetts Institute of Technology.

Fisher, D., Hogan, B., Brush, A.J., Smith, M., & Jacobs, A. (2006). Using social sorting to enhance email management. Microsoft Research. Retrieved from http://www.connectedaction.net/wp-content/uploads/2010/04/2005-HCIC-Using-Social-Sorting-to-Enhance-Email-Management.pdf

Johri, A. (2011). Look Ma, no email! Blogs and IRC as primary and preferred communication tools in a distributed firm. Proceedings of the ACM Conference on Computer Supported Cooperative Work. Retrieved from http://filebox.vt.edu/users/ajohri/publications/Johri%20no20email%CSCW%202011.pdf

Kennedy, A., & Clinton, C. (2009). Identifying the professional development needs of early career teachers in Scotland using nominal group technique. *Teacher Development, 13*(1), 29–41.

Nworie, J. (2011). Using the Delphi Technique in educational technology research. *TechTrends, 55*(5), 24–30.

Owen, J. (2002). *Making quality sense: A guide to quality, tools and techniques, awards and the thinking behind them*. London: Learning and Skills Development Agency.

Song, M., Halsey, V., & Burress, T. (2007). *The Lamster revolution: How to manage your email before it manages you*. San Francisco, CA: Berrett-Koehler.

Soucek, R., & Moser, K. (2010). Coping with information overload in email communication: Evaluation of a training intervention. *Computers in Human Behavior, 26*, 1458–1466.

Turnbull, B. J., Haslam, M. B., Arcaira, E. R., Riley, D. L., Sinclair, B., & Coleman, S. (2009). *Evaluation of the school administration manager project*. Retrieved from http://www.wallacefoundation.org/knowledge-center/school-leadership/effective-principal-leadership/Pages/The-School-Administration-Manager-Project.aspx

Walton, M. (1986). *The Deming management method*. New York, NY: Putnam.

Yu, B., & Zhu, D.-h. (2009). Combining neural networks and semantic feature space for email classification. *Knowledge-Based Systems, 22*, 376–381.

Chapter 14

Durlak, J. A., & DuPre, E. P. (2008). Implementation matters: A review of research on the influence of implementation on program outcomes and the factors affecting implementation. *American Journal of Community Psychology, 41*, 327–350.

Fetterman, D. M., & Wandersman, A. (Eds.) (2005). *Empowerment evaluation principles in practice*. New York: Guilford Press.

Fetterman, D., & Wandersman, A. (2007). Empowerment evaluation: Yesterday, today, and tomorrow. *American Journal of Evaluation, 28*, 179–198.

Fixsen, D. L., Naoom, S. F., Blase, K. A., Friedman, R. M., & Wallace, F. (2005). *Implementation research: A synthesis of the literature.* Tampa, FL: University of South Florida, Louis de la Parte Florida Mental Health Institute, The National Implementation Research Network.

Gordon, S. P. (1999). Ready? How effective schools know it's time to take the plunge. *Journal of Staff Development, 20*, 48–53.

Greene, J. C. (1986). *Participatory evaluation and the evaluation of social programs: Lessons learned from the field.* Paper presented to the annual meeting of the American Educational Research Association, San Francisco, April.

Hall, G. E., & Hord, S. M. (2006). *Implementing change: Patterns, principles, and potholes.* Boston, MA: Allyn & Bacon.

Kwok, P. W. (2014). The role of context in teachers' concerns about the implementation of an innovative curriculum. *Teaching and Teacher Education, 38*, 44–55.

Lendrum, A., & Humphrey, N. (2012). The importance of studying the implementation of interventions in school settings. *Oxford Review of Education, 38*, 635–652.

Llosa, L., & Slayton, J. (2009). Using program evaluation to inform and improve the education of young English language learners in U.S. schools. *Language Teaching Research, 13*(1), 35–54.

Stiegelbauer, S. M. (2008). The dimensions of implementation: From plans to action. In S.P. Gordon (Ed.), *Collaborative action research: Developing professional learning communities* (pp. 112–133). New York: Teachers College Press.

Swain-Bradway, J., Pinkney, C., & Flannery, K. B. (2015). Implementing SWPBIS in high schools: Contextual factors and stages of implementation. *Teaching Exceptional Children, 47*, 245–255.

Wolfe, R. (1969). A model for curriculum evaluation. *Psychology in the Schools, 6*, 107–108.

Wood, F. H., McQuarrie, F. Q., & Thompson, S. R. (1982). Professors and practitioners agree on effective staff development practices. *Educational Leadership, 43*(1), 63–66.

Chapter 15

Biss, J. L., DuFrene, D. D. (2006). An examination of reverse mentoring in the workplace. *Business Education Digest, 15*, 30–41.

Bullough, R. (2012). Mentoring and new teacher induction in the United States: A review and analysis of current practices. *Mentoring & Tutoring: Partnership in Learning, 20*, 57–74.

Cogan, M. (1973). *Clinical supervision.* Boston: Houghton Mifflin.

Forbes, C. T. (2004). Peer mentoring in the development of beginning secondary science teachers: Three case studies. *Mentoring & Tutoring: Partnerships in Learning, 12*, 219–239.

Gilles, C., Carrillo, L. T., Wang, Y., Stegall, J., & Bumgarner, B. (2013). Working with my mentor is like having a second brain/hands/feet/eyes: Perceptions of novice teachers. *English Journal, 102*(3), 78–86.

Glickman, C. D. (2002). *Leadership for learning: How to help teachers succeed.* Alexandria, VA: Association for Supervision and Curriculum Development.

Goldhammer, R. (1969). *Clinical supervision: Special methods for the supervision of teachers.* New York: Holt, Rinehart and Winston.

Hooker, T. (2013). Peer coaching: A review of the literature. *Waikato Journal Of Education, 18*(2), 129–139.

Kissau, S. P., & King, E. T. (2014). Peer mentoring second language teachers: A mutually beneficial experience? *Foreign Language Annals, 48*(1), 143–160.

Klinge, C. M. (2015). A conceptual framework for mentoring in a learning organization. *Adult Learning, 26*(4), 160–166.

LoCasale-Crouch, J., Davis, E., Wiens, P., & Pianta, R. (2012). The role of the mentor in supporting new teachers: Associations with self-efficacy, reflection, & quality. *Mentoring & Tutoring: Partnerships in Learning, 20*, 303–323.

Maor, D., & McConney, A. (2015). Wisdom of the elders: Mentors' perspectives on mentoring learning environments for beginning science and mathematics teachers. *Learning Environment Research, 18*, 335–347.

Nidus, G., & Sadder, M. (2011). The principal as formative coach. *Educational Leadership, 69*(2), 30–35.

Pajak, E. (2008). *Supervising instruction: Differentiating for teacher success* (3rd ed.). Norwood, MA: Christopher-Gordon.

Saphier, J. (2011). Outcomes: Coaching, teaching standards, and feedback mark the teacher's road to mastery. *Journal of Staff Development, 3*(4), 58–62.

Silva, J., & Contreras, K. (2011). The year we learned to collaborate. *Educational Leadership*, 69(2), 54–58.

Silva Dias, T., & Menezes, I. (2013). The role of classroom experiences and school ethos in the development of children as political actors: Confronting the vision of pupils and teachers. *Educational & Child Psychology*, 30(1), 26–37.

Zwart, R. C., Wubbels, T., Bergen, T., & Bolhuis, S. (2009). What characteristics of a reciprocal peer coaching context affect teacher learning as perceived by teachers and their students? *Journal of Teacher Education*, 60, 243–257.

Chapter 16

Allison, D. J. (1981). *Process evaluation: Some summarizing and integrating notes on the organizational implications of this form of teacher evaluation.* (ERIC ED 235 580)

Behrent, M. (2016). More than a score: Neoliberalism, testing, & teacher evaluations. *Workplace: A Journal for Academic Labor*, 26, 50–62.

Bolyard, C. (2015). Test-based teacher evaluations: Accountability vs. responsibility. *Philosophical Studies in Education*, 46, 73–82.

Champ, C. H. (2015). Measuring teacher effectiveness: The impact of institutional culture on initial implementation of New York's Annual Professional Performance Review. *AASA Journal of Scholarship and Practice*, 12(2), 34–43.

Croft, S. J., Roberts, M. A., & Stenhouse, V. L. (2016). The perfect storm of education reform: High-stakes testing and teacher evaluation. *Social Justice*, 42(1), 70–92.

Danielson, C. (2010/2011). Evaluations that help teachers learn. *Educational Leadership*, 68(4), pp. 35–39.

Danielson, C. (2013). *The framework for teaching evaluation instrument.* Princeton, NJ: The Danielson Group.

Danielson, C. (2015). Framing discussions about teaching. *Educational Leadership*, 72(7), 38–41.

Darling-Hammond, L., Amrein-Beardsley, A., Haertel, E. W., & Rothstein, J. (2011). *Getting teacher evaluation right: A background paper for policy makers.* American Educational Research Association. Retrieved from http://www.njea.org/njea-

Derrington, M. L., & Campbell, J. W. (2015). Principal concerns and superintendent support during teacher evaluation changes. *AASA Journal of Scholarship and Practice*, 12(3), 11–22.

Dodson, R. L. (2015). Kentucky principal perceptions of the state's new teacher evaluation system. *Educational Research Quarterly*, 39(2), 53–74.

Duffett, A., Farkas, S., Rotherham, A. J., & Silva, E. (2008). *Waiting to be won over: Teachers speak on the profession, unions, and reform.* Washington, DC: Education Sector.

Grissom, J. A., Loeb, S., & Master, B. (2013). Effective instructional time use for school leaders: Longitudinal evidence from observations of principals. *Educational Researcher*, 42(8), 433–444.

Kowalski, T. J., & Dolph, D. A. (2015). Principal dispositions regarding the Ohio Teacher Evaluation System. *AASA Journal of Scholarship & Practice*, 11(4), 4–20.

Marshall, K. (2006). The why's and how's of teacher evaluation rubrics. *Edge: The Latest Information for the Education Practitioner*, 2(1), 2–19.

Marzano, R. J. (2012). Reducing error in teacher observation scores. *Educational Leadership*, 70(3), 82–83.

Maslow, V. J., & Kelley, C. J. (2012). Does evaluation advance practice? The effects of performance evaluation on teaching quality and system change in large diverse schools. *Journal of School Improvement*, 22, 600–632.

McGrath, M. J. (2006). Dealing positively with the nonproductive teacher: A legal and ethical perspective on accountability. In J. H. Stronge (Ed.), *Evaluating Teaching* (pp. 253–267). Thousand Oaks, CA: Corwin Press.

McGreal, T. L. (1982). Effective teacher evaluation systems. *Educational Leadership*, 39(4), 303–305.

McGreal, T. L. (1983). *Successful teacher evaluation.* Alexandria, VA: Association for Supervision and Curriculum Development.

McGreal, T. L. (1988). Evaluation for enhancing instruction: Linking teacher evaluation and staff development. In S. J. Stanley & W. J. Popham (Eds.), *Teacher evaluation: Six prescriptions for success.* Alexandria, VA: Association for Supervision and Curriculum Development.

Morgan, G. B., Hodge, K. J., Trepinski, T. M., & Anderson, L. W. (2014). The stability of teacher performance and effectiveness: Implications for the policies concerning teacher evaluation. *Education Policy Analysis Archives*, 22(95), Retrieved from http://epaa.asu.edu/ojs/article/view/1619

Murphy, J., Hallinger, P. & Heck, R. H. (2013). Leading via teacher evaluation: The case of the missing clothes? *Educational Researcher*, *42*(6), 349–354.

National Board for Professional Teaching Standards (1989). *What teachers should know and be able to do.* Retrieved from http://www.nbpts.org/sites/default/files/what_teachers_should_know.pdf

National Board for Professional Teaching Standards (2014). *Five core propositions.* Retrieved from http://www.nbpts.org/five-core-propositions.

National Institute for Excellence in Teaching (2012). Career teaching handbook: TAP instructional rubrics. Retrieved from http://wep.edgefield.k12.sc.us/wp-content/uploads/2015/07/Career_Teacher_Handbook-TAP_Instructional_Rubrics.pdf

Noddings, N. (2007). *When school reform goes wrong.* New York: Teachers College Press.

Popham, J. (1988). The dysfunctional marriage of formative and summative evaluation. *Journal of Personnel Evaluation in Education*, *1*, 269–273.

Schachter, R. (2012). Brave new world of teacher evaluation. *District Administrator*, *48*(10), 43–47.

Smylie, M. A. (2014). Teacher evaluation and the problem of professional development. *Mid-Western Educational Researcher*, *26*(2), 97–111.

The Free Dictionary (n.d.). Retrieved from www.thefreedicttionary.com/driver.

Toch, T. (2008). Fixing teacher evaluation. *Educational Leadership*, *36*(2), 32–37.

Tucker, P. D., & DeSander, M. K. (2006). Legal considerations in designing teacher evaluation systems. In J. H. Stronge (Ed.), *Evaluating Teaching* (pp. 69–97). Thousand Oaks, CA: Corwin Press.

Wheeler, P. H., & Scriven, M. (2006). Building the foundation: Teacher roles and responsibilities. In J. H. Stronge (Ed.), *Evaluating Teaching* (pp. 27–53). Thousand Oaks, CA: Corwin Press.

Young, S., Range, B. G., Hvidston, D., & Mette, I. M. (2015). Teacher evaluation reform: Principals' beliefs about newly adopted teacher evaluation systems. *Planning and Changing*, *46*(1/2), 158–174.

Zepeda, S. J. (2016). *The leader's guide to working with underperforming teachers.* New York: Routledge.

Chapter 17

Allen, J. A., & Rogelberg, S. G. (2013). Manager-led group meetings: A context for promoting employee engagement. *Group & Organization Management*, *38*(5), 543–569.

Beebe, S. A., & Masterson, J. T. (2015). *Communication in small groups: Principles and practices* (11th. ed.). Boston: Pearson.

Benne, D. D., & Sheats, P. (1948). Functional roles of group members. *Journal of Social Issues*, *4*(2), 41–49.

Biech, E. (2008). A model for building teamwork. In E. Biech (Ed.), *Pfeiffer book of successful team-building tools: Best of the annuals* (pp. 13–26). San Francisco: John Wiley.

Bonebright, D. A. (2010). 40 years of storming: A historical review of Tuckman's model of small group development. *Human Resource Development International*, *13*(1), 111–120.

Chen, M. H. (2006). Understanding the benefits and detriments of conflict on team creativity process. *Creativity and Innovation Management*, *15*(1), 105–116.

Corey, G., & Corey, M. (1982). *Groups: Process and practice.* Monterey, CA: Brooks/Cole.

Eckstein, N. J. (2005). Making a lion into a pussycat: Working with difficult group members. *Communication Teacher*, *19*(4), 111–115.

Fairchild, J., & Hunter, S. T. (2014). 'We've got creative differences': The effects of task conflict and participative safety on team creative performance. *Journal Of Creative Behavior*, *48*(1), 64–87.

Franz, T. (2012). *Group dynamics and team interventions: Understanding and improving team performance*, Hoboken, NJ : John Wiley & Sons.

Fullan, M. (2000). *Change forces: The sequel.* Philadelphia, PA: George H. Buchanan.

Johnson, D. W., & Johnson, F. P. (2013). *Joining together: Group theory and group skills* (11th ed.). Boston: Pearson.

Kemp, C. G. (1970). *Perspectives on the group process: A foundation for counseling with groups* (2nd ed.). Boston, MA: Houghton Mifflin.

Levi, D. (2014). *Group dynamics for teams* (4th ed.) Thousand Oaks, CA: Sage.

Mickan, S., & Rodger, S. (2000). Characteristics of effective teams: A literature review. *Australian Health Review*, *23*(3), 201–208.

Necsoi, D.V., (2015). Team and team management: A practical approach. *Journal Plus Education*, *12*, 307–310.

Sheard, A. G., & Kakabadse, A. P. (2002). From loose groups to effective teams: The nine key factors of the team landscape. *Journal of Management Development*, 21(2), 133–151.

Tekleab, A. G., Quigley, N. R., & Tesluk, P. E. (2009). A longitudinal study of team conflict management, cohesion, and team effectiveness. *Group and Organization Management*, 34, 170–205.

Thistlethwaite, J., & Jackson, A. (2014). Conflict in practice-based settings: Nature, resolution and education. *Practice-Based Learning*, 2(2), 2–13.

Tuckman, B., & Jensen, M. (1977). Stages of small group development revisited. *Group and Organizational Studies*, 2, 419–427.

Wheelan, S. A. (2016). *Creating effective teams: A Guide for members and leaders* (5th ed.). Los Angeles: SAGE.

Woods, J. G. (2012). Using cognitive conflict to promote the use of dialectical learning for strategic decision-makers. *Learning Organization*, 19(2), 134–147.

Chapter 18

Bullough, R. (2012). Mentoring and new teacher induction in the United States: A review and analysis of current practices. *Mentoring & Tutoring: Partnership in Learning*, 20(1), 57–74.

Comas, P. C., & Barufaldi, J. P. (2011). The effective research-based characteristics of professional development of the National Science Foundation's GK–12 program. *Journal of Science Teacher Education*, 22, 255–272.

Gordon, S. P. (2004). *Professional development for school improvement: Empowering learning communities*. Boston, MA: Allyn & Bacon.

Guskey, T. R. (2002). Does it make a difference? Evaluating professional development. *Educational Leadership*, 59(6), 45–51.

Guskey, T. R. (2003). Analyzing lists of the characteristics of effective professional development to promote visionary leadership. *NASSP Bulletin*, 87(637), 4–20.

Holen, M., & Yunk, D. (2014). Benefits of 25 years of school district-university partnerships to improve teacher preparation and advance school renewal. *Educational Considerations*, 42(1), 49–54.

Howell, J. B., & Saye, J. W. (2016). Using lesson study to develop a shared professional teaching knowledge culture among 4th grade social studies teachers. *The Journal of Social Studies Research*, 40(1), 25–37.

Johnson, D. W., & Johnson, R. T. (2009). An educational psychology success story: Social interdependence theory and cooperative learning. *Educational Researcher*, 38(5), 365–379.

Kagan, S., & Kagan, M. (2009). *Kagan cooperative learning*. San Clemente, CA: Kagan.

Lambeth, D. (2012). Effective practices and resources for support of beginning teachers. *Academic Leadership*, 10(1), 1–13.

Lewis, C. (2009). What is the nature of knowledge development in lesson study? *Educational Action Research*, 17(1), 95–110.

Lieberman, J. (2009). Reinventing teacher professional norms and identities: The role of lesson study and learning communities. *Professional Development in Education*, 35(1), 83–99.

Poekert, P. (2012). Teacher leadership and professional development: Examining links between two concepts central to school improvement. *Professional Development in Education*, 38(2), 169–188.

Reeves, D. (2012). *Transforming professional development into student results*. Alexandria, VA: Association for Supervision and Curriculum Development.

Chapter 19

Banks, J. A. (2014). *An introduction to multicultural education* (5th ed.). Boston: Pearson.

Banks, J. A. (2010). Approaches to multicultural curriculum reform. In J. A. Banks & C. A. Banks (Eds.), *Multicultural education: Issues and perspectives* (7th ed., pp. 233–256). Hoboken, NJ: Wiley.

Bigham, G., & Riney, M. (2014). Trend analysis techniques to assist school leaders in making critical curriculum and instruction decisions. *Current Issues In Education*, 17(1), 1–12.

Bloemraad, I., & Wright, M. (2014). 'Utter failure' or unity out of diversity? Debating and evaluating policies of multiculturalism. *International Migration Review*, 48(S1), S292–S334.

Bloom, B. (1956). *Taxonomy of educational objectives. Handbook 1: The cognitive domain*. New York: David McKay.

Boote, D. N. (2006). Teachers' professional discretion and the curricula. *Teachers and Teaching: Theory and Practice*, 12(4), 461–478.

Coe, R. (2009). School improvement: Reality and illusion. *British Journal of Educational Studies*, 57, 363–379.

Crocco, M. S., & Costigan, A. T. (2007). The narrowing of curriculum and pedagogy in the age of accountability: Urban educators speak out. *Urban Education, 42*(6), 512–535.

Crowder, Z. (2014). From the editorial board: The politicization of the common core. *High School Journal, 98*(1), 1–4.

Drake, S. M., Bebbington, J., Laksman, S., Mackie, P., Maynes, N., & Wayne, L. (1992). *Developing an integrated curriculum using the story model.* Toronto: The Ontario Institute for Studies in Education.

English, F. W. (1980). Curriculum mapping. *Educational Leadership, 37*(7), 558–559.

Eppley, K. (2015). Seven traps of the Common Core State Standards. *Journal of Adolescent and Adult Literacy, 59*(2), 207–216.

Fitzharris, L. H. (2005). Making all the right connections. *Journal of Staff Development, 26*(1), 24–28.

Ford, D. (2014). Why education must be multicultural. *Gifted Child Today, 37*(1), 59–62.

Gay, G. (2005). Standards for diversity. In S. P. Gordon (Ed.), *Standards for instructional supervision: Enhancing teaching and learning.* Larchmont, NY: Eye on Education.

Gordon, S. P., & Boone, M. (2012, August). *Conflicting models and the future of educational leadership preparation: A call for integration.* Paper presented at the annual meeting of the National Council of Professors of Educational Administration, Kansas City, MO.

Gunzenhauser, M. G. (2006). Normalizing the educated subject: A Foucaultian analysis of high-stakes accountability. *Educational Studies, 39*(3), 241–259.

Hallinger, P., & Heck, R. H. (2010). Collaborative leadership and school improvement: Understanding the impact on school capacity and student learning. *School Leadership and Management, 30*(2), 95–110.

Handler, B. (2012). Teacher as curriculum leader: A consideration of the appropriateness of that role assignment to classroom-based practitioners. *International Journal of Teacher Leadership, 3*(3), 32–42.

Jacobs, H. H. (1989). *Interdisciplinary curriculum: Design and implementation.* Alexandria, VA: Association for Supervision and Curriculum Development.

Jacobs, H. H. (1997). *Mapping the big picture: Integrating curriculum and assessment K-12.* Alexandria, VA: Association for Supervision and Curriculum Development.

Jenkins, R. A. (2005). Interdisciplinary instruction in the inclusion classroom. *Teaching Exceptional Children, 37*(5), 42–48.

Johnson, A. (2010). Rachel's literacy stories: Unpacking one preservice teacher's moral perspectives on literacy teaching. *Teachers and Teaching: Theory and Practice, 16*(1), 97–109.

Kern, D. (2014). Common core-less?: A critical review of the Common Core State Standards research. *Review of Research in the Classroom, 50*(1), 75–77.

Kilpatrick, W. H. (1925). *Foundations of method.* New York: Macmillan.

Knoester, M., & Parkinson, P. (2015). Where is citizenship education in the age of common core state standards? *Critical Education, 6*(22). Retrieved from http://ojs.library.ubc.ca/index.php/criticaled/article/view/185901

Massell, D., Goertz, M., & Barnes, C. (2015) Engaging practitioners in state school improvement initiatives. *Peabody Journal of Education, 90*(1), 113–127.

Miller, J. P., & Seller, W. (1985). *Curriculum: Perspectives and practice.* New York: Longman.

Mongon, D., & Chapman, C. (2012). *High-leverage leadership: Improving outcomes in educational settings.* New York: Routledge.

Murphy, A. F., & Torff, B. (2016). Growing pains: The effect of common core state standards on perceived teacher effectiveness. *The Educational Forum, 80*(1), 21–33.

National Council of Teachers of English. (2014). *How standardized tests shape—and limit—student learning.* Author. Retrieved from http://www.ncte.org/library/NCTEFiles/Resources/Journals/CC/0242-nov2014/CC0242PolicyStandardized.pdf

Noddings, N. (2007). *When school reform goes wrong.* New York: Teachers College Press.

Oliva, P. F. (2008). *Developing the curriculum* (7th ed.). Boston, MA: Allyn & Bacon.

Ornstein, A. C., & Hunkins, F. P. (2012). *Curriculum: Foundations, principles, and issues* (6th ed.). Upper Saddle River, NJ: Prentice Hall.

Pace, J. (2015). *The charged classroom: Predicaments and possibilities for democratic teaching.* New York: Routledge.

Sergiovanni, T. (1987, August). *Introduction to the Breckenridge Conference on restructuring schools.* San Antonio, TX.

Shilling, T. (2013). Opportunities and challenges of curriculum mapping implementation in one school setting: Considerations for school learners. *Journal of Curriculum and Instruction*, 7(2), 20–37.

Tanner, D., & Tanner, L. N. (2007). *Curriculum development: Theory into practice* (4th ed.). Upper Saddle River, NJ: Prentice Hall.

Ukpokodu, O. (2010). How a sustainable campus-wide diversity curriculum fosters academic success. *Multicultural Education*, 17(2), 27–36.

Valli, L., & Buese, D. (2007). The changing roles of teachers in an era of high-stakes accountability. *American Educational Research Journal*, 44(3), 519–558.

Wiggins, C., & McTighe, J. (2005). *Understanding by design* (2nd ed.). Upper Saddle River, NJ: Pearson.

Wiggins, C., & McTighe, J. (2011). *The understanding by design guide to creating high quality units*. Alexandria, VA: ASCD.

Chapter 20

Allen, L., & Calhoun, E. F. (2009). Schoolwide action research: Findings from six years of study. In R. A. Schmuck (Ed.), *Practical action research* (2nd ed.). Thousand Oaks, CA: Corwin Press.

Bushe, G. R., & Kassam, A. F. (2005). When is appreciative inquiry transformational? A meta-case analysis. *The Journal of Applied Behavioral Science*, 41(2), 161–181.

Calhoun, E. F. (2009). Action research for school improvement. In R. A. Schmuck (Ed.), *Practical action research: A collection of articles* (2nd ed., pp. 99–108). Thousand Oaks, CA: Corwin Press.

Castro Garcés, A. Y., & Granada, L. (2016). The role of collaborative action research in teachers' professional development. *Profile: Issues In Teachers' Professional Development*, 18(1), 39–54.

Clauset, K. H., Lick, D. W., & Murphy, C. U. (2008). *Schoolwide action research for professional learning communities: Improving student learning through the whole-faculty study group approach*. Thousand Oaks, CA: Corwin Press.

Congreve, R. (2015). Using dialogic lesson observations and participatory action research to support teacher development. *Education Today*, 65(3), 16–20.

Cooperrider, D. L., & Srivastva, S. (1987). Appreciative inquiry in organizational life. In R. W. Woodman & W. A. Passmore (Eds.), *Research in organizational change and development* (Vol. 1, pp. 126–169). Stanford, CT: JAI

Corey, S. M. (1953). *Action research to improve school practices*. New York: Teachers College, Columbia University.

Glickman, C. D. (1993). *Renewing America's schools. A guide for school-based action*. San Francisco: Jossey-Bass.

Gordon, S. P. (Ed.). (2008). *Collaborative action research: Developing professional learning communities*. New York: Teachers College Press.

Gordon, S. P., Stiegelbauer, S. M., & Diehl, J. (2008). Characteristics of more and less successful action research programs. In S. P. Gordon (Ed.), *Collaborative action research: Developing professional learning communities* (pp. 79–94). New York: Teachers College Press.

Hadfield, M. M. (2012). Becoming critical again: Reconnecting critical social theory with the practice of action research. *Educational Action Research*, 20(4), 571–585.

Hubbard, R. S., & Power, B. M. (1993). *The art of classroom inquiry: A handbook for teacher-researchers*. Portsmouth, NH: Heinemann.

Kapachtsi, V. B., & Kakana, D. D. (2012). Initiating collaborative action research after the implementation of school self-evaluation. *International Studies in Educational Administration (Commonwealth Council for Educational Administration & Management [CCEAM])*, 40(1), 35–45.

Keen Wong, A. C. (2014). Moving from a transmission to a social reform teaching perspective: Using teachers' action research as critical pedagogy in higher education. *Canadian Journal of Action Research*, 15(3), 48–64.

Lewin, K. (1948). *Resolving social conflicts*. New York: Harper and Brothers.

López-Pastor, V. V., Monjas, R., & Manrique, J. C. (2011). Fifteen years of action research as professional development: Seeking more collaborative, useful and democratic systems for teachers. *Educational Action Research*, 19(2), 153–170.

Ludema, J. D., Cooperrider, D. L., & Barrett, F. J. (2001). Appreciative inquiry: The power of the unconditional positive question. In P. Reason & H. Bradbury (Eds.), *Handbook of action research: Participative inquiry and practice* (pp. 189–199). Thousand Oaks, CA: SAGE.

Pine, G. V. (2009). *Teacher action research: Building knowledge democracies*. Thousand Oaks, CA: Sage Press.

Sagor, R. (1993). *How to conduct collaborative action research*. Alexandria, VA: Association for Supervision and Curriculum Development.

Sagor, R. (2009). Collaborative action research and school improvement: We can't have one without the other. *Journal of Curriculum and Instruction, 3*(1), 7–14.

Schaefer, R. (1967). *The school as the center of inquiry*. New York: Harper and Row.

Schmuck, R. A., & Runkel, P. J. (1994). *The handbook of organizational development in schools and colleges* (4th ed.). Prospect Heights, IL: Waveland Press.

Shapiro, B. B. (2014). Engaging novice teachers in semiotic inquiry: Considering the environmental messages of school learning settings. *Cultural Studies of Science Education, 9*(4), 809–824.

Tschannen-Moran, M., & Tschannen-Moran, B. (2011). Taking a strengths-based focus improves school climate. *Journal of School Leadership, 21*, 422–448.

Chapter 21

Akmansoy, V., & Kartal, S. (2014). Chaos theory and its application to education: Mehmet Akif Ersoy University Case. *Educational Sciences: Theory & Practice, 14*(2), 510–518.

Allen, L., & Glickman, C. D. (1998). Restructuring and renewal. In A. Lieberman, M. Fullan, & D. Hopkins (Eds.), *International handbook of educational change* (pp. 505–528). Dordrecht, The Netherlands: Kluwer Academic.

Ambika, G. (2015). Ed Lorenz: Father of the 'butterfly effect'. *Resonance: Journal of Science Education, 20*(3), 198–205.

Atkinson, E. (2002). The responsible anarchist: Postmodernism and social change. *British Journal of Sociology of Education, 23*(1), 73–87.

Bain, A. (2007). *The self-organizing school: Next generation comprehensive school reforms*. Lanham, MD: Rowman and Littlefield Education.

Barnett, B. G., & O'Mahony, G. R. (2006). Developing a culture of reflection: Implications for school improvement. *Reflective Practice, 7*(4), 499–523.

Beabout, B. R. (2010). Urban school reform and the strange attractor of low-risk relationships. *School Community Journal, 20*(1), 9–30.

Boyd, V. (1992). *School context: Bridge or barrier to change?* Austin, TX: Southwest Educational Development Lab.

Chatterjee, A. (2013). Causality: Physics and philosophy. *European Journal of Physics Education, 4*(2), 1–5.

Cilliers, P. (1998). *Complexity and postmodernism: Understanding complex systems*. New York: Routledge.

Day, C., Gu, Q., & Sammons, P. (2016). The impact of leadership on student outcomes: How successful school leaders use transformational and instructional strategies to make a difference. *Educational Administration Quarterly, 52*(2), 221–258.

Eilers, A. M., & Camacho, A. (2007). School culture change in the making: Leadership factors that matter. *Urban Education, 42*(6), 616–627.

Evans, R. (1996). *The human side of change: Reform, resistance, and the real-life problems of innovation*. San Francisco, CA: Jossey-Bass.

Fullan, M. (1997). The complexity of the change process. In M. Fullan (Ed.), *The challenge of school change*. Arlington Heights, IL: Skylight Professional Development.

Fullan, M. (2002). The change leader. *Educational Leadership, 59*(8), 16–20.

Fullan, M. (2003). *Change forces with a vengeance*. London: Routledge-Falmer.

Fullan, M. (2005). Eight forces for change. *Journal of Staff Development, 26*(4), 54–58, 64.

Fullan, M. (2006). The future of education change: System thinkers in action. *Journal of Educational Change, 7*(3), 113–122.

Fullan, M. (2007). *The new meaning of educational change* (4th ed.). New York: Teachers College Press.

Fullan, M. (Ed.). (2009). *The challenge of change: Start school improvement now!* (2nd ed.). Thousand Oaks, CA: Corwin.

Gleick, J. (1987). *Chaos: Making new science*. New York: Penguin Books.

Gleick, J. (2008). *Chaos: Making new science* (rev. ed). New York: Penguin Books.

Gordon, S. P. (1992). Paradigms, transitions, and the new supervision. *Journal of Curriculum and Supervision, 8*(1), 62–76.

Gordon, S. P. (Ed.). (2008). *Collaborative action research: Developing professional learning communities*. New York: Teachers College Press.

Gordon, S. P., Stiegelbauer, S. M., & Diehl, J. (2008). Characteristics of more and less successful action research programs. In S. P. Gordon (Ed.), *Collaborative action research: Developing professional learning communities* (pp. 79–94). New York: Teachers College Press.

Hall, G. E., & Hord, S. M. (2006). *Implementing change: Patterns, principles, and potholes.* Boston, MA: Allyn & Bacon.

Hargreaves, A., & Goodson, I. (2006). Educational change over time? The sustainability and nonsustainability of three decades of secondary school change and continuity. *Educational Administrative Quarterly*, 42(1), 3–41.

Hargreaves, A., Lieberman, A., Fullan, M., & Hopkins, D. (1998). *International handbook of educational change.* Dordrecht, The Netherlands: Kluwer Academic.

Hart, K. (2004). *Postmodernism: A beginner's guide.* Oxford, UK: One World.

Hayles, N. K. (1990). *Chaos bound: Orderly disorder in contemporary literature and society.* Ithaca, NY: Cornell University Press.

Hopkins, D. (2007). *Every school a great school: Realizing the potential of system leadership.* Maidenhead, Berkshire, UK: Open University Press.

Johnson, C. (2013). Educational turbulence: The influence of macro and micro-policy on science education reform. *Journal of Science Teacher Education*, 24(4), 693–715.

Keedy, J. L. (1995). Teacher practical knowledge in restructured high schools. *Journal of Educational Research*, 89(2), 76–89.

Keedy, J. L., & Achilles, C. M. (1997). The need for school-constructed theories in practice in U.S. school restructuring. *Journal of Educational Administration*, 35(2), 102–121.

Krishnamurthy, V. (2015). Edward Norton Lorenz. *Resonance: Journal of Science Education*, 20(3), 191–197.

Larsson, J., & Dahlin, B. (2012). Educating far from equilibrium: Chaos philosophy and the quest for complexity in education. *Complicity: An International Journal of Complexity & Education*, 9(2), 1–14.

Levin, B., & Fullan, M. (2008). Learning about system renewal. *Educational Management Administration Leadership*, 36(2), 289–303.

Louis, K. S. (2007). Trust and improvement in schools. *Journal of Educational Change*, 8(1), 1–24.

Lukacs, K. (2015). 'For me, change is not a choice': The lived experience of a teacher change agent. *American Secondary Education*, 44(1), 38–49.

Mason, M. (2008). Complexity theory and the philosophy of education. *Educational Philosophy and Theory*, 40(1), 4–18.

Mitchell, C. E. (1995). *Teachers learning together: Organizational learning in an elementary school.* Unpublished doctoral dissertation, University of Saskatchewan, Saskatoon, Saskatchewan, Canada.

Murphy, D. (2011). "Chaos rules" revisited. *International Review of Research in Open and Distance Learning*, 12(7), 116–134.

Nelson, S. (2008). Becoming a critical friend. In S. P. Gordon (Ed.), *Collaborative action research: Developing professional learning communities* (pp. 26–45). New York: Teachers College Press.

Nolan, J. F. (2007). Five basic principles to facilitate change in schools. *Catalyst for Change*, 35(1), 3–8.

Patterson, J. L., Purkey, S. C., & Parker, J. V. (1986). *Productive school systems for a nonrational world.* Alexandria, VA: Association for Supervision and Curriculum Development.

Reigeluth, C. M. (2004, April). Chaos theory and the sciences of complexity: Foundations for transforming education. Paper presented at the American Educational Research Association, San Diego, CA.

Saphier, J., & King, M. (1985). Good seeds grow in strong cultures. *Educational Leadership*, 42(6), 67–74.

Sarason, S. B. (1990). *The predictable failure of educational reform.* San Francisco, CA: Jossey-Bass.

Senge, P., Cambron-McCabe, N., Lucas, T., Smith, B., Dutton, J., & Kleiner, A. (2000). *Schools that learn: A fifth discipline field book for educators, parents, and everyone who cares about education.* New York: Doubleday.

Stiegelbauer, S. M. (2008). The dimensions of learning: From plans to action. In S. P. Gordon (Ed.), *Collaborative action research: Developing professional learning communities* (pp. 112–133). New York: Teachers College Press.

Uzun, L. (2014). Raising awareness of educational philosophy: Learning and education on posthumanistic philosophy. *Journal of Theory & Practice in Education*, 10(3), 613–626.

Wheatley, M. J. (1992). *Leadership and the new science: Learning about organization from an orderly universe.* San Francisco, CA: Berrett-Koehler.

Zmuda, A., Kuklis, R., & Kline, E. (2004). *Transforming schools: Creating a culture of continuous improvement*. Alexandria, VA: Association for Supervision and Curriculum Development.

Chapter 22

Adamson, F. A., & Darling-Hammond, L. L. (2012). Funding disparities and the inequitable distribution of teachers: Evaluating sources and solutions. *Education Policy Analysis Archives*, 20(37), 1–42.

Amatea, E. S., Cholewa, B., & Mixon, K. A. (2012). Influencing preservice teachers' attitudes about working with low-income and/or ethnic minority families. *Urban Education*, 47(4), 801–834.

Amos, J. (2008). *Dropouts, diplomas, and dollars: U.S. high schools and the nation's economy*. Washington, DC: Alliance for Excellent Education.

Bae, S., Halloway, S. D., Li, J., & Bempechat, J. (2008). Mexican-American students' perceptions of teachers' expectations: Do perceptions differ depending on student achievement levels? *The Urban Review*, 40(2), 210–225.

Banks, J. A. (2000). The social construction of differences and the quest for educational equality. In R. S. Brandt (Ed.), *Education in a new era* (pp. 21–45). Alexandria, VA: Association for Supervision and Curriculum Development.

Banks, J. A. (2010). Approaches to multicultural curriculum reform. In J. A. Banks & C. A. Banks (Eds.), *Multicultural education: Issues and prospects* (7th ed., pp. 233–256). Hoboken, NJ: Wiley.

Batt, E. G. (2008). Teachers' perceptions of ELL education: Potential solutions to overcome the greatest challenges. *Multicultural Education*, 15(3), 39–43.

Bauer, K. S. (2000). Promoting gender equity in schools. *Contemporary Education*, 71(2), 22–25.

Bennett, M. J. (1993). Towards ethnorelativism: A developmental model of intercultural sensitivity. In M. Paige (Ed.), *Cross-cultural orientation* (pp. 27–69). Lanham, MD: University Press of America.

Bensimon, E. M. (2007). The underestimated significance of practitioner knowledge in the scholarship on student success. *The Review of Higher Education*, 30(4), 441–469.

Bernhard, J. K., Diaz, C. F., & Allgood, I. (2005). Research-based teacher education for multicultural contexts. *Intercultural Education*, 16(3), 263–277.

Birkett, M., Espelage, D. L., & Koenig, B. (2009). LGB and questioning students in schools: The moderating effects of homophobic bullying and school climate on negative outcomes. *Journal of Youth and Adolescence*, 38(7), 989–1000.

Boisjoly, J., Harris, K., & Duncan, G. (1998). Initial welfare spells: Trends, events, and duration. *Social Service Review*, 72(4), 466–492.

Brown, D. F. (2004). Urban teachers' professed classroom management strategies: Reflections of culturally responsive teaching. *Urban Education*, 39(3), 266–289.

Brown, M. R. (2007). Educating all students: Creating culturally responsive teachers, classrooms, and schools. *Intervention in School and Clinic*, 43(1) 57–52.

Carlisle, L. R., Jackson, B. W., & George, A. (2006). Principles of social justice education: The social justice education in schools project. *Equity and Excellence in Education*, 39(1), 55–64.

Cartledge, G., & Kourea, L. (2008). Culturally responsive classrooms for culturally diverse students with and at risk for disabilities. *Exceptional Children*, 74(3), 351–371.

Castro, E. L. (2014). "Underprepared" and "at-risk": Disrupting deficit discourses in undergraduate STEM recruitment and retention programming. *Journal of Student Affairs Research & Practice*, 51, 407–419.

Chamberlain, S. P. (2005). Recognizing and responding to cultural differences in the education of culturally and linguistically diverse learners. *Intervention in School and Clinic*, 40(4), 195–211.

Chigeza, P. (2011). Cultural resources of minority and marginalized students should be included in the school science curriculum. *Cultural Studies of Science Education*, 6, 401–412.

Codrington, J. (2014). Sharpening the lens of culturally responsive science teaching: A call for liberatory education for oppressed student groups. *Cultural Studies of Science Education*, 9, 1015–1024.

Cushner, K., McClelland, A., & Safford, P. (2009). *Human diversity in education: An integrative approach* (6th ed.). New York: McGraw-Hill.

De Gaetano, Y. (2007). The role of culture in engaging Latino parents' involvement in school. *Urban Education*, 42(2), 145–162.

De Valenzuela, J. S., Copeland, S. R., Qi, C. H., & Park, M. (2006). Examining educational equity: Revisiting the disproportionate representation of minority students in special education. *Exceptional Children, 72*(4), 425–441.

Dee, T. S. (2007). Teachers and the gender gaps in student achievement. *The Journal of Human Resources, 42*(3), 528–554.

Delpit, L. (2006). *Other people's children: Cultural conflict in the classroom.* New York: New Press.

Dworin, J. E. (2006). The families stories project: Using funds of knowledge for writing. *The Reading Teachers, 59,* 510–520.

Espelage, D. L., Aragon, S. R., Birkett, M., & Koenig, B. W. (2008). Homophobic teasing, psychological outcomes, and sexual orientation among high school students: What influence do parents and schools have? *School Psychology Review, 37*(2), 202–216.

Fiedler, C. R., Chiang, B., Van Haren, B., Jorgensen, J., Halberg, S., & Boreson, L. (2008). Culturally responsive practices in schools. *Teaching Exceptional Children, 40*(5), 52–59.

Frankenberg, E., Lee, C., & Orfield, G. (2003). *A multicultural society with segregated schools: Are we losing the dream?* Cambridge, MA: Harvard University, The Civil Rights Project.

Fry, S. W. (2003). Bite like a flea and keep them scratching: Steps to gender equity in America's schools. *Multicultural Education, 11*(1), 11–16.

Garcia, S. B., & Dominguez, L. (1997). Cultural contexts that influence learning and academic performance. *Academic Difficulties, 6*(3), 621–655.

Glimps, B. J. (2005). Students who are gay, lesbian, bisexual, or transgender. *Current Issues in Education, 8*(16). Retrieved from http://cie.ed.asu.edu/volume8/number16

Goldring, E., Cohen-Vogel, L., Smrekar, C., & Taylor, C. (2006). Schooling closer to home: Desegregation policy and neighborhood contexts. *American Journal of Education, 112*(3), 335–362.

Goodenow, C., Szalacha, L., & Westheimer, K. (2006). School support groups, other school factors, and the safety of sexual minority adolescents. *Psychology in the Schools, 43*(5), 573–589.

Grayson, D. A. (1987). Emerging equity issues related to homosexuality in education. *Peabody Journal of Education, 64*(4), 132–145.

Griner, A. C., & Stewart, M. L. (2013). Addressing the achievement gap and disproportionality through the use of culturally responsive teaching practices. *Urban Education, 48*(4), 585–621.

Gruber, J. E., & Fineran, S. (2007). The impact of bullying and sexual harassment on middle and high school girls. *Violence Against Women, 13*(6), 627–643.

Guerra, P. L., & Nelson, S. W. (2008). Cultural proficiency: Begin by developing awareness and assessing readiness. *Journal of Staff Development, 29*(1), 67–68.

Hamilton-Jones, B. M., & Vail, C. O. (2014). Preparing special educators for collaboration in the classroom: Pre-service teachers' beliefs and perspectives. *International Journal of Special Education, 29*(1), 76–86.

Hansen, A. L. (2007). School-based support for GLBT students: A review of three levels of research. *Psychology in Schools, 44*(8), 839–848.

Hoff, D. J. (2008). States to face uniform rules on grad data. *Education Week, 27*(32), 1, 21.

Howard, T. C. (2002). Hearing footsteps in the dark: African American students' description of effective teachers. *Journal of Education for Students Placed at Risk, 7*(4), 425–444.

Hudiburg, M., Mascher, E., Sagehorn, A., & Stidham, J. S. (2015). Moving toward a culturally competent model of education: Preliminary results of a study of culturally responsive teaching in an American Indian community. *School Libraries Worldwide, 21*(1), 137–148.

IDEA Funding Coalition Offers Proposal. (n.d.). Retrieved from http://www.nea.org/home/18750.htm

Individuals With Disabilities Education Improvement Act. (2004). Retrieved from http://idea.ed.gov/download/statute.html

Kidd, J. K., Sanchez, S. Y., & Thorp, E. K. (2007). Defining moments: Developing culturally responsive dispositions and teaching practices in early childhood preservice teachers. *Teaching and Teacher Education, 24,* 316–329.

Kim, S., Chang, M., Singh, K., & Allen, K. R. (2015). Patterns and factors of high school dropout risks of racial and linguistic groups. *Journal of Education for Students Placed at Risk, 20*(4), 336–351.

Kirsch, L., Braun, H., Yamamoto, K., & Sum, A. (2007). *America's perfect storm: Three forces changing our nation's future.* Princeton, NJ: Educational Testing Service.

Kommer, D. (2006). Boys and girls together: A case for creating gender-friendly middle school classrooms. *The Clearing House, 79*(6), 247–251.

Kumar, R., & Hamer, L. (2013). Preservice teachers' attitudes and beliefs toward student diversity and proposed instructional practices: A sequential design study. *Journal of Teacher Education, 64*(2), 162–177.

Ladson-Billings, G. (1995a). But that's just good teaching! The case for culturally relevant pedagogy. *Theory into Practice, 34*(3), 159–165.

Ladson-Billings, G. (1995b). Toward a theory of culturally relevant pedagogy. *American Educational Research Journal, 32*(3), 465–491.

Ladson-Billings, G. (2009). *The dreamkeepers: Successful teachers of African American children.* San Francisco: Jossey-Bass.

Lee, J. S., & Bowen, N. K. (2006). Parent involvement, cultural capital, and the achievement gap among elementary school children. *American Educational Research Journal, 42*(2), 193–218.

Lindsey, R. B., Roberts, L. M., & Campbell Jones, F. (2005). *The culturally proficient school: An implementation guide for school leaders.* Thousand Oaks, CA: Corwin Press.

Liu, G. (2006). How the federal government makes rich states richer. In *Funding gaps* (pp. 2–4). Washington, DC: Education Trust. Retrieved from www2.edtrust.org

Madsen, J. A., & Mabokela, R. O. (2005). *Culturally relevant schools: Creating positive workplace relationships and preventing intergroup differences.* New York: Routledge.

Mayberry, M. (2006). School reform efforts for lesbian, gay, bisexual, and transgendered students. *The Clearing House: A Journal of Educational Strategies, Issues, and Ideas, 76*(6), 262–264.

McLaughlin, M. J. (2010). Evolving interpretations of educational equity and students with disabilities. *Exceptional Children, 76,* 265–278.

McLeskey, J., & Waldron, N. (2002). School change and inclusive schools: Lessons learned from practice. Phi Delta Kappan, 84(1), 65–72

Michael, C. N., & Young, N. D. (2005). *Seeking meaningful school reform: Characteristics of inspired schools.* (ERIC ED 490 677)

Milner, H. R., & Ford, D. Y. (2007). Cultural considerations in the underrepresentation of culturally diverse elementary students in gifted education. *Roeper Review, 29*(3) 166–173.

Moll, L. C., Amanti, C., Neff, D., & González, N. (1992). Funds of knowledge for teaching: Using a qualitative approach to connect homes and classrooms. *Theory into Practice, 3*(2), 132–141.

Mullen, C. A., & Tuten, E. M. (2004). A case study of adolescent female leadership: Exploring the "light" of change. *Journal of Educational Thought, 38*(3), 287–313.

National Center for Educational Statistics. (2015). Retrieved from http://nces.ed.gov/programs/coe/indicator_cgg.asp

National Center for Education Statistics. (n.d.). *NAEP Data Explorer.* Retrieved from http://nces.ed.gov/nationsreportcard/NDE

Neild, R. C., Balfanz, R., & Herzog, L. (2007). An early warning system. *Educational Leadership, 65*(2), 28–33.

Orfield, G., & Frankenberg, E. (2014). Increasingly segregated and unequal schools as courts reverse policy. *Educational Administration Quarterly, 50,* 718–734.

Ormerod, A. J., Collinsworth, L. L., & Perry, L. A. (2008). Critical climate: Relations among sexual harassment, climate, and outcomes for high school girls and boys. *Psychology of Women Quarterly, 32*(2), 113–125.

Passel, J. S., & Cohn, D. (2008). *U.S. population projections: 2005–2050.* Washington, DC: Pew Research Center. Retrieved from http://pewsocialtrends.org/pubs/703/population-projections-united-states

Payne, E. C. (2007). Heterosexism, perfection, and popularity: Young lesbians' experiences of the high school social scene. *Educational Studies, 41*(1), 60–79.

Peske, H. G., & Haycock, K. (2006). *Teacher inequality: How poor and minority students are shortchanged on teacher quality.* Washington, DC: Education Trust. Retrieved from www2.edtrust.org

Richards, H. V., Brown, A. F., & Forde, T. B. (2007). Addressing diversity in schools: Culturally responsive pedagogy. *Teaching Exceptional Children, 39*(3), 64–68.

Rios-Aguilar, C. (2010). Measuring funds of knowledge: Contributions to Latina/o students' academic and nonacademic outcomes. *Teachers College Record, 112,* 2209–2257.

Risko, V. J., & Walker-Dalhouse, D. (2007). Tapping students' cultural funds of knowledge to address the achievement gap. *The Reading Teacher, 61,* 98–100.

Rothstein, R. (2004). *Class and schools.* New York: Teachers College Press.

Saifer, S., & Barton, R. (2007). Promoting culturally responsive standards-based teaching. *Principal Leadership, 8*(1), 24–28.

Sanders, J., & Cotton Nelson, S. 2004. Closing gender gaps in science. *Educational Leadership*, *62*(3), 74–77.

Schifier, L. (2011). High school graduation of students with disabilities: How long does it take? *Exceptional Children*, 77, 409–422.

Skiba, R. J., Simmons, A. B., Ritter, S., Gibb, A. C., Rausch, M. K., . . . Chung, C. (2008). Achieving equity in special education: History, status, and current challenges. *Exceptional Children*, *74*, 264–288.

Smith, D. D., Robb, S. M., West, J., & Tyler, N. C. (2010). The changing education landscape: How special education leadership preparation can make a difference for teachers and their students with disabilities. *Teacher Education & Special Education*, *33*(1), 25–43.

Spaulding, L. S., & Pratt, S. M. (2015). A review and analysis of the history of special education and disability advocacy in the United States. *American Educational History Journal*, *42*(1/2), 91–109.

Stritikus, T. T. (2006). Making meaning matter: A look at instructional practice in additive and subtractive contexts. *Bilingual Research Journal*, *30*(1), 219–227.

Swanson, C. B. (2004a). *Projections of 2003–04 high school graduates: Supplemental analyses based on findings from* Who graduates? Who doesn't? Washington, DC: Urban Institute.

Swanson, C. B. (2004b). *Who graduates? Who doesn't? A statistical portrait of public high school graduation, class of 2001*. Washington, DC: Urban Institute.

Taylor, D., & Lorimer, M. (2003). Helping gays succeed: Which research-based strategies curb negative trends now facing boys? *Educational Leadership*, *60*(4), 68–70.

Tyson, K. (2011). *Integration interrupted: Tracking, black students, and acting white after Brown*. New York: Oxford University Press.

University of Washington. (2015). *What is the individual with disabilities education act?* Retrieved from http://www.washington.edu/doit/what-individuals-disabilities-education-act

Valenzuela, A. (1999). *Subtractive schooling: U.S. Mexican youth and the politics of caring*. Albany, NY: State University of New York Press.

Van Den Bergh, N., & Crisp, C. (2004). Defining culturally competent practice with sexual minorities: Implications for social work education and practice. *Journal of Social Work Education*, *40*(2), 221–238.

van Wormer, K., & McKinney, R. (2003). What schools can do to help gay/lesbian/bisexual youth: A harm reduction approach. *Adolescence*, *38*, 409–420.

Villa, R. A., Thousand, J. S., Nevin, A., & Liston, A. (2005). Successful inclusive practices in middle and secondary schools. *American Secondary Education*, *3*(3), 33–50.

Villegas, A. M., & Lucas, T. (2007). The culturally responsive teacher. *Educational Leadership*, *64*(6), 28–33.

Walls, N. E., Kane, S. B., & Wisneski, H. (2010). Gay-straight alliances and school experiences of sexual minority youth. *Youth and Society*, *41*(3), 307–332.

Weiler, E. M. (2003). Making school safe for sexual minority students. *Principal Leadership (Middle School Ed.)*, *4*(4), 11–13.

Wells, A. S., Duran, J., & White, T. (2008). Refusing to leave desegregation behind: From graduates of racially diverse schools to the Supreme Court. *Teachers College Record*, *110*(12), 2532–2570.

Whelan, D. L. (2006). Out and ignored. *School Library Journal*, *52*(1), 46–50.

Wiener, R., & Pristoop, E. (2006). How states shortchange the districts that need the most help. In *Funding gaps 2006*. Washington, DC: Education Trust. Retrieved from www2.edtrust.org

Zhang, D., Katsiyannis, A., Ju, S., & Roberts, E. (2014). Minority representation in special education: 5 year trends. *Journal of Child and Family Studies*, *23*, 118–127.

Chapter 23

Akiba, M. (2008). Predictors of student fear of school violence: A comparative study of eighth graders in 33 countries. *School Effectiveness and School Improvement*, *19*(1), 51–72.

Anderson-Butcher, D., Stetler, G., & Midle, T. (2006). A case for expanded school-community partnerships in support of positive youth development. *Children and Schools*, *23*(3), 155–163.

Arrington, H. J., & Moore, S. D. (2001). Infusing service learning into instruction. *Middle School Journal*, *32*(4), 55–60.

Biag, M. (2016). A descriptive analysis of school connectedness. *Urban Education*, *51*(1), 32–59.

Beane, J. A. (2002). Beyond self-interest: A democratic core curriculum. *Educational Leadership, 59*(7), 25–28.

Bleazby, J. (2006). Autonomy, democratic community, and citizenship in philosophy for children: Dewey and philosophy for children's rejection of the individual/community dualism. *Analytic Teaching, 26*(1), 30–52.

Brown, A. L., & Campione, J. C. (1994). Guided discovery in a community of learners. In K. McGilly (Ed.), *Classroom lessons: Integrating cognitive theory and classroom practice* (pp. 229–270). Cambridge, MA: MIT Press.

Christenson, J. A., Fendley, K., & Robinson, J. W. (1989). Community development. In J. A. Christenson & J. W. Robinson (Eds.), *Community development in perspective* (pp. 3–25). Ames: Iowa State University Press.

Cranston, J. (2011). Relational trust: The glue that binds a professional learning community. *Alberta Journal of Educational Research, 57*(1), 59–72.

Darling-Hammond, L. (1997). *The right to learn: A blueprint for creating schools that work.* San Francisco: Jossey-Bass.

Dewey, J. (1916). *Democracy and education.* New York: Macmillan.

Dooner, A., Mandzuk, D., & Clifton, R. A. (2008). Stages of collaboration and the realities of professional learning communities. *Teaching and Teacher Education, 24,* 564–574.

Dryfoos, J. G. (1994). *Full-service schools.* San Francisco: Jossey-Bass.

DuFour, R. (2005). What is a professional learning community? In R. DuFour, R. Eaker, & R. DuFour (Eds.), *On common ground: The power of professional learning communities.* Bloomington, IN: National Educational Service.

DuFour, R., Eaker, R., & DuFour, R. (2005). Recurring themes of professional learning communities and the assumptions they challenge. In R. DuFour, R. Eaker, & R. DuFour (Eds.), *On common ground: The power of professional learning communities.* Bloomington, IN: National Educational Service.

DuFour, R., & Reaves, D. (2016). The futility of PLC lite. *Phi Delta Kappan, 97*(6), 69–71.

Earl, L. M., & Katz, S. (2006). *Leading schools in a data-rich world: Harnessing data for school improvement.* Thousand Oaks, CA: Corwin Press.

Elbers, E. (2003). Classroom interaction as reflection: Learning and teaching mathematics in a community of inquiry. *Educational Studies in Mathematics, 54,* 77–99.

Flanagan, C., Cumsille, P., Gill, S., & Gallay, L. (2007). School and community climates and civic commitments: Patterns for ethnic minority and majority students. *Journal of Educational Psychology, 99*(2), 421–431.

Garrison, D. R., & Arbaugh, J. B. (2007). Researching the community of inquiry framework: Review, issues, and future directions. *The Internet and Higher Education, 10*(3), 157–172.

Giles, C., & Hargreaves, A. (2006). The sustainability of innovative schools as learning organizations and professional learning communities during standardized reform. *Educational Administration Quarterly, 42*(1), 124–156.

Glanz, J. (2010). Justice and caring: Power, politics, and ethics in strategic leadership. *International Studies in Educational Administration, 38*(1), 66–86.

Glickman, C. D. (1998). Revolution, education, and the practice of democracy. *The Educational Forum, 63,* 16–22.

Goodlad, S. J. (2004). Democracy, schools, and the agenda. *Kappa Delta Pi Record, 41*(1), 17–20.

Gordon, S.P. (2001). The good school. *Florida Educational Leadership, 1*(2), 13–15.

Gordon, S. P. (2008). Dialogic reflective inquiry: Integrative function of instructional supervision. *Catalyst for Change, 35*(2) 4–11.

Gordon, S. P., Stiegelbauer, S. M., & Diehl, J. (2008). Characteristics of more and less successful action research programs. In S. P. Gordon (Ed.), *Collaborative action research: Developing professional learning communities* (pp. 79–94). New York: Teachers College Press.

Harris, A. (2008). Distributed leadership: According to evidence. *Journal of Educational Administration, 46*(2), 172–188.

Hiatt-Michael, D. (2006). Reflections and directions on research related to family-community involvement in schooling. *The School Community Journal, 16*(1), 7–30.

Hipp, K. K., Huffman, J. B., Pankake, A. M., & Olivier, D. F. (2008). Sustaining professional learning communities: Case studies. *Journal of Educational Change, 9,* 173–195.

Hord, S. M. (2008). Evolution of the professional learning community. *Journal of Staff Development, 29*(3), 10–13.

Hord, S. M., & Sommers, W. A. (2008). *Leading professional learning communities.* Thousand Oaks, CA: Corwin Press.

Huddy, S. (2015). Vulnerability in the classroom: Instructor's ability to build trust impacts the student's learning. *International Journal of Education Research*, 10(2), 96–103.

Isac, M. Maslowski, R., Creemers, B., & van der Werf, G. (2014). The contribution of schooling to secondary-school students' citizenship outcomes across countries. *School Effectiveness & School Improvement*, 25(1), 29–63.

Joyce, B. J., Wolf, J., & Calhoun, E. (1993). *The self-renewing school*. Alexandria, VA: Association for Supervision and Curriculum Development.

Lawson, H. A. (1999). Two new mental models for schools and their implications for principals' roles, responsibilities, and preparation. *NASSP Bulletin*, 83(611), 8–27.

Lawson, H. A., Claiborne, H., Hardiman, E., Austin, S., & Surko, M. (2007). Deriving theories of change from successful community development partnerships for youths: Implications for school improvement. *American Journal of Education*, 114(1), 1–40.

Louis, K. S., Kruse, S. D., & Marks, H. M. (1996). Schoolwide professional community. In F. M. Newmann & Associates (Eds.), *Authentic achievement: Restructuring schools for intellectual quality* (pp. 179–203). San Francisco: Jossey-Bass.

Mallory, B. J., & Reavis, C. A. (2007). Planning for school improvement: Closing the gap of culture with democratic principles. *Educational Planning*, 16(2), 8–18.

Marri, A. R. (2005). Building a framework for classroom-based multicultural democratic education: Learning from three skilled teachers. *Teachers College Record*, 107(5), 1036–1059.

Martin, G., & MacNeil, A. (2007). *School as community versus school as factory*. Retrieved from http://cnx.org/content/m14666/1.3

Martin, L. A., & Chiodo, J. J. (2007). Good citizenship: What students in rural schools have to say about it. *Theory and Research in Social Education*, 35(1), 112–134.

Meier, D. (1995). *The power of their ideas: Lessons for America from a small school in Harlem*. Boston, MA: Beacon Press.

Molinari, L. Speltini, G., & Passini, S. (2013). Do perceptions of being treated fairly increase students' outcomes? Teacher–student interactions and classroom justice in Italian adolescents. *Educational Research & Evaluation*, 19(1), 58–76.

Nash-Ditzel, S., & Brown, T. (2012). Freedoms in the classroom: Cultivating a successful third space for literacy growth. *Language & Literacy: A Canadian Educational E-Journal*, 14(3), 95–111.

National Commission on Service Learning. (2002). *Learning in deed*. Battle Creek, MI: W. K. Kellogg Foundation and the John Glenn Institute for Public Service. (Available from the W. K. Kellogg Foundation, wkkford@iserv.net)

Newmann, F. M., Marks, H. M., & Gamoran, A. (1995). Authentic pedagogy: Standards that boost student performance. *Issues in Restructuring Schools*, 8, 1–11.

Noddings, N. (2005). *The challenge to care in schools: An alternative approach to education* (2nd ed.). New York: Teachers College Press.

Noddings, N. (2010). Moral education in an age of globalization. *Educational Philosophy and Theory*, 42(4), 390–396.

Oser, F. K., Althof, W., & Higgins-D'Alessandro, A. (2008). The just community approach to moral education: System change or individual change? *Journal of Moral Education*, 37(3), 395–415.

Osterman, K. F. (2000). Students' needs for belonging in the school community. *Review of Educational Research*, 70, 323–367.

Powers, A. L. (2004). An evaluation of four place-based education programs. *The Journal of Environmental Education*, 35(4), 17–32.

Rhoads, R. A. (1998). In the service of citizenship: A study of student improvement in community service. *The Journal of Higher Education*, 69(3), 277–297.

Santiago, E., Ferrara, J., & Blank, M. (2010). A full-service school fulfills its promise. In M. Scherer (Ed.), *Keeping the whole child healthy and safe: Reflections on best practices in learning, teaching, and leadership*. Alexandria, VA: ASCD.

Schultz, B. (2007). Not satisfied with stupid Band-Aids: A portrait of a justice-oriented, democratic curriculum serving a disadvantaged neighborhood. *Equity and Excellence in Education*, 40(1), 166–176.

Schultz, B. (2008). Strategizing, sustaining, and supporting justice-oriented teaching. *Democracy and Education*, 17(3), 8–19.

Schussler, D. L., & Collins, A. (2006). An empirical exploration of the who, what, and how of school care. *Teachers College Record*, *108*, 1460–1495.

Scribner, J. P., Cockrell, K. S., Cockrell, D. H., & Valentine, J. W. (1999). Creating professional communities in schools through organizational learning: An evaluation of a school improvement process. *Educational Administration Quarterly*, *35*(1), 130–160.

Scribner, J. P., Hager, D. R., & Warne, T. R. (2002). The paradox of professional community: Tales from two high schools. *Educational Administration Quarterly*, *38*(1), 45–76.

Scribner, J. P., Sawyer, R. K., Watson, S. T., & Myers, V. L. (2007). Teacher teams and distributed leadership: A study of group discourse and collaboration. *Educational Administration Quarterly*, *43*(1), 67–100.

Sergiovanni, T. J. (1994a). *Building community in schools*. San Francisco: Jossey-Bass.

Sergiovanni, T. J. (1994b). Organizations or communities? Changing the metaphor changes the theory. *Educational Administration Quarterly*, *30*, 214–226.

Sergiovanni, T. J. (1999). Changing our theory of schooling. In T. J. Sergiovanni (Ed.), *Rethinking leadership: A collection of articles*. Arlington Heights, IL: Skylight Training and Publishing.

Sergiovanni, T. J. (2004). Building a community of hope. *Educational Leadership*, *61*(8), 33–37.

Servage, L. (2008). Critical and transformative practices in professional learning communities. *Teacher Education Quarterly*, *35*(1), 63–77.

Shields, C. M., & Seltzer, P. A. (1997). Complexities and paradoxes of community: Toward a more useful conceptualization of community. *Educational Administration Quarterly*, *33*, 413–439.

Simons, L., & Cleary, B. (2006). The influence of service learning on students' personal and social development. *College Teaching*, *54*(4), 307–319.

Smith, G. A. (2002). Going local. *Educational Leadership*, *60*(1), 30–33.

Smith, G. A. (2007). Place-based education: Breaking through the constraining regularities of public-school development. *College Teaching*, *54*(4), 307–319.

Smith-Maddox, R. (1999). An inquiry-based reform effort: Creating the conditions for reculturing and restructuring schools. *The Urban Review*, *31*, 283–304.

Spillane, J. P. (2005). Distributed leadership. *The Educational Forum*, *69*(2), 143–150.

Stoll, L., Bolam, R., McMahon, A., Wallace, M., & Thomas, S. (2006). Professional learning communities: A review of the literature. *Journal of Educational Change*, *7*(4), 221–258.

Strike, K. A. (2000). Schools as communities: Four metaphors, three models, and a dilemma or two. *Journal of Philosophy of Education*, *34*, 617–642.

Teague, G., & Anfara V. (2012). Professional learning communities create sustainable change through collaboration. *Middle School Journal*, *44*(2), 58–64.

Timpane, M., & Reich, B. (1997). Revitalizing the ecosystem for youth. *Phi Delta Kappan*, *78*, 464–470.

Vescio, V., Ross, D., & Adams, A. (2008). A review of research on the impact of professional learning communities on teaching practice and student learning. *Teaching and Teacher Education*, *24*, 80–91. Retrieved from www.sciencedirect.com

Name Index

Subject Index

Abuse, of sexual and gender minority students, 430–433
Accountability
  in culturally responsive teaching, 422
  and teacher evaluation, 286–288
Achievement gaps
  race/ethnicity and, 412–428
  socioeconomic status and, 412–428
  special needs students and, 434–435
Acquisition goals, in curriculum development, 364, 365f
Action, in community of inquiry, 451–452, 451f
Action research, 18f, 19, 47–48, 266
  and action plan design, 370, 370f, 372
  and action plan implementation, 370, 370f, 372
  alternative approaches to, 375–379
  appreciative inquiry approach, 377–379
  assisting, suggestions for, 384–385
  collaborative, 47–48
  collective, 371
  critical, 376–377
  and cultural responsiveness, 438
  and direct assistance to teachers, 370–371
  distributed instructional leadership and, 15t
  in education, 368
  and evaluation, 370, 370f, 372
  focus area for, 370, 370f
  and instructional improvement, 373, 373f
  interpretive, 376
  Lewin's concept of, 368
  needs assessment in, 370–371, 370f
  operational model for, 381–384, 382f
  phases of, 370–373, 370f
  schoolwide project, planning (small-group exercise), 380
  shared governance for, 379–384
  by students, 45
  successful, characteristics of, 374–375
  teacher-led, 44–45, 368–369
  and technical tasks of supervision, 371–373, 373f
  and traditional research, comparison of, 368–369, 369t
Additive approach, to multicultural curriculum reform,
  357–359, 358f
Adult development. *See also* Adult learning
  ebb and flow of, 91–92
  gender and, 88–89
  high stage of, 81–83, 82f
  low stage of, 81, 82f
  moderate stage of, 81, 82f
  and occupational development of teachers, 84–85
  race/ethnicity and, 89–90
  and selection of supervisory approach, 173–175, 175t
  sociocultural context of, 87–91
  stage theories of, 75–83, 82f
  theories of, 87–88, 91, 91t
  transition events and, 85–86
Adult learning, 63–75, 74f. *See also* Adult development
  andragogy theory of, 65–66
  critical perspectives on, 71–72
  experience and, 68–70
  heutogogy and, 67

  holistic, 70–71
  life events and, 86–87
  narrative in, 71
  and occupational development of teachers, 85
  self-determined, 67
  self-directed, 66–67
  situated, 68–70
  teachers and, 72–75. *See also* Professional development
  theories of, 65–68
  transformative, 67–68
  work-related, 87
Adult role(s), 86–87
Affinity diagrams, 239, 240f–241f
Agenda, for group meeting, 320–321, 320f
Analysis, in clinical supervision, 270, 272t
Andragogy, theory of, 65–66
Anticipatory principle, of appreciative inquiry, 378
Appreciative inquiry, 377–379
  5-D cycle of, 378–379
  phases of, 378–379
  principles of, 378–379
Apprenticeship, cognitive, 69
Assertiveness, 131
  in culturally responsive teaching, 422
Assessing, 221
Assessment. *See also* Needs assessment
  authentic, 45–46, 59–60
  culturally sensitive, 49
  and planning, combining, 244–246
  of student learners, 342
Assets-based approach, in culturally responsive teaching, 421
Atomism, 34–35

Beginning teacher(s). *See* Teacher(s), beginning
Behaviorism, 99
Belief(s)
  about education, 96–97
    and effective teaching, 94–95
    and instructional goals, 94–95
  culture and, 107–109
  shared, in professional learning communities, 449
  supervisory, 94, 97–99
    and decision-making responsibility, 106, 106t
    educational philosophy and, 99–103
Bicultural competence, 90
BIE. *See* Bug-in-ear technology
Blind self, 118–119, 118f, 120. *See also* Johari window
Bloom taxonomy, 197, 341, 341t, 345
Broad field, 356
Bug-in-ear technology, 216–217
Bureaucracy, 35–36
Butterfly effect, 393, 408t

Care, as moral principle, 445
Categorical frequency instrument(s), 196–198, 196f, 197f
Cause-and-effect diagram, 234–236, 235f
Cause beyond oneself, 41–42, 59, 63, 256
CCSS. *See* Common Core State Standards

Thinking
  abstract, 79
  adult forms of, 76
  dialectical, 79
  essentialist view of, 100–102
  experimentalist view of, 101–102
  higher-order, 44
  level of. *See* Bloom taxonomy
  reflective, 76
Time
  allocations of, changing, 225–228, 226*f*, 227*f*
  use of, assessing, 222–224, 223*f*
Transfer goals, in curriculum development, 364, 365*f*
Transformation approach
  in culturally responsive schools, 426
  in culturally responsive teaching, 422
  to multicultural curriculum reform, 357–359, 358*f*
Transformative/transformational learning, 67–68, 79
Transition events, 85–86
Trust
  building, and capacity for change, 399
  as moral principle, 448
Turbulence, change and, 394–395, 408*t*

UbD. *See* Understanding by design
Uncertainty principle, 54–55, 59
Understanding by design, 363–364, 365*f*
Unknown self, 118*f*, 119, 120. *See also* Johari window

Values, shared, in professional learning communities, 449
Verbatim observation, 204–205, 214*f*, 215
Video recording
  for observation, 216
  in teacher evaluation, 296
Vision
  authentic shared, 42
  shared, and capacity for change, 400
Visual diagramming, as observation instrument, 200–203, 202*f*, 204*f*, 214*f*, 215

Walkthrough, classroom
  collaborative, 217–218
  in teacher evaluation, 287
Webcam, for observation, 216
Wholeness, as moral principle, 445–446
Wisdom, 65
  balance theory of, 65
  dimensions of, 65
  emergent, 65
  practice, 65
Women's Ways of Knowing (Belenky et al.), 88
Work, and family life, linkages of, 86–87
Work environment
  novice teachers and, 28–29
  school as, 24–32
Writers, teachers as, 330